THE SUBJECTIVE DIMENSION OF MARXIST HISTORICAL DIALECTICS

THE SUBJECTIVE DIMENSION OF MARXIST HISTORICAL DIALECTICS

By Zhang Yibing

Translated by He Huiming

CANUT INTERNATIONAL PUBLISHERS

Istanbul ▪ Berlin ▪ London

Originally published as *The Subjective Dimension of Marxist Historical Dialectics* in 2003 by Nanjing University Press

Original Chinese Copyright © 2003, revised in 2008
ISBN: 978-7-305-03803-2

Canut International Publishers
Published by Canut International Publishers
Canut Int. Turkey, Balipaşa Cad. 155a, Tel : 0-212-5124356, İstanbul, Turkey
Canut Int. Germany, Heerstr. 29, D-47053, Duisburg, Germany
Canut Int. UK, 12a Guernsay Road, London E11 4BJ, England
Web: http://www.leftreader.com
E-Mail: canut@leftreader.com

English Print edition: *The Subjective Dimension of Marxist Historical Dialectics*, November 2013

ISBN: 978-3-942575-25-6

English Digital Edition:

ISBN: 978-3-942575-28-7

Printed in England
Lightning Source UK Ltd.
Chapter House
Pitfield
Kiln Farm
Milton Keynes
MK11 3LW
United Kingdom

To My Beloved Mother Huang Lingzhi

CONTENTS

For a Flourishing Marxist Philosophy   *ix*
Preface for the Third Edition   *xiii*
Preface for the Second Edition   *xvii*
Preface for the First Edition   *xxv*
Acknowledgements   *xli*

INTRODUCTION

A GENERAL LOGICAL CLUE OF THE THEORY OF
SOCIO-HISTORICAL DEVELOPMENT BEFORE MARX   **43**

I. *46*
II. *51*
III. *55*

CHAPTER I

THE SUBJECTIVE DIALECTICS IN THE PHILOSOPHICAL
HORIZON OF THE YOUNG MARX   **65**

I. The Human Essence is to Surpass the Restriction of Nature *68*
II. The Logical Contradiction Beneath the Eliminated Subject-Object Reversal *80*
III. The Economic Estrangement: Man is the Slave of His Own Creation *88*

CHAPTER II

THE HUMAN SUBJECT AND THE DEVELOPMENT OF
SOCIAL HISTORY BY THE NEW PHILOSOPHICAL HORIZON   *111*

I. The Conversion of the Dominant Logical Framework in Philosophical Changes *114*
II. The Natural Process and the Social-Historical Process
by the New Philosophical Horizon *129*
III.The Subjective Status of Man from the Perspective of Historical Dialectics *153*

CHAPTER III

THE AD HOC STIPULATION BY MARX ON 'NATURAL-NESS'
AND MATERIAL-SUBJUGATION IN SOCIAL HISTORY   *179*

I. The Absence of the Subjective Dimension of Historical Dialectics and the
Conventional Misunderstandings on Marx *182*
II.'Natural-ness' as the Special Mode in the Development of Social History
and its Alienation *201*
III. 'Natural-ness' & Material-Subjugation *213*
IV. The Economic Fetishism: Man Kneels down Before the Material
Created by Himself *226*

CHAPTER IV

RE-COGNITION OF THE WHOLE SOCIO-HISTORICAL DEVELOPMENT OF HUMAN BEINGS 237

I. Marx's Division of History and Material Subjugation 240
II. The Profound Transformation from the "Realm of Necessity" to the "Realm of Freedom" 260

CHAPTER V

ENGELS AND THE SOCIO-HISTORICAL DIALECTICS 281

I. Man and Nature in the Eyes of the Young Engels 284
II. The Only Perspective to Observe the World: Social Practice 291

CHAPTER VI

WESTERN MARXISM AND THE DIALECTICS OF SOCIAL HISTORY 313

I. The Internal Logical Conflict in the Theory of Social History in Contemporary Western Marxism 316
II. The "Humanist" Marxism and the Theory of 'Natural-ness' 334
III. The "Humanist" Marxism and the Theory of Material-Subjugation 343

CHAPTER VII

MODERN NATURAL SCIENCE AND THE MARXIST DIALECTICS OF SOCIAL HISTORY 361

I. The Modern Scientific Revolution and the Marxist View of History 364
II. Self-Organizing Theory of Complex Systems and 'Natural-ness' 372
III. The Deep Logic of the Contemporary Ecological Horizon and Marxist Historical Dialectics 383

CHAPTER VIII

CONTEMPORARY PRACTICES OF SOCIALISM AND HISTORICAL DIALECTICS 401

I. A Historical Reflection on the Road of Socialist Practices 404
II. Philosophical Thought behind Deng Xiaoping's Socialist Road 425

Appendix 1 453
Appendix 2 459
I. 459
II. 463
III. 471

Bibliography 477
About the Author 485
Index 487

FOR A FLOURISHING MARXIST PHILOSOPHY

Since its birth about 150 years ago, there have been endless debates on Marxist philosophy. There has been no agreement in comprehension among supporters, much less between supporters and opponents. Nevertheless, varieties of dissensions differ from each other in one way or another. Some of them are within the bounds of reason in that the disputes between each other do not conceal their agreement on basic orientation. Such dissensions are in the majority and common. On the contrary, the other type of dissensions exceed the above bounds of reason, one side or both of which, wittingly or unwittingly, gradually widens the gap between stands in the disputes so as to engender an open opposition between their basic orientation. The latter are in a minority and uncommon. As for the former category of dissensions: we should be tolerant of them and accept them with an open mind in order to learn from each other to complement each other, whereas concerning the latter, we must distinguish between right and wrong, making compromises on basic orientation by no means.

The developments and changes in Marxist philosophy are not only closely related to political practice but also strongly influenced by the changing trends of thought. It has undergone the high and low tides of revolution, the turbulent time of changes and the tranquil period of development. It has experienced both the phase of aggression and the phase of retreat in politics, seeing both the change of strategic goals and the shift of the focus of efforts. The approach of any strategic change endowed with the characteristics of the times is inevitably accompanied by the division and reorganization of people's political orientations and practice as well as the change of political concepts. In order to promote and solve the change, people are bound to advance the comprehension and interpretation of Marxism, especially its theoretical basis- the demand of Marxist philosophy. It was during the time of the strategic change that the upsurge in the discussion on Marxist philosophy among the Chinese academia arising in the early 1980s was going on. As far as the background is concerned, it was also exposed to the influence of the flooding of various contemporary western social thought.

It must be seen that history is always developing in the direction of advancement however tortuous it is. The purpose of retreating from old positions is to develop and consolidate new positions. The adjustment of strategic task means neither abandoning the ultimate goal nor ideologically refuting the ideas that were previously looked upon as the principles for political practice without analysis or purging them totally. All should be examined from the changing macroscopic historical perspective. We need to face more actual conditions and the main strategic goal and strategic task in every historical stage, accordingly investigating whether the principles and ideas dominating the philosophical spirit of the stage are of historical inevitability and rationality. According to this idea, Marxist philosophy tends to take on diverse styles and features and perform different social functions with both the change of the times and the turn of history. It guides and regulates human historical practice and in turn enriches, reforms and develops itself through human historical practice. However, this development does not aim at totally sublating the past history, much less radically changing its principles. Hence, when a succession of new historical challenges must be met on a large scale in the face of the change of the times, it is wrong to follow the beaten track and refuse to make either further exploration or timely changes; however, it is even worse to attempt to totally deny or play tricks with the basic ideas and dominant principles with the easy excuse of exploration and changes. It is a pity that both tendencies are shown to different degrees in the present situation of the Chinese academia.

Any development is the extension of history- not the simple extension, though. Not only is the course of development full of twists and turns, but also there are seeming returns to the starting point though the returns aim at seeking a new starting point to advance towards a higher goal instead of abandoning all that is attained fruitfully. When mentioning that the proletarian socialist revolutions cannot but make its way through hardships and frustration, Marx said, "proletarian revolutions, like those of the nineteenth century, constantly criticize themselves, constantly interrupt themselves in their own course, return to the apparently accomplished, in order to begin anew; they deride with cruel thoroughness the half-measures, weaknesses, and paltriness of their first attempts, seem to throw down their opponents only so the latter may draw new strength from the earth and rise before them again more gigantic than ever, recoil constantly from the indefinite colossalness of their own goals – until a situation is created which makes all turning back impossible [...]"[1] Marxist philosophy has gone through a similar course of development to that mentioned above. "Return to Marx," as well as "returning to the original texts of Marx," is the common orientation of those who are committed to the study of Marxist philosophy. As Marx vividly described above, it is certainly correct and sensible to redo the work without hesitation so as to advance Marxist thought and cause stoutly and thoroughly.

We return to both a real Marx and his original works for the purpose of further exploring the real essence of the change of Marxist philosophical revolution by employing the rich experience of the history of revolution and theory (both successful and unsuccessful, both positive and negative) for over a century together with abundant and vivid facts in the historical development of the world after Marx. Through the exploration we further delve deep into the new theoretical level and spiritual connotation so that Marxist theories can not only be applied to destroying an old order of the world, but also to successfully establish a new world order; additionally, they can be successfully employed not only during the old era of revolution and war but also during the new era of peace and development, which is the call of the times as well as a new historical mission of Marxist philosophy. A big issue that the present Chinese Marxist philosophers concentrate on is whether Marxist philosophy is able to face the challenge of the times and shoulder heavy historical responsibilities.

The present book of Zhang Yibing was written with his above ideological background after over ten years' study. In this book the author aims at restoring the principles of subjectivity of Marxist philosophy with no ignorance of its principles of objectivity; he intends carrying forward the humanistic spirit of Marxist philosophy without any derogation from its scientific spirit. Objecting to mechanistic philosophy, the book firmly defends the materialist stand. Emphasizing the basic role of practice in Marxist philosophy, it does not deny the priority of nature over human social practice and argues the priority will be maintained forever. The author refers to a variety of achievements in "Western Marxist" studies, but he remains sober to notice and resist many of their wrong basic orientations.

---

1   Marx, Karl. *Karl Marx on Society and Social Change*. University of Chicago Press, 1973. p. 169.

Despite special emphasis laid on reforming and improving the expositive system of Marxist philosophy, this book also aims at making a philosophical exploration to the China's political context.

I believe the publication of this book will vigorously promote the further study and discussion on Marxist philosophy in China.

Sun Bokui

Nanjing University, August 1994

PREFACE FOR THE THIRD EDITION

The year of 2009 means special to me. My *Back to Marx*[1] composed 10 years ago will be published as the second edition by Jiangsu People's Publishing House. And my *Subjective Dimension of Marxist Historical Dialectics* will be published as the third edition by Wu Han University Press. The work of revision makes me turn back and enter the past once again, in which I was excited to pass by my previous self, ideas, discussions, arguments and other characters in my books. Despite the rapid changes in the past ten years, it is pleasant to see that these works of mine have been receiving wide attention in the Chinese academic circles, which might also explain an important renaissance of China's contemporary thought, that is, a re-presence of Marxist scientific social criticism generated from and co-existent with the commodity-market world. This academic situating contains very complex historical values and meanings by itself.

The Subjective Dimension of Marxist Historical Dialectics, completed in 1993, is my first monograph on Marxist philosophical thought. The "Preface to the Second Edition" mainly explains the historical background of the situating logics in the book. This time, I want to illustrate its specific historical context and central ideas. I believe that the key words here are the pairs of general historical materialism and special historical material-ism, of foundation and dominance, of the subjective dimension and the objective dimension, and of 'quasi-natural-ness' and material-subjugation. Although 15 years have gone since 1993, during which time I published several other books, such as *Back to Marx* and *The Spiritual Meeting with*

---

1 Yibing, Zhang. *Back to Marx: The Philosophical Discourse in the Context of Economics, 2nd Edition.* Nanjing: Jiangsu People's Press, 2009.

Marx[2], today's journey to the thought of home is still fascinating, with the same deep questions and logical interpretations as before.

All in all, this book is to correct some mistakes in the traditional framework of Marxist philosophical illustration.

Firstly, the different basic and dominant principles of general historical materialism and special historical materialism. Marxist historical materialism holds a negative criticism of the phenomenon that under specific historical conditions, the economic forces become the external power to dominate social existence. However, the Second International theorists reversed it into a positive foundation for general socio-historical existence and development. Despite the serious disapproval by Engels shortly before his death, this misconception has become a "basic principle" in the traditional framework of philosophical interpretation. Hence, my first issue is to deal with the complicated logical relationship in the theoretical situating of Marxist historical materialism, especially, the difference between Marx's positive recognition of the actual *foundation* of socio-historical existence and development in general historical materialism and his historical identification of socio-historical existence and development under certain conditions in special historical materialism. For Marx and Engels, only the production and reproduction of the material living condition become the general foundation of the existence and development for human society, which appears as an *eternal natural necessity*. On the other side, different times and phases in history would always generate some special social relations, forces, and even concepts that historically become the *dominant* relationship and ideology in social life, for example, the production of humans themselves in primitive society, the symbolic myths in tribe life, the feudal political structure and divinity in the Middle Ages, and the economic control and fetishism in the bourgeois world. In the eyes of Marx, the rise and demise of these dominant social forces under certain conditions are all *historical*. His special historical materialism mainly targets the economic-material relationship in capitalism. Thus, the traditional framework of philosophical interpretation failed to delineate the real relationship of the basic and dominant forces of social history in Marx's general historical materialism and special historical materialism. (A century later, Baudrillard still made the same mistake in his opposition to Marxist historical materialism.)[3]

---

2 Zhang, and Meng Mujia. *The Spiritual Meeting with Marx: A Contemporary Interpretation of Original Marxism.* Beijing: China Renmin University Press, 2004.
3 Zhang Yibing. *Contra Baudrillard: Deconstruction of a Postmodern Myth.* Beijing: The Commercial Press, 2009.

Secondly, due to the impact of the Second International theorists, people used to interpret Marxist historical materialism as an *objective reflection* on the essence and movement of social existence but I think it is a *revolutionary and critical* theory when Marx and Engels established historical materialism and historical dialectics. (This important point was first put forward by Karl Korsch in his *Marxism and Philosophy*.) If the revolution of thought started in 1845 let Marx and Engels escape the humanistic alienation view of history and observe the socio-historical existence and development based on objective reality for the *scientific objective dimension* of a new worldview, their exploration on this objective dimension rightly aimed at a scientific criticism of capitalism and the final liberation of the proletarian class and all the people in the world as well. It is the *subjective dimension* that Marx and Engels never abandoned and always pursued. Nevertheless, the emphasis on the scientific subjective dimension is not intended for a return to the humanistic subjective logic. Therefore, it is an important theoretical question to differentiate my view from the humanistic school in Western Marxism.

Thirdly, in the capitalist society, the economic power temporarily and historically dominates the human subject, which is the phenomenon of economic material-subjugation. While in the development of social history, there emerges the spontaneous social movement similar to that of nature, which is the phenomenon of 'quasi-natural-ness' in certain historical conditions. Marx and Engels always negated those abnormal phenomena of material-subjugation and 'quasi-natural-ness' throughout their philosophical thought, with the wish to sublate the historical subject-object reversal in the free realm of human liberation. However, the traditional textbook of historical materialism continually extended such an ad hoc negative doctrine into a general law of social history. And the process of human society is consequently misinterpreted as a "natural historical process" independent of human will. In fact, when Marx made a metaphorical reference to the capitalist mode of production as something similar to nature, his cognition essentially contained a more important theoretical meaning, which precisely accorded with his validation of the historicality of capitalism. In other words, Marx's illustration of the social economic 'quasi-natural-ness' and material-subjugation is intended to explain that the capitalist mode of production *has not fundamentally gone beyond the natural world (animals) and thus not been the real beginning of human social development.* The traditional framework of philosophical interpretation was not aware of this deep analysis. Instead, they made a literal and simplified illustration to mistakenly extend the *specific distortion* before the capitalist mode of production to a general law of social development. (This new theoretical question and reflection was first put forward in "Is the Development of Human Social History Always a Process of Social History?" published in *Tian Fu New Idea*, which immediately aroused heated discussions across the academic circle in China[4]. In 1992, I published another essay "On Marx's Ad Hoc Stipulation of 'quasi-natural-ness' in the Development of Social History" to deepen the understanding of this issue.)

Those are the major points proposed in *The Subjective Dimension of Marxist Historical Dialectics* firstly composed 15 years ago.

In the third edition, there are not any substantial changes except for some editing works. In addition, I have included in the appendix two relevant essays respectively published in *Tian Fu New Idea* in 1988 and in *Philosophical Researches* in 1992. For this Edition, Meng Qingbin and Chen Peng made great effort in literature revision and Dr. Luo Huilin took the work of editing the whole book. I would like to express my deep thanks to them. And, I would specially acknowledge my debt to Director Tao Jialuo and his staff in the Academic Branch of Wuhan University Press. Without their hard work, the third edition would not have met the reader.

Zhang Yibing

Nanjing, End of 2008

---

4   During the years from 1989 to 1992, *Philosophical Researches* published many essays by such authors as Chen Zhiliang, Yang Geng, Liu Senlin, Wang Guiming, Tao Fuyuan, Liu Chengkui. In addition, Wang Jinfu wrote an essay on the same topic published in the *Journal of Suzhou University* in 1993.

PREFACE FOR THE SECOND EDITION

For a person engaged in academic study, nothing is more gratifying than learning that his ideas have attracted interest or want understanding and criticizing yet. Naturally, I was greatly gratified at the republication of The *Subjective Dimension of Marxist Historical Dialectics* that was finished in 1993. Opening the book on such a peaceful night, my memory extended as the pages being turned one after one.

Time always swiftly passes before one is aware. In retrospect, when I started composing the book over ten years ago, I was in the middle of the experimental ideological process of "returning to Marx." By then I had surely read all the works of both Marx and Engels more than once and even reaped initial benefits of textual study of such treatises as Lenin's "Philosophical Notes" and Marx's *The German Ideology*, but regrettably, I had neither noticed the latest data group of *MEGA2* (the second edition of *Die Marx-Engels Gesamtausgabe*) nor truly developed my unique historical approach to textual study. Although I insisted on "getting rid of the traditional framework of philosophical interpretation" and had some specialized opinions on Marxian theories on natural history, my theoretical discourse was, deep in theoretical framework, ultimately trapped in the old system. That may be what Polanyi called focal awareness and implicit paradox in the context of support. In order to make it clear, I would like to start with a brief review of my philosophical thinking and study.

It might be remembered that in the late 1970s, corresponding to the theoretical reflection and political correction, the domestic academia tried its best to banish the haze the full-scale ten-year calamity had brought to people's mind as well. Unsatisfied with the "left" ideological opinions, quite many scholars appealed to the reversion from "the philosophy of struggle" that the Gang of Four threw into disorder to Marxist philosophical system before "the Cultural Revolution," which can be considered as the theoretical "radical reform," or as it were, a kind of clarification. However, shortly afterwards in 1982, at a seminar on "Modern Natural Science and Marxist Epistemology" held in Guilin, seven academics from the Department of Philosophy of Fudan University, Shanghai such as Yu Wujin and Wu Xiaoming submitted an outline on Marxist epistemology in which they raised enlightening questions in the Marxist philosophical world at that time: Is the so-called "original Marxist" that we once considered absolutely correct and tried to "revert to" exactly a stagnant system? Does it need to develop further in the face of new achievements in natural science and western philosophy? You can imagine what a great shock those unconventional questions have brought to us Chinese scholars. It could even rank among the significant "events" in Chinese philosophical circles in the early 1980s. Though the event later ended against all expectations, it is a chance for me to develop a new line of thought.

Another thing that struck me deeply was the vigorous study groups on "the modernization of philosophy" that the Institute of Philosophy of Chinese Academy of Social Sciences took the lead in holding in 1985. Going through three rounds, the study groups spread from Beijing to other places. The participants consisted of nearly all the young and middle-aged scholars in the whole Chinese philosophical academia of the time. Certainly, "the modernization of philosophy" here particularly denotes the modernization of Marxist philosophy in a context related to Deng Xiaoping's "Three Orientations" of education. The lectures were mostly given by some well-known scholars from the Institute of Philosophy of Chinese Academy of Social Sciences and the academia of Beijing, covering significant development in both natural and social science of the day. Through the long duration of study, with no exception every lecture led off with such extreme remarks: "The thirty-year continuous Soviet Stalinist system has far lagged behind reform and development. Confronted with new achievements in natural science and the situation of reform and opening-up, philosophy is supposed to be modernized." Actually, the main purpose and study approach of all the lectures were nothing but injecting some new concepts into the original theoretical system. In spite of that, such practice was of revolutionary significance and theoretical charm at that time.

It was impacted by both above that I was determined to devote myself to "the modernization" of Marxist philosophy at one time.

First of all, I paid great attention to the discussion on such newborn disciplines as the methodology of natural science and modern cognitive science and was so keen on the attempt to modernize Marxism by grafting such new ideas on natural science as system theory and science of complexity onto the fundamental principles of "Marxism" (actually the explanation of traditional textbooks) that I even published a series of articles in which many new terms like the "field of practice," the "pattern of practice," the "construction of practice," and the "functionality of practice" were coined. However, the further my study went on, the harder I felt it to expand the theoretical dimension. The difficulty does not lie in techniques but precisely in the shake of "Marxism" which I considered as established foundation because Marxist theories that we were always thinking "at hand" cannot actually be immediately connected with contemporary natural science that has undergone profound qualitative changes. Such embarrassment in theoretical logics obliged me re-examine the former classical systematic philosophy that was firmly believed to be equal to "Marxism." I must make it clear whether something is wrong with *Marxist theories*, which is tantamount to my doubts about the solidity of the theoretical basis under my own foot (I knew well that once my doubts were proved right, the illegitimacy of all classical bases of Marxism would be declared. Neither other scholars, especially those of the older generation who devoted their life to the theories, nor I was willing to see such a result. However, truth is always being presented in its own way even if the way is too ruthless as far as its accepters are concerned).

I found, after in-depth study, that the validity of the textbook system of former Soviet and Eastern European pattern we inherited and added Chinese characteristics to, or at least the validity of its basis had been an unproved presupposition within the sphere of discourse in the whole Chinese Marxist academia since the founding of our People's Republic. In people's mind, the edifice of Marxian theories had been completed by former Soviet and Eastern European scholars (who owned first-hand literature). Our task was no more than adding something with Chinese characteristics to the construction to elaborate on and complement details. The so-called modernity and modernization of Marxist philosophy referred to nothing but the external joining of the fundamental principles of the existing systematic philosophy, new concepts of natural science and contemporary western philosophical culture. Thus, the "new development" of Marxist philosophy within such a presupposition tended to be the reproduction of new concepts plus the reorganization of subsystems within some existing system. However, self-evident presuppositions in theoretical logic sometimes exactly deserve to be questioned. My realization came that basic Marxist theories is not a problem solved and not only a "contemporary" one that develops in a simple way. If the development of Marxist philosophy is confined to the previous prejudiced views of dogmatism, whether Marxist philosophy is combined with the latest natural science, western philosophy and trend of thought in present society or the reality of Chinese reform, it will necessarily lead to either a weirder theoretical product or futilely bypassing Marxism. If that is served as the truth of Marxism to guide the practice of reform, you can imagine what the result is. I am fully confident that facing the new social reality and academic problems in earnest, above all, calls for a careful, detailed and even thorough examination of Marxist historical Circumstance, which is also my motive for "returning to Marx" suddenly in the last few years.

Next, I encountered a greater blow of thought when I set foot in the study of Marxism in the middle and late 1980s. In 1990, I published a booklet entitled *Broken Wings of Reason - Criticism of Western Marxism* (Nanjing Publishing House, 1990), from which, however, my stronger academic unease started. In the book, I assumed the airs of criticizing scholars of Western Marxism from a right standpoint of Marxism, discussing all their faults. Nevertheless, I felt indescribable embarrassment in my heart of hearts. As an academic school of "Marxism," a considerable number of exponents of Western Marxism made it their theoretical logic to graft various modern western trend of philosophical and cultural thought onto Marxism, constructing a variety of radical opposed discourse outside the mainstream of modern bourgeois academia, which is exactly based on elaborate interpretation of Marxist classics. As I pointed out,

"Like the young Lukacs's understanding of Marx's *Das Kapital* and the *Critique of Political Economy* prior to his writing *History and Class Consciousness*, Fromm's study of the Young Marx's *Economic and Philosophical Manuscripts of 1844* when writing Marx's *Concept of Man*, and Alfred Schmidt's *Cognition of Marx's Economic Manuscripts* during 1857 and 1858 when composing *The Concept of Nature in Marx*, Louis Althusser's *Reading Capital* is, as far as it goes, a considerable accomplishment in textual study."[1]

Regardless of their underlying framework of interpretation that was proved to be potentially false, if we did not personally study Marx's texts carefully that scholars of Western Marxism had carefully studied but simply focused

---

1   See Zhang Yibing. "An In-depth Interpretation: Western Marxism and Georg Lukács." *Philosophical Trends.* 8 (1999).

on their explicit conclusion, it would be difficult to judge whether they were right or wrong accurately. As a consequence, I realized the validity of my "criticism" was doubtful. Accordingly I further take the position that the Circumstance of criticizing Western Marxism remains to be broaden in both depth and extent until our own accomplishments are enhanced, which, likewise, requires us to fulfill the historic task of "returning to Marx."

Thirdly, in order to avoid such academic dilemma we have another option for escaping from it; that is, we can simply conclude that classical "dialectical materialism and historical materialism" can be out of date, independently procure new systematic philosophy without clarifying the historical circumstance of Marxist philosophy, and then act on our own within the system rather than get access to Chinese social changes and the contemporary world culture "face to face". That is really a gross self-deception like an ostrich burying its head in the sand, which is described in my academic argumentation as "practical materialism." Although I later found it actually an unsuccessful production still conditioned by systematic philosophy, at that time I was excited at it for quite a long time and spared no effort to speak highly of it, asserting to what a large extent the expression of "practical materialism" is a great reform. But soon I was aware that even with the same slogan of constructing "practical materialism" the theoretical orientations expressed by different exponents were widely divergent. What is more, people could establish various new systems at their pleasure, for instance, "humanism," "quasi-philosophy" or "practical humanism," and then simply designate the systematic philosophy as "the present form of Marxist philosophy." Is there any authentic ground for such designation? Are they just expressing their own philosophical ideas in the name of Marxism? The introspection is adequate to prevent me from making such theoretical transgress as the systematic philosophy called "the present form of Marxist philosophy" any more.

By then I had fully recognized that I still had a superficial and one-sided grasp of Marxist philosophy as a whole. If we want to be competent to communicate with "the present age," introduce Marxism to the present age, and respond to as well as solve new problems in the proper perspective, one historic task to be accomplished is to clarify afresh the Circumstance of Marxist theories. Though I had expected it is likely to be a tremendous theoretical project, what happened were still far beyond my expectation.

In the late 1980s, I began to make a systematic study of Marxian texts. But by the beginning of writing the present book, I had not found an independent way of thinking to accomplish such a theoretical project. Despite my definite rejection of the traditional framework of philosophical interpretation, what attracted my greater attention is a dispute on specific academic opinions rather than *new approaches to interpretation or heterogeneous fields of study* (which was achieved in the later *Back to Marx - the Philosophical Discourse in the Context of Economics*)[2]. To be specific, what I focused on was a key issue in the study of historical materialism that I showed an interest in as early as in the middle 1980s, that is to say, some fatal misinterpretation in the conventional understanding of Marxian theory of the spontaneous process of society. It was obvious that both Marx and Engels demonstrated the abnormal "process of natural history" in the negative and critical context, in the hope that the particular historical "inversion" of the subject and object could be subject to sublation in the realm of freedom of human liberation, when confronted with spontaneous economy (especially the situation in capitalist society in which economic power dominates humans as subjects) in the development of social history analogous to blind movements in nature. However, such a special statement of theirs was misinterpreted as the general law of the development of social history in classical textbooks on historical materialism. The so-called spontaneous historical process of society was mistaken for the common state of the whole development of social history. The development of human social history was thereby interpreted as a process of natural history independent of the human will and submissive to "the order of nature" in society. Simultaneously, I further discovered two opposite opinions on the development of social history in the development of modern western Marxist philosophy: the humanistic school from the young Lukacs to Sartre vs. the scientistic school from Althusser to analytical Marxism. The former is called "critical Marxist" from the perspective of the subject while the latter is provided with a positivist orientation proceeding from objective laws. According to the two extreme opinions, Marxist historical dialectics is "divided into two sides": it either emphasizes nothing but subjectivity and critical nature or simply highlights decisive objective factors in social existence, resulting in a metaphysical logical confrontation.

Facing the academic dilemma, I set such a temporary academic goal as exploring the overall Circumstance of Marxist historical dialectics: it uplifts the revolutionary critical spirit of historical dialectics again on the basis of the principles of historical materialism as well as sticks to the principles. As I claimed at that time, "it not only illustrates the initiative and dominant position of humans as subjects in a scientific way but also adheres

---

2   Zhang Yibing, *Back to Marx: The Philosophical Discourse in the Context of Economics*. Nanjing: Jiangsu People's Press, 2009.

to the common basis of material production and objective necessity of the development of social history. Marxist scientific concept of history is supposed to be the all-sided unity of historical dialectics that historically affirms the human role as the subject and historical materialism that insists on proceeding from the considerations of practical material production." Meanwhile, I defined my academic attempt as "the subjective dimension of Marxist historical dialectics" in a special sense as distinguished from the humanistic concept of subject in Western Marxism. Thus, I initiated the differentiation of general historical materialism from special historical materialism, the confirmation of the basic and dominant issues in the logics of historical materialism. I also originated the basic idea of employing the theory of 'quasi-natural-ness' and the theory of material-subjugation as the facade of construction, and discussed the historical and practical significance of my theory respectively from diverse angles such as the historical study and monographic study of developmental study. From the current point of view, the theories of 'quasi-natural-ness' and material-subjugation are still a kind of crucial theoretical identification. Because only through the establishment of the categories of 'quasi-natural-ness' and material-subjugation was I able to correct the serious misinterpretations of the major ideas of Marx and Engels made by the traditional framework of philosophical interpretation and to reunify the historical dialectics which had lopsidedly been split into the two logical extremes of subjectivity and objectivity by Western Marxism as well. Such an academic attempt is supposed to be of considerable academic value and practical significance whether at that time or at present.

However, some limitations must be pointed out. In the first place, the research methods I adopted in the present book are tentative. The description of the development of Marxian philosophical thought in Chapter One and Chapter Two contains my historical analysis and textual interpretation to some degree, which are, however, neither comprehensive nor standardized. Secondly, I did not get access to the crucial recent data of *MEGA2*, especially volumes of economic notes associated with the comprehension of the real context of changes in Marxian philosophical thought. Thirdly, while analyzing the theory of 'quasi-natural-ness' and the theory of material-subjugation, I was indulging in the method of "making matches" between homogeneous subjects that I myself later definitely criticized. In view of the above, readers need to critically discriminate among the discussions in the book. If possible, it would be better to have my subsequent book *Back to Marx - the Philosophical Discourse in the Context of Economics* for reference.

In preparing this second edition of the book, I have kept the book entirely the same as before except polishing it in language, correcting a few obvious printing errors and revising notes and references. I am happy to express my thanks to Professor Wu Yufang and my students, Wu Jing and Meng Mugui, for their painstaking help in reading and checking the text of this book.

Finally, I would like to acknowledge my debt to Henan People's Press, who published the first edition of this book in 1995. Meanwhile, my heartfelt thanks also go to the relevant personnel of Nanjing University Press, especially, Mr. Huang Jidong, the editor, for the opportunity they offered to publish the second edition of this book.

It is believed that one is lucky to witness a transition between two centuries and one is happy to encounter a change of the millennium. And we surprisingly have the two opportunities at a time. Life is like morning dew and time flies like an arrow! Isn't it enough to cause sorrow for the limitedness of our existence? In the first spring of the millennium, we have no reason not to be optimistic about the future. Let us make joint efforts to testify our genuine existence as Oriental thinkers.

Zhang Yibing

Hei Jialong (Wuchang), February 2001

PREFACE FOR THE FIRST EDITION

After reading the abstract of this book, quite many readers may feel deeply shocked: Isn't it what Marx argued, "The development of human social history is a process of natural history"? Aren't you criticizing Marx? Here, I can tell readers with clearness and exactness that I am not criticizing Marx but correcting some misinterpretation of Marxist conception of history within the traditional framework of philosophical interpretation[1].

Obviously, this issue is deeply rooted in complexity and thus very difficult to discern. I would like to start with the confusion over the issue and the resolution of the confusion. As Walter Benjamin writes in *Berlin Childhood around 1900*, "the predilections for seeing everything I care about approach me from a distance."[2] Similarly, the roads of academic exploration approach me from all sides and gradually become clear in my mind map.

More than ten years ago when I was still a graduate who majored in philosophical principles at the Department of Philosophy of Nanjing University, my instructor, Prof. Li Huayu, chaired our seminars on historical materialism. Then each of us was required to collect data on our own and make a presentation on a certain subject of historical materialism. The topic I selected was "As to the Logical Base of Historical Materialism." In this assignment, I viewed the subject from the perspective of historical

---

1 The "the traditional framework of philosophical interpretation" is a special term to indicate our conventional textbook discourse. See "Historical Restoration and New Theoretical Construction of Marxist Philosophy." *Jianghai Academic Journal.* 3 (1989).

2 Walter Benjamin. *Berlin Childhood Around 1900.* Harvard University Press, 2006. pp. 14-15.

investigation instead of stopping on the plane of the debate on the subject in the academia of the time (in 1980). Although in the discussion, I, based on the analysis of historical philosophy prior to Marxism, properly argued that the logical base of the conception of history of Marxist philosophy is the production and reproduction of material life, there was still some indescribable regrettable imperfection in my argument, which always haunted me in faint traces. I first started with the historical pivot beyond man that ancient "natural determinism" followed by a transition from "creationism" to humanistic conception of history that stresses human subjective initiative. In my opinion of the day, what is the closest to Marxist conception of history is the objective logical foothold established by excluding human nature once again from the cause of the historical development in Hegelian philosophy. The scientific conception of history in Marxist philosophy was established by means of Marx's and Engels' historical establishment of practice – the active material creation of human subject, resulting in the true revelation of the objective laws of the development of human social history. Marx's first great discovery is precisely the dynamic role that scientifically identifies humans as subjects in historical realistic concrete social material life[3]. Up to this point I strongly became aware of two essential logical layers in Marxist scientific conception of history: *It not only scientifically illustrate the dynamic and dominant role of humans as subjects, but also adheres to both the basis of general material production and the objective necessity of the development of social history.* It is a unity of historical dialectics that historically affirm man's subjective role and historical materialism that insists on proceeding from realistic material production. However, the above ideas are hard to find out within the traditional framework of philosophical interpretation adopted as my theoretical context of the time.

At that time, Marxist historical materialism is always interpreted as something almost unrelated to the real subject of history, "man." Within the framework, the colourful social being of humans is reduced to the simple addition of three substances: geographical environment, the population decreasing to a natural quantity, and the modes of material production seemingly unrelated to "man," which appears a dry statement. The basic contradiction and "dialectic movement" between the productive forces and the relations of production as well as between the economic base and the superstructure in the social movement appear to be objective processes separate from man (, which is virtually only the interpretation

---

3   Zhang Yibing. "The Historical Examination of the Logical Starting Point of Historical Materialism." *Journal of Nanjing University.* 2 (1982).

of dogmatism on the *objective dimension* of Marxist historical dialectics). Most importantly, the Marxian theory that the economic force represents the leading force dominating humans as subjects at a certain historical stage is interpreted as the general condition of social history; accordingly, the development of human social history is considered as a "process of natural history" both *independent of the human will and submissive to the "natural laws"* of society. As far as these points are concerned, the traditional framework seems to stick to materialist principles in the development of social history indeed, give prominence to scientific *epistemological* and *methodological* characters of historical materialism indeed, and abolish the root of idealist conception of history. Nevertheless, the general dialectics of the development of social history is totally "vaporized" within the framework; so is Marx's statement that "history does nothing" but the practice of humans as subjects, historically, concretely and realistically, *creates* the fundamental course of human social history from the lower level to the higher and from realm of necessity to realm of freedom. Human *subjective initiative* in social history simply remains to be the reaction of social consciousness, gradually withering in the aspect of subjective initiative. In the final analysis, Marxist conception of history is retrogressed into the Hegelian argumentation that "history is an objective course beyond man."

At that moment, I felt a dull but growing pain by a deep consciousness of imperfectness, but I could never scientifically discern the sticking point deep in the traditional framework of philosophical interpretation.

However, where there is confusion, there may be the impulsive sparks of thinking. My subsequent thought arose in the seminars on the history of Marxist philosophy chaired by Prof. Sun Bokui. The study of classical texts on Marxist philosophy offered me the first-hand data I needed and spurred me on to start a long and tough time of study (1983-1988) as well. Although the study was really beset with difficulties and was even suspended for a time after my graduation, I staggered and at last found a way out. Finally came the realization that the significance of the ideological revolution that Marxist philosophy accomplished is, above all, that it establishes a practical, active and revolutionary scientific conception of the world, namely *practical materialism*, whose theoretical essence is not the intuitive reflection of external objects as interpreted within the traditional framework of philosophical interpretation, but *the scientific cognition based on the historical change of external objects and humans by the subjects through objective material practice.* In particular, as Marx's first great discovery, materialist conception of history is by no means just the so-called onlooking intuitive reflection of the objective social laws beyond humans as subjects, but the scientific comprehension that is constructed by historical, concrete and realistic human social practice and with which man scientifically understands nature, human beings and the historical course of society. Marxist conception of history, in the first place, discloses the general *base* of objective material production in the development of human social history and scientifically clarifies the objective laws of historical dialectics, which is the objective angle of historical materialism (as well as the Marxist conception of history in a broad sense). Based on this premise, Marx also started from the subject of human society to seek the dominant factors in different historical phases of society. While investigating the history of human civilization, he pointed out that the economic force in social-economic formation is a decisive and dominant factors independent of the human will (, which is the Marxist conception of history in a narrow sense). However, it is not a constant state of the development of human social history. As the productive forces of human society develop, humans as subjects will ultimately transcend the passively determined historical status and become the master who creates history on his own initiative.

Therefore, historical materialism cannot be simply understood as the negative spontaneous determinism, for it is the *spiritual power to inspire people to struggle* rather than the "empirical science" that brings inertia to people and deprives the practical and dynamic role of humans as subjects with commandment of "having a high regard for objective laws". It calls for the change of the world and the establishment of human initiative on the basis of practical historical dialectics, which both aim at exerting human objective subjectivity better. With this general theoretical orientation, I tried to have a fresh understanding of Marx and his practical materialism based on my independent study. Thus, I discovered Marx's theory on 'quasi-natural-ness' in the logical perspective of subjective dimension in the dialectics of the development of social history that had been misinterpreted and neglected by the traditional framework of philosophical interpretation for a long time, and found the key joint of the theory and modern social development. In the following study, I made a further discovery of the intrinsic basis of Marxian theory of 'quasi-natural-ness', that is, the significant doctrine of material-subjugation in his theory of social criticism. I was greatly gratified at these discoveries. The following are the main arguments of my study, also an abstract of this book.

I first started with the interpretation of Marx's statement that "the development of human social history is a process of natural history" within the traditional framework of philosophical interpretation. It seems to me that in the present study of historical materialism when defining the objectivity of the development of social history, researchers mostly tend to quote Marx's statement that "the development of social-economic formation is a process of natural history" from the preface in Volume One of his *Das Kapital*. In my opinion, the purpose to quote such a statement within the traditional framework of philosophical interpretation is actually biased and additionally the statement is garbled to represent the general features of the whole development of human social history, resulting in far more difference between the quotation and what Marx originally meant, which is exactly where the initial deviation of the major misinterpretation lies.

Hence, I have to proceed with Marxian historical delimitation of so-called "social-economic formation." Certainly, in the preface in the first volume of *Das Kapital* Marx clarified that his book is aimed at disclosing the economic laws of capitalism ("modern society"). When defining the economic necessity of capitalist modes of production, he claimed that humans as subjects are nothing but the "personifications of economic categories"[4] under such a specified historical condition. Meanwhile, he further pointed out "the evolution of the economic formation of society is viewed as a process of natural history."[5] Herein Marx originally meant to explicate certain *particularity* in capitalist modes of production that *the social life of humans as subjects reversely assume the non-subjective spontaneous course enslaved by the materialized economic forces created by themselves* (, which I define as material-subjugation in the development of social history herein to distinguish it from the Young Marx's humanistic doctrine of "estrangement"). Since humans as subjects are extrinsically presented by the personification of the object of economic process, the social-historical development of humans as subjects becomes a process analogous to the history of nature independent of the human will like the spontaneous course without the subject (, which is described as "'quasi-natural-ness'" in my book). Such is Marx's elaboration on specific economic laws in the development of capitalist society, from which he, however, did not derive and extend the argument that "the development of human social history is a process of natural history forever." (The latter is the misinterpretation of theoreticians from the Second International, which has been distorted into the existing false stereotype within the traditional framework of philosophical interpretation via the "legal" verdict given by the academia of the Soviet Union.)

Apparently, according to the historical materialist interpretation of the traditional framework, social-economic formation is defined as the

---

4   Marx, Karl. *Das Kapital: A Critical Analysis of Capitalist Production*. Appleton, 1889. p. xix.
5   *Ibid.*, p. xix.

economic base together with the superstructure (the productive forces are also involved in some definitions), becoming the general social formation or structure. Then the conclusion that "the development of human social history is a process of natural history forever" is logically drawn from Marx's statement mentioned above. From my point of view, this is a serious theoretical misinterpretation because it practically confuses the developmental laws during specific periods of human social history (the special historical materialism, Marx disclosed that the external control of economy over humans leads to a state in history identical with that dominant in unconscious nature) with the general laws of social development, mistaking the historical phenomenon that the historical laws of human society are manifested by a constant natural law of the development of human society in general.

As a matter of fact, the term "social-economic formation" (which should be translated into "the economic formation of society," to be exact, for the original German is Ökonomische Gesell-schaftsformation) employed by Marx has a specified connotation. It refers not *generally* to the economic formations in the whole social history but to the specific historical stage since human history developed into civilization, especially in the developmental form of capitalist society. The essential point of this historical stage is the intrinsic "*antagonism*" of the development of social history dependent on private ownership (See the preface of *Marx's Critique of Political Economy*, but the italicized words are the emphasis given by the author of this book). As to the division of historical stages, we are familiar with Marxian doctrine of "Five Major Forms" that the development of human society is divided into primitive society, slave society, feudal society, capitalist society and communist (or socialist) society. This abstract summarization is at the cost of necessary richness. Moreover, in accordance with the *practical* and *specific historical* position of humans as subjects in the development of social history. Marx divided the development of human society into three great forms (types). For my part, it is a doctrine on Marxist conception of social history from the perspective of historical dialectics that is of great importance but has been ignored.

Marx developed his analysis of the three great forms from different theoretical perspectives as follows: Firstly, from the perspective of the position of humans as subjects in the historical development, Marx came up with the social forms of "the Relations of personal dependence," of "personal independence founded on objective dependence" and of "free individuality, based on the universal development of individuals and on their subordination of their communal, social productivity as their social wealth."[6] Next, in term of human social relations, social forms can be classified into that of "a local connection resting on blood ties, or on primeval, natural or master-servant relations," that with the manifestation of "objective bond" as well as that of "universally developed individuals, whose social relations, as their own communal relations."[7] Thirdly, in view of objective laws of social development, there appears society of natural necessity, society of economic necessity and "society of free human development." The first two are "realm of necessity" in the "prehistoric" development of human society, while the last is "realm of freedom." The second great social form designated by Marx above is precisely the model of the *economic formation of society*.

For Marx, the economic formation of society is not the general form of the development of human history but the product of a specific phase of the development of human social history. In ancient society dominated by natural necessity, it is personal production of humans rather than material production that predominates in the existence and development of human society (, which does not exclude social material production from the general decisive basis of society). When the productive forces reach a certain point, material production will be independent of and dominant over human production. Material production appears as a special economic power, forcing man, as the subject of history, subjected to the rule of external economic necessity. Though man is no longer a slave to natural necessity, showing his independence of nature in the economic force, he becomes a slave to the new objective force created by himself ("the invisible hand" arising from the pell-mell development of commodity economy). Human society, in a sense, exceeds nature (or animality), creating history on its own, but this process of creation is still an activity-in-itself inevitably restricted and therefore blindly developed because, with humans being materially controlled and remaining "economic animals" while history occurring beyond humans as before, the development of human social history still seems analogous to the development of nature (contemporaneous with "manuscripts written in Paris" of 1844). In earlier stages, Marx defined that phenomenon as the "alienation" of history, and he still acknowledged the historic "alienation" (, which should, to be exact, be "material-subjugation") according to the scientific conception of history after the establishment of historical materialism. Nevertheless, he

---

6   Marx, Karl. *Grundrisse: Foundations of the Critique of Political Economy (rough draft)*. Trans. Martin Nicolaus. London; New York: Penguin, 1993. p. 158.

7   *Ibid.*, p. 162.

here specified further that the rule of economic necessity over man is not permanent but temporary. With the development of the productive forces, when personal production regains the predominance, that of the economic force over individuals will not exist. That is to say, by the end of the prehistoric phase of human society the economic formation of society is bound to be transcended; in other words, *the similarity of the development of human society to that of nature as well as material-subjugation is bound to be transcended!*

A careful reader may find some similar ideas held by certain western "humanistic" Marxists: Lukacs's objection to "economic priority" and the subsequent concept of "economic individuals" as well as such propositions by Lefebvre and Fromm as that it is the spontaneous domination of economic laws over social history that is supposed to be transcended. They alleged that the human liberation predicted by Marx precisely refers to the sublation of lopsided "economic individuals (animals)" in conjunction with the realization of universally developed individuals, and that the society in which economy predominates will certainly be replaced by a real historical stage of human society, and otherwise. In view of that, we need to make careful differentiation. On the one hand, it should be acknowledged that western Marxists paid justifiable attention to Marx's important statement on historical dialectics, a perspective undergoing a period of long neglect in historical materialism; on the other hand, it must be noticed that on account of their failure to scientifically understand the progressive relationship between the special and the general Marxist scientific conceptions of history and correctly distinguish the dialectical relationship between the foundation and dominant factors of social history, their perspectives cannot but move from negating economic necessity to negating material production, the general social base, eventually deviating from historical materialism in essence and retrogressing to subjective dialectics of humanism.

Now we can return to and have a close look at Marx's argument that "the economic formation of society should be viewed as a process of natural history." Marx specified the 'quasi-natural-ness' in the development of the economic formation of society (he had never referred to the whole development of social history), from which the proposition can be deduced on no account that "the whole development of social history becomes the process of natural history independent of man." In fact, this statement of Marx's simply confirms that only after the emergence of private ownership, especially the society of class antagonism can the society after the emergence of class society belong to the economic formation of society (in high antiquity man depended immediately on nature so that the development of social history at that time was virtually sub-natural). Marx once clearly stated that the "the Asiatic, ancient, feudal and modern bourgeois modes of production may be designated as epochs marking progress in the economic development of society."[8] In these social forms, there exist various blind external necessities, such as the laws of social history alienated as the laws of nature. As we know, Marx was always prudent in the issue of "natural laws." For one thing, he objected to bourgeois classical economists' eternalizing the historical laws of the development of capitalist society and defining them as "natural laws"; for another thing, he employed "natural laws" in a sense opposite to the real human social history. What he stated above evidently bears the second meaning.

Marx argued that the pell-mell development of the economic formation of society (capitalist society in particular) similar to natural development is nothing but a transitional historical state, a certain stage of social development, which accounts for limitation and spontaneity of the development of capitalist society. As the productive forces have improved, the "natural laws" implemented by means of blind destruction are bound to be substituted by the real "laws of social production"; so is the material-subjugation created by man bound to be radically transcended! By then, the development of human social history will no more appear as a process of natural history but a process of human social history in the real sense; moreover, the human role as the subject of history will not fulfilled in *a resultant form of blind multi-dimensional forces* but of a unified conscious creative power. Sublating the external economic necessity, human society will enter realm of freedom from realm of necessity.

It should equally be specified that though Marx's view on the leap from the realm of necessity to the realm of freedom have been frequently cited in previous studies, the deep structure and true significance of such a key point of Marx and Engels' have not been really grasped theoretically. The external necessity of social history, namely the economic laws *functioning blindly* "independent of the human will, has been mostly taken as eternal historical laws so that man seems to be permanently restricted by the objective world, which, however, is quite inaccurate. Historical laws are generally different from natural laws. The latter cannot be created; the former are spontaneous in prehistoric society (, which is what Marx called the first and second social forms) and unlikely to be created consciously likewise. In this sense, man is locked in the social realm of necessity. However, in the future communist society Marx imagined, a real human society with both highly developed material production and universal and free development

---

8   Marx, Karl. *Early Writings*. Harmondsworth: Penguin Books, 1992. p. 426.

of individuals, sublating and presupposing necessity, history will be on the threshold of realm of freedom. At that point man will be the master of his own history, not only correctly understanding and choosing historical laws but also creating his own history wholly consciously in accordance with his own scientific will and practical intention (instead of enslaving nature against ecology!). That is exactly where communism in essence surpasses any previous society. Hence, a succession of Marx's discussion on "real human society" (the overall historical process), "the capital human" (the subject of history), "realm of freedom" (the status and position of human beings in history), and "the union of free individuals" (social structure) all needs careful examination with a *new discourse framework of Marx's own.* Deepening that subject will certainly have considerable theoretical influence over grasping the essence of the development of social history on the basis of historical materialism, learning basic differences between communism and all previous class societies, investigating the latest changes of the present capitalism as well as studying strategically the direction and historical course of current modern socialist construction and all-round reform with Chinese characteristics.

In conclusion, Marx indeed stated in the preface of *Das Kapital* that the development of "the economic formation of human society" is similar to that of natural history. But his "economic formation of society" herein does not generally designate all human social forms, but only in particular the stage in the development of human social history where the economic force historically determines humans as subjects. Marx originally meant to clarify that in the specific historical phases the objective economic force created by humans as subjects is reversely expressed in the dominator of social history ("material-subjugation"), while humans as subjects, unable to be the master of their own activities, abnormally develop into the personification of economic relations; history appears to occur and operate excluded from human beings in a state similar to the pell-mell movement of nature ("'quasi-natural-ness'"). Consequently, social history with humans as the subjects is abnormally objectified by the natural historical process; human subjective activities constituted by human beings themselves turn into objective activities independent of the human will; human history *often* manifests the antihuman nature. The most representative form is capitalist mode of production (Surely, what Marx here expounded is still laissez-faire capitalism and the social forms prior to capitalism).

Such is the original implication of Marx's original idea that the development of social-economic formation in human social history is similar to the process of natural history. However, within the traditional framework of philosophical interpretation such a proposition has been interpreted as something totally contrary to Marxist thought. Seemingly, Marx contended that the economic formation of society is just the general social form so that the whole development of human social history will appear as the process of natural history. In that case, it is better to claim that the dominance of the economic force over man and social history arising from capitalist mode of production is a permanent and unchangeable objective natural phenomenon, which is of no difference from an idealistic bourgeois view. Or rather, the traditional framework of philosophical interpretation seems to argue that capitalism is unsurpassable!

To be sure, we should acknowledge that the starting point of the argument within the traditional framework of philosophical interpretation is not completely wrong. It is known to us all that the development of human social history differs from the unrestrained movement of nature mainly in that the former consists of intentional activities of humans as subjects. That is why in the light of idealism among all previous conceptions of history human subjective motives are viewed as the essence of social history. Definitely opposed to various idealist deterministic views, Marxist materialist conception of history demonstrates scientifically that in the development of human social history exist inherent objective laws, which is the *materialist* principle of Marxist conception of history (including the *objective dimension* of historical dialectics). It is on the basis of Marx's proposition above that the traditional framework of philosophical interpretation illustrates the objective necessity in the development of social history. Such a basic orientation is not wrong. However, Marx only specified certain phases in the development of human social history that are analogous to the process of natural history rather than designated the whole historical course in general; what's more important, herein he certainly demonstrated objective necessity, but he did not prove the *general* necessity of the development of human social history; instead, he *specially* criticized non-subjective economic necessity represented by capitalism in which objects dominate humans, an abnormal state only in the economic formation of society where economy determines everything. Furthermore, both human material-subjugation man himself creates and natural alienation of human activities are destined to be transcended by further development of social history, which is precisely Marxist proletarian value orientation as well as the base of communism.

In my opinion, the traditional framework of philosophical interpretation has only put a theoretically superficial interpretation on this idea. Anyhow, it is generally acceptable to illustrate objective laws of the development of human social history simply in view of this statement of Marx's in the preface of *Das Kapital*. However, Marx took capitalist mode of production as a metaphor for something similar to the movement of nature, which, in essence, has greater theoretical significance, which just accords with the historic significance of his establishment of capitalist system. Alternatively, in order to clarify the proposition that *the capitalist mode of production has not essentially overstepped nature (animals) and nor is it the real beginning of the development of human society*, Marx defined 'quasi-natural-ness' and material-subjugation of the economic formation of society. Nevertheless, the traditional framework of philosophical interpretation has failed to figure out the deep meaning of Marx's analysis, simply generalizing his argument according to its surface meaning and misinterpreting the particular distortion of the development of human history only prior to capitalist mode of production that Marx defined as the general rule of social development.

Next, paying close attention to only one aspect of Marxist conception of social history, namely the *fundamental* principles of historical materialism, the traditional framework of philosophical interpretation has to a large extent ignored the *subjective dimension of historical dialectics*, a deep theoretical logic that Marx equally attached great importance to and applied to the exploration into the dominant factors of the socio-historical course. Historical dialectics is not the contradictory development of objective dialectics in the abstract historical course, but *the logic of practical dialectics based on the realistic and concrete historical status of humans as subjects*. In my judgment, failure to have a scientific understanding of the dialectical relation between two different logical perspectives in Marxist scientific conception of history is critical to the misunderstanding of the essence of Marxist conception of history. The theorists of the Second International initiated the misinterpretation of Marxist philosophy as a kind of "onlooking empirical science" beyond the development of human social history. With the practical initiative of humans as subjects, the core of Marxist philosophy, greatly weakened, Marxist conception of social history seems to focus on no more than the material conditions of the development of social history, whereas the real subject of historical development – real people under given historical conditions – simply shrinks back to have one-sided "subjective initiative" (the opposite of western Marxist humanism). It goes without saying that it is a total deviation from Marxist scientific conception of the world – practical materialism. Such a theoretical misinterpretation has been refuted by both the Russian Revolution (1917) led by Lenin and the socialist revolutionary road with Chinese characteristics inaugurated by Mao Zedong in successful practical socialist movement.

Marxist scientific conception of history, above all, certainly acknowledges that the development of social history follows objective laws and that production and reproduction in human life represent the general foundation of the development of social history; however, all of these are practically and actively constructed by humans as subjects and in no case the natural growth of things beyond people. Marxist philosophy is in essence revolutionary and practical, whose theoretical logic is definitely communism, which is oriented towards the establishment of human roles as subjects along with the ultimate liberation of human beings, and specific ways to achieve communism as well. Marxist philosophy aims not only to interpret the world, but, more importantly, to change it, which is the only slogan written in the banner of Marxist practical materialism! Practical and dynamic dialectics of social history is the essence of Marxian doctrines of 'quasi-natural-ness' and material-subjugation Such is the theoretical gist of the present book.

In addition, there is a need for me to give an account of both principles and conceptions of writing this book. In the book, *refutation* is the first theoretical principle I have established. Since this book tries to correct the misinterpretation of Marxian relation between the development of human social history and the historical course of nature within the traditional framework of philosophical interpretation, I am always telling some of Marx's propositions from something else among quantities of expositions, which is a major theoretical thread. The second one is *radical reform in theoretical logics*, that is, proceeding from authenticity of Marx's theoretical texts and expounding their essence of historical theory in a scientific way. Some researchers are inclined to impose some arguments of their own upon the object of study, leading to theoretical deviations. In this book, I am always as careful as possible to define the logical orientation in the original context and the initial sense of Marxism (although it is impossible according to modern interpretative theories). I did label explicitly all my viewpoints (for example, the terms like "'quasi-natural-ness'" and "material-subjugation"). The third is adhering to a *historical and logical unity* of theories, especially highlighting the historical perspective in studying Marxist philosophy. From my point of view, not least among the main faults in the traditional framework of philosophical interpretation is exactly its failure to study Marxism in accordance with Marxist viewpoints, namely, in a word, the failure to historically study the texts of classical Marxist writers. The overall theoretical framework of this book is proceeding from the considerations of historical thread of the development of Marxist philosophy and establishing the logic of Marxist theories in the context of the history of Marxist philosophy. Fourthly, I persist in the *scientific approach of starting from the internal logic development of theories* to free myself from superficially stringing volumes of external data together in the study of Marxism. As readers can see, the motive force of theoretical construction of this book lies in the quest for two different logical perspectives in Marxist scientific conception of history (the materialist conception of history in a general sense defining material production as the basis of social history vs. the materialist conception of history in a special sense seeking the dominant factors of the development of social history, the logic of the objective description in the objective dimension of historical materialism and historical dialectics vs. the logic of the initiative in the subjective dimension of historical dialectics) as well as the internal connection between them. Apparently, the argument of this book is based on the latter essential logic that has been ignored for long (, which, admittedly, is present *in a metaphorical* way to a considerable degree in Marxian texts). Fifthly, this book does not make a *comprehensive* discussion on Marxist scientific conception of history, but centres on the subjective dimension of practical Marxist historical dialectics, to which little attention has been paid in our theoretical study over a long period of time, that is, showing concern and the ultimate solicitude for the living conditions of humans as subjects pertinent to Marx's criticism of capitalism and scientific socialism. Accordingly, this book is the one on a special subject. The sixth is the integration of theory and practice, which is, likewise, the practical purpose of writing this book. In comparison with the theoretical flowers that are easy to wither, practice is always the evergreen tree. For the study of Marxist scientific theories tends to call forth its internal vitality only when combined with socio-historical practice. Indeed, Marxist philosophy is *a movement of scientific thought* that never ceases developing itself in historical practice.

I am expecting that the book can activate some hard thinking of everyone who intends to be freed from the traditional framework of philosophical interpretation and to adopt a serious attitude towards Marxist theories on social history. Finally yet importantly, I want to clarify that my instructor, Prof. Sun Bokui in Nanjing University, has had considerable influence on the fundamental academic orientation of this book, especially the developmental logic of Marxist philosophy as the basic framework of the book. In the book, the discussion on both the two transitions in the revolution of Marxist philosophy and double logical contradictions derives inspiration directly from similar views in Prof. Sun's *An Exploration of the Explorers' Road*. The two books can be considered to be in direct line of academic descent. For my part, Prof. Sun is an inaugurator in constructing a *discourse of deep historical logic* in Chinese study of the history of Marxist philosophy. We did not have access to Althusser's "epistemological rupture" in the discourse of Pan-structuralism until early in the 1980s. Despite the similarity between Althusser's doctrine of historical stages of Marxist philosophy and our positions in the span of each stage, the two theoretical discourses are still definitely heterogeneous. In this book, I collate and stipulate such a crucial theoretical distinction. Of course, all the arguments of the book reflect my personal points of view, and thus I remain fully responsible for any errors that remain.

Zhang Yibing

City of Stone, March 1993

ACKNOWLEDGEMENTS

Marxist theory of 'quasi-naturalness' and material-subjugation about the phenomena comes forth in a definite historical period of human social development, which, pointed out herein, is a significant content of the subjective dimension of historical dialectics in Marxist scientific view of history. However, for quite a long time this important scientific and critical discourse of Marx has been overlooked. The following important doctrine is advanced and demonstrated de novo by the writer of this book whose study is based on a careful reading of a great quantity of classical literature: the development of human society and history, which is not always a natural historical process, unfolds itself as a historical phenomenon something like the blindfold movement of nature only with a definite functionality of human social practice; in this specific historical period, the human subject becomes aberrant as the slave of external forces (nature and the materialized world created by humans), and the development of the social history is externalized to "a process without subject" similar to the natural historical movement; the phenomena of 'quasi-natural-ness' and material-subjugation in this specific social history cannot be the eternal order of nature, and with the development of human social practice, humankind will surpass this historical existential status in the end, i.e., making for the period of all-round free development, the realm of freedom, from the pre-historical period of human social development, the realm of necessity. Furthermore, the writer held a vivid and thorough discussion of the modern signification of this doctrine from the theoretical perspective of contemporary thought history and the view of natural science, especially, combined with the socialist praxis in China.

This book, which has a new and deep implication and an uppermost expression in such aspects as initiative thoughts and contextual mutual-motion, as history distinguishing and tractatus, as logical penetration and simple lifelikeness, and as theoretical research and reality reflection, offering a creative work on the re-investigation of fundemental theories of Marxism by Zhang Yibing. I hope this book will contribute to greater global communication and dialog among Marxist philosophy researchers. Finally I would like to thank to Nanjing University Press, for their efforts in realizing this book.I also thank Mr. He Huiming for his tireless translation work.

Dennis Simon

Berlin, June 2011

INTRODUCTION

A GENERAL LOGICAL CLUE OF THE THEORY OF SOCIO-HISTORICAL DEVELOPMENT BEFORE MARX

INTRODUCTION

When the dust of years is gently brushed and the grand book of human thought is slowly opened, we see the image of "man" floating between the lines of almost all the pages, making a really fantastic walking scene. The discovery of man's own secrets and his historical development seems to be a constant focus or an inescapable theme for every philosopher. Today, the philosophers and sages are still wrestling with this riddle of the Sphinx that becomes more attractive as time goes by. However, the long cognitive process of human beings and history discouragingly tells us that a fruitless outcome is destined to wait ahead. Every time a mantle of mist is scattered and a faint light glimmers before, a heavier haze will immediately take the vacancy. A deep, old call "Know thyself" echoes in our ears. It seems to come afar, repeating and rebounding between heaven and earth from everlasting to everlasting. The "prehistorical" process of understanding man and history has a real hard period before Marxist scientific view comes into being. Here, I attempt to make a logical introduction before the full extension of the major themes of this book from the perspective of the relation between man and the external world in the general process of cognition.

I.

The ancient outlook of the socio-historical existence and development can be generally regarded as an *external determinism* centred on the worship of nature. As in the analysis of Marx and Engels, the subjectivity of man has not been established and people are completely submissive to nature at that time.

> **It is consciousness of nature, which first appears to men as a completely alien, all-powerful and unassailable force, with which men's relations are purely animal and by which they are overawed like beasts; it is thus a purely animal consciousness of nature (natural religion) just because nature is as yet hardly modified historically.**[1]

Whether in the East or West, whether as an individual or in a group, the man has not found his own strength. The survival of mankind at this time takes the major form of *group life* where the individual subject has not yet been separated. The individual is cast in a bleak corner of oblivion. Although the people of that time produce a number of the means of subsistence and production for survival, they are limited to their own basic needs and confined within a small place. The primitive tools of production, monotonous labours, clumsy methods…All these constraints render man unable to become the master of himself and his surroundings, so much so that the whole social and historical movement seems *irrelevant* to him and becomes an independent progress governed by some objective super force. Thus, the decisive part for the foundation of history becomes an objective natural process of the *superhuman*. And man knees down before the sacrosanct nature.

The early anthropomorphic and animistic worship of nature does contain an *unconscious* projection of the *subjective initiative* against the subdued status before the natural objects in reality. Humans are awed by the magic of nature, the insoluble mysteries of the natural phenomena. Therefore, they treat the natural objects as divine. At the same time, the natural force is assimilated by personification. The natural objects are not only powerful but also endowed with human characteristics. These gods possess both the external shapes and internal feelings of humans. At first view, humans seem to kneel down before the objects. After rational analysis, we see that the human initiative is realized by *a concealed form of alienation*, that is, the projection of the *subjective myths*. If the myth is an imaged fairy tale, the

---

1   Marx, and Friedrich Engels. *The German Ideology.* Ed. Christopher John Arthur. New York: International Publishers Co, 1970. p. 51.

wings of imagination carry the wildest dreams of people. The weakness in reality gives rises to the sublimation and transcendence of the subjective fantasy. Therefore, the earliest *paradox of the objective constraints and the subjective initiative* is born, though it hides in virtuality.

It should be noted that from the angle of the process of social and historical development there is a deeply entwined paradox between the human subjectivity and the external objectivity, which actually represents the reality of the relations between people and nature, the subject and the object in the social and historical development. It also runs through the basic logic of philosophy and later becomes the theoretical focus of the prehistorical logic clue of Marx's 'natural-ness' and material-subjugation.

When people enter the early period of "civilization," they have accumulated a certain degree of power in comparison with the natural existence of other creatures. Within a very limited sphere of production and living, humans can rely on the group strength to confront nature and make use of the natural forces for their interest. The contemporary agricultural tools have made a substantial leap forward with the extensive use of bronze and iron, which enables them to gain some initial advantages over the natural objects. Of course, man is still subjugated by nature on the overall level of the social and historical development. Meanwhile, the certain development of the productive forces improves their quality and capability, expands their living space and starts the establishment of a structural life of society. In my view, it is the real progress of the subjective force of humans that considerably lifts up their subjective initiative once again. Accordingly, there comes the *heroic view of history* centred on the grand characters. It is true with both eastern and western cultures.

For example, the Chinese myths have made many impressive portrayals of the towering heroines and heroes, such as Nu Wa, Da Yu and Hou Yi, who are extolled with their gallant fights against nature, like Nu Wa replenishing the skies, Da Yu preventing the floods, Hou Yi shooting down the extra suns. Still shining today, their presence is a virtual transcendence of nature, in which people achieve the expected but unrealistic goals through the human heroes in the myths. Similarly, in ancient Greek mythology, there are such figures as Zeus, Apollo, Venus, and Prometheus, the hero who steals fire for mankind. In comparison with the Chinese human heroes, they belong to the deities. According to Feuerbach, god is the generic nature of the alienated subject of man. The Greek gods are all imbued with the human features. They have our common emotions and they even provoke war for a golden apple. Most of all, they have weaknesses that are difficult to be ridded of, which is, of course, the very character of human beings. I consider them as demigods across human heroes and gods. There is a big difference between man and god, in which the human hero *struggles against nature* while god already *dominates nature and man*. Beneath the social and cultural phenomena is a paradox of the belief of fate beyond man's own control and the heroic conception that represents the human subjectivity. Here, the most significant external force that determines the survival of mankind is no longer nature, which is imaginatively replaced by the alienated *quasi-human*, the god. It is an undeniable exaggeration of the human subjectivity as well as a deep *self-division* of man. Moreover, it reflects the actual division of society on the cross-section of social and historical reality: the emergence of private ownership and classes, the division of the "strong" and "weak" persons, etc. From a historical point of view, I think the early people who are lost in mythology lack the necessary knowledge of the internal connections within the social and historical process of mankind. As a result, they cannot develop a generally progressive view to observe history.

In ancient Greek philosophy, a rational division is clearly seen: on one side is the natural substances valued by the materialists, for instance, "fire" by Heraclitus and "water" by Thales; on the other is the human reason upheld by the idealists, such as "Eidos" by Plato. The paradox comes into being from the very beginning between the thought of the natural objects as the universal origin and the proud conclusion that "man is the measure of all things." It is noteworthy that these Greek philosophers took great effort to pursue the fixed sources and "logos" behind the changeable and miscellaneous phenomena. Among the naturalist philosophers were the Eleatics, who held that "all is one" from the perspective of the real ontological existence while motion is exiled to phenomena, like "the arrow paradox" proposed by Zeno. It is easy to see the contradiction of *essence* and *phenomenal existence* here. Their thought is quite different from the ancient Chinese wisdom, in which the communication, change and switch of *Yin* and *Yang* in Tai Chi is the fundamental force to create all. Although the motion still appears in the closed form of iteration, the reality constantly reveals the truth, the unanimity of existence and essence. At this time, there cannot be the real freedom for man's historical development that is only subject to the universal forces of nature.

In addition, I find that the status of contemporary human subject rises in the cognitive process of society and history. (According to the theories of post-modern thought, it is from here that logocentrism and the implicit anthropocentrism are instituted.) The "fire" of Heraclitus and the "water" of Thales *belong to the personified abstraction rather than the intuitionistic objects.* Their fire and water express the vivacity of life with warmth and humidity. In the same way, the Chinese "Qi" does not refer not to the natural air but to an anthropomorphic abstract. Therefore, whether it is "fire," "water," the Eleatic "one," or Plato's "Eidos," they are consistent with each other on the logical level of philosophy. Even more critical is their potential tendency towards *the absolute essence and subject that are supernatural and superhuman*, that is, a monotheistic God.

The theory of Creationism completely dominates in the long years of medieval history and the East. God, the superhuman and supernatural objective force is the master of the world. Heaven and earth are left with God's traces and legends. In addition to the sacred paradise, there are churches to spread Christianity in the West and Tianzi, "the son of heaven" to act for God in the East. Nature, people and society bathe in the divine light of God. Obviously, the above view of the historical development of human society is a direct negation of the ancient conception of history. The change is contributed by the considerable growth of the material production in reality. For example, with agricultural development, humans begin to *transform nature as an overall object to be conquered*, or at least, they have realized the possibility of getting the upper hand of the natural object, despite the fact that the people of that time are still bound by land and dependent on seasons for food, and the human subject remains a "slave" of Nature, the necessity of which brings people at the command of material objects with its mighty forces. However, it is resisted by man, who adds nature, together with himself, to the subjects of God.

As to the almighty God that sits on the top of the world, Engels says, "All religion, however, is nothing but the fantastic reflection in men's minds of those external forces which control their daily life, a reflection in which the terrestrial forces assume the form of supernatural forces."[2] We can see that by the monotheistic religion, people have gradually discovered their own strength. They no longer let themselves simply placed in an external, enslaved condition. Instead, they endow their own image and all the initiatives that they know to God, although in an unconscious way. If the world is regarded as an external process in early natural determinism, and

---

2   Marx, and Friedrich Engels. *On Religion*. Chicago: Scholars Press, 1982. p. 147.

humans begin to struggle against the objective world in the heroic view of history, here the world is defined as a *created* existence. Hence, creationism is essentially made by man that virtually apotheosizes his own capabilities in pursuit of an absolute essence that is independent. It represents a subjective attempt to conquer the world and realize what they cannot achieve in reality through a master in "heaven." In this regard, God is actually a subjective illusion or a hubristic expectation to control the world. Therefore, it is safe to conclude that creationism is *a human creation* in essence. Only it happens in an unconscious way, *reflecting the malformed transference and mapping of the human subjectivity*. (Later, it is echoed in Nietzsche's statement that "God is dead" and the subject rolls "away from the centre toward an X.")

While God's initiative is the reflection of man's initiative, "the alienation of man," in the words of Feuerbach, the existence of man at that time – which has been converted into "being" *on a deeper level of logic* – is still denied for the reason that the essence of man takes the form of an illusory God, the *ethical "ought"* on a deeper philosophical level. As the theological concept of society and history is based on the almighty God who creates the world and life, it inevitably reflects a tendency towards idealism. Besides, the City of God is a projection of the "secular world," the feudal hierarchy, which is essentially *antihuman*. In the reality of the existence of humans, only one, the emperor, is free and the others live in the negated group of patriarchal dependency. Also, the monarchical power derives from God; there will be no "human" in reality. Therefore, in the theological concept of history, the historical process does not reflect the purpose of mankind but represent the implementation of the will of God, whose spokesman is the feudal monarch on earth. The secular existence of humans is unsurprisingly contaminated by the built-in blindness, the desire that is rooted in the original sin. The "guilt" driven by the individual desire is defined as the *blind necessity*, an inherent quality of man; and the "crime" contained in the existence of mankind, together with their final return, is nothing else but a way to achieve their own objectives under the guise of God. After all, the theological conception of history acknowledges that history is created by mankind as the world's secondary master and the ultimate expression of God's will. (We will soon discover that this view of history is later re-explored by Hegel.) Here, we should pay attention to the significant progress of the theological concept of history in the logic of historical cognition: Firstly, a view of the dialectical movement of history that takes the form of teleology, that is, the original subject, e.g. Adam and Eve in the Garden of Eden, is misled by the serpent, banished to earth, and allowed to enter heaven after death. It is a prototype of the metaphorical alienation of the subjective dialectic in the theological concept of history, "negation of negation." Secondly, in the halo of God, man finally makes a progressive step in history. Christianity begins a conscious history. Thirdly, the theological concept of history indicates that the internal driving force of historical development comes from the *contradictory* movement of good and evil, God and the devil. Obviously, it is an important advance compared to the ancient concept of society and history.

II.

With amazing improvement of natural sciences and the social productivity in the 17th century West, the social practice capability of humans obtains a strategic pass, that is, people strides the initial step to become the master of the real world. Nature, for the first time, is taken as the passive object to be transformed in reality. (In comparison, this decisive step in the East is never fully realized.) Thus, it begins a new mode of production with the emergence of the bud of capitalism. First of all, the capitalist economy needs the free men composed of *individual* labours, unquestionably dominated by the new idol, capital. Moreover, it is in the development of capitalist industry and commerce that the subject affirms himself in practical activities for the first time. By the statement of the Enlightenment, man has already regarded himself as the creator of the world history, being a true god. As a result, God is overthrown and man "ought" to *be* man. The above self-awareness generated in the activities of transforming the world begins from the 13th-15th century Renaissance. Divinity is replaced by humanity; theology becomes a human science; and the concept of society and history is filled by "people." It opens an age that needs secular giants and eventually creates giants.

We see an interesting phenomenon with many Renaissance humanists, who do not directly esteem people and confirm their real existence but adopt an indirect mode, the "revival" and reaffirmation of humanities in ancient literary works, so as to ask for human liberation in actual life. There are two important logical points that deserve our attention. Firstly, the nascent bourgeoisie are not strong in the political reality, which forces them to make refracted critics of divinity within the last tension of the theological framework. Secondly, the humanistic "cultural revival" is in fact a glorification of humans in the excuse of those ancient or mythological heroes. It has another indication, viz., if the subjective generalization – religion of nature – and the myths in the early days are an unconscious projection of the subjective initiative, the Middle Ages is the alienation of the subjective initiative, and then, here in renaissance, the subject makes a *conscious* endorsement of itself. "History thus became the history of human passions, regarded as necessary manifestations of human nature."[3] In fact, in the late period of Renaissance, people start throwing away the "retro" cover and directly demand for "human." It should be noted that it is the establishment of *truly human history* for the first time in the logic of the social and historical development as well as the real beginning of the humanistic view of history, the dominance of anthropocentricism. At the same time, it is this confirmation of humanistic eternity that the concept of history again loses the progressive tendency and ends in a tragic prevalence by cyclicism.

Furthermore, when the entire industry obtains full expansion later or after the completion of the industrial revolution, especially the gradual development of modern natural sciences, the basic view of the social and historical development experiences considerable changes. People begin to face the reality of their own strength. The mode of industrial production, unlike the agricultural civilization, can be regarded as the real commencement of man in the overall triumph and domination over the external nature. The power of human knowledge – "instrumental rationality" – and social activities gradually come into light. They become a rip in the path of human history, gushing flares of thoughts out of the old crust. The first impressive phenomenon is the 16th-17th century European movement of scientific thought. Francis Bacon initiated the human subjectivity by his famous aphorism, "knowledge is power," which also accounts for the bud of the earliest reason-determinism of science and technology. In his view, as long as humans develop industry and the technology is based on scientific experiments, they can control themselves and dominate the natural objects. Thus, the slogan that man is his own God is no longer abstract but an accessible reality by man through the activities of the subjective initiative. The idea is further developed and logically confirmed by Descartes and Leibniz.

At the same time, a new objective force *opposed to humans* looms amid the growing industrial production created by people, especially, the ensuing economic kingdom based on it. Again, man sees an "external" force that *dominates* the social movement. This time it is not the natural object. In this regard, the *logical opposition between the subject and the natural object outside* in philosophic concept of history *is turned into the conflict between*

---

3   Collingwood, Robin George. *The Idea of History.* Oxford University Press, 1956. p. 57.

the subject and the objective force in social and historical process. It is an incremental change from the perspective of theoretical logic. It should be noted that until the 18th century the philosophers generally take man as the ultimate factor that decides everything although many of them begin to look for the key of social and historical development from the objective social role that is external to the subject. For example, for Enlightenment thinkers in the 18th century France, the *foundation* for the social and historical development is clearly placed above the social environment of mankind. They believe that the whole social life with every phenomenon results from the effect of the surroundings on human beings. Furthermore, the surroundings are nothing but the product of social education created in accordance with the ideas of mankind. In this way, the ultimate determinants of social history are reduced to a few thinkers' minds. It is the first time for human beings to observe society from an objective perspective of history per se, that is, the theoretical logic of *objective description.* Although this theoretical point is incomplete, it is the project of a *materialistic concept* of history.

Among the Enlightenment thinkers, Rousseau stands out with his unique view of negative romanticism. He unequivocally demonstrates his standpoint of anthropocentrism to seek the *dominant* element in social history. In my opinion, his perspective is very different from the objective description above. He wisely discovers the paradox in the historical development of human reason, and profoundly discovers the contradictions between good and evil, progress and regress. (It can be regarded as *the actualization and logical transformation* of the contradiction-impetus theory in theology.) Rousseau idealizes the early natural state of humans as a golden age of mankind because due to the full freedom and equality among people while with the advance of new reason and civilization, people fall into the abyss of misery and suffering despite their enhanced capabilities, because "all ulterior improvements have been so many steps, in appearance towards the perfection of individuals, but in fact towards the decrepitness of the species."[4] The growth of human capacity and civilization bring people the yoke. The more socialized they are, the further people slip away from their own nature; the more conquest and wealth, the more burden they take. It is a very insightful critic.

---

4   Rousseau, Jean-Jacques. *The Social Contract and The First and Second Discourses.* Yale University Press, 2002. p. 271.

Behold, Rousseau's point here amounts to saying *the material strength created by humans has turned into something that enslaves themselves*. Later, Hegel echoes it with his view of materialization represented by the objectivism of logic object, from which traces Marx's prehistoric thought of material slavery in a certain social and historical development. Rousseau earnestly says, "Mankind thus debased and harassed, and no longer able to retreat, or renounce the unhappy acquisitions it had made."[5] There is no turning back. Furthermore, Rousseau regards property as the real basis for various inequalities and sufferings in society. As he states,

> **All that which we now behold owes its force and its growth to the development of our faculties and the improvement of our understanding, and at last becomes permanent and lawful by the establishment of property and of laws.[6]**

In the eyes of Rousseau, we look like the master of the world but actually come down to slaves. "One thinks himself a master of others, and still remains a greater slave than they."[7] Of course, Rousseau still points a way out to the bright future, a new "social contract" that abrogates private ownership and all the evils.

I have noted that there is another major theoretical point in Rousseau's idea, the heritage to Samsāra, the circle of birth, death and rebirth, and a degraded natural right with the alienation of society and history proposed by Thomas Hobbes. It already paves *the way for Hegel's discourse of alienation and negation of negation*. No wonder Engels makes the following comment, later. "Already in Rousseau, therefore, we find not only a line of thought which corresponds exactly to the one developed in Marx's *Das Kapital*, but also, in detail, a whole series of the same dialectical turns of speech as Marx used."[8] It is easy to see that Rousseau's concept of history contains a strong teleology of human will, which asks for the self-confirmation, for the due historical place in the development. More importantly, Rousseau relates it with the movement of *the subjective dialectics* and highlights the contradiction between the "ought" – man's natural state – included in the theological logic and the "is," man's confused nature in reality. He proposes *the historical paradox between the real existence and the*

---

5   Rousseau, Jean-Jacques. *Discourse on the Origin of Inequality*. Minneapolis: Filiquarian Publishing LLC., 2007. p. 75.

6   *Ibid.*, p. 97.

7   Rousseau, Jacques. *The Social Contract Or Principles Of Political Right*. Kessinger Publishing, 2004. p. 2. Here, it seems to be the source of the postmodern "de-subjectification" and the "discourse of domination" by the Frankfurt School later.

8   Marx, and Friedrich Engels. *On Literature and Art*. Moscow: Progress Publishers, 1976. p. 282.

transcendental essence. It forms one of the most important *logical elements* of the entire humanistic concept of history.

Here, we should not forget the contemporary Italian historian and philosopher, Giambattista Vico, who, in *Scienza Nuova*, clearly states that the history of mankind is created by themselves and differentiated from the history of nature. It is later confirmed by Marx. Vico regards the human history as a *spiral development* of three ages: the human, the heroic, and the divine, which firstly opens a gap in the closed-circle theory of modern society and history. Indeed, this is an outstanding opinion. In addition, he puts forward another profound argument: it is true that man intentionally "plans" history but the historical object is not always in line with our particular wishes, whose inconsistence and contradiction generates a more general objective that better expresses the mind of human beings[9]. It is an *objective teleology* of history not conditioned by the individual goals, which can be almost deduced to such a theoretical view: during the historical development of society, *there exists an objective trend that is created by the human subject – instead of nature or God – but independent of the wish of the individuals*. It transforms the original contradiction between man and the object of the external nature into the paradox of man and society, the individual and the generic in the history of mankind. And the false historical conflicts between God and human, God and nature represented in the theological malformation are refurbished. This opinion is near the gate to expose the objective rules of history. Later, it is deepened by Kant and Hegel, and anticipates Marx's 'natural-ness' theory of the historical and social development.

III.

In the 19th century, the rise of big industries makes it possible for a refreshed perceptible process of history and society. Man leaps to a new level as to the understanding of nature and the laws of social development. As we know, before the formation of the scientific view of history of Marx, the major theoretical trends that he faces in contemporary social and historical thoughts of the European philosophy are as follows, the historiographical thoughts in French Restoration, the utopian socialist view of history in France, the natural and economic concepts of history in the British classical economics, as well as the philosophical view of history in German classical philosophy.

---

9   See Vico, Giambattista . *The New Science*. 1725.

In the first half of the 19th century, the field of European historiography produces a group of French historians with progressive ideas. The revolutionary process in reality and the ongoing events make people doubt the abstract reason. As a result, the perception from the wish of the human subject or the superstructure itself begins to change, and the politics and laws are taken as something derivative because the system is decided by our civic life and relations of property. In addition, the contemporary thinkers also grasp the crucial point, the class struggle centred on the objective relations of interest, which is seen as the immediate driving force of history. For example, François-Pierre Guillaume Guizot, Louis-Adolphe Thiers, and François Auguste Marie Mignée. They offer definite descriptions of this view in their writings. For them, the key to understand the historical events is the property system and class struggle. Furthermore, they begin to observe the social life and historical development *from the basis of objective conditions of society and history*, which, of course, is undoubtedly a pleasant leap forward. However, as to what further decides the property relations and the development of classes, they do not have clear answers. The conclusion from all their theoretical premises is still "the nature of man." Therefore, they fall into the old ruts of the previous century. In the struggle against feudalism, they see the *class slavery of humans* while to capitalism, "man" is already liberated. Correspondingly, man with his nature in the bourgeois society is sacred and supreme despite that different interpretations of them do exist. All in all, the nature of man should be regarded as fixed and *unchanging* in playing the role of the highest criterion. In this point, they are certainly unanimous.

At the same time, those French utopian socialists with similar opinions begin to *speak for the proletariat*. Among them, Saint-Simon is a typical one, He says that the parliamentary form of government is better than any other forms but it still turns out to be mere formality and wants the essential establishment of the system of ownership that is the cornerstone for society. In his eyes, the existence of society is determined by the saving of the ownership instead of the initial law that stipulates that right. These views of Saint-Simon are well developed in comparison with those thinkers like Guizot and even better than the contemporary ideas of "man's passion" and "the basic principles of man's nature" proposed by Fourier and Owen. Unlike the past historians who often more or less regard the history of mankind as a result of accidental events, Saint-Simon starts to discover regularities in history.

It is safe to conclude that the thought of Saint-Simon represents an important step in the development of the European philosophical concept of history. There are two reasons: on one side, as Engels says, "The knowledge that economic conditions are the basis of political institutions appears here only in embryo"[10]; on the other side, Saint-Simon views history as a connecting and regular process of development, the division of which into the theological, metaphysical and empirical stages only appear in modern time. Before that, especially in the ancient and medieval ages, history is always considered as a circular motion. Therefore, Saint-Simon unquestionably starts a new era after Vico. What is the driving force of society and history, then? According to him, the cause of ownership should be uncovered from the industrial development. His analysis might have straightly come to a materialist assumption. However, he goes to the opposite. In his eyes,

For production the implements of labour are necessary. These implements are not provided by nature ready-made, they are invented by man. The invention or even the simple use of a particular implement presupposes in the producer a certain degree of intellectual development. The development of "industry" is, therefore, the unquestionable result of the intellectual development of man-kind...The development of knowledge is for him the fundamental factor of historical advance.[11]

It can be seen that this view still, in essence, belongs to the historical idealism. At the same time, the role of man in Saint-Simon's view is not only an abstract nature and reason but also the great boost by sciences in society and history. However, he is incorrect in attributing science to the movement of subjective knowledge and the exaggerated idealism. In the historical and logical process of the view of history, some thinkers are often very close to the scientific truths, especially in their search for the basis of the social and historical existence, but once they want to determine the *dominant* factor in the development of social history, they tremble again and fall back to idealism. It is a problem we should guard against.

At that time, a new movement of reason buds in the British classical economics that is in close proximity to the reality of life. During his study of the economic movement of human society, Adam Smith finds a very strange situation in which people cannot completely or independently control their social life among the socio-economic functioning created

---

10   Marx, and Friedrich Engels. *Karl Marx, Friedrich Engels: Marx and Engels Collected Works 1874-83*. New York: International Publishers, 1989. p. 292.

11   Plekhanov, Georgiǐ Valentinovich. *The Development of the Monist View of History*. Прогресс Публишерс, 1972. p. 41.

by themselves. Although they just want to achieve their purpose, making money, they seem to be manipulated by "an invisible hand" indeed, "without intending it, without knowing it."[12] This time, it seems to return to the non-subjective natural process! Smith's view stems from the 18th century French Physiocrats, who try to discern from the economic affairs of mankind "the natural order," vis-à-vis "man's order." While the latter refers to that hyper-economic coercion to restrict the freedom of people and contradict the nature, the former means a humane social/economic law by which man can freely pursue his own interest and the social life runs smoothly under an ideal and objective/natural order. Francois Quesnay points out that the law of the natural order does not limit but enhance the freedom of human beings with its advantages. Adam Smith further develops it. He discovers that the commodity production appears in a spontaneous operation and regulation on various levels of the capitalist economy. Man is primarily concerned with his own interests. "He intends only his own gain, and he is in this, as in many other cases, led by an invisible hand to promote an end which was no part of his intention."[13] It should be noted that Smith holds a positive attitude in his statement. If the Physiocrats take the natural order merely as an ideal, Smith has noticed the actual "behaviour" in the economic reality of capitalism. Clearly, the significance of this bourgeois economic theory cannot be exaggerated. In fact, it already touches the principle of *the profound subject-object contradiction in which man is subject to the objective economic force created by himself* in modern social and historical development. In addition, it almost touches the key to the correct view of history that the objective economic rules independent of individual human wills still exist in the development of *modern* society. However, those economists who stand in the bourgeois position make assumptions to argue for the eternal and "natural" attribute of this historical phenomenon, which starts the very critical point for Marx's 'natural-ness' in special historical materialism and the subjective dimension of historical dialectics.

Finally, the German classical philosophy that is nearest to Marxist view of history. Its exploration of the dialectical thinking on the subject of social and historical development starts from Kant, whose major achievements in history are, as we all know, the definition of the rational capability and scientific analysis of the form of knowledge by human beings, another "Copernican revolution" in the epistemology of modern intellectual

---

12   Smith, Adam. *The Theory of Moral Sentiments.* London: H. G. Bohn, 1853. p. 265.

13   Smith, and Kathryn Sutherland. *An Inquiry Into the Nature and Causes of the Wealth of Nations.* Oxford University Press, 1998. p. 292.

history. According to Kant, reality and experience that remain in natural space and time is left to empirical science while the understanding of the hyperspace eternality, freedom and absolute by man's intellect is generalized into the value and beauty of the subject. Obviously, it causes a binary division in reason. However, even in Kant's intuitive phenomena, the subject still "legislates laws for nature" through the a priori framework of comprehensive judgment. The perceptible nature is actually restructured by the subject's idea, especially in good and beauty that are dominated by human morality and created by human reason and will. Kant's philosophy sings high of the initiative and freedom of mankind.

To Kant, the historical process is constructed by human reason and will not go beyond the scope of experience, so it belongs to phenomena. And behind history, there is the "ideal of pure reason" beyond phenomena. The actual activities in history reflect the limited nature of the individuals while the ideal reason represents infinity and liberty. Ontologically, the human behaviours are regulated and guided by moral imperatives. Therefore, there seems to be the freedom of the will but what actually happens in history is not dominated by the individual purposes. In the words of R. G. Collingwood, "Nor does it mean that a man is free to do what he chooses… each doing what he set out to do and each assuming full responsibility for the consequences, captain of his soul and all that. Nothing could be more false."[14] In Kant's view, freedom to the subject is not the condition of practice but the possibility of changing to reality. As a result, Heinrich Cunow says that what the people holding the free idea with metaphysical intention can do is still the phenomena of will, the human behaviour, like any other natural event that is decided by the universal laws.[15] It means *the human society remains a natural process controlled by Necessity.*

In the opinion of Kant, during the historical process created by mankind, the individual inevitably enters their own limitations to realize the intentions; consequently, history is presented in *the casual and disordered phenomena.* However, those seemingly accidental events must abide by a certain "natural rule," in this way, history nevertheless has a *regular* movement, because in the historical activities of the individual, they "unconsciously move forward in line with a natural intention of which they are not aware and for which they work."[16] At the same time when "philosophers examine people and their activities; they are fundamentally unable

14   Collingwood, Robin. George. *The Idea of History.* Hesperides Press, 2008. p. 316.
15   See Heinrich Cunow's *Marx's Theories of History, Society and State.*
16   Translated from Immanuel Kant. *Kant's Collected Writings, Vol. 8* (Chinese Version). The Berlin-Brandenburg Academy of Sciences and Humanities, 1968. p. 17.

to be equipped with a general premise of the intention of reason. Thus, they attempt to discover a natural intention through the absurd things of man, from which the unplanned creature can have a planned history according to some natural intention."[17]

What Kant means to say is, as the natural development has its inherent rules, the social and historical development of humans also has its own laws and although people have their own goals and plans, they are but the realized purposes and programs by "nature." Hence, Kant says, "People can generally view history as a secret implementation of nature's plan, which is to produce an innate (with apparent purposes), perfect, and unique social condition."[18]

It should be noted that the natural intent in Kant's sense cannot be simply regarded as the domination of the natural object in phenomena over the human subject. In fact, it is used from the perspective of Necessity and Nature, always with the *ontological* meaning of the thing-in-itself behind the historical process. Here, we can observe the deep marks left by Kant's dualism. In any case, we find in Kant what Vico once pointed out: man cannot handle himself in his own history. Furthermore, Kant philologically foresees that "invisible hand" in classical economics, which anticipates the Hegelian "cunning of reason" that unconsciously dominates human history.

It is admitted that the philosophical ideas of Johann Gottlieb Fichte and Friedrich Schelling build a bridge for the German classical philosophy to re-enter the subjective unification. Through the *free* "I," Fichte establishes a new noumenon with the absolute action that has a unified "subject-object" structure. In order to realize "self (ego)," it sets a "non-self (non-ego)" in the opposite and positively returns to itself during the process of realization for the inner identification of subject and object. This is the dynamic and organic movement of returning to the subject with strong ontological hues, and a purely subjective *negation of negation* of the dialectics. In my opinion, this view is the first description of an abstract negation of negation (theory of alienation) in the logic of philosophy. It is here that Schelling unifies reality with possibility, theory and action or "practice." Moreover, that the action/practice originated from the subject/I and containing the internal self-contradiction is regarded as the way to ontology almost approaches the view that admits the priority of practice. He seems to unify Kant's dualistic doctrine with the *empiricism of practice*. Also,

17   *Ibid.*, p. 17.
18   *Ibid.*

Schelling says that the actual history lays the foundation for the consciousness of self and it is nothing but the implementation process of an absolute "I." The above idea already edges towards the Hegelian unification of the objective reality with the subject.

Before Marxist scientific view of history, Hegel has climbed to the summit of the development of social and historical view and become an epitome of social studies in the West. As we know, the Hegelian philosophy takes the essence of the world and the only subject as an absolute idea that first objectifies itself and returns to itself through a concrete and vivid self-consciousness after the material degradation of natural object and social history to achieve its own realization.(In the words of today's post-modernist, it is but a hegemonic discourse of reason.) It is not difficult for us to discover that Hegel makes a *historical evolution* of the idea. He turns Fichte's "self" into an objective general idea and unifies Schelling's reason of history. In essence, Hegel's absolute idea is only a mystified metaphor of the performance of human beings, or a caricatured inversion of the actual historical dialectics. It is in the logic deduction of Hegel's idea that the view of history undergoes a fundamental change.

First of all, since the Renaissance, "man" has been considered the subject of initiative in historical development with the abstract human nature as the basis of the concept of history. With Hegel, the nature without history and the society with history is differentiated. However, as to the basis for the human social and historical development, the essential point is again ascertained *outside* "man," that is, an objective idea completely independent of man. As far as I know, although the absolute idea in Hegelian philosophy is by and large an objective distortion of the human knowledge and its development; in essence, it is still an inverted reflection of the development of the objective world. More importantly, the man in Hegelian thought is not the subject of the historical movement but a false agent of the objective spirit. Man's consciousness dissolves in the totality of idea and the individual bows before the reification of idea, the state. Of course, Hegel's thought is not groundless but a result from the observation of the looming presence of the objective economic force and the laws of its movement in modern history.

Secondly, in completion of his own dialectical system of absolute idea, Hegel uncovers *the objective historical dialectics* that is driven by the inherent movement of contradictions in the historical development from lower to higher stages, from bound to free positions, from limited to unlimited statuses.

> **From this point of view, the history of mankind no longer appeared as a wild whirl of senseless deeds of violence, all equally condemnable at the judgment seat of mature philosophic reason and which are best forgotten as quickly as possible, but as the process of evolution of man himself. It was now the task of the intellect to follow the gradual march of this process through all its devious ways, and to trace out the inner law running through all its apparently accidental phenomena.[19]**

For the first time, a complete objective logic independent of the individual will of the subject is identified in the social and historical development. Here, we should pay attention to the following theoretical perspectives of logic by Hegel: one *with ontological basis* to ascertain the historical existence and development and the other of the dominant force during the exploration of different historical stages, each of which *identifies with the other* and has the same significance in the idealistic logic of the Hegelian absolute idea. It is also the twin structure of the famous "cunning of reason" in his view of history and the alienation and return of the subject.

First, the "cunning of reason" in historical development put forward by Hegel. In his view, the absolute idea is the essence of history while man is only a tool to realize the idea in the development of society and history that follows an intrinsically decisive and self-realizing law. It can be regarded as *the ontological foundation* of "spirit" for everything to develop. The absolute spirit "has the History of the World for its theatre, its possession, and the sphere of its realization." "*It* is not of such a nature as to be tossed to and fro amid the superficial play of accidents, but is rather the absolute arbiter of things; entirely unmoved by contingencies, which, indeed, it applies and manages for its own purposes."[20] "The special interest of passion" in the limited existence of the individual and "particularity contends with its like." Therefore, "some loss is involved in the issue. It is not the general idea that is implicated in opposition and combat, and that is exposed to danger." It remains in the background, untouched and uninjured. This may be called the cunning of reason – that it sets the passions to work for itself, while that which develops its existence through such impulsion pays the penalty, and suffers loss.[21] I note that Hegel discusses the non-human factor inherent in the human history from a positive point. He calls the

---

19 Marx, and Friedrich Engels. *Karl Marx, Friedrich Engels: Marx and Engels Collected Works* 1874-83. New York: International Publishers, 1989. p. 302.
20 Hegel, Georg Wilhelm Friedrich. *Philosophy of History*. New York: Barnes & Noble Publishing, 2004. p. 60.
21 *Ibid.*, p. 36.

reality of human life spread by reason the historical "phenomena," part of which is valueless because "the particular is for the most part of too trifling value as compared with the general: individuals are sacrificed and abandoned."[22] On contrary, the individual or nation "performs" the necessity of the idea in the conscious wills, they acquire the freedom of survival.

From this, we can see that this raving "cunning of reason" by Hegel, to a certain extent, inherits Vico's, or especially, Kant's "natural intent." In my opinion, it also provides Marx with the theoretical source of 'natural-ness' in the capitalist economic development.

The second point is Hegel's theory of historical alienation. It is influenced by Fichte, who believes that "self" is objectified into the object of "non-self" during confirmation. In comparison, Hegel's absolute idea also alienates self into the object for realization. Initially, for the realization of idea, self loses the *dominant* status and falls into the material process; later, it makes subjective returns through sublation and transcendence of objectivity in the gradual development of society, and finally completes the restoration in man's self-consciousness. With Hegel, the idea gets concrete and enriched by undergoing various hardships as a result of objective alienation. In the *objectified* realms of necessity composed by the process of natural object and human social history, it finally reaches the pinnacle of the absolute spirit after many hard experiences despite its status of being dominated and decided as well as the material disturbance, limitation and enslavement. It is a negation of negation of the subject per se. Hence, the idea *transcends* the objectified necessity and enters the "realm of freedom."[23] This is very important to understand the theory of material-subjugation and the relation between the realm of necessity and the realm of freedom in Marx's historical dialectics.

Here, in Hegel's view, objectification means alienation; accordingly, alienation becomes the logic framework of the development of idea. Obviously, it is a *positive* ascertainment. Following Hegel, Feuerbach stands at *a negative position* of humanity and proposes that the essence of religion is the essence of man while God is only the alienation of man. Again, he points out that there is a logic contradiction between the generic nature of man,

---

22   *Ibid.*

23   Hegel tends to use the negation of negation in the conceptual development and alienation to confirm the relations of the subject and object. In his philosophy, alienation logically accords with the negation of negation. See Zhang Yibing. "On the Source of the Negation of Negation and the Philosophical Thought History." *Academic Journal of Zhongzhou.* 3 (1987).

"ought," and his alienated existence, "is." (A reconsideration of Rousseau's view of history.) Later, Moses Hess, one of the Young Hegelians, proposes the thought of economic alienation in the reality of social life, especially, the important idea that money is the alienation of man's nature. The theoretical clue makes a profound impact on the concept of history of the Young Marx.

Although Hegel's theory of the historical development makes great progress, close to almost many aspects of the scientific view of history. Despite his enormous influence, he ultimately defines the foundation of historical development as the objective spirit, whose nature is only the arbitrarily objectified structure of human knowledge and its development. Of equal importance is that Hegel negates the man in historical reality with the movement of dialectic reason; thus, man miserably becomes the shell of objective spirit and history is turned into a "non-human" process. This opinion is clearly incompatible to the advocated freedom, equality by the rising German bourgeois democrats. Consequently, the Hegelian system comes to the verge of collapse after the enhanced contradictions proposed by his disciples. This is the introduction to the basic status of the development of thought history before Marx enters the social and historical studies.

CHAPTER II

THE SUBJECTIVE DIALECTICS IN THE PHILOSOPHICAL HORIZON OF THE YOUNG MARX

1 *The Human Essence is to Surpass
   the Restriction of Nature*
2 *The Logical Contradiction Beneath
   the Eliminated Subject-Object Reversal*
3 *The Economic Estrangement:
   Man is the Slave of His Own Creation*

CHAPTER ONE

INTRODUCTION

To determine any scientific theory on the philosophical horizon of Marxism, we should adhere to the principle of historicality, instead of marking the logical points postulated in certain times as some fixed or universal rules. Hence, in our understanding of the Marxist historical dialectics, in particular, the inter relations between the human subject and the external world, we need to first get clear of the previous historical clues of his thought, that is, the transformation and evolution of the subjective dialectics in the development of Marxist philosophy.

I. THE HUMAN ESSENCE IS TO SURPASS THE RESTRICTION OF NATURE

First, it should be noted that Marx, the great man who created the noble cause of humankind and sacrificed his life for it, does not represents an inflexible formula deified in traditional interpretations, in which every word of him is once a magic wand that directs our behaviours. The supremely honoured Marx is actually shoved off his established theory. Instead, we should know that the Young Marx is not a born Marxist. He, like any of us, is a living person, experiences a vigorous youth and ordinary development. The same is with his theoretical advancement, which also goes through a complicated course of initiation, fracture, enrichment and transformation. Although the first philosophical points of the Young Marx do not contain great ideas, his high regard for and pursuit of the noble cause of humanity from the outset make his thought distinctive. The early progression of his philosophy is explored here to understand the original clues and the inherent logical conflicts in this period.

A. THE SELF-TRANSCENDENCE AND CREATIVITY OF THE HUMAN SUBJECT

The school essays of the Young Marx provide the earliest text of theoretical significance. One of them was composed on August 10, 1835, from which we can see that the Young Marx is still restricted within the theological discourse of Christianity. To comment on the disciples and Christ, he writes:

When we consider also the history of individuals, when we consider the nature of man, it is true that we always see a spark of divinity in his breast, a passion for what is good, a striving for knowledge, a yearning for truth. But the sparks of the eternal are extinguished by the flames of desire.[1]

Here, man stays religiously created and his relation with God is compared with the branches and tendrils of vines. Two days later, in "Reflections of a Young Man on The Choice of a Profession," he has a little change. Man seems to attain a comparatively independent *subjectivity* that derives from God, who dictates the general goal that man must progress to nobility. Man should not work for himself. Although one may choose to be a scholar or a poet, it is far from enough to become a great figure. The Young Marx wants to be "the man who has made the greatest number of people happy."[2] He passionately writes, "but our happiness will belong to mil-

---

1   Marx, and Friedrich Engels. *Karl Marx, Friedrich Engels: Collected Works*. New York: International Publishers, 1975. p. 637.
2   *Ibid.*, p. 4.

lions, our deeds will live on quietly but perpetually at work, and over our ashes will be shed the hot tears of noble people."[3] Here, we see an evident confirmation of the *subjective initiative* by the Young Marx: the difference between man and animals is defined as *the self-transcendence* and *creativity* of the subject. In his eyes, "nature herself has determined the sphere of activity in which the animal should move."[4] In comparison, man is superior to other animals because of the continual wish and activities of "ennobling mankind and himself." The goal before man constantly guides his transcendence. "We are not servile tools, but in which we act independently in our own sphere."[5] To the Young Marx, it is a divine guidance. In the same text full of youthful enthusiasm, I find his exceptional sobriety.

But we cannot always attain the position to which we believe we are called; our relations in society have to some extent already begun to be established before we are in a position to determine them.[6]

"Our relations in society" here refers to the "pre-existing" objective reality faced by each new generations, which dominates man's creation and transcendence. The real existence – the logical "is"- *restricts* the nature of man's transcendence – the axiological "ought" – and thus, the survival of the subject must be *an ongoing process of breaking the external restriction.* In my opinion, the thought of *the conflicts between the potential subjective initiative and the external objective restriction, between the individual and society, between the basis and dominant element*, seems to be the Young Marx's major development in the relations between man and the natural history, and a prelude in the logic of the *subjective dialectics* from the perspective of human beings.

In October 1835, the Young Marx followed his father's will and entered the University of Bonn to study law. In the early stage of university studies, his romanticism and the subjective consciousness was mainly expressed in the literary writings, intertwined with his love for Jenny. Though not completely shaking off the influence of the theological discourse, he started to be attracted by the subjective philosophy of Kant and Fichte. Poetry was used to embody his youthful desire and gently play the beautiful music in his young mind. The impulse of idealism seems to saturate the entire world of his.

---

3   *Ibid.*, p. 5.
4   *Ibid.*, p. xxxvii.
5   *Ibid.*, p. 3.
6   *Ibid.*, p. xxxviii.

In a poem titled "Feelings" composed in 1836, the Young Marx writes the following lines:

Never can I do in peace
That with which my Soul's obsessed,
Never take things at my ease;
I must press on without rest.
Others only know elation
When things go their peaceful way,
Free with self-congratulation,
Giving thanks each time they pray.
I am caught in endless strife,
Endless ferment, endless dream;
I cannot conform to Life,
Will not travel with the stream.
Heaven I would comprehend,
I would draw the world to me;
Loving, hating, I intend
That my star shines brilliantly.
That my star shines brilliantly.
All the blessings Gods impart,
Grasp all knowledge deep within,
Plumb the depths of Song and Art.
......
Then let us traverse with daring
That predestined God-drawn ring,
Joy and Sorrow fully sharing
As the scales of Fortune swing.
Therefore let us risk our all,
Never resting, never tiring;
Not in silence dismal, dull,
Without action or desiring;
Not in brooding introspection
Bowed beneath a yoke of pain,
So that yearning, dream and action
Unfulfilled to us remain.[7]

It is palpable to feel Marx's fervour and ambition here with his calls to grasp the entire world. In face of the powerful external force and the difficulties that may occur in one's life, the Young Marx demonstrates an outstanding boldness. Then, what exactly supports the subjective initiative of the Young Marx during this period? In my opinion, it is the impetus of "I" created with the *subjective spirit* of Kant and Fichte. In another poem titled "Human Pride," Marx eulogizes the proud heart of the subject.

7   Marx, and Friedrich Engels. *Collected Works*. London: Lawrence & Wishart, 1975. p. 527.

But the Soul embraces all,
Is a lofty giant flame that glows,
Even in its very Fall
Dragging Suns in its destructive throes.
And out of itself it swells
Up to Heaven's realms on high;
Gods within its depths it lulls,
Thunderous lightning flashes in its eye.[8]
This time, without God's guidance, the subject flashes the thunderous lightening to drag "suns" from the sky and "swells up to" the heaven of God.

If in 1836, the surging passion of the Young Marx was articulated in three books of love songs for Jenny, in 1837, he set sail for *the objective* Hegel, departing from Kant and Fichte who emphasize the *subjective initiative*. In the anthology written to his father, Marx still lauds man's creativity but the theme is turned into an "objective spirit."

Creator Spirit uncreated
Sails on fleet waves far away,
Worlds heave, Lives are generated,
His Eye spans Eternity.
All inspiriting reigns his Countenance,
In its burning magic, Forms condense.
Voids pulsate and Ages roll,
Deep in prayer before his Face;
Spheres resound and Sea-Floods swell,
Golden Stars ride on apace.
Fatherhead in blessing gives the sign,
And the All is bathed in Light divine.[9]

Needless to say, a vivid *objective* spirit that *transcends the individual* dangles between the lines. It is the creative evolution of the subject that transcends the whole world, which, of course, refers to the Hegelian philosophy.

At this time, the Young Marx begins to accept Hegel through other philosophers such as Eduard Gans. For him, it is like a New World slowly emerging from the boundless ocean. With the Hegelian philosophy, the Young Marx says he finds the sublime wisdom and understands its profound mysteries. However, he is not a capture of Hegel; instead, he ambitiously wants to surpass Hegel. After careful studies, he finds that the Hegelian philosophy may not be as great as God may in his initial imagination. In fact, he wants to adopt that pure wisdom to explore this world. Here, we can see

---

8   *Ibid.*, p. 585.
9   *Ibid.*, p. 534.

the process of the Young Marx's attention: from Kant, Fichte to Hegel. It is an adventure from the subjective *heaven to the earthly reality.*

When the Young Marx begins to be engaged in Hegel's philosophy, he stops his theological romanticism and literal ideals and formally steps into the philosophical palace[10]. A sentence in the mail of November 1837 reveals this change: "There are moments in life which mark the close of a period like boundary posts and at the same time definitely point in a new direction."[11] Here, he wants "to view the past and the present with the eagle eye of thought." The new perspective is like "a memorial to what we have once lived through" and presents a fresh world[12]. The future lies ahead but the past still clings. Marx deeply feels the pain interwoven by birth and death. "My heaven, my art, became a world beyond, as remote as my love."[13] His "heaven" refers to the theological discourse, where Kant and Fichte fly; art means his literal writings; and love is for Jenny. He even treats the poems of the first three volumes to Jenny as "a longing that has no bounds," which displays the "characteristic of idealism." It can be regarded as his first serious reflection, in which there is "the same opposition between what is and what ought to be."[14] To my discovery, the Young Marx senses the contradiction between "ought" and "is" for the first time in his own theoretical development. He needs a kind of *liberation* that breaks loose all shackles, a *connecting point* of the internal human desire with reality. He wants to create a surging sea out of the boundless lava. During his inclination towards the Hegelian philosophy, in particular, *the concrete objective dialectics that utilizes the idea to appropriate the reality of history*, he gets "to know Hegel from beginning to end, together with most of his disciples."[15] And "through a number of meetings with friends in Stralow,"[16] he comes across the Hegelian "Doctors' Club." It seems a virtual rebirth to him. Marx says, "A curtain had fallen, my holy of holies was rent asunder." He manages to arrive "at the point of seeking the idea

---

10   Some critics hold that the Young Marx's acceptance of the Hegelian philosophy is his "first change." However, before his study of Hegel, Marx does not form his own independent doctrine. In addition to the theological discourse, Kant and Fichte are the external logical tools that Marx uses in his early period. In a strict sense, the establishment of the Young Marx's philosophy happens after his investigation of Hegel. See Chen Xingping's "On Marx's First Change of Thought." *Journal of Nanjing University.* 2 (1993).

11   Marx, and Friedrich Engels. *Karl Marx, Friedrich Engels. Collected Works.* New York: International Publishers, 1975. p. 6.

12   *Ibid.*, p. 6.

13   *Ibid.*, p. 7.

14   *Ibid.*, p. 8.

15   *Ibid.*, p. 19.

16   *Ibid.*

in reality itself" from the idealism. "If previously the gods had dwelt above the earth, now they became its centre."[17]

Does the turn to reality mean abandoning his early quest for man's creative evolution? Does something "ought," the logical *domination*, really yield to something "is," the *foundation* for external reality? Does the subject lower his noble head before the external force? For answers to these questions, we shall cruise to his new world.

B. THE MODERN WORLD ORIGINATED FROM THE SPIRIT

It should be noted that Hegel does provide the first theoretical steps for the Young Marx. However, with the unique thinking and strong sense of reality, Marx's development of philosophy has always been an independent process of internal changes.

We know that the Hegelian philosophy deconstructs the entire world with the super- natural and -human absolute spirit. Nature, society and man become only the objective phases to gradually realize the absolute idea. Here, the problem of "ought" and "is" that previously frequented the mind of the Young Marx is solved. Nevertheless, Hegel *adopts the absolute essence to beat and appropriate the existence of reality*, which is but the objectification and externalization of the essence. The fundamental negation of reality at most affirms that reality is a positive object in the sense of realizing the essence. Therefore, in the eyes of Hegel, *"ought" means "is"* where there is nothing new under the sun. All in all, the Hegelian philosophy makes an actual distortion of the subjective spirit into an objective absolute noumenon. The initiative of people, especially, the role of the individual, is greatly weakened. However, Hegel's absolute spirit external to man is in nature an alienated subjectivity despite its confusing mode of reversing the objectified historical dialectics. Thus, Hegel's philosophy is still the highlight of human subjectivity but taking a very tortuous or obscure form instead of offering the clear definition or confirmation as Kant and Fichte do. Accordingly, the creative evolution of the subject appears as a thoroughly *anti-human phenomenon*. I believe that the most profound contradiction in Hegel's philosophy is not between form and content but that between the subjective initiative (dialectics) and the objectification of the subject. It is also the theoretical point to be developed by the young Hegelians later.

---

17   *Ibid.*, p. 18.

The 19th century Germany is still under the rule of the feudal autocracy while the actual strength of the bourgeoisie grows with the economic development and the revolution lurks in the depths of the whole society. It is no more natural for the bourgeoisie to seek the parallel response in political and conceptual fields. Then, the young Hegelians hold high the banner of "man" to resist the Prussian feudalism by the radical trend of democracy. Their thought is born out of the very Hegelian system and rightly separates the abstract entity of logic that consumes the subjective (the individual) initiative. It highlights the representation of the personal self-consciousness to create the premise of reason (the Enlightenment) that is necessary for the bourgeoisie. The intention to extol man's subjectivity has a natural *fit* for the Young Marx who has just entered the hall of Hegel's philosophy. The enthusiasm for democracy meets with a critical understanding of Hegel's philosophy by him, thus, Marx's doctoral dissertation, *The Difference Between the Democritean and Epicurean Philosophy of Nature,* came into being in 1841 after two years of preparation and writing. The core idea is about the subjective dialectics of the self-consciousness. The new discourse of the Young Marx now focuses on man. In the study notes, the Young Marx displays a theoretical tendency of the young Hegelians that emphasize the initiative of the self-consciousness. He sees the alienation of the spiritual entity as the necessary way to realize self because alienation means objectification and through which the union of essence and existence can be reached. Undoubtedly, the spell of Hegel still hovers over Marx and his basic logic *affirms* the essential alienation, objectification, of the spiritual subject. However, like a stream running towards the sea while the tides desire the land, every time Marx's attention is drawn to history, the other view stubbornly pops up.

> **Antiquity was rooted in nature, in materiality. Its degradation and profanation means in the main the defeat of materiality, of solid life; the modern world is rooted in the spirit and it can be free, can release the other, nature, out of itself. But equally, by contrast, what with the ancients was profanation of nature is with the moderns salvation from the shackles of servile faith.**[18]

In ancient times, people cannot rid themselves of the influence by Mother Nature that restricts them. As time goes by, people gradually stand up and become the master of nature with their internal development of reason. In the eyes of the Young Marx, "the premise of the ancients is the act of nature, that of the moderns the act of the spirit"[19] and nature must be

---

18   Marx, and Friedrich Engels. *Collected Works.* London: Lawrence & Wishart, 1975. p. 423.
19   *Ibid.,* p. 431.

split in two for the spirit to be one in itself. "The Greeks broke it up with the Hephaestan hammer of art, broke it up in their statues; the Roman plunged his sword into its heart."[20] These acts belong to the creative evolution of the human subject (spirit). His approval of the *dominant status* of man's initiative is clearly not compatible with the ontological logic of Hegel.

At that time in the philosophical logic of the Young Marx, the major part is not Hegel's objective idealism but the tendency towards the emphasis on the *self-consciousness* with objective idealism held by the young Hegelians. The "self-consciousness" here alludes to the individual *subjective initiative* required by the bourgeois reason. Marx says the nous is active and is resorted to where there is no natural determination. "It is itself the *non ens* [Not-being] of the natural, the ideality."[21] He evidently notes that man should *surpass nature*. Of course, it is "in a form which raises natural energy to ideality and does not consume it, but processes it and leaves it intact in the determination of the natural,"[22] and the subject naturally detaches itself from the substantial, and hence naturally determined, life. At this point, the Young Marx obviously pays more attention to the superior social and historical development of the human subject (spirit), and places it in a position vis-à-vis the natural historical development. The context of Marx's thought includes both Hegel's philosophy and his own theoretical purpose of stressing the subjective initiative.

On the other side, his dissertation illustrates the philosophical differences of nature between Democritus and Epicurus. In his studies, we find the deep implications and important positioning of the two. In general, the Epicurean view of man and nature filled with the subjective consciousness is more appealing to the Young Marx.

The natural philosophy of Democritus belongs to the materialistic determinism because the world is composed of the atoms constantly falling from the void and their combination and separation determine the birth and death of the world. During the movement of atoms, any event or phenomenon inevitably takes place according to specific reasons. In contrast, Epicurus focuses on the subjective freedom and works hard to abandon the inflexible determinism, observing the occasional declination in the atomic movement. In addition to the motions of falling and exclusion, Epicurus highlights a kind of declination that deflects from the straight line, which

---

20   *Ibid.*
21   *Ibid.*, p. 435.
22   *Ibid.*, p. 436.

represents the independent spiritual essence of the atoms that transcend the material. Declination breaks the bounds of fate. For illustration, Marx cites the words of Titus Lucretius Carus, "declination represents the real soul of the atom, the concept of abstract individuality."[23] Marx further commends that "while the atom frees itself from its relative existence, the straight line, by abstracting from it, by swerving away from it; so the entire Epicurean philosophy swerves away from the restrictive mode of being wherever the concept of abstract individuality, self-sufficiency and nega-tion of all relation to other things must be represented in its existence."[24] In other words, the declining movement of atoms stands for a *non-material transcendence of the subject*, a spiritual essence. Because of the deflection from the straight line, the material Dasein, the atom, discards the non-free mode of existence and establishes its own independence and free creation. The Young Marx points out that Democritus only recognizes the material existence of atoms, the necessary Dasein while Epicurus really understands the spiritual essence of the atom, declination. For example, *"when I relate myself to myself as to something which is directly another, then my relationship is a material one."*[25] It is only man's external status of superior existence and only when he breaks the relative Dasein, transcends the pure force of nature that he ceases to be a product of nature. Obviously, the Young Marx fully approves of the "rebellious" atoms.

Here, we can see the continual extension of the original idea of the Young Marx that the subject surpasses the natural restriction and individuality de-velops in creative evolution. However, Marx's thought contains a contra-diction, one between the conceptual determinism and the initiative of the individual consciousness, which actually accounts for the contradiction that goes through the young Hegelians. Marx also discusses the contradictions between existence and essence, material and form within the concept of at-oms at a deeper level. In Chapters 2 and 3 of the second part, he discovers Epicurus' interest in the conception of atom and the contradiction of setting it as a Dasein that is externalized and differentiated from its own essence. It is clear that Marx makes use of the young-Hegelian logic of self-consciousness to "fry" Epicurus the materialist. The atom is now turned into the logical subject of the self-consciousness. Here, the key role is played by the Hegelian thought that Idea produces a world through alienation. "The atom is con-ceptually the absolute, essential form of nature." Due to its substance, the atom betrays its own concept; and thus the phenomenal world – the world

---

23   *Ibid.*, p. 50.
24   *Ibid.*.
25   *Ibid.*, p. 52.

of nature – comes into being. But it realizes the concept per se. In the process of realization, "*this absolute form has now been degraded to absolute matter, to the formless substrate of the world of appearance.*"[26]

In the eyes of the Young Marx,

> **The atoms are, it is true, the substance of nature, out of which everything emerges, into which everything dissolves; but the continuous annihilation of the world of appearance comes to no result. New appearances are formed; but the atom itself always remains at the bottom as the foundations.**[27]

He sees the natural material "as the bearer of a world of manifold relations."[28] It never exists but in forms which are indifferent and external to it. Nature is only "the counter-image of the nature of essence, the atom."[29] In fact, "just as the atom is nothing hut the natural form of abstract, individual self-consciousness, so sensuous nature is only the objectified, empirical, individual self-consciousness, and this is the sensuous."[30] Here, the Young Marx adopts the Hegelian logic to fully confirm that self-consciousness (nature) realizes itself through alienation.

> **Thus, as long as nature as atom and appearance expresses individual self-consciousness and its contradiction, the subjectivity of self-consciousness appears only in the form of matter itself. Where, on the other hand, it becomes independent, it reflects itself in itself, confronts matter in its own shape as independent form.**[31]

The alienation theory is not taken as a critical tool of negation. It is true that Marx borrows the words of Epicurus to confirm the condition of the subject of self-consciousness that is alienated into the Dasein of the natural material *will be eventually surpassed* but that is, at most, a return of the Idea. At that time, the philosophical logic of the Young Marx is still idealistic. His emphasis of the transcendence of the subject stems from the limitation of the self-consciousness of the absolute idea, which is far from the social and historical reality. Hence, the logic based on the subjective idea and the natural object is impossible to be scientifically defined. However, we do see the creative evolution of the subject always held high by the Young Marx.

---

26   *Ibid.*, p. 62.
27   *Ibid.*
28   *Ibid.*
29   *Ibid.*, p. 64.
30   *Ibid.*, p. 65.
31   *Ibid.*, p. 72.

C. THE ABJECT MATERIALISM

In a sense, school education is like a shallow river that lies distant from the sea of social life. One that is stranded will become a dried shell on the sand. The Young Marx did not want to be the shell; he desired to cruise in the deep sea. After he left college, he began to face the practical issues during his work for *Rheinische Zeitung* (Newspaper). He strode into the political life as a fighter of democracy. It proved a hard process, just like the experience from previous overlooking by the riverside to jumping into water for feeling the social reality. It was also a period when he began to abandon his idealistic ideas.

When criticizing the Prussian authoritarian suppression of the press freedom, the Young Marx insists, "The essence of the spirit is always *truth itself.*"[32] In his mind, the general independence of thought, or, the "ought" of reason, is a fundamental requirement. In addition, he says, "We must therefore take the essence of the inner idea as the measure to evaluate the existence of things. Then we shall less allow ourselves to be led astray by a one-sided and trivial experience, since in such cases the result is indeed that all experience ceases."[33] From a deeper perspective, the Young Marx still starts from the Hegelian objective spirit and reason that represent the human subjectivity rather than the subject and individual.

While in dealing with a series of practical problems, like the "Third Article Debates on the Law on Thefts of Wood in Rhine Province Assembly,"[34] the Young Marx finds that the alienation of spirit in real life is not achieved through the objectification of the sublime advocated by Hegel but by the materialization of a despicable consciousness – a negative "is." As to this pursuit for material interest, he scornfully calls it "the erudition of a penny magazine" or "the *religion of sensuous desire.*"[35] For him, this material experience not under the control of man's reason is the "*abject materialism*" or the "*gold fetish.*" Strongly against this automatic worship of *material* that places man among animals, he comments that the abuse arises from a period when the history of humankind is still a part of natural history, the medieval of feudalism. According to the Young Marx, the feudal system is the spiritual world of animals because only the animals make their body a place for combination, fusing and liaison of different things, and man degrades into animals with *his principles of survival under the mercy of the law*

---

32   *Ibid.*, p. 112.
33   *Ibid.*, p. 154.
34   *Ibid.*, p. 224.
35   *Ibid.*, p. 189.

of the natural materials. Tragically, it is a *historical reversal* of human reason. To this end, the Young Marx cites a very interesting example.

> **A coarse person who regards a passer-by as the most infamous, vilest creature under the sun because this unfortunate creature has trodden on his corns. He makes his corns the basis for his views and judgment; he makes the one point where the passer-by comes into contact with him into the only point where the very nature of this man comes into contact with the world. But a man may very well happen to tread on my corns without on that account ceasing to be an honest, indeed an excellent, man. Just as you must not judge people by your corns, you must not see them through the eyes of your private interest.[36]**

The Young Marx calls the private interest as something that "cannot bear the light of publicity."[37] He still believes that "the crude desire of the fetish-worshipper smashes the fetish when it ceases to be its most obedient servant."[38] It needs to be reminded that the Young Marx *always holds a negative view towards the phenomenon that the human subject bows to the external material object or the objective force.* It also accounts for his early wording of "fetish" to ascertain the reversed relationship between man and material. However, he does not explore the reason why such reversal takes place, which is only correctly handled in his scientific view of history later. An extremely important change occurs in the logic of the Young Marx at this time. If his dissertation still pursues Hegel's *confirmation* of the alienation value of the spiritual essence, here, the Young Marx no longer regards the second part of the essence-existence-essence logic, that is, the alienation of the spirit or the material reality, as the realization of reason. Instead, he negates it as a sin that violates the human spirit. Only the human history is real while *the historical materialization or alienation that is similar to nature is anti-human.* The Young Marx tends to make a consistent combination of the thought on the relation between human society and nature with the perspective of observing history (the view of alienation). In my opinion, what dominates his philosophical logic then is not the Hegelian idealism as generally seen but a profound *new discourse of the subjective dialectics of humanism.* Here appears the first negative critic of the social history by the potential subjective dialectics in the philosophical development of the Young Marx. At the same time, we find that this critic is not inherently unified with his own philosophical logic. Despite it, the idea is indeed another important theoretical point for development.

---

36   *Ibid.*, pp. 235-236.
37   *Ibid.*, p. 261.
38   *Ibid.*, p. 189.

In addition, the Young Marx has already admitted, although reluctantly, that the law is "outvoted" by the material interest.[39] It is a vital theoretical intuition and a *start* that anticipates his new scientific theory. Despite it, his major logic at that moment is still about what *dominates* the social history. From the idealistic angle, he negates the phenomenon that the material force dominates the human beings, which precisely disproves the general material *foundation* of the history in reality. It is his principle farewell to the idealistic reason, only that the contradiction is not yet apparent in the generally Hegelian philosophy held by the Young Marx for the time being.

II. THE LOGICAL CONTRADICTION BENEATH THE ELIMINATED SUBJECT-OBJECT REVERSAL

In fact, after 1842, the Young Marx begins to be influenced by Feuerbach's humanism. At first, he has only a passing reference to Feuerbach; gradually, he feels the weakness of the "sublime" slogan of the Hegelian reason, equality and freedom before reality. Not able to sublate the spiritual estrangement, the Young Marx is aware that only Feuerbach's materialism may lead to the road of truth in the heated social life and struggles. As a result, he starts to say goodbye to and ring the knell of idealism. Another cause that explains the change of the Young Marx is the humanistic nature of Feuerbach's materialism, which contains a certain structure similar to the discourse of Marx's subjective dialectics. Hence, the Young Marx falls to a deeper theoretical contradiction, that is, the separation between the basic and dominant factors in history.

A. A RETURN TO THE FOUNDATION: THE NEGATION OF THE "REVERSED WORLD" AND THE "REVERSED WORLDVIEW"

Early in 1842, the Young Marx says in an article that if one wants to study things according to their nature in reality, he must first be liberated from the idealistic philosophy and only through the "fire brook," the literal meaning of Feuerbach the name can freedom be achieved. From the summer in 1843 to early 1844, the Young Marx wrote the *Critique of Hegel's 'Philosophy of Right'*, and publishes *On the Jewish Question* and the *Introduction to the Critique of Hegel's 'Philosophy of Right'* in *Deutsch-Französische Jahrbücher*. This time, his critique of Hegel's idealism changes to the position of Feuerbach's materialism, but he never becomes a real Feuerbachian. This is the *first transition of philosophical framework* in the

---

39   *Ibid.*, p. 261.

theoretical development of the Young Marx. He makes a *return* to the real objective *foundation* of social existence in his understanding of social history.

As we know, early in the *Kreuznach Manuscripts of 1843*, he abandons the hypothesis based on the "law of reason." By Feuerbach's materialism, he criticizes Hegel's reversed subject-predicate relation of spirit and material, or the relation between law, nation and civil society, and exposes the mystical nature of the Hegelian philosophy. The Young Marx points out the features of Hegel's philosophy as follows.

> **Hegel makes the predicates, the object independent, but independent as separated from their real independence, their subject. Subsequently, and because of this, the real subject appears to be the result; whereas one has to start from the real subject and examine its objectification. The mystical substance becomes the real subject and the real subject appears to be something else, namely a moment of the mystical substance.[40]**

This is the secret of Hegel's idealism. The Young Marx wants to overthrow idealism and make a *self-criticism* of his reversed worldview. More importantly, he has begun to observe the existent structure of the social and historical reality with the new logic of materialist philosophy.

To his discovery, there is also a thorough reversal in the logic of the Hegelian philosophical view of history. (For Hegel, because the reality of social history is produced by the Idea, "it is not their own life's course which unites them into the state, but rather the life's course of the Idea, which has distinguished them from itself."[41] In this way, "Hegel at all times makes the Idea the subject and makes the proper and actual subject, like 'political sentiment', the predicate. But the development proceeds at all times on the side of the predicate."[42] In the eyes of Marx, Hegel "makes the cause the effect and the effect the cause, the determining that which has been determined and that which has been determined the determining."[43] The Idea is given the status of a subject, and the actual relationship of family and civil society to the state is conceived to be its inner imaginary activity. In fact, "family and civil society are the presuppositions of the state; they are the really active things; but in speculative philosophy it is reversed."[44]

---

40   Marx, and Joseph O'Malley. *Critique of Hegel's 'Philosophy of Right.'* CUP Archive, 1977. p. 24.
41   *Ibid.*, p. 9.
42   *Ibid.*, p. 11.
43   *Ibid.*, p. 100.
44   *Ibid.*, p. 8.

Here, indeed, we see an *innovative* clue of logic in Marx's socio-historical observation, which is the *materialistic perspective based on the reality of social history.* However, this is by no means Feuerbach's natural materialism or the traditional materialism in a general sense. The Young Marx takes hold of the fundamental core of materialism, and thus for the first time discovers a materialistic foothold in the field of social history, which, interestingly, turns out to be the logic of "is" that he previously *opposes.* At first, he unconsciously finds that it always takes the upper hand in the reality of life; now he already agrees *in a philosophical sense.* It is a very interesting *inversion of logic.* In this connection, he goes far beyond Feuerbach. Obviously, his thought can be compared with Saint-Simon's philosophical view of history in the 17th century France but the Young Marx goes further to lay the foundation of social history upon the economic "civil society" and family. In my opinion, it means a *generally negative* birth of the upcoming revolutionary view of history from the old framework. Nevertheless, at that time, this sober observation does not reach the height of the overall conception of history but remains a common theoretical explanation of social history. In the belief of the Young Marx, neither the Idea nor the law and political conception of nation can determine and produce the social reality. It is but the "civil society" and family in reality that generate the Idea. At the same time, the "true philosophical criticism of the present state constitution not only shows the contradictions as existing, but clarifies them, grasps their essence and necessity. It comprehends their own proper significance."[45] Without doubt, this different logical point can also be viewed as the *initial development* of Marx's change in his historical view.

It should be noted that in Marx's logic then, the above view to offer an objective description of social history mainly appears in the synchronic *structural analysis of the social existence,* in other words, it is the train of thought formed from the *perspective of reality* during the exploration of existence of social history that we discuss before. To keep it in mind is of great importance for our next discussion. In addition, I do not think it is the dominant *power discourse* in Marx's philosophical thought of that time.

B. REQUIREMENT-ORIENTED MAN IS THE VERY FOUNDATION OF THE WORLD

As mentioned before, the Young Marx's critique of the Hegelian philosophy is inspired by Feuerbach, who makes the whole world oriented towards the human subject. Marx is deeply touched by this view because

---

45   *Ibid.,* p. 92.

Feuerbach's humanistic logic that demands the ontological existence of *man*, the species essence that man *ought to have, inadvertently coincides* with Marx's precious focus on the status of the human subject. Therefore, in the Young Marx's knowledge of the social history, particularly, his diachronic or progressive observation of the development of social history to determine its *dominant aspect*, there is a logic clue that starts with man, which, we shall discover, proves to be an *old idealistic view of history*. It is the logical framework that plays the *dominant role* and the real inner power discourse in the Young Marx's philosophy. In other words, although he turns from Hegel's idealism to Feuerbach's natural materialism, he does not give up his main philosophical reflection, the subjective dialectics; he just *changes from the conceptual subjective dialectics of self-consciousness to the humanistic subjective dialectics centred on the abstract nature of man*. As a result, the conceptual subject is transformed to that of the "species man," and the teleological logic of the old control of Idea and surpassing reality has become a practical thought that "man" requires and criticizes the *non-human* reality. The new subject "should" stay opposed to the estranged "is." In comparison with the aforementioned synchronic perspective, a humanistic *theory of value* is highlighted. In his critique of the Hegelian idealism, the Young Marx argues that from the very beginning "the true method is turned upside down" by Hegel's philosophy. What is most simple is made most complex and vice versa. What should be the point of departure becomes the mystical result, and what should be the rational result becomes the mystical point of departure."[46] Then, what is Marx's point of departure at that time? It is "Man." The Young Marx always observes from the angle of "man" and it becomes the functional discourse that subtly dominates his philosophical development. More importantly, he has far surpassed Feuerbach's logical framework at that time. However, this "man" in the eyes of the Young Marx does not mean the natural one that Feuerbach believes but indicates the combined consideration of such specific social relations as family, property and the "civil society." He offers an interesting example, "the nature of the particular person is not his beard, his blood, his abstract Physis, but rather his *social quality*."[47] In my opinion, it is the old bottle branded with the name of "man" but poured with the new wine. There is a very significant difference. The Young Marx tries to "translate this entire paragraph into common language."[48] He never stops his effort to stress the *subjectivity* but that is then replaced by the

---

46   *Ibid.*, p. 40.
47   *Ibid.*, p. 22.
48   *Ibid.*, p. 16.

"man" instead of Hegel's abstract reason. If Feuerbach attempts to eliminate Hegel's subject/object reversal and the self-estrangement of religion,
the bad "is," while restoring God and man in the original sense, the Young
Marx believes that the key to beat down idealism and correct the inversion
of religion lies with the true recognition of the reversed man in reality, a
new bad "is." Here, we once again see the continual stirs of the inner conflict in the Young Marx's theory.

In regards to the authoritarian state and social estrangement confirmed by
Hegel, the Young Marx writes, "Man is man's world, the state, society. This
state, this society, produces religion, a distorted consciousness of the world,
because the world is distorted."[49] Most of all, here man must "undertake an
essential schism within himself."[50] It assumes a profound inconsistency in
political and social life, namely, the separation of the "state" and the "civil
society." "It is a development of history that has transformed the political
classes into social classes such that, just as the Christians are equal in heaven
yet unequal on earth, so the individual members of a people are equal in the
heaven of their political world yet unequal in the *earthly existence of society*."[51]

> **Where the political state has attained its true development, man
> – not only in thought, in consciousness, but *in reality, in life*
> – leads a twofold life, a heavenly and an earthly life: life in the
> *political community*, in which he considers himself a communal
> being, and life in *civil society*, in which he acts as *a private in-
> dividual*, regards other men as a means, degrades himself into a
> means, and becomes the plaything of alien powers.[52]**

Obviously, it is *a new estrangement*. At this point, the Young Marx puts
forward a very important issue of the relation between the *political emancipation* and the *human liberation*. According to his understanding here,
the political emancipation by which the human society shakes off the authoritarian system is not human emancipation yet.

> **Political emancipation is, of course, a big step forward. True, it
> is not the final form of human emancipation in general, but it is
> the final form of human emancipation within the hitherto exist-
> ing world order. It goes without saying that we are speaking here
> of real, practical emancipation.[53]**

49   Marx, and Eugene Kamenka. *The Portable Karl Marx*. New York: Viking Press, 1983. p. 115.

50   Marx, and Joseph O'Malley. *Critique of Hegel's 'Philosophy of Right.'* CUP Archive, 1977. p. 77.

51   *Ibid.*, p. 80.

52   Löwy, Michael. *The Theory of Revolution in the Young Marx*. Chicago: Haymarket Books,
2005. p. 14.

53   Marx, and Friedrich Engels. *Karl Marx, Friedrich Engels: Collected Works*. New York:
International Publishers, 1975. p. 155.

The political liberation does not really get rid of certain restrictions. It is not a method without contradictions because it still maintains a new social estrangement, in which "it separates man from his universal nature; it makes him an animal whose being coincides immediately with its determinate character."[54] In the authoritarian system, people cannot be themselves; they are but animals. "The Middle Ages constitutes the *animal history* of mankind, its zoology."[55] "In this system, nature immediately creates kings, peers, etc. just as it creates eyes and noses. This is, of course, why we find in the aristocracy such pride in blood and descent, in short, in the life history of their body. It is this zoological point of view which has its corresponding science in heraldry... The secret of aristocracy is zoology."[56] In "modern times, civilisation, commits the opposite mistake. It separates man's objective essence from him, taking it to be merely external and material. Man's content is not taken to be his true actuality."[57] "He acts as a private individual, regards other men as a means, degrades himself into a means, and becomes the plaything of alien powers."[58] He is the meretricious "man who has lost himself, been alienated, and handed over to the rule of inhuman conditions and elements – in short, man who is not yet a real species-being."[59] If in the Middle Ages, the constraints in reality come from nature that, together with his natural determination, has deprived him of the subjective status, here, *the non-subjectification of man is dominated by a non-human force*. The Young Marx first discovers the phenomenon of man's *self-created material domination and slavery*, which is, of course, influenced by Rousseau and Hegel.

It is not difficult to see that the main logical framework of the Young Marx is still the humanistic subjective dialectics pillared by the relation of the subject-object estrangement. In other words, although Hegel's theory of alienation remains an important *inner driving force* but is now changed to the estrangement of the *essence of man* instead of the *spiritual* subject. It belongs to the materialist and humanist *estrangement view of history* held by Feuerbach, who intends to overthrow God, restore man out of God (the estrangement of man's essence), and let God descend from the sacred heaven to the secular world. For Feuerbach, the establishment of "man"

---

54   Marx, and Joseph O'Malley. *Critique of Hegel's 'Philosophy of Right.'* CUP Archive, 1977. p. 82.
55   *Ibid.*, p. 82.
56   *Ibid.*, p. 106.
57   *Ibid.*, p. 82.
58   Löwy, Michael. *The Theory of Revolution in the Young Marx*. Chicago: Haymarket Books, 2005. p. 14.
59   Kiss, Artúr. Marxism and Democracy: *A Contribution to the Problems of the Marxist Interpretation of Democracy*. Akadémiai Kiadó, 1982. p. 110.

and his living world amount to the sublation of estrangement. The Young Marx strides a big step forward. With him, *man is still estranged in his own world of reality*, which is but a more subtle estrangement in the existing political system. If positioned in the humanistic philosophy, the "ought" to restore man's species essence required by the Feuerbachian theory becomes *again* a bad "is" once entering reality, because, in the real life of the capitalist society, people are no longer God's slaves but *enslaved by their own life*. In this connection, the Young Marx directs the humanistic critique of the bourgeoisie *to themselves*. He uncovers a more profound point, or a new axiological "ought." His *political stance is changed*. Along the dimension of exploring the *major factors* of the social history, *the Young Marx's subjective dialectics highlight a negative and critical analysis of capitalism*.

In the Introduction to the *"Critique of Hegel's Philosophy of Law*, the Young Marx takes a generally humanistic view and chants a series of astounding slogans, like "to be radical is to grasp the root of the matter, but for man, the root is man himself,"[60] "man is the highest essence for man,"[61] or "*all* emancipation is a *reduction* of the human world and relationships to *man himself*."[62] For the bourgeoisie, the "political emancipation is the reduction of man, on the one hand, to a member of civil society, to an egoistic, independent individual, and, on the other hand, to a *citizen*, a juridical person."[63] It leads to the separation and estrangement among people on a deeper level. The Young Marx desires for the *complete* liberation of the human subject, "with the *categorical imperative to overthrow all relations* in which man is a debased, enslaved, abandoned, despicable essence."[64] In his eyes, the ideal kingdom of the bourgeoisie still represents "the *complete loss* of man and hence can win itself only through *the complete re-winning of man*."

Only when the real, individual man re-absorbs in himself the abstract citizen, and as an individual human being has become a *species-being* in his everyday life, in his particular work, and in his particular situation, only when man has recognized and organized his "own powers" as *social* powers, and, consequently, no longer separates social power from himself in the shape of *political* power, only then will human emancipation have been accomplished.[65]

---

60   Marx, and Friedrich Engels. *On Religion*. Chicago: Scholars Press, 1982. p. 50.

61   *Ibid.*, p.50.

62   Marx, Karl. *Early Writings*. Harmondsworth: Penguin Books, 1992. p. 234.

63   Marx, and Friedrich Engels. *Karl Marx, Friedrich Engels: Collected Works*. New York: International Publishers, 1975. p. 168.

64   Marx, and Friedrich Engels. *On Religion*. Chicago: Scholars Press, 1982. p. 50.

65   Marx, and Friedrich Engels. *Karl Marx, Friedrich Engels: Collected Works*. New York: International Publishers, 1975. p. 168.

As a result, such an estranged status of man in the capitalist society is bound to be eliminated. The ultimate liberation of people will be realized by the opposite of the bourgeoisie, the proletariat. Then, he points out the features of liberation:

> It "cannot emancipate itself without emancipating itself from all other spheres of society and thereby emancipating all other spheres of society, which, in a word, is the *complete loss* of man and hence can win itself only through the *complete re-winning of man.* This dissolution of society as a particular estate is the proletariat."[66]

Now, the fog gradually disperses and we can have a clear look at the political stance of the Young Marx: it is changed *from democratism to the proletarian position, from criticizing feudalism to the direct critique of capitalism.* In other words, the "ought" in the humanistic theory of the Young Marx should be interpreted as that the proletariat ought to be *humans* and capitalism ought to be beaten down. The man in the subjective discourse of the Young Marx no longer means the "man" in the general ideological sense but specifically refers to the proletarian. We must pay a serious attention to this modification because it indicates that the Young Marx begins to accept *the communist* ideology, although it is not a *scientific socialism* yet. It also marks the corresponding change of the first transformation for the Marxist philosophy.

Last but not least, despite his sombre consideration of the proletarian revolution and the fate of workers in capitalist society, the Young Marx's major weapon of critique at that time, the Feuerbachian humanistic estrangement, is essentially idealistic. Moreover, this humanistic discourse of the subjective dialectics and axiology are actually externalized as his primary theoretical framework. Here, the Young Marx does NOT base his train of thought on the materialist idea that should have been the foundation of social history. Why? Because at that moment he cannot draw from the real situation of the capitalist social history the revolutionary supposition that he needs, namely, the critical and negative conclusions of capitalism. Consequently, he cannot make the confirmatory observations from the reality of social economy but places his logical start with the abstract "man," which is indeed the "individual in the civil society," *for further criticism.* Thus, the essence of history is some kind of a priori human nature and the ideal realization of "ought." The modern capitalist society is irrational

---

66   Marx, & Engels. *K. Marx and F. Engels on Religion.* Moscow: Foreign Languages Pub. House, 1957. p. 57.

in that it violates humanity instead of the objective necessity of the social and historical movements, which, obviously, cannot be a scientific view of history. At the same time, we can sense that the humanistic view of estrangement in the Young Marx's logical development *subtly and historically corresponds* to the dynamic discourse of the human subject that he has been building, despite that this humanistic theory is far from a completed system.

In the philosophical logic of the Young Marx, there are two trends with a binary separation at different levels: on the general level of determining *the structural foundation* of the social history, his negation of the Hegelian conception of history almost approaches the materialist principles; on the level of exploring the *dominant* factors of the development of society and history, he adheres to the humanistic estrangement view of history and value critique *for the sake of the proletarian revolution*. It should be noted that the theoretical principles of these two aspects are mutually contradictory, but the Young Marx is not aware of it. While the former is only a theoretical principle, the latter involves his wholehearted impulse to put into practice, which naturally becomes his main theoretical framework and power discourse. Meanwhile, the framework gets further strengthened and systematized in the new economic theory of estrangement, reaching an unprecedented peak in his thought.

III. THE ECONOMIC ESTRANGEMENT: MAN IS THE SLAVE OF HIS OWN CREATION

If the above thought of estrangement by the Young Marx is from the socio-political perspective and relatively limited within the specific analysis of the objective criticism, his critical thinking about the discourse of the subjective dialectics in which man is conditioned by his own creation gets more profound once he steps into the reality of social economy, especially, with his scrutiny of the capitalist mode of production. Next, I am going to discuss the idea of economic estrangement, in particular, the famous theory of labour estrangement, created by the Young Marx during his critique of the capitalist economy, which also reaches the peak of his subjective dialectics and axiological philosophy.

A. THE CONSTRUCTION OF THE ECONOMIC ESTRANGEMENT THEORY: MONEY IS THE ESTRANGED ESSENCE OF MAN

As to the idea of the economic estrangement, the Young Marx was under the influence of the German philosopher Moses Hess, who discussed about the essence of money in the *Twenty-One Sheets from Switzerland*. In *On the Jewish Question* of 1843, the new theory of estrangement came up. For the Young Marx, in the economic life, money is both the object outside the human subject and the external expression of the essence of man. It is a man's creation but it has deprived the subject and the entire world of their value with its "universal and self-constituted value set upon all things." More importantly, the estranged subject has to kneel down in front of this man-made material. Here, unlike the attack on the phenomenon of merely pursuing material interest–"the vulgar materialism"–waged during his work for *Rheinische Newspaper*, the Young Marx regards it as an important aspect of the capitalist economic life, "the civil society." The matter unconsciously comes up: *the estrangement in the economic life is the foundation of the estrangement of social politics*. Here, the Young Marx makes a big leap forward. He says, "Money is the estranged essence of man's work and man's existence, and this alien essence dominates him, and he worships it."[67] The *discourse of reference* here is nothing more than a reversed relation of man and his own material creation, which manifests itself with an illusory necessity in the capitalist economic reality.

Selling [Veräusserung] is the practical aspect of alienation [Entäusserung]. So under the domination of egoistic need he can be active practically, and produce objects in practice, only by putting his products, and his activity, under the domination of an alien being, and bestowing the significance of an alien entity – money – on them.[68]

The Young Marx only explains the reversed relation of the subject and the external object by a concrete aspect of the capitalist economic process, which is the perspective of the fetishism of the universal money. Only when he carries out a comprehensive and systematic study of the process of the capitalist economy, the question can be observed on a deeper level.

After February 1844, he seriously turned to the economic researches that were more "realistic" than politics. His purpose was very clear: to find the

---

67   Marx, and Friedrich Engels. *Karl Marx, Friedrich Engels: Collected Works*. New York: International Publishers, 1975. p. 172.
68   *Ibid.*, p. 174.

theoretical foundation for the proletarian revolution. However, his concern with the economic theory was still *projected from the perspective of the philosophical logic.*

His initial plan was to publish two volumes of the *Critique of Political and National Economics* but he did not finish it. Despite it, he has left us with the preparatory notes and manuscripts. It is from his studies in this period that we see a further development of the economic theory of estrangement. In the *Paris Notebooks*, the most important text is his notes addressing James Mill's book, *Elements of Political Economy*, hereinafter referred to as the *Comments on James Mill.* In those important manuscripts, we find his estrangement theory greatly extended in both logical scope and degree, making a sudden leap forward of his theoretical understanding. *The Comments on James Mill* can be viewed as the *logic laboratory* for building the theory of economic estrangement because the entire model *in the classical sense* is initially constructed here.

We can see that the Young Marx actually puts his notes into the four parts of production, distribution, exchange and consumption in his reading of Mill's works. From the beginning to page 137, Section 8 of Part III, he never writes any commentary. His first *logical activation* appears in Section 6 of the same part. We should bear in mind the topic of Section 6: money. Marx inserts a word "medium" in the beginning of the section to arouse attention. In the part that Mill thinks the metal value and relation are decided by the cost of production, the Young Marx abruptly stops extraction and unexpectedly writes a long comment. That the personal argument occupies a considerable part is not a very common practice in other manuscripts of his. Indeed, the Young Marx is *making use of it for his own thought.*

With the comment as a beginning, Marx first criticizes that Mill makes the same mistake as that of the classical Bourgeois economists, that is, a non-historical approach to fossilize certain economic laws. Then, he makes a swift return to Section 6, where Mill calls money as the "medium of exchange." In a confirming tone, Marx says it is a very successful concept to express the essence of the matter. Why? Because money, as a medium, looks like an exchange link but people have lost themselves in the medium that alienates man's nature. Hence, Money acquires the "power" to dominate the subject and becomes the "*real god*" that is worshiped by man. With a Christian metaphor that Christ is the medium between man and God, Marx illustrates that the essence of money is the estrangement and reversal of man's nature. In fact, it is nothing but Marx's own mind exercise. I find that it is also buried here a tendency to *go on with* the above logic that money is the estrangement of man's essence in the text of "On the Jewish Question." However, this is no longer a simple continuation but an in-depth sublimation of the theoretical construction of the Young Marx.

According to the Young Marx, the nature of money does not lie with that transference through which property moves but the intermediary activity or movement on which the man-made products rely to complement each other. The *personal* and social activities are estranged and become the *material being* external to man.

> **Since man alienates this mediating activity itself, he is active here only as a man who has lost himself and is dehumanised; the relation itself between things, man's operation with them, becomes the operation of an entity outside man and above man. Owing to this alien mediator – instead of man himself being the mediator for man – man regards his will, his activity and his relation to other men as a power independent of him and them. His slavery, therefore, reaches its peak.[69]**

Here, man mainly refers to the labour that creates the social history. However, in reality, money acquires *the dominant position* as a mediating relation, by which the capitalist obtains the control of the labours. Therefore, it is a serious reversal.

Clearly, the Young Marx starts to jump from a specific question in economic studies to a general theoretical logic, that is, from the phenomenon of monetary estrangement upgraded to the study of the whole economic estrangement in capitalism. In this way, his theoretical research quite differs from the previous researches. It is not a step-by-step progress but a qualitative advancement. Because he *is consciously constructing his own complete logical framework of the economic estrangement.* The potential discourse quietly coincides with the consciously developed theory. Here, the Young Marx firmly grasps a very important issue that he notices not long ago, viz. man's change from the slave of nature to that of the material created by himself. In both conditions, *man is enslaved* and cannot master his own fate. It is clear to see a strong ethical and romantic hue in the humanistic view of history held by the Young Marx.

At the same time, it is discernible that Feuerbach's philosophy subtly plays a supportive role in the background. As we know, for Feuerbach, God is the reversed essence of man who creates the almighty deity but empties

---

69   *Ibid.*, p. 212.

the subject himself; accordingly, the incompetent *hollow man* crawls before the powerful material created by himself. In comparison, Marx stands higher than Feuerbach does in that he has reached the conclusive evidence of man's social essence from his natural humanity and essence, which is clearer than the estrangement logic proposed by him not long before.

> **Since human nature is the true community of men, by manifest-ing their nature men create, produce, the human community, the social entity, which is no abstract universal power opposed to the single individual, but is the essential nature of each in-dividual, his own activity, his own life, his own spirit, his own wealth.**[70]

Please note that this is the *designation of man's nature* by the Young Marx at that time, the a priori and authentic status that the subject *ought to* have *before being estranged*. This view has a more specific reference when compared to his previous thought of estrangement. It is also his first logical component in the theory of the economic estrangement.

Furthermore, when the Young Marx takes the *man-ought-to-have* scale to measure the contemporary capitalist economic life, he immediately finds that the nature of the subject, the labour, is completely estranged in his own economic life (another bad "is," just as in the process of the religious alienation). Here, "ought" and "is" become contradictory.

> **To say that *man* is estranged from himself, therefore, is the same thing as saying that the society of this estranged man is a cari-cature of his *real community*, of his true species-life, that his activity therefore appears to him as a torment, his own creation as an alien power, his wealth as poverty, the *essential bond* link-ing him with other men as an unessential bond, and separation from his fellow men, on the other hand, as his true mode of existence, his life as a sacrifice of his life, the realisation of his nature as making his life unreal, his production as the produc-tion of his nullity, his power over an object as the power of the object over him, and he himself, the lord of his creation, as the servant of this creation.**[71]

It becomes his second logical component. Now we understand that the Young Marx undergoes a series of philosophical changes, from the notice of the social and political separation/estrangement to the concern about the phenomenon of estrangement in the economic field, and then from the specific criticism of the monetary estrangement to the general logic

---

70   *Ibid.*, p. 217.
71   *Ibid.*

of the economic estrangement. As a Chinese saying goes, while dancing on the waves in retrospection, the boat has already passed the stretching mountains. With the ongoing steps of exploration, the Young Marx gradually alters his vision and thinking.

Marx's general logical construction of the estrangement theory already appears in his first discussion. From then on, the train of thought runs forward like an unbridled horse. After extracting the last half of Part III and Section III in Part IV, he once again addresses the inner connection between the capitalist private ownership and the economic estrangement, further confirming his complete logic framework of the estrangement theory. He sharply points out that production is done for the selfish material possession on the foundation of private ownership in reality. Hence, in production and exchanges, the relation between men, the essence of people, is no longer real and the products are no more "the link between the products we make for one another" but "a *different* selfish need, independent of him and alien to him," and "the *means* for giving me power over you."[72] Therefore, in the reality of the capitalist economy, "we are to such an extent estranged from man's essential nature that the direct language of this essential nature seems to us a *violation of human dignity*, whereas the estranged language of material values seems to be the well-justified assertion of human dignity that is self-confident and conscious of itself."[73] This is highlighted in two ways:

1) Each of us actually behaves in the way he is regarded by the other. You have actually made yourself the means, the instrument, the producer of your own object in order to gain possession of mine;

2) Only the sensuously *perceptible covering*, the *hidden shape*, of my object; for its production *signifies and seeks to express the acquisition* of my object. In fact, therefore, you have become for yourself a means, an instrument of your object, of which your desire is the *servant*.[74]

The Young Marx rebuts such estrangement of man's essence and the reversal of the human subject. According to him, the estranged subject is nobody else but the proletarian under the rule of the bourgeoisie. As analyzed above, he is now standing with the proletariat to seek the revolutionary basis and demands the critique of weapon to abandon the irrational social

---

72   *Ibid.*, p. 225.
73   *Ibid.*, p. 227.
74   *Ibid*

and historical phenomenon for the final return of the human subject to the normal state. However, as the revolution still begins from the mind of the philosopher at the moment, the elimination of estrangement and the emancipation of the human beings remain a philosophical conclusion of the humanistic values. It also accounts for the last logical component of his complete theory of the economic estrangement, namely, the *sublation of estrangement and the return of the subject from estrangement to his nature.* This is the logical expansion of the negation of the negation but within the *logical advancement* of the humanistic subjective dialectics. It should be noted that for the first time the Young Marx combines the negation of the negation with the historical development, especially, the critical tension of the existence in reality caused by the necessary negation of the negation, which is useful to understand his later logical transition of the criticism of capitalism based on the practice of the historical dialectics. Here, the Young Marx does not specify that the return of the subject mean communism. He just starts from the species nature of "man" to describe an ideal scene:

> Let us suppose that we had carried out production as human beings. Each of us would have in two ways *affirmed* himself and the other person. 1) In my *production* I would have objectified my *individuality*, its *specific character*, and therefore enjoyed not only an individual *manifestation of my life during* the activity, but also when looking at the object I would have the individual pleasure of knowing my personality to be *objective, visible to the senses* and hence a power *beyond all doubt.* 2) In your enjoyment or use of my product I would have the *direct* enjoyment both of being conscious of having satisfied a *human* need by my work, that is, of having objectified *man's* essential nature, and of having thus created an object corresponding to the need of another man's essential nature. 3) I would have been for you the *mediator* between you and the species, and therefore would become recognised and felt by you yourself as a completion of your own essential nature and as a necessary part of yourself, and consequently would know myself to be confirmed both in your thought and your love. 4) In the individual expression of my life I would have directly created your expression of your life, and therefore in my individual activity I would have directly *confirmed* and *realised* my true nature, my *human nature,* my *communal nature.*[75]

---

75   *Ibid.*, pp. 227-228.

To be frank, it is an idealized human context as if floating among the rosy clouds. The Young Marx then makes an immediate comparison of the different conditions in which the subject is estranged and not estranged. First, when the subject is not estranged, "my work would be a *free manifestation of life*, hence an enjoyment of life. Presupposing private property, my work is an *alienation of life*, for I work in order to live, in order to obtain for myself the *means* of life. My work is not my life."[76] Second, for the subject, "the specific nature of my *individuality*, therefore, would be affirmed in my labour, since the latter would be an affirmation of my *individual* life. Labour therefore would be *true, active property*."[77] Preconditioned by the context of private ownership, labour becomes a *forced* activity, a miserable task for man; so in the activity of the subject, the human individuality is but alienated. It is close to say that *labour is the essence of the subject* and the true nature of man acquired through abandoning the estrangement of labour is the fundamental foundation of human liberation. However, the Young Marx does not further explain the *concrete* aspects of the new point. In my view, he has finished the initial steps of constructing his first complete logic of estrangement. After all, the three logical components of the classical estrangement smoothly work. To my discovery, in the construction of the economic estrangement, the Young Marx seldom touches on the social and historical *foundation in reality* while the theoretical intention to seek the major elements in the social and historical development, that is, the inner discourse perceived from the position of the human subject and the humanistic speculative logic becomes his *main theoretical model*. In addition, it is a specific implementation of his humanistic dialectics in the field of social history, achieved through the operation of the *diachronic self-contradiction* of the subject's nature. And this achievement mainly concentrates on the critique of the reality of the capitalist economy.

The Young Marx is aware that he needs an opportunity to fully expound his new theory, which may account for the intrinsic theoretical impulses in the later development of the train of thought when writing the *Economic and Philosophical Manuscripts of 1844*.

B. THE QUADRUPLE ESTRANGEMENT OF THE LABOUR ESSENCE OF THE HUMAN SUBJECT

It is known that the economic estrangement theory is fully expanded in the *1844 Manuscripts*, the last major works during his early philosophical development. The Young Marx makes an intense criticism and negation

---

76 *Ibid.*, p. 228.
77 *Ibid*

of the economic estrangement in which the man or the proletarian has lost the historical subjective status in the social development. For the purpose of *finding the foundation for the proletarian revolution*, he naturally connects the analysis with the communist movement, which also forms the logical framework with the dominant elements of society and history as the main thread *centred on the estrangement of labour and its sublation*. Marx adopts the logical scale to make a more profound and systematic axiological and ethical critique of the capitalist economic life. First, the Young Marx always holds that the natural limits mainly account for the loss of the subjective status while spirit is the essence of man and thus the spiritual freedom can liberate man. Then, he begins to notice that that "abnormal" phenomenon of history originates not only from nature but also from the reversal of man's power, viz. the force of the man-created God or the political coercion. Finally, he is aware that in modern society man cannot be man not because he is subject to the external nature or the power outside him but that he is enslaved by the power made by himself. Here, the Young Marx says, "Not the gods, not nature, but only man himself can be this alien power over men."[78] The astounding statement inherits the critical reflection on the religious and authoritarian rule; it also demonstrates that the Young Marx eventually gets the essence of the de-subjective estrangement in the objective economic world created by man. Meanwhile, he finds that it is labour–instead of the previous spiritual power of reason–that creates the material world; therefore, all this de-subjective estrangement stems from the estrangement of man's creative evolution. "What was previously being external to oneself – man's actual externalisation – has merely become the act of externalising – the process of alienating."[79] "The domination of the land as an alien power over men is already inherent in feudal landed property."[80] This is "the complete domination of dead matter over man."[81] Today, this dominating force is neither the land nor the illusory gods, but an objective materialized world of economy created by man. The Young Marx says, "The *devaluation* of the world of men is in direct proportion to the increasing value of the world of things ... Labour produces, its product, stands opposed to it as something alien , as a power independent of the producer."[82]

---

78   *Ibid.*, p. 278.
79   *Ibid.*, p. 291.
80   *Ibid.*, p. 266.
81   *Ibid.*, p. 267.
82   *Ibid.*, p. 272.

In capitalism, "this realization of labour appears as *loss of realization* for the workers, objectification as *loss of the object and bondage to it*; appropriation as *estrangement, as alienation*."[83] Therefore, "the more the worker exerts himself in his work, the more powerful the alien, objective world becomes which he brings into being over against himself, the poorer he and his inner world become, and the less they belong to him."[84] Next, the Young Marx makes a very important systematic delineation of man's nature. Although his thinking has initially turned from Feuerbach's narration of man and nature to the "actual" social relationship of man, he does not specify its forms; and despite his talk of labour and the estrangement of labour, labour is still not identified as the ideal essence of the subject. This is changed in the *1844 Manuscripts*: *man's nature is further classified as the labour activities of the subject, the worker*. Here, labour does not mean the empirical activity in the reality of a specific historical process but a humanistic *hypothesis of subjective values*. According to the Young Marx, the labour here as man's nature shakes off all the subjective activities *in the original sense (the "ought")* of specification. It is the *creative activity that is free, independent and conscious as the real life action and the personification of the human subject*. It is the real species nature of man. In the *Comments on James Mill*, there is the Hegelian influence along with the impact of Feuerbach's philosophy. The Young Marx states "Hegel grasps *labour* as the essence of man – as man's essence which stands the test. The *real, active* orientation of man to himself as a species-being, or his manifestation as a real species-being (i.e., as a human being)."[85] However, he rejects Hegel's mistake of confusing the objectification with the estrangement and keenly captures the "negative aspect" of labour ignored by Hegel, that is, the *de-subjective* estrangement of labour, which undoubtedly brings philosophical vigour to Marx's thought. In his view, the subjective essence of man's labour ought to be the *dominant aspect* of history (Marx is not establishing the general *foundation* of social history here). Nevertheless, the specific labour in the past based on the private ownership "is" always estranged so that man loses his dominant aspect. It does not represent the subjective essence that man *ought to have possessed* but reverses and drops one's nature. The estrangement of the subject is noticeable in current capitalist economy, especially, the labour estrangement of the proletariat and the capital power generated from the estrangement of the essence of labour but growing

---

83   Ibid., p. 272.
84   Marx, Karl. *Early Writings*. Harmondsworth: Penguin Books, 1992. p. 324.
85   Marx, and Friedrich Engels. *Collected Works*. New York: International Publishers, 1975. p. 333.

to control the subject. During the capitalist process of production, the worker is regarded "only as a working animal – as a beast reduced to the strictest bodily needs."[86] In the *1844 Manuscripts*, Marx examines the four aspects of the worker's labour estrangement. First, the worker is *estranged from the product of labour* created by himself. In the philosophical logic of the Young Marx, the product of labour is the objectification of the worker subject that should realize himself through the product and naturally possess it. On the contrary, in the capitalist production, the worker cannot own that product; in addition he loses himself and "becomes a slave of his object." "The *externalisation* of the worker in his product means not only that his labour becomes an object, an *external* existence, but that it exists *outside* him, independently of him and alien to him, and begins to confront him as an autonomous power; that the life which he has bestowed on the object confronts him as hostile and alien."[87] Inevitably, it leads to the misleading and confusing consequences as described below.

> **The more the worker produces, the less he has to consume; the more value he creates, the more worthless he becomes; the more his product is shaped, the more misshapen the worker; the more civilized his object, the more barbarous the worker; the more powerful the work, the more powerless the worker; the more intelligent the work, the duller the worker and the more he becomes a slave of nature.[88]**

The Young Marx denies Hegel's confusion of objectification with estrangement, seizes the abnormal estrangement in which the worker is enslaved by his own created material, the objectified product of labour, and obtains the truth after painstaking investigations.

Another question is about *the estrangement of the labour activity per se*. The Young Marx further explores that the reason why the worker is dominated by his own product is the estrangement of his own creative activity. The labour as man's subjective essence "does not belong to his essential being; that he, therefore, does not confirm himself in his work, but denies himself, feels miserable and not happy, does not develop free mental and physical energy, but mortifies his flesh and ruins his mind."[89] In this condition, "external labour, labour in which man alienates himself, is a labour of self-sacrifice, of mortification."[90] Labour should have expressed the essence of

---

86   *Ibid.*, p. 242.
87   Marx, Karl. *Early Writings*. Harmondsworth: Penguin Books, 1992. p. 324.
88   Marx, and John C. Raines. *Marx on Religion*. Temple University Press, 2002. p. 120.
89   *Ibid.*, p. 121.
90   Marx, Karl. *Early Writings*. Harmondsworth: Penguin Books, 1992. p. 326.

the living subject and the activity to realize oneself in the subject's creation of the object. However, "this relationship is the relationship of the worker to his own activity as something which is alien and does not belong to him, activity as passivity, power as impotence, procreation as emasculation, the worker's own physical and mental energy, his personal life – for what is life but activity? – as an activity directed against himself, which is independent of him and does not belong to him."[91] It is the *self-estrangement*.

Then, *man and the estrangement of his species being*. According to the Young Marx, the free and conscious labour activity is the manifestation of life, and the species being of man as well. Man is different from the animal, which is immediately one with its life activity. Man makes his life activity itself an object of his will and consciousness. "Conscious life activity directly distinguishes man from animal life activity. Only because of that is he a species-being."[92] Although the animal is also involved in certain production, it is fundamentally different from that of man.

> But they produce only their own immediate needs or those of their young; they produce only when immediate physical need compels them to do so, while man produces even when he is free from physical need and truly produces only in freedom from such need; they produce only themselves, while man reproduces the whole of nature; their products belong immediately to their physical bodies, while man freely confronts his own product. Animals produce only according to the standards and needs of the species to which they belong, while man is capable of producing according to the standards of every species and of applying to each object its inherent standard; hence, man also produces in accordance with the laws of beauty.[93]

Similarly, man's product and his created world of object world become the species being of the human objectification, or the humanized natural world.

The meaning of human existence is to continuously create and transform the world, through which man can truly prove his species being. This life is the active species living and through such production, nature is represented as man's product and becomes man's reality. Therefore, the object of labour is the objectification of man's species living: man not only makes a rational copy of himself as in the consciousness but also dynamically and actually realizes himself so he can take an intuitive perception of himself

---

91   *Ibid.*, p. 327.
92   *Ibid.*, p. 327.
93   *Ibid.*, p. 328.

in his own world. However, the estranged labour reverses that relationship and converts this representation of man's life into a mere means of survival; at the same time, the estranged labour deprives man of his productive object and thus exterminates his species life, turning all the merits that man has over the animals into disadvantages. Their estrangement, together with that of man, becomes the estranged species being of man. Here, the "species" is the antithesis of the human individuals.

Last but not least, due to man's estrangement with his own product, life activities and species being, *he is naturally estranged with others*. No personality, no creation, no life, only repetitions and mechanic productions. When the worker is opposed to his own product and activities, those things must belong to another person, who, of course, is the capitalist. It then generates the confrontation and estrangement of man with the other.

> **So through estranged labour man not only produces his relationship to the object and to the act of production as to alien and hostile powers; he also produces the relationship in which other men stand to his production and product, and the relationship in which he stands to these other men. Just as he creates his own production as a loss of reality, a punishment, and his own product as a loss, a product which does not belong to him, so he creates the domination of the non-producer over production and its product.[94]**

The "non-producer" indicates the capitalist, who, in the eyes of the Young Marx, is not the "man"- the subject, but the thing, the incarnation of the capital – the dead labour. The capitalist is thus an estranged existence and a materialized false subject. Accordingly, the Young Marx says "each man is estranged from the others and that all are estranged from man's essence" in the estrangement of labour.[95]

In short, the human subject creates a new material world–"is" by means of labour but loses everything that he *ought to have possessed* in that world. This is a battle without fire, in which everything is destroyed while the culprit proves to be man himself. Ironically, the necessary right of the subject is reversed to the dominant power of the material capital; man loses himself and allows his own created material, the capital, to acquire life. It is the estrangement of man's labour essence.

---

94   *Ibid.*, p. 331.
95   *Ibid.*, p. cccxxxi.

Here, we clearly see the philosophical framework initiated in the *Comments on James Mill*, a humanistic Estrangement view of history based on the a priori subject. In the *1844 Manuscripts*, he first sets an idealized labour as the essence of the subject, which, unsurprisingly and fully, illustrates the subjective initiative surpassing the external object. When the species being of man, with our familiar standard of "ought" as an important inner logical component in the traditional humanism, is taken to measure the capitalist production, the Young Marx finds the reversion of man and the material, the loss of man's species essence and the self-estrangement of man that he already sees in the social political field. It demonstrates the actual operation of the axiological philosophy that is inseparable from the estrangement view of history. I would like to point out that the humanistic estrangement theory is *greatly enhanced* and becomes the power discourse that absolutely dominates his *1844 Manuscripts*. In addition, another big step forward is that the estrangement theory has become a conscious tool of logic in his mind.

We should also pay attention to the substantial *sameness* of the estrangement theory of labour with the humanistic subjective dialectic. With Hegel, the estrangement relation corresponds to the negation of the negation, which is in fact the diachronic extension of a certain contradiction between the subject and the object. By comparison, we find a relativity in Marx's text here. From the standpoint of the humanistic subjective dialectics, he criticizes the abstract *affirmation* in Hegel's idealistic stipulation of the negation of the negation with the purpose to change the actual foundation from idea to "the real history of man as a given subject" and as "only *the act of creation, the history of the origin of man*."[96] He intends to confirm the *criticism and true negation* of the capitalist reality from the negation of the negation about the historical evolution of man, the subject. Therefore, the Young Marx's subjective dialectic is driven by the contradiction of the subject-object estrangement and the historical process of the estrangement and restoration of labour is the negation of the negation about the subject's self-realization, during which, the first stipulation of the subjective movement, the idealized *confirmation* of labour, is a logic hypothesis of value and an authentic ought in the ethical sense but without true existence; the second point is the actual living condition of man, estranged and alienated in the context of private ownership. It is a *negation* of the status that the subject should have had (It "is" also the reality); the last is the sublation of estrangement, that is, "the real appropriation of the human essence by

---

96   *Ibid.*, p. 382.

and for man; therefore as the complete return of man to himself as a *social* (i.e., human) being." It is the communist "appropriation of the human essence through the intermediary of the negation of private property."[97] Fundamentally, it is a negation of the negation achieved by the necessity of the process of the theoretical logic. Accompanied by the stipulations of the labour estrangement, it ushers in the critical and negative reality of capitalism.

In my opinion, there is an astute accomplishment contained in the theory of the labour estrangement of the Young Marx: 1) the *direct completion* of his estrangement theory; 2) the *historical completion* of the discourse of the subjective dialectics with the impulses of the subject's initiative stressed in his philosophical thought; 3) the *preliminary formation* of his first critical theory on the social values of the proletariat. It can be interpreted as his philosophical "trinity," to be exact, *the logic of the estrangement view of history, the discourse of the subjective dialectic and the fusion of humanism with the philosophical critique of value.*

It is true that his philosophy at this time is inspired by Hegel and Feuerbach but for the most part, it is from his own theoretical gushes. The Young Marx is never confined by a certain philosophical trend. Although various thoughts have left impacts on him, he still flies high in the theoretical sky of his own and makes all those influences his logical tools. Therefore, we can obviously feel the striking theoretical features of the Young Marx at different times. As for the discussions here, it refers to his constant concern of the *initiative with which the human subject surpasses and dominates the object.* If interpreted in the postmodern discourse, it contains a very strong anthropocentrism here. The theory of labour estrangement is the most complete logical confirmation of the discourse of the subjective dialectics in the theoretical development of the Young Marx as well as a systematic verification of the estrangement after his specific analysis of the Hegelian estrangement of self-consciousness, social politics and money because here come all the theoretical components of the *classical* estrangement theory, namely, the *a priori subject*–the species being of man's labour, the *estrangement* of the subject's labour and the *return* to the subject after the *sublation* of estrangement. It reaches the *theoretical summit* after the logic of alienation initiated by Hegel, worthy of many high regards later.

---

97   Marx, and Friedrich Engels. *Karl Marx, Friedrich Engels: Collected Works.* New York: International Publishers, 1975. p. 313.

It is not difficult to find that the Young Marx only catches a phenomenon of reversal in the process of the capitalist society and economy with his theory of estrangement as the *result*. He does not go further to find the historical reason and the necessity that generate this social phenomenon. He seems to know that the private ownership in capitalism is *not good* but unable to see the objective historical rationality of this capitalist mode of production. Consequently, he cannot draw the right revolutionary conclusion here. In short, an ethical criticism naturally leads to a theoretical fantasy.

C. COMMUNISM: THE COMPLETED HUMANISM IN A SUBJECTIVE SENSE

As noted above, the Young Marx already turns to the political stance of the working class and begins to seek the foundation for the proletarian revolution to overthrow capitalism. Early in the *1844 Manuscripts*, the theory of estrangement points to the capitalist economic life in reality; this time it is bound to become the important tool for the introduction of communism. We can perceive that the Young Marx makes the profound criticism and negation of the estrangement of labour with the hope of sublating the estrangement and returning to the true essence of man. Here, the sublation of the labour estrangement, the private ownership, means communism, which is the axiological "ought." The Young Marx has not yet determined its objective necessity in the reality of the economic development. In particular, he has not found the *realistic road* towards the realization of the objective. In his analysis of the capitalist mode of production, he says:

> Through *estranged, alienated labour*, the worker creates the relationship of another man, who is alien to labour and stands outside it, to that labour. The relation of the worker to labour creates the relation of the capitalist – or whatever other word one chooses for the master of labour – to that labour. *Private property* is therefore the product, result, and necessary consequence of *alienated labour*, of the external relation of the worker to nature and to himself.[98]

According to him, "estranged labour is the immediate cause of private property."[99] And "the emancipation of society from private property, etc., from servitude, is expressed in the *political* form of *the emancipation of the workers*. This is not because it is only a question of their emancipation, but because in their emancipation is contained universal human

---

98   Marx, Karl. *Early Writings*. Harmondsworth: Penguin Books, 1992. p. cccxxxiii.
99   *Ibid.*, p. 333.

emancipation."[100] Therefore, "the positive transcendence of private property as the appropriation of *human* life, is therefore the positive transcendence of all estrangement – that is to say, the return of man from religion, family, state, etc., to his *human*, i.e., *social* existence."[101] The presence of such society means the living existence of man as the subject, which also expresses the main affirmation of the communist revolution by the Young Marx.

> **Communism as the *positive transcendence of private property as human self-estrangement*, and therefore as the real appropriation of the human essence by and for man; communism therefore as the complete return of man to himself as a *social* (i.e., human) being – a return accomplished consciously and embracing the entire wealth of previous development. This communism, as fully developed naturalism, equals humanism, and as fully developed humanism equals naturalism; it is the *genuine* resolution of the conflict between man and nature and between man and man.[102]**

It needs to be stressed that the sublation of the estrangement and the restoration of the reversed relationship between man and the material do not result in the new *dominance and enslavement of nature and the object by man* but lead to a final solution to the relation between man and nature, the object. (The point is also related by the ecological Marxism and the Frankfurt School in its later stage.) Obviously, the Young Marx paints a humanistic colour on communism and his conclusion is not the objective law of the social development but a *logical result* of the subjective dialectics in the ethical sense. Communism is a positive sublation of the private property; it does not negate the objectified labour but abandons the estranged labour. The world in reality is the objectification of man's essence while repossessing the objectified world means the restoration of the lost essence of man. Of course, such repossession is no longer partial or individual but takes the social form "in a comprehensive manner" to fully and truly hold one's essence, not that self-interested ownership and dominance. Meanwhile, communism is also a natural generation for man. Nature becomes man's nature through man's producing activities while only as a social being can, he really possess nature. The future expectations are always full of pleasant melodies. In a *futurological* sense, Marx passionately writes:

100   Marx, and John C. Raines. *Marx on Religion.* Temple University Press, 2002. p. 126.
101   Marx, and Friedrich Engels. *Karl Marx, Friedrich Engels: Collected Works.* New York: International Publishers, 1975. p. 297.
102 *Ibid.*, p. 296.

> Thus the social character is the general character of the whole movement: *just as* society itself produces *man as man*, so is society *produced* by him. Activity and enjoyment, both in their content and in their *mode of existence*, are social: social activity and social enjoyment. The *human* aspect of nature exists only for *social* man; for only then does nature exist for him as a bond with man – as his existence for the other and the other's existence for him – and as the life-element of human reality. Only then does nature exist as the *foundation* of his own human existence. Only here has what is to him his *natural* existence become his *human* existence, and nature become man for him. Thus *society is the complete unity of man with nature* – the true resurrection of nature – the consistent naturalism of man and the consistent humanism of nature.[103]

For this, he cites another example. "When I am active *scientifically*, etc. – an activity which I can seldom perform in direct community with others – then my activity is *social*, because I perform it as a man. Not only is the material of my activity given to me as a social product (as is even the language in which the thinker is active): my *own* existence is social activity, and therefore that which I make of myself, I make of myself for society and with the consciousness of myself as a social being."[104] Here, the consciousness is used in a general sense, that is, "only the theoretical shape of that of which the living shape is the real community, the social fabric,"[105] and under the condition of the labour estrangement the "general consciousness is an abstraction from real life and as such confronts it with hostility. The activity of my general consciousness, as an activity, is therefore also my theoretical existence as a social being."[106]

Moreover, the Young Marx makes an analysis with a *comparative logical scale*, which is deeper than that in the *Comments on James Mill*. In his view, if in the previous condition of estrangement and private property, "man becomes objective for himself and at the same time becomes to himself a strange and inhuman object; just as it expresses the fact that the manifestation of his life is the alienation of his life, that his realisation is his loss of reality, is an alien reality," while in the communist society where the private ownership is abandoned, his activities become "the perceptible appropriation for and by man of the human essence and of human life, of objective man, of human achievements," and thus "man appropriates

103   *Ibid.*, p. 298.
104   *Ibid.*
105   *Ibid.*
106   *Ibid.*, p. 299.

his comprehensive essence in a comprehensive manner, that is to say, as a whole man."[107] "The appropriation of the object, the appropriation of *human* reality" and their "orientation to the object is the *manifestation of the human reality... it is human *activity* and human *suffering*, for suffering, humanly considered, is a kind of self-enjoyment of man."[108] Here, the Young Marx makes another explanation by liberating man's sense. For him, "the abolition of private property is therefore the complete *emancipation* of all human senses and qualities have become, subjectively and objectively, human."[109] And the position of the material is also restored: "In practice I can relate myself to a thing humanly only if the thing relates itself humanly to the human being."[110] "The care-burdened, poverty-stricken man has no sense for the finest play; the dealer in minerals sees only the commercial value but not the beauty and the specific character of the mineral."[111] In short, the capitalist society reverses the relationship between men to a material one, a typical expression of estrangement.

> **Estrangement is manifested not only in the fact that my means of life belong to *someone else*, that which I desire is the inaccessible possession of *another*, but also in the fact that everything is itself something different from itself – that my activity is *something else* and that, finally (and this applies also to the capitalist), all is under (the sway) of *inhuman* power.[112]**

After quoting the famous lines about the gold in Shakespeare's *Timon of Athens*, the Young Marx comments, "the *divine* power of money – lies in its character as men's estranged, alienating and self-disposing species-nature."[113] It is "the visible divinity – the transformation of all human and natural properties into their contraries, the universal confounding and distorting of things: impossibilities are soldered together by it."[114] "Money is the *alienated ability of mankind*."[115] "It transforms fidelity into infidelity, love into hate, hate into love, virtue into vice, vice into virtue, servant into master, master into servant, idiocy into intelligence, and intelligence into idiocy."[116] In summary, money reverses all the relations of man. However,

---

107   *Ibid*
108   *Ibid.*, p. 300.
109   *Ibid*
110   *Ibid*
111   *Ibid.*, p. 302.
112   *Ibid.*, p. 314.
113   *Ibid.*, p. 325.
114   *Ibid.*, p. 324.
115   *Ibid.*, p. 325.
116   *Ibid.*, p. 326.

when it comes to communism, the heavy haze of money will be dispersed and the sun will shine again in the blue sky.

> **Assume *man* to be *man* and his relationship to the world to be a human one: then you can exchange love only for love, trust for trust, etc. If you want to enjoy art, you must be an artistically cultivated person; if you want to exercise influence over other people, you must be a person with a stimulating and encouraging effect on other people.**[117]

Here comes the *first* comprehensive and systematic argument about communism in the logic of the Young Marx. But it is only *an ideal that the reality ought to accord with*, or a beautiful illusion of rationality. In that ideal state, the human subject regains the dominant position, surpasses the material objects again, and wins the complete freedom and liberation.

D. AN IMPORTANT THEORETICAL CLARIFICATION

The study of the economic estrangement has been an important issue in the philosophical development of the Young Marx. My discussion here is basically extended in accordance with the evolution of the inner logic in the Young Marx's philosophy. Due to the complexity of the question as such, I have to make a demarcation here.

First, the recent textual research reveals that the *1844 Manuscripts* only composes a part of the 12 notebooks made by the Young Marx who extracted and made notes after reading a large amount of economic literature in 1844. Besides, writing was not an uninterrupted process. Three notebooks among them are believed to be written with continual reading. We should pay a serious attention to it. In the explanation of Volume 2 in Part I of the latest Marx/Engels Collected Works (MEGA2), the editors assume that it was after the completion of the *1844 Manuscripts* that the Young Marx made the economic notes of David Ricardo and James Mill. The assumption is based on the observation that there is no direct extracts of the words of Ricardo and Miller in the last half of the Manuscripts, the last pages of the second notebook and the whole third notebook.[118] However, it contradicts my analysis here. This book does not take that conclusion for granted. In my opinion, the writing of the *1844 Manuscripts* indeed happened during Marx's initial study of the economics. However, due to his adoption of the philosophical perspective to observe the economic questions, he was not entirely occupied by the reading materials. More impor-

---

117   *Ibid.*
118   See *Materials for the Study of Marxism.* 2 (1984): 37.

tantly, his own philosophical development demonstrates that the idea of the economic estrangement in the *Comments on James Mill* is only the embryo of the labour estrangement theory. As noted above, the framework of the estrangement view of history in the classical sense was first established in the *Comments on James Mill* but fully developed and systematically corroborated in the *1844 Manuscripts*.

Second, the theoretical analysis so far in this section has been centred on the humanistic estrangement view of history and the discourse of the subjective dialectics in the philosophical thought of the Young Marx, which, as clearly mentioned before, is also the dominant logical framework of his theoretical development at that time. However, in the *1844 Manuscripts*, we easily see another theoretical logic, which *inherits the materialist thought that proceeds from the objective reality* in the *Critique of Hegel's Philosophy of Law*. It is also his theoretical perception to ascertain the *foundation in reality* of the social history with the scale of materialism. (That theoretical development is not treated as a major subject in this book.)

In fact, the *1844 Manuscripts* adopts a general humanistic logic to criticize the phenomenon of the labour estrangement and the oppression of the human subject, the worker, and expose other irrational things existent in the capitalist society. However, the delicate theory can only develop by relying on the evergreen practice. During his in-depth studies of the economic phenomena, the more he approaches the economic reality, the further he involuntarily deviates from his original theoretical logic, that is, to abandon the a priori setting of logic and proceed from reality, from the real foundation of the development of social history. Many theoretical points of the Young Marx unconsciously approach the first great discovery of his philosophical revolution: the historical materialism. While in the specific analysis, his view can be interpreted as follows: the production of material goods is the most fundamental production while "the realisation or the reality of man," and "religion, family, state, law, morality, science, art, etc., are only *particular* modes of production, and fall under its general law."[119] Here, the "general law" does not refer to the "species essence" of man but the objective rule of the social development. He also notes that "the history of industry and the established *objective* existence of industry are the *open book of man's essential powers*."[120] If the industrial history is the "book" of man's essence, that book must be turned page by page. It then leads to the

---

119   Marx, and Friedrich Engels. *Karl Marx, Friedrich Engels: Collected Works*. New York: International Publishers, 1975. p. 297.
120   *Ibid.*, p. 302.

trend as described by Marx: "natural science has invaded and transformed human life all the more *practically* through the medium of industry; and has prepared human emancipation," and "*industry* is the *actual*, historical relationship of nature, and therefore of natural science, to man,"[121] while "the *entire so-called history of the world* is nothing but the creation of man through human labour, nothing but the emergence of nature for man."[122] At that moment, the Young Marx actually grows out of the humanistic estrangement logic that is dominant in the *1844 Manuscripts*. After going through a long night of exploration, he comes to the edge of the new philosophical vision. In his eyes, "the resolution of the *theoretical* antitheses is only possible in a practical way, by virtue of the practical energy of man. Their resolution is therefore by no means merely a problem of understanding, but a *real* problem of life."[123] Indeed, the Young Marx almost touches on the *realistic road* of how to eliminate the estrangement of labour and the private ownership.

There are actually two theoretical clues in the *1844 Manuscripts*: one is the logic/discourse of the subjective dialectics with the humanistic estrangement view of history based on the a priori subject; the other is the logic based on the material production – practice and industry – in reality to observe social history – "is." Here, I want to reiterate that the first is the dominant logical framework of the Young Marx at that time while the latter is only a negative element of the new theoretical clue, but he is still unable to identify the objective necessity of "is" in the latter with the negative bad "is" in the former clue due to a profound paradox between them. This accords with what we see in the *Critique of Hegel's 'Philosophy of Right'*. If examined from a historical perspective, it is still the continuation of the two views that have been existent in the inner philosophical development of the Young Marx. Therefore, I cannot agree with the philosopher Louis Althusser, who makes a simplistic conclusion of the Young Marx's development of thought, especially his later philosophical reform, as an "epistemological break." In fact, the scientific worldview of the Young Marx also undergoes a historical process. Early in the *1844 Manuscripts*, we see the initial clue of that scientific thread.

In addition, I want to draw attention to some significant sparks in his deeper logic here. First, when the Young Marx exiles nature from reality to the logical framework in the *1844 Manuscripts*, he changes his idea

---

121   *Ibid.*, p. 303.
122   *Ibid.*, p. 305.
123   *Ibid.*, p. 302.

and begins to esteem nature. Man's essence is nature and the personified nature, naturalized man and history is the true natural history of man. It goes without saying that the nature here is honoured as the object of man after casting off the estrangement. In fact, it is an *inflated natural human- ism*, which is not contradictory to Marx's previous negation of man con- strained by nature and his placement of the history of nature in antithesis to that of man. Strictly speaking, it is not a view revealed by contemporary ecological studies.

Second, we also find the impact of classical economics in this book. It puts forward the non-subjective problem that is characteristic of the capitalist economy from the angle of positive economics. For example, the Young Marx once confirms that Ricardo exposes the *blind control of the world* by the capitalist economic laws, which develops the opinion that the capitalist economic rules are determined by their opposite, irregularity, identified in the *Comments on James Mill*. Moreover, he proposes the natural tendency of the capitalist movement: "it is precisely through competition that the way is cleared for this natural disposition of capital."[124] The "natural dispo- sition" here refers to the non-human power out of man's control. It should be noted that it is an economic fact instead of a humanistic logical conclu- sion. We shall see a major theoretical expansion in the later development of the philosophical and economic thought of the Young Marx.

---

124   *Ibid.*, p. 251.

CHAPTER II

THE HUMAN SUBJECT AND THE DEVELOPMENT OF SOCIAL HISTORY BY THE NEW PHILOSOPHICAL HORIZON

1 *The Conversion of the Dominant Logical Framework in Philosophical Changes*
2 *The Natural Process and the Social-Historical Process on the New Philosophical Horizon*
3 *The Subjective Status of Man from the Perspective of Historical Dialectics*

CHAPTER TWO

INTRODUCTION

Marx's philosophy with new horizon finally emerged in the spring of 1845. The important philosophical revolution came into being through a gradual development. He first makes a scientific solution of the basic logic to observe social history, establishes the dominant discourse with social practice as the foundation, expedites the great discovery of historical materialism (historical dialectics) and externalizes it into a general view of the world at long last. With the complete new theory, Marx unlocks a series of important paradoxes on deeper philosophical levels and finally obtains the scientific existence and development for the philosophy of humankind. It is here that many questions are finally solved, such as the issues of man and nature, the individual and society, the foundation and dominance of social history, the value requirements of the proletariat and the scientific road of realizing communism, etc.

I. THE CONVERSION OF THE DOMINANT LOGICAL FRAMEWORK IN PHILOSOPHICAL CHANGES

Marx's new philosophical horizon took form in 1845. In the same year, his two books, *Theses on Feuerbach* and the *German Ideology*, marked the birth of a new Marxist worldview. It is, of course, not a simplistic continuation of the *1844 Manuscripts* but a major qualitative leap forward, a "break," as the French philosopher Louis Althusser describes in an almost meta-physical expression, because it is here that the logical framework of Marx's philosophy experiences a Gestalt transformation. He generally abandons the logical context of the estrangement view of history based on the transcendental essence of the human subject and discovers a different foundation – the historical, concrete and actual social practice. From that, a new philosophical horizon of practical materialism is created.

A. THREE MAJOR PROBLEMS IN THE CONVERSION OF MARX'S PHILOSOPHICAL LOGIC

In the eyes of Althusser, the *1844 Manuscripts* represent the darkness before dawn for the Young Marx.[1] The book, despite its temporal closeness to the beginning of the new worldview, is logically the most distant from the sun of truth. Although not in total agreement with Althusser's opinion, I think the *1844 Manuscripts* is written during a chaotic but creative period when the dominant logical framework and power discourse are, without doubt, still with the humanistic estrangement view of history, a paradigm proceeding from the main logic of the subjective essence of "man" to manipulate all the theoretical stipulations. As we know, at that time, Marx is also seeking the foundation for the proletarian revolution. However, the more he is rooted in reality, the further he is forced to comply with another line of thought that is oriented towards the real foundation of social history. We can see the traces of the potential logical conflict in the *1844 Manuscripts*. I hereby repeat that they are not equivalent and parallel logics. The former is Marx's logical framework per se while the latter is a new general negativity included in the former. But Marx does not realize it himself. Once he knows, a fundamental theoretical change naturally ensues.

I disagree with Althusser in that Marx's new philosophical horizon does not abruptly come up from nowhere. Moreover, his conversion of philosophical logic is not a change of fields but a solution to the deep logical paradox in his own philosophy. As we know, in the first change around

---

1   Althusser, Louis. *For Marx*. London: Verso, 2005. p. 36.

1843, the Young Marx's philosophical thought covers the multiple logical contradictions that are interwoven with each other. He turns from the Young Hegel's idealism to Feuerbach's materialism, from the bourgeois democratism to communism; meanwhile, his own philosophical thinking drives the criticism of Feuerbach's naturalistic humanism and religious alienation to the critique of labour estrangement with a concern with the subjective status in social history, which then becomes the foundation for the proletarian revolution. The subjective requirement contains his affirmation of Hegel's dynamic dialectics. On a deeper level, Marx's attention to the historical condition of the proletariat in reality synchronizes the return of his philosophical logic to the objective historical process. Thus, he has a new perception based on the industrial production in reality, another theoretical development of the new horizon of historical materialism that we shall discuss.

We should not stop with the general conflicts of the above logical tendencies. Instead, Marx faces several compound challenges at that time. As we know, the dominant part of the Young Marx's philosophical discourse from 1838 to 1842 preaches the creative abilities of the human subject. However, the severe reality shakes his initial theoretical standpoint to subject the initiative of the subject to the subjective spirit (the Hegelian self-consciousness). Therefore, he has to rely on Feuerbach's materialism but he does not pause at the naturalistic materialism after being a materialist philosopher. Despite his reversal of the previous position of material and spirit, he returns to the initiative of the social subject's standard discourse from Feuerbach's passive naturalistic human subject because Marx cannot bear the de-subjective status of the subject enslaved by the external force, which is exactly of the same theoretical value in his search for the foundation of the proletarian revolution! Therefore, Marx seems to be confined to the traditional Feuerbachian camp but actually yearns to leave and press on. His dominant logical framework is Feuerbach's humanistic estrangement view of history but he is reluctant to give up the Hegelian dialectics that conform to his inner thoughts; in addition, once he approaches the objective economic process, he unconsciously embarks on a logical way to face the historical reality. Nevertheless, the moment he enters the actual rationality – "is," it contradicts his basic political stance – "ought" – to beat down capitalism – the bad "is." Marx is stranded in the vacillating comparison of multiple viewpoints and collision of manifold forces. He finds it a very hard task to make the final decision. As analyzed above, the *1844 Manuscripts* are still aimed at developing his own thought on the basis of communist perception. And Marx still puts the subjective essence as an "ought," the ideal labour, opposed to the real existence, the estranged status of the species essence of man; thus, communism becomes the logical result of the abstract axiological hypothesis and the sublation of the estranged labour. Here, Marx's philosophical logic remains a hidden idealistic view of history because the inner driving force of the social and historical development still lies with the idealized "species" requirement of the subjective reason.

To break the logical obstacle, Marx needs a new entry that must have the following attributes at a time:

(1) To proceed from the human subject, in particular, to maintain the function of the self-established creativity of the human subject. It is both the potential discourse that runs consistently in Marx's philosophical logic and the Hegelian dynamic dialectics most prone to self-certification in his own logical structure. However, in the *1844 Manuscripts*, the validation of the subjective initiative changes shape and precisely transforms into the humanistic estrangement view of history.

(2) To proceed from the objective reality, especially, to make the theoretical framework comply with the foundation of social life in reality. It is the basic position of Marx's materialism at that time and a general materialist doctrine of Feuerbach, on which Marx relies after his disapproval of Hegel's idealistic subjectivity. This principle is unconsciously weakened in the emphasis on the subjective status of man in the *1844 Manuscripts*.

(3) To proceed from the social revolution, particularly, to enable the real establishment of the sense of calling for the proletarian revolution. For the time being, it remains a communist impulse to demand ethical values and Feuerbach's alienation of history is an important theoretical basis for that request, which, has long been ignored in our research. However, it is Marx's most concerned issue and theoretical objective at that time.

Although the previous logic of Marx has eliminated Hegel's idealism, his methodological and structural dialectics are apparently undermined at the same time. The operation of affirming the subjective initiative discourse is made through a meandering theoretical requirement: the humanistic dialectical discourse with the logical tool of Feuerbach's alienation of history. Instead of fully accepting the Feuerbachian naturalistic humanism, Marx extols man on a social critical level, and thus, with intention or not, weakens Feuerbach's doctrine. In particular, the "unfinished" idealistic view of history that intends to dictate the history in reality with the subjective reason recesses to the depths of Marx's theoretical logic at the moment.

Here, Marx's Communism also continues the same utopian "ought" and the criticism of capitalism becomes an ethical slogan that is romantic and empty. In short, Marx has to solve the three theoretical questions at once: to eliminate idealism and carry forward the dialectical initiative; to reject mechanicalism in the naturalistic materialism and adhere to the basic stand of materialism; and to criticize capitalism and found the scientific communism.

In my opinion, Marx's solution stems from the negation and transcendence of his own dominant framework and power discourse, which is first represented in a direct denial of Feuerbach's logical structure of humanism and aims to resolve the above issues on a new theoretical level. Of course, Marx's new philosophical logic does not come out of nowhere but comes into being during a gradual theoretical development, especially the connection of theory with reality. It means that dilemma is broken in the actual struggles. We see an important pre-clue of the theoretical development in *The Holy Family* written by Marx and Engels in late 1844.

The book mainly targets the idealistic view of history by Herr Bruno Bauer and others in the German philosophical circle. It proceeds from Feuerbach. In other words, although *The Holy Family* remains in the theoretical framework of the Feuerbachian humanism, a new dynamic pattern already emerges in the statements of Marx and Engels. First, the more objectively Marx and Engels examine man in reality, the further away they depart from Feuerbach's abstract man; second, the more their view is based on the social history and the actual development, the less dominant is the general logic of estrangement and restoration of the subject's essence. When the new theory is being improved systematically, the old restriction still lingers on. The theoretical revolution has to wait for the dawn.

The idealistic philosophy of Hegel and Bauer is put in perspective by the deep engagement of thought with reality in the field of social history. First of all, in the previous philosophical logic, Marx adopts the humanistic stand to stress that only man restores the estranged essence or realizes the unification of man and nature as well as man and man can he become the real man in reality. Thus, in Marx's reflection of reality, he criticizes the in- and anti-human nature in the capitalist society. That theoretical clue still plays a supportive role now. Marx and Engels further point out that the loss of the means of existence indicates the loss of man per se, and his essence. Therefore, the eradication of the real estrangement between man and his objective essence means the actual change of the real existence and the condition of existence; hence the repossession of the means of existence. It can be interpreted that the "objective essence" above is very close to the important stipulation of the material means of subsistence. Furthermore, "the object as being for man, as the objective being of man, is at the same time the existence of man for other men, his human relation to other men, the social behaviour of man to man."[2] And the "change of the condition of existence" in reality is actually arguing for the realistic way to eliminate the estrangement or realize communism. Here, we can see that the philosophical framework of Marx and Engels is still dominated by Feuerbach's humanism but they often make some theoretical logical shifts in their operation of the concrete discourses, for instance, their fundamental return to the process of social history in reality, which appears harmonious but is actually inconsistent.

In addition, when Marx and Engels criticize the exclusion of the industrial research in the natural science to the understanding of history, they carry out a profound analysis:

> **Or does Critical Criticism believe that it has reached even the beginning of a knowledge of historical reality so long as it excludes *from* the historical movement the theoretical and practical relation of man to nature, i.e., natural science and industry? Or does it think that it actually knows any period without knowing, for example, the industry of that period, the immediate mode of Production of life itself?[3]**

Needless to say, Marx and Engels have actually surpassed Feuerbach here. The stipulation of practice already takes the specific form of "industry" on their theoretical horizon.

Most importantly, Marx does not focus on the positive aspects of production and labour in the *1844 Manuscripts*, where, instead, lies his concern about the negative aspect of labour, estrangement. He does not validate labour with the objectification of production and the creativity in reality, that is, not from the perspective of productive forces but from the angle of social relations to analyze the nature of capitalist employment and oppose the full support to labour by Hegel and other bourgeois economists. Here, they begin a serious affirmation of the huge creative role that the worker plays in the reality of history. In their eyes, the workers construct the world through labour and production, even including the generation of people himself. "Ideas can never lead beyond an old world order but only beyond

---

2   Marx, and Friedrich Engels. *Marx and Engels Collected Works* 1844-45. New York: International Publishers, 1975. p. 43.

3   *Ibid.*, p. 150.

the ideas of the old world order. Ideas cannot carry out anything at all. In order to carry out ideas men are needed who can exert practical force."[4] The only way to eliminate the estranged subjugation of the proletariat is practice. Obviously, the philosophical thought of Marx and Engels is greatly developed in *The Holy Family*. The old humanistic logic is riddled with problems while the new thought based on the reality of social history approaches the critical change out of the overall negation. However, the previous three problems have not been solved. It is even believable that *The Holy Family* represents the most chaotic status of his philosophical thought because of the incomplete deletion of the former Feuerbachian humanistic ideology from it despite their recognizable preference for the reality of social history, the subject-emphasized dialectics unable to find the real historical foundation despite their in-depth criticism of Hegel's idealism, and, most of all, the proletarian revolution only as a philosophical requirement, the real integration of which with the process of social history remains unsolved. In short, the original problems still persist and wait for a breakthrough aground. The establishment of a new world necessitates a different set of coordinates. With the removal of the old thoughts by fresh ideas, the truth will be revealed in an innovative theoretical framework. The new philosophical horizon is about to emerge with a theoretical revolution.

B. MARX'S INITIAL DECONSTRUCTION OF THE LOGICAL FRAMEWORK OF THE ESTRANGED LABOUR

Marx blew the horn of philosophical revolution in the spring of 1845. In that year, his logical framework of the estranged labour with humanistic characters came across a sudden deconstruction, which was a crucial signal of changes. In my judgment, that theoretical deconstruction takes place in the "Draft of an Article on Friedrich List's book: Das Nationale System der Politischen Ökonomie" written by Marx in March. In that important but long ignored essay, we see a strange situation: It is the same relation of the bondage of the human subject (the worker) by the external object (the capital) in the capitalist condition, or man's activity is not the free expression of his life, and the same call to beat down private ownership, but there is a conspicuous absence of the logical tool of estrangement used in the *1844 Manuscripts* and *The Holy Family* not long ago. He only says, "Private property is nothing but objectified labour." And in the representation of the servant position of worker in capitalism, Marx carefully chooses the word

---

4   *Ibid.*, p. 119.

"labour" with quotation marks to emphasize that it "is the living basis of private property."[5] We should bear in mind that his previous wording here is nothing else but the estrangement of labour. Here, Marx abandons the power discourse of the estrangement of labour. However, his real theoretical direction, the requirements of the proletarian revolution, does not alter. In his eyes, the "free labour" in modern capitalism is only an indirect subjugation that offers itself for sale and the purpose of the capitalist production is for man or man's development but "an external aim" or "an exchange value, money."[6] In short, the entire capitalist system is "the baseness of people being sacrificed for things"[7], where "we have made industry into a power over us"[8] and man is degraded "to a 'force' capable of creating wealth."[9] The capitalist regards the proletarian as a thing instead of a man. And labour is only a productive force of materials. The key issue is that Marx's understanding of the productive forces here is not the traditional conception of historical materialism but the validation of List's view in the negative sense. Marx intends to break the mysterious beautification of the productive forces. For the bourgeois economists, manpower is juxtaposed with waterpower, steampower, and horsepower. "All these are "productive forces." He questions, "Is it a high appreciation of man for him to figure as a "force" alongside horses, steam and water?" It is here that Marx attempts to negate the anti-human social system of capitalism, the bad "is" but he discards the important logical component, the "ought" used by him a short time ago. Despite the remaining traces of the humanistic discourse, Marx does not make an a priori stipulation to tell what man should do but expresses an important view, "It is one of the greatest misapprehensions to speak of free, human, social labour, of labour without private property."[10] Marx validates that today's so-called labour, conditioned by capitalism, has become the aforementioned estranged labour instead of one in its common sense. Labour "by its very nature is unfree, unhuman, unsocial activity, determined by private property and creating private property."[11] Is it not a certain self-reflection of Marx? Now he is consciously deserting the logical framework and axiology of the estrangement view of history adopted in his *1844 Manuscripts*. The change of discourse is often accompanied with that of logic; hence, here emerges a new discourse and theoretical context. Another piece of evidence further

---

5   *Ibid.*, p. 278.
6   *Ibid.*, p. 284.
7   *Ibid.*, p. 284.
8   *Ibid.*, p. 283.
9   *Ibid.*, p. 286.
10   *Ibid.*, p. 278.
11   *Ibid.*, p. 279.

consolidates this belief: Marx surely wants to negate the reversed relation between the human subject and his own creation but it is not done through the
sublation of estrangement. He says, "Hence the abolition of private property
will become a reality only when it is conceived as the abolition of 'labour'
(an abolition which, of course, has become possible only as a result of labour
itself, that is to say, has become possible as a result of the material activity
of society and which should on no account be conceived as the replacement
of one category by another)."[12] Here, Marx is approaching a new overall
view of history, that is, the original objective logic based on social reality. As
we know, Marx has noticed the practice of "industry, of the by now almost
exhausted development."[13] In my view, the validation of "industry" as the
social foundation is a crucial breakthrough. If Marx's previous logical framework is mainly concerned about the "ought" in the humanistic axiology,
here he begins to notice the realistic way through which the necessary "is" of
the real existence of history reaches the "ought" (in a borrowed sense) via the
elimination of the bad "is." For the first time, the "ought" and "is" reconciles
with each other because in the industrial practice, "man first takes possession
of his own forces and the forces of nature, objectifies himself and creates for
himself the conditions for a human existence."[14] Man will be scientifically
interpreted. Marx is now very close to the discovery of the necessary reason
why labour is generated from the historical development of the material
production per se, which means he not only sees the result caused by the unreasonable phenomenon of labour but also starts to explore the deep reason
why such result is generated in the capitalist mode of production. After the
long journey of adventures, the ship mast of the Marxist philosophy and the
scientific socialism gradually rises on the horizon.

Marx sharply points out:

> **When industry is regarded in this way, one abstracts from the
> circumstances in which it operates today, and in which it exists
> as industry; one's standpoint is not from within the industrial
> epoch, but above it; industry is regarded not by what it is for
> man today, but by what present-day man is for human history,
> what he is historically; it is not its present-day existence (not
> industry as such) that is recognized, but rather the power which
> industry has without knowing or willing it and which destroys
> it and creates the basis for a human existence.[15]**

---

12 Ibid., p. 279.
13 Ibid., p. 274.
14 Ibid., p. 281.
15 Ibid., p. 281.

A new theoretical thought based on the industrial reality begins to prevail in his mind. He says,

> **The hour has come for it to be done away with, or for the abolition of the material and social conditions in which mankind has had to develop its abilities as a slave. For as soon as industry is no longer regarded as a huckstering interest, but as the development of man, man, instead of huckstering interest, is made the principle and' what in industry could develop only in contradiction with industry itself is given the basis which is in harmony with that which is to be developed.**[16]

Once again, Marx's theoretical logic makes a turn here, that is, from exploring the major elements in the development of social history to the verification of the social and historical foundation, which is a very important step for Marx's change of the historical view. At the same time, he directly connects this theoretical corroboration with the quest for the proletarian revolution. Thus, the axiological logic of "man" is doomed. To seek the foundation of the proletarian revolution, Marx says, "Breaking the spell cast on industry was to abstract from the conditions, the money fetters, in which the forces of industry operate today and to examine these forces in themselves. This was the first call to the people to emancipate their industry from huckstering and to understand present-day industry as a transitional epoch."[17] The second sentence highlights a significant context. Marx has already had a thorough understanding of what he is doing: To eliminate the capitalist form of industry instead of industry itself (the development of material productive forces), which is but a transition to the later negation of capitalism. While his revolutionary theory still borrows the slogan of "man," the actual discourse is no longer about the inference of the humanistic labour estrangement, the "ought" but the objective development of industry, the "is." The objective capitalistic enslavement of labour remains but the negation of the negation with humanistic logic already disappears. In my opinion, Marx's philosophy already begins the concrete transition from the humanistic subjective dialectics to the objective historical dialectics.

Now, communism (the proletarian revolution) grows out of the logical requirement of abstract values into a necessary trend of the actual history. Marx concludes:

---

16   *Ibid.*, pp. 281-282.
17   *Ibid.*, p. 283.

> The forces of nature and the social forces which industry brings into being (conjures up), stand in the same relation to it as the proletariat. Today they are still the slaves of the bourgeois, and in them he sees nothing but the instruments (the bearers) of his dirty (selfish) lust for profit; tomorrow they will break their chains and reveal themselves as the bearers of human development which will blow him sky-high together with his industry, which assumes the dirty outer shell – which he regards as its essence only until the human kernel has gained sufficient strength to burst this shell and appear in its own shape. Tomorrow they will burst the chains by which the bourgeois separates them from man and so distorts (transforms) them from a real social bond into fetters of society.[18]

It almost validates a practical road to communism in the real process of the development of social history. The objective social rules in the scientific view of history are about to be revealed.

Please note that at this time Marx's previous process of multiple logics still continues but the two different logical threads quietly lose their importance with the functional changes of his original subjective discourse. The three problems are still there to be solved. The historical development of "industry" in reality begins to dominate Marx's theoretical evolution while the estrangement logic of man and his essence is marginalized. This is a breakthrough moment. Once the old hurdle crashes, a fresh logical framework is bound to emerge and rise to a new height.

C. NEW THEORETICAL FOUNDATION: THE OBJECTIVE MATERIAL PRACTICE BASED ON THE HUMAN SUBJECT

In April 1845, Marx made a concise outline in pages 51 to 55 of his *1844-1847 Philosophical Notebook*, which became the famous *Theses on Feuerbach*. We can see the gestalt transition of Marx's philosophical logic. A complete new logic now comes up, in which Marx finally solves the previous problems.

The *Theses* is composed of eleven logical points. Feuerbach's logical framework of humanism becomes the major target of criticism, and his abstraction of humanism and the logical structure of the humanistic estrangement view of history, including the slogan of man, are completely abandoned. A new philosophical starting point is established, that is, the dynamic social and historical practice represented by the objective material creation of the

---

18   *Ibid.*, p. 282.

human subject. It should not be confined to the field of a specific "industry." The *Theses*, written in the spring of 1845, marks a holistic conversion of Marx's theoretical logic, which is not the presentation of an already existing thought of Materialism undergoing a slow accumulative change but rather a structural revolution. In this connection, Althusser is wise. Nevertheless, when he regards Marx's conversion as an "epistemological break" that seems to completely differ from all the previous things, he is not entirely correct. In my opinion, the new worldview highlights a scientific solution of the internal conflicts in Marx's philosophical logic via cognitive integrations. All his theoretical concerns are re-evaluated on a new level of unity to reach a scientific conclusion. Hence, there is a way out for the conundrum of philosophy and politics.

In beginning of the *Theses*, Marx directs his criticism to the old materialism of Feuerbach and others.

> **The chief defect of all hitherto existing materialism – that of Feuerbach included – is that the thing, reality, sensuousness, is conceived only in the form of the *object or of contemplation*, but not as *sensuous human activity*, *practice*, not subjectively.[19]**

In fact, an intuitional contemplation of the object as material is not right. "Feuerbach wants sensuous objects [Objekte], differentiated from thought-objects, but he does not conceive human activity itself as objective [gegenständliche] activity."[20] Feuerbach cannot observe the object from the perspective of the subjective practice. Therefore, he is wrong. This is an unprecedented saying that Materialism is wrong. However, it proves Marx's breakthrough of the old materialism. He still insists on the subjective discourse and makes it the dominant line of his thought. However, the discussion here is no longer about man's essence and the logical subjectivity but the real, historical, concrete, practical subjectivity.

Obviously, Marx's criticism of the old materialism is not meant to return to idealism that is still wrong in his eyes because "the active side, in opposition to materialism, was developed by idealism – but only abstractly" and "idealism does not know real, sensuous activity as such"[21], which accounts for the decisive foundation of the subject's initiative. In the above analysis, Marx proceeds from the subjective and objective activities of material practice to offer a unified solution to the first and second problems on a

---

19   Marx, and Friedrich Engels. *The German Ideology*. Ed. Christopher John Arthur. New York: International Publishers Co, 1970. p. 121.
20   *Ibid.*, p. 121.
21   *Ibid.*, p. 121.

deeper philosophical level. He maintains the full recognition of the active role of the subject and objectifies it into a sensuous material activity. Thus, the Hegelian initiative is retained while the idealistic base is abandoned; the Feuerbachian materialist premise is kept and materialism is pushed onto the new dimension of the revolutionary practical materialism.

It is clear that the theoretical significance of the aforementioned aspects has been recognized in traditional researches. If there is anything to add, it is Marx's realization that the philosophical reform is not a simple mixture of the rational parts of Hegel and Feuerbach, or an organic combination of materialism and dialectics. Here, the so-called "dialectical materialism" does not represent the essential features of the Marxist philosophy. Practical materialism sticks out as a completely new creation of Marxism. In addition, Marx achieves an unprecedented transcendence in the logical point of scientific practice. The relation between material and spirit deemed by Engels as the basic question of the traditional philosophy is re-examined in the new framework. Practical materialism is neither sided with the abstract spirit, the development of abstraction, nor assimilated into the old abstract material, the objective or sensuous form. Both material and spirit are reassessed and redefined on a historical, concrete, actual, subjective and practical scale. In my opinion, when the innate drive of Marx's new vision turns from a general subjectivity to practice, it means that the new discourse is a practical initiative. Once the material object enters the social history of humans, it undergoes the historical reform by man's practice. The natural object as the foundation for human life becomes the "human nature" after certain mediation of practice while the social material life transforms to a hierarchical survival for the new man. Spirit results only from practice conditioned by certain historical society. Therefore, the natural cognitive schema is historical and the social and historical consciousness belongs to the product of history. The innovative foundation of Marx's philosophical horizon is nothing else but the scientific relationship between the material life and social consciousness perceived through the prism of practice. Dialectics and materialism are not just put together as separate parts of a philosophical system but generated with unified functional characters from the initiative of material practice. What Marx establishes here is the logic of practical materialism and the objective dialectics of practice.

Marx's profoundness will reappear in Kant's paradox – contradiction between the objective world and the human world – covered and mediated by the Hegelian absolute monism, and gets truly and finally consolidated with the new measurement of the objective and material activities of the initiative human subject.[22] What a wonderful budding of thought and a great leap forward!

In fact, I am not only concerned about the basic logical points demonstrated above but also the foundation, the "ought" of the proletarian revolution in his original philosophical thought, or, the third problem in his previous theoretical line. It should be noted that Marx's recognition of the reasonableness of social practice as such indicates the necessary phenomenon in which the proletariat is subjugated and suppressed in the reality of capitalist society. Criticizing Feuerbach's humanistic conception of history means losing the axiological hypothesis of man's essence and the criticism of the capitalist contradictions is lost as a result, which is often overlooked by later researchers. I think Marx's emphasis in the *Theses* means nothing else but the solution of the third problem in his previous philosophical logic. More importantly, his logical breakthrough is also obtained on the basis of practice.

In my opinion, Marx does not make a thorough negation of the basic theories and the critical line of thought of the estranged subjective essence in religion held by Feuerbach, that is to say, Feuerbach is not wrong when he "resolves the religious essence into the human essence" and "starts out from the fact of religious self-alienation, of the duplication of the world into a religious world and a secular one," but he makes the mistake of taking man's essence as "abstraction inherent in each single individual."[23] For Feuerbach, the essence of human subject becomes naturality and "religious sentiment," and thus, he is compelled to "abstract from the historical process" and "to presuppose an abstract – isolated – human individual."[24] According to Marx, the standpoint of the new worldview is "human society, or social humanity" instead of an abstract individual because "all social life is essentially practical."[25] Feuerbach's abstract man belongs to a certain social form and the alleged "religious sentiment" is itself a social product. The essence of man is in its reality "the ensemble of the social relations."[26] Obviously, Marx discusses about the unscientific philosophy of Feuerbach

---

22　Here, Marx's new philosophical horizon is absolutely not a return to Kant's empiricism. Marxism cannot be concluded as some practical empiricism. It is very important for us to carry out a correct materialist research. We shall discuss this topic later in the understanding of nature by Marx's practical materialism.

23　Marx, and Friedrich Engels. *The German Ideology*. Ed. Christopher John Arthur. New York: International Publishers Co, 1970. p. 122.

24　*Ibid.*, p. 122.

25　*Ibid.*, p. 122.

26　*Ibid.*, p. 122.

from a new standpoint. At the same time, Marx is committed to a profound theoretical construction. He intends to carry on the banner of liberation for all human subjects with his new philosophy.

In Marx's stipulation of practice, we see a repeated use of such adjectives
as "revolutionary" and "critical." He claims that his new worldview differentiates from all the old ones with the purpose of not only explaining
the world but also changing it. Proceeding from the objectivity of practice,
this new view is not attributed to the Hegelian affirmation of the existing world but to the actual change of the unreasonable survival status of
the human beings. In other words, Marx adopts the actual requirement
of the value of practice to substitute the "ought" of subjective value in a
humanistic logic while the "ought" is reached via the "is" that is constituted of the reality of practice. Here, the "ought" and "is" begin to approach each other. Marx does not proceed from the old passive material
existence; instead, he starts from the practice that contains a humanistic
actual initiative to stipulate that the "ought" of the proletarian revolution
is the actual value of practice instead of an abstract humanistic hypothesis
of value. Hence, Marx finishes the turn from the philosophical criticism
of humanistic values to the scientific proletarian value-orientation based
on the real historical practice. The consistent change of conditions and
human beings can only be reasonably regarded as the practice of revolution. Despite criticism against the secular world and its irrationality, Marx
does not adopt the humanistic logic of estrangement and the negation of
the negation in the subjective dialectics. "But that the secular basis detaches itself from itself and establishes itself as an independent realm in
the clouds can only be explained by the cleavages and self-contradictions
within this secular basis."[27] Here, Marx employs a metaphorical means
to show that the contemporary capitalism still leaves the human subject
in a reversed condition similar to that of the religious estrangement. The
economic life created at the hands of man is separated from the subject
himself, forming an "independent kingdom" above and opposed to the
human subject. This is of course unreasonable. However, Marx already
abandons the estrangement logic for the judgment of such condition. He
has not found an appropriate way to articulate it but he knows it must be
solved from the unreasonable situation per se, that is, to "be both understood in its contradiction and revolutionized in practice."[28] Obviously, the
third problem is also addressed according to the practical dialectics in the
socio-historical process. On the new philosophical horizon, Marx proposes

---

27   *Ibid.*, p. 122.
28   Marx, and John C. Raines. *Marx on Religion.* Temple University Press, 2002. p. 183.

that he is to seek the real cause for the social "self-division," the original "estrangement," in the capitalist economy, especially, the objective contradiction in the actual process. Moreover, this social conundrum can only be explained with the eradication of the cause through the revolutionary practice of the proletarians.

Here, we see the second important transformation in Marx's philosophical logic, that is, to turn from the humanistic dialectics to the historical dialectics based on objective practice. He no longer draws criticism from the general negation-of-the-negation logic but focuses on the innate contradictions and the settlement of the socio-historical practice. The specific construction of historical dialectics is later carried out in the *German Ideology*. In this way, the negation of the negation loses the dominant position in the previous subjective dialectics and gives way to the objective contradiction of practice. It is often ignored in the traditional philosophical framework. In my opinion, a scientific solution to this question has a far-reaching impact on the ensuing Marxist economics and socialistic theories.

At the same time, due to the innate stipulation of practice, the new philosophical line generally begins with specific conditions in history, by which Marx can achieve his third transformation in his philosophical worldview: a change from the humanistic estrangement view of history to the scientific view of historical materialism. He gives up the rational logic to assess nature and social history while engages himself in revealing the development laws of the material world[29]. Therefore, in the eyes of a real Marxist philosopher, the history of human society is no longer the negation-of-the-negation process of man's estrangement and restoration but the actual development of the objective historical dialectics of the human social practice that constantly moves forward. In this way, Marx eventually overcomes the hidden nub of historical idealism. It should be noted that Marx's focus on the criticism of historical idealism, especially of those "semi-materialists," does not indicate that spirit simply generates the reality of social history but refers to the abstract doctrine that human will is the drive. In other words, since the essential difference between human society and nature lies with the fact that social history is composed of human activities dominated by human wills, social history transcends nature in that the human society is always driven by man's spirit. It is through a scientific description of the historical development rules that Marx's historical materialism corrects

---

29 In this connection, the practical materialism established in the Thesis is by no means a historical view or another statement of historical materialism. Instead, it represents the overall epistemology and methodology of observing and solving the problems of the objective world by Karl Marx.

this erroneous view of history and reveals such historical dialectics as that man's social existence (the material practice) decides his ideology, that the development of the social practice of the subject, or the productive forces, is what drives the human historical movement, and that the masses are the creators and masters of social history. However, for a long time, in the traditional philosophical framework of the social and historical development, Marx's difference from the idealistic drive of human wills is defined as an external social-historical process that is forever independent of man's will, or more precisely, free of the individual will. This is a misunderstanding of Marx, whose new philosophical horizon is much more than historical materialism. It also includes the historical dialectics and the foundation for communism, the liberation of the human subject, in particular, the first emancipation of the proletarians.

As noted above, it is with the new materialist vision; Marx establishes the stipulation of practice, constructs a new philosophical discourse and achieves his great philosophical transformation. For the first time, he offers a scientific solution to the three major problems, combines the emphasis on the initiative practice of the human subject and the necessary insistence on the materialist principle of proceeding from the reality of social history, and thus turns the fight for the freedom of the proletariat, the communism, into science. In my opinion, Marx and Engels' description of the new philosophical vision as "revolutionary" and "practical-critical" materialism contains a profound implication: It starts the trinity of historical materialism, historical dialectics and the scientific socialism based on practical materialism. Finally, it finds a unified and scientific solution to the three theoretical questions always in Marx's concern. It indicates the first scientific unification of the two philosophical logics that direct his thought: the objective logic of respecting the social reality and the active logic of highlighting the dominant role of the human subject in the social and historical development, which is especially worthy of our attention.

II. THE NATURAL PROCESS AND THE SOCIAL-HISTORICAL PROCESS BY THE NEW PHILOSOPHICAL HORIZON

We believe that the *Theses* are the symbol of the new philosophical horizon. Through solving the key problems in his philosophical logic, Marx undergoes an overall philosophical turn based on practice and establishes the Marxist philosophical worldview. At the same time, the new line of thought is still for self-clarification and in the form of sporadic points, not ready to emerge in a theoretical formula. The systematic elucidation of the new worldview is finished in the *German Ideology*, a book co-authored by Marx and Engels in 1845 and 1846, which focuses on the objective thought of historical materialism and historical dialectics.

A. *THE GERMAN IDEOLOGY*: THE INITIAL THEORETICAL HORIZON OF THE NEW WORLDVIEW

The *Theses* is called by Engels "a work of genius" whilst *Germany Ideology* is the first systematic and detailed exposition of the new worldview, mainly in the form of a scientific view of history. They are organic parts of the same logical body. I think that the initial form of the basic Marxist framework is clearly expressed in the first chapter of Volume 1, which occupies a very important position in the entire development of Marxism.

German Ideology was not published during the lifetime of Marx and Engels. In 1932, 37 years after the death of Engels in 1895, the book first appeared in the Soviet Union. Marx and Engels first take the standpoint of a scientific socialism to carry out a comprehensive criticism of various radical trends of thought in Germany and thus establish the basic positions, viewpoints and the methodology of Marxism. In fact, the word "ideology" mainly refers to the fallacy of a conceptual system after Destutt de Tracy and Georg Wilhelm Friedrich Hegel. Marx and Engels further point out that ideology is an illusion in which the ruling class makes use of false relations to cover up reality. In *German Ideology*, Marx and Engels profoundly expose the ideological essence of Feuerbach, Stirner and Bauer who apparently criticize capitalism but actually adopt the idealistic view of history to replace reality with concepts. They are well aware that any true criticism of capitalism needs abandoning the false idealistic conception that only targets the shadow of reality and explaining the relationship between "criticism" and the material situation in reality, so as to establish a scientific worldview. Thus, Marx's newly established philosophy of practical materialism becomes the major content of the first chapter in *German Ideology*.

Chapter One focuses on the frontal illustration of the important philosophical view of history, that is to say, it is the first and the only theoretical explication of the new logical vision held by Marx and Engels since the establishment of Marxism. Therefore, this chapter is one of the most important classic books in the overall Marxist framework. Unfortunately, the manuscript of this part is unfinished and damaged, with 12 pages missing in Chapter One and 20 pages lost in Chapter 20. The Soviet scholars rearranged the manuscripts in order to make it a completed works, which became today's text we see in Vol. 3 of MECW.

However, people gradually realize that the above layout is not satisfactory in subsequent studies. In 1962, three missing pages of *German Ideology* were found in Amsterdam, Netherlands and published in the same year. In the meantime, researchers began to notice the importance of recovering the initial logical clue in the original manuscripts of Marx and Engels. As a result, in 1965 the Institute of Marxism-Leninism under CC CPSU reprinted the first chapter of the *German Ideology*. In the following year, a similar monograph was published, which restored the original coding sequence of Marx and Engels, re-separated the manuscripts into 27 sections in four parts, and provided 25 sub-titles according to the understanding of the editor. In 1966, East Germany generally adopted the aforementioned Russian version, but deleted the additional 26 subtitles. In 1988, the new version of the first chapter of Ideology was published in China. It mainly follows the East Germany version of 1966 and retains the original 26 subtitles of the Russian version[30].

The material available shows that the manuscripts of *German Ideology* are incomplete. Judging from the situation when they were composed, the first chapter consists of five relatively independent manuscripts. They are: 29 pages of the first manuscripts explains the new philosophical horizon, now included in the second part; 43 pages of the second and the third manuscripts are extracted from the finished Chapter Three, now compiled into Part Three and Part Four; and the last is about the fourth and fifth manuscripts, now integrated into Part One, composed of two drafted introductions and an overall summary of the new worldview written when Marx and Engels almost finished their whole manuscripts. The first manuscript, or the second part of the current edition, covers the major elements of the new worldview. It is also the most systematic and comprehensive relation about the basic Marxist framework in the early time. In this part, Marx and Engels have two tasks in mind: To have a thorough criticism of Feuerbach and correct their previous philosophical thought and to elucidate their newly established philosophical horizon. However, the first task is not completed, which, of course, does not mean little criticism of Feuerbach is involved but shows the absence of concrete criticism of Feuerbach's doctrines per se as made in Chapters Two and Three.[31] Obviously, this task needs great extra amount of effort.

---

30 For more discussion on the theoretical structure of the new version, see "On the Structure of the First Chapter in *German Ideology*." *Theoretical Studies Monthly* 10 (1992).

31 Later Engels writes, "To Feuerbach, who after all in many respects forms an intermediate link between Hegelian philosophy and our conception, we never returned." See Marx, and Friedrich Engels. *Karl Marx and Friedrich Engels: Selected Works in One Volume*. New York: International Publishers, 1968. p. 594.

The present first manuscript can be viewed as two parts. The first part, pages 1 to 10, starts from solving problems, covers the German philosophy, especially, Feuerbach's natural materialism, transcends the abstract "natural" foundation of the old materialism, and validates the logical base of the new worldview: Practice and the starting point of practical materialism. In the second part, pages 11 to 29, Marx and Engels turn the general logical expression in the *Theses* into a historical, concrete, actual, systematic theory so that the new worldview takes its initial form.

I must add that there is a slight difference between the consideration of the *Theses* and the words of Marx and Engels here. The former is the overall logical structure of Marx's new theory. During his denial of the previous logical framework, Marx grasps the innate unification of the objective real base of social history and the dominant historical status of the proletariat (the subject). In comparison, by *German Ideology*, Marx and Engels underscore the real base of social history that is openly, or secretly, rejected by historical idealism.[32] Therefore, Marx and Engels lay their emphasis on the foundation of social history while, to their intention or not, appear to weaken the dominant elements of the process of social history. As expected, they are concerned about the objective material aspect as the real base of the existence of human social history and their logical plan is to first reassess the abstract nature as the foundation of society and then validate the real base of social history: the production and reproduction of the material means of subsistence. It leads to historical materialism and the objective aspect of historical dialectics.

B. THE HUMANIZED NATURE MEDIATED THROUGH THE SUBJECTIVE PRACTICE

It is a great pity that the first part of the manuscripts has five pages missing while the content of which is very critical. Generally speaking, that part demonstrates the essential errors of Feuerbach but is not an exclusive criticism against the entire philosophy of his. Instead, it takes the standpoint of the new worldview, lays the important premise of the new philosophy by disproving Feuerbach and the surrounding nature mediated through the practice of the human subject. As we know, the core of Feuerbach's philosophy contains the "natural" object, "man," and man's intuition (consciousness), which also accounts for the major theoretical points in Marx's *Theses*. And this part almost amounts to an explication of the *Theses*.

---

32   In a letter to J. Bloch in Königsberg, Engels says, "We had to emphasise the main principle vis-à-vis our adversaries, who denied it…" See Marx, Friedrich Engels, and Gareth Stedman Jones. *The Communist Manifesto*. Penguin, 2002. p. 144.

In my interpretation, *Theses* provides an outline of thought for *German Ideology*. It is an entrance to the new philosophy, and of course a premise for the first manuscripts. To my discovery, the first part of the first manuscripts coincides with the basic line of thought in the *Theses*. Thus, the two parts are put together for discussion.

Here, the first important point of the *Theses* is extended and Feuerbach's incorrect perception of the "sensuous world" (the natural object) is analyzed in detail. According to Marx and Engels, "Feuerbach's conception of the sensuous world is confined on the one hand to mere contemplation of it, and on the other to mere feeling"[33] because he "wants sensuous contemplation [Anschauung]; but he does not conceive sensuousness as practical, human-sensuous activity."[34] Marx is extremely precise. He does not say that the natural material as such is the production of man but means to express that the sensuous nature or man's sensuous world around him that he intuitively faces is the production of man. Marx never says that the entire material existence of nature is produced by man, which is actually an unscientific proposition. Instead, Marx and Engels reject Feuerbach's view that the practice-mediated nature surrounding men becomes a sensuous picture, like being cast through the historical prism of practice into an imaginary natural material existence. Thus, Marx and Engels say that Feuerbach "always takes refuge in external nature, and moreover in nature which has not yet been subdued by men."[35] This proposition needs a careful identification because it is used later as a weapon against the materialist nature of Marxism and the first step toward the logical mistake of humanism for certain western "humanistic" Marxists.

According to Marx, Feuerbach's limitation inevitably leads to the observation of the external world with a non-historical view. "As far as Feuerbach is a materialist he does not deal with history, and as far as he considers history he is not a materialist."[36] "He does not see how the sensuous world around him is, not a thing given direct from all eternity, remaining ever the same, but the product of industry and of the state of society; and, indeed, in the sense that it is an historical product, the result of the activity of a whole succession of generations, each standing on the shoulders of the preceding one."[37] Obviously, the above statements correspond to the first and fifth parts in the *Theses*.

---

33   Marx, and Friedrich Engels. *The German Ideology*. Ed. Christopher John Arthur. New York: International Publishers Co, 1970. p. 62.
34   *Ibid.*, p. 122.
35   *Ibid.*, p. 61.
36   *Ibid.*, p. 64.
37   *Ibid.*, p. 62.

It is interesting to careful study these sentences. In fact, Marx's surrounding nature contains two stipulations: The "earth-centred" natural condition of man, which, of course, does not mean all the natural material existence; and the surrounding natural conditions that now exist in the reality of man's social history, or the nature as the material base of social existence. It accounts for the connotations of man's sensuous world mentioned by Marx. The key is that, to Marx's discovery, "the priority of external nature remains unassailed, and all this has no application to the original men produced by generatio aequivoca [spontaneous generation]."[38] For the survival of primitive people, nature remains almost unaffected by the historical process. Thus, the natural surroundings cannot be regarded as a result of man's practice at that time.

Marx and Engels also point out:

> **For that matter, nature, the nature that preceded human history, is not by any means the nature in which Feuerbach lives, it is nature which today no longer exists anywhere (except perhaps on a few Australian coral-islands of recent origin) and which, therefore, does not exist for Feuerbach.**[39]

By "no longer exists," Marx does not mean the non-existence of the nature without being mediated by practice but indicates that Feuerbach regards a historically affected man's nature as some idealized natural existence and that specific, false, unaltered nature does not exist. In a similar way of criticizing Stirner's "fantastic relation of man to nature," Marx and Engels mean the non-existence of that subjective relation of imagination but they admit that it is "the actual relation of man to nature, determined by industry and natural science."[40] This is a clear ad hoc explanation, which has neither the least denotational extension nor any deductive possibility of the assumption that the natural material external to man's practice does not exist. It is very obvious that the being-in-itself nature is continually diminishing in the process of human history. "But every new invention, every advance made by industry, detaches another piece from this domain, so that the ground which produces examples illustrating such Feuerbachian propositions is steadily shrinking."[41] Today, the situation is quite different for the social man in reality. The surrounding nature for human existence is the inevitable outcome of practice. Marx and Engels

---

38 *Ibid.*, p. 63.
39 *Ibid.*, p. 63.
40 Marx, Karl. *Early Writings by Karl Marx*. Harmondsworth: Penguin Books, 1992. p. 355.
41 Marx, and Friedrich Engels. *The German Ideology*. Ed. Christopher John Arthur. New York: International Publishers Co, 1970. p. 61.

particularly emphasize that "this differentiation has meaning only insofar as man is considered to be distinct from nature," in other words, that the surrounding nature – the sensuous world – becomes the result of practice is different from the nature of animals and means the real establishment of man's social history. It is an important objective logical relationship. On one aspect, even nature is mediated through practice, it does not lose its objective sense due to man's activities; as a result, "in all this the priority of external nature remains unassailed."[42] It only loses the "thing-in-itself" of the natural material per se but acquires a new "mediated" objective form of existence by practice, that is, the natural existence of man's mediation of practice. Not a few researchers only pay attention to the first aspect and neglect the second feature of Marx's statement on the sensuous world and our surrounding nature – the artificial "natural" part (that he once mentions as the product of man). The first aspect refers to the removal of "a few Australian coral-islands of recent origin" or some virgin land in a forest, where man collectively uses and chooses nature in practice, for instance, the "cherry-tree" mentioned in the script is only possible to be perceived by Feuerbach's "sensuous certainty" because of certain social and periodical activities.[43] The fruit tree is natural growth and they are planted in an orchard because of commerce and industry. On the other aspect, it refers to the new material form of existence created by man's practice. However, man does not create new material by practice. In fact, the natural material undergoes an objective reconstruction according to man's usage. For this, Marx offers a metaphorical example: "In Manchester, for instance, Feuerbach sees only factories and machines, where a hundred years ago only spinning-wheels and weaving-rooms were to be seen, or in the Campagna of Rome he finds only pasture lands and swamps, where in the time of Augustus he would have found nothing but the vineyards and villas of Roman capitalists."[44] Here, everything is a direct result of man's practice except the vineyards. This is about the second aspect of the "sensuous world" of Marx and Engels, the material condition of which provides the more important and direct foundation for the survival of human society in the process of practice. It reflects the quantity of the productive forces and the entity of the material living condition in social existence. I attempt to summarize the theoretical intention of Marx and Engels into a logical formula: The sensuous world that surrounds us is in constant changes from the nature in itself to man's natural condition during the development of

---

42   *Ibid.*, p. 63.
43   *Ibid.*, p. 62.
44   *Ibid.*, p. 63.

social practice. Nature generally pre-exists man but his practice becomes a new prerequisite of the sensuous world on another level.

> **So much is this activity, this unceasing sensuous labour and creation, this production, the basis of the whole sensuous world as it now exists, that, were it interrupted only for a year, Feuerbach would not only find an enormous change in the natural world, but would very soon find that the whole world of men and his own perceptive faculty, nay his own existence, were missing.**[45]

As to the understanding of this point, we cannot retrogressively resort to Kant. It seems as if Marx again divides the external object into the ontological world beyond man – "things in themselves" and the phenomenal world of experience and practice[46]. In fact, neither Marx constructs a different ontological model with the practice of man nor he defines a new "binary split." In the objective perspective of Marx's philosophical logic, the natural objects have their own objective reality and historical priority, which is absolute and does not change with occurrence of practice. At the same time, that to what extent the natural object becomes the foundation and object of practice (knowledge) for human beings is conditioned by the historical development of practice. It forms the subjective perspective of Marx's philosophical logic. Here, the latter is simply highlighted on a certain theoretical level by the criticism of Feuerbach's intuitive materialism. The connection between man and nature by practice is in actual unification, instead of binary opposition. As a soaring eagle needs two balanced wings, either of Marx's angles should not be exaggerated. We must guard against the exaggeration of the former by traditional hermeneutics and the overemphasis of the latter by some "practical materialists."

Judging from the existing materials, the first part of the first manuscripts mainly employs an argument against Feuerbach to reveal the true essence of "nature" and "intuition" as his prerequisite, and thus lays the foundation of practice for a new scientific materialistic worldview. This part is driven by a palpable innate force of the *Theses*. It is almost a reiteration of Marx and Engels when they say, "In reality and for the practical materialist, i.e. the communist, it is a question of revolutionising the existing world, of practically attacking and changing existing things."[47] Practice is the logical

---

45   *Ibid.*, p. 63.

46   When some Chinese researchers of practical materialism attempt to walk out of the incorrect field of "practical ontology," they often, consciously or not, edge toward the Kantian duality, that is, they put the objective *nature-in-itself* in antithesis with the natural phenomena in empirical practice (the *objective* schema).

47   Marx, and Friedrich Engels. *The German Ideology*. Ed. Christopher John Arthur. New York: International Publishers Co, 1970. p. 62.

start of Marx's new philosophical horizon, where nature is sublated and assimilated into the social practice of human beings as a pre-existent material premise. In Marx's view, nature is no longer an abstract object in antithesis to the subject as in old materialism but a basic precondition of the human social history. The object on the new Marxist philosophical horizon is already a historical, real social existence. While in the new philosophical logic, practice replaces the abstract material and the sensuous nature in old materialism, and makes the initiative of human from the abstraction of the subjective concreteness into an objective creative activity. As a result, the new philosophy sees practice versus nature (the material), practice versus man, and the subject versus the idea. The practice of human society historically, realistically, and concretely leads to a different philosophical framework, which is used as a revolutionary weapon for the proletarians and a theoretical guide for the communist movement. It goes without saying that this new philosophical worldview still has the general standpoint of Marx's logical "trinity" in the *Theses*.

After a specific analysis of the text in the manuscripts, I would like to make an ad hoc explanation. In the philosophical validation of nature by Marx and Engels, there is a clear contrast: his different attitudes towards nature here and in the *1844 Manuscripts*. When Marx gets out of Feuerbach's logical framework of natural humanism, his view of nature loses that form of logical generalization and abstract unification; he no longer sees nature as man's return to himself but another target of change. In a certain sense, it seems a high-level return to the subjective-transcendence of nature held by him before.[48] Of course, this is the re-validation of his view of nature by the scientific practical materialism.

C. THE ESSENCE AND MECHANISM OF THE SOCIO-HISTORICAL PROCESS OF HUMAN BEINGS

The first part of the first manuscripts focuses on the criticism of the premise of Feuerbach's old materialism but also validates the true position of the natural material in the new worldview as the general objective base for the entire social life. After Marx and Engels stride over the first logical step, they begin to construe the major part of the new philosophical horizon.

---

48   It should be noted that Marx's view of nature and the productive forces should never be understood as a simple "natural view of dominant instrumental rationality" held by the Frankfurt School and the Eco-Marxian scholars. Marx never puts the human subject against nature in his scientific theories of nature. We shall come to this subject several times again in later discussions.

In the following part of the first manuscripts, the basic framework of the new philosophical horizon is illustrated with the real historical logic, in which Marx and Engels switch to the true unification of a general logical abstraction and the real development of historical process from their previous theoretical alliance with the humanistic subjective logic. Moreover, they even abandon the scientific validating of the dominant elements in the historical progress during their philosophical exploration. This practice of thought is a complete exposition of the scientific framework of worldview founded on the objective practice – the logic of historical materialism and the historical dialectics in the field of social history. Of course, this exposition gravitates towards the main line of establishing the real foundation of the existence and development of social history. Thus, the new philosophical worldview possesses the general epistemological and methodological function for a scientific reflection of the external world. In the mean time, Marx and Engels reveal the general law of the existence and movement of social history. In my opinion, it is the major foundation for the traditional philosophical framework to interpret Marxism, epically, historical materialism.

The fundamental structure of the new philosophical horizon starts by validating a point, that is, the production and reproduction of man's real life. It should be noted that this idea is not the same as Hegel's "pure" idea; instead, it accords with the initial occurrence of social history. The new philosophical horizon is always unified with history. At this point, we have an important logical delimitation: The relationship between the theoretical starting point and the logical starting point of the new philosophical horizon.

In fact, in the above teleological discourse, the analysis of the *Theses* is put together with the discussions of Marx and Engels, which inadvertently obscures another important point already existent in Chapter One of the manuscripts of the *German Ideology*, that is, the construing of the new philosophical horizon does not start with practice as proposed in the *Theses* but from the material production in social history. This important point has been neglected or even forgotten by some enthusiasts of "practical materialism" in our traditional philosophical framework. It is true that Marx does base his general logical starting point of the new worldview on practice but he makes an abrupt turn in further establishment of his own theory and gives up the abstract paradigm with generality as his theoretical starting point. The reason is simple.

First, once entering the specific historical process, the social practice itself is further broken down and transformed into a complex system of multi-dimensional behaviours of human beings; while through the historical, real, specific, social practice, the process of the human subject's using the material activity to change the production and reproduction of the natural objects becomes the concrete real base and the central reference of textual construction. In my opinion, the transition from a general paradigm of practice to the paradigm of production and reproduction is actually a return from a general logic to the specific theoretical operation. The former is the logical starting point of the overall Marxist framework and the latter is the theoretical beginning of constructing such concrete principles into historical materialism and historical dialectics. These two are not contradictory.

Secondly, in the *Theses*, to proceed from the subject has an ad hoc sense of the objective material practice of man's initiative. It defines the difference between the new horizon and the old materialism. Although the general objective material activities have the same priority with the historical, real, specific, sensuous material activities with which man changes the material objects, Marx seems to lay more emphasis on the logical foundation of the latter. This is an "ontological" standpoint for Marx's observation of the world. However, when it comes to returning to the specific social life, the general subjective aspect (the practical activities) in antithesis to the object previously mentioned in the *Theses* undergoes, once again, a micro-division: The material production and reproduction as the fundamental elements in the social existence of man, which Marx considers as a prerequisite to the natural material and the starting point of history itself. Here, the material production activity as the subjective aspect (opposed to the external object) in the old logic is designated as the special objective aspect of social history, in particular, as the "first" part of that social object (Marx's special social object includes all the social activities and the existence of human beings built upon the natural materials mediated by practice; in comparison, there is the special subject different from that general social subject of human, viz., the real, historical, concrete individual). By "first," it not only means the material objectivity but also suggests the basic and ultimate decisiveness of the social material existence.[49] It is no more important to clarify the above logical heterogeneity. The error of the so-called "practical ontology," especially its difference from the new philosophical horizon, is highlighted here. The former moves from a general

---

49   Later, in the *Economic Manuscripts of 1857-1858*, Marx regards it as the first grade and the third aspect of the primary in social existence.

subjectivity to that of an abstract man whereas the latter from practice toward the historical objective base.

In the second part of the first manuscripts, Marx and Engels make further specific arguments for their new philosophy. First, they set forth from "the first premise of all human existence."

> **Men must be in a position to live in order to be able to "make history." But life involves before everything else eating and drinking, a habitation, clothing and many other things. The first historical act is thus the production of the means to satisfy these needs, the production of material life itself. And indeed this is an historical act, a fundamental condition of all history, which today, as thousands of years ago, must daily and hourly be fulfilled merely in order to sustain human life. [50]**

This is the starting point of the scientific view of history. "In any interpretation of history one has first of all to observe this fundamental fact in all its significance and all its implications and to accord it its due importance."[51] Obviously, the new view stems not from the speculations of philosophers but from the common sense known to all. The real starting point of human history is the production of material means of subsistence and thus the foundation of social existence is the specific production in different epochs, which is precisely the theoretical starting point of Marxism. A proof is that Marx and Engels no longer employ the general philosophical designation of practice but build their theory on man's real, specific and historical material production and reproduction in the development of social history. Without doubt, it is a return to the historical reality from the philosophical and logical abstraction of stipulations. In their view, man's material production and reproduction form the most important and fundamental objective practical activities.

Moreover, material production is not an isolated event; its occurrence and movement have a complex process.

> **The second point is that the satisfaction of the first need (the action of satisfying, and the instrument of satisfaction which has been acquired) leads to new needs; and this production of new needs is the first historical act.[52]**

---

50   Marx, and Friedrich Engels. *The German Ideology*. Ed. Christopher John Arthur. New York: International Publishers Co, 1970. p. 48.

51   *Ibid.*, p. 49.

52   *Ibid.*, p. 49.

The "new needs" is the result of production and an innate requirement of the smooth progress of production; its realization constitutes the process of reproduction, which has undoubtedly obtained a qualitative development composed by the "new needs" instead of a simple repetition of itself. It is a dynamic pivot of the social foundation.

In addition, material production is the real starting point of human history instead of a direct goal of social existence. Production is carried out to maintain one's survival and enable him to live on; therefore, the third aspect (relationship) of production as such in the beginning of the early history is but the production and reproduction of the subject himself. "Men, who daily remake their own life, begin to make other men, to propagate their kind."[53] The propagation of men involves two factors: The natural production of the human subjects themselves and some natural relationship among the subjects (the natural inter-subjective connections). The natural production of men is done by propagation while the subjective relationship begins from the very natural production of men, their blood relation.

> **The relation between man and woman, parents and children, the family. The family, which to begin with is the only social relationship, becomes later, when increased needs create new social relations and the increased population new needs, a subordinate one.**[54]

In fact, the family is also the first production unit. In the primitive stage of human history, the material production is only subsidiary. The situation is gradually changed. For a scientific explanation of these two kinds of relations, Marx and Engels make a more detailed analysis years later. In this connection, I agree with the Chinese scholars Sun Bokui and Yao Shunliang.[55] Here, Marx and Engels make an ad hoc explanation:

> **These three aspects of social activity are not of course to be taken as three different stages, but just as three aspects or... three "moments," which have existed simultaneously since the dawn of history and the first men, and which still assert themselves in history today.**[56]

---

53   *Ibid.*, p. 49.
54   *Ibid.*, p. 49.
55   See Bo Liang. "Special and General Understandings of Historical Materialism from the Theoretical Perspective of 'Two Kinds of Production.'" *Academic Journal of Jinyang.* 5 (1982).
56   Marx, and Friedrich Engels. *The German Ideology.* Ed. Christopher John Arthur. New York: International Publishers Co, 1970. p. 50.

Marx and Engels want to point out that the content of the above three aspects actually means the three major co-existing factors of man's production in the "primary historical relationships."

After explaining the historical foundation in reality, they turn to the ensuing fourth factor, the objective social relationships between men outside the natural relations. According to Marx and Engels, "the production of life, both of one's own in labour and of fresh life in procreation, now appears as a double relationship: on the one hand as a natural, on the other as a social relationship."[57] Here, Marx and Engels want to introduce the social relationship but they inadvertently produce a perfect logical formula, which is illustrated as follows:

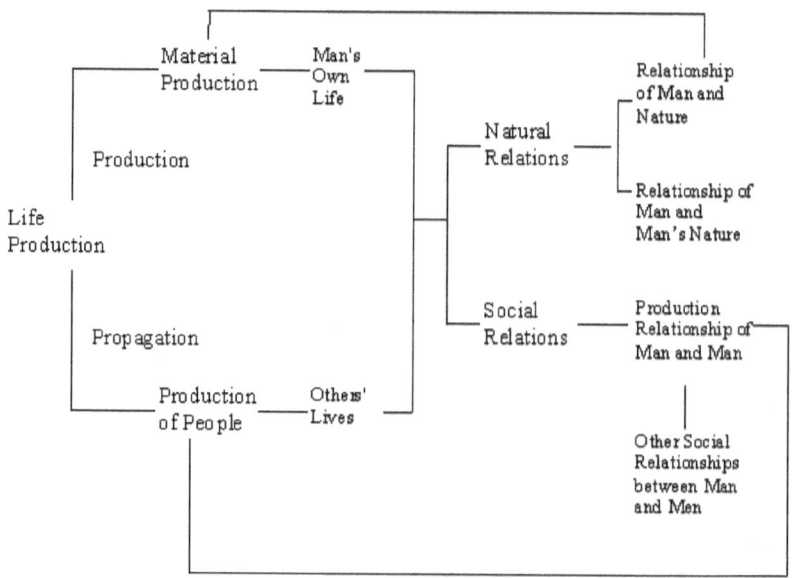

The traditional researchers have a misinterpretation of the above statement mainly because the social relationship here is simply understood as the relationship between man and nature (the productive forces) and between man and man (the relations of production). It is inconsistent with the meaning of the original text. By "life," Marx and Engels refer to the human subject, the establishment of which is achieved through production, or labour. The subtlety here is the identification of a very complex system of social relationships built on productive labour.

---

57   *Ibid.*, p. 50.

As the fourth factor of the early historical process (the second general factor), the social relationship mainly refers to the "co-operation of several individuals, no matter under what conditions, in what manner and to what end."[58] The social relationship mentioned here is in its general sense, sometimes called by Marx and Engels as the "social condition." It actually includes the relations of production and other social relations. In addition, there is a passivity of the social relations here. Where does it come from, then?

> It follows from this that a certain mode of production, or industrial stage, is always combined with a certain mode of co-operation, or social stage, and this mode of co-operation is itself a "productive force." Further, that the multitude of productive forces accessible to men determines the nature of society, hence, that the "history of humanity" must always be studied and treated in relation to the history of industry and exchange.[59]

The mode of how people carry out their production is called the productive force, that is, the functionality of practice possessed by man in his relationship to nature. The productive forces determine the relations of production, and thus condition the entire social nature and human history. In addition, in the human history, "there exists a materialistic connection of men with one another, which is determined by their needs and their mode of production, and which is as old as men themselves. This connection is ever taking on new forms, and thus presents a 'history.'"[60]

The fifth factor (the third general factor) is man's consciousness corresponding to all the social existence mentioned above. The explanation of consciousness by Marx and Engels is made from the perspective of historical genetics.[61]

So far, Marx and Engels have outlined five basic factors of the primitive society on the new philosophical horizon (or three general factors). They form a synchronic structure of the human social history. In the following discussion, the general outline of history is replaced by a deeper analysis of the historical logical contradictions. To their discovery, the real basic composition of society is not of some simple combinations, driven and dominated by things like "fantasies," the "supreme existence" and so on.

---

58 *Ibid.*, p. 50.
59 *Ibid.*, p. 50.
60 *Ibid.*, p. 50.
61 Zhang Yibing. "The Relationship of Me to My Condition is My Consciousness." *Tianfu New Idea.* 5 (1992).

Instead, the true essence of social history is decided by the specific, real, historical innate contradictions during the development of production. They point out that (the three factors of) the productive forces, the social condition and consciousness are not easily connected in the historical process; they "must come into contradiction with one another."[62] They are unified in the synchronic and diachronic contradictions, a dialectical movement with the social history developed to a certain level. It is not difficult to find that, when Marx and Engels construe history, they do not approach it with an abstract theory but make the historical, real, concrete observation to grasp the internal pulse of the development of history.

Here, the lucid explanation of historical materialism is also the historical dialectics on Marx's new philosophical horizon. This is just a specific subjective dimension of historical dialectics for observing the general base of social history (which also dominates the interpretation of the Marxist historical dialectics in the traditional philosophical framework).

We need to have further theoretical clarifications here. First of all, in Marx's objective description of the dialectics of social history, the historical development is not viewed as Hegel's external process that is deemed independent of man. The social contradictions centred on the mode of production are composed of man's real activities on the historical cross section of man's productive forces. Without man, there is no socio-historical existence. Those productive forces and modes of productions external to man's movement only find their way leading to "God" or the "absolute idea." Secondly, in the historical dialectics observed on this objective dimension, the real man and his subjective activities appear as the scientific object of cognition. In other words, the man on the objective dimension of historical dialectics is not a self-subject but an objective subject. Hence, Marx starts from neither the subjective dimension of historical dialectics nor the request for dominant elements in social history but from the objective dimension of observing the historical process to understand historical dialectics, which is very crucial for the in-depth discussions later.

So far, we have made clear of the most important logical thought of historical materialism on the new philosophical horizon. Marx and Engels attempt to illustrate what the real human social history is.

---

62   Marx, and Friedrich Engels. *The German Ideology*. Ed. Christopher John Arthur. New York: International Publishers Co, 1970. p. 52.

D. TWO IMPORTANT STATEMENTS ON THE BASIC PRINCIPLES OF THE SCIENTIFIC VIEW OF HISTORY

In a systematic illustration of the basic framework of their scientific view of history on the new philosophical horizon, Marx and Engels make two principle arguments. The first one is in the second part of the first manuscripts, the second in the fifth manuscripts (the latter half of the first part now).

Beginning from page 24, it has four points. The first is a classic summary of the new historical worldview.

> **This conception of history depends on our ability to expound the real process of production, starting out from the material production of life itself, and to comprehend the form of intercourse connected with this and created by this mode of production (i.e. civil society in its various stages), as the basis of all history; and to show it in its action as State, to explain all the different theoretical products and forms of consciousness, religion, philosophy, ethics, etc...).[63]**

Here, Marx and Engels actually explain the basic outline of the new worldview: (1) The starting point of the entire theory is "the material production of life itself." We are already familiar with the "real process of production" that contains the material production and reproduction and the propagation of people centred on the core of material production that is the most general basis for the existence of social history. (2) The inter-people relations (the civil society) generated from a certain mode of production form the structural foundation for the "whole history." In this point, "history" is not in its ordinary sense. As they state on page 13 of the manuscripts, "this connection is ever taking on new forms, and thus presents a 'history.'"[64] In fact, it indicates that the economic structure with the core of material relations is the foundation of all other social structures. (3) The whole social structure conditions the form and development of consciousness.

The second point is a general principle of the new worldview. "It has not, like the idealistic view of history, in every period to look for a category, but remains constantly on the real ground of history; it does not explain practice from the idea but explains the formation of ideas from material practice."[65] Interestingly, when Marx and Engels argue for the general principle of their philosophical framework, the paradigm of practice turns

---

63   *Ibid.*, p. 58.
64   *Ibid.*, p. 50.
65   *Ibid.*, p. 58.

up once again. The implication here is very profound. Neither do they employ a general materialist method from the material and the sensuous object to construe the idea, nor do they use the production in their specific exposition. Instead, they take the "material practice" as the origin of the whole logic to explain their idea. And Marx adds an underlined marginal note: "Feuerbach" to show the ad hoc reference of this principle, that is, the new worldview is not only in opposition to a general theory of social history driven by spirit but is also put to avoid the trap that the origination of material leads again to a hidden historical idealism due to the intuitive and non-historical problem under the guise of materialism. Without doubt, it is a very important theoretical point.

The third principal argument is about the decisive premise of the historical development of human society:

> **It shows that history does not end by being resolved into "self-consciousness as spirit of the spirit," but that in it at each stage there is found a material result: a sum of productive forces, an historically created relation of individuals to nature and to one another, which is handed down to each generation from its predecessor; a mass of productive forces, capital funds and conditions, which, on the one hand, is indeed modified by the new generation, but also on the other prescribes for it its conditions of life and gives it a definite development, a special character.[66]**

Thus, historical determinism persists on the new philosophical horizon because in each stage of social history we are inevitable to meet the real productive forces generated during man's transformation of nature and himself and the material surroundings (man's natural situation and social condition) caused by certain historical practice. It is the objective premise for the existence and activities of the human subject; it preconditions the certain development and special characters of the subjective activities. However, Marx and Engels do not stick to the mechanical determinism for social history develops only with the practical changes of the "new generation" in the objective condition. History is created by the dynamic practice of the human subject.

Naturally, after a thoughtful voyage, Marx and Engels come back to the starting point: the general relationship, or the historical dialectics of the social object (the entire social existence built on the foundation of the material production) and the subject (the "social humanity"– the real individual). Marx and Engels emphasize, "Circumstances make men just

---

66 *Ibid.*, p. 59.

as much as men make circumstances."[67] Obviously, this corresponds to the third point in the *Theses* and marks a double cut-off point of the new philosophical horizon from all the previous materialist and idealist views. In an unambiguous statement, they say:

> **History is nothing but the succession of the separate genera-tions, each of which exploits the materials, the capital funds, the productive forces handed down to it by all preceding gen-erations, and thus, on the one hand, continues the traditional activity in completely changed circumstances and, on the oth-er, modifies the old circumstances with a completely changed activity.**[68]

Here, I want to stress that their coordinates are still historical dialectics and the objective dimension.

In the last part of the second "Introduction" (the fifth manuscript) as the draft of Chapter One, we see a clarification of the second aspect of the new philosophical horizon in that "definite individuals who are produc-tively active in a definite way enter into these definite social and political relations."[69] This is a wonderful classic statement of the new philosophical view except a little imprecision. Unaware of the Ancient Society by Lewis H. Morgan, they do not know a classless primitive society where there is no "ownership." Therefore, whether the "political relations" or the "states" in his first classic statement, they are but produced in a certain socio-historical phase and thus generalized here. Later, Marx and Engels perfect this argument. At the same time, in accordance with the above-mentioned line of thought, "the social structure and the State are continually evolv-ing out of the life-process of definite individuals, but of individuals, not as they may appear in their own or other people's imagination, but as they really are; i.e. as they operate, produce materially, and hence as they work under definite material limits, presuppositions and conditions independ-ent of their will."[70]

In addition, a key issue of the second summary is to answer the relation-ship between consciousness and social existence, which should not be in-terpreted as the opposition between the abstract consciousness and mate-rial in previous philosophical explanations. Social existence refers not to the material entity existent in social life but the social life itself composed

---

67   *Ibid.*, p. 59.
68   *Ibid.*, p. 57.
69   *Ibid.*, p.46.
70   *Ibid.*, pp. 46-47.

of practical activities. It certainly contains all the real practical activities of the human subject in transforming the external object, including the political practice–the class struggles. In later works of Marx, his transforming of surroundings means to a large extent the change of the unreasonable social system. In my opinion, it is an important supplement to the principal statement of the overall historical materialism in the first manuscripts. This principle is the foundation to disprove idealism but it does not suggest the more basic material production in the social life or the dominance of the economic power under certain social conditions, like the capitalist society, which we need to carefully discern.

This principle scientifically explains the essence of social consciousness. In the *German Ideology*, consciousness, sometimes the misnomer for "religion" or "man's essence," is falsely put as a premise of history, which is held by almost all the previous thinkers to observe the human social history. Just as Marx and Engels point out, consciousness becomes an egregious point for the German philosophers to define man's social existence. In their view, the natural process, like the animals, is non-subjective and unconscious while human consciousness is the torch to light the long nights, in other words, the historical progress is put forward only through man's conscious activities of creation. Therefore, the fire of consciousness enlightens the whole world and becomes the starting point and premise of the existence and development of social history; without it, there is no history. Even such materialist as Feuerbach sides with the camp of idealists. This, of course, becomes a major target of Marx and Engels to criticize.

Their critical concern is how to restore consciousness to its due status. First of all, "the production of ideas, of conceptions, of consciousness, is at first directly interwoven with the material activity and the material intercourse of men, the language of real life. Conceiving, thinking, the mental intercourse of men, appear at this stage as the direct efflux of their material behaviour."[71] Although politics, religion, philosophy and the other phenomena of consciousness seem to obtain their independence and self-disciplined functions in present life, the initial historical consciousness is closely related with the material production. Man's conscious interactions stem from and accompany the production exchanges. Secondly, "men are the producers of their conceptions, ideas, etc. – real, active men, as they are conditioned by a definite development of their productive forces and of the intercourse corresponding to these, up to its furthest forms."[72] That

---

71   *Ibid.*, p. 47.
72   *Ibid.*, p. 47.

is to say, people produce their own consciousness but today the production of consciousness is ultimately conditioned by the form of man's material production and exchange. Thirdly, "consciousness can never be anything else than conscious existence, and the existence of men is their actual life-process."[73] It is here that our traditional framework of interpretation is completely wrong. The proposition puts consciousness in opposition to the material abstraction, which is the philosophical conclusion that Marx tries to deny on the new philosophical horizon. It means the content of consciousness contains man's real social life with the natural material being historically perceived by men in different social lives.

Therefore, Marx and Engels write, "the phantoms formed in the human brain are also, necessarily, sublimates of their material life-process."[74] Therefore, "morality, religion, metaphysics, all the rest of ideology and their corresponding forms of consciousness, thus no longer retain the semblance of independence."[75] In fact, they just reflect life with more abstract forms.

In the end, the development of consciousness is decided by the actual life. As for consciousness, "they have no history, no development; but men, developing their material production and their material intercourse, alter, along with this their real existence, their thinking and the products of their thinking." In short, "life is not determined by consciousness, but consciousness by life."[76]

The last theoretical explanation is the methodological principle of the new worldview. For Marx and Engels, the new worldview is differentiated from all the old philosophical ideas by that it is not an abstract philosophical speculation but able to be validated by a purely empirical method. "Where speculation ends – in real life – there real, positive science begins: the representation of the practical activity, of the practical process of development of men."[77] To understand this point is very important because it explains the essence of the scientific epistemology and methodology on the new philosophical horizon, with an emphasis on the fundamental difference between the new worldview and the old subjective logic with humanistic values. It no longer starts from the transcendental logic to criticize the historical reality but from the reality in every historical era to have an

73   *Ibid.*, p. 47.
74   *Ibid.*, p. 47.
75   *Ibid.*, p. 47.
76   *Ibid.*, p. 47.
77   *Ibid.*, p. 48.

objective description and revelation of the true process and movement of history. In addition, it is not about a simple perceptual experience but based on the actual scientific abstraction, "a summing-up of the most general results."[78] It is also different from the natural science because the abstraction itself loses the least value once segregated from the reality of human history. Lastly, the new worldview is by no means like "a recipe or schema, as does philosophy, for neatly trimming the epochs of history" but "can only serve to facilitate the arrangement of historical material, to indicate the sequence of its separate strata."[79] There is no universal law or formula here, only a "scientific guide."

Above is the first comprehensive exposition and systematic validation of their new philosophical horizon: The fundamental ideas of historical materialism and historical dialectics on the foundation of practical materialism.[80]

E. THE OBJECTIFICATION OF PRACTICAL MATERIALISM: THE CONCLUSION OF THE CONCLUSION

It is necessary to point out two ad hoc definitions here. One, the historical context explained before. According to Engels' later explanation, "we had to emphasise the main principle vis-á-vis our adversaries, who denied it."[81] In other words, when Marx and Engels establish the new philosophical horizon, their major objective is against the historical idealism dominant in the research of social history; therefore, they mainly stress the historical materialism that starts from the objective practice and decides the idea, and the logic of historical dialectics to have an objective description of the movement of social history. For Marx and Engels, it is the main line of thought as well as the dominant aspect of the most important basic logic and the scientific text. Nevertheless, in my opinion, it is not the only logical consideration in *German Ideology*. Second, more importantly, Marx and Engels relate the general principle of historical materialism: The general base (the production of the material means of subsistence) and the ultimate decisive factor (a certain level of the productive forces) of the existence and development of the entire social history. To understand it,

---

78 *Ibid.*, p. 48.
79 *Ibid.*, p. 48.
80 In the specific critiques of "German Ideology" that appear in the later part of this book, Marx and Engels illustrate the basic points of historical materialism for several times.
81 Marx, Friedrich Engels, and Gareth Stedman Jones. *The Communist Manifesto*. Penguin, 2002. p. 144.

we must remove such historical phenomena as "state" and "political relations," which can be viewed as the general form of historical materialism. Furthermore, it should be noted that in their scientific historical research we see a viewpoint of the special historical materialism that plays a major and dominant role in modern social development, especially in the social material relations and the economic forces of the capitalist society. In particular, we see a certain subjective dimension of historical dialectics related to the proletarian criticism of capitalism and struggles for communism. It is in this dimension that the individual subjective status in modern social history is re-explained in a scientific way. Of course, this is not the major part but an unseen theoretical discourse in the frontal argument of Marx and Engels. Hence, there seems to be a perceptible logical structure in Marxism that is fundamentally different from the linear schema in the traditional philosophical framework. It is a very complex clue with multiple theoretical levels. At this point, we might as well make a logical analysis of the principle statements in Marx's philosophy, a conclusion of the conclusion.

I think that Marx created a new worldview by his philosophical change in the spring of 1845. It contains a rather complicated logical structure, covering several theoretical levels as follows:

First, the general logic of practical materialism. When Marx wrote the *Theses* in the spring of 1845, he obtained a gestalt conversion of the philosophical logic: The three previous conundrums are scientifically combined and solved for good in the objective material practice of the subjective initiative. With practice as a new philosophical point, he builds a fresh materialism of practice. Marx's revolution contains three aspects of "insistence" and "sublation": Insistence for the dialectics by expurgating the Hegelian idealistic impurities and the initiative by rejecting Feuerbach's individual subject of humanism (commonly neglected in our traditional framework of philosophical interpretation), for the materialist base by erasing Feuerbach's mechanism and non-historicity along with the objective historical logic(law) by removing Hegel's speculation, and for a scientific communism by eradicating the imaginary and abstract ethical theories off the proletarian revolution; and his sublation (mainly targeted on Feuerbach and all the old materialism) of the abstract material (the nature in sensuous intuition) to obtain an intermediary validation for the external object in the process of historical practice, of the abstract consciousness (the sensuous intuition) to restore it with its social and historical essence only existent in practice, and of the abstract transcendental essence between men to re-establish the real individual as the subject of practice existent in specific history. The first two aspects of "sublation" abandon the old philosophical question of the abstract opposition between material and consciousness to build the new basic point of the historical relations of social life and man's social consciousness on the foundation of practice. Despite that the natural materials and human practice are both objectively existent and primary, with the former as the prerequisite base of man's social existence, the pre-existing object can be historically present only through the objective progress of practice. Therefore, in the discourse of Marx's practical materialism, practice has a logical priority while the actual individual as the subject of practice is certainly the most real subject and the ultimate goal of the historical development. In my opinion, Marx's logic is rather comprehensive instead of a narrow theoretical focus displayed by the *Theses*, which is different from the *German Ideology* that emphases historical materialism.

Second, the material production as the real base of social history in practical materialism. To my discovery, the 1845 revolution of practical materialism is an overall turn of his philosophical logic. Marx never attempts to rebuild the world with practice ("the ontology of practice"). When he co-authored with Friedrich Engels in writing *German Ideology*, their thought changed: The new philosophical horizon is further objectified and specified; the purpose is to criticize the contemporary "German Ideology" (mainly, Feuerbach's view of history in hidden idealism), which deepens the logical evolution in their philosophy and causes a theoretical shift. The former moves from a general evolution of the logical essence of practice to an orderly structure inside the process of practice and the latter underscores the objective dimension of historical materialism and historical dialectics. Hence, in *German Ideology*, Marx and Engels further validate the material production and reproduction as the originality of the specific structure in the primary objective practice. He later calls it a first-class and indigenous structure in the practical construction. The inner structure of practice is laid as the foundation of the social building, which then deduces the superstructure. This is the general historical materialism emphasizing a common objective base of the social life; it is also the objective dimension of historical dialectics. Although we see the dialectics of the subject and object ("man and the environment"), base and superstructure here, their human subject and social consciousness are both perceived as the object of the objective dialectics.

Third, the subjective dimension of historical dialectics in practical materialism. As Marx says, the essential point that his practical materialism possesses to transcend all the old philosophical trends is that it not only explains and interprets the world but also intends to change the world. It is to me a hidden but important discourse that runs through Marx's entire theoretical quest. Hence, Marx is not only contented with a clarification of the general material base and the objective historical dialectics but also aims to serve the final emancipation of human kind. Naturally, he turns his philosophical angle and restarts from the perspective of the leading elements in the development of social history to narrate historical dialectics and make a scientific call of waking up the oppressed people. Thus, a new aspect silently comes into being: The subjective dimension of historical dialectics on the foundation of the special historical materialism. It mainly targets at certain historical conditions, where social life produces the phenomena of leading and dominant economic forces and the subjugation of the real men (the proletariat) by the material (the capital). With a standpoint of the proletarian revolution, Marx certainly opposes these historical phenomena. As spring rain gently moistens the earth, the social criticism on his new philosophical horizon has quietly become the logic of the objective historical dialectics based on the mass production of capitalism.

In my opinion, the above three aspects are independent on each other in Marx's philosophical logic. In the *German Ideology*, the second aspect is his focus while the first aspect only appears in his relation of practice, social consciousness and the general logic, and the third aspect of his thought is still noticeable in an implicit discourse.

It should be noted that the main clue of this book evolves from the third theoretical aspect of Marx's new philosophical horizon. In the next section, we are going to discuss that important theoretical clue in the *German Ideology*.

III. THE SUBJECTIVE STATUS OF MAN FROM THE PERSPECTIVE OF HISTORICAL DIALECTICS

Some of the Marxist researchers have a correct understanding of the theoretical revolution in the spring of 1845. In the *Theses* and *German Ideology*, Marx and Engels turn from Feuerbach's humanistic alienation to the new worldview and from a general communism to the scientific socialism. However, it must be particularly noted that these scholars make a mistaken assertion by saying Marx's logic in the *1844 Manuscripts* (the concern about the subjective status of man's own development: communism) is completely abandoned. It may account for our long-time neglect of that important theoretical clue. For me, Marx and Engels have been focusing on the dominant position of man in the development of social history; it is thus not deserted at all with the establishment of the new worldview but is re-explained on a fresh theoretical foundation. The issue of the development and the dominant status of the human subject (the proletariat) in the reality of the capitalist society, and its relation with the goal of communism become another important theoretical clue in *German Ideology*, which also explains a crucial logical aspect of the entire Marxist philosophy, especially, the special perception of historical materialism and the subjective dimension of historical dialectics. However, at this point, that logical clue still lurks under their frontal clarification of the major theoretical contents and needs to be corroborated from the specific analysis of Marx and Engels.

A. THE MISTAKES OF THE HUMANISTIC VIEW OF HISTORY

In fact, in *German Ideology*, there is another key issue in the criticism of Feuerbach besides the aforementioned "nature" and "consciousness," that is, "man." In other words, a theoretical subject that Marx and Engels endeavour to prove from both the positive and negative aspects is on the denial of the abstract humanistic logical structure by Feuerbach, Stirner and others. It also proves a major self-reflection of their previous philosophical beliefs.

For the integrity of a theoretical argument, the relation of Marx and Engels will be analyzed together with the study of "man" in the *Theses on Feuerbach* that provides the outline for *German Ideology*. In the *Theses*, Marx points out that Feuerbach's humanistic logic begins from "human": first, his "human" is "to abstract from the historical process... and to presuppose an abstract – isolated – human individual"; then, the logical definition of the essence of human, which "can be comprehended only as 'genus', as an internal, dumb generality which naturally unites the many individuals."[82] In *German Ideology*, Marx and Engels display Feuerbach's error.

> **He never arrives at the really existing active men, but stops at the abstraction "man," and gets no further than recognising "the true, individual, corporeal man," emotionally, i.e. he knows no other "human relationships" "of man to man" than love and friendship, and even then idealised.[83]**

---

82   Marx, Karl. *Early Writings*. Harmondsworth: Penguin Books, 1992. p. 52.
83   Marx, and Friedrich Engels. *The German Ideology*. Ed. Christopher John Arthur. New York: International Publishers Co, 1970. p. 64.

In the eyes of Feuerbach, the essence of human nature is an idealized common abstraction for the individual, an emotional relationship shared by everybody. Moreover, this relationship transforms to some "religious sensualism" during the historical changes. Feuerbach opens a door but closes a window. Despite his criticism that the essence of religion is man's inversion, he actually falls on to another abstracted essence of human. "That 'man', 'pure, genuine man', is the ultimate purpose of world history, that religion is externalised [entäusserte] human essence, that human essence is human essence and the measure of all things."[84] He does not see that the "religious sensualism" is itself a product of society while the abstracted individual belongs to a certain social form. Nor does he understand that the essence of human in real existence is only the sum of all social relations under certain historical conditions. Marx and Engels write, "now we shall find the same thing recurring in connection with Feuerbach, whose illusions 'Stirner' faithfully accepts in order to build further on their foundation... and he constantly foists 'Man' on history as the sole dramatis persona and believes that 'Man' has made history."[85] Sancho regards man as the active subject on which the whole of previous history is based. "The holy as a person is 'man,' which for Sancho is only another name for the concept, the idea."[86] As a result, the actual human is scolded by that strange shadow of man: You are not people. "You have always been people, but you were not conscious of what you were, and for that very reason you were not in reality True People. Therefore your appearance was not appropriate to your essence." In other words, "you should be different from what you really are."[87] It means the human in real existence is involved in an inhuman relation compared with the essence that should have existed. It is similar to Feuerbach's criticism of the nature of religion. Obviously, Sancho intends to "present all actual relations, [and also] actual individuals, [as alienated] (to retain this philosophical [expression] for the time being), to [transform] them into the wholly [abstract] phrase of alienation."[88] Just as Marx and Engels point out, what Feuerbach and Sancho adopt is the abstract human, the essence of the transcendental human.

At every historical stage "Man" was substituted for the individuals and shown as the motive force of history. The whole process was thus conceived as a process of the self-estrangement of

84   Marx, and Friedrich Engels. *Karl Marx, Friedrich Engels: Collected Works*. New York: International Publishers, 1975. p. 486.
85   *Ibid.*, p. 234.
86   *Ibid.*, p. 293.
87   *Ibid.*, p. 250.
88   *Ibid.*, p. 281.

"Man," and this was essentially due to the fact that the average individual of the later stage was always foisted on to the earlier stage, and the consciousness of a later age on to the individuals of an earlier. Through this inversion, which from the first is an abstract image of the actual conditions, it was possible to transform the whole of history into an evolutionary process of consciousness.[89]

Hence, history is always measured with a scale outside it; the real life and production are viewed as something non-historical while the historical thing is regarded as something out of everyday life, something in the outside or transcendental world. For Feuerbach and Sancho, "history becomes a mere history of illusory ideas, a history of spirits and ghosts." In fact, "the speculative idea, the abstract conception, is made the driving force of history."[90] Needless to say, it is an idealistic opinion, a deeper ideology! According to Marx and Engel, in both religious critiques and previous reflections of human beings, "people make their empirical world into an entity that is only conceived, imagined, that confronts them as something foreign."[91] The cause of that inverted relations (estrangement) in reality should not be found in something like "man's essence," "species," and others but be explained "in the material world which each stage of religious development finds in existence"[92] and "from the entire hitherto existing mode of production and intercourse."[93] Marx offers his keen comment:

This so-called "inhuman" is just as much a product of present-day relations as the "human" is; it is their negative aspect, the rebellion – which is not based on any new revolutionary productive force – against the prevailing relations brought about by the existing productive forces, and against the way of satisfying needs that corresponds to these relations. The positive expression "human" corresponds to the definite relations _predominant_ at a certain stage of production and to the way of satisfying needs determined by them, just as the negative expression "inhuman" corresponds to the attempt to negate these predominant relations and the way of satisfying needs prevailing under them without changing the existing mode of production, an attempt that this stage of production daily engenders afresh.[94]

---

89 _Ibid._, pp. 88-89.
90 _Ibid._, p. 130.
91 _Ibid._, p. 159.
92 _Ibid._, p. 160.
93 _Ibid._, p. 159.
94 _Ibid._, p. 432.

Here, the criticism of Feuerbach's abstract estrangement logic of human-ism by Marx and Engels represents a profound self-criticism (clarifica-tion) as well. As mentioned above, the first turn of the Marxist worldview from Hegel's inverted logic to the real civil society for the explanation of state and law (the "materialistic worldview" based on experience to study the "material premise" of history), starts from the writing for *Deutsch-Französische Jahrbücher* (the 1843 "Introduction to the Critique of Hegel's 'Philosophy of Right'" and "On the Jewish Question").

But since at that time this was done in philosophical phraseol-ogy, the traditionally occurring philosophical expressions such as "human essence", "species", etc., gave the German theoreti-cians the desired reason for misunderstanding the real trend of thought and believing that here again it was a question merely of giving a new turn to their worn-out theoretical garment.[95]

True, it is the materialistic position of the Young Marx in understanding the general foundation of social history; but when he turns to seek the lead-ing elements in social history for the establishment of the theoretical basis of the proletarian revolution, the dominant role is played by Feuerbach's humanistic subjective dialectics and axiology. As explained above, the the-oretical core of that subjective dialectics, the estrangement logic of labour remains essentially idealistic. This logical clue exactly contradicts the line of thought rooted from the material foundation of social history.

In the *1844 Manuscripts* and *The Holy Family*, the contradiction reach-es its peak and produces a clear transitional image of Marx's turn from Feuerbach to the new worldview. The immediate result of that contradic-tion is the deconstruction of the entire humanistic estrangement of his-tory: "Draft of an Article on Friedrich List's book: Das Nationale System der Politischen Ökonomie." The previously recessive scientific objective logic becomes dominant. Therefore, a prerequisite theoretical emphasis in the *Theses* and *German Ideology* is on the criticism of Hegel and then the philosophical framework generally driven by the logic of the humanistic "ought" held by Feuerbach and themselves before, for the highlight of a new revolutionary worldview. Accordingly, some important logical points in the criticism of Feuerbach's humanistic estrangement of history are, in fact, the sparks of self-reflection by Marx and Engels.

The reason is that in the *1844 Manuscripts*, the abstract and idealized la-bour is also a "species essence" pre-existent to history, which amounts to the saying that "you should be different from what you really are." As a

---

95   *Ibid.*, p. 236.

result, the history of human society becomes the history of estrangement and the restoration of labour. Marx attempts to address reality with a scale outside history, "labour," to reveal the irrational private ownership from the conception of man's estranged essence, and to realize communism, an ideal status of "ought" with the sublation of the estranged labour. In my opinion, the above profound self-reflection shows the hearty determination to break away from the old philosophies by Marx and Engels. It becomes a crucial step for them to establish their new worldview. Here, we should care less about whether or not Marx abandons his previous philosophical beliefs (we have solved this question) than the question of whether or not he gives up his long-concerned issue of the subjective status of the development of man himself in the establishment of his specific theories (e.g. in *German Ideology*), and he keeps the ultimate communist liberation of the human subject, led by the proletarian emancipation, in the philosophical field.

For me, to correct the humanistic estrangement view of history and a scientific explanation of the dominant status of the human subject in the reality of history are two essentially different questions. However, in the previous research of Marxism, they are seriously mistaken for each other and are both deserted as the remnant shell of the old philosophies. In fact, Marx does stop that general estrangement view of history and the humanistic criticism of axiology but he never denies the significant fact that the human subject (the proletarians) has an unreasonable historical condition in the capitalist society; he makes a scientific re-explanation of that issue in the framework of a new horizon. It also accounts for another important recessive clue from the philosophical construction of *German Ideology* that the new subjective dimension of historical dialectics is based on the theoretical logic of historical materialism and in replacement of the humanistic subjective dialectics and axiology. This train of thought is isomorphic to Marx's points in the special historical materialism of modern society: The economic forces obtain a decisive role in the development of social history.

Last but not least, it is noteworthy to understand that Marx and Engels do not neglect the dialectical movement of the development of social history during their clarification of the new philosophical horizon. They do reveal the objective dialectics in the movement of social history when elucidating the principles of historical materialism, only with a theoretical emphasis on the objective dimension: The innate contradictory movement that forms out of the material production and then conditions the whole structure of social functions. It is a theoretical perspective complementary to our conclusive logic of historical dialectics here that is based on the subjective dimension and mainly concerned with the certain survival status of the human subject in the historical process of capitalism. They are two aspects of the same dialectical movement of social history, with the latter as a continuation of Marx's concern of the dominant historical role of man on the new philosophical horizon.

B. WHAT IS THE ACTUAL MAN ON THE OBJECTIVE DIMENSION OF HISTORICAL DIALECTICS?

For a firm grasp of the subjective dimension of Marx's historical dialectics, in particular, a full knowledge of Marx's scientific rewriting of the human subject, we have to first make clear of the human subject scientifically explained from the objective perspective in Marx's historical materialism. It is a theoretical premise of the subjective dimension. If the last section illustrates what man is not in historical materialism, this part deals with what man is.

In the fourth manuscripts of the first chapter in the *German Ideology* (the first half of the present first part in the first rewritten "Introduction"), Marx and Engels actually answer three graduated questions to the issue of the "German Ideology": What is the real subject of the development of social history? What is the essence of man's social existence? What decides man's social existence? In a succinct statement, Marx and Engels answer, "they are the real individuals, their activity and the material conditions under which they live, both those which they find already existing and those produced by their activity."[96]

When Marx and Engels take the "the existence of living human individuals" as "the first premise of all human history,"[97] there are specific meanings. Individuals are trying to be minimized in the general evolution of Hegel's philosophy; human beings become the logical start of the philosophy of Feuerbach and others, hence, Marx and Engels do not want to avoid the apparent cornerstone of social history, "man." This logical step is a stunning and wonderful debut. They put it bluntly that, that natural existence ("the physical organizations of these individuals") of man as man held by Feuerbach and others, along with man's dependency on nature, is not the essential aspect of man's social history because the individual human being needs sunshine, air, fire and water, which is very similar to those of animals. Even from this perspective, the social history ("the writing of history")

---

96   *Ibid.*, p. 31.
97   *Ibid.*, p. 31.

"must always set out from these natural bases and their modification in the course of history through the action of men."[98] In this way, Marx and Engels first deny the philosophical base of Feuerbach and others: the natural human individual. Thus, it needs to re-argue about the issue that people have taken for granted: What is human? Or, more precisely put: What is the essential difference between human and other animals?

At this point, Marx and Engels are engaged in a deep logical argument. In the nearby *1844 Manuscripts* by Marx and the *Outlines of a Critique of Political Economy* by Engels, "man" is rightly the transcendental subject of social history and his species essence is defined as an ideal labour. Now they want to criticize Feuerbach's humanistic logic and have a self-correction, the key issue of which is to make a clear demarcation. It also explains their theoretical focus on "man" in the establishment of the new horizon.

What is the real historical innate requirement (quality) of man, then? Marx and Engels state that "men can be distinguished from animals by consciousness, by religion or anything else you like."[99] Idealism is centred on consciousness while Feuerbach and Bauer take the emotional relationships and alienated religions as the basic difference between men and animals. This is not wrong in a general understanding. At the same time, that demarcation can extend to a boundless space. However, they are not the qualitative stipulation to differentiate men from other animals. In Marx's new philosophy, people "begin to distinguish themselves from animals as soon as they begin to produce their means of subsistence, a step which is conditioned by their physical organisation."[100] Here, there is nothing like the alleged abstract species essence that human beings ought to have (even "production" is no exception). Only when the humankind makes the historical step from the animal survival (driven by the physical and biological organization) to the readiness of production, can man, the real individual, historically, concretely and actually obtain the new qualitative stipulation for social subsistence. Like a bolt out of the blue, the existence of social history is historically realized through the actual production in a certain phase of material development.

First of all, the real individual is no longer dependent on nature. Man has grown out of the baby image crying for milk in the cradle of nature (the direct natural dependency). They now use the medium of production

---

98   Marx, and Friedrich Engels. *The German Ideology.* Ed. Christopher John Arthur. New York: International Publishers Co, 1970. p. 42.
99   *Ibid.*, p. 42.
100 *Ibid.*, p. 42.

(practice) to acquire their necessary means of subsistence, including both "their modification in the course of history" (of course, the ensuing loss of nature's thing-in-itself to become their new material condition of survival) and "those produced by their activity" (which, mainly refers to the new artificial "nature" and the social condition of men). Secondly, the actual men no longer belong to the total natural process itself but yield to "their actual material life" indirectly produced with the means of subsistence.[101] It is necessary to add that in the early stages, the human social history is not a direct and conscious construction but a spontaneous occurrence. Therefore, the wording of "indirectly" by Marx and Engels is quite accurate.

Their attempt to define the innate stipulation of "production" results in a new category of man's social existence at the same time. Man is less a physical organization of natural existence than a novel form of survival. He is his own social life. It is the historical production that lifts man out of the animals and makes him the "essence of the universe and the soul of all things." It is production that enables humankind to leave the initial ignorance of chaos for the opening light of glory. It is production that gives man what the animals have not: consciousness, language, religion and other unique things in social life. Marx and Engels want to tell us that man is indeed the real individual but man's general stipulation is not the coupling of individuals but a new group life formed by production. Man is individual; the combination of whom in social life makes the historical, real and concrete man. It is the movement of social production that establishes man as the historical subject. Therefore, in Marx's view, man can only belong to "human society, or social humanity." The individual is unified with species in the human subject.

During production, man is obviously separated from the natural barriers for the creation of the unique subject; in the same way, the man-mediated nature and man-created material condition produce the historical object (in a similar demarcation of the objective material existence). In other words, production segregates the subject and object in the chaotic objective process, which signifies that a new colourful page is turned and the real human social history starts. In comparison with the subject-object, production plays the role of medium outside; by deeper analysis, it is actually inside because it separates the subject from the object and glues them on a new basis. In this process of unification, production transforms from the initial relationship to the later real subject.

---

101   *Ibid.*, p. 42.

The movement, or the relation, which *originally* appears as mediatory between the extremes necessarily develops dialectically to where it appears as mediation with itself, as the subject [Subjekt] for whom the extremes are merely its moments.[102]

A normal re-interpretation of the above statement shows that in the process of social history, man is indeed the subject but his real subjectivity is realized due to production (practice). Hence, in the historical existence of social history, man's natural existence in antithesis to the abstract subject (not only the population), man's social material condition in antithesis to the abstract object (not only the geographic condition but also the industrial and cultural surroundings), and the combined people in the practical activities of social production, especially their material activities and relations per se for the construction of history itself, consist of the general social subject that is unconscious at first. At the same time, the individual and the subjective activities in comparison to the human subject are the most important and decisive objective existence in society. Without doubt, the above argument glows with the profound light of historical dialectics.

Needless to say, that Engels and Marx define man by production is only a general stipulation on the primary level of social phenomena. Production segregates men from the animals, and separates the object from the subject that has certain socio-historical characteristics. However, the attention to production seems to be always attracted to a new target in the spreading philosophical field, like an arrow shot into the sky but far missing the target of man's essence and the specific nature of society. Nevertheless, Marx and Engels further develop their logic. In line with the above analysis, man's production plays the most important role in social existence. It is neither a chaotic totality nor a general stipulation of abstraction. Any kind of production is specific, orderly and a functional realization of its structural organization and dynamic pattern inside. This is the means of production. As Marx says, in the activities of social production, men "produce their means of subsistence," which is first decided by the features of the means of subsistence that they obtain at present and need to reproduce. At the same time, it is related with the reproduction of the individual physical existence. More importantly, this mode of production is the mode of the individual activities to a greater extent, a certain mode of expressing their life, and their certain way of life. That is to say, on one side, the orderly structure of production is decided by the historical material means; on the other, the mode of production more expresses the new orderliness of the subjective activities during their creation of social history.

---

102 *Marxian Sociology, Volume 1.* Delhi: Ajanta Publications, 1979. p. 99.

It is the mode of production formed in the activities of human beings that historically conditions the real individuals, the whole social and various exchange relations (including the ideological relations) outside the individual production. The total specific social relations conditioned by a certain mode of production constitute the specific, real, and historical essence of man.[103] It is a transition from the qualitative stipulation of man to his social essence. Hence, men's social mode of production is also the specific essence of social existence. In my opinion, the core paradigm of the new Marxist philosophical horizon is nothing else but the mode of production as the internal structure of the production-practice.[104] "As individuals express their life, so they are. What they are, therefore, coincides with their production, both with what they produce and with how they produce."[105]

Now, Marx's idea is extended from the line of "man" to the "production" (man's species stipulation), and to the "mode of production" (the essence of man and society). Thus, he finishes the gradual and profound development of the human subject as an aim of objective cognition on the objective dimension of historical dialectics. It is clear that the scientific validation of man by Marx and Engels is completely consistent with their description of the objective historical process in general historical materialism. There are two points worthy of our attention: First, Marx validates the general actual human subject, instead of an abstract human subject or one on a specific historical stage, which differs from what we see in the subjective dimension; second, in line with the scientific logic, the human society experiences the development from primitive communes to capitalist society, which is also a process in which the human subject realizes himself with the material advancement and historically establishes the real subjectivity of himself with the capitalist culmination of a humanized world and a full achievement of man's real subjectivity.

---

103   It also truly reflects Marx's saying that the essence of man is "in its reality the ensemble of the social relations."

104   The mode of production can be specifically understood as the functional structure of production, or the practical pattern of material production. See Zhang Yibing. "The Practical Pattern: The Deep Restrictive Structure of the Historical Process of Human Society – On the New Philosophical Horizon" *Social Science Research*. 4 (1991).

105   Marx, and Friedrich Engels. *The German Ideology*. Ed. Christopher John Arthur. New York: International Publishers Co, 1970. p. 42.

C. DO MARX AND ENGELS NOT CARE OF THE EXISTENTIAL STATUS OF THE HUMAN SUBJECT?

As we know, in the frontal explanation of general historical materialism, Marx and Engels illustrate the common situation of the real man, their activities and development. Production, the mode of production and superstructure are composed of the real activities of the individuals, not some objective material progress independent of men. This is the scientific base for the new logical clue that is to be dealt with here. In the first section of the book, we see the major explanation of what "man" is not in the criticism against Feuerbach and others; in the second section, Marx and Engels make a confirmatory argument that men are "not in any fantastic isolation and rigidity, but in their actual, empirically perceptible process of development under definite conditions."[106] They can only obtain the essence of social existence that differentiates them from other animals through the actual occurrence of production. Therefore, men are their actual process of production and what they are is decided by what and how they produce, their material condition of production.

In this way, the so-called essence of man is naturally the whole social relations under certain conditions. As for the theoretical validation and reflection of man himself, it can only be drawn from the actual life, instead of vice versa. Marx and Engels point out:

> **The conditions, independent of them, in which they produced their life, the necessary forms of intercourse connected herewith, and the personal and social relations thereby given, had to take the form – insofar as they were expressed in thoughts – of ideal conditions and necessary relations, i.e., they had to be expressed in consciousness as determinations arising from the concept of man as such, from human essence, from the nature of man, from man *as such*. What people were, what their relations were, appeared in consciousness as ideas of man as such, of his modes of existence or of his immediate conceptual determinations.[107]**

More importantly, "'natural human affinity' is a historical product which is daily changed at the hands of men; it has always been perfectly natural, however inhuman and contrary to nature it may seem, not only in the judgment of 'Man,' but also of a later revolutionary generation."[108] In a similar way, the historical development of the human subject is conditioned by a

---

106   *Ibid.*, p. 47.
107   Marx, and Friedrich Engels. *Karl Marx, Friedrich Engels: Collected Works.* New York: International Publishers, 1975. p. 184.
108   *Ibid.*, p. 479.

certain productive force and mode of production. Marx says:

> **Individuals have always and in all circumstances "proceeded *from themselves*", but since they were not *unique* in the sense of not needing any connections with one another, and since their *needs*, consequently their nature, and the method of satisfying their needs, connected them with one another (relations between the sexes, exchange, division of labour), they *had to* enter into relations with one another. Moreover, since they entered into intercourse with one another not as pure egos, but as individuals at a definite stage of development of their productive forces and requirements, and since this intercourse, in its turn, determined production and needs, it was, therefore, precisely the personal, individual behaviour of individuals, their behaviour to one another as individuals, that created the existing relations and daily reproduces them anew. Hence, it certainly follows that the development of an individual is determined by the development of all the others with whom he is directly or indirectly associated, that development takes place and that the history of a single individual cannot possibly be separated from the history of preceding or contemporary individuals, but is determined by this history.[109]**

For example, one's ability is neither something pre-existing that one should have nor a given from God but the result of the historical development of certain social productive forces. Therefore, the abilities to change nature, to interact with each other, to create and imagine, depend "also on the relations of production and intercourse in which he lives."[110] The desire of people is also a historical existence for it, along with needs, occurs under certain conditions in a certain social form. The desire to land on moon can only be fulfilled in the condition of industrial and technical advancement to create the space rockets; otherwise, it remains a poetic imagination. Hence, the realization of one's desire "depends on whether material circumstances, 'bad' mundane conditions permit the normal satisfaction of this desire and, on the other hand, the development of a totality of desires. This latter depends, in turn, on whether we live in circumstances that allow all-round activity and thereby the full development of all our potentialities."[111] The freedom of man is the same. "People won freedom for themselves each time to the extent that was dictated and permitted not

---

109   *Ibid.*, pp. 437-438.
110   *Ibid.*, p. 209.
111   *Ibid.*, p. 255.

by their ideal of man, but by the existing productive forces."[112] Their right of options is always conditioned by their existential status. As to the reality that man faces, "it in no way depends on him whether he 'accepts' these things or not; all the same, even if for an instant we accept his premises, he has only the choice between definite things which lie within his province and which are in no way posited by his peculiarity."[113] Marx cites an example. "As an Irish peasant, for example, he can only choose to eat potatoes or starve, and he is not always free to make even this choice."[114] In short, the development of one's subjective feature is driven by the progress of history itself. "If the circumstances in which the individual lives allow him only the [one]-sided development of one quality at the expense of all the rest, [if] they give him the material and time to develop only that one quality, then this individual achieves only a one-sided, crippled development. No moral preaching avails here."[115]

A reader may reach the conclusion that Marx abandons the idea of man, the entire abstraction of man's essence and makes the logical judgment of man's real subsistence and the inverted subject and object as an "inhuman" theory. Or, in Althusser's opinion, Marxism is to deny the theoretical humanism. The question is, in the philosophical revolution in the spring of 1845, does Marx remove his previous attention to the subjective status, especially, the unreasonable ("inhuman") position of the human subject in capitalism or any other society of private ownership from the scientific philosophical logic? Judging from the actual critical discourse in *German Ideology*, the answer is no. Marx and Engels are still very concerned about the dominant position of humankind in the actual development of society and history. Based on a scientific theory, they make a historical analysis of the loss and the possibility of recovery for humankind (the proletarians) in the capitalist society. The theoretical thought is the kernel of subjective dimension with the foothold of special materialism, as well as their critical discourse of the scientific socialism to deny the capitalist social reality and the bourgeoisie ideology. However, the theory is not obviously pointed out but assumes a recessive discourse.[116]

---

112 *Ibid.*, p. 431.
113 *Ibid.*, p. 312.
114 *Ibid.*, p. 312.
115 *Ibid.*, p. 262.
116 It is the neglect of this point by the leaders of the Second International that results in the mechanical economic determinism. Although the Western Marxian scholars correctly find this mistake, they go to the other extreme by overstating it to the opposite humanistic subjective dialectics. See Zhang Yibing. *The Broken Wings of Rationality: Criticism of the Western Marxian Philosophy*. Nanjing: Nanjing Press, 1990. pp, 317-319.

For a clearer grasp of Marx's thought, a retrospective way will be discussed to reproduce the important clue. Certain historical phenomena in capitalism perceived from the analysis of Hegel and Feuerbach are now redescribed in a scientific and objective logic. According to Marx, in the history of social development, (Marx calls the pre-capitalist society naturally formed and the capitalist society spontaneously formed.) the social division of labour in its special sense is not on a voluntary base but historically formed. "As activity is not voluntarily, but naturally, divided, man's own deed becomes an alien power opposed to him, which enslaves him instead of being controlled by him."[117] In such a social development, "this consolidation of what we ourselves produce into an objective power above us, growing out of our control, thwarting our expectations, bringing to naught our calculations."[118] Marx makes an ad hoc explanation that it "is one of the chief factors in historical development."[119] It still means that the unreasonable state where man is subjugated is nothing else but what the bourgeois ideology tries to maintain. We should cautiously discern the real meaning of Marx's statement here. First, the controlling, reactionary and subject-degrading "objective power" is obviously about neither the general objective foundation for social existence nor the explanation of the general material conditions of man's historical activities. As analyzed above, it means the "definite material limits, presuppositions and conditions independent of their will" or a new pre-stipulated condition of living so as to obtain certain development and special features in the historical phase of society. The reason is that, as long as humankind exists, the prerequisite material foundation is never to be neglected or surpassed (which, Marx and Engels later define as the eternal natural necessity). It is not difficult to find that the actual discourse operation here departs from the old direct illustration of the total historical progress, the general historical materialism (including the objective dimension of the historical dialectics), to the re-examination of the relation between man and his object from the subjective perspective. Moreover, the theoretical ground of historical materialism is already the special understanding of Marx and Engels who believe that the economic power dominates man and the development of modern social history. If the former establishes a general foundation and law of the existence and development of social history, here it validates the dominant elements in the historical process, that is, emphasizing the stipulation of

---

117 Marx, and Friedrich Engels. *The German Ideology.* Ed. Christopher John Arthur. New York: International Publishers Co, 1970. p. 53.

118 *Ibid.,* p. 53.

119 *Ibid.,* p. 53.

the subjective dimension of historical dialectics. From the new theoretical perspective, they explain the control of man by the economic necessity (not a general material production) in a negative sense, and request man's actual subjective status from the historical reality created by the capitalist material production. This time, it is not man's transcendental essence of "ought" but the inevitable result of the actual social and historical development. Second, it is also noticeable that the present concern of the transformation of the individual force (relationship) into a material force is the same estranged essence of man that Marx already reprimands in the *1844 Manuscripts*. We must carefully define the crucial point. Some Western Marxian theoreticians believe that Marx still holds the philosophical framework of the *1844 Manuscripts* here, only under another guise. It is a big mistake. In my understanding, what Marx keeps is not the humanistic estrangement view of history but the criticism of the specific historical inversion of subject and object in the capitalist society to confront the unreasonable phenomena of private ownership, which is actually examined in a new theoretical vision. He makes it clear that the previous humanistic estrangement view of history (although more close to reality than those of Feuerbach, Stirner and others) is a general idea to be discarded from mind. Then, he borrows the term "alienation" for an easy understanding of the German philosophers and adds an ad hoc explanation: The logic of "of describing [actual] individuals in their [actual] alienation and in the empirical relations of this alienation."[120] Another similar logical point is that, Marx still opposes, just as he does in the *1844 Manuscripts*, the bourgeoisie conclusion that the capitalist system of exploitation is an eternal natural law. Marx tries to correct the contemporary historical ideological mistake that eradicates man's subjective status. More importantly, in the *1844 Manuscripts*, Marx adopts the logic of alienation (along with the negation of the negation of the subjective dialectics) to illustrate the reality of private ownership (social division) but now he starts from the mode of production in social development to explain private ownership and alienation. Thus, he says in a "borrowed" sense that:

> **The positive expression "human" corresponds to the definite relations predominant at a certain stage of production and to the way of satisfying needs determined by them, just as the negative expression "inhuman" corresponds to the attempt to negate these predominant relations and the way of satisfying needs prevailing under them without changing the existing mode of**

---

120 Marx, and Friedrich Engels. *Karl Marx, Friedrich Engels: Collected Works*. New York: International Publishers, 1975. p. 281.

production, an attempt that this stage of production daily engenders afresh.[121]

It is a really insightful statement. By comparison, we see two different logical conclusions: One is in the *1844 Manuscripts*, where the Young Marx takes the logical perspective of abstract ethics and axiology to critique the unreasonable subjective loss of status and the phenomena of alienation; the other is in *German Ideology*, where Marx first makes a historical explanation of the necessity (historical rationality) of the subjective loss of man in certain material development of social history, reveals the unreasonable subjective loss in the innate drive (the proletarian demand to overthrow the "new intention" of capitalism) that stems from society and represents the new productive force, and demonstrates an actual possibility of recovering the subjective status and a scientific road to achieve that goal in the new social tendency towards communism. The former proceeds from result to cause while the latter is vice versa. Marx's description of "division" here is not very satisfactory, but he is on a scientific road anyway.

The above analysis shows that Marx and Engels still negate the subjugation of the human subject by their own creation in the *German Ideology*. Judging from their main theoretical purpose, it is not a dominant logic in their mind but the important discourse does exist as a recessive support in the background.

D. "SELF-ACTIVITY": A NEW SCIENTIFIC SCALE TO MEASURE THE SUBJECTIVE STATUS

As we know, in the *1844 Manuscripts*, the Young Marx takes the measurement of the subject's labour essence to validate the estranged essence of the proletarian labour in the capitalist system. Here, what is the logical scale as a reference to indicate the inversion of the human subject and his creation in capitalism? This is a very crucial question that we cannot afford to ignore.

In the *German Ideology*, we see the first statement about the historical forms of society after their new establishment of the worldview. According to the materials available at that time, Marx takes the scale of the innate structure of the mode of production to make a little imaginary description of the historical progress of human beings. He puts forward four forms or stages of the development of social ownership: 1) tribal [Stammeigentum] ownership; 2) the ancient communal and State ownership; 3) feudal or

---

121 *Ibid.*, p. 432.

estate property; 4) the capitalist ownership and the future communist society. Following the historical description is an important logical explanation by the historical dialectics of the subject-object relationship.

It is a pity that the first part of this logical explanation (pages 36-39 of the third manuscript) is destroyed by the gnawing criticism of the mice. We have to begin our analysis with the middle part. The tool of production used by Marx as the analytical base is also actually measured with the real development of the productive forces. Here, they regard the first three forms of ownership (the tribal, ancient and feudal ownership) as natural generation and the human history since the capitalist society as a civilized social form and communism as a new social form in fundamental antithesis to all the previous "ownership" societies. It is safe to say that in the missing part Marx may have made a comparative analysis of the above (naturally generated and culturally created) social forms from the angle of their production and objective development, and carefully explained their major differences.

There are eight different points here. One, the naturally generated tools of production (land, water, etc.) keep the individuals gather together and the culturally created tools render man part of the production tools, combined with other tools. Man depends on his own power in the former condition but he has to depend on the external tools created by him in the latter situation. Two, thus, every individual is dominated by nature in the first case while they are controlled by the labour products in the latter. The former indicates that man's subjective status is still unstable and generally limited by nature; in the latter, man already establishes himself in the material economic situation created by himself but on a deeper level, he begins to be enslaved by his own production despite that the actual social progress from natural generation to civil creation is not a "humanistic" loss. In such a social advancement, the human subject is still a false image. Three, in the former condition, "property (landed property) appears as direct natural domination, in the second, as domination of labour, particularly of accumulated labour, capital."[122] This is a further explanation of the second point. The former means some of the people can directly control others because of their possession of land while in the latter case some indirectly dominate the others via their private capital. It is the loss of the subjective status again for most of the people, the doubled "subjugation" of man by man in addition to the external domination. It forms the third aspect of Marx's comparative analysis.

---

122   *Ibid.*, p. 63.

The next five comparisons cover the differences of these generally different social forms: The human relations (the kinship and exchange relations; exchanges between humans and nature and exchanges among people), division (the manual and mental labour; the division-based industries or small workshops), and the social control (of man and money), etc.

Then, Marx pays his sole attention to the "latter case." He starts from the social nature of capitalism, examines division, exchanges and the ensuing private phenomena in a certain phase of social history, and the resultant division of labour. After that, Marx returns to the human subject standard (the leading element in history), and thus inspects the subject-object relationship in the capitalist society. Soon, he discovers two facts of modern society: "First the productive forces appear as a world for themselves, quite independent of and divorced from the individuals, alongside the individuals"; second, they have "taken on a material form and are for the individuals no longer the forces of the individuals" but of inverted material forces.[123] In other words, the forces of human beings are misrepresented by material forces. Hence, the subject-object position is inverted. However, in what sense is it defined or by what scale is the subject-object inversion validated? The answer cannot be found from the species essence ("labour") that man ought to have. It is a very critical issue.

In fact, Marx puts forward a new scientific concept to measure the subject-object relationship of historical dialectics: Self-activity. At first sight, it is similar to the idealized "labour" in the *1844 Manuscripts*. However, here Marx intends to explain a new actual scale of the subjective status on the new philosophical horizon. (In my opinion, the concept of "self-activity" is not a final stipulation on this logical level. Marx later makes a scientific definition of it as man's complete free development in social history. See Section III of Chapter IV.)

The paradigm of self-activity has two unified aspects. First, self-activity is man's actual, specific and historical creative activity to change the outside world. According to Marx, the real condition of our self-activity in history is a constant process of historical establishment and realization instead of a transcendental species essence (or the subjective status) that people ought to have. In every specific development of human history, their actual self-activity will always meet certain material conditions.

Conditions under which these definite individuals, living under definite relationships, can alone produce their material life and

---

123   *Ibid.*, p. 86.

what is connected with it, are thus the conditions of their self-activity and are produced by this self-activity.[124]

This is the dialectical subject-object relationship that Marx describes as the expression of their life and the "definite material limits, presuppositions and conditions independent of their will." Obviously, it is the validation of the self-activity on the objective dimension of historical dialectics.

Second, the self-activity refers to a real discernible possibility of man himself in the industrial material production, or his conscious free activity and the historical dominant status. It is a logical determination that stems from the new values on the subjective dimension of historical dialectics. According to Marx, in the past social development (the first three forms of ownership that are naturally or spontaneously generated), it is an illusion that man owns the self-activity and his power (simply collected) directly faces the material (natural) power. In the past history, "self-activity and the production of material life were separated, in that they devolved on different persons."[125] Slave-owners and landlords are the real subjects while their slaves and peasants are degraded to the talking tools. Meanwhile, "the production of material life was considered as a subordinate mode of self-activity."[126] Only the controlling class can own the self-activity based on the material production by the subordinate working people. However, it is completely different in modern capitalist society, "they now diverge to such an extent that altogether material life appears as the end, and what produces this material life, labour (which is now the only possible but, as we see, negative form of self-activity), as the means" because "the individuals must appropriate the existing totality of productive forces, not only to achieve self-activity, but, also, merely to safeguard their very existence. This appropriation is first determined by the object to be appropriated, the productive forces, which have been developed to a totality and which only exist within a universal intercourse."[127] In other words, the actual self-activity becomes the means of material production, with the denial of their self-activity and the subjective status. Man is enslaved by material; the subjective status of human activities is reversed into the objective status.

Marx points out that in past history the non-subjective status (the inhuman condition) in which man's life departs from self-activity is nothing else but the actual result of history. The reason is as follows.

---

124 Marx, and Friedrich Engels. *The German Ideology.* Ed. Christopher John Arthur. New York: International Publishers Co, 1970. p. 87.
125 *Ibid.,* p. 92.
126 *Ibid.,* p. 92.
127 *Ibid.,* p. 92.

**The definite condition, under which they produce, thus corre-
sponds, as long as the contradiction has not yet appeared, to the
reality of their conditioned nature, their one-sided existence,
the one-sidedness of which only becomes evident when the contradiction enters on the scene and thus exists for the later individuals. Then this condition appears as an accidental fetter, and
the consciousness that it is a fetter is imputed to the earlier age
as well... These various conditions, which appear first as conditions of self-activity, later as fetters upon it, form in the whole
evolution of history a coherent series of forms of intercourse,
the coherence of which consists in this: in the place of an earlier
form of intercourse, which has become a fetter, a new one is put,
corresponding to the more developed productive forces and,
hence, to the advanced mode of the self-activity of individuals–
a form which in its turn becomes a fetter and is then replaced
by another.**[128]

It is History, the history of the development of man's own power. Please
note that, Marx does not generally negate man's dominant status, self-
activity, but makes a scientific explanation that the human subject and the
actual dominant state are not an ontological status and that the establishment and realization of self-activity are a historical process of the dynamic
development of man's objective practice. It needs special notice that Marx
never takes the condition that human beings cannot truly establish their
subjective status (the subject-object inversion in pre-historical societies) as
the eternal law of history because it is precisely the essence of the capitalist
ideology. He profoundly argues that "in this process of private interests
acquiring independent existence as class interests the personal behaviour
of the individual is bound to be objectified [sich versachlichen], estranged
[sich entfremden], and at the same time exists as a power independent
of him and without him, created by intercourse, and is transformed into
social relations, into a series of powers which determine and subordinate
the individual, within the framework of definite modes of production,
which, of course, are not dependent on the will, alien [fremde] practical
forces, which are independent not only of isolated individuals but even
of all of them together, always come to stand above people."[129] From the
proletarian standpoint, Marx certainly negates that external control of
man. However, that negative criticism is no longer an abstract ethical requirement of "human," "not a question of the Hegelian 'negative unity' of

---

128   *Ibid.*, p. 87.
129   Marx, and Friedrich Engels. *Karl Marx, Friedrich Engels: Collected Works*. New York:
International Publishers, 1975. p. 245.

two sides of a contradiction, but of the materially determined destruction of the preceding materially determined mode of life of individuals, with the disappearance of which this contradiction together with its unity also disappears."[130] That is to say, in Marx's belief, it is the dynamic historical development of the social practice itself that opens up the actual possibility for man to truly obtain his dominant position. The idea is built on the special understanding of Marx's historical materialism. The traditional philosophical framework just confuses these different theoretical aspects of historical materialism; as a result, the dominant economic power, or the economic necessity is interpreted in a special sense as an invisible hand and a universalized historical phenomenon independent of the subjective will of human beings in modern social history. It will be discussed in detail in the next chapter. Here, there is a vital theoretical ad hoc explanation: as long as Marx talks about the human subject, it does not refer to the humankind but is limited to the proletariat (which is consistent with the reference of the human subject in the *1844 Manuscripts*). It means that, on the high development level of modern industrial production, only after the proletarian revolution deleting all the capitalist system, especially the denial of the capitalist private ownership, can the real historical development of human society begin. Communism is the starting point for this new era in human history. I think the practical subjective dimension (discourse) of Marx and Engels is always oriented toward the ultimate liberation of humanity, communism.

E. "COMMUNISM IS NOT AN IDEALIZED STATE THAT OUGHT TO BE ESTABLISHED"

According to Marx, although the development of modern capitalism enables men to change the naturally generated relations in previous historical phases via their own effort and form a new social power (the expanded productive forces) composed of common activities, it still leaves a difficult legacy behind:

> **Since their co-operation is not voluntary but has come about naturally, not as their own united power, but as an alien force existing outside them, of the origin and goal of which they are ignorant, which they thus cannot control, which on the contrary passes through a peculiar series of phases and stages independent of the will and the action of man.**[131]

---

130   *Ibid.*, p. 247.
131   *Ibid.*, p. 48.

It is what Marx previously calls the "estrangement," that is, the real invert-ed subject-object relationship when the subject has not established his own subjective status. Marx still requests the negation of the historical phenom-ena peculiar to capitalism and looks forward to the future communism. This time, he starts from the logic of the scientific historical materialism to validate the objective necessity of that modern social development and pays more attention to the actual road of the liberation of humankind. Capitalism has created a huge materialized system. This development cre-ated by man but represented by an inhuman force is spontaneously carried forward, or it does not obey the common plan of the freely united indi-viduals; at the same time, the development is very slow, with the produc-tive forces encountering a contradictory power; finally, man's development in capitalism cannot change the general status of being controlled by the object but, on the contrary, dramatically intensifies that inversion. On the other side, the capitalist development creates and provides in itself an actual possibility to fully establish the subjective status of human beings. Nevertheless, due to the nature of the capitalist mode of production, the ultimate emancipation of people cannot be obtained. According to Marx, the bourgeoisie revolution only finishes the political liberation. As a result, there must be another revolution to solve this problem. For Marx, "the transformation, through the division of labour, of personal powers (rela-tionships) into material powers, cannot be dispelled by dismissing the gen-eral idea of it from one's mind, but can only be abolished by the individuals again subjecting these material powers to themselves and abolishing the di-vision of labour."[132] In this actual revolution based on the historical devel-opment, "all-round dependence, this natural form of the world-historical co-operation of individuals, will be transformed by this communist revo-lution into the control and conscious mastery of these powers, which, born of the action of men on one another, have till now overawed and governed men as powers completely alien to them."[133] Only at this new historical stage, are human beings "in a position to achieve a complete and no longer restricted self-activity, which consists in the appropriation of a totality of productive forces and in the thus postulated development of a totality of capacities."[134] "Only at this stage does self-activity coincide with material life, which corresponds to the development of individuals into complete individuals and the casting-off of all natural limitations."[135] Similarly, in

132 Ibid., p. 78.
133 Marx, and Friedrich Engels. *The German Ideology*. Ed. Christopher John Arthur. New York: International Publishers Co, 1970. p. 55.
134 Ibid., p. 93.
135 Ibid., p. 93.

this new era of human self-development, the individuals choose to associate (of course, based on the already developed productive forces), which places the condition of the individual freedom and movement under their control. "In a real community the individuals obtain their freedom in and through their association."[136] We can clearly see that realizing communism and eliminating private ownership (and the division of labor in the special sense) form the last logical link of the subjective dimension in the historical dialectics of man's self-development as well as the only real standpoint. However, it is not the communism described as a theoretical argumentation and axiological critique in the *1844 Manuscripts* but a reflection of the real historical objective trend. "Communism is for us not a state of affairs which is to be established, an ideal to which reality [will] have to adjust itself. We call communism the real movement which abolishes the present state of things."[137] "Now, the communists do not preach morality at all."[138] The negation of the private ownership is no longer based on the inhuman reason, which certainly invites some axiological and moral criticism but is, in fact, an objective requirement of change after the private ownership developed into an advanced stage. Marx also criticizes his previous humanistic communism (the "true socialism" in contemporary Germany) because "with perfect consistency they transform the relations of these particular individuals into relations of 'Man,'" which is then used to criticize reality and thus makes the final communism with imaginary features. Naturally, "they have abandoned the realm of real history and returned to the realm of ideology."[139] Consequently, it falls into the bourgeois ideology. Marx is shrewd to find that:

> **That private property is a form of intercourse necessary for certain stages of development of the productive forces; a form of intercourse that cannot be abolished, and cannot be dispensed with in the production of actual material life.**[140]

Here, it runs in the opposite direction to the line of thought in the *1844 Manuscripts*. Marx does not generally negate the phenomena of the estranged inhuman in the private ownership but first explains the necessity of it. Thus, the communist negation of the private ownership grows out of the "moral demand" and the unreasonable subject-object inversion

---

136 *Ibid.*, p. 83.
137 *Ibid.*, pp. 56-57.
138 *Ibid.*, p. 104.
139 *Ibid.*, p. 119.
140 Marx, and Friedrich Engels. *Karl Marx, Friedrich Engels: Collected Works.* New York: International Publishers, 1975. p. 366.

"is in definite circumstances a necessary form of the self-assertion of individuals."[141] Marx believes that the liberation of humankind is by no means an abstract theoretical revolution.

It is only possible to achieve real liberation in the real world and by employing real means, that slavery cannot be abolished without the steam-engine and the mule and spinning-jenny, serfdom cannot be abolished without improved agriculture, and that, in general, people cannot be liberated as long as they are unable to obtain food and drink, housing and clothing in adequate quality and quantity. "Liberation" is an historical and not a mental act, and it is brought about by historical conditions, the development of industry, commerce, agriculture, the conditions of intercourse... [142]

However, "in all revolutions up till now the mode of activity always remained unscathed and it was only a question of a different distribution of this activity, a new distribution of labour to other persons, whilst the communist revolution is directed against the preceding mode of activity, does away with labour, and abolishes the rule of all classes with the classes themselves."[143] Marx points out that the modern individuals must rise to wipe out the private ownership. It is an objective requirement because "in the development of productive forces there comes a stage when productive forces and means of intercourse are brought into being, which, under the existing relationships, only cause mischief, and are no longer productive but destructive forces."[144] That is to say, the capitalist mode of production has become an obstacle to the development of the productive forces because "the existing form of intercourse and the existing productive forces are all-embracing and only individuals that are developing in an all-round fashion can appropriate them, i.e., can turn them into free manifestations of their lives."[145] Naturally, it leads to a completely new mode of production according to the full development of the productive forces: Communism.

Hence, communism is not an imaginary product of some concept like man's essence. Nor is it in abstract contradiction to the private ownership. Most of all, it is not described as the case in which the "universal lack of

---

141 *Ibid.*, p. 247.
142 Marx, and Friedrich Engels. *The German Ideology.* Ed. Christopher John Arthur. New York: International Publishers Co, 1970. p. 61.
143 *Ibid.*, p. 94.
144 *Ibid.*, p. 94.
145 Marx, and Friedrich Engels. *Karl Marx, Friedrich Engels: Collected Works.* New York: International Publishers, 1975. p. 439.

property or destitution results, or else the lack of property is abolished."[146] (The above view is a continual development of the similar opinion in the *1844 Manuscripts*. It reminds me of the Chinese Cultural Revolution when the Gang of Four preached the poor socialism and Deng Xiaoping concluded that poverty was not socialism.) Marx's communism here is the objective result of the development of the modern capitalism that corresponds to the productive forces. At the same time, "communism differs from all previous movements in that it overturns the basis of all earlier relations of production and intercourse, and for the first time consciously treats all natural premises as the creatures of hitherto existing men, strips them of their natural character and subjugates them to the power of the united individuals."[147] "When the impact of the world which stimulates the real development of the abilities of the individual is under the control of the individuals themselves," communism is no longer ideal but becomes the reality.[148] It is clear that in the actual historical development only man can establish his subjective status and become the master of history. It should be noted that Marx's scientific explanation of communism is made in the innate unity of the two logical aspects of historical materialism: Critique of the reality of capitalism is based on the subjective dimension of historical dialectics; the argumentation of the historical law and the actual road for the inevitable demise of capitalism and the foreseeable communism is done on the objective dimension of historical materialism and historical dialectics. To understand that is very important. In addition, we have neglected for a long time an important theoretical problem: The intrinsic theoretical relationship of communism (the scientific socialism) and the logical thinking of subjective dimension in Marx's historical dialectics, which also explains the lack of attention to the real historical foundation of the subject himself in our socialist practice. This is the first actual historical explanation of man's real dominant status on the new scientific foundation and a very important theoretical part of historical dialectics in Marxist philosophy. Later, it is gradually developed to the scientific social criticism of 'natural-ness', material-subjugation and three fetishistic beliefs in the socio-historical development.

---

146   Marx, and Friedrich Engels. *Marx and Engels Collected Works 1845-47*. New York: International Publishers, 1976. p. 469.

147   Marx, and Friedrich Engels. *The German Ideology*. Ed. Christopher John Arthur. New York: International Publishers Co, 1970. p. 86.

148   Smart, Paul. *Mill and Marx: Individual Liberty and the Roads to Freedom*. Manchester University Press ND, 1991. p. 141.

CHAPTER ⫴

THE AD HOC STIPULATION BY MARX ON 'NATURAL-NESS' AND MATERIAL-SUBJUGATION IN SOCIAL HISTORY

1 *The Absence of the Subjective Dimension of Historical Dialectics and the Conventional Misunderstandings on Marx*
2 *'Natural-ness' as the Special Mode in the Development of Social History and its Alienation*
3 *'Natural-ness' and Material-Subjugation*
4 *The Economic Fetishism: Man Kneels down Before the Material Created by Himself*

CHAPTER THREE

INTRODUCTION

During his further theoretical and practical explorations, Marx deepens the critical discourse concerning the existential status of humans on the subjective dimension of historical dialectics. Especially, when he studies the economic process in the capitalist mode of production, his theoretical thought edges toward criticizing the inverted relationship between humans and material in capitalism, which also suggests a special understanding of the ideological criticism of society and consciousness by historical materialism, and of the phenomena of 'natural-ness' and material-subjugation in certain conditions of socio-historical development.

I. THE ABSENCE OF THE SUBJECTIVE DIMENSION OF HISTORICAL DIALECTICS AND THE CONVENTIONAL MISUNDERSTANDINGS ON MARX

In Marx's philosophical revolution, the original consideration of the subjective status has transformed to an important aspect of the subjective dimension in historical dialectics based on historical materialism. This philosophical discourse is rapidly developed into a historical theory of social criticism with his research of scientific socialism and the capitalist economics. However, it has been long ignored or mistaken as a "process of natural history" in the conventional philosophical framework. Therefore, I think it is necessary to first carry out a theoretical and logical overhaul.

A. THE DOUBLE STRUCTURE OF HISTORICAL MATERIALISM AS THE PREMISE OF MARX'S ECONOMIC RESEARCH

After establishing the scientific philosophical worldview, Marx instantly applies it to the practical process of the proletarian revolution and lays the foundation for scientific socialism. In the year of 1847, he and Engels co-wrote the glorious Communist Manifesto. Almost at the same time, Marx was fully involved in the scientific study of the actual economic structure in capitalism to further validate the *preliminary conclusion of scientific socialism in the philosophical view of history* by an empirical economics. As we all know, almost all of Marx's later life was dedicated to the scientific exploration and the revolutionary cause of the working class. After the long nights of winter, spring finally comes, bringing with it the beautiful fruits of continuous thought. He revealed the economic essence and the secret exploration of the capitalist mode of production in the 1850s and 1860s: *The theory of surplus value.* Then, his *Das Kapital* marked a theoretical breakthrough. It was deemed by Engels as the second greatest discovery in Marx's scientific theories after the establishment of materialism. It should be noted that Marx's economic research was made under the guidance of the scientific standpoints and the methodology of historical materialism; at the same time, the scientific historical view was enriched and developed with the in-depth economic discussions. Immediately after the *German Ideology*, Marx began his serious economic studies (no longer a philosophical projection onto economics). In a letter to Pavel Annenkov, Marx criticizes the historical idealistic premise held by Proudhon, the petty-bourgeois socialist scholar. Once again, Marx stresses the principles of the newly established historical materialism. He first points out that society is not formed by "mankind's impersonal reason." "What is society, irrespective of its form? The product of man's interaction upon man."[1] Marx continues:

> **If you assume a given state of development of man's productive faculties, you will have a corresponding form of commerce and consumption. If you assume given stages of development in production, commerce or consumption, you will have a corresponding form of social constitution, a corresponding organisation, whether of the family, of the estates or of the classes- in a word, a corresponding civil society. If you assume this or that civil society, you will have this or that political system, which is but the official expression of civil society.[2]**

We can see that Marx adroitly uses the attributive word "corresponding" here to emphasize the *objective principle of historical materialism and the historical determinism of the development of productive forces*. He notes that man cannot freely choose a particular form of society although they already know a social form is "not good" (e.g. alienation) or another one is reasonable (e.g. socialism). Why? Because people cannot freely choose their own productive forces. It is his second important point. In the following analysis, Marx says that the material productive forces form the foundation for the complete human history.

> **For every productive force is an acquired force, the product of previous activity. Thus the productive forces are the result of man's practical energy, but that energy is in turn circumscribed by the conditions in which man is placed by the productive forces already acquired, by the form of society which exists before him, which he does not create, which is the product of the preceding generation. [3]**

History is created by the subjective *ability of practice*; the productive forces lay the foundation for history but they are *determined* by the historical condition, which *is just decided* by the previous productive forces and the current social form. The serial determination here centres on a *certain historicality* of the level of the productive forces. *The human subject creates history by practice, the process of which is conditioned by the historical development*. This important view of historical dialectics is especially worthy of notice for those addicted to "practical materialism" because it correctly reflects an *actual, historical, concrete dialectical materialist* relationship. In

---

1   Marx, and Friedrich Engels. *Collected Works 1844-1851: Marx Engels*. New York: International Publishers Company, Incorporated, 1982. p. 96.

2   *Ibid.*, p. 96.

3   *Ibid.*, p. 96.

Marx's scientific view of history, practice, as a logical base, is not a historical "ontology" but the dual construction of the *condition* of productive forces and the creation of new reality in history. For Marx, the material productive forces make up the general foundation of the first grade and the primary of the objective society, which then provides a possibility to form the secondary and the tertiary social levels and structure.[4] Therefore, Marx believes that on a certain cross section of history people make use of the productive forces available for the new production to form a historical connection, the history of humankind. Hence, the development level of the productive forces becomes the only logical start. In the third point, Marx explains the *objective essence* of the historical progress from the perspective of the dynamic development of social history. He says:

> **Thus, the economic forms in which man produces, consumes and exchanges are *transitory and historical*. With the acquisition of new productive faculties man changes his mode of production and with the mode of production he changes all the economic relations which were but the necessary relations of that particular mode of production.[5]**

In particular, Marx says, "Mr. Proudhon confuses ideas and things" because his historical "evolution" and the economic categories "are arranged within his mind." Marx believes it is the Hegelian eternal rationality (the instrument for the development of self). Proudhon's misunderstanding of the different issues of division, machinery and ownership as the abstract economic categories comes from his failure "to understand the *historical* and *transitory* nature of the forms of production in any one epoch."[6] The historical progress (including socialism) is not decided by the *good or bad* ideas in the mind of people (the ethical axiology). Instead, "in developing his productive faculties, i.e. in living, man develops certain inter-relations, and that the nature of these relations necessarily changes with the modification and the growth of the said productive faculties."[7] He cites an extreme example of slavery to illustrate the *historical rationality and necessity* of certain relations of production, which amounts to saying that the capitalist mode of production is unreasonable ("bad") but is a *necessary result* of the certain development of productive forces. This historical necessity is

4 Marx, Karl. *Grundrisse: Foundations of the Critique of Political Economy (rough draft)*. Trans. Martin Nicolaus. London; New York: Penguin, 1993. p. 109.

5 Marx, Karl. *The Letters of Karl Marx*. Ed. Saul Kussiel Padover. Englewood Cliffs, N.J.: Prentice-Hall, 1979. p. 46.

6 Marx, and Friedrich Engels. *Karl Marx, Friedrich Engels: Collected Works*, Volume 38. London: Lawrence & Wishart, 1982. p. 100.

7 *Ibid.*, p. 100.

also historically transitory, only to be eliminated with further development of productive forces (the *objective prerequisites* of socialism). Capitalism can never be changed or abolished in the mind. Hence, the fourth point naturally goes that those who produce social relations in conformity with their material productivity also produce the ideas, categories, i.e. the ideal abstract expressions of those same social relations. "Indeed, the categories are no more eternal than the relations they express. They are historical and transitory products."[8] It is the first time for Marx to state the premise of the scientific view of history in his research of the capitalist economy. In the *Poverty of Philosophy* published not long after, he makes a detailed description of the same view that the social relations are closely related to the productive forces:

Social relations are closely bound up with productive forces. In acquiring new productive forces men change their mode of production; and in changing their mode of production, in changing the way of earning their living, they change all their social relations. The hand-mill gives you society with the feudal lord; the steam-mill society with the industrial capitalist. The same men, who establish their social relations in conformity with the material productivity, produce also principles, ideas, and categories, in conformity with their social relations. "Thus the ideas, these categories, are as little eternal as the relations they express. They are *historical and transitory products*."[9]

There are two important points we should notice. First, the previous criticism of Proudhon's economic methodology: the Hegelian *negation of the negation*. Historical materialism opposes proceeding from the idea. Naturally, Marx is against the *methodological tool* of the ideal negation of the negation[10], which is his dominant logical tool a few years ago. In my opinion, the negation of the negation is no longer an innate logical drive or "core" of historical dialectics but appears as a result and a general character of the objective movement of the social-historical contradictions.[11] For the Young Marx, the negation of the negation, together with alienation, is the theoretical foundation of criticizing and negating reality. Communism is the negation of the negation. Now, the critical point of capitalism has been

---

8   *Ibid.*, p. 102.
9   Marx, and David Caute. *Essential Writings of Karl Marx*. New York: Macmillan, 1967. p. 97.
10   *It needs to be pointed out that the old framework of philosophical interpretation positively* confirms the Hegelian stipulation of the negation of the negation that Marx negatively criticizes.
11   Together with Marx's application of this dialectic in the *Das Kapital*, the concept is adopted and used with certain characters and in certain forms, where such words as "restoration" and "similar" have not the least meanings of logical subjective transformation. I shall deal with this topic later.

converted to the confrontation of the social and historical contradictions themselves, that is, the contradictions of the capitalist mode of production also form the premise of Marx's methodology and criticism of the capitalist economy. Therefore, we can see that Marx's historical dialectics stem from the objective *contradictory* movement of the historical development of the productive forces and the mode of production. As indicated in the *German Ideology*, any study of the actual individual and society must start from a certain condition of the productive forces that the individual or society has, in particular, the contradictions of the mode of production that the socio-historical development has. "To understand these contradictions one must examine the particular mode of production, together with the whole set of social conditions based upon it; and that only by actually changing the mode of production and the entire social system based upon it can these contradictions be solved."[12]

Second, the dual theoretical structure of a general *foundation* of historical view and the premise of a *direct* historical view in Marx's economic studies. It is safe to say that after Marx's specific economic research of the capitalist production relations, he has been holding the basic ground of the above scientific historical view, especially, of the *objective logic* of historical dialectics and the general historical materialism oriented towards the *objective social and material development* of production. I believe that the theoretical premise for Marx's direct research into the capitalist economic reality is the special historical materialism as we have known. If we carefully follow his thoughtful steps, we shall understand it. In his first works on economics, *A Contribution to the Critique of Political Economy*, Marx details a *philosophical premise* of the "guiding principle" of his studies, which still appears as that objective logic to describe the socio-historical development but a departure waits in the near future because there is already a fine difference between them. Marx points out:

> **In the social production of their existence, men inevitably enter into definite relations, which are independent of their will, namely relations of production appropriate to a given stage in the development of their material forces of production. The totality of these relations of production constitutes the economic structure of society, the real foundation, on which arises a legal and political superstructure and to which correspond definite forms of social consciousness. The mode of production of material life conditions the general process of social, political and intellectual life. It is not the consciousness of men that determines**

---

12 Marx, and Friedrich Engels. *The German Ideology: Including Theses on Feuerbach and Introduction to The Critique of Political Economy*. Buffalo, N.Y: Prometheus Books, 1998. p. 543.

their existence, but their social existence that determines their consciousness. At a certain stage of development, the material productive forces of society come into conflict with the existing relations of production or – this merely expresses the same thing in legal terms – with the property relations within the framework of which they have operated hitherto. From forms of development of the productive forces these relations turn into their fetters. Then begins an era of social revolution. The changes in the economic foundation lead sooner or later to the transformation of the whole immense superstructure.[13]

Indeed, the above paragraph can be regarded as the one of most classic and concise statements of the scientific view of history by Marx after the mid-1850s. From an integrated synchronic and diachronic perspective of social history, he makes a precise explanation of the *orderly structure* as well as the *innate drive and the objective mechanism* of the historical progress in human *civilization*. It is also his basic ground and philosophical premise to observe the capitalist reality and economy. By further analysis, I find that Marx's statement here is not the same as the frontal explanation of the general historical materialism in *German Ideology* and even the *Letter to Pavel Annenkov*. Marx focuses on the basic condition of the social existence and development when people enter the eras of civilization after his validation of the first and primary foundation of the social development, the material production, because his "economic structure" and "legal and political superstructure" here can only appear after the disintegration of the primitive communities.[14] Moreover, the communism with the future relations of production will not appear as something "independent of their will."[15] I have reason to believe that Marx's historical materialism mainly accords with specific historical reality after humans enter the *social-economic forms*. It is not the universal status of the social existence of human beings. Thus, the *dominant position* of the economic relations and forces upheld by Marx in social history cannot possess a general necessity as the material production does in social history.

In other words, there are actually two different theoretical aspects in Marx's historical materialism here. First, a validation of the general foundation of the material production that runs through all human societies, which is an eternal universal law (called by Marx as the "natural necessity" later). It is a *general understanding* of historical materialism defined in my explanation

---

13   Marx, and John C. Raines. *Marx on Religion.* Temple University Press, 2002. p. 109.

14   *Ibid.*, p. 109.

15   *Ibid.*, p. 109.

above. Second, an impartial description of the existence and development of the social-economic forms where the economic forces become the major historical elements before the demise of capitalism. The second aspect is not a general law of the entire social history of humankind but a *special one* that works across a broad range of historical periods. It is the special understanding of historical materialism. If the former takes the perspective of validating the general foundation of socio-historical existence and development, the latter mainly explores the major elements of society and history. (Marx already notices that the dominant elements and roles *vary* according to the different development levels of material production in the process of human history, for example, man and nature, subject and object, and the two kinds of production, etc.) They are not *contradictory* but form a dual structure in a *unified* theoretical logic, only that Marx does not have a clear demarcation of them.[16]

In my opinion, historical materialism is indeed the premise of his entire economic studies. However, Marx's historical criticism of the capitalist society is mainly based on the special understanding of the latter. In addition, he often directly transits from this theoretical aspect to the validation of major historical elements in some specific theoretical discussions, that is, to come onto the *subjective dimension* of historical dialectics, which, of course, targets capitalism and illustrates the theoretical base of the proletarian revolution. Here, we see another highlighted theoretical point: "No social order is ever destroyed before all the productive forces for which it is sufficient have been developed, and new superior relations of production never replace older ones before the material conditions for their existence have matured within the framework of the old society."[17] "Mankind thus inevitably sets itself only such tasks as it is able to solve, since closer examination will always show that the problem itself arises only when the material conditions for its solution are already present or at least in the course of formation."[18] Marx's scientific view of history is developed to oppose any abstract, non-historical, ethical *requirement of value* in the criticism of capitalism. He now adopts the law of social and historical development to reveal the *historical trend* of the inevitable demise of capitalism and the necessary victory of socialism.

---

16   The opinion is also perceptible in *German Ideology* and the *Letter to Pavel Annenkov*. It is not further clarified until Marx deepens his economic studies later, especially, his observation of the newly discovered materials about the primitive human societies. It is a pity that Marx never again relates it in general historical materialism.

17   Marx, and John C. Raines. *Marx on Religion*. Temple University Press, 2002. p. 109.

18   Marx, Karl. *Early Writings by Karl Marx*. Harmondsworth: Penguin Books, 1992. p. 426.

In broad outline, the Asiatic, ancient, feudal and modern bourgeois modes of production may be designated as epochs marking progress in the economic development of society. The bourgeois mode of production is the last antagonistic form of the social process of production – antagonistic not in the sense of individual antagonism but of an antagonism that emanates from the individuals' social conditions of existence – but the productive forces developing within bourgeois society create also the material conditions for a solution of this antagonism. "The prehistory of human society accordingly closes with this social formation." [19]

Thus, Marx intends to find the specific laws of social-economic forms by the special understanding of historical materialism, in particular, the historical necessity of the capitalist mode of production and the new irreconcilable "contradiction" with the further development of the productive forces, and to validate the negative condition created in the capitalist material production: The new socialized industrial production and its representative historical subject, the proletariat.

The premise of the scientific view of history dominates all the process of Marx's economic studies. He exposes the objective laws of the capitalist movement, discovers the capitalist secret of exploiting the workers in the theories of surplus value, and accordingly, finds the *root cause* of various unreasonable phenomena in capitalist society, such as the subjugation of man by nature, the productive forces becoming a blind destructive power, and so on. Finally, his socialism is based on the achievements of *empirical science*.

So far, we have dealt with the theoretical premise used by Marx to guide his studies of economics and scientific socialism, that is, the basic principles of historical materialism and its development, in particular, the binary logical structure in this theoretical premise. It is the basic logical premise for all the studies of Marx, which has been sufficiently noticed by previous Marxist researchers and is therefore not a major concern of this book. Here, my concern is: The traditional philosophical framework does not include the different aspects of the general and special meanings of historical materialism; it does not start from the different theoretical angles of a general foundation and the major elements of the historical existence of society validated by Marx; nor does it tell the difference between the objective and subjective dimensions of historical dialectics; in addition, it generalizes the special understanding of historical materialism into a universal description of social history, that is, to take a historical phenomenon

---

19   *Ibid.*, p. 426.

in a certain period of social history as a general law so that it completely removes the subjective dimension of observing social development with historical dialectics, leading to a succession of serous misconceptions of the basic logics of historical materialism.

The purpose of this book is to restore the truth of the Marxist conception of history, especially, to understand historical materialism from the subjective dimension of historical dialectics and to validate Marx's scientific criticism of the capitalist society. To achieve this aim, we have to take a roundabout way. From now on, our theoretical vision will be undergoing a *significant shift*. We shall bid farewell to the old confusion of the special and general meanings of historical materialism, and rediscover Marx's later economic theories that do *not provide a generalized foundation* but do occupy a very important position in his new worldview, that is, the *subjective dimension* of historical dialectics. It also reflects Marx's critical thought of the unreasonable phenomena *resulted from* the capitalist mode of production in his later economic and social studies. However, the important thought is just overlooked and misinterpreted by the traditional philosophical researchers. In my opinion, the conventional negligence causes a serious logical *absence* of the subjective dimension of historical dialectics.

For a clear understanding of the theoretical issue, let us first return to the general difference between the historical development of human society and the natural progress.

B. RECONSIDERING THE RELATIONSHIP BETWEEN THE PROCESS OF NATURAL HISTORY AND THE DEVELOPMENT OF HUMAN SOCIAL HISTORY

We have already known that the humanistic framework based on a transcendental subjective essence no longer exists in Marx's new horizon of historical materialism with the core conception of practice; instead, there is a scientific mapping of the specific conditions of social history. At the same time, Marx is concerned about the existence of the human subject. The question is: What exactly happens in Marx's change of the general relationship between man and nature in the new philosophical horizon? Especially, what is the real meaning of that view in his further economic studies? The answer to these questions is a prerequisite for us to go on with the discussion.

As mentioned above, the Young Marx circumscribes the field of nature and the social life of humankind with the initiative of the human subject, with an emphasis on the latter. The opposition to the control of humans by nature, to the external confinement of people is always his pursuit. In his theoretical development, the negative thought is always based on some *abstract logical requirement of subjective dialectics*. (Initially, it is the creativity of self-consciousness; then, it is the humanistic tool of alienation.) In the new philosophical vision, Marx puts his logical starting point on the creative material activity of the human subject: Practice. He reviews and makes a scientific validation of three major theoretical issues. Finally, Marx realizes a fundamental philosophical change via three chief logical shifts. The key point of Marx's philosophical revolution is the great discovery of historical materialism, the core of which is the recognition of the unique laws of the development of social history that is different from the natural historical progress. To truly understand the essence of the problem and decode the mysterious password, we must put Marx's scientific discoveries into the dimensions of the development of social history.

As we know, the relationship between nature and social history is always an important question in conception of history. When the subject begins to rise from the natural evolution, his historical existence and development is still cramped and tenuous before the strong Mother Nature. People cannot understand nature and their own existence. Inevitably, there come the ideas of natural determinism and creationism. Giambattista Vico for the first time defines the fundamental difference of the human history from the natural history in that it is created by humans themselves. Social history is that of the human subjects, generated and driven by the constant activities of people. This view marks the establishment of self in the socio-historical view (the dominant "anthropocentrism"). It is an improvement compared to natural determinism and creationism.

In the progress of social history, the special quality derived from the initiative of the human subject is also closely connected to the epistemology of historical idealism. Not a few philosophers intuitively regard nature as the existence external to the human subject and admit its own objective movement and laws, which, as expected, leads to natural determinism. However, some others think that people cannot be excluded from social history due to their living existence in it. The process of social life is completely different from that of nature. Without human subjects, there would be no social history. Meanwhile, the words and deeds of any individual in the process of social history are all driven and controlled by the motives of the subjective consciousness, which unsurprisingly causes an illusion, that is, the dominant historical idealism takes the subjective motives of the humans as the innate drive of social history because it is comprised of and created by the activities of the subjects themselves that are just inseparable from the subjective motives. That non-determinism in socio-historical view often prevails over other general doctrines. Thus, many philosophers, including the materialists, fail to climb out of the logical trap.

In my view, it is a small number of philosophers holding *historical determinism* that lead the way out of the above labyrinth, for example, Vico, Kant, and Hegel. Some of their invaluable ideas essentially belong to historical determinism. Vico differentiates the socio-historical process from the natural process with man's creation; at the same time, he points out a "common plan" hidden in social history that is independent of, even contrary to, an individual plan. Although Vico attributes that common objective of history to the will of God being carried out via human beings, he puts forward a clue of socio-historical determinism that is different from creationism.

In a similar way, it is also a great step forward for Kant to separate a "natural will" in itself from the totality of the subjective activities for themselves. At first glance, this idea seems strange because in Kant's philosophical framework the subject of man is higher than the noumenon of nature in the phenomenal realm and the perceptible object is restructured in the paradigm of knowledge by the subject; while from the social and historical view, Kant discovers the controlling hand of non-human Nature. However, Kant's idea is not a paradox. Epistemological explanation shows that what the human subject knows is not the nature-in-itself but the "phenomena" that nature represents and people acquire through their subjective framing. It is an antinomy of knowing and not knowing. Kant still criticizes the abstract subjectivity of people. In his eyes, the individual activity in the process of social history is creative but the general process of society is already determined, often embodying a non-individual "natural will." Therefore, man is free; at the same time, man is not free while everything of his is but the necessity of nature. Here, nature does not simply equate with the natural world. It first refers to the essence of things and the law of the thing in itself. Its semantic explanation leads to Kant's use of the "natural necessity" in a similar sense of social history and the natural development in itself and notes the deterministic character of social history.

Hegel's great achievement is, for Marx and Engels, the first establishment of the idea of the historical development. As we see, in his deformed historical view, the object of nature is marginalized despite that the natural existence is a necessary link of alienation for the absolute idea to realize itself. They are only set as an arrangement and combination of the external material phenomena. "There is nothing new under the sun!"[20] In contrast, human society is a dialectical development of the absolute-idea-subject's self-consciousness, and an evolutionary upgrade, in which, the necessary thing (that is, the universal subjective idea) is historically achieved through a special purpose (the individual interests and enthusiasm). Hegel's view that the "cunning of reason" dominates history is destined to produce a teleological determinism. It is noteworthy that despite being teleological and deterministic, Hegel sticks to the innate law of the subjective development itself instead of following Kant to rely on the external nature in itself when exploring the necessity of social history. It proves Hegel's outstanding wisdom.

In addition, there is another *wonderful point* in the depths of Hegel's view of history: The specific historical unification (identification) of such contradictory pairs as history and logics, necessity and freedom, materialization and transcendence, and "is" and "ought." Hegel eliminates the Kantian dualism and establishes the monistic absolute idea as the essence of the world. His absolute idea is at first a logical framework, which undergoes the materialization of nature (the subjugation of the subject by nature) to realize itself; in later development, it becomes human society and is under the control of the social material created by the human. During *these* periods, in order to realize itself, the idea has to descend to the status of *materialization: The realm of necessity* (inversely represented as the object). However, it struggles on to break the heavy chains, presses foreword with the material development in reality (the "is"), gradually goes out of necessity, and approaches the final realization of itself: *The realm of freedom.* Here, the "ought" for the ideal return to the subjective status is actually acquired in the "is." Therefore, for the whole Hegelian logical development, there is only *one* thing: The absolute idea, which, for its own realization, sets and creatively evolves into the external material object that is only a phenomenon of the ideal essence (the material shell). For idea, the world of the material object is the actual realm of necessity ("is") and that it cannot avoid and the process of experiencing the materialized world is also the real road to the realm of freedom (the "ought"). Accordingly, *the pairs of logics and freedom, the "ought" and "is," necessity and freedom, materialization and transcendence meet their ends.*

To my discovery, when Marx begins to accept Hegel, he only grasps the Hegelian change of self-consciousness and the subject himself. Even when Marx comes to admit Feuerbach's humanistic estrangement view of history, he is still far away from the general philosophical clue of the Hegelian

---

20   Marx, and Friedrich Engels. *Karl Marx, Friedrich Engels: Collected Works*, Volume 4. London: Lawrence & Wishart, 1991. p. 14.

unification of logics and history. It is not until 1845 when Marx establishes the new philosophical vision, especially, historical materialism and solves his own multiple logical complexes that he somewhat *returns* to the general *historical logics* of Hegel and correct them by practical materialism, forming his own *historical dialectics*. In his later economic studies, many important methodological logics derive from the Hegelian dialectics, which, in fact, proves the famous inversion of dialectics in the postscript of his *Das Kapital* and explains why Lenin says that without the comprehension of Hegel's *Science of Logic*, it is impossible to understand the meaning of Marx's *Das Kapital*.[21] In my opinion, Lenin's reference to the "capital Logic" in *Das Kapital* has a very profound connotation, essential for the following analysis and discussions.

The natural movement and social history from the perspective of practical materialism is demarcated by the labour for material production. As we have discussed in the previous chapter, nature consists of the unaffected nature, which exists outside the objective world faced by man (including a few number of virgin lands) and the natural surroundings mediated by man's practice, again divided into the changed natural objects and the reconstructed artificial materials by practice. In any case, people can only discover and use the objective laws of the material movements in the process of transforming nature, instead of creating those laws. The material development of nature in its *ontological sense* is beyond the subjective will. However, the social history of humankind is different. It seems that "history does nothing."[22] It is a dynamic growth of material production by labour. With productive labour, the human subject establishes himself and rises out of the natural process. Thus, the social history of humankind is certainly different from the "subjectless" process of nature. Here, Marx and Engels do not employ the subjective essence (as held by Feuerbach) to validate the difference between society and nature; nor do they take the ideological motivation of the subject (as Hegel) as the driving force for the movements of social history. Instead, they apprehend practice as the key point. This historical, actual, concrete, social practice (the material production) *makes the social history of humankind clearly separated from the natural history due to its historical subjectivity and declares the determinism of socio-historical dialectics via the progress of practice.*

---

21 See Zhang Yibing. "A Big Leap for Lenin in His Deepened Understanding of Materialistic Dialectics: Notes of *Philosophical Notes*." *Philosophical Researches*. 5 (1992).

22 Marx, and Friedrich Engels. *The Holy Family*, or, *Critique of Critical Critique*. Moscow: Foreign Languages Pub. House, 1956. p. 125.

We must also recognize that the objective essence and laws to determine the process of social history form the major logical aspect and the *general theoretical foundation* of the new worldview of Marx and Engels for their theoretical task is against the idealist conception of history and the determinism of ideological motivations. Therefore, in the above changing of thoughts, the emphasis on the objective necessity of social history is a major logical clue. Objectivity is also a *dominant* theoretical stipulation in their philosophical text. The traditional researchers tend to pay more attention to this aspect while ignoring the *discourse centred on the subjective initiative* that is still existent in their new ideological vision, that is, the theoretical clue that stems from the subjective dimension of historical dialectics. This big mistake leads to the attenuation of the *objective dimension* of historical dialectics into a relevant and abstract "reaction" limited to the movements of social object.

Still worse, by citing an *ad hoc economic explanation*, the traditional philosophical researchers *follow Kant's* reliance on natural *thing-in-itself*. They put forward the proposition that the social history of humankind is a process of natural history, which seems to serve for the utmost purpose of establishing the objectivity of the development of social history. By a *nominal* generalization, the social history of humankind becomes forever a process of natural history, which is a point of view that we absolutely deny. As the issue involves the comprehension of Marx's important conclusions in his economic research and the misunderstanding hides a deeper logical crux, we have to pay a serious attention here and re-present Marx's original logical vision and context. (Although it is almost impossible from the perspective of modern Hermeneutics, we can at least follow the Confucian saying to "do it even though we know it is impossible to succeed.")

C. IS THE DEVELOPMENT OF SOCIAL HISTORY ALWAYS A PROCESS OF NATURAL HISTORY?

As we know, the traditional misinterpretation stems from the misunderstanding of a theoretical statement in the preface of Vol. 1 in *Das Kapital* that "in this work I have to examine the *capitalist mode of production*, and the *conditions of production and exchange* corresponding to that mode."[23] As to the capitalist economic process, Marx says, "Intrinsically, it is not a question of the higher or lower degree of development of the social antagonisms that result from the natural laws of capitalist production. It is a question of these *laws themselves*, of these *tendencies* working with iron necessity

---

23   Marx, Engels, Moore, etc. *Das Kapital: The Process of Capitalist Production.* H. Kerr & Company, 1906. p. 13.

towards inevitable results."[24] Marx's explanation of the "natural laws" and the "inevitable results" indicates the sense of the objective necessity. He further clarifies that "even when a society has got upon the right track for the discovery of the *natural laws of its movement* – and it is the ultimate aim of this work, to lay bare the economic law of motion of modern society – it can neither clear by bold leaps, nor remove by legal enactments, the obstacles offered by the successive phases of its normal development. But it can shorten and lessen the birth-pangs."[25] Here, Marx has two important categories: The "natural laws" and the "natural development" in human society. He seems to say that the objective necessity in social history is also the law of the natural development and the movement of social history is like that of nature.

Then, Marx makes a new argument to explain how to deal with "man" in his studies of the economic process (which also plays a crucial role in the traditional philosophical framework).

> **But here individuals are dealt with only in so far as they are the personifications of economic categories, embodiments of particular class-relations and class-interests. My standpoint, from which *the evolution of the economic formation of society is viewed as a process of natural history*, can less than any other make the individual responsible for relations whose creature he socially remains, however much he may subjectively raise himself above them.[26]**

Marx tries to illustrate two points: Man in social history is only a personification of the economic relations, a bearer of certain social relations, thus being weakened in history; the human social history also becomes a process of natural history that can exclude people, "independent of man's will" if interpreted in the traditional philosophical framework. They probably form the later general view that takes the human socio-historical development as a natural historical process.

However, it is *not a scientific view*. The above comprehension of the preface to Marx's *Das Kapital* is not accurate. We have to make a theoretical re-definition that will pave the way for our next discussions.

First of all, to put Marx's statement here in the correct dimensions, we must hold in mind a premise that Marx does not define the foundation of the development of social history in a general meaning of historical

---

24 *Ibid.*, p. 13.
25 *Ibid.*, p. 15.
26 *Ibid.*, p. 15.

materialism; instead, he mainly refers to the special mechanism of his target, the function of the capitalist society. Marx never intends to generalize his theory here to a universal law of the entire social history. The "capitalist mode of production" and the "capitalist natural laws" are of course specific references. In addition, the "natural laws" and the "natural development" existent in the process of social history here are not in positive validation of the essence of social history but used with an ad hoc category in theory and logics since he certainly knows the fundamental difference between the process of social history and that of the natural movement. Lastly, the real meaning of the third statement means that in capitalist economy, the activities of the subjects are materialized into the economic relations and material forces against themselves; humans are but the personified economic forces (the economic men). This is by no means a positive theoretical validation because man is not always being degraded to a material (economic) representation in all societies. Moreover, that famous sentence does not mean the entire human social history is a natural progress. In fact, it has two implied meanings. What Marx relates here is only of the "social-economic forms" in the development of society, in which appears the phenomenon similar to the development of natural history during this period. A careful reader may require a detailed analysis of this opinion.

I shall start with a theoretical misinterpretation on a shallow technical level. First, it is the misunderstanding of Marx's "social-economic forms." With Marx, the meaning of the social economic forms (its original German is the "economic social forms") has been changed by the stipulation of the traditional philosophical framework into the total of the productive forces and the relations of production, the economic base and superstructure. In fact, Marx only refers to certain periods in the process of social history when with the development of the productive forces, the economic relations and forces have become the major socio-historical elements, producing unique *contradictions* in societies of private ownership. Marx never calls the primitive and communist societies as the "social-economic forms," which are but clearly divided by him as "the Asiatic, ancient, feudal and modern bourgeois modes of production."[27] It is the first reason to cause the erroneous generalization. Second, Marx's statement in German is mistranslated. Originally, it means the social and economic forms that are viewed as a process of natural history but the Chinese version directly equates the former with the latter.

---

27   Marx, Karl. *Early Writings by Karl Marx.* Harmondsworth: Penguin Books, 1992. p. 426.

Although the slight error of translation causes a big theoretical misunderstanding, the fundamental reason lies in the traditional negligence of the dual theoretical structure in Marx's scientific view of history, especially, the logic of the subjective dimension in historical dialectics to value the existence of the human subject with the scales of major historical elements. The specific laws in the special understanding of historical materialism are generalized to the universal essence of social history, which is again described as a material evolutionary process without "man" by a mechanical economic determinism. Consequently, the human social history is *simplified* into a process of natural history external to humankind. What a big mistake! I would like to point out that the deep concerns with man in Marx's new philosophical vision and the logical clue of the hidden subjective dimension in historical dialectics of his early scientific philosophical text (*German Ideology*) always take up an important position in his historical view as well as the economic studies and the practice of scientific socialism. It is true that he regards the objective process of material production in social history as the foundation for social existence but that situation is to be changed by man. Marx obviously attaches great importance to the dynamic practice of the human subject in social history and makes it the base for his revolutionary, critical historical dialectics. In the later development of his scientific socialist practice and economic studies, the revolutionary historical dialectics and the discourse to validate the practical initiative of the human subject are *highlighted* instead, forming the unique *social critical theory* of the capitalist society.

Marx no longer makes an ethical negation of the unreasonable alienation of man by the social-economic forms of the human historical development, especially, the capitalist society, which is regarded, instead, as a more "reasonable" and advanced mode of production than that of the previous historical periods from the perspective of the development of social production. In the *Communist Manifesto*, Marx and Engels say, "The bourgeoisie, during its rule of scarce one hundred years, has created more massive and more colossal productive forces than have all preceding generations together."[28] The view here is quite different from that in the *1844 Manuscripts*. As noted above, in the objective dimension of historical dialectics defined in the *German Ideology*, the historical process is the result of the subjective material production and creation; therefore, a certain condition of productive forces necessarily fosters a commensurate human existence (which includes the early human history dominated by natural

---

28   Marx, Karl. *Early Writings by Karl Marx*. Harmondsworth: Penguin Books, 1992. p. 426.

forces and the later phases controlled by the human's own materials, called by Marx as the pre-historical periods of the human social development and the "realm of necessity"). Even if this state reverses the human subject, it is a *necessary phase* for human beings to actually realize themselves in social history. It reminds us of the Hegelian *objective logic* and seems to be a dialectical logic of the "is" and "necessity." Nevertheless, our traditional philosophical framework comes to a stop here. But what causes the halt?

It seems those researchers only pay attention to the objective aspect of historical dialectics while ignoring a subjective dimension oriented towards the actual cause of the proletarian revolution. In other words, in the objective historical process, the human subject proceeds from necessity to freedom, from today's "is" (the objective status of the material domination) to the "ought" already constructed by the capitalist material production (the large-scale industries), man's actual subjective status of full freedom and development. This is what Marx already knows: With the development of productive forces, the capitalist mode of production starts to *transform from the historically reasonable to the historically unreasonable* due to its deep innate contradictions, and will be replaced by communism. It is not a logical conclusion of the previous abstract negation of the negation (the essential sublation of man's estranged labour is communism) but an exposition of the necessary trend of the objective social laws. For Marx, such scientific conceptual pairs as necessity and freedom, base and domination, is and ought, materialization and transcendence, and history and logics are unified in the historical, actual and concrete practice. It is on the foundation of practical materialism that Marx reverses Hegel's historical dialectics. Marx reaches the true and immediate unification of theory and history in comparison to the Hegelian caricatured identification. It is also the *theme of this book* to illustrate that Marx starts from the subjective dimension of historical dialectics to carry out the negative criticism of the representation of the capitalist social history as a non-subjective natural process and the subjugation of man by the external forces. They form Marx's scientific stipulation of the social and historical phenomena of '*natural-ness*' and *object-subjugation* that we are going to re-explore.

To my discovery, it is during Marx's critical studies of the capitalist social and political economy that he puts forward an abnormal non-subjective blind status in certain socio-historical movements of humankind, just similar to that in the natural field, which can be simply called "'natural-ness'." In essence, it indicates the *unreasonable condition where the human subject is subjugated and controlled by his own created material*, which can also be called the phenomenon of "material-subjugation." It embodies the *historical* and *unreasonable* capitalism that Marx attempts to validate in his *theories* of political economics and practice of scientific socialism.[29] It also explains the true indication of his preface to the *Das Kapital*.

Unfortunately, our traditional philosophical framework alters it into a general proposition separated from the specific context and further pushes it away from the original theoretical vision of the author. The laws of specific historical periods ("entirely analogous to that prevailing in the realm of unconscious nature"[30]) revealed by Marx are simply mistaken as the general laws of social development; thus, the historical alienation of social laws into natural ones becomes an eternal law by itself. This big mistake leads to a series of significant theoretical deviations in the traditional framework of philosophical interpretation.[31]

Hence, it is no more important for us to clarify the theoretical question by a *comprehensive* and precise understanding of the authentic meanings of the theory of socio-historical development in Marx's historical materialism. It is also the major concern of this book. Then, how exactly does Marx define 'natural-ness' and material-subjugation in the development of social history? What is its innate relevance to his new philosophical vision? In this regard, let us return to Marx's own scientific theories for the right answers.

---

29   I want to particularly remind the reader that Marx discovers the *fundamental reason* of generating the unreasonable phenomena mentioned above, on which our traditional political economy and scientific socialism has laid enough emphasis and is therefore no longer a major topic of this book. I attempt to dig out the ignored and distorted historical "result" and "phenomenon" in capitalism to illustrate the theoretical error of turning them into a general law.

30   Marx, and Friedrich Engels. *Karl Marx and Friedrich Engels: Selected Works in One Volume.* New York: International Publishers, 1968. p. 623.

31   In 1988, I published the essay titled "Is the Development of Human Social History Always a Process of Natural History?" in *Tianfu Xinlun*, which has drawn continual attention from many Chinese scholars. However, most of them are still confined in the traditional framework of *philosophical interpretation*, for which I have to treat them as a whole in our philosophical dialogue.

II.'NATURAL-NESS' AS THE SPECIAL MODE IN THE DEVELOPMENT OF SOCIAL HISTORY AND ITS ALIENATION

To confirm Marx's theory of 'natural-ness' in the development of social history, it is necessary to first explain his later validation on the categories of nature and the natural laws. Marx's references to these two concepts are rich and varied, with multiple semantic interpretations. Here, "'natural-ness'" is used within a specific theoretical stipulation. Moreover, Marx's logical starting point is established on his negation of the ideological conclusion that advocates: capitalist mode of production is eternal as a natural law. He then develops the theory of 'natural-ness' in the development of the capitalist social history.

A. THE DIFFERENT SEMANTIC ASPECTS OF MARX'S "NATURE" AND "NATURAL LAWS"

By a careful reading of Marx's philosophical texts, there is a slight but perceptible logical inclination: Marx often uses the same category with different semantic meanings. If we are unable to tell the difference, the theoretical chaos is sure to follow. Not a few misconceptions by the traditional framework of philosophical interpretation start from here. **Therefore, a prerequisite to study Marx's 'natural-ness' is to define the research domain. Above all, we should make clear what our research object is Not.**

First, from a historical point of view, we exclude Marx's view of nature before 1845. In the first chapter of this book, we have seen several basic references to nature in the early theoretical studies of the Young Marx. One is a general category as the human subject transcending the object in the logic of idealistic philosophy. Marx often puts nature in opposition to the subjective spirit of human beings. Nature, for him, often represents the objectivity of the object and the ascendancy of the external natural materials over the human subject. Moreover, he tends to establish the subject on the transcendence of the external nature. We can see that Marx's nature here actually bears a deep imprint of Hegel. This view of nature mainly exists in his works before 1842. Second, in the *1844 Manuscripts*, his stipulation of nature undergoes a significant change. Except for the sense of subjective possession of the objects, Marx suddenly praises nature that it actually corresponds to the sensual existence of man's essence and becomes the ontological base of restoration for the human subject. At first look, Marx has a big change in his attitude toward nature (under the influence of the Humanistic scholar Feuerbach) but he is actually generalizing the connotations of nature by the humanistic subjective ontology (the humanized nature after the subjectification of nature). Third, Marx uses the concepts of "nature" and the "natural laws" in their normal sense, which is unnecessary to discuss here.

After the 1845 philosophical revolution, the old speculative logic devouring the natural object disappears from his text but his discourse on nature and the natural laws is still with multiple semantic interpretations. Generally speaking, Marx's use of nature and the natural laws is a scientific explanation at this period, without much semantic connotation or metaphoric inclination. Of course, Marx and Engels always put nature (the natural objects around us) in the scope of the historical development of social practice. It must be pointed out that this "common" usage of nature and the natural laws does not need special validation. They can be temporarily put into brackets.

At the same time, Marx is occasionally seen using nature in a general sense (or the natural history, natural necessity and natural laws) to explain the *objectivity* of a certain social phenomenon and process. For example, in his explanation of the general material production as the foundation of the existence and development of the human social history, he says, "Natural laws cannot be abolished at all. The only thing that can change, under historically differing conditions, is the form in which those laws assert themselves."[32] When discussing the elements of labour as use-value, the use-labour, Marx says, "It is a necessary condition, independent of all forms of society, for the existence of the human race; it is an eternal nature-imposed necessity, without which there can be no material exchanges between man and Nature, and therefore no life."[33] We shall find that Marx's use of natural history or natural necessity here is in an analogous or borrowed sense, that is, referring to the same social phenomena on the dimension of the *objective thing-in-itself* and the foundation of the natural movement, instead of a direct validation of the real *emergence* of the natural movement in social existence. Obviously, this semantic borrowing is in a very limited sphere. An excess step forward will make the right become wrong. The traditional interpretaion expands the above *limited smeaning*. However, Marx's discourse is not the theme of our discussion yet.

---

32   Marx, and Friedrich Engels. *Karl Marx, Friedrich Engels: Collected Works*. New York: International Publishers, 1975. p. 68.
33   Marx, Friedrich Engels, and Hugh Griffith. *Karl Marx & Friedrich Engels*. London: Collector's Library, 2009. p. 151.

What on earth is it, then? Frankly, it is not in Marx's general sense of nature and the natural laws but used in a very special meaning, a critical reflection of the non-subjective status represented by the social life composed of the subjective activities during a certain development of social history. It is an *ad hoc* logical stipulation, in which Marx employs the conceptions of "nature" and the "natural laws" to describe the pre-historical periods of the human social development on a metonymical level. Precisely, he tries to show that in a certain development period in social history there appears an objective process similar to the blind movement of nature, the essence of which is branded as an abnormal subjugation and dominates over the human subject by the external objective forces or materials. History develops in a tragic way sacrificing the human subject. In my opinion, this points to the *non-subjective phenomena in capitalist society omitted by Marx's early alienation theory, thus becomes the first thought forward to the newborn scientific worldview: a new humanistic alienation theory burrying from the non-scientific speculative thinking structure.* It will finally become an important theoretical advance in Marx's later economic exploration, the scientific practice of socialism and the subjective dimension of historical dialectics. The following discussion will focus on the process and basic content of the important theory of 'natural-ness' in Marx's social criticism.

B. THE THEORETICAL OUTSET: FALSIFYING THE CAPITALISTIC "ETERNAL LAW OF NATURE"

Marx's initial validation of the stipulation of 'natural-ness' begins from his defining the historicality of the capitalist mode of production. Meanwhile, he wages his critical sword toward the bourgeois economists who stand for the capitalist system and ideology. As we all know, in classical economics, the bourgeois scholars defend their ideology and celebrate capitalism as an eternal system. The major economic aim is to find the rules of production, distribution and exchange that decide the material wealth. As we know, early in the *1844 Manuscripts*, Marx employs the labour-estrangement theory against the postulation that the bourgeois private ownership is a natural and eternal condition. In later works, he further points out that it is unscientific for the bourgeois scholars to view the capitalist mode of production as universal and perpetual. This critique first appears in his early study of economics. For example, in the "Comments on James Mill," he criticizes Mill's interpretation of the special economic law in capitalism as "a constant law."[34] And in the *1844 Manuscripts*, the Young Marx deepens

---

34   Marx, and Friedrich Engels. *Karl Marx, Friedrich Engels: Collected Works*. New York: International Publishers, 1975. p. 211.

his thought by saying that the capitalist economy "grasps the material process of private property, the process through which it actually passes, in general and abstract formulae which it then takes as laws."[35] His theoretical motivation here is plain: He has to argue against the immortality of capitalism for the proletarian revolution.

After 1845, this view is more conspicuous in his scientific economic studies and obtains a systematic explanation in the Poverty of Philosophy, by which he criticizes the petty bourgeois scholar Proudhon. For the bourgeois economists, there seems to be two social systems: The artificial feudal system and the natural capitalist system. (See the ideas of the bourgeois economics by the physiocrats and Adam Smith.) Marx is very clear by saying that "when the economists say that present-day relations – the relations of bourgeois production – are natural, they imply that these are the relations in which wealth is created and productive forces developed in conformity with the laws of nature. These relations therefore are themselves natural laws independent of the influence of time. They are eternal laws which must always govern society. Thus, there has been history, but there is no longer any."[36] Please note that the above use of "natural laws" is Marx's quote from the bourgeois scholars for a new semantic meaning, the *natural status* in antithesis to the man-made things (which is not identical to Marx's stipulation of 'natural-ness' in the development of social history).

In later economic studies, Marx makes a specific analysis of the physiocrats: "It was their great merit that they conceived these forms as physiological forms of society: as forms arising from the natural necessity of production itself, forms that are independent of anyone's will or of politics, etc. They are material laws; the error is only that the material law of a definite historical social stage is conceived as an abstract law governing equally all forms of society."[37] For Marx, they essentially regard the certain *social relations of material production* as the natural attributes of these materials themselves. In his view, any bourgeois economic book contains a theoretical inversion where land, capital and labour are the "general elements" of the process of production. "On one side we name the elements of the labour process enmeshed with the specific social characteristics they possess at a particular historical stage of development (*landed property, wage labour*); and on the other side we add an element which is attributable to the labour process,

---

35   Marx, Karl. *Early Writings by Karl Marx.* Harmondsworth: Penguin Books, 1992. p. 123.
36   Marx, Pierre-Joseph Proudhon, and Friedrich Engels. *The Poverty of Philosophy.* Chicago: C.H. Kerr & Company, 1910. p. 131.
37   Oakley, Allen. *Marx's Critique of Political Economy: Intellectual Sources and Evolution.* London: Routledge & Kegan Paul, 1985. p. 36.

independently of all specific social formations, as an eternal process be-tween man and nature in general."[38] It actually means, "The appropria-tion of the labour process by capital is confused with the labour process itself."[39] Marx sharply goes on to say, "It can be stated immediately that this is a very convenient method of demonstrating the eternal character of the capitalist mode of production, or of showing that *capital* is a *permanent natural element* of human production in general"[40], which demonstrates a striking *ideological* falsification. According to Marx, "their intention is to prove in this manner the eternal natural necessity for capital; but instead of this, it is rather the opposite that is proved. Capital's necessity even for a particular historical stage of development of the social production process is thereby negated."[41]

It is noticeable here that Marx's fundamental intent of criticizing the bour-geois economy is to illustrate the *historicality* and *transitoriness* of the capi-talist mode of production, and to expose the deceptive and illusory bour-geois ideology. They are his most important *practical purpose and theoretical premise* of scientific socialism. We can never attach enough significance to them in Marx's theoretical logics. This critical and argumentative discourse often runs through Marx's specific economic analysis. For example, in the comment on the Ricardian economics, he says, "The bourgeois form of labour is regarded by Ricardo as the eternal natural form of social labour. Ricardo's primitive fisherman and primitive hunter are from the outset owners of commodities."[42] Essentially, "the value form of the product of labour is not only the most abstract, but is also the most universal form, taken by the product in bourgeois production and stamps that production as a particular species of social production, and thereby gives it its special historical character. If then we treat this mode of production as one eter-nally fixed by Nature for every state of society, we necessarily overlook that which is the *differentia specifica* of the value form, and consequently of the commodity form, and of its further developments, money form, capital form, etc."[43] Marx finds that the bourgeois scholars extract the "fair" ideal from the reality of social commodity production and attempt, in vain, to

---

38 Marx, and Friedrich Engels. *Karl Marx, Friedrich Engels: Collected Works*, Volume 34. London: Lawrence & Wishart, 1994. p. 406.
39 *Ibid.*, 406.
40 *Ibid.*, 406.
41 *Ibid.*, 407.
42 Marx, Karl. *Contribution to the Critique of Political Economy*. New York: International Publishers, 1979. p. 60.
43 Marx, Engels, Moore, etc. *Das Kapital: The Process of Capitalist Production*. H. Kerr & Company, 1906. p. 93.

argue for this "eternal and fair" production. However, their effort is only about whitewashing. In a humorous example, Marx describes:

What opinion should we have of a chemist, who, instead of studying the actual laws of the molecular changes in the composition and decomposition of matter, and on that foundation solving definite problems, claimed to regulate the composition and decomposition of matter by means of the "eternal ideas," of "naturalité" and "affinité"?[44]

The above phenomenon in capitalism, of course, leads to a logical confusion. This bourgeois economic view does not stem from nowhere but represents the *ideological essence* of the entire bourgeoisie (which complies with the characters of fetishism). The issue is, this natural capitalist mode of production seems to be "encased in eternal natural laws independent of history, at which opportunity bourgeois relations are then quietly smuggled in as the inviolable natural laws on which society in the abstract is founded."[45] Marx once concludes that when the classical political economists take the transient process of production as a permanent natural form, they are lying.

Now we are clear of the *ad hoc context*. In Marx's criticism of the capitalist mode of production as the eternal "natural laws," he develops a negative innate logical tendency, that is, to *explain the historicality and essence of the capitalist mode of production from the deep levels of economical and historical development*. Indeed, Engels comments in his review of Marx's first volume of *Das Kapital* it as "the sense of history which pervades the whole book and forbids the author to take the laws of economics for eternal truths, for anything but the formulations of the conditions of existence of certain transitory states of society."[46] Marx certainly opposes the views of the bourgeois scholars. In his new philosophical vision, he always accepts that "the mode of production, the relations in which productive forces are developed, are anything but eternal laws, but that they correspond to a definite development of men and of their productive forces, and that a change in men's productive forces necessarily brings about a change in their relations of production."[47] So is the capitalist system itself, whose innate contradictions necessarily lead to the death of such mode of production and

44 Marx, and Friedrich Engels. *Das Kapital: A Critique of Political Economy (Vol. I-Part I): The Process of Capitalist Production*. New York: Cosimo, Inc., 2007. p. 97.
45 Marx, Karl. *Early Writings*. Harmondsworth: Penguin Books, 1992. p. 27.
46 Marx, and Friedrich Engels. *Marx and Engels Collected Works 1864-68*. New York: International Publ., 1986. p. xxxi.
47 Marx, and Allen W. Wood. *Marx Selections*. New York: Macmillan, 1988. p. 118.

the replacement of socialism (communism) corresponding to the development of new productive forces. This standpoint of observing the process of historical development has never been altered by Marx.

C. THE SEMANTIC METONYMY: THE SPECIFIC "NATURAL LAWS" IN THE CAPITALIST PROCESS OF PRODUCTION

Later in his critical analysis of the bourgeois economy, Marx has a new **semantic change** in the logic of the "natural laws," which is specifically validated in the *Economic Manuscripts of 1861-1863*. As usual, Marx analyses that "the bourgeois economists who regard capital as an eternal and natural (not historical) form of production then attempt at the same time to legitimize it."[48]

It is necessary to point out that Marx's "natural laws" here are endowed with a new metonymic sense to replace the old simplified negation of the bourgeois opinion. Marx compares the special laws in capitalism to some "natural laws." Of course, his comparison is to validate that the capitalist mode of production is not a natural permanent law but a blind one similar to the natural movement and functions during a certain period of human social development, which is the immediate meaning of Marx's stipulation of 'natural-ness'. Obviously, it is not a universal character of social history but an ad hoc explanation of a certain historical period in human social history.[49] Marx shrewdly argues that the capitalist system has indeed some characters similar to the laws of nature with its economy appearing in a *status of the non-subjective development dominated by the blind forces*. It shows that humankind still remains in the realm of animals, only becoming more advanced economic *animals*. Noticeably, it is another continuation of the previous historical view of the Young Marx, which we have seen in the *1844 Manuscripts*. It also corresponds to that of the *Critique of Political Economy* by the Young Engels (which we shall have a special discussion in Chapter Five). In my opinion, in line with the above consideration, 'natural-ness' in the capitalist economic development exposes the historicality and "incompleteness" of the capitalist mode of production. Marx profoundly observes that in the capitalist system, social production reflects an uncontrollable blindness. It is the "mode of production whose inherent laws impose themselves only as the mean of apparently lawless

---

48   Marx, Karl. *Grundrisse: Foundations of the Critique of Political Economy (rough draft)*. Trans. Martin Nicolaus. London; New York: Penguin, 1993. p. 460.
49   I do not imply that only in this time does Marx have that semantic transformation. In fact, it is but Marx's special stipulation in his own text, which I particularly note.

irregularities that compensate one another."[50] Here, the "lawless" "laws" refer to those of the human socio-historical development and the "mean" "laws" can be viewed as the description of the natural laws. Hence, the laws of production are represented by the "natural laws of production."[51] With Marx, the laws of the capitalist development seem to be "metamorphosed by economists into pretended law of Nature."[52] As a result, it is of the contradictory characters of the capitalist mode of production that Marx writes, "These forms conform to its nature and have come into being in the natural evolution of competition, and on the surface competition appears to be simply the movement of this inverted world."[53]

In the above validation, we see a *negative* and *critical* use of the "natural laws" and "naturality." Careful analysis shows that it is not a direct logical stipulation but a *semantic metonymy*. In retrospect of the famous statement in the preface to *Das Kapital*, the original clouds of doubt disperse. When Marx researches the economy of the capitalist mode of production, he does not regard the human socio-historical development as a *permanent* process of natural history but negatively validates the "pre-historical" character of the capitalist society from the angle of social criticism. He points out that the movement of the capitalist socio-economic forms is still with the natural characters due to their common "similarity."

It should be noted that Marx himself does not put forward the concept of "'natural-ness'." It is *my theoretical conclusion on Marx's important ideas in this period*[54]: During the human socio-historical development, there is an abnormal blind status similar to the non-subjective movement of nature because of certain historical limitations. It does not mean the socio-historical process is the natural historical progress but that there are "natural laws" in human society that are independent of the will of humankind and similar to those dominating nature. Marx does not directly identify the semantic metonymy. Nor does he formally use the concept of 'natural-ness'. However, he does call the objective laws of capitalism (and the pre-historical period) the "natural laws." The point is not about the apparent

---

50   Marx, and Friedrich Engels. *Das Kapital: A Critique of Political Economy (Vol. I-Part I):* The Process of Capitalist Production. New York: Cosimo, Inc., 2007. p. 115.

51   *Ibid.*, p. 809.

52   *Ibid.*, p. 680.

53   Marx, and Friedrich Engels. *Karl Marx, Friedrich Engels: Collected Works.* New York: International Publishers, 1975. p. 514.

54   I am inspired by the psychological term of instinctoid coined by Abraham H. Maslow, who uses it to illustrate the special human attributes *resembling* the instincts. My adoption here is in a negative sense, contrary to Maslow's original affirmative or neutral usage.

existence of this theoretical stipulation but the fact that Marx's specific reference is very clear.

During his critical understanding of the capitalist economy, Marx obtains a new perspective, which improves the classical interpretation of the capitalist economy. That "invisible hand" behind the market economy proposed by Adam Smith is now specifically proved. More importantly, in Marx's study of the socio-historical process, the logic of historical dialectics based on subjectivity is scientifically reconstructed and theoretically highlighted, which means Marx's theory of 'natural-ness' is established on his later achievements on economics. In my opinion, it is not only an important accomplishment of the political economy but also a great theoretical leap forward of his historical dialectics. Marx's discovery of 'natural-ness' of the social movement in capitalism is, indeed, a historical continuation of his estrangement view on history where the human subject transcends the natural object, the artificial nature, and a *positivistic and scientific* extension of his concern for the human subject in his past philosophical exploration. It is a major logical advance of the subjective dimension in his historical dialectics. Marx adheres to the *basic premise* of historical materialism, raises the revolutionary and critical banner of historical dialectics, and achieves his purpose to "change the world." In short, if his view of history canot validate the practical initiative of the human subject and prove the inevitable overthrow of capitalism by the proletariat, it is not scientific! It is here that he generates the impediment for the theoreticians of the Second International and for our traditional philosophical understanding, which then falls to the economic historical view tainted with mechanical determinism and follows suit of the bourgeois ideology.

D. 'NATURAL-NESS': IN WHAT SENSE IS THE SOCIO-HISTORICAL DEVELOPMENT SIMILAR TO THE NATURAL PROCESS

What are the basic characteristics of the capitalist 'natural-ness' in Marx's special discourse? In other words, in what sense is the human socio-historical development similar to the natural process?

First, the human socio-historical development possesses a *non-subjectivity external to man*. As we know, natural movement is an objective process in itself if excluding the influence of humankind. There is no super-natural subject external to nature, for instance, God, in the existence and development of nature. Therefore, the natural movement is certainly an objective process independent of the human will. As noted above, on Marx's new philosophical horizon, the human socio-historical development is different from the natural process: Social history is created by humans and the historical process reflects the productive labour development of the human subjects; hence, the human socio-historical development is certainly different from the subjective activities of the process of natural history. However, Marx finds that in the productive process of capitalism, "there reigns complete anarchy within which the social interrelations of production assert themselves only as an overwhelming natural law in relation to individual free will."[55] Later, Engels comments, "according to Marx's views all history up to now, in the case of big events, has come about unconsciously."[56] Here, the word "unconsciously" has a rich implication, indicating that the laws of human social activities in the historical process become the natural laws *independent of man's* will and thus the social movement seems to transform into a *non-subjective* natural process external to humankind. Marx analyses that the internal division of social labour in the capitalist process of production can only be viewed as "an *a posteriori*, nature-imposed necessity, controlling the lawless caprice of the producers, and perceptible in the barometrical fluctuations of the market-prices."[57]

Second, the human socio-historical development presents an inverted *external compulsion contrary to the will of the individual.* The law of the material movement in the development of natural materials is objective necessity, which firmly works, not susceptible to any requirement of the material object. In comparison, the subject in the human social development is always a conscious and intentional individual to create their social history. They are "the authors and the actors of their own drama."[58] When it comes to the capitalist economic process, the artificial economic power is presented as an external coercion contradictory to the individual will. For example, "free competition brings out the *inherent laws* of capitalist production, in the shape of *external coercive laws having power over* every individual capitalist."[59] It means that the inherent laws of capitalist society perform like the natural laws and the rules of the human social development are inversely represented as the external mandatory rules. Marx

---

55 Marx, and Friedrich Engels. *Das Kapital: The Process of Capitalist Production.* Moscow: Foreign Languages Pub. House, 1959. p. 859.

56 See *Engels' Letter to W. Sombart*, March 11, 1895.

57 Marx, Engels, Moore, etc. *Das Kapital: The Process of Capitalist Production.* H. Kerr & Company, 1906. p. 391.

58 Marx, Pierre-Joseph Proudhon, and Friedrich Engels. *The Poverty of Philosophy.* Chicago: C.H. Kerr & Company, 1910. p. 125.

59 Marx, Engels, Moore, etc. *Das Kapital: The Process of Capitalist Production.* H. Kerr & Company, 1906. p. 297.

profoundly points out:

> **In the midst of all the accidental and ever fluctuating exchange relations between the products, the labour time socially necessary for their production forcibly asserts itself like an over-riding law of Nature. The law of gravity thus asserts itself when a house falls about our ears.**[60]

This is a very important statement. With Marx, the law of gravity is a natural law while the law of value on commodity exchanges in capitalism takes the same effect as the aimless natural laws.

Third, the socio-historical process composed of the subjective activities appears in a *blind* movement. During the process of natural development, the material movement blindly evolves among the aimless but mutually affected factors. Even the evolution of animals is but driven by the immediate needs of survival. For the human social development, the historical progress is in the charge of the human subjects who intentionally direct it. However, in capitalist society, "only as an inner law, vis-à-vis the individual agents, as a blind law of Nature, does the law of value exert its influence here and maintain the social equilibrium of production amidst its accidental fluctuations." According to Marx, "the point of bourgeois society is precisely that, a priori, no conscious social regulation of production takes place. What is reasonable and necessary by nature asserts itself only as a blindly operating average."[61] He also cites the opinion of Engels in the *Critique of Political Economy*: when it comes to the bourgeois economic process, it is not a spiritual law "but a law of Nature founded on the want of knowledge of those whose action is the subject of it."[62]

Fourth, the human socio-historical development presents a *destructive tendency* of its own process. During the objective natural process, there are often destructive forms of the material development, such as earthquakes, volcanoes droughts, and various killings, struggles for survival in the biosphere. The development of human society is centred on man's active construction; the development of the productive forces and the improvement of material living standards form the main clue of history. However, in capitalist society, the situation is reversed: The development of the productive forces poses a destructive force against itself. With Marx, during the

---

60   *Ibid.*, 86.
61   Marx, and Friedrich Engels. *Collected Works, Volume 43*. London: Lawrence and Wishart, 1988. p. 69.
62   Marx, Karl. *Das Kapital: A Critique of Political Economy (Vol. I-Part I)*: The Process of Capitalist Production. New York: Cosimo, Inc., 2007. p. 86.

capitalist economic process, "variation of work at present imposes itself after the manner of an overpowering natural law, and with the blindly destructive action of a natural law that meets with resistance at all points."[63] "In existing society, in industry based on individual exchange, anarchy of production, which is the source of so much misery, is at the same time the source of all progress."[64] In addition, there is a malignant tumour growing with the whole process of the capitalist production. It forms a vicious circle, in which "production is inevitably compelled to pass in continuous succession through vicissitudes of prosperity, depression, crisis, stagnation, renewed prosperity, and so on."[65] Without destruction, the capitalist economy cannot move forward.

In short, the process of the capitalist economy is similar to that of the natural sphere. The subjective activities are represented as objective operations; the individual is in serious confrontation with society; the social progress demonstrates at the same time self-harm, and so on. For Marx, they are all abnormal historical conditions. Thus, his explanation of 'natural-ness' represented by the capitalist development is carried out in a negative sense instead of a general law for the entire human social development as perceived by the traditional framework of philosophical understanding. More importantly, he does not treat the unique capitalist phenomenon as the premise for an abstract ethical criticism (as he does in his early period), but regards it as an objective result of the capitalist mode of production. To remember this is particularly important.

63   Marx, and Friedrich Engels. *Collected Works, Volume 35*. London: Lawrence & Wishart, 1996. p. 490.

64   Marx, Pierre-Joseph Proudhon, and Friedrich Engels. *The Poverty of Philosophy*. Chicago: C.H. Kerr & Company, 1910. p. 73.

65   Marx, Karl. *The Poverty of Philosophy*. Charleston, South Carolina: Forgotten Books. p. 59.

III. 'NATURAL-NESS' & MATERIAL-SUBJUGATION

I have already explained that Marx's stipulation of 'natural-ness' in the capitalist social development generally describes the whole social process, which is, to be precise, a theoretical validation through a general comparison between the social development and the natural process. What is the essence of the phenomenon of 'natural-ness' in the capitalist social movement, then? Marx later proposes that it is the historical material-subjugation together with subject-object inversion in social life. In my opinion, the theory of material-subjugation stems from the second aspect of the social critical theory/discourse transformed from the estrangement theory of the Young Marx. It is also the other theoretical premise of his criticism of the bourgeois ideology.

A. OBJECTIFICATION AND ALIENATION; MATERIALIZATION AND MATERIAL-SUBJUGATION

Before understanding the basic points of Marx's material-subjugation theory, we have to first define two important categories: The relationship between *objectification* and *alienation* in his new philosophical logics and the relationship between *materialization* and *material-subjugation* on his new philosophical horizon and we should also understand the theoretical correlation between the former and the later.

As mentioned earlier, in his writing of the doctoral dissertation, the Young Marx still holds the Hegelian philosophical position and accepts the default objectification from atoms to reality (the emerging affirmative logic of alienation). When it comes to the writing for *Deutsch-Französische Jahrbücher* and the *Critique of Hegel's 'Philosophy of Right'*, he begins to negate the status of alienation and differentiate it from objectification. When the Young Marx constructs his own logic of labour alienation in the *1844 Manuscripts*, he already makes a conscious criticism of the idealistic confusion of objectification and alienation concept of Hegel, for whom, the ideal objectification of self-creation and self-realization is only a movement toward the material self-externalization and self-alienation; therefore, the process of alienating and externalizing the absolute idea into nature and history is also an objectified and spiral increment from abstraction to concreteness, from limitedness to infinity. In the eyes of Hegel, alienation is objectification; therefore, he is positive towards alienation. Marx thus comments: "In Hegel, therefore, the negation of the negation is not the confirmation of the true essence, effected precisely through negation of the pseudo-essence."[66] Marx stands with the proletarians, and he

---

66 Marx, and Friedrich Engels. *Karl Marx, Friedrich Engels: Collected Works*. London: Lawrence & Wishart, 1975. p. 339.

must negate alienation for the phenomenon of labour alienation is closely connected with the irrational reversal of man and material that he criticizes in capitalism. However, his criticism is not based on a scientific theory.

I have already noted that Marx's logic of labour alienation loses its dominance as early as in the "Draft of an Article on Friedrich List's book: *Das Nationale System der Politischen Ökonomie*" in March, 1845, when he no longer uses the logical tool of labour alienation but makes an objective explanation of that special phenomenon of *the materialization of people* in the same criticism of the inverted man and material in the capitalist economic life. He says, "The worker is the slave of capital, that he is a 'commodity', an exchange value. If I characterise man as an 'exchange value', this expression already implies that social conditions have transformed him into a 'thing'."[67] In this condition, "his activity is not a free manifestation of his human life that it is, rather, a huckstering sale of his forces, alienation (sale) to capital of his one-sidedly developed abilities, in a word, that it is 'labour'."[68] Marx now replaces the previous term "estranged labour" with an underscored word "labour," which is a semantic signal worth of our serious attention. In my opinion, Marx first sheds off the ethical requirement of the humanistic logic and makes an objective explanation of the unreasonable phenomenon in his criticism of the reversed relationship of man and material in capitalism. He points out that "free labour, that is to say, indirect slavery which offers itself for sale, is its principle."[69] To take an example from the productive forces in the capitalist condition, "the bourgeois sees in the proletarian not a *human being*, but a *force* capable of creating wealth."[70] For a worker in capitalism, "if a crooked spine, twisted limbs, a one-sided development and strengthening of certain muscles, etc., make you more capable of working (more productive), then your crooked spine, your twisted limbs, your one-sided muscular movement are a productive force."[71] A human here is used as a material force. Thus, Marx asks in fury, "Is it a high appreciation of man for him to figure as a 'force' alongside horses, steam and water?"[72] He calls it the "baseness of people" "being sacrificed for things."[73]

---

67   *Ibid.*, p. 286.
68   *Ibid.*, p. 278.
69   *Ibid.*, p. 284.
70   *Ibid.*, p. 286.
71   *Ibid.*, p. 285.
72   *Ibid.*, p. 285.
73   *Ibid.*, p. 284

Here, Marx leaves a very important demarcation between the materialization in the process of production and the special "material" ascendancy over man in the same process. First, people are objectified in their materialized activities of industrial production. "Industry can be regarded as a great workshop in which man first takes possession of his own forces and the forces of nature, objectifies himself and creates for himself the conditions for a human existence."[74] Marx calls the industry "the development of man."[75] Second, "as industry is no longer regarded as a huckstering interest that degrades him to a 'force' capable of creating wealth mankind has had to develop its abilities as a slave. The whole of human society becomes merely a machine for the creation of wealth."[76] In contrast to the first materialization consented by Marx, the second form of materialization leads to "the productive force that industry creates unconsciously and against its will" and becomes "a power over us."[77] The special materialization refers to the phenomenon of *man's subjugation by his own creation* in capitalist society.

According to Marx, in modern capitalism, the productive force has two attributes: It makes man's labour more efficient or the natural and the social power more effective; it also becomes a tool for the bourgeois to get rich and realize their selfish/dirty profits. Obviously, Marx affirms the former and negates the latter. His attempt is to eliminate and shake off the chain of money, not the industry itself. This attitude accounts for his final rejection of Rousseau's romanticism and embracing the scientific logic. Marx does not use the estrangement logic but still follows the discourse of the "human principle." He makes it clear that he is not against the general material development but against the "labour" (essence) that turns humans into animals. For Marx, in capitalism, "'labour' by its very nature is unfree, inhuman, unsocial activity, determined by private property and creating private property."[78] He calls on the proletarians to fight against this "labour" as the foundation of private property. At the same time, Marx offers a passionate imagination of the future.

> **Tomorrow they will break their chains and reveal themselves as the bearers of human development which will blow him sky-high together with his industry, which assumes the dirty outer shell – which he regards as its essence – only until the human**

---

74   *Ibid.*, p. 281.
75   *Ibid.*, p. 282.
76   *Ibid.*, p. 286.
77   *Ibid.*, p. 283.
78   *Ibid.*, p. 279.

kernel has gained sufficient strength to burst this shell and appear in its own shape.[79]

However, it is perceptible that Marx has not found a suitable concept to express his idea at this time, which lasts until the establishment of his scientific theory.

In 1845 *German Ideology*, we see the new philosophical horizon started by Marx and Engels. As noted earlier, here, the theoretical construction was based on the establishment on the objective logics of historical materialism. Meanwhile, although Marx abandons the logic of alienation, he is still concerned with the human existence in capitalism employing the subjective dimension of historical dialectics. Thus, he is preoccupied with the unreasonable status quo in the capitalist historical development and the bourgeois ideology to maintain that reality (the unreasonable phenomenon previously attacked by Marx employing the negative logic of alienation). Marx points out that if people were subject to the mercy of nature in previous ages, they are now controlled by their own labour products and the "past labour" in capitalist society. In socio-historical development, "this consolidation of what we ourselves produce into an objective power above us, growing out of our control, thwarting our expectations, bringing to naught our calculations, is one of the chief factors in historical development up till now."[80] In this condition, the social activities become "an alien power opposed to him, which enslaves him instead of being controlled by him."[81] In the process of social movement, those practical forces "are independent not only of isolated individuals but even of all of them together."[82] Moreover, these forces "born of the action of men on one another, have till now overawed and governed men as powers completely alien to them."[83] Marx further says that it is like "a relation which, as an English economist says, hovers over the earth like the fate of the ancients, and with invisible hand allots fortune and misfortune to men, sets up empires and overthrows empires, causes nations to rise and to disappear."[84] For him, "in the present epoch, the domination of material relations over individuals, and the suppression of individuality by fortuitous circumstances, has assumed its sharpest and most universal form."[85] Meanwhile, the productive forces

---

79 *Ibid.*, p. 282.

80 Marx, and Friedrich Engels. *The German Ideology.* Ed. Christopher John Arthur. New York: International Publishers Co, 1970. p. 53.

81 *Ibid.*, p. 53.

82 *Ibid.*, p. 104.

83 *Ibid.*, p. 55.

84 *Ibid.*, p. 55.

85 Marx, and Friedrich Engels. *Karl Marx, Friedrich Engels: Collected Works.* New York: International Publishers, 1975. p. 438.

come to a stage where their development only bring damages and become a power of destruction instead of production.

Obviously, the unreasonable phenomenon in capitalism is what Marx previously negates with the logic of alienation. He specially uses "a term which will be comprehensible to the philosophers": "alienation." But now, it is a new re-evaluation by historical materialist view. As we know, the fundamental meaning of the communist revolution is to *correct the material oppression and subjugation of humans in capitalism*, to re-control and consciously direct the forces of alienation. "With the abolition of the basis of private property, with the communistic regulation of production (and, implicit in this, the destruction of the alien relation between men and what they themselves produce), the power of the relation of supply and demand is dissolved into nothing, and men get exchange, production, the mode of their mutual relation, under their own control again."[86]

Frankly, Marx's critical discourse here is not systematic and complete, probably due to the uncertainty of his recent theoretical transformation. Nevertheless, his replacement of the alienation logic with the new philosophical horizon is still perceptible here. It has two important points: First, the oppression and subjugation of people by their created materials and material relations in the capitalist economic process, which presents an unreasonable subject-object reversal on the subjective dimension of historical dialectics; second, in this specific historical condition, the human socio-historical development seems to become a blind and self-destructive process external to humankind. Any development is sacrificed with destruction and catastrophes. It is very clear now that the latter indicates what Marx regards as 'natural-ness' in socio-historical development and the former is his *theory of material-subjugation* equally ignored by most of the researchers.

B. MATERIAL-SUBJUGATION: WE ARE DRIVEN BY THE MATERIAL FORCES CREATED BY OURSELVES

The above social critical theories get further systematic explanation in Marx's subsequent research, mainly in his social economic research and the practice of scientific socialism

As we see, Marx still separates the different aspects of the capitalist materialization in his economic studies. One is the materialization with a "*natural characteristic*," which generally means, "All production is appropriation of nature on the part of an individual within and through

---

86   Marx, and Friedrich Engels. *The German Ideology*. Ed. Christopher John Arthur. New York: International Publishers Co, 1970. p. 55.

a specific form of society."[87] Or, from the perspective of socio-historical development, the human "labour is, in the first place, a process in which both man and Nature participate, and in which man of his own accord starts, regulates, and controls the material re-actions between himself and Nature."[88] Labour is employed to "appropriate Nature's productions in a form adapted to his own wants."[89] Here, materialization is actually transformed from Marx's previous objectification; it means the active process of the human subjects to realize their own aims through changing the object with their labour production.

In the other type of materialization that Marx discovers in the capitalist production, "the individual is not objectified in his natural quality, but in a social quality (relation) which is, at the same time, external to him."[90] In this respect, "the producer is therefore controlled by the product, the subject by the object, labour which is being embodied by labour embodied in an object, etc." Hence, Marx says, "the relationship of labour to the conditions of labour is turned upside-down."[91] Essentially, materialization leads to the *irrational subjugation of people by their own created material*. In his eyes, it is the unique phenomenon of material-subjugation in the development of the capitalist social history.[92]

Marx particularly points out:

The emphasis comes to be placed not on the state of being objectified, but on the state of being alienated, dispossessed, sold [Der Ton wird gelegt nicht auf das Vergegenständlichtsein, sondern das Entfremdet-, Entäussert-, Veräussertsein]; on the condition that the monstrous objective power which social labour itself erected opposite itself as one of its moments belongs not to the worker, but to the personified conditions of production, i.e. to capital.[93]

---

87   Marx, Karl. *Grundrisse: Foundations of the Critique of Political Economy (rough draft)*. Trans. Martin Nicolaus. London; New York: Penguin, 1993. p. 87.

88   Marx, Karl. *Das Kapital: A Critique of Political Economy: The Process of Capitalist Production*. New York: Cosimo, Inc., 2007. p. 197.

89   *Ibid.*, 198.

90   Marx, Karl. *Grundrisse: Foundations of the Critique of Political Economy (rough draft)*. Trans. Martin Nicolaus. London; New York: Penguin, 1993. p. 226.

91   Marx, Karl. *Theories of Surplus Value, Volume 3*. London: Lawrence & Wishart, 1969. p. 276.

92   Georg Lukács does not understand this important identification in his History and Class Consciousness. He neither differentiates the two types of materialization nor sees a logical upgrade from alienation to material-subjugation. See III of Chapter Six in this book.

93   Marx, Karl. *Grundrisse: Foundations of the Critique of Political Economy (rough draft)*. Trans. Martin Nicolaus. London; New York: Penguin, 1993. p. 831.

Marx describes the true *confusion* and *inversion* in the reality of the capitalist economic life. Contrary to the bourgeois scholars, he says, "But obviously this process of inversion is a merely *historical* necessity, a necessity for the development of the forces of production solely from a specific historic point of departure, or basis, but in no way an *absolute* necessity of production; rather, a vanishing one, and the result and the inherent purpose of this process is to suspend this basis itself, together with this form of the process."[94] The above statement lays the foundation for his theory of scientific socialism. "The bourgeois economists are so much cooped up within the notions belonging to a specific historic stage of social development that the necessity of the *objectification* of the powers of social labour appears to them as inseparable from the necessity of their *alienation vis-à-vis* living labour."[95] This is decided by their class position. Marx sharply concludes that the bourgeois scholars try to maintain the inversion of human and material with the ideological intention to validate the eternalness of the capitalist mode of production.

Here, Marx does not negate the active materialization brought up by the development of the productive forces in the capitalist process of production (the general foundation of social history). His old abstract ethical criticism and romanticism have vanished. Now, he targets at the subjugation of and blind dominance over the subject, that is, he is *still* against the material control of man and the dominant element of the economic power. Marx says, "As, in religion, man is governed by the products of his own brain, so in capitalistic production, he is governed by the products of his own hands."[96] "The rule of the capitalist over the worker is therefore the rule of the object over the human, of dead labour over living, of the product over the producer."[97] In the reality of social life, there is a relationship identical to that of *religion* in the field of ideology, the inverted condition of subject and object. It, *historically*, creates wealth at the expense of the majority and anticipates the creation of endless productive forces that construct the material base of free human beings. This contradictory experience is a necessary throe, not different from the initial religious experience when people have to antagonize themselves by their own spiritual power as if it were independent. This is the *process of labour "alienation."*

---

94 *Ibid.*, p. 832.
95 *Ibid.*, p. 832.
96 Marx, Karl. *Das Kapital: A Critique of Political Economy: The Process of Capitalist Production.* New York: Cosimo, Inc., 2007. p. 681.
97 Marx, Karl. *Grundrisse: Foundations of the Critique of Political Economy (rough draft).* Trans. Martin Nicolaus. London; New York: Penguin, 1993. p. 46.

To that extent, the worker here stands higher than the capitalist from the outset, in that the latter is rooted in that alienation process and finds in it his absolute satisfaction, whereas the worker, as its victim, stands from the outset in a relation of rebellion towards it and perceives it as a process of enslavement.[98]

Marx actually adopts the subjective dimension of historical dialectics to criticize the unique human-material inversion in capitalism, which, fundamentally, reflects *the control and subjugation of the human subject by his own created material.* In short, it is the material-subjugation of the subject in the process of social history.[99] In the capitalist mode of production, it is by *material-subjugation that the capitalists indirectly dominate and control people.* It is, understandably, Marx's profound exposition of the *suppressive nature* of wage labour in capitalism. In my opinion, Marx's material-subjugation theory is not only important for the social criticism but also valuable for the subjective dimension of historical dialectics. Unfortunately, together with the theory of 'natural-ness' (the mechanical economic determinism, which will be dealt with later), it is only ignored and seriously distorted in our traditional framework of philosophical illustration.

In addition, Marx's theory of material-subjugation is *based on the new scientific historical view of history for an immediate transformation of the old humanistic alienation theory.* As mentioned earlier, in the philosophical change of 1845, Marx abandons Feuerbach's alienation logic but retains his concern for the subject-object inversion in social history from the perspective of subjective dialectics. It is clearly reflected in the discourse of the "Draft of an Article on Friedrich List's book: *Das Nationale System der Politischen Ökonomie*" and *German Ideology.* For Marx, the negation of the inverted phenomenon of man and material in the socio-historical process remains a significant content in the logics of his new philosophical horizon and the theory of communism. Here, the more he reflects and questions the essence of the capitalist economy, the more importance he attaches to the criticism that he previously made only on a philosophical level. I think the idea of material-subjugation is in fact a *central discourse* of the social criticism formed in Marx's economic studies and practice of scientific socialism.

98　Marx, and Friedrich Engels. *Karl Marx, Friedrich Engels: Collected Works,* Volume 34. London: Lawrence & Wishart, 1994. p. 399.

99　Marx does not put forward a clear definition of "material-subjugation." It is *my theoretical summary of this important Marxist idea.* This concept is also formed under the influence of the ancient Chinese thinkers who preach not to be "tormented by material gains."

Here, I would like to point out another theoretical issue: Marx does not have any humanistic element in his criticism of the capitalist material-subjugation. He abandons the simple inversion of humankind and material but first admits the historical necessity of the phenomenon of material-subjugation and then validates its transitoriness by the internal contradictions in the movement of social history. This may be a big difference between Marx's theory of material-subjugation and his previous alienation theory. Although his material-subjugation does not boil down to a well-defined theory, his basic thought is very clear. Sometimes, Marx still uses the word *"alienation" to replace material-subjugation* in his manuscripts, only in a scientific sense that has outgrown the *classical humanistic framework of logics.*[100] Sometimes, Marx juxtaposes alienation with such categories as *confrontation and contradiction, inversion and confusion.* They are not really the same. Instead, the use of "contradiction" and "inversion" is limited to the specific *subject-object relationship in the economic process, especially, in the illustration of the material subjugation of people.* In my opinion, the concept of material-subjugation is more precise. However, due to the complexity of the issue, the idea never assumes an easy perceptibility, and thus misleads not a few Marxist researchers.

C. THE FUNDAMENTAL ASPECTS OF MATERIAL SUBJUGATION IN THE SOCIAL PROCESS OF CAPITALISM

Marx carries a comparative and systematic analysis of the phenomenon of material-subjugation in the capitalist social life. In summary, there are several aspects as follows:

The first aspect indicates that the productive forces of the human labour become the material power to oppress the individuals. Marx points out:

> **In our days, everything seems pregnant with its contrary: Machinery, gifted with the wonderful power of shortening and fructifying human labour, we behold starving and overworking it; The newfangled sources of wealth, by some strange weird spell, are turned into sources of want; The victories of art seem bought by the loss of character. At the same pace that mankind masters nature, man seems to become enslaved to other men or to his own infamy. Even the pure light of science seems unable to shine but on the dark background of ignorance. All**

---

100 It is commonly seen in Marx's later economic manuscripts. Here, the conception of "alienation" actually refers to the meaning of *material-subjugation* in his scientific social criticism.

our invention and progress seem to result in endowing material forces with intellectual life, and in stultifying human life into a material force.[101]

It means that the human social productive forces transform from the previous subjective power of changing the external object to the opposite side: A material power to subjugate the individuals in the capitalist process of production. To be specific, firstly, it is the ability of labour that undergoes the change of material-subjugation. In human history, "labour is the living, form-giving fire; it is the transitoriness of things, their temporality, as their formation by living time," that is, "to posit their usefulness."[102] However, in the process of capitalist production, labour is inverted to the power of capital because of the essence of wage. Therefore, Marx says:

In this contradiction, political economy merely expressed the essence of capitalist production or, if you like, of wage-labour, of labour alienated from itself, which stands confronted by the wealth it has created as alien wealth, by its own productive power as the productive power of its product, by its enrichment as its own impoverishment and by its social power as the power of society.[103]

Therefore, the more labour is objectified, the further the world of objective values as the property of the other will expand in antithesis to labour. In this way, labour is represented "as negated property, or property as negation of the alien quality of alien labour"[104], and "the necessary process of positing its own powers as *alien* to the worker."[105] Second, it is the material-subjugation of the labour products. Marx considers the difference between the capitalist mode of production and all the previous forms is that "the capitalist does not rule the worker in any kind of personal capacity, but only in so far as he is 'capital'; his rule is only that of objectified labour over living labour; the rule of the worker's product over the worker himself."[106] The products made by humans appear "as capital; objectified labour as mastery, command over living labour."[107]

---

101   Marx, and Friedrich Engels. *On Literature and Art*. Moscow: Progress Publishers, 1976. pp. 159-160.

102   Marx, Karl. *Grundrisse: Foundations of the Critique of Political Economy (rough draft)*. Trans. Martin Nicolaus. London; New York: Penguin, 1993. p. 361.

103   Marx, Karl. *Theories of Surplus Value, Volume 3*. London: Lawrence & Wishart, 1969. p. 259.

104   Marx, Karl. *Grundrisse: Foundations of the Critique of Political Economy (rough draft)*. Trans. Martin Nicolaus. London; New York: Penguin, 1993. p. 470.

105   *Ibid.*, p. 308.

106   Marx, and Friedrich Engels. *Karl Marx, Friedrich Engels: Collected Works, Volume 34*. London: Lawrence & Wishart, 1994. p. 123.

107   Marx, Karl. *Grundrisse: Foundations of the Critique of Political Economy (rough draft)*. Trans. Martin Nicolaus. London; New York: Penguin, 1993. p. 453.

The product of labour appears as *alien property*, as a mode of existence confronting living labour as independent, as *value* in its being for itself; the product of labour, objectified labour, has been endowed by living labour with a soul of its own, and establishes itself opposite living labour as an *alien power*.[108]

In the capitalist process of reproduction, it is surplus value that drives the material labour forward and becomes the power over the living labour by the personified capital. As a result, "it realizes itself in the objective conditions, it simultaneously repulses this realization from itself as an alien reality, and hence posits itself as insubstantial, as mere penurious labour capacity in face of this reality alienated [entfremdet] from it, belonging not to it but to others; that it posits its own reality not as a being for it, but merely as a being for others, and hence also as mere other-being [Anderssein], or being of another opposite itself."[109]

Third, it is the material-subjugation of the forms of labour, like tools and technologies, whose structure, as we know, is originally the intermediary condition used by the human subject to affect the object, and the functional expansion of the human activities. However, in the capitalist mode of production, not only the material things are directly against the worker but also the historically development forms of labour, such as the social cooperation and division are magically turned into the forms of capital, even with science and technologies as the representation of the capital's productive forces.

In fact, unity in cooperation, combination in the division of labour , the application of the forces of nature and science, as well as the products of labour in the shape of machinery, for the purpose of production, are all things which confront the individual workers themselves as *alien and objective*...[110]

According to Marx, the most striking thing in modern capitalist process of production is that the tools used by humans to change the external object have become the forces to subjugate people. Capitalism has changed the previous situation that "the worker animates and makes into his organ with his skill and strength, and whose handling therefore depends on his virtuosity" because now "it is the machine which possesses skill and strength in place of the worker, is itself the virtuoso, with a soul of its own

---

108   *Ibid.*, p. 453.
109   *Ibid.*, p. 454.
110   Marx, and Friedrich Engels. *Karl Marx, Friedrich Engels: Collected Works, Volume 34.* London: Lawrence & Wishart, 1994. p. 123.

in the mechanical laws acting through it."[111] Especially in the capitalist industrial production, "objectified labour materially confronts living labour as a ruling power and as an active subsumption of the latter under itself, not only by appropriating it, but in the real production process itself."[112] "Here too past labour – in the automaton and the machinery moved by it – steps forth as acting apparently in independence of [living] labour, it subordinates labour instead of being subordinate to it, it is the iron man confronting the man of flesh and blood."[113]

Furthermore, science and technologies changes in the capitalist process of production. At first, it is created by humans as a new productive force. Then, in capitalism, "here we have it as a direct antagonism, in that past labour; hence the general social powers of labour, including natural forces and scientific knowledge, appear directly as weapons, used partly to throw the worker onto the streets, to posit him as a *surplus object*."[114] "The science which compels the inanimate limbs of the machinery, by their construction, to act purposefully, as an automaton, does not exist in the worker's consciousness, but rather acts upon him through the machine as an alien power, as the power of the machine itself."[115] Therefore, "science appears as a potentiality alien to labour, hostile to it and dominant over it."[116]

In the second aspect, Marx points out the characters of material-subjugation in the capitalist relationships. He says, "Thus the participants in capitalist production live in a bewitched world and their own relationships appear to them as properties of things, as properties of the material elements of production."[117] In the capitalist economic process, interpersonal relations cannot be really achieved until they are inversely represented by the commercial relationships of goods. In the world of capitalism, money is the benchmark of everything. The human existence and value can be realized only through the refraction of money. Marx says that "a social relation, a definite relation between individuals, here appears as a metal, a stone, as a

---

111   Marx, Karl. *Grundrisse: Foundations of the Critique of Political Economy (rough draft)*. Trans. Martin Nicolaus. London; New York: Penguin, 1993. p. 693.

112   *Ibid.*, p. 693.

113   Marx, and Friedrich Engels. *Karl Marx, Friedrich Engels: Collected Works, Volume 34*. London: Lawrence & Wishart, 1994. p. 30.

114   *Ibid.*, p. 29.

115   Marx, Karl. *Grundrisse: Foundations of the Critique of Political Economy (rough draft)*. Trans. Martin Nicolaus. London; New York: Penguin, 1993. p. 693.

116   Marx, and Friedrich Engels. *Karl Marx, Friedrich Engels: Collected Works, Volume 34*. London: Lawrence & Wishart, 1994. p. 34.

117   Marx, and Friedrich Engels. *Karl Marx, Friedrich Engels: Collected Works*. New York: International Publishers, 1975. p. 514.

purely physical, external thing which can be found, as such, in nature, and which is indistinguishable in form from its natural existence."[118] For Marx, the essence of money is a social relationship of the exchange value. Only by possessing it can people appropriate the material. Hence, the relationship between humans can only be realized through the "media" of material relations that now ascend over people. According to the aforementioned definition of humankind from the objective perspective of Marxist historical materialism and historical dialectics, the essence ("species") of human is the sum of the real social relations. However, in capitalist society, the real social relations of humans are distorted to the material ones, independent of and even put against the individuals as a false "species." With Marx, "the exchange relation establishes itself as a power external to and independent of the producers. What originally appeared as a means to promote production becomes a relation alien to the producers."[119]

The third aspect is the material-subjugation inversion of the entire socio-historical process. Social history is the result of the human activities; thus, the general historical process is mainly a creative development of the human subjects themselves. However, in capitalist society, it "appears as something independent of the individuals, but not only as, say, in a coin or in exchange value, but extending to the whole of the social movement itself"[120] because "as much, then, as the whole of this movement appears as a social process, and as much as the individual moments of this movement arise from the conscious will and particular purposes of individuals, so much does the totality of the process appear as an objective interrelation, which arises spontaneously from nature; arising, it is true, from the mutual influence of conscious individuals on one another, but neither located in their consciousness, nor subsumed under them as a whole. Their own collisions with one another produce an alien social power standing above them, produce their mutual interaction as a process and power independent of them."[121] The view becomes a supportive background for a "resultant forces" theory developed by Engels later.[122]

---

118   Marx, Karl. *Grundrisse: Foundations of the Critique of Political Economy (rough draft)*. Trans. Martin Nicolaus. London; New York: Penguin, 1993. p. 239.
119   *Ibid.*, p. 146.
120   *Ibid.*, p. 197.
121   *Ibid.*, p. 197.
122   The traditional framework of philosophical illustration cannot correctly take the specific indications here, thus, leading to the later misunderstanding of Engels' "resultant" forces theory. Moreover, we must know Marx's negative conception of the phenomenon independent of the individual will because it also undergoes interpretive shifts by conventional researchers.

Marx noticeably comments, "Society does not consist of individuals, but expresses the sum of interrelations, the relations within which these individuals stand."[123] He does not consent to the general material-subjugation of the capitalist society. For example, as to the worker in the cooperation of production, he says, "His function is one-sided, abstract, partial. He has himself become a mere detail."[124] The production process "confronts the workers as an external power, dominating and enveloping them."[125] Obviously, Marx firmly opposes the general character of material-subjugation in capitalist society.

In short, "the barrier to *capital* is that this entire development proceeds in a contradictory way, and that the working-out of the productive forces, of general wealth etc., knowledge etc., appears in such a way that the working individual *alienates* himself [sich entäussert]; relates to the conditions brought out of him by his labour as those not of his own but of an *alien wealth* and of his own poverty."[126] Furthermore, "the transformation of production under the sway of capital, means, at the same time, the martyrdom of the producer; the instrument of labour becomes the means of enslaving, exploiting, and impoverishing the labourer; the social combination and organisation of labour-processes is turned into an organised mode of crushing out the workman's individual vitality, freedom, and independence."[127] In my opinion, Marx's theory of material-subjugation is essentially a doctrine against the abnormal phenomenon of the control of humans by their own created material in capitalist society.

IV. THE ECONOMIC FETISHISM: MAN KNEELS DOWN BEFORE THE MATERIAL CREATED BY HIMSELF

The material-subjugation phenomenon in capitalism revealed by Marx also accounts for the essential 'natural-ness' of the capitalist form. As a result, the bourgeois scholars need to fully affirm material-subjugation and adroitly cover up its essence in their maintenance of the capitalist mode

---

123   Marx, Karl. *Grundrisse: Foundations of the Critique of Political Economy (rough draft)*. Trans. Martin Nicolaus. London; New York: Penguin, 1993. p. 265.

124   Dussel, and Fred Moseley. *Towards an Unknown Marx: A Commentary on the Manuscripts of 1861-63*. London; New York: Routledge, 2001. p. 35. Quoted from MECW.

125   Bidet, David Fernbach, and Alex Callinicos. *Exploring Marx's Das Kapital: Philosophical, Economic and Political Dimensions*. Boston: BRILL., 2007. p. 192.

126   Marx, Karl. *Grundrisse: Foundations of the Critique of Political Economy (rough draft)*. Trans. Martin Nicolaus. London; New York: Penguin, 1993. p. 541.

127   Marx, Karl. *Das Kapital: A Critique of Political Economy: The Process of Capitalist Production*. New York: Cosimo, Inc., 2007. p. 555.

of production. In my opinion, the phenomenon of material-subjugation is reflected in the conception of the bourgeois fetishism, which is the most important ideology for the bourgeois to maintain their social political control. Marx will not overlook it in his critical fire. He makes three famous conclusive points of fetishism, developing the third important semantic level based on the critical discourse of scientific socialism in the subjective dimension of historical dialectics, that is, the aspect of the subjective consciousness.

A. THE ESSENCE OF FETISHISM IS BOURGEOIS IDEOLOGY

For Marx, material-subjugation is closely connected with another important concept, viz. *fetishism*. In my view, fetishism is *the conceptual presentation of material-subjugation*. Etymologically, fetishism derives from the Latin word "facticius," which refers to something made by man and cast with a spell. In early time, fetishism was a religious belief to own power over some sacred objects. Marx employs its particular meaning and applies it to other fields, making a general explanation and analogy of the special upside-down phenomenon in social life. However, this concept has different connotations in several periods of his theoretical development.

Before 1844, the Young Marx employed it to criticize the view confirming the subject-object inversion in political economic life. He showed his contempt by calling it "the erudition of a penny magazine."[128] Meanwhile, under the influence of Moses Hess, Marx first construes the essence of money *fetishism*: "Money is the estranged essence of man's work and man's existence, and this alien essence dominates him, and he worships it."[129] While in the *1844 Manuscripts*, he takes the logical perspective of labour alienation to criticize the phenomena of fetishism that *subjectively* reflects the reality of the capitalist economic life. The Young Marx believes that the capitalist economic estrangement certainly generates the idea of keeping that labour alienation, which he calls "a servile art."[130] Here, Marx still follows Feuerbach's religious criticism, unable to recognize the nature of commodity fetishism only existent in the capitalist mode of production. His scientific critique of the capitalist fetishism doe not really start until after his deep study of the essence of the capitalist economic structure based on the scientific historical view.

---

128 Marx, and Friedrich Engels. *Collected Works*. London: Lawrence & Wishart, 1975. p. 189.
129 Marx, Karl. *Early Writings*. Harmondsworth: Penguin Books, 1992. p. 239.
130 Marx, Karl. *Early Writings*. Harmondsworth: Penguin Books, 1992. p. 361.

In the repeatedly mentioned "Draft of an Article on Friedrich List's book: *Das Nationale System der Politischen Ökonomie*," Marx points out the "sordid materialism" used by the bourgeoisie in cheating and "subjecting this majority to the wholly material conditions of exchange value."[131] He already makes a conscious connection between fetishism and the bourgeois ideology, thus revealing the root of the problem. I believe the theory of fetishism is an important component of his social criticism of capitalism as well as a profound explanation of material-subjugation in his 'natural-ness' theory. Its theoretical significance lies in revealing the actual subject-object inversion in the capitalist economic life and the ideological essence concealed by the capitalist economy. It is the *third semantic aspect* of Marx's scientific critical discourse, an *aspect of subjective consciousness* as well.

As analyzed above, in his later economic research, Marx resolutely opposes the bourgeois scholars' attempt to eternalize the capitalist mode of production by tearing the veil off the bourgeois fetishism and thus breaking the capitalist myth of the "automatic fetish," the self-expanding value. This is also a significant part of his scientific socialism. The deep theoretical themes are but regrettably ignored in the traditional framework of philosophical illustration. In a certain sense, the major points of the old historical view slip to the *standpoint of the bourgeois fetishism* that Marx just opposes. It is a very serious question worthy of our attention. At the same time, we must guard against another tendency to overstate the importance of this point. In fact, even in Marx's early works, the concept of fetishism does not enter the core. It is only a *conceptual reflection* of "alienation." In later works, fetishism becomes a subjective verification of the phenomenon of material-subjugation, criticized by Marx as the bourgeois ideology.

B. THE THREE CRITIQUES ON FETISHISM BY MARX

I think that Marx's critical theory of fetishism is completed in his later economic studies. As to this scientific category, Marx has several other names, like, magic, spiritism, mystification, unreasonable form, and so on. They are all meant to illustrate the special subject-object inversion and the bourgeois ideological attempt to mystify and eternalize the historical phenomenon. His critical theory has three basic aspects: *Commodity fetishism, money fetishism, and capital fetishism.*

Marx assigns a special section in the later chapter of Vol. One in *Das Kapital*, with the title of "The Fetishism of Commodities and the Secret thereof" analyzing the general nature of commodities. For him, at first

---

131   Marx, and Friedrich Engels. *Marx and Engels Collected Works 1844-45*. New York: International Publishers, 1975. p. 279.

glance, a commodity is trivial and common. There is nothing mysterious in its use value or attribute as man's product of labour. Marx cites the example of a table, which is "a very queer thing, abounding in metaphysical subtleties and theological niceties"[132] when the table appears as a commodity. "But, in relation to all other commodities, it stands on its head, and evolves out of its wooden brain grotesque ideas, far more wonderful than 'table-turning' ever was."[133]

Then, why does it have the mysterious feature once the product of labour assumes the form of a commodity? Marx discovers that it stems from the special nature of the commodity itself. The equivalent human labour generates the value of the products. This social relationship makes the products become commodities. And there is a lack of direct common interest for all these independent commodity producers; thus, their social associations can only be reversed into the commodity relations. The relationships between human beings are represented by the material relationships. Hence, the commodity exhibits a mysterious feature. In a careful analysis, Marx says:

> In the same way, the light from an object is perceived by us not as the subjective excitation of our optic nerve, but as the objective form of something outside the eye itself. But, in the act of seeing, there is at all events, an actual passage of light from one thing to another, from the external object to the eye. There is a physical relation between physical things. There, the existence of the things *quâ* commodities, and the value relation between the products of labour which stamps them as commodities, have absolutely no connection with their physical properties and with the material relations arising therefrom. There it is a definite social relation between men, which assumes, in their eyes, the fantastic form of a relation between things. In order, therefore, to find an analogy, we must have recourse to the mist-enveloped regions of the religious world. In that world the productions of the human brain appear as independent beings endowed with life, and entering into relation both with one another and the human race. So it is in the world of commodities with the products of men's hands. This I call the Fetishism which attaches itself to the products of labour, as soon as they are produced as commodities, and which is therefore inseparable from the production of commodities.[134]

132   Marx, Karl. *Das Kapital: A Critical Analysis of Capitalist Production.* Appleton, 1889. p. 41.
133   Marx, Karl. *Das Kapital: A Critique of Political Economy: The Process of Capitalist Production.* New York: Cosimo, Inc., 2007. p. 82.
134   *Ibid.*, p. 83.

Marx concludes that the *essence* of fetishism is to *maintain and affirm material-subjugation in the capitalist economic life.* "In the form of society now under consideration, the behaviour of men in the social process of production is purely atomic. Hence, their relations to each other in production assume a conscious individual action and the material character independent of their control. These facts manifest themselves at first by products as a *general rule* taking the *form of commodities.*"[135] Marx captures the core of the issue.

Marx then makes an in-depth analysis of money fetishism. To him, money is nothing but the manifestation of commodities, or the material to achieve social representation by the commodity value. But money is mistaken as a pure value; in particular, the metallic currency is almost equivalent to value (the social relations). Marx observes that money obscures the social relations. There is a false impression here.

> **We followed up this false appearance to its final establishment, which is complete as soon as the universal equivalent form becomes identified with the bodily form of a particular commodity, and thus crystallised into the money-form. What appears to happen is, not that gold becomes money, in consequence of all other commodities expressing their values in it, but, on the contrary, that all other commodities universally express their values in gold, because it is money from the intermediary role of sport in its own results, disappeared and left no trace. The intermediate steps of the process vanish in the result and leave no trace behind. Commodities find their own value already completely represented, without any initiative on their part, in another commodity existing in company with them. These objects, gold and silver, just as they come out of the bowels of the earth, are forthwith the direct incarnation of all human labour. Hence the magic of money.**[136]

Marx believes that the mystery of money fetishism is that of commodity fetishism, only more striking or conspicuous. Because the exchange value of commodities is still represented by the exchange relations with other goods, it is possible to get a glimpse into some social relations hidden within. The forms of money, however, do not bear even the least trace of social relations. Consequently, the fetishistic nature is covered deep inside.

The last is the most confusing capital fetishism. After criticizing the bourgeois theory of major factors of production, Marx grasps the key point that capital, land and labour form the sources of profit, rent and wages. Capitalism is, in his words, "the distorted form in which the *real inversion*

---

135   *Ibid.*, p. 105.
136   *Ibid.*, p. 105.

is expressed."[137] And, "the form of revenue and the sources of revenue are the *most fetishistic* expression of the relations of capitalist production."[138] "It is their form of existence as it appears on the surface, divorced from the hidden connections and the intermediate connecting links."[139] As we all know, the bourgeois economists always preach the trinity formula: "Capital–interest, land–ground-rent, labour–wages."[140] "In this economic trinity represented as the connection between the component parts of value and wealth in general and its sources, we have the complete mystification of the capitalist mode of production, the conversion of social relations into things, the direct coalescence of the material production relations with their historical and social determination. It is an enchanted, perverted, topsy-turvy world."[141] "However, of all these forms, the most complete fetish is interest-bearing capital. This is the original starting-point of capital – money – and the formula M–C–M' is reduced to its two extremes – M–M' – money which creates more money. It is the original and general formula of capital reduced to a meaningless résumé."[142] "The transubstantiation, the fetishism, is complete."[143] "In interest-bearing capital, therefore, this automatic fetish, self-expanding value, money generating money, are brought out in their pure state and in this form it no longer bears the birth-marks of its origin."[144] "Thus capital becomes a very mysterious being."[145] Marx argues that the above inverted ideas of fetishism cover up the real relations in the capitalist economic process.

In the capital-relation – to the extent that it is still considered independently of its circulation process – what is essentially characteristic is the mystification, the upside-down world, the inversion of the subjective and the objective, as it already appears in money. Corresponding to the inverted relation, there necessarily arises, already in the actual production process itself, an inverted *conception*, a transposed *consciousness*.[146]

---

137   Marx, Karl. *Theories of Surplus Value, Volume 3*. London: Lawrence & Wishart, 1969. p. 453.

138   *Ibid.*, p. 453.

139   *Ibid.*, p. 453.

140   Marx, and Friedrich Engels. *Karl Marx, Friedrich Engels: Collected Works, Volume 37*. New York: International Publishers, 1975.p. 801.

141   Ibid., p. 817.

142   Marx, Karl. *Theories of Surplus Value, Volume 3*. London: Lawrence & Wishart, 1969. p. 450.

143   *Ibid.*, p. 494.

144   Marx, and Friedrich Engels. *Das Kapital, a Critical Analysis of Capitalist Production*. Moscow: Foreign Languages Pub. House, 1959. p. 384.

145   Marx, and Friedrich Engels. Karl Marx, Friedrich Engels: *Collected Works, Volume 34*. London: Lawrence & Wishart, 1994. p. 125.

146   Marx, and Friedrich Engels. *Collected Works*. London: Lawrence & Wishart, 1991. p. 73.

It is clear now that the essence of fetishism is the inverted subjective reflection of the capitalist material-subjugation, in which "the social relations of individuals appear in the perverted form of a social relation between things." "It is a relation hidden by a material veil."[147] In fact, it is an inverted from of human relations, only deified in fetishism. Therefore, Marx says, "social relations of production should assume the shape of things, so that the relations into which people enter in the course of their work appear as the relation of things to one another and of things to people."[148] In his eyes, "the crude materialism of the economists who regard as the natural properties of things what are social relations of production among people, and qualities which things obtain because they are subsumed under these relations, is at the same time just as crude an idealism, even fetishism, since it imputes social relations to things as inherent characteristics, and thus mystifies them."[149] From an economic perspective, the fundamental purpose of fetishism is to hide the essence of the capitalist exploration of the worker and unlimited appropriation of surplus value. By the scientific theory of surplus value, Marx exposes the nature of the capitalist mode of production and the secret of utilizing the worker, thus, breaking the bourgeois myth of fetishism and laying the foundation for the practice of scientific socialism.

Standing by the proletarians, Marx holds an obviously negative attitude towards the bourgeois fetishistic conception. To him, fetishism cannot be finally erased until a complete denial of the capitalist mode of production and the objective condition that generates the inverted relations.

> The *alien property* of the capitalist in this labour can only be abolished by converting his property into the property of the non-individual in its independent singularity, hence of the *associated, social individual.* This naturally brings to an end the fetishistic situation when the product is the proprietor of the producer, and all the social forms of labour developed within capitalist production are released from the contradiction which falsifies them all and presents them as mutually opposed.[150]

---

147 Marx, Karl. *Contribution to the Critique of Political Economy.* New York: International Publishers, 1979. p. 34.

148 *Ibid.*, p. 34.

149 Marx, Karl. *Grundrisse: Foundations of the Critique of Political Economy (rough draft).* Trans. Martin Nicolaus. London; New York: Penguin, 1993. p. 687.

150 Marx, and Friedrich Engels. Karl Marx, Friedrich Engels: *Collected Works*, Volume 34. London: Lawrence & Wishart, 1994. p. 109.

In other words, "the religious reflex of the real world can, in any case, only then finally vanish, when the practical relations of every-day life offer to man none but perfectly intelligible and reasonable relations with regard to his fellowmen and to Nature. The life-process of society, which is based on the process of material production, does not strip off its mystical veil until it is treated as production by freely associated men, and is consciously regulated by them in accordance with a settled plan."[151] The above comment really brushes aside the confusing clouds and lets the truth of sunshine come in.

C. IS THE PHENOMENON OF THE ECONOMIC DOMINANCE OVER MAN A PERPETUAL LAW OF HISTORY?

In my view, Marx's criticism of the capitalist fetishism is also an essential exposition of the bourgeois ideology by de-mystifying the nature of the capitalist mode of production.

> **But this definite, *specific*, historical form of social labour which is exemplified in capitalist production is proclaimed by *these* economists as the general, eternal form, as a natural phenomenon, and these relations of production as the absolutely (not historically) necessary, natural and reasonable relations of social labour.**[152]

This is the Achilles' heel of the bourgeois defence for the capitalist system. In the eyes of Marx, the essence of bourgeois ideology lies in its cover-up of the capitalist's secret exploitation of workers, attempt for the necessity of the man-material inversion in the capitalist development and persuasion for the supremacy of the material (economic) power. Marx spares no effort to criticize the specific phenomena of 'natural-ness' and material-subjugation in social history and reveal the essence of fetishism to validate the non-scientific nature of bourgeois ideology.

With Marx, the criticism of 'natural-ness', material-subjugation and fetishism (the bourgeois certification of the subject-object inversion) consists of three developing aspects of the discourse of social criticism targeted at the capitalist reality. The entire theoretical logic begins from the establishment of the scientific view of history, which is then used to guide Marx's economic research. After that, he discovers the secret of the capitalist mode of

---

151   Marx, Karl. *Das Kapital: A Critique of Political Economy: The Process of Capitalist Production.* New York: Cosimo, Inc., 2007. p. 92.
152   Marx, Karl. *Theories of Surplus Value, Volume 3.* London: Lawrence & Wishart, 1969. p. 259.

production: The theory of surplus value, which substantially negates the foundation of capitalism. His scientific socialism leads to the overthrow of capitalism and the realization of communism. In my opinion, the afore-mentioned 'natural-ness' and material-subjugation form the inner dialecti-cal drive of Marx's scientific economic discussions and practice of scientific socialism, that is, his *potential critical discourse* projected from the subjec-tive dimension of historical dialectics, which is just neglected in our con-ventional research of philosophy, economics and socialism. Nevertheless, that neglected aspect is crucial for our understanding of Marx's essential criticism of capitalism from a *general historical* view.

Marx makes a relevant summary in *Das Kapital* about the bourgeois at-tempt to validate the eternality and naturality of the capitalist mode of production.

> **On the other hand, scientific analysis of the capitalist mode of production demonstrates the contrary, that it is a mode of pro-duction of a special kind, with specific historical features; that, like any other specific mode of production, it presupposes a given level of the social productive forces and their forms of de-velopment as its historical precondition: a precondition which is itself the historical result and product of a preceding process, and from which the new mode of production proceeds as its given basis; that the production relations corresponding to this specific, historically determined mode of production–relations which human beings enter into during the process of social life, in the creation of their social life–possess a specific, historical and transitory character; and, finally, that the distribution rela-tions essentially coincident with these production relations are their opposite side, so that both share the same historically tran-sitory character.** [153]

The reason is that "the capitalist system is past its prime in the West, ap-proaching the time when it will be no more than a regressive social regime." [154]

We have repeatedly pointed out that Marx's observation of the human social history has two theoretical foundations: The general perspective of social existence in historical materialism on the objective dimension of historical dialectics; the logical perspective on the subjective dimen-sion of historical dialectics based on the determination of major historical

153   Marx, and Friedrich Engels. *Das Kapital, a Critical Analysis of Capitalist Production.* Moscow: Foreign Languages Pub. House, 1959. p. 856.
154   Shanin, Teodor. *Late Marx and the Russian Road.* London: Routledge & Kegan Paul, 1983. p. 103.

elements. Although the above perspectives do not have identical focuses, the utmost aim of Marx's scientific view of history is without doubt, to negate capitalism, which also guides his practice of scientific socialism and studies of political economy.

With the first logical perspective, Marx mainly focuses on the objective progress of historical development, reveals the innate contradictions of the capitalist mode of production, and steps on the realistic road to prove the inevitable demise of capitalism and the necessary triumph of communism. We have been concerned with this aspect. As to the latter, Marx stands on the revolutionary position of the real social practice in historical dialectics to criticize 'natural-ness' and material-subjugation in the historical development of capitalist society, hence, exposing the irrational subject-object inversion in its mode of production. It forms the *major and essential* aspect of Marx's later economic studies and scientific socialism. In the postscript of *Das Kapital*, Marx makes a specific statement of the essence of historical dialectics:

> **It includes in its comprehension and affirmative recognition of the existing state of things, at the same time also, the recognition of the negation of that state, of its inevitable breaking up; because it regards every historically developed social form as in fluid movement, and therefore takes into account its transient nature not less than its momentary existence; because it lets nothing impose upon it, and is in its essence critical and revolutionary.[155]**

Unfortunately, the special phenomena of 'natural-ness' and material-subjugation in the development of capitalist society are not correctly illustrated in the traditional Marxist research. Under the influence of such views as economic determinism and that the human social development is a natural process, it actually confirms the legitimacy of the above historical phenomena that the bourgeois scholars try to maintain while Marx *criticizes*. In the old framework of interpretation, the human social development seems forever a monolithic "natural process" independent of man's will as well as a blind economic power that dominates humans and society. To a certain extent, this kind of explanation echoes, consciously or not, the fetishistic stance of the bourgeois ideology. What a sad mistake! Of course, I am not saying that traditional philosophical researchers directly argue for the bourgeoisie. However, due to its simplified interpretation of and flimsy

---

155 Selsam, and Harry Marte. *Reader in Marxist Philosophy.* New York: International Publishers Co, 1987. p. 99.

argument for Marx's historical materialism, it just results in a *hidden logical shift* toward the bourgeois ideological discourse.

In summary, in Marx's philosophical vision, whether it is 'natural-ness' in social history or material-subjugation in the social economic form, they are certainly not the eternal phenomena of historical development but rather transitory things existent in the capitalist ("pre-historical") society. They are destined to be surpassed and laid aside after their historical roles have been played; only leaving their trances in the gold rays of the communist morning sun. However, the traditional philosophical framework indeed causes serious theoretical errors that, with a domino effect, leading to significant misunderstandings on the Marxist view of history. The grave consequences will be discussed in the next chapter.

CHAPTER IV

RE-COGNITION OF THE WHOLE SOCIO-HISTORICAL DEVELOPMENT OF HUMAN BEINGS

1 *Marx's Division of History and Material-Subjugation*
2 *The Profound Transformation from the "Realm of Necessity" to the "Realm of Freedom"*
3 *'Natural-ness' and Material-Subjugation*
4 *The Economic Fetishism: Man Kneels down Before the Material Created by Himself*

CHAPTER FOUR

INTRODUCTION

It should be noted that Marx's subjective dimension of scientific historical dialectics not only validates the phenomena of 'natural-ness' and material-subjugation but also further indicates that the material dominance over man and its deformation into a natural movement are not exclusive to capitalism but the common character of the pre-historical periods of human beings. Moreover, both the ultimate purpose and the practical stance of Marx's historical dialectics are about the full and free development of humans after their transcendence of the material-subjugation status, that is, communism. For a deep analogical examination, we can draw on his theoretical analysis of the different forms of socio-historical development.

I. MARX'S DIVISION OF HISTORY AND MATERIAL SUBJUGATION

From the perspective of scientific practical materialism, Marx never admits there is an eternal law of the development of social history. Instead, he believes that there are specific and real social laws and historical forms corresponding to the different social productive forces. Therefore, the alleged unified "general way" of social development is just an imagined castle in the air, an impossible existence. With historical materialism, Marx attempts to reveal the general trend through specific historical progresses. He never proposes a linear mode of historical development; thus, there is no rigid and universal division of social history. Despite his differentiation of the socio-historical progresses from several aspects, the theoretical significance is far more important than the identification of historical forms.

A. TWO LOGICAL PERSPECTIVES IN MARX'S THEORY ON THE DIVISION OF HISTORY

There is a debate of the "five great forms" and "three great forms" in present Marxist research of social history. Many researchers tenaciously hold one view against the other while some others try to reconcile them. Generally, these discussions and debates display a lot of theoretical originality. More importantly, they begin to note the *different perspectives* in Marx's division. For instance, some researchers classify the "three major forms" into a "macro-description" of social history while regarding the "five great forms" as a "micro-depiction" of the historical process; still others take the former as the guide of a general law of the human relations and development and the latter as the mechanism of a general law of the human relations and development applied in reality.[1] However, all these opinions regrettably miss the innate logical clue of the theory, which, in my view, is not abstruse at all, if we observe in the objective dimension of historical *materialism* and the subjective dimension of historical dialectics. To be more concrete, one way of division is based on the general social history and centred on the mode of production and the real economic structure with the main line of social relations, which is also the *objective logical description* of historical materialism; the other is established on the major elements of historical development and centred on the concrete historical status of the subject in reality with the main line of the subject-object relationship (the natural

---

1 See Liu Youcheng. *Three Forms of Social Development.* Zhejiang People's Publishing House, 1987. p. 20. See also Liu Jiongzhong and Ye Xianming. "Two Major Theoretical Structures of Historical Materialism and the Methodological Functionality of Three Great Social Forms and Five Great Social Forms" in *Journal of Renmin University of China.* 6 (1990).

object at first, then, the social and economic object), which is the *dynamic discourse of the subjective dimension* in historical dialectics.

I find that it is very complicated to precisely define the historical forms in Marx's text. He does not put forward a universal mode of human development. If we only stop with the literal meaning of the theory, we shall certainly be confused in the various specific analyses of Marx. I have sorted out them as follows.

Before 1843, the Young Marx's basic point is the spiritual reason of the human subject; he employs the relationship between man and nature to divide history into the ancient society in which nature dominates and the modern society or a "new world" where man's spirit rules.

In the *Critique of Hegel's 'Philosophy of Right'* written in 1843, Marx proposes the historical division of the ancient society, middle ages and the new age (democracy).

In the *1844 Manuscripts*, Marx adopts the logical axis of the human essence and labour to divide history into the periods when there is no labour alienation, when there is labour alienation and property, and when labour alienation is sublated (communism).

In *German Ideology* in 1845, Marx divides the phases of social production into the tribal ownership, the ancient ownership, the feudal ownership, the bourgeois ownership and communism.

In 1847, Marx talks about the ancient society, the feudal society and the capitalist society.

In the *1857-1858 Economic Manuscripts*, Marx proposes the three major social forms: That based on man's reliance that founded on material reliance, and that offering the full and free development for humankind.

In the preface to *A Contribution to the Critique of Political Economy* in 1859, Marx puts forward the Asiatic, ancient, feudal and capitalist modes of production as well as the two major historical periods: The pre-historical human society and the real human history, communism.

In the 1860s, Marx further suggests the "realm of necessity" and the "realm of freedom" in human social history.

In the *Letter to Vera Zasulich* in 1881, Marx points out there are "primary, secondary and tertiary types" of society.[2]

---

2   Marx, and Friedrich Engels. *Karl Marx, Friedrich Engels: Marx and Engels Collected Works 1874-83*. New York: International Publishers, 1989. p. 358.

Judging from the above analysis, we can see that there is no unified or fixed illustration of historical forms in Marx's theory of historical division, not to mention the identical mode of historical development advocated in the traditional philosophical interpretation, that is, the primitive, the slavery, the feudal, the capitalist and the communist societies. Marx just indicates several different clues of historical development on various research levels. We cannot stop with a specific discussion and regard it as a universal formula. However, it does not mean that Marx's theory of historical forms is confusing. I intend to have a more scientific comprehension on a deeper level. In other words, besides the different social forms in historical development proposed by Marx, is there a hidden logical clue that has not been found?

Let us first track the source of Marx's theory of historical forms. As mentioned earlier, in the Notebooks on Epicurean Philosophy in 1839, the Young Marx relies on the human possession of rationality to suggest the ancient society where the natural force dominates and the modern society where the subjective spirit dominates. It cannot be taken as Marx's full view of historical division but it contains a basic point: The scale of the *subject-object relationship* (the subjective self-consciousness of the individual) to measure different historical forms. When it comes to 1843, in the articles of the *Critique of Hegel's 'Philosophy of Right'* and *Deutsch-Französische Jahrbücher*, Marx draws the materialistic conclusion that the "civil society" decides the state and the law. For the first time, he makes a clear division of the ancient society, the medieval autocracy or the "animal period" in human history, the capitalist age after man's political emancipation and the future communism when the true human liberation and democratic system are achieved. Here, we can see that the alienated social and political existence of the human subject is still in the concern of Marx.

In 1844, the Young Marx has almost completed his humanistic alienation view of history. In the *1844 Manuscripts*, he makes a social and historical analysis by the logical line of the *subjective* transcendental essence, labour, which seems to reveal a vague clue of historical division with the innate movement of contradictions in the discourse of subjective dialectics. In this logical framework, social history is set as the existential status of the subject that has not experienced alienation, the modern society of private ownership and labour alienation (capitalism), and the future society (communism) where labour alienation and property are sublated and eliminated. This is a dialectical negation of the negation about the objective historical development. Here, Marx does not identify a *pre-alienation* period of human development, only leaving a hypothetical option (an abstract confirmation of "ought").

Hence, the alleged theory of division in Marx's subjective dialectics can be illustrated as follows:

The "Division" in the Discourse of Subjective Dialectics by Young Marx				
Period of Dissertation Writing (Dominant Status)	Ancient Society (Dominance of Nature)		Modern Society (The "New World") (Man's Subjective Spirit)	
Period of Writing the Critique of Hegel's 'Philosophy of Right' and Deutsch-FranzösischeJahrbücher	Ancient Times	Middle Ages (The Animal Period of Human Society)	Modern society ("Political emancipation" and alienation)	Future Society (Human Liberation)
Period of Writing the Economic and Philosophic Manuscripts of 1844	Un-alienated Human Existence (Logical Stipulation)		Capitalism (Private Ownership and Labour Alienation)	Communism (Sublation of Labour Alienation and Property)

From the above analysis, we can see that the Young Marx has a constant logical main line (the dialectical relationship of the subject-object contradictions) despite his transformation from the idealistic division to a general materialist view. Meanwhile, the human subject always dominates the logical "ought" in the social and historical development.

Marx's theory of historical division gradually came into being after the spring of 1845. In *German Ideology*, he first uses the "forms of ownership" and divides the forms of property into the "tribal, ancient, feudal," capitalist and communist by the historical materialist criteria that production decides social division and social division decides ownership. Now, Marx attempts to make a careful description of the objective historical process to replace his previous criticism of social history with logical structure. However, it is still an *inferential* conclusion due to lack of necessary research materials. It is noteworthy that the positive description of historical materialism (including historical dialectics) here is no longer based on the relationship of subject and object but on the general *objective structure* of social history, which forms a new logical clue in Marx's division of history: The logic of the objective description of historical materialism. As analyzed above, it is here that Marx achieves the discourse transformation from *subjective dialectics to objective historical dialectics*. The new logical clue is concerned with the process of the objective social practice, in particular, the different stages of social forms with the criteria of the social structure conditioned by the material productive forces. It is a necessary theoretical point in Marx's new philosophical vision. Nevertheless, does he abandon the logic based on the subject-object relationship after the establishment of the scientific conception of history? My answer is No.

As mentioned in Chapter 2, Marx still keeps his concern for the subject's status in history in *German Ideology*. He calls the first three social forms the natural society where the human subject is dominated by the force of nature; in comparison, the capitalist ownership is "created by civilization" and humankind is again subjected to the products made by them.[3] In the eyes of Marx, they all belong to the abnormal situation of social and historical development in which the alien material forces determine and subjugate humankind, that is, the phenomenon of material-subjugation. Hence, he proposes communism in which the human subject, as the core of the system, can scientifically re-control the material power. Here, we see the previous initiative discourse based on the contradictory relationship of the human subject and the external object in Marx's division of history, which, of course, has developed from the abstract humanistic "ought" to the scientific idea founded on historical materialism, that is, it gives up the a priori human essence and adopts a certain subjective level of objective practice and specific historical development of the social productive forces. It also means the logical thought of the subjective dimension in historical dialectics through ascertaining the major elements of historical development.

Therefore, we can draw a new conclusion here: There are actually *two different logical perspectives* in Marx's scientific division of history, which is not a simple difference between the "macro" and "micro" clues but contains two distinctive logical dimensions. The former Soviet Union scholar Ter-Akopian also notices this point. He says that the first thought focuses on "man" while the latter is about "society." Unfortunately, he only offers a concrete and narrow comment, without further exploration of this issue.[4] In the discussion about the anthropological notes (to be precise, the *study of ancient history*) and the alleged "eastern road" in Marx's late years, some

---

3   Marx, and Friedrich Engels. The *German Ideology*. Ed. Christopher John Arthur. New York: International Publishers Co, 1970. p. 68.

4   Ter-Akopian. "On the History of the Concept of 'Original Society.'" *Marxist-Leninist Study Materials*. 2 (1987).

Chinese scholars put forward the issues of the relationship between the scales of economy and ethics in Marx's historical view. They are correct in some points. However, due to the limited discussion, especially, the classification of the "scale of the productive forces" and the "scale of the rationality of the relations of production," their reasoning is susceptible to doubt.[5] And the consideration of Marx's late intention to restore the "humanistic standard" is only a logical copy of Western Marxist humanism. In my understanding of the objective perspective of historical materialism, Marx mainly studies the specific laws of social history, from which he then defines different social forms; in the subjective dimension of historical dialectics, his main concern is the dominant elements of modern social history, that is, the human liberation. Therefore, he uses the basic clue of the real and concrete status of the subject in the objective socio-historical process to classify different historical periods. The latter is the logical background that I am going to discuss.

With the help of such a theoretical frame of reference, it is easy to study Marx's theory of historical division now. It is clear that his *Wage Labour and Capital* starts from the logic of objective description to address the issue of historical forms. Here, he completely excludes the old concepts of "civil society," "ownership" and so on; instead, he makes a direct employment of such categories as "society" and "social forms." In the new division of history, he abandons the inferential "tribal ownership" once again and puts forward the theory of ancient society, feudal society, capitalist society, and communist society.

When it comes to the 1850s and 1860s, Marx endeavours to deepen and prove the theory of historical division in his economic research, which is but finally achieved by historical studies. To be precise, it is not until then that Marx begins to explore historical division in a truly scientific sense.

First of all, we see two important theoretical categories on the "social economic forms" and the "Asiatic mode of production" proposed in the *Preface to the Critique of Political Economy* in 1859. When Marx observes the pre-capitalist social forms, in particular, the primary human social patterns, he employs the Indian social and historical materials to validate the communal economy without land ownership in early human civilization and regards the Asiatic mode of production as the first prototype of the social economic form after the disintegration of the primitive communes.[6]

---

5   See Qi Liang. "The Anthropological Notes of Marx and Historical Materialism" in *Contentions* (Zheng Ming). 4 (1990).
6   Marx, Karl. *Early Writings*. Harmondsworth: Penguin Books, 1992. p. 426.

As pointed in the last chapter, Marx's social economic forms do not cover the entire human history. It is just a theoretical misinterpretation by the traditional philosophical framework. With Marx, the division of social economic forms is meant to represent the antagonistic societies in human history. He seldom directly calls the primitive society and communist society as social economic forms (which we shall prove in our next discussions). He says:

> In broad outline, the Asiatic, ancient, feudal and modern bourgeois modes of production may be designated as epochs marking progress in the economic development of society. The bourgeois mode of production is the last antagonistic form of the social process of production – antagonistic not in the sense of individual antagonism but of an antagonism that emanates from the individuals' social conditions of existence – but the productive forces developing within bourgeois society create also the material conditions for a solution of this antagonism. The prehistory of human society accordingly closes with this social formation.[7]

Here, we capture another clue of Marx's historical division: The primitive society (commune) – the social economic forms (including the ancient, feudal and modern bourgeois modes of production) – the communist society. Meanwhile, the societies prior to capitalism are identified as the pre-historical period of human history while communism ushers the real historical development of human beings. It is also Marx's theoretical result based on the logic of the objective description of social history.

However, in Marx's 1850s manuscripts of economics, he proposes another division theory from the same historical status of the human subject in the subjective dimension of historical dialectics: The idea of **three great social forms**. Marx considers the reality of the human subject in history and divides the entire human history (excluding the primitive society) into three major forms. First, the natural pre-capitalist society that is dominated by the "relations of personal dependence"; second, the capitalist society of "personal independence founded on objective [sachlicher] dependence.[8] The two social forms possess the common feature that the human subject is dominated by external forces, displaying a pattern similar to natural movement. To deny this non-subjective status of historical development, Marx abandons the ethical "ought" as used in his *1844 Manuscripts*; instead, he relies on the condition generated from the capitalist development

---

7 *Ibid.*, p. 426.
8 Marx, Karl. *Grundrisse: Foundations of the Critique of Political Economy (rough draft)*. Trans. Martin Nicolaus. London; New York: Penguin, 1993. p. 158.

of the productive forces and the historical transcendence of material-sub-jugation to enter the third historical stage: "Free individuality, based on the universal development of individuals and on their subordination of their communal, social productivity as their social wealth."[9]

Then, in Marx's *Das Kapital (Volume 3)*, he still starts from the subject-object relationship to ascertain the "realm of necessity" with the first two historical forms where the human subject is in material-subjugation and the "realm of freedom" with the ultimate liberation and full development of human beings.[10] In the *Letter to Vera Zasulich* in the 1880s, Marx studies the new historical materials and gives an objective description of "a whole series of primary, secondary, tertiary types, etc,"[11] which is perhaps the most *mature* division of history in the logic of the objective description of historical materialism.

So far, we have Marx's theoretical achievement in his new philosophical vision. For a clear illustration of my point, the following table is used to display a summary of the various divisions from different logical perspectives.

Marx's Theory of Historical Division in the Objective Dimension of Historical Dialectics						
German Ideology	Ancient Ownership	Tribal Owner-ship	Feudal Owner-ship	Capitalist Owner-ship	Communism	
Wage Labour and Capital	Ancient Society	Feudal Society	Capitalist Society	Communist Society		
Preface to the Critique of Political Economy	Primitive Society	Asiatic Society	Ancient Society	Feudal Society	Capi-talist Society	(Com-mu-nism)
		Antagonistic Socio-Economic Forms				
Letter To Vera Zasulich	Primary Type		Secondary Type		Tertiary Type	

9   *Ibid.*, p. 158.
10   Marx, and Friedrich Engels. *On Literature and Art.* Moscow: Progress Publishers, 1976. p. 183.
11   Marx, and Friedrich Engels. *Karl Marx, Friedrich Engels: Marx and Engels Collected Works 1874-83.* New York: International Publishers, 1989. p. 358.

Marx's Theory of Historical Division in the Subjective Dimension of Historical Dialectics				
	Pre-capitalist Period		Capitalism	Communism
German Ideology	Formation of Nature	Formation of Civilization		
	Material Forces Dominate Humans			Realization of Independent Activities
The Economic Manuscripts in the 1850s-1860s and Das Kapital	(Primitive Society)	Society of Personal Dependence	Society of Material Dependence	Full and Free Social Development of Humans
	Realm of Necessity			Realm of Freedom

Marx's theoretical standpoint of historical division obviously varies. From the perspective of the subjective dimension in historical dialectics that stresses the subjective initiative, Marx is not strict about the division of historical forms; instead, he reflects on the unique situation of the human subject in different social and historical forms to explore the innate social logic of development from the unreasonable mode of production in capitalism to communism. In other words, Marx intends to *discover the scientific foundation for the proletarian revolution*, which is not different from the purpose of writing the *1844 Manuscripts*, but based on another theoretical point. In the latter logic of the objective description, he really abides by the law of historical development to divide different socio-historical periods with the scale of the mode of production. It will be a mistake if we cannot grasp the innate logical clue of Marx's division and compare his analysis here with other logical clues of historical division. Furthermore, it only leads to a far-fetched conclusion if Marx's different perspectives of division were treated with the same logical scale of "maturity" and "development link."

Clearly, there are two logical perspectives in Marx's research of historical division: One is the dynamic logic concerned with the dominant socio-historical elements in the subjective dimension of historical dialectics founded on the relationship of the human subject and the external object; the other is the logic of the objective description in historical materialism concerned with the qualities of different social forms based on the objective structure of socio-historical development. In my opinion, the first logical aspect is neglected in the traditional framework of philosophical interpretation, which necessarily leads to a series of theoretical mistakes. Thus, to deal with this problem is one of the major tasks of the book.

Here, Marx's first logical clue will be analyzed to study the existence of the human subject in *different social and historical conditions* (which mainly means the first two periods of the three great social forms) as well as its relationship with the theories of 'natural-ness' and material-subjugation. However, for a clear explanation of this issue, it is necessary to first understand the latest scientific achievement of the other basic logical clue of Marx.

B. THE DIFFERENT HISTORICAL PERIODS IN MARX'S LOGIC OF THE OBJECTIVE DESCRIPTION

As early as in the 1850s, Marx began his research of social and historical divisions from the perspective of the objective description; but his theory only became mature after the 1870s, indicating that his research was a complicated process and many of his ideas were in constant changes. Therefore, we can make a brief conclusion by comparing the ultimate achievement of the perspective of the objective description in historical materialism.[12]

First of all, it is about the "primary society" confirmed by Marx or the primitive society in the five major social forms in the traditional framework of philosophical illustration. In fact, Marx does not concentrate on historical research here but reaches a *historical origin* when exploring the *premise* of capitalism. By the materials available at that time, Marx thinks that the initial form of human existence is the tribal community expanded with families, which is also a "naturally formed" human community. There is a primitive relation of *natural sameness* in the human subject and the natural object along with the individual and the community. Thus, Marx believes that in primitive tribes, the subject of human production (the human body) and the objective condition (the land) are naturally formed in the same state of primary chaos.

---

12 In our textual research, there is a serious confusion about Marx's division of history. Many researchers do not understand Marx's different theoretical starting points in his study of economics and history. Therefore, they overstate his specific perspective and semantic situation, which leads to the transgression of multiple semantic domains. This issue is worth our careful consideration. At this point, I think my teacher, Mr. Sun Bokui and my contemporary Yao Shunliang have scientific discussions of it. See Sun Bokui and Yao Shunliang. "Section Three, Chapter Two" in *History of Marxist Philosophy*, Volume 2. Beijing Publishing House, 1991.

> **Just as the working subject appears naturally as an individual, as natural being- so does the first objective condition of his labour appear as nature, earth, as his inorganic body; he himself is not only the organic body, but also the subject of this inorganic nature. This condition is not his product but something he finds to hand- presupposed to him as a natural being apart from him.**[13]

Obviously, the existence and development of human social history at this period is consubstantial with nature. For the same reason, Marx regards this initial natural community as the "primary" society of social history, the first establishment of human existence in nature, which actually means the "process of natural history" of human society in a general and essential sense. It can be safely recognized as a *sub-natural period* in early human history.

Then, it is Marx's "secondary type" in socio-historical development, which consists of the Asiatic, ancient, feudal and capitalist periods.

According to Marx, the primary natural community begins to disintegrate with the development of the material productive forces, closely followed by the "Asiatic type." It undergoes some mutation but keeps its land ownership based on the primitive community relationship. In my view, Marx's understanding of this Asiatic mode of production goes through a gradual development. In the early 1850s, he discovers that some Asian countries still have rural communes of land ownership after studying those countries as India. At first, he uses "Asiatic society" to show the particular economic and political system in Asia. When it comes to the *Critique of Political Economy*, his thought becomes more profound and the "Asiatic mode of production" is taken as a pre-capitalist historical development. This view is proved after Marx's research of Georg Ludwig von Maurer's works on the ancient European history and the *Ancient Society* by Lewis H. Morgan. He spends more attention to details with meticulous effort. The Asiatic mode of production is regarded as a transition from the primitive society to the social and economic form. Meanwhile, it is also the last phase in the *disintegration* of the primary social type and the *first prototype* of the established social economic formation. In Marx's words, "the period of the agricultural commune appears as a period of transition from communal property to private property, as a period of transition from the primary form to the secondary one."[14]

---

13   Marx, Karl. *Grundrisse: Foundations of the Critique of Political Economy (rough draft)*. Trans. Martin Nicolaus. London; New York: Penguin, 1993. p. 488.
14   *Ibid.*, p. 352.

The second social economic formation is the ancient ownership, which is the slavery society founded on a city-centric system of land privatization in the early period (mainly in ancient Greece and Rome). At this point, the commune still acts as the premise of this land ownership but has grown out of the independent entity into an economic coalition because such private ownership as land and property already happens despite the partial co-existence with the commune system. The Third is the "Germanic" form of ownership, in which land is "shared" by the commune members, losing the real sense of property. The "economic entity" at this time is actually an independent family economy. It is regarded by Marx as the starting point of the feudal land ownership.

In my opinion, Marx focuses not on the linear types of human history but on the discussion of several situations from the initial disintegration of primitive communes all the way down to capitalism. With an inherent link, the above three forms of land ownership certainly take place in different places and periods. Therefore, Marx regards them as several *evolutionary* economic ages in human history. More importantly, he finds that the above social forms have an important point in common: *The original and natural unification of labour and land.* Thus, man has established his subjectivity through material production at this time; however, the scale and depth of social production are still small and shallow. People are still attached to land (nature); the process of human social history is still dependent on the natural blood ties; and the human dependency relationship dominates society. It is the separation of labour from the means of labour that leads to the occurrence of capitalism.

Marx believes that the capitalist mode of production is a special stage in the evolution of the "secondary" social economical form, and the result of all the previous historical development. It presupposes the separation of the means of production from the producer, which "has no natural basis."[15] "Neither is its social basis one that is common to all historical periods. It is clearly the result of a past historical development, the product of many economic revolutions, of the extinction of a whole series of older forms of social production."[16] After history meets such requirements as the unification of land (all the natural condition for labourer), labourer and his own labour tools as well as the disintegration of the slavery and feudal systems where the labourer acts as the condition of production, there emerge two necessary conditions for the capitalist production: Free labourers losing

---

15 Marx, Karl. *Capital: Marx and Engels.* New York: International Publishers, 1984. p. 169.
16 *Ibid.*, p. 169.

their objective condition of production and the capital that plays the necessary role of objective condition. Marx takes the perspective of the objective description in historical materialism, compares the capitalist mode of production ("man") with the previous social forms ("ape"), and for the first time validates the *grand historical rationality* of capitalism, that is, the effective and proficient development of the productive forces in this system.

In the past narrow social communities, the working condition is regarded as individually possessed; the productive forces slowly develop in separate directions; the economic performance is confined to a naive stage. The capitalist mode of production breaks the old system that constrains the development of the productive forces, turning the previous simple production and reproduction on the level of single use value into social production that aims at value, especially, surplus value. The innate law of surplus value and competition drive the capitalists in desperate expansion of production, creating an unprecedented social productivity. At the same time, it also creates the truly comprehensive social relations as well as human capacities and needs. Marx says in a positive tone, "The bourgeoisie, during its rule of scarce one hundred years, has created more massive and more colossal productive forces than have all preceding generations together."[17] This grand civilization of capitalism, "in comparison to which all earlier ones appear as mere *local developments* of humanity and as *nature-idolatry*."[18]

It is true that Marx starts from the perspective of the objective description in historical materialism to confirm the great advancement of the social productive forces in the capitalist mode of production; instead of following the bourgeoisie scholars to take it as the eternal natural law or an immortal magic, Marx discovers in its development the contradiction that leads to the demise of capitalism, that is, the contradiction between the expanding social production and the capitalist private ownership. It also signals that the objective development of capitalism will again encounter its own historical boundary; the eventual dirge will be heard when the stage curtain falls down. Once the capitalist relation of production hinders the development of productive forces, capitalism must be *objectively overthrown*! According to Marx, capitalism is the last social economic form of "antagonism." "The prehistory of human society accordingly closes with this social formation." [19]It is the conclusion of his "secondary" type in human social history. From here, a real development of new human *social history* is ushered, that is, the "tertiary type" or communism, which will be discussed in the last part of this chapter.

---

17   Marx, Karl. *Karl Marx: A Reader*. Ed. Jon Elster. Cambridge University Press, 1986. p. 229.

18   Marx, Karl. *Karl Marx's Economics, Volume 1*. London: Routledge, 1988. p. 275.

19   Marx, Karl. *Early Writings*. Harmondsworth: Penguin Books, 1992. p. 426.

C. MARX'S THEORY OF THREE GREAT SOCIAL FORMS AND 'NATURAL-NESS' AND MATERIAL-SUBJUGATION

In the above analysis, we observe different historical periods and the basic historical trend of human societies from Marxist perspective of objective description in historical materialism. Marx mainly starts from the general movement and the objective law of material production in social and historical development to adopt the objective structure of social history (the relationship of production) as the scale and theoretical axis in the division of different historical forms, which provides the *foundation* for his analysis of the general social and historical development. However, once we change the perspective to the subjective dimension of historical dialectics and the major elements in historical development, our context will be greatly modified and a new picture of the social and historical process will emerge. It is nothing else but Marx's theory of three great social forms as well as his analysis of the phenomena of 'natural-ness' and material-subjugation in the entire pre-historical periods from the perspective of historical dialectics, especially, his critique of 'natural-ness' and material-subjugation of the specific subject-object inversion in the sense of major social elements within the capitalist society.

As we know, Marx used to employ alienation to represent the inverted subject and object. After 1845, he begins to put forward the issues of material-subjugation and 'natural-ness' in the "pre-historical" period of human societies. As noted above, in the first chapter of *German Ideology*, Marx starts from the nature of the productive tools to relate the three major social forms: The pre-capitalist society with "natural instruments of production" (Marx was not aware of the primitive society at that time), the modern capitalist society with tools "created by civilization" and the future communist society.[20] For Marx, in the first and second social forms, the major aspect of social history is not the human subject but the material. Both of them present certain material-subjugation phenomena, with different qualities. "In the first case, that of the natural instrument of production, individuals are subservient to nature; in the second, to a product of labour. In the first case, therefore, property (landed property) appears as direct natural domination, in the second, as domination of labour, particularly of accumulated labour, capital."[21]

---

20 Marx, and Friedrich Engels. *The German Ideology*. Ed. Christopher John Arthur. New York: International Publishers Co, 1970. p. 68.
21 *Ibid.*, p. 68.

This idea is further developed in *Das Kapital* and his Manuscripts. From multiple perspectives, Marx reaffirms different qualities of the major elements of human social history in three great social forms.

Relations of personal dependence (entirely spontaneous at the outset) are the first social forms, in which human productive capacity develops only to a slight extent and at isolated points. Personal independence founded on objective [sachlicher] dependence is the second great form, in which a system of general social metabolism, of universal relations, of all-round needs and universal capacities is formed for the first time. Free individuality, based on the universal development of individuals and on their subordination of their communal, social productivity as their social wealth, is the third stage.[22]

The new theory of three great social forms bears some obvious changes from the idea contained in the *German Ideology*; now Marx begins to exclude the primitive society from the *civil society* that has the written record of history. As analyzed earlier, the subject and object in the initial period of human social history exist in an original *identical* sub-natural state, which means it is just illegal to discuss their relationship in the sense of social history. In fact, the three great social forms only include the "secondary" (the first two) and the "tertiary" (communist) social forms. Therefore, our major purpose here is to discuss how Marx analyzes the phenomenon of 'natural-ness' along with the situation and status of the subjective material-subjugation in the *first two* historical periods.

First of all, judging from the subjective role in the historical development, man's activity is based on the dependent relationship that is "entirely spontaneous at the outset" in the first social form; in the second social form, there is the "personal independence founded on objective [sachlicher] dependence"; and the "free individuality, based on the universal development of individuals and on their subordination of their communal, social productivity as their social wealth, is the third stage."[23]

Marx points out that in the first social form, man's natural production (including the human multiplication and use of raw materials) dominates and the production of the material means of subsistence is at most "a peripheral matter."[24] Whether in agriculture, fishing or hunting, man's labour only plays an *assistant* role in nature. Moreover, the human subject

---

22   Marx, Karl. *Grundrisse: Foundations of the Critique of Political Economy (rough draft)*. Trans. Martin Nicolaus. London; New York: Penguin, 1993. p. 158.
23   *Ibid.*, p. 158.
24   *Ibid.*, p. 223.

only "directly and naturally reproduces himself"[25] in his own living process because his living is to "make not the acquiring of wealth his object, but self-sustenance."[26] At this point, the human existence, like that of the animals, just stays on the level of mere survival in natural production, with no power to create a huge surplus of wealth. Once wealth appears, the situation changes. "The outgrowth of property has been so immense; its forms so diversified, its uses so expanding and its management so intelligent in the interests of its owners, that it has become, on the part of the people, an unmanageable power."[27]

In the second form, man's material production takes the lead and drives the social development; at the same time, the human subject makes use of it to produce a new condition of social existence directly founded on his own created materials; and man makes real realization of his subjectivity in the material production. The economic world is thus differentiated from the natural world as man's creation. However, Marx discovers that in this constantly expanding and growing economic kingdom man's material production "appears as something alien to them, autonomous, as a thing" to himself.[28] The economic force created by the human subject is now reversed to become an objective external power that subjugates and dominates people. Moreover, both of these social forms contain the phenomenon of material-subjugation. The passive man is still determined by the external condition, and the process of society itself is "a natural relation, as it were, external to the individuals and independent of them."[29] What is different between them is, "in all forms where landed property rules, the natural relation still predominant. In those where capital rules, the social, historically created element."[30] In this way, social history obtains a *double natural and economic* material-subjugation. We realize that Marx's discussion here makes a specific development of the same thought in his *German Ideology*.

However, when Marx turns to take the perspective of social relations of people, the three great social forms respectively take on "a merely local connection resting on blood ties, or on primeval, natural or master-servant

---

25   *Ibid.*, p. 157

26   *Ibid.*, p. 476.

27   Marx, and Friedrich Engels. *Collected Works, Volume 26*. London: Lawrence & Wishart, 1990. p. 276.

28   Marx, Karl. *Grundrisse: Foundations of the Critique of Political Economy (rough draft)*. Trans. Martin Nicolaus. London; New York: Penguin, 1993. p. 157.

29   *Ibid.*, p. 158.

30   *Ibid.*, p. 107.

relations," a form that misrepresents the human social relations with the "objective bond" and the "universally developed individuals, whose social relations, as their own communal [gemeinschaftlich] relations."[31] The first social form is "founded either on the immature development of man individually, who has not yet severed the umbilical cord that unites him with his fellowmen in a primitive tribal community, or upon direct relations of subjection."[32] For Marx, this idea would be rather expressed as "earlier historical periods make him the accessory of a definite and limited human conglomerate."[33] At this time, the human relations are still "spontaneous" and in regional tribal groups, the individuals are bonded by simple blood relations. They are "in a still quite natural way in the family and in the family expanded into the clan [Stamm]; then later in the various forms of communal society arising out of the antitheses and fusions of the clan."[34] When it comes to the Middle Ages later, "personal dependence here characterizes the social relations of production just as much as it does the other spheres of life organised on the basis of that production forms the groundwork of society."[35] That personal dependence is dominated by control and obedience is due to "a low stage, and when, therefore, the social relations within the sphere of material life, between man and man, and between man and Nature, are correspondingly narrow."[36] Nevertheless, personal relations are always represented as their own relationships instead of between things and products.

It is much different in the second social form. The original "ties of personal dependence, of distinctions of blood, education, etc, are in fact exploded, ripped up"[37] and "the social connection between persons is transformed into a social relation between things; personal capacity into objective wealth."[38] "The various forms of social connectedness confront the individual as a mere means towards his private purposes, as external necessity."[39] This social form is more advanced than its predecessor is. "And, certainly, this objective connection is preferable to the lack of any connection, or to

---

31   *Ibid.*, p. 162.
32   Marx, Karl. *Capital: Marx and Engels.* New York: International Publishers, 1984. p. 79.
33   Marx, Karl. *Grundrisse: Foundations of the Critique of Political Economy (rough draft).* Trans. Martin Nicolaus. London; New York: Penguin, 1993. p. 83.
34   *Ibid.*, p. 84.
35   Marx, Karl. *Karl Marx: A Reader.* Ed. Jon Elster. Cambridge University Press, 1986. p. 69.
36   *Ibid.*, p. 71.
37   *Ibid.*, p. 54.
38   *Ibid.*, p. 49.
39   Marx, Karl. *Grundrisse: Foundations of the Critique of Political Economy (rough draft).* Trans. Martin Nicolaus. London; New York: Penguin, 1993. p. 84.

a merely local connection resting on blood ties, or on primeval, natural or master-servant relations."[40] In particular, these material links are no longer "spontaneous" but become the non-natural relations created by people. However, in his in-depth analysis, Marx says that the individual obtains not true independence through this material relation but the dependent external relations of the human subject. "These external relations are very far from being an abolition of 'relations of dependence'[41]; they are rather the dissolution of these relations into a general form; they are merely the elaboration and emergence of the general foundation of the relations of personal dependence." Moreover, during their historical process, "these conditions, in turn, are independent of the individuals and, although created by society, appear as if they were natural conditions, not controllable by individuals."[42]

This argument of Marx's is very important. It practically illustrates 'natural-ness' and material-subjugation in the capitalist economic relations. "The definedness of individuals, which in the former case appears as a personal restriction of the individual by another, appears in the latter case as developed into an objective restriction of the individual by relations independent of him and sufficient unto themselves."[43] Nevertheless, this human histori-cal development "has still a limited, primitive character."[44] In this particular state, "the social interrelations of production assert themselves only as an overwhelming natural law in relation to individual free will."[45]

The third point is that Marx starts from the objective laws of social history to further propose three corresponding characters of social movement, the "natural necessity," the "economic necessity" and the independent devel-opment of human freedom. In the first form of society, the human sub-jects as a whole are still under the direct control of natural laws; in the second social form, people are manipulated by the "invisible hand" behind the economic process created by themselves. "Individuals are subsumed under social production; social production exists outside them as their fate."[46] The status of the first social movement is called as natural necessity

---

40   *Ibid.*, p. 161.
41   *Ibid.*, p. 164.
42   *Ibid.*, p. 164.
43   *Ibid.*, p. 164.
44   *Ibid.*, p. 165.
45   Marx, and Friedrich Engels. *Capital, a Critical Analysis of Capitalist Production.* Moscow: Foreign Languages Pub. House, 1959. p. 859.
46   Marx, Karl. *Grundrisse: Foundations of the Critique of Political Economy (rough draft).* Trans. Martin Nicolaus. London; New York: Penguin, 1993. p. 158.

and the latter, the economic necessity. In both conditions, the social and historical activities of human beings have a spontaneous non-subjective status, which I shall deal with in the next section.

Furthermore, Marx classifies the existential aspects of the human subject itself into the "natural existence," the economic "participants" and the social "Freeman." In the first social form, the natural element still dominates the subjective existence, which means man and the animals are alike in their existential context; in the second form, human apparently becomes the master of nature with the economic power but is inversely presented as an economic personification at the same time, called by Marx as the "economic animal." Therefore, in these two conditions, the human subject is still unable to shake off the various shackles and truly rise. From the perspective of social structure, Marx also makes the definitions of the "natural community," the "social formation" and the "free association." In the first form, the vulnerable people have to turn to the community, spontaneously based on the natural blood relationships. In the second form, the human subjects have created an economic society but still obtain integration via the inverted material association independent of their subjective wills. It is by defining the first two social forms that Marx uncovers the early human status of being-in-itself in Mother Nature and the non-human status of a personified capital with the social structure presented in the natural formation of blood relationship groups and the spontaneous composition of the economic relations in the market network. As for Marx's three great social forms, we find that people in the first period are heavily reliant on nature, so the external objective force (natural necessity) dominates humans and their social activities; in the second period, the social productive forces generate a huge system of material production while the economic power becomes a supernatural force above man. In this new world, there is again an inverted *quasi-religious* image: Although man displays his independence of nature in the economic life, no longer a slave to nature now, he is at the same time subjected to the material forces created by himself, under the control of the "invisible hand" among the blind economic movements. Undoubtedly, it is a new economic necessity that exists outside man himself. In a certain sense, human society surpasses nature (other animals) and begins creating their own history, which is only achieved through a resultant force of blind and spontaneous activities. Marx makes a sharp comment on the fault of this period.

> **As much, then, as the whole of this movement appears as a social process, and as much as the individual moments of this movement arise from the conscious will and particular purposes of**

individuals, so much does the totality of the process appear as an objective interrelation, which arises spontaneously from nature; arising, it is true, from the mutual influence of conscious individuals on one another, but neither located in their consciousness, nor subsumed under them as a whole. Their own collisions with one another produce an alien social power standing above them, produce their mutual interaction as a process and power independent of them.[47]

We should pay special attention to the point that man is still the economic animal abiding by the jungle law in the economic process although he grows out of the dependence on nature that is similar to other animals in the first social form. History has not become true yet (no humanistic implication here) for it still runs outside the domain of human beings like nature.

Thus, we can see that Marx makes a scientific description that in the entire capitalist and pre-capitalist development of human social history the phenomena of material-subjugation and 'natural-ness' *appear and exist in different forms* due to specific levels of the productive forces in history. In this way, Marx attaches further historical importance to this theory. On the other side, Marx's theory is based on his subjective perspective of historical dialectics, which means he will never behave like those bourgeois scholars to maintain an eternal existence of material-subjugation and 'natural-ness'. In fact, the innate logical requirement is to negate such unreasonable historical phenomena. He points out that the non-subjective 'natural-ness' and material-subjugation dominant in "pre-historical" social economical forms are only historical by themselves. All the "pre-historical" societies, especially, the capitalist system, are *narrow* and *historical*. With the development of the productive forces, this "natural law" carried out through blind destruction is sure to be replaced by a true social law. To be specific, it refers to the replacement of the blind commodity economy by the *planned and proportional development of social production*, that is, the achievement of socialism (communism). It also demonstrates the real historical process of human beings striding from the realm of necessity into the fully developed realm of freedom from the general perspective of social history.[48]

---

47 *Ibid.*, p. 196.
48 Here, I want to mention another point of Alvin Toffler's: The theory of three "waves" and three forms of power. In the Powershift published in 1991, Toffler believes the powers that dominate human life and development in the three stages of social history are different. First, it is violence that dominates in the agricultural society; second, it is wealth that directs the industrial society; third, it is knowledge (intelligence) that controls the information society. In addition to this non-scientific division of history and its conspicuous defense of the contemporary capitalist ideology, the view contains an evident

II. THE PROFOUND TRANSFORMATION FROM THE "REALM OF NECESSITY" TO THE "REALM OF FREEDOM"

In the previous section, two kinds of external necessity issues in Marx's three great social forms have been dealt with. In fact, it is also relevant with the theory of the realm of necessity and the realm of freedom on the development of human social and historical activities. As for this matter, the traditional framework of philosophical interpretation contains many mistakes, too. Here, I attempt to make another investigation into this theoretical point by integrating the illustrated theories of 'natural-ness' and material-subjugation with the division of three great social forms from the subjective perspective of historical dialectics,

A. THE REALM OF NECESSITY: THE NATURAL NECESSITY AND THE ECONOMIC NECESSITY

In the last part of *Das Kapital, Vol. 3*, after a complete research of the capitalist reproduction process, Marx makes a general outline of the entire socio-historical development of human beings and reaches the famous conclusion of the realm of necessity and the realm of freedom. He wisely writes,

> The realm of freedom actually begins only where labour which is determined by necessity and mundane considerations ceases; thus in the very nature of things it lies beyond the sphere of actual material production. [...] Freedom in this field can only consist in socialised man, the associated producers, rationally regulating their interchange with Nature, bringing it under their common control, instead of being ruled by it as by the blind forces of Nature; and achieving this with the least expenditure of energy and under conditions most favourable to, and worthy of, their human nature. But it nonetheless still remains a realm of necessity. Beyond it begins that development of human energy which is an end in itself, the true realm of freedom, which, however, can blossom forth only with this realm of necessity as its basis.[49]

---

error, that is, it fails to differentiate *the general foundation from the dominant elements* in social history. A logical inversion occurs: The dominant elements become the general foundation. Thus, the violence-dominant and knowledge-deciding doctrine. This view is popular among some scholars both at home and abroad, which we should carefully guard against. See Alvin Toffler. *Powershift: Knowledge, Wealth and Violence at the Edge of the 21st Century*. New York: Bantam Books, 1990.

49 Marx, and Friedrich Engels. *On Literature and Art*. Moscow: Progress Publishers, 1976. p. 183.

Obviously, Marx is influenced by Hegel's conceptual evolution of the realm of necessity and the realm of freedom (See "Introduction" of this book). It is noteworthy that Hegel's absolute idea has been substituted by the process of real practice of human society at this point. There is in fact an ontological difference: Marx's theoretical discourse here is still concerned with the existential status of the human subject in the subjective dimension of historical dialectics. He takes the criterion of man's subjective activities to divide social life into two spheres: One is the material production centred on *man's means of survival*; the other is the free activities centred on the self-development of the human subject. The former is the *realm of necessity* for human survival, while the latter is the *realm of freedom* for the advanced development of human beings.

In the domain of survival, man's subjective activities are mainly about material production, which has *two logical levels*.

First, it is the physical need of human survival. As long as people live, they should eat, drink, wear clothes, and have shelter; they have to carry out the material production. As mentioned above, in his establishment of the scientific historical view, Marx says,

> **Men must be in a position to live in order to be able to "make history." But life involves before everything else eating and drinking, a habitation, clothing and many other things. The first historical act is thus the production of the means to satisfy these needs, the production of material life itself. And indeed this is an historical act, a fundamental condition of all history, which today, as thousands of years ago, must daily and hourly be fulfilled merely in order to sustain human life.[50]**

According to Marx's historical materialism, the existence of human history is the necessary objective premise that man *cannot shake off*. In other words, the physical needs of survival determine the human production. Man is subject to this necessity once he enters the historical process. Therefore, Marx says, "Every child knows that any nation that stopped working, not for a year, but let us say, just for a few weeks, would perish."[51] It is the first level of the realm of necessity as well as the logic in the objective dimension of historical materialism and dialectics as the general foundation of social history.

---

50   Marx, and Friedrich Engels. *The German Ideology*. Ed. Christopher John Arthur. New York: International Publishers Co, 1970. p. 48.
51   Marx, and Friedrich Engels. *Karl Marx, Friedrich Engels: Collected Works*. New York: International Publishers, 1975. p. 68.

Please note that Marx deems the activities of material production as a *general base* for the existence and development of human social history, which is what we call Marx's general interpretation of historical materialism. He also makes a special note that "just as the savage must wrestle with Nature to satisfy his wants, to maintain and reproduce life, so must civilized man, and he must do so in all social formations and under all possible modes of production."[52] He says,

> **As labour is a creator of use value, is useful labour, it is a necessary condition, independent of all forms of society, for the existence of the human race; it is an eternal nature-imposed necessity, without which there can be no material exchanges between man and Nature, and therefore no life.**[53]

It is the first theoretical level of the realm of necessity.

Marx's "realm of necessity" indicates another *deeper historical* meaning : The historical unreasonable situation of the dominating elements in the development of human social history, that is, the phenomenon of material-subjugation in which the human subject is dominated and enslaved by the external objective force (necessity) in their own activities of survival. It is a historical phenomenon that should be surpassed in the development of human beings. It is worth noting that this dynamic discourse in the subjective dimension of historical dialectics is based on the specific understanding of historical materialism. At this point, Marx's theory of the realm of necessity contains an actual inherent indication of the *entire pre-historical period of human social development, including capitalism and the pre-capitalist time*, which also means the first two (along with the primitive period) social forms in Marx's division, that is, the periods of historical development under the control of the natural and economic necessity of material-subjugation.

According to Marx's theory of history, man's subjective power is weak in the beginning of social history and his survival becomes the sole purpose of all his activities with labour and production being the means of "living." Therefore, "wealth does not appear as the aim of production" at that time.[54] However, at this time, man's labour and production is under the mandatory provisions of the "necessity" of natural existence. He is driven by the external necessity of nature. In later historical process, the human subject works on his own labour and production to gradually wean himself

---

52   Marx, and Friedrich Engels. *On Literature and Art*. Moscow: Progress Publishers, 1976. p. 183.
53   Marx, Engels, Moore, etc. *Capital: The Process of Capitalist Production*. C. H. Kerr, 1908, p. 50.
54   Marx, Karl. *Grundrisse: Foundations of the Critique of Political Economy (rough draft)*. Trans. Martin Nicolaus. London; New York: Penguin, 1993. p. 487.

off the external force of natural necessity and create a new artificial materi-al world: The industrial society based on the commodity economy. In this new world, it is true that human subjectivity rings high and man begins to become the real master of nature in the historical process, but he actually suffers a loss of subjectivity in a deeper sense because he is no longer the *purpose* of social development, only "as mere means of production, objec-tive wealth as an end in itself."[55] In other words, the original material pro-duction/means generated by man's needs of survival is turned into the aim while man becomes the *means* of production/means. Marx once compares the human activities in these two social forms as follows: "Thus the old view, in which the human being appears as the aim of production, regard-less of his limited national, religious, political character, seems to be very lofty when contrasted to the modern world, where production appears as the aim of mankind and wealth as the aim of production."[56]

The production of wealth should have been an absolute exertion of man's creative power, a true realization of man's subjective essence. However, it is quite contrary to reality.

In bourgeois economics – and in the epoch of production to which it corresponds – this complete working-out of the hu-man content appears as a complete emptying-out, this universal objectification as total alienation, and the tearing-down of all limited, one-sided aims as sacrifice of the human end-in-itself to an entirely external end.[57]

Here, man's labour and production become a non-subjective process stipu-lated by the material desire (external purpose) under the control of an "invisible hand." Man is a slave to the external process again. In the eyes of Marx, if man is dominated by the natural necessity in the first social form, he is driven by the economic necessity in the second social form.

Hence, during the entire *pre-historical ages* from primitive society to capi-talism, it is actually impossible for the human subject to achieve true freedom; man cannot obtain a strong pair of wings to fly high, but is historically anchored in the mandatory "realm of necessity" composed of the external forces. The primitive society and the first great social form still belong to the natural realm of necessity. The humble human subject is confined to his instinctive labour and production for the needs of sur-vival. Like other animals, his production "is originally restricted to the

---

55   *Ibid.*, p. 461.
56   Marx, Karl. *Karl Marx: A Reader.* Ed. Jon Elster. Cambridge University Press, 1986. p. 200.
57   *Ibid.*, p. 200.

reproduction of his own body through the appropriation of ready objects prepared by nature itself for consumption."[58] In the critical situation that completely depends on the natural world, the human subject cannot be free. Later, the capability of practice is increased in the first great social form but the corresponding labour and production are still confined to the dependence on land.

While in the second great social form, or the capitalist economic society, the natural realm of necessity is surpassed.

> **Hence the great civilizing influence of capital; its production of a stage of society in comparison to which all earlier ones appear as mere *local developments* of humanity and as *nature-idolatry*. For the first time, nature becomes purely an object for human-kind, purely a matter of utility; ceases to be recognized as a power for itself; and the theoretical discovery of its autonomous laws appears merely as a ruse so as to subjugate it under human needs, whether as an object of consumption or as a means of production.[59]**

Finally, there comes the relevant freedom of man from nature in history. Meanwhile, the human subject begins a comprehensive relationship with society to discover, create and satisfy the new needs generated by society itself. This is a fresh human kingdom turned out by the commodity economy and industrial society.

In capitalism, the human subject starts "to replace the detail-worker of to-day, grappled by life-long repetition of one and the same trivial operation, and thus reduced to the mere fragment of a man, by the fully developed individual, fit for a variety of labours, ready to face any change of production."[60] Now, it is possible for "the cultivation of all the qualities of the social human being, production of the same in a form as rich as possible in needs, because rich in qualities and relations—production of this being as the most total and universal possible social product a system of general social metabolism, of universal relations, of all-round needs and universal capacities is formed."[61] It is in this situation that the original "natural necessity in its direct form has disappeared; because a historically

---

58   *Ibid.*, p. 204.

59   Marx, Karl. *Grundrisse: Foundations of the Critique of Political Economy (rough draft)*. Trans. Martin Nicolaus. London; New York: Penguin, 1993. p. 410.

60   Bredel, Ralf. *The Ethical Economy of Conflict Prevention and Development: towards a Model for International Organizations*. Boston: Martinus Nijhoff Publishers, 2007. p. 51.

61   Marx, Karl. *Grundrisse: Foundations of the Critique of Political Economy (rough draft)*. Trans. Martin Nicolaus. London; New York: Penguin, 1993. p. 409.

created need has taken the place of the natural one."[62] At the same time, all relations are "posited by society, not as determined by nature."[63] "Thus capital creates the bourgeois society, and the universal appropriation of nature as well as of the social bond itself by the members of society."[64] And the human subject also acquires more freedom in the sense of social existence, that is, he is liberated from the old relationship of dependence, obtaining the freedom of commodity exchange and competition.

On one side, in the economic realm created by human beings, they achieve liberation from the natural confinement and produce a wider range of living conditions on the social level of existence; on the other side, they lose their subjectivity, freedom, and fall before the economic necessity created by them in a deeper sense. For Marx, the capitalist freedom is not a true emancipation as propagandized by the bourgeois scholars but the freedom of the objective economic power, especially, the movement of capital. Marx points out that there is nothing true about the view of the free competition in the process of capitalist economy as "the ultimate development of human freedom" because "it is nothing more than free development on a limited basis – the basis of the rule of capital" where "it is not individuals who are set free by free competition; it is, rather, capital which is set free."[65] For human beings, "this kind of individual freedom is therefore at the same time the most complete suspension of all individual freedom, and the most complete subjugation of individuality under social conditions which assume the form of objective powers, even of overpowering objects – of things independent of the relations among individuals themselves."[66] People escape the external necessity of nature only to find themselves falling into the *hand of economic necessity*. Here, the relationship of man and material is still inverted, which is the second meaning of Marx's "realm of necessity."

However, the realm of necessity is sure to be surpassed with the development of human social history. The system of capitalism is not eternal; man's subjective development cannot be trapped in this reverse state forever. Marx firmly believes:

> **But obviously this process of inversion is a merely historical necessity, a necessity for the development of the forces of production solely from a specific historic point of departure, or basis,**

---

62   *Ibid.*, p. 325.
63   *Ibid.*, p. 276.
64   *Ibid.*, p. 409.
65   *Ibid.*, p. 650.
66   *Ibid.*, p. 652.

> **but in no way an absolute necessity of production; rather, a vanishing one, and the result and the inherent purpose of this process is to suspend this basis itself, together with this form of the process.**[67]

What is the next after the sublation of the realm of necessity? The paddle strokes and the other side are visible in the distance: The realm of freedom in the socio-historical development of human beings.

B. THE REALM OF FREEDOM: SELF-REALIZATION AND EMANCIPATION OF THE HUMAN SUBJECT

Marx puts forward the second domain of human activities: The field of *non-instrumental* production, where the purpose of man's living activities is centred on his existence and development. Labour and all human activities are for the internal needs of the subject himself. Man is both the goal and the instrument. The activities per se reflect the unified purpose and means as well as realization and creation of man's value. The harmonious unification gives rise to the realm of freedom for human activities; its actual content is the development of the subject's ability into the purpose of society. In my opinion, this important idea further confirms the previous idea of the "self-activity" in human social history in *German Ideology*, only replaced by *man's comprehensive development of freedom* here.

I think that Marx's realm of freedom has two meanings: One, the human subject previously confined in the realm of necessity obtains freedom after eliminating the control of the external necessity (material-subjugation); two, in the advanced stage of historical development, man can only enter the true realm of freedom after the internal sublation of the eternal natural necessity (the base of material production).

First of all, when Marx mentions "the associated producers, rationally regulating their interchange with Nature, bringing it under their common control, instead of being ruled by it as by the blind forces of Nature"[68], he mainly refers to eliminating the pre-historical material-subjugation and 'natural-ness' that control people as an external objective power and a distortion of human social history, which, of course, contains man's scientific knowledge and usage of the objective laws to transform the "invisible hand" in the economic laws of social development to a "visible hand" (common control). That external law, the "cunning of reason" in Hegel's words (especially, the historical law that represents the new social

---

67   *Ibid.*, p. 831.
68   Marx, and Friedrich Engels. *On Literature and Art. Moscow.* Progress Publishers, 1976. p. 183.

production) will be dominated by the human subject again. Marx says, "We do not mistake the shape of the shrewd spirit that continues to mark all these contradictions. We know that to work well the newfangled forces of society, they only want to be mastered by newfangled men."[69] In his wish for the future society, the development of social history will transit from the spontaneous and nature-like process to the period of self-realization, full development and conscious creation of the human subject. No matter what it is, that domain (the material field) is always a realm of necessity. In later discussion of this book, we shall see that Engels puts more emphasis on this aspect in his opinion of Marx's realm of freedom (See Chapter V) because it is the *general foundation* of the existence and development of social history. However, the outlook of the future realm of freedom does not indicate whether or not people will abandon the general foundation of material production (the realm of necessity in the first sense) but refers to the subject's re-achievement of the dominant status in the process of historical development.[70]

In addition, *once man's capacity is fully developed as his own purpose*, the true realm of freedom will be approached from the other side of material production. A theoretical error must be pointed out here: The realm of necessity is regarded by some only as material production and correspondingly, the realm of freedom, as "non-material production." Please note that Marx's view here is not a simplified distinction of material or non-material production but with a deep incremental logical sense, that is, the realm of freedom is premised on the great affluence with the full development of the social productive forces when people are no longer troubled by the issue of mere survival and the material production is not for the single purpose of subsistence but "the development of human productive forces, in other words the development of the richness of human nature as an end in itself."[71]

Naturally, in his discussion of man's freedom, Marx says, "the external aims become stripped of the semblance of merely external natural urgencies, and become posited as aims which the individual himself posits–hence as self-realization, objectification of the subject, hence real freedom, whose

---

69   Marx, and Friedrich Engels. *Karl Marx and Friedrich Engels: Selected Works in Two Volumes, Volume 1.* Moscow: Foreign Languages Publishing House, 1958. p. 360.
70   The "dominant status" here differs from enslaving nature with the "instrumental reason" accused by the Frankfurt School and eco-Marxism. Marx never adopts an inverted logic to oppose the domination of man by material. A scientific recognition of the objective natural and social laws is to reach a new reasonable modulation. Of this point, Marx's logical discourse is very clear, although he is not equipped with the modern ecological vision.
71   Marx and Friedrich Engels. *Collected Works.* London: Lawrence & Wishart, 1989. p. 347.

action is, precisely, labour." [72]Marx is in agreement with Adam Smith on this point. "In its historic forms as slave-labour, serf-labour, and wage-labour, labour always appears as repulsive, always as external forced labour; and not-labour, by contrast, as 'freedom, and happiness.'"[73] Therefore, he calls it the "contradictory labour" in contrast to the "free labour" that "becomes attractive work, the individual's self-realization."[74]

Another important issue is: What does Marx exactly mean by his labour here? In my opinion, it is, first of all, neither a general reference to the activities of the human subject (the non-historical specific labour) nor an ontological abstract labour in his humanistic historical view of alienation in the *1844 Manuscripts*. Moreover, this kind of labour is not a material process of practice already combined with the object, that is, not a general material production with the theme of creating goods and use value. Marx's definition of labour as objectification and self-realization of man's freedom here means the human subject's action at a certain historical stage *to achieve full play of man's creative intelligence based on* the general material production under the conditions of the highly developed social productive forces when the subject completely escapes the subjugation of the external objective necessity. It is also a *historical phenomenon* under certain conditions instead of an abstract essence or ontological stipulation. Marx shows no sign of withdrawing to humanism.

However, under what conditions can the free labour of self-realization appear? In a specific analysis, Marx says,

> **The work of material production can achieve this character only (1) when its social character is posited, (2) when it is of a scientific and at the same time general character, net merely human exertion as a specifically harnessed natural force, but exertion as subject, which appears in the production process not in a merely natural, spontaneous form, but as an activity regulating all the forces of nature.[75]**

> **Of course, we should not mistake Marx's free labour as something like a game, something post-Wittgenstein.**

> **Free time – which is both idle time and time for higher activity – has naturally transformed its possessor into a different subject, and he then enters into the direct production process as this**

---

72   Marx, Karl. *Grundrisse: Foundations of the Critique of Political Economy (rough draft)*. Trans. Martin Nicolaus. London; New York: Penguin, 1993. p. 611.

73   *Ibid.*, p. 611.

74   *Ibid.*, p. 611.

75   *Ibid.*, p. 612.

different subject. This process is then both discipline, as regards the human being in the process of becoming; and, at the same time, practice [Ausübung], experimental science, materially creative and objectifying science, as regards the human being who has become, in whose head exists the accumulated knowledge of society. For both, in so far as labour requires practical use of the hands and free bodily movement, as in agriculture, at the same time exercise.[76]

Later, it becomes the stipulation of labour in *Critique of the Gotha Program*: "Labour has become not only a means of life but life's prime want."[77]

Only at this time can the human subject become the true master of history under the condition of free labour as the main content of the entire social existence; hence, the development of human social history shakes off its previous blindness and enters a true historical process of Human's free activities; consequently, man can truly eliminate material-subjugation, obtain the final emancipation, and achieve the great transformation from the realm of necessity to the realm of freedom.

C. THE HISTORICAL LEAP FROM THE "REALM OF NECESSITY" TO THE "REALM OF FREEDOM"

The process from the realm of necessity to the realm of freedom means, in fact, transforming from the first two great social forms (the pre-historical period in the complete human social history) to the third one. Obviously, it is, first of all, *a result from the objective development* of the material production instead of a conceptual or political *logical requirement*, such as Hegel's logic of coercion and the political "advance running" strategy in China during the 1950s. To understand this is crucial because in Marx's vision both the transformation from the natural necessity to the economic necessity and the riddance of external necessity to reach the full freedom of human social development are *objectively constructed* through the real, historical, concrete practice of material production (the "is") by the human subject. It does not contain any non-realistic "ought" with *subjective values* (not even a privileged "excellence" in socialism). Therefore, the change from the realm of necessity to the realm of freedom is mainly premised on the reality generated with the development of the productive forces. Man practically achieves the comprehensive freedom *from the economic relations* in the advanced stage of material production and then truly liberates

---

76   *Ibid.*, p. 712.
77   Marx, and Friedrich Engels. *Karl Marx, Friedrich Engels: Marx and Engels Collected Works 1874-83*. New York: International Publishers, 1989. p. 87.

himself with the newly developed productive forces. It is a great leap in the development of human society.

Judging from its specific mechanism, the transformation has several features as follows. First, the human subject creates the huge productive forces in the advanced stage of material production when man can take material production as a *general natural foundation* of his own development and sublate it into an innate prerequisite for his improvement. Second, the human subject thus surpasses the capitalist material-subjugation, re-obtains the control of the economic process and thoroughly eliminates 'natural-ness' from the development of social history, which then becomes a *conscious and independent* progress to achieve the final liberation of the human subject. According to Marx, the two aspects of this process are *in a sequential order of irreversible premise and result*. In other words, the phenomena of 'natural-ness' and material-subjugation characteristic of the economic necessity in capitalist society only occur with certain developed productive forces and have to be removed only after a corresponding occurrence of the necessary material condition generated with the *economic development per se*. Marx never imagines to blow up the reality of capitalism and transcend the stage of 'natural-ness' and material-subjugation of the socio-historical development on an underdeveloped level of material production. He says,

> **If we did not find concealed in society as it is the material conditions of production and the corresponding relations of exchange prerequisite for a classless society, then all attempts to explode it would be quixotic.**[78]

Regrettably, this beautiful and insightful statement has been misunderstood by some of us.

Thus, the social transformation from the realm of necessity to the realm of freedom is an objective evolution decided by the material development of the productive forces in the process of social history. The change only happens on an advanced level. The period of the realm of necessity in human history is, essentially, a time when human beings take labour as their means of survival and the central issue of social activities is to survive and satisfy the biological needs of the human subjects; in comparison, in the realm of freedom where the material productive forces reach a certain level, the human subject begins to aim at production and social activities while the central life shifts from the natural material needs to the satisfaction of spiritual and cultural needs, from passive possession of the external

---

78   Marx, Karl. *Grundrisse: Foundations of the Critique of Political Economy (rough draft)*. Trans. Martin Nicolaus. London; New York: Penguin, 1993. p. 159.

material objects to the creative activities that are neither instrumental nor material. By that time, with a turnaround from the labour of survival to the labour of freedom, the human subject achieves consistency with the object during his development of capabilities; the material shift of production is at the same time man's self-creation; thus, the objectification of production directly becomes the self-confirmation of the subject.

As we know, during the first period of the realm of necessity, the social production dominated by the necessity of nature is for the use values of specific commodities and the human subject has to carry out production for survival; thus, he is subjugated by the object. In the society where the economic necessity dominates, production aims for the *exchange values* of the products and people live for money; thus, they are subjugated by the goods and money created by themselves. In the realm of freedom, social production is intended for the comprehensive development of human beings themselves, which is also the direct purpose of the historical movement. Marx says, "The absolute working-out of his creative potentialities, with no presupposition other than the previous historic development, which makes this totality of development, i.e. the development of all human powers as such the end in itself, not as measured on a predetermined yardstick? Where he does not reproduce himself in one specificity, but produces his totality? Strives not to remain something he has become, but is in the absolute movement of becoming?"[79] Hence, man's comprehensive development is premised on the highly developed productive forces because only in the stage of large-scale social production, especially of the modern production, where the question of producing enough material means of subsistence is solved and the human subject no longer needs to pay exclusive attention on production, can he probably turn his purpose to the full capability development. Therefore, it is really possible "for the development of human abilities and social potentialities (art, etc., science) which have no directly practical purpose."[80]

The full development of human capacity is premised on the condition of abundant free time. It is safe to say that the existence of the realm of freedom relies on free time, of which Marx also gives his further discussion. In his view, during the early historical development when the productive forces are developed to a certain level, surplus labour occurs and then there is the contradiction between labour time and free time, that is, the human beings are able to assign part of their time to be engaged in the activities

79 Marx, Karl. *Karl Marx: A Reader*. Ed. Jon Elster. Cambridge University Press, 1986. p. 200.
80 Marx, Karl. *Economic Manuscripts of 1861-63*. New York: Intl Pub, 1989. p. 190.

other than material production. However, in the societies based on private ownership, free time and labour time are divided and distributed to the ruling class and the ruled class. The working class create free time but they cannot enjoy it while the exploiting class occupy the surplus labour of the labourers and enjoy free time.

Marx points out that in the historic realm of necessity, especially, in capitalism, wealth is based on stealing other people's labour time.

> *Labour time as the measure of value* **posits wealth itself as founded on poverty, and disposable time as existing** *in and because of the antithesis to surplus labour time*; **or, the positing of an individual's entire time as labour time, and his degradation therefore to mere worker, subsumption under labour.**[81]

Here, we can see that the fundamental analysis of the realm of necessity is to indicate the material production of "wealth itself as founded on poverty," which means in the whole realm of necessity, the human subject *is objectively locked in the economic necessity where material production is a means of livelihood*. Man is not able to objectively produce any free time as the direct form of his own development. For Marx, "the whole of human development, so far as it extends beyond the development directly necessary for the natural existence of human beings, consists merely in the employment of this free time and presupposes it as its necessary basis."[82] In capitalism, "the free time of society is produced through the production of unfree time, the labour time of workers prolonged beyond that required for their own subsistence. Free time on one side corresponds to subjugated time on the other side."[83]

Therefore, Marx believes that material production itself must first be developed to minimize the unfree time or the necessary labour time, generate enough free time and the *real* possibility to surpass the kingdom of necessity.

In this way, "as soon as labour in the direct form has ceased to be the great well-spring of wealth, labour time ceases and must cease to be its measure, and hence exchange value [must cease to be the measure] of use value."[84] Thus, the production based on the exchange value will collapse and the

---

81 Marx, Karl. *Grundrisse: Foundations of the Critique of Political Economy (rough draft)*. Trans. Martin Nicolaus. London; New York: Penguin, 1993. p. 708.
82 Marx, Karl. *Economic Manuscripts of 1861-63*. New York: Intl Pub, 1989. p. 191.
83 Marx, and Friedrich Engels. *Collected Works*. London: Lawrence & Wishart, 1988. p. 192.
84 Marx, Karl. *Grundrisse: Foundations of the Critique of Political Economy (rough draft)*. Trans. Martin Nicolaus. London; New York: Penguin, 1993. p. 705.

process of material production will grow out of the old contradictory form of poverty. Only during the objective process of material production can the realm of necessity be truly transcended; similarly, 'natural-ness' and material-subjugation can be eliminated only with the developed productive forces. That is to say, the human subjects cannot obtain their individual development of freedom until the real liberation in the domain of material production. Hence, "not the reduction of necessary labour time so as to posit surplus labour, but rather the general reduction of the necessary labour of society to a minimum, which then corresponds to the artistic, scientific etc. development of the individuals in the time set free, and with the means created, for all of them."[85]

"For real wealth is the developed productive power of all individuals. The measure of wealth is then not any longer, in any way, labour time, but rather disposable time."[86] And "time is in fact the active existence of the human being. It is not only the measure of human life. It is the space for its development."[87]

It is the social transition from the realm of necessity to the realm of freedom. Marx profoundly points out:

> **In this transformation, it is neither the direct human labour he himself performs, nor the time during which he works, but rather the appropriation of his own general productive power, his understanding of nature and his mastery over it by virtue of his presence as a social body – it is, in a word, the development of the social individual which appears as the great foundation-stone of production and of wealth.[88]**

Only in this way can human beings (the social individuals) really achieve their full development of freedom and truly complete a great transformation in the historical process: The liberation of *humanity*.

I think that Marx's theory of the realm of necessity and the realm of freedom is not about the specific forms of human history but an insightful revelation of the fundamental nature of social history. It is also an important principle of historical division: The pre-historical societies belong to the realm of necessity while the future communist society, the realm of freedom.

---

85   *Ibid.*, p. 706.
86   *Ibid.*, p. 708.
87   Marx, and Friedrich Engels. *Karl Marx, Friedrich Engels: Collected Works: Karl Marx, 1861-63.* New York: Intl Pub, 1992. p. 493.
88   *Marx, Karl. Grundrisse: Foundations of the Critique of Political Economy (rough draft).* Trans. Martin Nicolaus. London; New York: Penguin, 1993. p. 705.

D. TRANSCENDENCING MATERIAL SUBJUGATION: THE HUMAN EXISTENTIAL STATUS IN THE FUTURE COMMUNIST SOCIETY

In my opinion, I think the most important logical point to explain the phenomenon of 'natural-ness' occurring in specific historical conditions during the socio-historical development is to validate the true meaning of this assumption in that it essentially puts in perspective the capitalist historicality and irrationality so as to explore the inevitable trend of socialism or communism. For Marx, the logical provisions of 'natural-ness' and material-subjugation precisely define the basic difference between the development of socialist society and the historical movement of capitalism, which is also very important and profound for today's theoretical constructions.

It is necessary to confirm that the most significant meaning of Marx's 'natural-ness' and material-subjugation lies in its collective embodiment of the objective logic of historical materialism and the subjective logic of historical dialectics, that is, the dialectical unity of such grand social contradictions as the objective historicality and subjectivity principles, the basic conditions and the dominant elements, man and nature, the individuals and society. It is also a fundamental point of Marxist historical materialism. The first two social forms in the pre-historic ages, especially, 'natural-ness' and material-subjugation generated during the capitalist society (the private ownership), rightly expose the temporary and historical nature of the capitalist mode of production and even all the exploitative systems; thus, only socialism (communism as the third great social form) that corresponds with the development of the new productive forces can really start the fresh history of human society. It is here that the development of human history finally ends its pre-historicality and thoroughly eliminates 'natural-ness'; hence, man completely escapes the animal domain (including the economic animal or the economic man), and steps into the period of the true historical advancement of "Man": The realm of freedom for the social history.

As for this point, the traditional philosophical interpretation has a generalization of Marx's idea of 'natural-ness' in a certain historical period into a law of human history as if our social development is forever a "process of natural history," which has indeed been proved a mistake. In addition, it is once criticized by Marx in the statement that "the error is only that the material law of a definite historical social stage is conceived as an abstract law governing equally all forms of society."[89] Just imagine that if human society was always a process of natural history, we would accept the eternity of the inverted materialization in capitalism and man would be subjugated by the external force forever. How can this idea be Marx's original intention? Moreover, judging from the socialist practice, it is absolutely impossible for the existence of 'natural-ness' and material-subjugation in the future communist society. Needless to say, the traditional philosophical framework fails to explain Marx's scientific verification of the essence of communism.

Here, it is the *third time* to describe the vision of future communism. The previous discussions are carried out in the *1844 Manuscripts* where communism is still a humanistic theoretical conclusion of subjective values and in *German Ideology* co-authored by Marx and Engels where the scientific view of history is established and communism is transformed from fantasy into science. When Marx confirms 'natural-ness' and material-subjugation in capitalism and even all the pre-historical ages, his philosophical thought becomes increasingly comprehensive and mature. In my view, communism is the *practical foothold* of Marx's *revolutionary, critical* historical dialectics.

If we proceed with the scientific thought of historical materialism, it is clear that in the ancient times when the social productive forces are on a very low level of development, the human history is fundamentally a part of the history of nature. With the economic improvement and the productive forces developing to a certain level, material production protrudes and departs from the production of human beings. It then takes control of the socio-historical development and makes man once again a slave to the economic power. As a result, history is presented in a blind, non-subjective status, similar to that of the natural development. However, the economic society is not equivalent to the general form of social history. It is but a specific stage of human history. Therefore, the control of the economic necessity over man, that 'natural-ness' of historical development is only a temporary phenomenon. When the productive forces are developed and the production of human beings themselves is re-raised to the dominant status, the controlling role of the economic power over man no longer exists. In other words, with the end of human's prehistory, the phenomenon of 'natural-ness' and the status of material-subjugation are certain to be surpassed. Therefore, the human history in its real sense cannot begin until the end of the pre-historical periods (the "past history", in Marx's words), which is a critical step from the realm of necessity, both of the natural

---

89   Marx, Karl. *Theories of Surplus Value, Volume 1*. London: Lawrence & Wishart, 1969. p. 44.

necessity and the economic necessity, to the realm of freedom where human society freely develops. Its destination is, of course, communism!

As we know, the phenomenon of 'natural-ness' presented in pre-historical societies, especially, the capitalist society, is replaced by Marx's expectation of the future. In his eyes, capitalism is indeed once the advanced mode of production that significantly improves the productive forces by destroying all the local development and the worship of nature, "tearing down all the barriers which hem in the development of the forces of production, the expansion of needs, the all-sided development of production, and the exploitation and exchange of natural and mental forces."[90] Nevertheless, it "encounters barriers in its own nature, which will, at a certain stage of its development, allow it to be recognized as being itself the greatest barrier to this tendency, and hence will drive towards its own suspension."[91]

> **These barriers to production based on capital are even more strongly inherent in the earlier modes of production, in so far as they rest on exchange. But they do not form a law of production pure and simple; [and,] as soon as exchange value no longer forms a barrier to material production, as soon as its barrier is rather posited by the total development of the individual, the whole story with its spasms and convulsions is left behind.[92]**

Human society is to embrace a fresh historical period and bid farewell to the days of poverty, the times of ignorance and all the old forms. "A new mode of production, which is founded not on the development of the forces of production for the purpose of reproducing or at most expanding a given condition, but where the free, unobstructed, progressive and universal development of the forces of production is itself the presupposition of society and hence of its reproduction; where advance beyond the point of departure is the only presupposition."[93]

According to Marx's diagnosis, "the point of bourgeois society is precisely that, a priori, no conscious social regulation of production takes place. What is reasonable and necessary by nature asserts itself only as a blindly operating average."[94] There will be a planned and purposeful production by the subject in the future society to put "an end to the constant anarchy and

---

90   Marx, Karl. *Grundrisse: Foundations of the Critique of Political Economy (rough draft)*. Trans. Martin Nicolaus. London; New York: Penguin, 1993. p. 410.
91   *Ibid.*, p. 410.
92   *Ibid.*, p. 623.
93   *Ibid.*, p. 540.
94   Marx, and Friedrich Engels. *Karl Marx, Friedrich Engels: Collected Works*. New York: International Publishers, 1975. p. 69.

periodical convulsions which are the fatality of capitalist production."[95] Hence, the previous "*all-round* dependence, this natural form of the world-historical co-operation of individuals, will be transformed by this communist revolution into the control and conscious mastery of these powers, which, born of the action of men on one another, have till now overawed and governed men as powers completely alien to them."[96] In other words, once the original economic power as the major element of domination and oppression in capitalism is controlled, its material-subjugation nature will be eliminated and it will become the subject's independent power as his own unification. Marx also comments, "In Communist society, accumulated labour is, but a means to widen, to enrich, to promote the existence of the labourer."[97]

Obviously, Marx would never regard communism as a process of natural history independent of man's operation; instead, in his eyes, it is a comprehensively and freely developed society that gets rid of 'natural-ness' and material-subjugation. And, the natural necessity and the economic necessity disappear; the spontaneous labour in the social process of material production becomes conscious; naturally, society is "organised as a conscious and planned association."[98]

Socialised man, the associated producers, rationally regulating their interchange with Nature, bringing it under their common control, instead of being ruled by it as by the blind forces of Nature; and achieving this with the least expenditure of energy and under conditions most favourable to, and worthy of, their human nature.[99]

Marx points out that the old macro-social process similar to that of the natural movement is turned into a conscious and planned one in the new life while "the planned distribution of labour time among the various branches of production, remains the first economic law on the basis of communal production."[100]

---

95   Marx, Karl. *Karl Marx: A Reader.* Ed. Jon Elster. Cambridge University Press, 1986. p. 291.

96   Marx, and Friedrich Engels. *The German Ideology.* Ed. Christopher John Arthur. New York: International Publishers Co, 1970. p. 55.

97   Marx, Karl. *Karl Marx: A Reader.* Ed. Jon Elster. Cambridge University Press, 1986. p. 261.

98   *Marx, and Friedrich Engels. Collected Works, Volume 37.* London: Lawrence & Wishart, 1998. p. 654.

99   Marx, and Friedrich Engels. *On Literature and Art.* Moscow: Progress Publishers, 1976. p. 183.

100   Marx, Karl. G*rundrisse: Foundations of the Critique of Political Economy (rough draft).* Trans. Martin Nicolaus. London; New York: Penguin, 1993. p. 173.

"In place of the old bourgeois society, with its classes and class antagonisms, we shall have an association, in which the free development of each is the condition for the free development of all."[101] This is "a higher form of society, a society in which the full and free development of every individual forms the ruling principle."[102] According to Marx's vision of communism, the real alternative to the system of alienated labour ownership in capitalism can only be the system of the associated, social individuals. It is "a community of free individuals, carrying on their work with the means of production in common, in which the labour power of all the different individuals is consciously applied as the combined labour power of the community."[103] Here, there is the Man in its real sense for the first time, the "free individuality, based on the universal development of individuals and on their subordination of their communal, social productivity as their social wealth"[104] as well as the "universally developed individuals, whose social relations, as their own communal [gemeinschaftlich] relations."[105] It is the true liberation of the human subject.

Thus, only in the future communist society can people obtain their *real, historical dominance*; only with a general base of highly developed productive forces and under the condition of understanding and utilizing the objective laws can man become the *real creator and master* of social history. It is, in my opinion, nothing else but the *historical essence* of the communist movement for a critical feature of communism as the *realistic* achievement of man's subjective status, which is the *advance beyond* the socio-historical 'natural-ness' and material-subjugation.

I would like to stress that the realization of communism, or the transcendence of historical 'natural-ness' and material-subjugation, is never a mere political transformation; it mostly reflects the highly developed productive forces.

According to Marx, communism is not preconditioned by a general political liberation from the social systems but by the liberation of the productive forces of the human subjects. We cannot do away with the capitalists only politically because they are just the personification of the economic power. "Except as personified capital, the capitalist has no historical

---

101   Marx, Karl. *Karl Marx: A Reader.* Ed. Jon Elster. Cambridge University Press, 1986. p. 266.
102   Marx, Karl. *Capital: A Critique of Political Economy: The Process of Capitalist Production.* New York: Cosimo, Inc., 2007. p. 649.
103   Marx, Karl. *Karl Marx: A Reader.* Ed. Jon Elster. Cambridge University Press, 1986. p. 70.
104   *Ibid.,* p. 149.
105   Marx, Karl. *Grundrisse: Foundations of the Critique of Political Economy (rough draft).* Trans. Martin Nicolaus. London; New York: Penguin, 1993. p. 162.

value."[106] In capitalism, "he is but one of the wheels."[107] It is more important for the human subject to increase the productive forces to eliminate material-subjugation in the process of material development. This is the way to achieve full liberation and free advancement of human beings, misunderstanding of which also accounts for the later detours of the practice of socialism in reality.

As analyzed above, in the early time of Marx's establishment of historical materialism, the key point of turning socialism from an Utopian thought to a scientific theory is transforming the idealized "ought" to the "is," the real material production. For example, in the "Draft of an Article on Friedrich List's book: *Das Nationale System der Politischen Ökonomie*" written in March, 1845, Marx abandons the old thought that begins from a theoretical logic. He stresses "the abolition of the material and social conditions in which mankind has had to develop its abilities as a slave"[108], and emphasizes "the abolition of private property has become possible only as a result of labour itself, that is to say, has become possible as a result of the material activity of society."[109] The view gets more distinct since the scientific view of history is created.

Marx's comment is brilliant. He says, "Communism differs from all previous movements in that it overturns the basis of all earlier relations of production and intercourse, and for the first time consciously treats all natural premises as the creatures of hitherto existing men, strips them of their natural character and subjugates them to the power of the united individuals."[110] He believes that the establishment of communism is, in essence, an economic practice because it is based on the prerequisite material conditions generated with the development of the productive forces, which also means the socio-historical 'natural-ness' and material-subjugation "cannot be dispelled by dismissing the general idea of it from one's mind, but can only be abolished by the individuals again subjecting these material powers to themselves."[111] That is to say, the eradication of the specific historical phenomenon (like "alienation") in which man is subjugated

---

106 Marx, Karl. *Capital: A Critique of Political Economy: The Process of Capitalist Production.* New York: Cosimo, Inc., 2007. p. 648.
107 *Ibid.,* p. 649.
108 Marx, and Friedrich Engels. *Marx and Engels Collected Works 1844-45.* New York: International Publishers, 1975. p. 281.
109 *Ibid.,* p. 279.
110 Marx, and Friedrich Engels. *The German Ideology.* Ed. Christopher John Arthur. New York: International Publishers Co, 1970. p. 86.
111 *Ibid.,* p. 83.

to the external object can only be achieved after he owns the real premise brought up by the development of the material production, the premise of the tremendous growth of the productive forces. Hence, "we call communism the real movement which abolishes the present state of things. The conditions of this movement result from the premises now in existence."[112] "In a real community the individuals obtain their freedom in and through their association."[113] For that association, industries should create necessary means to realize this new economy; first of all, it means the highly developed productive forces. "Without these conditions a communal economy would not in itself form a new productive force; lacking any material basis and resting on a purely theoretical foundation, it would be a mere freak and would end in nothing more than a monastic economy."[114]

Therefore, communism can neither be simply understood and illustrated as nor be distorted into an abstract egalitarianism in the backward condition of material production. It is of far-reaching significance for China's socialist practice today.

112   Marx, and Friedrich Engels. *Feuerbach–Opposition of the Materialist and Idealist Outlooks.* London: Lawrence and Wishart, 1973. p. 40.
113   Marx, and Friedrich Engels. *The German Ideology.* Ed. Christopher John Arthur. New York: International Publishers Co, 1970. p. 83.
114   *Ibid.,* p. 50.

CHAPTER V

ENGELS AND THE SOCIO-HISTORICAL DIALECTICS

1 *Man and Nature in the Eyes of the Young Engels*
2 *The Only Perspective to Observe the World: Social Practice*
3 *'Natural-ness', Material-Subjugation and the Independent Activities of Human Practice*
4 *Reinterpretation of the "Resultant Forces" Doctrine of Engels' Socio-Historical Vision*

CHAPTER FIVE

INTRODUCTION

It is especially important to confirm Engels' academic status for the whole research of the history of Marxism today. First, since the beginning of the 20th century, a few "Marxian" and "Western Marxist" scholars have always, intentionally or not, belittled or distorted Engels, in particular, his thought of the development of social history. In their eyes, Engels is simplified as an "objective naturalist" opposite to the "humanistic" Marx, or misrepresented as an old mechanical materialist negligent of man's leading role in social history. Second, it results from the deep logical error in the traditional interpretation of historical materialism that abstracts the socio-historical process into an eternal non-subjective natural history independent of man's will. This theoretical error just echoes the criticism of Engels by the Western scholars. For the reason above, we have to take a serious re-examination of the real logical process and the theoretical meaning of Engels' thought of social and historical development as well as its innate association with Marx's historical dialectics.

I. MAN AND NATURE IN THE EYES OF THE YOUNG ENGELS

Ideal is the spark to light the colourful lamp of youth. Like Marx, the Young Engels was idealistic and enthusiastic. His romantic attempt in literature was as impressive as his exciting effort in daily life. To be exact, he did not start from an exact natural scientist. In my opinion, the early rebel against the theological context by the Young Engels makes a humanistic and liberal soldier out of him. His drop out of school offers the opportunity to get more close contact with the major body of social life, the real creators of social history: the working people. Obviously, it is with the humanistic cry of democratism and the strong demand for the recovery of man's subjective status in history that Engels starts his theoretical career. In that initial stage, his thought beats with the impulse of the social reality, different from Marx's gushing fountain of philosophical ideas. But he also sings high praise of man, the subjective spirit and the enthusiastic attitude towards life. He regards the existence of man as the transcendence of nature. At this point, his early discourse of subjective dialectics is not unlike that of Marx.

A. "NIRVANA PHOENIX"

In contrast to the warm and democratic family environment that the Young Marx enjoyed, Engels was born in a conservative religious family. For him, childhood was not a beautiful fairy tale but the first meeting of hard life. The repressive family atmosphere combined with the poisoning of school education always depressed him. However, the suffering tempered his ideal. He made full use of the school learning, laid a solid foundation for his further development, and finally stepped onto the free and democratic road contrary to the general religious preaches.

In a similar way, the Young Engels loved literature very much. His free passion, proud heart and the will to esteem the subjective initiative were evident in the poems. For example, he wrote "On the Invention of Printing," in which he gave his freedom a pair of wings to fly high in the sky.

> And, with almighty voice,
> Called out to all the World: Mankind is free!
> And narrow boundaries no longer caged
> The sacred call: it rose up on the wing
> Of the great echo Gutenberg invented,
> Soared up, a wondrous thing,
> And swift, in mighty inspiration,

O'erleapt the mountains and the ocean wide
And o'er the very winds held domination.
It was not shouted down by Tyranny,
And loud and lusty rang on every side
The joyful cry of Reason: Man is free!
Oh, free, yes, free! Sweetest of words, the breast
Swells, beating faster at the sound of you;
My spirit, that you imbue,
O'erbrimming with your holy inspiration,
Soars to serene celestial dominions,
Bearing me on its fiery beating pinions.
Where are you all that hear
My singing, mortal beings? From on high,
I see the awesome prison doors of Fate
Open, the impenetrable veil of Time
Is torn apart – the Future lies before me![1]

Engel's pursuit of human freedom is prominent between the lines. In addition, he openly expresses his determination and confidence in opposing the feudal autocracy. Another poem of his, "An Evening" fully demonstrates his intention.

New wine shall fill your glasses to the brim,
Pure Freedom wine 's intoxicating brew:
Not the unwary senses to bedim,
But jaded senses to exchange for new,
That with revived perception you may hear
The spheres in heaven singing high and low;
That the blood coursing through your veins may clear,
Transformed into pure Aether, which flows through
The Infinities; that your eye-beams may spear
Primordial Space, like warriors bold that go[2]

Here, Engels' writing is in "the modern style with its proudly soaring rockets of enthusiasm which at their highest point dissolve in a gaily colored shower of poetical fire or burst in crackling sparks of wit."[3] Indeed, the bright intellectual sparks dance in the literary sky, creating a never-fading scene and an eternal legend. Literature is the study of human beings. With it, Engels displays the *subjective creativity* that can "storm the starry summits without fear."

---

1   Marx, and Friedrich Engels. *Collected Works*. London: Lawrence & Wishart, 1975. p. 60.
2   *Ibid.*, p. 110.
3   Marx, and Friedrich Engels. *Collected Works*. New York: International Publishers, 1975. p. 81.

For the same reason, Engels was deeply fascinated by Hegel's philosophy. The young man described his fervent feeling of the philosophical charm in the following words, "when for the first time the divine idea of the last of the philosophers [probably Hegel] this most colossal creation of the thought of the nineteenth century, dawned upon me, I experienced the same blissful thrill, it was like a breath of fresh sea air blowing down upon me from the purest sky; the depths of speculation lay before me like the un-fathomable sea from which one cannot turn one's eyes straining to see the ground below."[4] It is clear that after Engels has become a Young Hegelian warrior, his logical emphasis on the subjective initiative is both deepened and widened by a speculation of subjective dialectics. Like Marx, he op-poses the conservative part in Hegel's philosophy and concludes as a demo-cratic fighter: "There is nothing new under the sun!" In his eyes, whether it is "the feudalism," "the absolutism" or "the pietism," "they all disintegrate in conflict with one another and under the adamantine foot of the forward moving time."[5] He cries out, "I would rather have the surging ocean with its grand freedom than the narrow inland lake with its quiet surface, whose miniature waves are broken every three steps by a spit of land, the root of a tree, or a stone."[6] Then, he is in strong opposition to the belief that "as if human beings could thus be tied to the soil for all eternity."[7]

He gives high praise to the struggle of the Young Hegelians: "All the ba-sic principles of Christianity, and even of what has hitherto been called religion itself, have fallen before the inexorable criticism of reason, the absolute idea claims to be the founder of a new era."[8] It is practically a political struggle for the freedom of the human subject. Frankly, Engels writes, "And if we were to give up the spirit and its freedom, we should be denying ourselves, we should be betraying our most sacred possession, we should be murdering our own living strength."[9] "Man is born free, he is free!"[10] It is really a sincere call.

At the same time, the Young Engels pays attention to the general contact between the human subject and nature. In **"Wanderings in Lombardy"** written in 1841, he feels the "resistance of the power of nature to the hu-man spirit" from the labour and survival in the Alpine valley.[11] He calls

---

4   *Ibid.*, p. 99.
5   *Ibid.*, p. 48.
6   *Ibid.*, p. 147.
7   *Ibid.*, p. 147.
8   *Ibid.*, p. 197.
9   *Ibid.*, p. 197.
10 *Ibid.*, p. 456.
11 *Ibid.*, p. 177.

for a thoughtful awakening from nature, believing that "men have been stronger than nature" and his "spirit has conquered nature."[12] Here, the human transformation of the natural objects is regarded as the triumphant return of human subjectivity, the laurel of which unsurprisingly falls onto the "self-consciousness" of the Young Hegelians. The Young Engels passionately writes, "The Idea, the self-consciousness of mankind, is that wonderful phoenix who builds for himself a funeral pyre out of all that is most precious in the world and rises rejuvenated from the flames which destroy an old time."[13] Engels remains under the influence of the Young Hegelian School until around 1842. He stresses the human initiative, especially the spiritual activities but *denounces the human impulsion of material interests*. In his eyes, "the so-called material interests can never operate in history as independent, guiding aims."[14] It rightly shows that the Young Engels is to seek the *dominant elements* of the development of history, which is, of course, the spirit and reason of that time.

Clearly, the Young Engels starts with a different theoretical exploration from that of the Young Marx. Firstly, he does not form a *logical discourse* based on a philosophical system but simply accepts the democratic philosophy of the young Hegelians due to the impact in real life. In other words, during his early period, he does not have a consistent philosophical view of the outside world. Therefore, his later logical conversion is not such a difficult struggle as that of Marx. Secondly, judging from his initial development of thought, Engels' major tendency towards the human subject's initiative basically corresponds to that of Marx; both of them posit the subject *beyond nature and the external object*, although it is still within the domain of the Hegelian philosophy.

B. SEIZURE OF THE "HISTORICAL INITIATIVE"

Like Marx, the first philosophical change of Engels took place in the struggles of real life. In 1843, his political stance shifted from democratism to communism (not in a real scientific sense but tainted with a strong humanistic colour, similar to Marx at that time). In his opinion, "communism, however, was such a necessary consequence of New Hegelian philosophy."[15] Engels argues that communism is the "conclusion" of Europe. "The English came to the conclusion practically, by the rapid

---

12 *Ibid.*, p. 176.
13 *Ibid.*, p. 239.
14 *Ibid.*, p. 371.
15 Marx, and Friedrich Engels. *Collected Works, Volume 3*. London: Lawrence and Wishart, 1975. p. 406.

increase of misery, demoralisation, and pauperism in their own country: the French politically, by first asking for political liberty and equality; and, finding this insufficient, joining social liberty, and social equality to their political claims: the Germans became Communists philosophically, by reasoning upon first principles."[16] At this point, Engels' communism is "founded upon sound philosophical principles."[17]

In his view, "either all the philosophical efforts of the German nation, from Kant to Hegel, have been useless – worse than useless; or, that they must end in Communism; that the Germans must either reject their great philosophers, whose names they hold up as the glory of their nation, or that they must adopt Communism."[18] He also admits that his communist principles are received "from a system of philosophy embracing every part of human knowledge."[19]

His philosophical perspective also turns to Feuerbach's *natural* material-ism that worships human nature. This new theoretical tendency is shown in the *Outlines of a Critique of Political Economy* and the *Condition of the Working Class in England* in 1844. To my discovery, across Engels' basic thought, there is a natural inclination of perceiving from the objective reality and the proletarians, which just accords with the general principle of materialism. However, at this time, Engels still focuses on the discov-ery of the *dominant elements* of historical development. It is also achieved through Feuerbach's humanism.

Engels no longer holds to the self-consciousness esteemed by the Young Hegelians while "man" becomes the logical pivot. From a new theoretical perspective, he takes a serious materialist critique of the bourgeois eco-nomics. In his opinion, it essentially serves the interests of the bourgeoisie with property as the theoretical premise. And it has the "same hypocrisy, inconsistency and immorality which now confront free humanity in every sphere."[20] From a philosophical point of view, the logic "did not attack the Christian contempt for and humiliation of Man, and merely posited Nature instead of the Christian God as the Absolute confronting Man."[21]

---

16   *Ibid.*, p. 393.
17   *Ibid.*, p. 406.
18   *Ibid.*, p. 406.
19   Marx, and Friedrich Engels. *Collected Works.* New York: International Publishers, 1975. p. 407.
20   Marx, and Friedrich Engels. *The Economic and Philosophic Manuscripts of 1844 and the Communist Manifesto.* Buffalo, N.Y.: Prometheus Books, 1988. p. 173.
21   Marx, and Friedrich Engels. *Collected Works.* New York: International Publishers, 1975. p. 419.

The Young Engels finds that the so-called free trade and competition are enhanced because they do "not resolve the great antithesis which has been the concern of history from the beginning and whose development constitutes history, the antithesis of substance and subject, nature and mind, necessity and freedom." [22]This fierce struggle of winning the "historical initiative" aims at recovering the *dominant* status that the human subject *deserves*. Now, there is a slight difference in that the major role is no longer played by the abstract nature and spirit, nor by the separation of man and nature as the factor of production, but by the fact that man's activities are split into a new contradictory pair of *labour and capital*. Capital, the original result of the labour activities, becomes the premise and the controlling thing now. In the capitalist economy, human activities demonstrate an "unconscious condition," in which man is dominated by "material" (the materialized world of commodities).

Engels' conclusion is very profound: "It is certainly a natural law based on the unconsciousness of the participants."[23] This law is purely a law of nature and not a law of the mind. Here we can see, the Young Engels' *idea that the specific historical development of human society (capitalism) has something similar to the natural movement is formed before Marx.*

Next, Engels abandons the general subjective transcendence of nature and turns to the essential condition of man: Labour is the major aspect of production and the "free human activity" in the ontological sense. However, the subjective essence is alienated and man loses his status that he *should have owned*. The inverted non-subjective condition culminates in capitalism at present. For Engels, the periods prior to capitalism, like antiquity, know "nothing of the rights of the individual" and the "whole outlook" is "essentially abstract, universal and material." [24]By "material," Engels refers to nature. He even suggests that the ancient society does not belong to social history because human beings have not established their subjectivity at that time. Later, capitalism admits human subjectivity, which is only expressed in an abstract and "biased" way. Indeed, capitalism eliminates the feudal system and "the apparent acknowledgment of reason, and hence really the culmination of unreason," only makes "it more inhuman and more universal."[25] According to Engels, the property-based society holds high the banner of self-interest; the economic power in pursuit of benefits becomes the dominant factor of history, controlling and enslaving people,

22 *Ibid.*, p. 471.
23 *Ibid.*, p. 434.
24 *Ibid.*, p. 475.
25 *Ibid.*, p. 475.

which is, essentially, the subjugation of man by the non-human wealth. People are isolated and transformed "into a collection of mutually repelling atoms"[26] with the subject of a class essentially lost. Thus, human beings become the slaves of *things*, which is no longer natural but an artificial economic power created by people themselves, the money or property. The Young Engels points out that man seemingly creates an economic life that is different from nature but it only leads to a deeper loss of his original subjectivity by that objective force in-itself (the "invisible hand").

C. THE CLAIM FOR THE MEANING OF HISTORY

The Young Engels cries for the restoration of the human nature and the reclaiming of the meaning of history, which just indicates that people in the capitalist society generate a huge reality of economy. Although it is the realization of the human subjects, *they further lose themselves in that artificial material world.* Engels requires us to penetrate the fascinating illusion, reflect the subjective alienation, and re-understand the world with the humanistic logical scale.

He says, "We have no need, in order to see the splendour of the human character, in order to recognise the development of the human species through history, its irresistible progress, its ever certain victory over the unreason of the individual, its overcoming of all that is apparently supernatural, its hard but successful struggle against nature until the final achievement of free, human self-consciousness, the discernment of the unity of man and nature, and the independent creation – voluntarily and by its own effort – of a new world based on purely human and moral social relationships."[27] For that end, "man has only to understand himself, to take himself as the measure of all aspects of life, to judge according to his being, to organise the world in a truly human manner according to the demands of his own nature."[28] Only in this way can we truly eliminate alienation to regain our humanity and nature. It also constitutes Engels' theoretical base to criticize capitalism at that time.

Obviously, Engels takes a humanistic perspective to analyze history; his emphasis on human subjectivity is still *abstract and transcendental*; his illustration of the contradictory movement of historical subject and object is a humanistic *subjective dialectics* and *axiology*, an unscientific discourse, which lacks the theoretical integrity and completeness of the contemporary

---

26   *Ibid.*, p. 475.
27   *Ibid.*, p. 464.
28   *Ibid.*, p. 464.

Marx. Therefore, we cannot say that Engels' overall philosophical framework is scientific at that time. In my opinion, the Young Engels' subjective dialectics is actually not *completely humanistic* and his social criticism is at most a teleological drive of humanism instead of a socio-historical view of alienation with finished logical components because Engels offers neither the specific definition of the species being of man, like Marx's labour, nor a profound confirmation of the subject's alienation. Hence, Engels does not have a systematic *framework of the humanistic view of alienation*, which is his clear difference from Marx. His later development from the subjective dialectics to the new worldview seems quite spontaneous.

Here, we also notice that some new *logical points* already emerge in Engels' theoretical effort. For instance, he notices that industry is the driving force behind all social development and the industrial revolution lays the foundation for various social relations, which is very *close* to the view of historical materialism. However, he does not further explore the true laws of social and historical development, only taking the social revolution initiated by "industry" as a special point to differentiate the historical progress of England from the perspective of the political revolution of France and the philosophical revolution of Germany.

II. THE ONLY PERSPECTIVE TO OBSERVE THE WORLD: SOCIAL PRACTICE

As noted above, in 1845, Engels and Marx co-founded the scientific materialist worldview based on the historical, real social practice, which was the groundbreaking theory of historical materialism. In their new logical framework, the *German Ideology*, "human beings," or the "human essence," are no longer the starting point; the logic of reason to comment on the external world itself is also deserted; instead, they directly reveal the laws of the material world and the historical process of the human social practice. In this way, Engels and Marx fight side by side, finally transcend Feuerbach's "half-materialism" (the humanistic view of alienation) that is but a hidden idealistic view of history, and obtain a thorough victory over idealism. It should be noted that in their validation of the framework of historical materialism, they attach the same importance to the new special points in the social existence and development brought about by the creative activities (practice) of the human subjects as well as to the direct reflection of the objective process of socio-historical development.

A. CO-ESTABLISHMENT OF SCIENTIFIC WELTANSCHAUUNG BY ENGELS AND MARX

In the new philosophical vision, the only starting point is the historical social practice, which is also the theoretical prism used by Marx and Engels. Therefore, contrary to the criticism by some Western scholars, Engels, the true Marxist, definitely recognizes the leading role of human beings in social history. More importantly, the task is how to restore the present subjectivity hyperbolized by idealism and humanism to its historical, real functionality of practice.

With the new perspective of historical materialism, Engels believes that the determination of social existence over social consciousness indicates not a control of men by general material but that the objective activities and development level of the human subjects are conditioned by their subjective activities and abilities. Similarly, historical materialism resolutely rejects the conception of history as heroic determinism and claims that man is the creator and matter of social history. First of all, these basic principles collectively represent an objective stipulation of the general foundation of social history, viz., the logic of the objective description based on the contradictory movement and development of material production. It should be admitted that the focus on the general principles of historical materialism and the objective dimension of historical dialectics lasts for a long time in the explanation of Marxist philosophy by Engels and Marx. It is determined by the contemporary condition when the new worldview is established, that is, to oppose the idealistic premise for the view of history. Engels later says, "We had to emphasise the main principle vis-á-vis our adversaries, who denied it."[29]

However, on the other side, we must understand that the revolutionary critique by Marx and Engels clearly seeks the dominant status of the human subject from the initiative practice and starts with the subjective dimension of historical dialectics in their new worldview.

For a long time, some Western scholars degrade Marxism into an abstract historical determinism or a mechanical materialism. They are not totally wrong if the criticism is put against some theorists in the Second International or the old dogmatic illustration. However, it is quite ridiculous if they take it to deny the whole doctrine of Marxism. Their target is not real Marxism itself. I have repeatedly pointed out that many Western

---

29   Marx, and Friedrich Engels. *Karl Marx and Friedrich Engels: Selected Works in One Volume.* New York: International Publishers, 1968. p. 693.

Marxian researchers notice the tendency of weakening the dialectics of practice in Marxism and attempt at its recovery, but they just go to extremes and slip into a new idealistic trap of humanistic subjective philosophy and cultural criticism (See Chapter VI). In particular, they make a non-historical comprehension to attribute that theoretical error to Engels and put it in opposition to a so-called "humanistic" Marx obsessed with the subjective role. As a result, the very idea with fairly reasonable elements is now complicated, being rather chaotic on a higher level. This unexpected and unfortunate change needs our special vigilance. Since this book is not on a specific definition of this issue, a general explanation of Engels' historical dialectics about socio-historical development will be discussed here for an indirect validation of it.

The criticism against Engels by some Marxian and Western Marxist scholars is focused on his inattention to man's role of initiative in creating social history and changing nature, on his "advocacy" of the objective law outside human beings, like the dialectics of nature noumenon, while neglecting the practical nature of the subject in human history concerned by Marx, like the historical dialectics of interactive subject and object. That accusation is not fair. Although Engels does differ from Marx in theoretical logics, their general direction and essential points are basically the same. As we know, the early Engels attaches great importance to the subjectivity and initiative role, first the spiritual transcendence and later the initiative nature of man. Is it possible that his thought has a complete reversal after his new philosophical achievement? Does he throw out the baby of human initiative with the bath water of idealistic disturbance? After a careful analysis, I really doubt that conclusion. In fact, what Engels surpasses in his conversion of thought is the speculative subjective dialectics. He does not ignore the dominant historical status of human beings in social development but re-examines it on the subjective dimension of historical materialism and objective historical dialectics. Why? We shall soon see the all the proofs.

B. "THE NATURAL LAW" GRADUALLY BECOMES THE HISTORICAL LAW

As a co-founder of Marxist practical materialism, Engels cooperated with Marx in the writing of *German Ideology* in 1945. In the 1880s when Marx finished *Theses on Feuerbach*, Engels called the new worldview a genius outline. Meanwhile, as to Marx's *Das Kapital* and other economic works on 'natural-ness', material-subjugation and fetishism, Engels also showed his clear and affirmative attitude. It is thus hard to draw the conclusion that Engels generally goes in the opposite direction of Marx. Is it possible for him to propose a new logic in his later works, then? Let us first pay attention to his two independent works: *Anti-Dühring* and the *Dialectics of Nature*. At the same time, we shall analyze his most attacked aspect, the philosophical perspective of observing nature.

Engels illustrates his philosophical validation based on natural science. It seems inclined towards over-emphasizing the external natural law-*in-itself* during his argumentation, which also accounts for one of the major critical points by the Western scholars. However, it is not difficult to discover some important theoretical demarcations here after careful examination. First, we must make sure of Engels' starting point in his research of the natural object: Is it the original nature or man's nature mediated by practice? In my opinion, Engels' reference can be roughly identified with the nature changed by man's activities mentioned in the *German Ideology*. He is in clear opposition to the naturalistic conception that "as if nature exclusively reacts on man, and natural conditions everywhere exclusively determined his historical development, is therefore one-sided and forgets that man also reacts on nature, changing it and creating new conditions of existence for himself."[30] "There is devilishly little left of 'nature'"[31] before the subjective practice. In addition, Engels explains the foundation for a correct observation of nature.

Natural science, like philosophy, has hitherto entirely neglected the in influence of activity on their thought; both know only nature on the one hand and thought on the other. But it is precisely the alteration of nature by men, not solely nature as such, which is most essential and immediate basis of human thought.[32]

Obviously, as for the relationship between man and nature, the basic point for Engels' observation is neither the nature-in-itself in the old materialist view nor the abstract subjective consciousness but the practice of the human subject, especially, the *change of the natural object per se initiated by man's subjective activities.*

Even in his study of nature from a scientific perspective, Engels does not regard the "natural laws" as some external laws-in-themselves but makes a profound discovery of the historical sense and the projection of subjective practice in the scientific mapping of the world. In his opinion, "the

---

30 Engels, Friedrich. *Dialectics of Nature*. Moscow: Foreign Languages Pub. House, 1954. p. 306.
31 *Ibid.*, p. 306.
32 *Ibid.*, p. 306.

eternal laws of nature also become transformed more and more into histori-cal ones"[33] because "their imagined rigidity and absolute validity have been introduced into nature only by our reflective minds."[34] Engels' reflection originates from the historical practice of the human subject, "the alteration of nature by men."[35]

Engels points out:

Man alone has succeeded in impressing his stamp on nature, not only by shifting the plant and animal world from one place to another, but also by so altering the aspect and climate of his dwelling place, and even the plants and animals themselves, that the consequences of his activity can disappear only with the general extinction of the terrestrial globe.[36]

Undoubtedly, contrary to the distortion of some Western scholars, Engels is very concerned about role of man's *practical initiative* in nature. For him, animals merely change nature during their survival while man makes nature serve his own purpose via his activities so that nature is dominated by him, which makes the fundamental difference between man with ini-tiatives and the passive animals. Here, Engels' intention is to criticize the one-sided mechanical naturalism.

C. THE EXCLUSIVE GEOCENTRIC PROSPECT OF NATURE

Engels also says that our observation of nature is based on the real, spe-cific practice of the human subjects. Consequently, "we can only know under the conditions of our epoch and *as far as these allow.*"[37] Thus, with the improved functionality of practice, man can continually construct the historical and natural prospect of the world. Such a dynamic, historical perception constitutes the core of the dialectical view of nature.

Engels once employs the establishment of a causal concept to make an ex-planation. In his analysis, our validation of the external natural laws is not a direct reflection of the old materialist, whose "outlook on nature means nothing more than the simple conception of nature just as it is, without al-ien addition."[38] For a Marxist scientific view, "the proof of necessity lies in

---

33   *Ibid.*, p. 315.
34   Engels, Friedrich. *Anti-Dühring: Herr Eugen Dühring's Revolution in Science.* Moscow: Foreign Languages Pub. House, 1959. p. 21.
35   Engels, Friedrich. *Dialectics of Nature.* Moscow: Foreign Languages Pub. House, 1954. p. 306.
36   *Ibid.*, p. 47.
37   *Ibid.*, p. 320.
38   Engels, Friedrich. *Society and Revolution: Essays in Honour of Engels.* People's Pub. House, 1971. p. 155.

human activity, in experiment, in work: if I am able to make the post hoc, it becomes identical with the *propter hoc*."[39] That is to say, if I can generate the order between things, their causal relations are proved. Engels goes on to explain that we first see the mutual association and constraint between the individuals during our observation of the moving objects. However, we immediately discover one motion closely followed by another.

> **We find also that we can evoke a particular motion by setting up, the conditions in which it takes place in nature, that we can even produce motions which do not occur at all in nature (industry), at least not in this way, and that we can give these motions a predetermined direction and extent. *In this way*, by the *activity of human beings* the idea of *causality* becomes established, the idea that one motion is the cause of another.**[40]

It can be seen that we do not directly reflect the relationship of the natural object. Instead, the "laws" and relations in the prospect of nature are but an objective ontological structure mediated by man's practice. They are, simply put, *reflected by the prism of practice*.

Engels also notices that the necessary result of man's observation and the change of nature will generate the n*atural prospect with the axis of the role and result of human practice*, an "exclusively geocentric" prospect of nature. He points out that "our whole official physics, chemistry, and biology are exclusively geocentric, calculated only for the earth."[41] Here, by "exclusive geocentric," it means all our subjective practice happens on earth, the result in a certain condition that possesses no *universality* but an ad hoc meaning to the whole domain of the universe. The consequence of our practice here will not necessarily appear on other material levels. It is very similar to the modern theory of "anthropic principle."

Now we see that Engels' historical dialectical view of nature based on practice is essentially different from the mechanical dialectics of natural noumenon in the eyes of some Western scholars. It is nothing but the important foundation for Engels to further validate the development of nature and society.

---

39   Engels, Clemens Dutt and John B S Haldane. *Dialectics of Nature*. London: Lawrence & Wishart, 1941. p.230.
40   *Ibid.*, p. 171.
41   Engels, Friedrich. *Dialectics of Nature*. Moscow: Foreign Languages Pub. House, 1954. p. 316.

III. 'NATURAL-NESS', MATERIAL-SUBJUGATION AND THE INDEPENDENT ACTIVITIES OF HUMAN PRACTICE

Some may argue that Engels' major error lies in his application of the natural laws into the social development, leading to his ignorance of the subjective status in social history even the above explanation is correct. In my opinion, it is still an untenable accusation. As noted earlier, the Young Engels highly values the subjective role from the very beginning. After the birth of Marxism, this logical intention of him does not alter but obtains a solid scientific foundation, which is not only conveyed in his general view of history but is more collectively expressed during his explanatory process of the whole development of socio-historical dialectics. Moreover, Engels' view is consistent with Marx's 'natural-ness' and material-subjugation.

A. SIMILARITIES AND DIFFERENCES BETWEEN THE DEVELOPMENT OF SOCIAL HISTORY AND THAT OF NATURAL HISTORY

As analyzed in previous chapters, Marx and Engels co-authored the *Holy Family* and *German Ideology*, in which they took the historical development of man's dynamic practice as the basic perspective to enlighten and check the whole social process, drawing the conclusion that "history is *nothing but* the activity of man pursuing his aims."[42] It means the critical difference between social history and natural history is that the former cannot be separated from human beings to be independently operated by itself. Society is created by the initiatives of man's practice. At the same time, Marx and Engels also observe within the coordinates of history that under certain conditions the development of social history can mutate into a blind movement similar to that of nature. People create history but fall down before the external power in the real social process, first as slaves of nature and later as the subjects of the economic material world. Marx and Engels get to the core of the matter by saying that "this consolidation of what we ourselves produce into an objective power above us, growing out of our control, thwarting our expectations, bringing to naught our calculations, is one of the chief factors in historical development up till now."[43] The status of subjective loss is only a particular pre-historical phenomenon, after which, human beings can enter the independent development of the

---

42   Marx, and Friedrich Engels. *The Holy Family, or, Critique of Critical Critique*. Moscow: Foreign Languages Publishing House, 1956. p. 125.
43   Marx, and Friedrich Engels. *The German Ideology*. Ed. Christopher John Arthur. New York: International Publishers Co, 1970. p. 53.

realm of freedom from this passive realm of necessity. At that time, history will open a new chapter; the initiative role of humans will be brought into full play; social history can truly reflect man's own will.

Engels is not only in accord with Marx's thought in the early time but also sticks to the *logic of initiatives in the subjective dimension of historical dialectics* in Marx's practical materialism, like in the works of *Anti-Dühring, The Dialectics of Nature* and *Ludwig Feuerbach and the End of Classical German Philosophy*. In some respects, he even expands and deepens Marx's thought.

As in *Ludwig Feuerbach and the End of Classical German Philosophy*, Engels says, "In one point, however, the history of the development of society proves to be essentially different from that of nature. In nature – in so far as we ignore man's reaction upon nature – there are only blind, unconscious agencies acting upon one another, out of whose interplay the general law comes into operation." However, "the history of the development of society endowed with consciousness, are men acting with deliberation or passion, working towards definite goals; nothing happens without a conscious purpose, without an intended aim." It forms the most fundamental difference between social history and natural history. In a clear way, Engels opposes that error of special historical point sliding into idealism (the view of will-drive); he proposes that the process of history is governed by the innate general laws. Here, we are close to the brink of the traditional framework of philosophical illustration, which often runs this way: The misguided historical idealism goes from man's will and motivation in social life to the negation of the objective socio-historical process; therefore, historical materialism is to discover the objective laws "independent of man's will," or more precisely, "independent of the individual will" in social history. To validate the above point, Marx's statement in the preface of *Das Kapital* becomes an important *logical misunderstanding*: Social history is also a non-subjective historical process, for which, the French philosopher Louis Althusser makes a worse structuralist footnote of the "process without a subjective."

At first sight, that explanation from Louis Althusser seems to have no problem. However, it only stops on the primary understanding of Engels' statement about that important point of historical materialism. In fact, Engels has two ascending logical aims during his validation. First, he does refute the error of the idealistic view of "will-drive" and indicate the objectivity and innate necessity of the progressive social history, which is the logic of the objective description based on the *general foundation* of material production in socio-historical existence and development. However, for this proposition of historical materialism, Engels, like Marx, makes another validation on a micro level, that is, to seek the *real dominant elements* in the socio-historical development on the subjective dimension of historical dialectics. It is on that specific logical dimension that he analyzes the specific forms under different historical conditions.

That which is willed happens but rarely; in the majority of instances the numerous desired ends cross and conflict with one another... thus the conflicts of innumerable individual wills and individual actions in the domain of history produce a state of affairs entirely analogous to that prevailing in the realm of unconscious nature.[44]

Social history appears to be subject to contingency; in fact, behind those individual thoughts and drives, there exist "the real ultimate driving forces of history"[45], that is, the innate necessity presented as social forces, for instance, the class struggles in class societies. In other words, under certain historical conditions, people cannot obtain an independent perception of the objective laws of social development. These laws often take the external form separated from men, like the "invisible hand," and blaze a trail among numerous contingencies. As a result, they present a peculiar *'natural-ness'*, in the words of Engels, "a state of affairs entirely analogous to that prevailing in the realm of unconscious nature."[46] However, Engels does not consider 'natural-ness' as a general condition of history. He is explaining the *historical* phenomenon in a *negative* sense. The traditional framework of philosophical interpretation stops here, gradually sliding in an affirmative direction to a logical generalization.[47]

Second, there is a profound meaning in Engels' theoretical vision. The phenomenon of 'natural-ness' only occurs in the "pre-historical" period. In the future social development when people truly recognize the objective social laws with their own initiatives, they can scientifically create their social life in a planned, proportionate and independent way. That pre-historical status will disappear; the necessity of socio-historical development will be firmly grasped in the hand of the human subject; the objective necessity will become the innate premise of freedom; and humans will truly achieve

---

44   Marx, and Friedrich Engels. *Karl Marx and Friedrich Engels: Selected Works in One Volume.* New York: International Publishers, 1968. p. 623.
45   Marx, and Friedrich Engels. *On Religion.* Chicago: Scholars Press, 1982. p. 256.
46   Marx, and Friedrich Engels. *Karl Marx and Friedrich Engels: Selected Works in One Volume.* New York: International Publishers, 1968. p. 623.
47   See Wang Jinfu. "Another Discussion on the True Significance of the 'Natural Historical Process' by Marx" in *Journal of Suzhou University.* 3 (1993):16.

the *real dominant elements* in the socio-historical development. In this way, the realm of freedom in human history begins, like a new train going to the distance, spreading waves of rhythmic whistles. This is nothing but the theoretical perspective of the *subjective dimension* of historical dialectics based on practical materialism. Hence, it is safe to conclude that Engels does not eternalize the non-subjective status of social development, in particular, the economic laws of capitalism; on the contrary, he negates that historical condition, looking forward to the beautiful future of the free subjective development: Communism. At that time, the external necessity will no longer dominate people and the laws of social development will not be totally independent of humans. Man recognizes laws, making his own will in agreement with them; history opens a new chapter, being an *independent process of man's conscious creation*. While the past sleeps among the pages of history like a dried leaf mark, the future is buried as a seed in the earth to be awakened in the beautiful spring. Mankind will finally become the master of society, nature and themselves.

B. THE ABNORMAL PHENOMENON OF THE HUMAN SUBJECT DOMINATED BY THE EXTERNAL NECESSITY

In *Anti-Dühring*, Engels rebuts the ridiculous view that the capitalist economic laws are eternal and "natural." In the eyes of the bourgeois philosophers and economists, "the laws of production and exchange discovered by this science were not laws of a historically determined form of those activities, but eternal laws of nature; were deduced from the nature of man."[48] In my view, Engels is in the same position as Marx's "natural laws" of semantic transformation in socio-historical development. He says that in the past production without planning and connections, the economic laws act in *natural forms* above man's control and contrary to their will. By a negative wording of "natural" here, Engels reveals the *anti-human* and *non-subjective* essence of the capitalist production. It will be clearer with further analysis later.

For Engels, in the early development of human society, external nature dominates men's lives and activities and thus they become the servants of nature:

> **As men originally made their exit from the animal world- in the narrower sense of the term- so they made their entry into history: still half animal, brutal, still helpless in face of the forces**

---

48 Engels, Friedrich. *Anti-Dühring: Herr Eugen Dühring's Revolution in Science*. Moscow: Foreign Languages Pub. House, 1959. p. 209.

of nature, still ignorant of their own strength; and consequently as poor as the animals and hardly more productive than they.[49]

This is the *material-subjugation of natural necessity* in early historical development. However, man's dominant status is instead established as for the relationship between people and their own production. Engels says,

> **At all earlier stages of society production was essentially collective, just as consumption proceeded by direct distribution of the products within larger or smaller communistic communities. This collective production was very limited; but inherent in it was the producers' control over their process of production and their product. They knew what became of their product: they consumed it; it did not leave their hands. And so long as production remains on this basis, it cannot grow above the heads of the producers nor raise up incorporeal alien powers against them, as in civilization is always and inevitably the case.**[50]

However, things change with further social development. The journey of humankind extends to a wide and peaceful field with occasional bird chirps in the soft breeze while a storm is lurking not far away. With man's productive capability increasingly improved, the external natural object begins to be subject to human beings who gradually become the master of nature. At the same time, a new material-subjugation is inevitable to occur. **"But it is not long before, side by side with the forces of nature, social forces begin to be active – forces which confront man as equally alien and at first equally inexplicable, dominating him with the same apparent natural necessity as the forces of nature themselves."**[51]

It amounts to Marx's *material-subjugation of the economic necessity*. In the eyes of Engels, "the producers have lost control over the total production within their own spheres, and the merchants have not gained it. Products and production become subjects of chance."[52] People are still controlled by their economic relations, their means of production, just as the alien forces of nature before. "The producers have lost control over their own

---

49   *Ibid.*, 247.

50   Engels, West, and Eleanor Burke Leacock. *The Origin of the Family, Private Property, and the State, in the Light of the Researches of Lewis H. Morgan.* New York: International Publishers Co, 1972. p. 233.

51   Marx, and Friedrich Engels. *On Religion.* Chicago: Scholars Press, 1982. p. 147.

52   Engels, West, and Eleanor Burke Leacock. *The Origin of the Family, Private Property, and the State, in the Light of the Researches of Lewis H. Morgan.* New York: International Publishers Co, 1972. p. 233.

social inter-relations."[53] "Anarchy reigns in socialized production."[54] The special laws of social life "work, despite anarchy, in and through anarchy."[55] Therefore, they are "only like a law of Nature working blindly."[56] It is not the external expression or natural law as explained by Dühring or in the old framework of philosophical illustration. Instead, it is a certain relationship or expression, a law of economic form in a historical sense.

Hence, Engels observes that the human subject seems to return to nature in the capitalist economic life. "Advantages in natural or artificial conditions of production now decide the existence or non-existence of individual capitalists, as well as of whole industries and countries. He that falls is remorselessly cast aside. It is the Darwinian struggle of the individual for existence transferred from Nature to society with intensified violence. The conditions of existence natural to the animal appear as the final term of human development."[57] Engels' view that the socio-historical development contains something similar to nature and his observation of the phenomenon of material-subjugation are almost the same with Marx's theories of 'natural-ness' and material-subjugation. Engels is very clear in saying that "to the everlasting disgrace of modern bourgeois development that it has not yet progressed beyond the economic forms of the animal kingdom. The so-called 'economic laws' are not eternal laws of nature but historical laws that appear and disappear."[58]

In other words, the uncontrollable, unconscious status in socio-historical development should not be a universal law because in reality "the more that human beings become removed from animals in the narrower sense of the word, the more they make their own history consciously, the less becomes the influence of unforeseen effects and uncontrolled forces of this history, and the more accurately does the historical result correspond to the aim laid down in advance."[59] Engels believes that during the development of social production, the "economic laws can assert themselves in a society of private producers: as a blindly operating law of nature inherent

53   Marx, and Friedrich Engels. *Karl Marx and Friedrich Engels: Selected Works in One Volume.* New York: International Publishers, 1968. p. 421.

54   Engels, Friedrich. *Anti-Dühring: Herr Eugen Dühring's Revolution in Science.* Moscow: Foreign Languages Pub. House, 1959. p. 374.

55   *Ibid.,* p. 374.

56   Marx, and Friedrich Engels. *Karl Marx, Friedrich Engels: Marx and Engels Collected Works 1874-83.* New York: International Publishers, 1989. p. 319.

57   Marx, and Friedrich Engels. *Karl Marx and Friedrich Engels: Selected Works in One Volume.* New York: International Publishers, 1968. p. 423.

58   Mishra, Girish. *Malthus and his Ghost.* New Delhi: Manak Publications, 2001. p. 152.

59   Marx, and Friedrich Engels. *On Religion.* Chicago: Scholars Press, 1982. p. 168.

in things and relations, and independent of the will or actions of the producers."[60] The artificial material forces dominate the whole process of capitalist society, always "at work in spite of us, in opposition to us, so long they master us."[61] Engels also perceives that abnormal social phenomenon in his *Origins of the Family, Private Property, and the State* from the angle of the relationship between contingency and necessity.

> **The more a social activity, a series of social processes, becomes too powerful for men's conscious control and grows above their heads, and the more it appears a matter of pure chance, then all the more surely within this chance the laws peculiar to it and inherent in it assert themselves as if by natural necessity.[62]**

Especially in capitalism, the external laws "appear as alien, at first often unrecognized, powers, whose nature Must first be laboriously investigated and established."[63] And still to this day, the product rules the producer as incorporeal alien powers. "The total production of society is regulated, not by a jointly devised plan, but by blind laws, which manifest themselves with elemental violence, in the final instance in the storms of the periodical trade crises."[64] Do the defenders of the traditional framework of philosophical illustration believe that the condition of man's enslavement by the alien powers, of the human social development distorted into a non-subjective natural process is also eternal?

C. FROM THE REALM OF NECESSITY TO THE REALM OF FREEDOM

For Engels, it takes nature millions of years to have humans come into existence, while they it takes them only years to be able to organize common social activities. People are not only conscious of their individual activities but also collectively struggle for common goals. Engels' social development here is confined to the *future communist society without any social 'natural-ness' and material-subjugation* because "only conscious organisation of social production, in which production and distribution are carried on in a planned way, can mankind lift above the rest of the animal

60   Engels, Friedrich. Anti-Dühring: Herr Eugen Dühring's Revolution in Science. Moscow: Foreign Languages Pub. House, 1959. p. 430.

61   Marx, and Friedrich Engels. *Karl Marx, Friedrich Engels: Marx and Engels Collected Works 1874-83*. New York: International Publishers, 1989. p. 320.

62   Engels, West, and Eleanor Burke Leacock. *The Origin of the Family, Private Property, and the State, in the Light of the Researches of Lewis H. Morgan*. New York: International Publishers Co, 1972. p. 57.

63   *Ibid.*, p. 234.

64   *Ibid.*, p. 234.

world as regards the social aspect, in the same way that production in general has done this for men in their aspect as species."[65] It is a very insightful statement!

In Engels' view, the social power in the development of capitalist society is just like the natural forces, blind, coercive and destructive, bringing people under control. However, once its essence is revealed, in particular, with the social productive forces developed in socialism and communism, the alien power external to humans will be transformed from devil tyrants into meek servants. "The social anarchy of production" ('natural-ness') will disappear and "give place to a social regulation of production upon a definite plan, according to the needs of the community and of each individual."[66]

"In making itself the master of all the means of production to use them in accordance with a social plan, society puts an end to the former subjection of men to their own means of production."[67] "Therefore, productive labour will become a pleasure instead of being a burden."[68] Thus, that "former subjection of men" and one-sided development can be finally eliminated; historical 'natural-ness' and material-subjection can be surpassed and laid behind.

Engels asserts that the cruel control of man by the economic materialization will be eradicated only with the premise of the social possession of the means of production in the future non-natural historical development. And the old anarchical condition will be substituted by the planned, conscious and organized activities. The struggle for individual existence disappears. Then, for the first time, man, in a certain sense, is finally marked off from the rest of the animal kingdom, and emerges from mere animal survival into real human existence. The whole sphere of the living condition which environs man, and which has hitherto ruled man, now comes under the dominion and control of man who has become the real, conscious lord of nature and the master of social organization. The laws of his own social action, hitherto standing face to face with man, as laws of nature foreign to, and dominating him, will then be used with full understanding, and so mastered by him. Man's own social organization, confronting him as a necessity imposed by nature and history, now becomes the result of his

65   Marx, and Friedrich Engels. *Collected Works, Volume 25*. London: Lawrence & Wishart, 1987. p. 331.
66   Marx, Friedrich Engels, and Robert C. Tucker. *The Marx-Engels Reader*. New York: Norton, 1972. p. 634.
67   *Ibid.*, p. 323.
68   Engels, Friedrich. *Anti-Dühring: Herr Eugen Dühring's Revolution in Science*. Moscow: Foreign Languages Pub. House, 1959. p. 406.

own free action. The extraneous objective forces that have hitherto governed history pass under the control of man himself. "Only from that time will man himself, with full consciousness, make his own history – only from that time will the social causes set in movement by him have, in the main and in a constantly growing measure, the results intended by him. It is the humanity's leap from the kingdom of necessity to the kingdom of freedom."[69] How precise and brilliant the point is!

Similarly, it is worthwhile to notice another important issue. When criticizing the mistake that it is the idea and view that create people's living conditions, he believes that this view is being overthrown by all the past history. The result always differs from man's will, or even contrary during its development. The idea can only be realized in the distant future on the following conditions. That is to say, people will expect the necessity of changing social status due to the changed relations (if I am permitted to say) and will accept that change instead of being unconsciously forced to recognize and comely with it.

Engels clearly explains that the essential error of idealism is to use an abstract conception of humankind to drive the objective reality; in comparison, historical materialism holds that social existence decides consciousness, which is also a general principle of Marxist historical view. Nevertheless, on the logical level of the *subjective dimension of historical dialectics* or the dominant status of the human subject in social development, historical materialism accepts neither the ever-lasting non-subjective status of man in social life nor the perpetual inability to consciously and dynamically guide practice for the creative evolution of social life. Like Marx, Engels firmly opposes the "law of nature inherent in things and relations, and independent of the will or actions of the producers."[70] While recognizing the general foundation of the objective material production in social history, Marxist historical dialectics certainly establishes the dominant status of the human subject in historical development. Marxism is not a philosophy of slaves. For Marx and Engels, the social life in future communism must *accord with* man's scientific wills and with his mastery of the external laws, including those of social development. It is the true theoretical meaning of Marx's realm of freedom and the most important confirmation of the subjective dimension in historical dialectics.

---

69   Marx, and Friedrich Engels. *Karl Marx and Friedrich Engels: Selected Works in Two Volumes, Volume 1*. Moscow: Foreign Languages Publishing House, 1958. p. 432.
70   Engels, Friedrich. *Anti-Dühring: Herr Eugen Dühring's Revolution in Science*. Moscow: Foreign Languages Pub. House, 1959. p. 430.

Here, I have to remind the reader that Marx and Engels approach the same theoretical logic from different perspectives. Marx often explains by the economic research and critiques while Engels puts emphasis on the *political discourse of scientific socialism*, which explains why his above view is generally neglected and distorted by those Western Marxian scholars.

IV. REINTERPRETATION OF THE "RESULTANT FORCES" DOCTRINE OF ENGELS' SOCIO-HISTORICAL VISION

As we know, Engels is in agreement with Marx's philosophical vision. We can effectively rebut the misunderstandings by the Western scholars or those in the old framework of philosophical interpretations. Regrettably, many profound theories of Engels' have not been truly recognized by us. First of all, it is the traditional framework of philosophical interpretation that confuses Marxist ideas. Therefore, we have to step outside the old discourse and re-study every theoretical link of Engels' philosophy for the proper textual meanings. This section is then about Engels' "resultant" doctrine of human activities and roles in social history and its relationship with Marx's theory of 'natural-ness'.

A. THE REAL "RESULTANT FORCES" DOCTRINE

For a long time, Engels' "resultant" doctrine has been interpreted as follows: In any socio-historical process, the individual activities are always unable to obtain their purposes but only presented as something contingent. Different motives act upon each other (independent of the individual will), forming a general historical direction of necessity; thus, the objective *resultant* reality of various causal elements and impulsions. This doctrine of Engels then seems to become a *universal law* to describe individual activities and roles in historical materialism, which is very questionable to me. To get to the root of the issue, let us return to the original texts.

As we all know, Engels' most famous statements of the resultant doctrine are recorded in his correspondence written in his late years to illustrate historical materialism. First, it is in the letter to J. Bloch in 1890. He makes clear that humans create their own history while the historical determinants always come down to the production and reproduction of real life; furthermore, he puts forward two points. One, the creation of history can only happen "under very definite assumptions and conditions."[71]

---

71   Marx, and Friedrich Engels. *Karl Marx and Friedrich Engels: Selected Works in One Volume.* New York: International Publishers, 1968. p. 692.

Two:

> **History is made in such a way that the final result always arises from conflicts between many individual wills, of which each in turn has been made what it is by a host of particular conditions of life. Thus there are innumerable intersecting force, an infinite series of parallelograms of forces which give rise to one result-ant – the historical event. This may again itself be viewed as the product of a power which works as a whole unconsciously and without volition.**[72]

We can see that every individual will in social life is disturbed by another one or sociality; correspondingly, the final result is out of everybody's ex-pectation. Here, Engels does not mean the individual will is zero. Instead, each one of them contributes to and melts into the resultant direction. In his words, they "are merged into an aggregate mean, a common resultant."[73]

An illustration is used to display Engels' thought as follows:

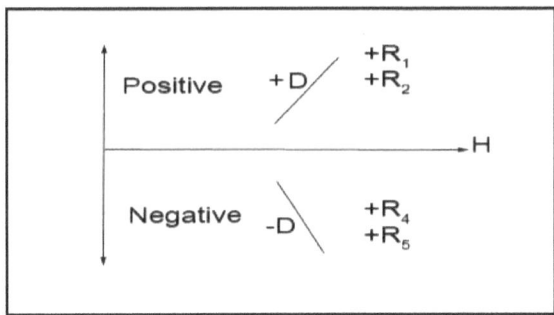

The above schema can be a historical section of individual activities and the resultant doctrine. "D" stands for the material foundation for man to create historical necessity or the level of the "production and reproduc-tion of the real life" in certain conditions, the historical functionality of practice, which is also Engels' "very definite assumptions and conditions." However, in reality, the premise ranges from "+D" that represents man's extra activities of creation to "-D" that corresponds to our regular rising and falling activities in the social frame, while the individual humans R1, R2, R3, R4, R5......Rn, can only act in certain conditions. Since each individual has a specific living condition, they have their own wills, in-dicated by different directions of Rs, which, according to Engels' under-standing, is often contradictory to or interactive with others. But history is not chaotic; "there are innumerable intersecting forces, an infinite series

72   *Ibid.*, p. 693.
73   *Ibid.*, p. 693.

of parallelograms of forces which give rise to one resultant–the historical event,"[74] or H (History). It points out the direction of history and with time goes on, those points are connected to form the general dimension of historical development.

In the letter to Borgius written in January 1894, Engels reiterates this idea:

> **Men make their history themselves, but not as yet with a collective will or according to a collective plan or even in a definitely defined, given society. Their efforts clash, and for that very reason all such societies are governed by *necessity*, which is supplemented by and appears under the forms of *accident*.**[75]

The issue is clearly approached from the unified perspective of contingency, the specific accidents of different individuals, and necessity, the innate laws and historical dimension of social development. If the aforementioned schema is employed again, the accidents now consist of contradictory Rs and float in the specific district D, the diagonals of the parallelogram are then the necessity (H) of the general law of social activities.

B. THE "RESULTANT" DOCTRINE IS AN AD HOC PROPOSITION

The above analysis basically explains Engels' theory. However, when the traditional framework of philosophical illustration posits it into the structure of historical materialism, the resultant doctrine is *universalized* into a common law of all the activities through social history. It is a critical logical error, with which Engels will probably not agree because the resultant doctrine cannot be right in all the social process; it works as a *special law* under *specific conditions*, that is, the pre-historical period with the phenomena of 'natural-ness' and material-subjugation. Even the original text does not openly demonstrate that it is a universal law. On the contrary, Engels adds an ad hoc comment in his first explanation: "Thus history has proceeded hitherto in the manner of a natural process and is essentially subject to the same laws of motion."[76] "The same laws" means the blind movement in social history that is similar to nature mentioned earlier in this book, the human laws alienated into natural laws. Here, the specific conditions refer to the "past history," including capitalism and the "pre-historical" periods. Thus, the resultant doctrine cannot be viewed as universally effective. In

---

74   *Ibid.*, p. 693.
75   Marx, and Friedrich Engels. *On Literature and Art.* Moscow: Progress Publishers, 1976. p. 10.
76   Marx, and Friedrich Engels. *Karl Marx and Friedrich Engels: Selected Works in One Volume.* New York: International Publishers, 1968. p. 693.

addition, Engels makes another two important *ad hoc* limitations. One, it is expressed in the words of "not as yet," by which he does not say the future communist society will have the same situation; two, it is in "all such societies," indicating that it does not unconditionally cover all societies. Hence, there is not the least trace to be found that Engels attempts to universalize the "resultant" doctrine into all social history of humankind.

In fact, this doctrine can be precisely interpreted when combined with the new logical vision of historical materialism and historical dialectics. To this end, let us go back to the clue in Engels' *Ludwig Feuerbach and the End of Classical German Philosophy*.

As noted above, in Chapter IV, Engels says, "In nature- in so far as we ignore man's reaction upon nature- there are only blind, unconscious agencies acting upon one another, out of whose interplay the general law comes into operation...In the history of society, on the contrary, the actors are all endowed with consciousness, are men acting with deliberation or passion, working towards definite goals; nothing happens without a conscious purpose, without an intended aim."[77] We already know that it is the essential difference between social development and natural process. Here, Engels clearly opposes the erroneous sliding into idealism from the special point of social history (the doctrine of will-drive). By the proposition that "socio-historical process is dominated by the innate laws," Engels reveals the objective premise of human development from the perspective of historical materialism and historical dialectics, which is called herein as the logic of the objective description in historical materialism that starts with the general foundation of material production. At this point, the traditional framework of philosophical illustration is not wrong.

Engels also attempts to explain that the objective progress of social history will adopt different forms under different conditions.

That which is willed happens but rarely; in the majority of instances the numerous desired ends cross and conflict with one another... thus the conflicts of innumerable individual wills and individual actions in the domain of history produce a state of affairs entirely analogous to that prevailing in the realm of unconscious nature.[78]

In the past, social life seems like floating fog, dominated by contingency (the random individual wills); nevertheless, behind all these chaotic

---

77   Marx, and Friedrich Engels. *On Religion*. Chicago: Scholars Press, 1982. p. 254.
78   Ibid., p. 254.

phenomena, there exist the objective laws of social history, "the real ultimate driving forces of history,"[79] that is, the innate necessity or resultant generated by the social forces like class struggles. Due to the specific historical conditions, it is still not possible for people at that time to perceive the objective foundation of social development (the economic structure and movement based on the productive forces); hence, those laws always take the form of external necessity (the resultant of the "invisible hand" and the blind natural forces), walking their way among numerous contingencies and demonstrating a peculiar 'natural-ness'. Here, Engels already makes a theoretical conversion to the discourse of the *dominant status* of the human subject and the *subjective dimension* of historical dialectics, which is unfortunately ignored in the traditional framework of philosophical interpretation. Therefore, there comes the deviating and conjectured explanation in which this ad hoc assertion is abstracted into a universal description of all social development.

Moreover, Engels' thought is very clear. In his view, 'natural-ness' and material-subjugation as well as the phenomenon of individual activities forced to be represented in a natural resultant only occur in the *specific* conditions of the "pre-historical" ages. With further social development in the future, people will truly recognize the objective laws of social development pushed by their own creative activities. Hence, they can make a planned and proportionate progress according to their own will. The pre-historical status of 'natural-ness' will disappear; the necessity of sociohistorical development will be returned to the hand of the human subject. The material production and objective necessity as a general foundation of social existence and historical development become the innate premise of our free development; thus, it comes true for the realm of freedom on earth. And the subjective purpose will be unified with the historical result, eliminating the blind resultant ('natural-ness') that ignores the individual roles. In this regard, Engels comments, "The more that human beings become removed from animals in the narrower sense of the word, the more they make their own history consciously, the less becomes the influence of unforeseen effects and uncontrolled forces of this history, and the more accurately does the historical result correspond to the aim laid down in advance."[80] Needless to say, what Engels opposes is nothing else but the abnormal phenomena in which humans are subject to the unconscious but controllable forces and men's purposes can only be achieved as exceptions.

---

79   Ibid., p. 256.
80   Engels, John Burdon and Sanderson Haldane. *Dialektik der Natur*. New York: International Publishers, 194. p. 18.

It is obvious that Engels does not externalize the non-subjective status in human social development; on the contrary, he negates that condition and expects communism in the beautiful future. In that free development of human individuals, the external necessity will not blindly dominate the subject and the social laws will cater to the needs of human beings because the will of people corresponds to the historical necessity and thus history becomes the process of conscious activities. The human subject really becomes the major aspect of social history and finally masters his own society and nature. In the same way, the human will is no longer realized through the unconscious resultant after people consciously plan their activities in an organic whole of social practice. At that time, the vitality of the creative power will become the engine of history.[81] People are no longer puppets controlled by the "invisible hand." Their activities are integrated into the necessary and conscious resultant to replace the precious blind one. The red sun slowly rises while the old parallelogram magically falls down and disappears on the horizon of new history.[82]

This is the true vision of Engels' resultant doctrine, which is much more profound than those traditional explanations.

---

81   Zhang Yibing. "Integration of Practice: The Functional System of the Orderly and Interactive Human Activities: A New Philosophical Vision." *Seeking Truth*. 5 (1989).

82   Liu Senlin coincides with me in this point.

CHAPTER VI

WESTERN MARXISM AND THE DIALECTICS OF SOCIAL HISTORY

1 *The Internal Logical Conflict of the Theory of Social History in Contemporary Western Marxism*
2 *The "Humanist" Marxism and the Theory of 'Natural-ness'*
3 *The "Humanist" Marxism and the Theory of Material-Subjugation*

CHAPTER SIX

INTRODUCTION

As mentioned earlier, the theories of 'natural-ness' and material-subjugation in socio-historical development on the subjective dimension of Marxist historical dialectics are always neglected by researchers, leading to logical errors in the understanding of Marx's scientific view of history. In comparison, western Marxism already notices, to a certain extent, Marx's 'natural-ness' and material-subjugation, in particular, the theoretical validation of some specific historical phenomena in social history. However, a few reasonable points cannot cover their bigger mistake. Here, I shall discuss their major logical aspects, which will guide us against falling into the logical error during our scientific interpretation of Marx's historical dialectics.

I. THE INTERNAL LOGICAL CONFLICT IN THE THEORY OF SOCIAL HISTORY IN CONTEMPORARY WESTERN MARXISM

After the 1920s, there was a trend in Marxist development against both the "dogmatic Marxism" and the so-called "third way" Western Marxism of the bourgeois ideology. In its early development, Western Marxism stressed the major elements of historical development from the perspective of the proletarian revolution but this reasonable theoretical advance went to extremes and then fell to the pit of "will-drive" doctrine; and when it came to the 1930s, some held high the banner of "humanistic Marxism"; after the 1950s, Western Marxism had a tendency of scientism as antithesis to the dominant theoretical trend, in which the Marxist view of history was led to another extreme.

A. A SUBJECTIVE TRANSCENDENCE: AGAINST ECONOMISM

In the 1920s, Western Marxism was born in the background when the alleged "orthodox Marxism" of the Second International was being reviewed.[1] As we all know, the Second International makes the fundamental mistake of regarding Marxist view of history as mechanic economism, to which Engels has already noticed in his later years. He makes two ad hoc points in the correspondences about historical materialism. One, during the early establishment of the new world-view when Marx and Engels mainly target at the dominant idealistic view of history, their initial focus is put on the decisive role of the economic life based on general material production. Two, the Marxist view of history is never equivalent to the economism that takes economy as the only decisive factor. "Hence, if somebody twists this into saying that the economic element is the only determining one, he transforms that proposition into a meaningless, abstract, senseless phrase."[2] The "material dependency" in socio-historical development is not a universal law and the essence of history is of *practical and dialectical initiatives*. "The whole vast process proceeds in the form of interaction" and what the believers of economism "all lack is dialectic," especially, the practical dialectic of socio-historical development.[3]

---

1 For the formation, development and basic logics of Western Marxism, see "Introduction" in Zhang Yibing's *Broken Wings of Reason—Criticism of Western Marxism*. Nanjing: Nanjing Publishing House, 1990.

2 Marx, and Friedrich Engels. *Karl Marx and Friedrich Engels: Selected Works in One Volume*. New York: International Publishers, 1968. p. 692.

3 Marx, and Friedrich Engels. *Literature and Art*. New York: International Publishers, 1947. p. 8.

But for the theorists in the Second International, the Marxist doctrine of social development is the pure *empirical* science of history and economics while the dialectics of practice are metamorphosed to the *natural occurrence* with positivist and economistic features. As the empirical and mechanic "sociology" that is isomorphic and homogeneous with natural science, Marxism is no longer essentially practical and revolutionary but scientifically "reasonable" and "predictable" (in the background of Newton's mechanics). Therefore, for Karl Kautsky and others, human history is attached to natural history while the law of historical movement is another biological manifestation. People can only look on before the objective development of social history. Hence, social history runs independently; Marx's *Das Kapital* is like an iron schedule of history; the growth of material production brings forth the economic changes and the ensuing revolution of the whole social superstructure. Accordingly, the collapse of capitalism is proved "inevitable"; revolution is to break out under certain conditions; the proletarians will become a conscious revolutionary force; and what people need to do is just waiting for proper opportunities. This opinion proves a fundamental betrayal to Marxist revolution and unsurprisingly leads to a mechanic standpoint of the Second International, which may account for their conflict against Lenin's real practice to exert the initiative of the proletarian revolution.

The early 20th century Russia was still in the initial phase of capitalism. In the eyes of the Second International that believed in economism, the underdeveloped Russia was not eligible for a proletarian revolution. But the success of Lenin's October Revolution broke their mechanic determinism of natural occurrence and demonstrated the great power of Marxist historical dialectics, giving rise to the Western "re-interpretation" of Marxist view of history, accompanied by other controversial views of the Russian revolution and considerations of the peculiar workers' movement in West Europe.

In the famous article entitled "The Revolution against Das Kapital", Antonio Gramsci criticizes the idea that "events must take a certain course in Russia "and calls the Second International's understanding of Marx as "positivist and naturalist incrustations."[4] Then, he makes a thorough analysis of the Russian revolution: "And this true Marxist thought has always identified as the most important factor in history not crude, economic facts, but rather men themselves, and the societies they create, as they

---

4   Gramsci, Antonio. Antonio Gramsci: *Pre-Prison Writings*. London: Cambridge University Press, 1994. p. 39.

learn to live with one another and understand one another; as, out of these contacts (civilization), they forge a social, collective will."[5] In my opinion, Gramsci is directly opposed to economism. He attaches more importance to the conscious power of the human subject in socio-historical development.

> **As they come to understand economic facts, and to assess them, and to control them with their will, until this collective will becomes the driving force of the economy, the force which shapes reality itself, so that objective reality becomes a living, breathing force, like a current of molten lava, which can be channelled wherever and however the will directs.[6]**

Gramsci is more concerned with man and his subjective will; he is at the same time against the unreasonable control of people by the economic reality. For him, "reality does exit on its own, in and for itself but only in an historical relationship with the men who modify it, etc."[7] He thinks that the Second International takes an economistic interpretation of Marx, which is but a mistaken perspective to observe things through a miserable prism. In that "linear" or "single-theme" economism, people feel there is a phantom-like thing independent of the individuals because they do little but something just occurs.[8] This is proper "historical mysticism." Gramsci believes that economism is reasonable in a certain sense. After all, it tells us that we shall finally win, which is an axiological hypothesis of "necessity." He compares it to a religious excitement but anesthetic "aroma" that strengthens one's will on one side but on the other wears out their resistance in the long run. Hence, for Gramsci, Marxism is the theory to dynamically revolve and change practice, a humanistic practical "monism."[9]

The Young Lukacs and Karl Korsch, as Gramsci's peers and the founders of Western Marxism, hold similar views. They believe that the decisions of the Second International turn socialism into "purely scientific observations, without any immediate connection to the political or other practices of class struggle."[10] It obviously leads to historical determinism and the cancellation of men and their social activities. For Lukacs and Korsch, that

---

5   *Ibid.*, p. 40.

6   *Ibid.*, p. 40.

7   Gramsci, Antonio. *Selections from the Prison Notebooks*. New York: International Publishers, 1992. p.346.

8   Gramsci, Antonio. *Further Selections from the Prison Notebooks*. London: Cambridge University Press, 1995. P XV.

9   Gramsci, Antonio. *Selections from the Prison Notebooks*. New York: International Publishers, 1992. p. 372

10   Korsch, Karl. *Marxism and Philosophy*. London: NLB, 1970. p. 54.

misinterpretation of Marxist historical materialism ignores the subjective initiative, which consequently eternalizes what Marx criticizes as the phenomenon of man's subjugation by the external forces. In fact, Marx never confuses social history with natural history because the human historical development is the result of the dynamic activities of the subject and correspondingly, the historical laws are enforced through the initiative role of human beings. Only in specific historical stages can people be dominated by the object, which is what we should overcome. Later, Henri Lefebvre comments that Marxist surpassing of this destined status is the most creative action in modern times.

The Young Lukacs frankly refers to Marxist philosophy as a socio-historical theory. In his eyes, the unilateral emphasis on the economic dominance and control is actually a bourgeois idea that dissolves the proletarian subjectivity and revolutionariness. "It is not the primacy of economic motives in historical explanation that constitutes the decisive difference between Marxism and bourgeois thought, but the point of view of totality."[11] He indicates that it is wrong to regard historical development as a merely spontaneous economic process independent of the human subjects. "This he achieved by focusing the known totality upon the reality of the historical process and by confining it to this. By this means he determined both the knowable totality and the totality to be known."[12] In the capitalist economy of materialization, the proletariat is alienated into an attachment to the economic forces, a distorted object separated from history. What Marx does is to re-unify the subject and object separated by capitalism, to unite "the class which was able to discover within itself on the basis of its life-experience the identical subject-object, the subject of action; the 'we' of the genesis: namely the proletariat."[13] For the Second International of mechanical determinism, "with the totality out of the way, the fetishistic relations of the isolated parts appeared as a timeless law valid for every human society."[14]

The Young Lukacs asserts that Marxism is centred on the historical dialectics of subject and object, whose "central problem is to change reality."[15] In his eyes, Engels "does not even mention the most vital interaction, namely the *dialectical relation between subject and object in the historical process*, let

---

11   Lukacs, Georg. *History and Class Consciousness: Studies in Marxist Dialectics.* MIT Press, 1972. p. 27.
12   *Ibid.*, p. 39.
13   *Ibid.*, p. 149.
14   *Ibid.*, p. 9.
15   *Ibid.*, p. 3.

alone give it the prominence it deserves. Yet without this factor dialectics ceases to be revolutionary."[16] For the Young Lukacs, it is the theoretical negligence of this important meaning by the Second International that turns Marxism into a pure scientific thing, which, in essence, amounts to saying that "the proletariat submits to the 'laws' of bourgeois society either in a spirit of supine fatalism (e.g. towards the natural laws of production) or else in a spirit of 'moral' affirmation (the state as an ideal, a cultural positive),"[17] which is "a thorough-going opportunistic theory, a theory of 'evolution' without revolution and of 'natural development' into Socialism without any conflict."[18]

It is not difficult to see that the first-generation Western Marxian theoreticians are actually correcting and restoring Marxist historical dialectics messed up by the Second International. In particular, their recovery of the practical initiative of the human subject is done with obviously *justifiable*. Against this background, Gramsci exerts the "philosophy of practice" of the proletarian will; the Young Lukacs emphasizes the "totality" principle of the proletarian consciousness; and Korsch grasps the "subject-object dialectics" as the base of the proletarian revolution. However, their efforts just lead to another distracted road by their philosophical impulsion to hyperbolize the subjective initiative behind. It is true that we do need a new theory for reflection, a new ideology to light the road ahead when the worldwide workers' movement suffers setbacks and the bourgeois forces are increasingly stronger. It is also right to criticize the mechanic Second International. But all this should not be done at the expense of scientific Marxism. In my opinion, these first-generation Western Marxian theoreticians do not actually understand the general and special meanings of Marxist historical materialism; they cannot differentiate material production as the foundation of certain socio-historical existence and development from the dominant economic forces under specific historical conditions but negate them in the same way. Their undifferentiated methodology, without doubt, results in an incorrect retreat to the subjective dialectics from the scientific Marxist historical dialectics. Just a step forward, truth often becomes false.

The second-generation Western Marxism rose in the 1930s. Because of the newly discovered *1844 Manuscripts* (first published in 1932), *Marxism was expressly interpreted as a humanistic philosophy*. Those Marxian theoreticians

---

16 *Ibid.*, p. 3.
17 *Ibid.*, p. 196.
18 *Ibid.*, p. 196.

were both unsatisfied with the revolutionary standpoint of the Second International and contrary to the "old" Marxist ideology.

Erich Fromm was one of such representatives who believe that in the period from Marx's death to the 1920s, philosophy was dominated by the positivist mechanism that influenced Lenin, Nikolai Bukharin and other thinkers. This twisted view of Marxism as economism made historical materialism a theory to treat the pursuit of material interests as the perpetual drive for the social development of human beings, with which Fromm absolutely disagreed.

In *Beyond the Chains of Illusion: my Encounter with Marx and Freud*, he writes, "The liberation of man from the strangle hold of economic conditions which prevented his full development was the aim of all Marx's thought and effort."[19] In *Marx's Concept of Man*, he points out, "Marx's aim was that of the spiritual emancipation of man, of his liberation from the chains of economic determination, of restituting him in his human wholeness, of enabling him to find unity and harmony with his fellow man and with nature."[20] People are subject to and suffering from the blind economic forces in capitalism, which dominate all the aspects of their lives. They adore their own created materials and turn themselves into the material objects. For Fromm, Marx coincides with Freud in that man is unconsciously controlled by the external power, like a puppet with the lines drawn by those unconscious forces. It is the inverted man-material relationship that Marx wants to eliminate.

Fromm firmly claims:

Marx's whole criticism of capitalism is exactly that it has made interest in money and material gain the main motive in man, and his concept of socialism is precisely that of a society in which this material interest would cease to be the dominant one.[21]

In this society, "the freedom in this field cannot consist of anything else but of the fact that socialized men, the associated producers, regulate their interchange with nature rationally, bring it under their common control, instead of being ruled by it as by some blind power."[22] Marx "is concerned with the liberation of man from a kind of work which destroys his

---

19   Fromm, Erich. *Beyond the Chains of Illusion: My Encounter with Marx and Freud.* New York: Continuum International Publishing Group, 2001. p. 142.
20   Fromm, Erich. *Marx's Concept of Man.* New York: Continuum International Publishing Group, 2004. p. 2.
21   *Ibid.,* p. 12.
22   *Ibid.,* p. 50.

individuality, which transforms him into a thing, and which makes him into the slave of things."[23]

It is discernible that the second-generation Marxians no longer stress the subjective initiative ignored by the Second International but openly turn Marxism into a humanistic philosophy, with the aim of *restoring the "deserved" status of man in socio-historical development that is lost in reality*. Fromm believes that Marxism is to liberate humanity, together with their innate initiative and autonomy. Human nature is a particular potentiality, which *abstractly* transcends the object external to himself. A gust of spring wind will blow off winter snow; a seed will finally break the earth; dreams will transcend the fence; hopes will transform the fetters; and humankind will continuously go beyond themselves with their initiative and subjectivity. J. Bloch defines the essence of Marxism as a transcending "hope" from which a humanistic "ought" directly emerges to the theoretical surface. "Ought" and "is" are put into contrast here. In "phenomenological Marxism" advocated by Graham Pechey and Paul Piccone, the Marxist thought boils down to the reconstruction of one's "daily life." Sartre's existentialism expressly ascertains Marxism as "Marxist-Humanist dialectics" that constantly transcend the external material shortages and inertia. Here, Marxist philosophy is once again *reversed* to the humanistic standpoint that the Young Marx holds in his *1844 Manuscripts* and transformed into a downright *subjective teleology* and *axiology*, a humanistic doctrine for the subject to demand his own liberation and freedom from historical reality, a discourse of humanistic *subjective* dialectics.

B. THE ANTI-HUMAN "PROCESS WITHOUT A SUBJECT": THE THEORETICAL BACKWASH OF SCIENTISM

Interestingly, there came a theoretical trend in the 1950s that was contradictory to the dominant humanistic thought of Western Marxism. Mainly represented by Althusser in France, they preached the scientistic logics against humanistic Marxism.

Althusser announced that he opposed the theoretical reversal of Marxism started by the Young Lukacs to "soften" it into a humanistic view of history. He pointed out that "scientific" Marxism was born in 1845, before which, the Young Marx did not write a few works with the idealistic and humanistic hues. However, these "early works have been a war-house for petty bourgeois intellectuals in their struggle against Marxism" since the

---

23 *Ibid.*, p. 40.

1930s[24]. Especially, after the 1950s, the radical wave set off by the 20th Congress of the CPSU made the scientific thought itself in great danger. Althusser then felt necessary to re-demarcate "ideology" and "science" in Marx's works for a lucid and right understanding to counterattack the humanistic trend and restore the original scientific meanings of Marxism, particularly, the truth of Marx's historical science.

Althusser approaches from the significance of Marx's scientific revolution, which is compared to three scientific "continents" closely connected with the development of philosophy. The first is the continent of mathematics opened up by the Greeks, like Plato, that gave birth to philosophy; the second is the continent of physics started by Galileo that brought forth profound changes; the third is Marx's continent of history, the end of all the classical philosophies and the great philosophical revolution that follows[25]. Here, Althusser treats Marx's view of history as, first of all, a historical science. According to him, the humanistic view of history takes the historical development as the realization of human subjects, in which social history is only the process of loss and recovery for a transcendental "human" subject that *should exist*. "It is to state: History is a *process of alienation which has a subject*, and that subject is man."[26] Althusser claims that when Marx wrote the *1844 Manuscripts*, he was for the subjective view of history despite that it was not a scientific one. The unconfirmed opinion held by Marx was to state "History is the 'History of the alienation of man.'"[27] After the outcome of the new scientific worldview in 1845, Marx abandoned that subjective view of social history and established the doctrine of the process "without a subject" based on the objective laws of historical development.

With Althusser, Marx's concepts of the "process" "without a subject" are borrowed from Hegel, who takes history as a process of alienation not that of the human subject but of the objective idea external to human beings. More importantly, Hegel never thinks alienation as some ethical impulsion, as humanism does, but believes that alienation is dialectic and "*the process itself in its teleology*."[28] Thus, alienation is not the loss of a transcendental subject for Hegel but a logical drive and inner stimulus of the Idea's self-movement. Meanwhile, if "existence" equals "nothing," the "absolute" "ought" to eradicate any origin and subject; it is the process

---

24   Althusser, Louis. *For Marx*. London: Verso, 2005. p. 10.
25   *Ibid.*, p. 14.
26   Althusser, Louis. "Marx's Relation to Hegel" in *Politics and History*. Montesquieu, Rousseau, Marx. London: NLB, 1972. p. 182
27   *Ibid.*, p. 182.
28   *Ibid.*, p. 183.

without a subject, the same in reality and scientific knowledge. In this way, "the process of alienation without a subject (or the dialectic) is the only subject recognized by Hegel. There is no subject to the process: it is the process itself which is a subject in so far as it does not have a subject." In teleology, there lies the true Hegelian Subject. "Take away the teleology, there remains the philosophical that Marx inherited: *the category of a process without a subject*."[29] Althusser, then alarms that Marx's previous subjective view of history "exploded." And "the result of this explosion was the evaporation of the notions of subject, human essence, and alienation, which disappear, completely atomized, and the liberation of the concept of a process (procès or processus) without a subject, which is the basis of all the analyses in Capital."[30]

Althusser holds that the concept of "process" replaces the category of "subject" in the later works of Marx because the former is scientific while the latter is ideological. The proposition is with strategic significance to oppose the doctrine of transcendental subject with abstract humanism. From the perspective of the scientific Marxist view of history, "history is a process without a subject, that the dialectic at work in history is not the work of any Subject whatsoever, whether Absolute (God) or merely human, but that the origin of history is always already thrust back before history, and therefore that there is neither a philosophical origin nor a philosophical subject to History."[31] He also cites Engels' "resultant" theory for illustration. In his eyes, it is a formula of physics to explain the role of the human subject in social history. "The resultant is, in essence, unconscious (it does not correspond to the consciousness of each will – and at the same time, it is a force without a subject, an objective force, but, from the outset nobody's force."[32]

At the same time, Althusser confirms that in the writing of *Das Kapital*, Marx still accepts the subject of history, which is not a transcendental subject of humanism but the process of the objective social relations and the structure in the development of human history.

> **The true 'subjects' (in the sense of constitutive subjects of the process) are therefore not these occupants or functionaries, are not, despite all appearances, the 'obviousnesses' of the 'given' of naïve anthropology, 'concrete individuals', 'real men' – but the**

29   *Ibid.*, p. 183.
30   Althusser, Louis. *Lenin and Philosophy and Other Essays.* Trans. Ben Brewster. New York: Monthly Review Press, 1971. p. 121.
31   *Ibid.*, p. 122.
32   Althusser, Louis. *For Marx.* London: Verso, 2005. p. 121.

definition and distribution of these places and functions. The true 'subjects' are these definers and distributors: the relations of production (and political and ideological social relations).[33]

In his view, we cannot investigate them within the subjective sphere since they are relations.

Now it is clear that Althusser's understanding of Marx is an anti-"human" historical process. He does not simply deny the subject of historical development but intends to cleanse the historical subject, man. Hence, he is against the structuralist opinion that man is the centre of the world, of the absolute vision and environment. He also opposes the ensuing humanistic proposition that human is the original essence and objective of the human world. Although he thinks Marx once accepted the humanistic issues proposed by Feuerbach and others, like in the *1844 Manuscripts*, Marx did achieve his own revolution of worldview by breaking away from Feuerbach. After that, the ideological discourse of "man" was practically wiped out from him.

Probably based on the observation that "if the category 'man' is meant here, then he has, in general, 'no' needs,"[34] Althusser comments in a very confident way that there is no category of man in Marx's scientific works, not even its trace. Marx no longer wastes time on the issue of man; he turns to certain social economic periods when faced with the development of social history. The decisive factor in Marxist view of history is neither the illusory essence or nature of man nor the abstract man and even the concrete man but the relations of production that "rests upon its economic infrastructure."[35] Marx's relation of production "is not a relation between men, a relation between persons, nor an inter-subjective or psychological or anthropological relation, but a double relation: a relation between groups of men concerning the relation between these groups of men and things."[36] "Marx considers men in this case only as "supports" of a relation, or "bearers" of a function in the production process, determined by the production relation."[37] For Althusser, Marx does not leave far away from specific person who acts in and constitutes of certain relationships, defined

---

33   Althusser, Louis. *Reading Capital*. Trans. Étienne Balibar. London: Verso, 1997. p. 180.
34   Marx, Karl. Marx: *Later Political Writings*. Ed. Terrell Carver. Cambridge University Press, 2002. p. 235.
35   Althusser, Louis. *Louis Althusser Philosophy and the Spontaneous Philosophy of the Scientists & Other Essays*. Ed. Gregory Elliot. London: Verso, 1990. p. 255.
36   Althusser, Louis. *Louis Althusser Essays in Self-Criticism*. Trans. Grahame Lock. London: NLB, 1976. p. 201.
37   *Ibid.*, p. 201.

by the comprehensive regulations of the same relationships. In addition, it is the capitalist relations that degrade "man" to the "bearers" of function, which is just opposed by Marx. One of the scientific objectives of Marxism is against the bourgeois ideology in the guise of "men."

For those who have similar views with Althusser, like Della Volpe and Lucio Colletti, Marxism is actually the dialectics of science. Unsurprisingly, there are no traces of "man" in the works of Nicos Poulantzas, a disciple of Althusser's, and the later "scientific" argumentations by such "analytical Marxists" as G. A. Cohen and Jon Elster. Hence, it is the "scientistic" interpretation of Marxism that accounts for the *reactionary logic* of the humanistic Western Marxist view of history.

In my view, Althusser and his companions hold the view very close to that of our traditional framework of philosophical interpretation. They only recognize the *objective logic* in Marx's scientific view of history, confuse this objective description of social history with the special interpretation of historical materialism in which the economic power dominates, and then ushers it to positivism, forming a partial, crippled metaphysical freak. Accordingly, in their mechanic determinism, social history becomes the objective movement of the anti-human non-subject with the human subject actually negated and historical process externally operated outside human beings. It is, of course, against Marxism. Moreover, it is only a *caricatured* expression of "scientific" Marxism and the traditional framework of philosophical illustration, only in the appearance of Western structuralism and positivism this time.

C. THE DECONSTRUCTION OF LOGICAL POLARITY: A THEORETICAL RECOGNITION

As to the two Western Marxian trends analyzed above, the former is based on the logic of humanism, emphasizing the subjective role in social history, especially, man's transcendence over the economic limits; the latter is centred on scientism, highlighting the objectivity of historical movement and submerging the human subject in the social structure created by the relations of production. These two views are *polarized* to each other. Although Western Marxism starts with a reasonable point, it tends to *cut short the curve of cognition and develop rationality to extremes,* only resulting in distraction and even mistakes. We should draw lesson from their fault.

The humanistic trend of Western Marxism was not totally wrong in its *initial* standpoint to correct the economism of the Second International. The first-generation Western Marxians, such as Gramsci, the Young Lukacs and Korsch, were all drawn by the proletarian revolution at the beginning and then sought the theoretical foundation calling on the workers to rise, which should be fully acknowledged. Meanwhile, in order to oppose the attempt of the Second International's leaders to stop the revolution and ignore the role of the subject, they all attached great importance to the subjective initiative and creativity, which almost touched on the logic of the subjective dimension in Marxist historical dialectics. This was no doubt a reasonable starting point. However, when they strode over certain theoretical limits to put human subjectivity on an inappropriate *base* of historical view, things began to develop in the opposite direction. Marxism can neither turn the abstract totality into its own premise nor let the essence of practice speak for the subject's will; in the same way, the objective historical dialectics are certainly different from the humanistic subjective dialectics. They really went too far in their erroneous way.

The second-generation Western Marxian humanists were completely wrong with their attempt to make whole Marxism humanistic by referring to the *1844 Manuscripts*. This fault cannot be mitigated despite some sensible elements in the historical background, like the criticism of Stalinism and the rise of Western humanism. Marx's theory is always concerned with humankind, which is but put on a *general foundation of material production in scientific historical materialism* to ascertain the true *dominant* position *(not the ontological status)* and the real prospects of human subjects in social history. Admittedly, certain points of Fromm and other similar researchers are correct, e.g. their negation of the "economic man" and economism, which exactly exposes a crucial problem of the traditional framework of philosophical interpretation: *Abstraction* and *fossilization* of the laws of social development, in particular, the historical laws under certain conditions where economic factors dominate. Herbert Marcuse is right to say that Marx "is principally fighting reification in political economy, which turns a particular kind of historical facticity into rigid 'eternal' laws and so-called 'essential relationships.'"[38] Indeed, Marx does perpetualize the capitalist status in which the economic power blindly dominates people and the human relationship is reversed to the material relationship; instead, his communist/socialist movement is to radically surpass the economic material-subjugation, which is already proved by the theories of 'natural-ness' and material-subjugation analyzed earlier in this book. However, on no account can Marx's historical dialectics lead to a humanistic logic centered on the idea of "ought to." Therefore, when Fromm, Marcuse, Lefebvre and

---

38   Marcuse, Herbert. Richard Wolin, John Abromeit. *Heideggerian Marxism*. University of Nebraska Press, 2005. p. 105.

others wanted to "develop" Marxism by the contemporary Western bourgeois philosophy, they only ended in attaining poor shams.

Similarly, we must admit that Althusser did make outstanding contributions when he rose to uphold scientific Marxism during a time of humanistic distraction and studied the division of Marxist historical in his critiques against the humanistic thought. After careful readings, he put forward the boundaries of the science of Marxism, like the issues of "science," "ideology," time border and problematic conversions, which effectively eliminated the constant confusion in the historical research of Marxist philosophy and resisted Fromm's incorrect use of the Young Marx's humanistic logic for a unified Marxism. In my opinion, the new worldview of Marxist philosophy was born in the spring of 1845 but, as has been repeatedly proved, there is no such absolute "epistemological rupture" in his theoretical development. And it is true that he abandons Feuerbach's old-style logical framework of humanism but in his new scientific thought, neither man nor the previous concerned issues are *entirely* negated, only re-solved on a new level. Because Marx's ultimate ideal is to achieve the all-round emancipation of human beings, he is certainly concerned about the existential status of man in reality (the proletarians and all other labourers) and the essence of his philosophical view should not be an objective reflection of the alleged process "without-a-subject" but the revolutionary historical dialectics calling for the change of the irrational reality. It is essentially a request to stand up against the capitalist reality instead of an affectionate inscription of history. His purpose is to break the so-called "eternal" laws and "objective" process, rather than maintain the present structure. In this connection, Lefebvre is right in saying that it is but a bourgeois view for Althusser's terminology of "technical rationality" being extended to "society as a whole."[39] Whether Althusser was consciously aware of it is not important any more for it did result in an awful consequence.

On the other hand, Althusser later admitted that his metaphysical doctrine of rupture was fallacious since he already noticed Marx was *concerned with humankind*, stressing the *logic of subjective dimension in historical dialectics of historical materialism* in such text as the *Preface to the Critique of Political Economy*, the *1857-1858 Manuscripts*, and even *Das Kapital*. As a result, he had to console himself by soothing remarks that the *Critique of the Gotha Program* (1875) and the *Critical Notes on the Economic Work of Adolf Wagner* (1882) completely got rid of Hegel's last influence. It indicates that Althusser already knew his logical failure.

---

39   Lefebvre, Henri. *Survival of Capitalism*. London: Allison & Busby, 1976. p. 26.

Indeed, it is not very difficult to define the theoretical essence of Western Marxian philosophy that apparently holds the banner of Marxism and bases its foundation on a large amount of Marx's texts. But it is very complicated and intriguing at the same time in contemporary research of Marxism. In my view, there is only one way out: *To start from the authentic logics of Marx*. I am to accept neither the humanistic interpretation of Marxism by Fromm and his fellow theoreticians nor the Althusserian support "for Marxism."

An important logical validation in *Theses On Feuerbach* is quoted in "Chapter Two" of this book, in which Marx mainly criticizes Feuerbach's old materialism as a mere conception of the external object and reality "in the form of the object [Objekts], or of contemplation [Anschauung]," a "thing-in-itself" outside man's existence. Marx wants us not to understand "objectively" but to perceive reality and existence from man's objective activities of practice. At the same time, he is also firmly opposed to the Hegelian abstract "development" of man's "initiative aspect." The essence of Marxist philosophy is defined as the creativity of the human subject but dynamically represented through the material activities of objective practice. It is, according to my previous analysis, a scientific logical *integration* of Marx's new worldview as well as the revolutionary nature of Marxism. We can employ this important definition to evaluate the Western Marxian trends on a more specific scale.

Judging from this point, Althusser clearly adheres to the materialism translated by positivism and structuralism, effectively combating and preventing the infiltration of humanism but he only takes the process and the law of social history as a non-human object and a material process "without a subject," that is, he *fails to observe from the subjective aspect*, just regarding them as sensuous human activities and practice. Consequently, he slips into the same error as that of our traditional framework of philosophical interpretation. In contrast to Althusser, the Young Lukacs and others make an *abstract development* of the initiative aspect of social history with their humanistic subjectivism. For these humanistic Marxians, the objective historical process becomes the contradictory movement between the unreasonable reality and the abstract essence of man with the a priori "proletarian consciousness" and an axiological hypothesis of subjective transcendence; the nature of history is not the historical, real, concrete production and practice but a subjective impulsion and an ethical requirement of value. It is also a theoretical setback. Such logical transgressions or traps abound in the Western Marxian trends, which we shall guard against.

Most of all, the real nature of Marxist historical materialism slips off the above radical trends. These researchers let go of the innate association of the different logical perspectives in Marx's new vision; they cannot wait but hold one end, thus turning the whole science of Marxist historical view into a biased and fragmented theory.

D. AN AD HOC EXPLANATION

There is another theoretical trend in Western Marxian development to re-merge "man" and "science," which is mainly represented by Ben Agger's eco-Marxism.

In *Western Marxism, an Introduction: Classical and Contemporary Sources*[40], Agger describes a new idea to understand Marx, which neither agrees with the mechanical and deterministic "scientism" by the Second International nor consents the distortion of Marxism into a subjective voluntarism by Lukacs and others. Agger wants to *unify* Marxism from the scientific and dialectical aspects. He divides Marxism into three parts: Alienation and man's liberation; capitalism and its innate contradictions; the mode of crisis in which the logic of innate contradictions is empirically transformed. The division seems to match the three Marxist aspects of philosophy, political economics and scientific socialism. The first two are regarded by Agger as the basic contents of Marxist dialectics. The former, as philosophical critiques, provides judgment for the fundamentally unfair phenomena in capitalism because labour is separated from the labourer and possessed and dominated by the other in that society; the latter, centred on practical analysis, gives a summary of the fixed laws and scientific theories in the process of capitalist production, revealing the self-contradictory and self-destructive social system of capitalism. Then, Marx uses the crisis theory for the realistic road of the proletariat revolutionary to overthrow capitalism. It is a "trinity" of the *axiological critique of humanistic emancipation, the positive science of epistemology and methodology and the realizing way of the crisis theory.*

For Agger, Marx associates alienation with the social and economic structures that produce this alienation. However, Marx's theory of alienation is not about cause and effect for he also illustrates the innate contradictions and possible crises in capitalism. Moreover, Marx analyzes the structural condition for the human liberation produced in the process when capitalism itself endeavours to suppress what he believes as the deep-rooted

---

40　See Ben Agger's *Western Marxism, an Introduction: Classical and Contemporary Sources.* Santa Monica, Calif. : Goodyear Pub. Co., 1979.

(ineradicable) contradictions. Marx does not give the didactic lecture to workers like a moralist but explains the mature contradictions and the subsequent planning and strategy for class struggles presented by the tendency of the capitalist crisis. Agger has something important and reasonable in this opinion.

In his eyes, Marx's dialectics combine the "structural role" of the objective laws with "man's role"; the alienation theory allows people to be aware of their subjugated status and calls on them to rise; the "science of 'innate contradictions'" demonstrates how to recognize the internal contradictions of capitalism and act to fight for socialism. It is about the know-how of revolution and the crisis theory provides an empirical, practical road. On the other hand, Agger rightly notices that Marx's development is not to be seen without understanding the background of constant changes in economics and politics. As a result, whether it is Marx's theoretical development or the subsequent history of Marxist thought, Agger tries to find out the cause from reality. For example, in the description of contemporary changes in Western Marxian theory, he finds that when contradictions become intense and lead to crisis, Marxist theory is taken with a scientific, deterministic standpoint; when contradictions get alleviated and crisis avoided, non-deterministic Marxism will appear. In both cases, there will always be the Marists exaggerating the role of determinism or amplifying the function of will. They reduce Marxism to either an almost fatalistic determinism or a philosophical pessimism. Hence, Agger believes it is necessary to propose a contemporary Marxism unifying the revolutionary determinism and will while dodging the sacrifice of either of them.

These opinions should be valued, especially, in comparison with the conspicuous errors of other Western Marxians. Regrettably, some of Agger's reasonable theoretical *characters* cannot justify the fundamental defect of the Western Marxian logics. In the first place, his "eco-Marxism" is still humanistic *in essence* because it boils down to anti-determinism despite his own consciousness of the rational humanistic problems and subsequent corrections. Then, he is blind to Marx's transformation from the humanistic alienation view of history to a scientific worldview, let alone a true authentic interpretation of the discourse of historical dialectics. Therefore, Marxist philosophy is inevitably attributed to a "theory of alienation" and even a certain voluntarism, like an intact book torn down page by page and then clumsily bound again. Finally, Agger misses the difference between the scientific historical dialectics and the humanistic subjective dialectics; he also fails to understand the theories of 'natural-ness' and material-subjugation used by Marx to replace the alienation theory and validate the real dominant status of humans in the development of social history after his philosophical revolution. Consequently, he is unable to integrate the objective and subjective dimensions of historical dialectics within a scientific logic of *practice*, leading to an eventual binary split of the "structural factors" of material conditions and the "subjective factors" of will and motivation, which reveals his theoretical problems on a deeper level.

Meanwhile, it is worthwhile to note a *recessive transformation* in the later development of Western humanistic thought, that is, a critical examination and self-reflection of humanism itself. It mainly occurs in the late Frankfurt School writings. I call this complex issue a "post-modern turn."

As we all know, since the late 1950s, a postmodern thought stirred the entire Western philosophical structure, including scientism based on positivist thought and all the new humanistic trends. When it came to the 1970s and 80s, postmodernism had become so fashionable that it almost constituted the "cultural logic of late capitalism" (Fredric Jameson). In this wave of philosophical rationality, the post-humanistic tendency of anti-anthropocentrism and non-subjectification was particularly noticeable. In my opinion, some important works of the late Frankfurt School were influenced by, or just integrated into this trend.

As early as in the *Dialectic of Enlightenment: Philosophical Fragments*, Theodor Adorno and Max Horkheimer leave an observable post-humanistic tendency that is substantially different from the interpretation of Marx's *1844 Manuscripts* in the 1930s. The authors are clearly against anthropocentricism because the purpose of enlightenment is to make man the "master." "Man's likeness to God consists in sovereignty over existence, in the lordly gaze, in the command."[41] From the domination over nature to the practice of subjugating society, enlightenment becomes a tool for the human subject to enslave nature and himself. Isn't this a more profound self-alienation? The logics of traditional humanism and rationalism are anything but the bourgeois ideology (The idea is further developed in *Domination of Nature* by William Leiss, an eco-Marxist).[42]

Adorno thoroughly demonstrates the postmodern critical and negative spirit in this point. The deconstructive non-integrity, non-identification

---

41   Horkheimer, Adorno, and Gunzelin Schmidt Noerr. *Dialectic of Enlightenment: Philosophical Fragments*. Stanford University Press, 2002. p. 6.
42   See William Leiss's *The Domination of Nature*. Montréal: McGill-Queen's Press—MQUP, 1994.

consists of the major discourse of his unique "atonal" thinking[43]. Below
that vast "atonal" sky, there is the glittering palace full of fairy tales, sur-
rounded by playful brooks. There lies the free castle, there is the eternal
other side! In fact, he is not only negating positivism, but also criticizing
the Hegel-Lukacsian collective meta-subject which amounts to a theory
of subjective dialectic and identity ("totality") without the least objectivity. For Adorno, the Young Lukacs, along with other Western humanistic Marxians, is actually repeating the idealistic subject-object concept.
In order to expose the structural and subjective error, he is to question
this "subjectivism" that is metaphysical or transcending the individual[44].
In Adorno's view, the critical point of the Young Lukacs's subjectivism is
the separation of subject and object, in which, the subject attributes it
to its own scale and submerges the object. It is a radical humanism and
"racial imperialism" because it demonstrates the subject's domination of
the object, in which the subject leaves to manipulate the object. This is
the subjective impulsion hidden behind the Young Lukacs's totality: "The
object is no more a subjectless residuum than what the subject posits."[45]
On a deeper level, it is a doctrine of totality with the domination of the
subject over the object. Adorno angrily says *totality* is hypocritical and
the liberated humankind should never be a totality. He advocates a fresh
"peace," "the state of distinctness without domination, with the distinct
participating in each other."[46] Now, this "atonal" postmodern thought has
gone far away from the Young Lukacs's humanistic logic.

Another example of the second-generation Western Marxian is Erich
Fromm, whose *To Have or to Be?* (1976) already gives up the abstract
subject-centralism, and differentiates the "possessive" humanistic survival
of the subject from the post-humanistic, non-possessive and non-central
totality of being. Fromm opposes that "narcissistic, self-involved, and possessive" humanism, in which man subjugates nature and holds a deep antagonistic attitude to it[47]. Despite his effort to unify the theoretical trend
with his own humanism, his original stress of the subjective dominance
and the logic of transcendence has been greatly compromised.

---

43   There are Western scholars who believe that Derrida actually inherits from Adorno.
See *"Adorno as the Devil"* by Jean-Francois Lyotard in TELOS 19 (Spring 1974).

44   Adorno, Theodor W. *Negative Dialectics*. London: Routledge, 1990. p. xi.

45   Gerhardt, Eike, and Andrew Arato. *The Essential Frankfurt School Reader*. New York:
Urizen Books, 1978. p. 505.

46   *Ibid.*, pp. 499-500.

47   Fromm, Erich. *To Have or To Be?* New York: Continuum International Publishing
Group, 2005. p.94.

II. THE "HUMANIST" MARXISM AND THE THEORY OF 'NATURAL-NESS'

If the points in the previous section are examined in abstract logical stipulations to represent the prospects of the Western Marxian trend, the following analysis will deal with their seemingly common interest with the subjective dimension of Marx's historical dialectics. First of all, it is the relationship of the humanistic Marxism with the theory of 'natural-ness'.

A. A MEDITATION ON THE HETEROGENEOUS RELATIONSHIP BETWEEN SOCIAL DEVELOPMENT AND NATURAL PROCESS

Most of the "humanistic" Marxians are concerned about the initiative of the human subject. Based on man's transcendence of nature, they also notice the heterogeneity of the human social history and the non-subjective natural processes.

First, Henri Lefebvre. He concludes that Marx goes beyond Feuerbach's naturalistic philosophy and all other idealistic thoughts with a real dialectical speculation of man's nature. To Lefebvre, man is a natural existence on the road of transcendence, the natural existence fighting against nature to govern it. Man protrudes from nature but his way of protruding, his governance of nature renders him more deeply rooted in nature. In ancient times, the alienated existence of man is essentially an antagonistic being; after man steps into social existence, the previous conflict with nature lingers on but assumes a new form.

In his view, the gradual growth of people's domination over nature cannot eliminate the remaining nature's control of man. Man's product works as a natural existence. He has to objectify himself. The social object turns into something against man, some fetishes. Here he is posited in a new conflict of history and humanity. Obviously, the natural contradiction continues, especially, in the aspect of its necessity and blindness. Man can only be self-separated through splitting, and humanized through self-division, like the division of activity and product, ability and fetishes, generated consciousness and spontaneous consciousness, structure and resistance, etc.

Lefebvre summarizes his opinion by a sentence from Marx that the human history is usually pushed forward by their dark side. He employs the capitalist market economy as an example. "A typical social object – the market–still exercises today a power over human beings exactly like that of the realities of the untrolled sector of Nature."[48] The market is often the

---

48   Lefebvre, Sturrock, and Kipfer. *Dialectical Materialism.* Uni. of Minnesota Press, 2009. p. 134.

decisive factor of human life, the natural presence within social existence. Social determinism is the natural determinism in society: On one hand, it provides the condition for human activities; on the other, it opposes and contains man's freedom. "It originates in natural objectivity, which is extended into the objectivity of Fetishes and the specific objectivity of social relations."[49]

Lefebvre makes an extension of the reversed human-object relationship in capitalism to an inevitable continuance of natural conflict, which gives this historical phenomenon an *abstract* necessity. Then, he turns Marx's metaphorical use of the social "naturalness" into its literal sense; thus, specific 'natural-ness' becomes an abstract non-historical logical stipulation.

Another second-generation thinker in Frankfurt School worthy of our attention is Alfred Schmidt, whose view seems the closest to Marx's theory of 'natural-ness' despite some critical misconceptions of his. The *Concept of Nature in Marx* observes the views of nature by Marx and Hegel. Schmidt says, for Hegel, the material world outside humankind is the "first" nature, "where blind necessity and blind chance coincide"; while people develop the forms of nation, society and economy, there comes the "second nature," which is still the material manifestation of reason and the objective spirit according to what Hegel says in his *Philosophy of Spirit*[50]. Thus, Marx's view that the historical development of human society forms the process of nature actually originates in Hegel's "second nature."

In Schmidt's view, "not the abstract nature of matter, but the concrete nature of social practice is the true subject and basis" of Marx's philosophical world[51]. Therefore, the aim of Marxism is "to help men out of their self-made prison of uncomprehended economic determination."[52] With Marx, "men have allowed themselves to be degraded into objects of the blind and mechanical process of its economic dynamic."[53] Moreover, the materialist part in Marx's theory is not to claim for the economic superiority but to mean that it is hostile to men, abstractly created by reality and thus independent of men. Marx thinks that "the economy was brought back again from its all-powerful position to a subordinate role."[54]

---

49   *Ibid.*, p. 135.
50   Schmidt, Alfred. *The Concept of Nature in Marx*, London: NLB, 1973. p. 43.
51   *Ibid.*, p. 40.
52   *Ibid.*, p. 41.
53   *Ibid.*, p. 41.
54   *Ibid.*, p. 41.

Schmidt points out, "In a wrongly organized society, the control of nature, however highly developed, remains at the same time an utter subjection to nature." [55]Noticeably, he is very precise when he says that when Marx takes the social history so far "as a 'process of natural history,' this had first of all the critical meaning that 'the laws of economics confront men in all [...] planless and incoherent production as objective laws over which they have no power...therefore in the form of laws of nature.'"[56]

Therefore, "Marx had in mind the experience gained in the course of the perennial 'prehistory' of man that, in spite of all technical triumphs, it is still always nature which is victorious in the last resort and not man."[57] Schmidt also cites Max Horkheimer's description of the capitalist anarchy: "The process is accomplished not under the control of a conscious will but as a natural occurrence. Everyday life results blindly, accidently, and badly from the chaotic activity of individuals, industries and states."[58] It is "merely nature tearing itself to pieces in that it is not socially controlled."[59]

In my opinion, Schmidt, as a Western Marxian, is closer to the authentic logic of Marx's theory of 'natural-ness' than that of our traditional framework of philosophical illustration. However, he does not fully understand the scientific significance of this argument. In particular, he fails to make a deep association of this point with Marx's ad hoc stipulation of the capitalist socio-historical laws. Regrettably, his exploring sail comes to a stop just in a short distance to the side of truth.

B. THE CRITIQUE OF THE CAPITALIST "ORDER OF NATURE"

As mentioned above, when Marx determines the phenomenon of material subjugation in capitalism, he uses the phrase "natural laws of production" in a figurative sense to illustrate the ridiculous blindness of human society similar to that of nature. The humanist Marxians begin to criticize and focus on these "natural laws" in capitalism[60], among whom, Karl Korsch and the Young Lukacs are the best representatives.

---

55   *Ibid.*, p. 42.
56   *Ibid.*, p. 43.
57   *Ibid.*, p. 43.
58   *Ibid.*, p. 41.
59   *Ibid.*, p. 43.
60   Probably, only Adorno and Habermas notice Marx's "natural laws" of capitalist society used in the sense of "similarity." They even adopt such expression as "naturwuchsigkeit" to describe the blind, unplanned phenomena in social history. See Jürgen Habermas's *Legitimation Crisis* (1975) and *John Keane's Public Life and Late Capitalism* (1984).

As with Gramsci, Korsch does not recognize the real significance of the natural substance independent of the human existence. He also disagrees with Gramsci's statement that there is no reality as itself, in itself and by itself, but the reality always existent in the mutual historical relations of people that change it. He believes that material nature does not directly affect human society and history. "Marxian materialism that 'pure' nature which is presupposed to all human activity (the economic *natura naturans*) is replaced everywhere by a "nature" mediated and modified through human social activity, and thus at the same time capable of a further change and modification by our own present and future activity, i.e., by nature as material production (or the economic *natura naturata*)."[61] It indicates that nature is *man's nature* in the social context, which has been paid much attention in our traditional research. However, Korsch's "nature" in the social process itself (or, the social laws of nature) is often been ignored.

In his view, Marx's research of the capitalist economy contains an important issue, that is, the "social laws of nature" during the process of production, which is *established in a negative sense*. Korsch notes that Marx is against the "general natural necessity" employed by the bourgeois economists who insist on the fallacy that the capitalist system continues to exist. Marx then validates the specific "social laws of nature" in capitalism from a "critical and revolutionary"[62] perspective. The laws "do not have within the new materialistic science of society that positive and final meaning which the real 'laws of nature' have for the physicist and which, according to their first discoverers and inventors, pertained also to those 'natural' laws which would in future govern the new 'civil' mode of existence emerging from the artificial fetters of mediaeval feudalism."[63] They are only used in a negative definition to illustrate the existent inhuman activities in the capitalist economic process. "The fact that the general conditions of bourgeois society which had been proclaimed as laws by the bourgeois economists, are restricted to a definite historical epoch, implies that in the further development of society all those apparent laws can be abrogated through the conscious social act of the class which is at present oppressed by them, to be replaced by another, a willed and planned form of the social activities of man."[64] Korsch is precise and penetrating.

---

61   Korsch, Karl. *Karl Marx*. Chapman & Hall, 1938. p. 191.
62   *Ibid.*, p. 110.
63   *Ibid.*, p. 247.
64   *Ibid.*, p. 247.

Later, Agger also sees this point. He says that Marx aims at revealing the capitalist "natural laws" (both Agger and Korsch put double quotes around the words "natural laws" to differentiate them with the general usage). However, for Agger, Marx does not intend to say capitalism is a typical scientific system with eternal characters that can be induced by observers who then propose assessable hypothesis of this system to seek the natural laws. And Agger believes that the so-called "natural laws" is only used by Marx to indicate the peculiar mode of capitalist development. In addition Marx holds that the capitalist natural laws suppress man and deprives him of his true autonomy; thus, he hopes to break the control of these natural laws over human beings.

In my opinion, the above opinion by Korsch and Agger shows their general understanding of Marx's theory of 'natural-ness', but they fail to go further to explore the contents of these "social laws of nature." The task is carried on by the Young Lukacs. His approach of the socio-historical "laws of nature" starts from Marx's exposition of the capitalist fetishism. Lukacs claims that "commodity fetishism is a *specific* problem of our age, the age of modern capitalism."[65] "The fetishistic illusions enveloping all phenomena in capitalist society succeed in concealing reality, but more is concealed than the historical, i.e. transitory, ephemeral nature of phenomena."[66] In his view, the generalization of the phenomenon of capitalist fetishism described in Marx's *Das Kapital* is the bourgeois aim to cover the true nature of capitalist society. It also accounts for an important aspect of the bourgeois defenders' claim for the eternal nature (naturalness) of capitalism. The Young Lukacs rightly points out: Marx conceives fetishism as the subjective reflection of the material-subjugation characteristic of the capitalist economic process and generally presents 'natural-ness' in the social history of capitalism. Judging from the perspective of criticizing the capitalist system, the Young Lukacs rightly hits the nail right on the head. According to him, Ricardo and other modern vulgar economists attempt to argue that the capitalist existence seems to "correspond to the nature of human reason and the 'laws of nature.'"[67] One of their most important points is that the capitalist economic laws are objective and independent of man's will, wherein, like nature, the economic laws promote the social development as an "invisible hand" does. Thus, the bourgeois economics establishes the economic laws as the laws of "nature." To oppose this view,

---

65   Lukács, Georg. *History and Class Consciousness: Studies in Marxist Dialectics*. MIT Press, 1972. p. 86.

66   *Ibid.*, p. 14.

67   *Ibid.*, p. 30.

the Young Lukacs puts forward three forms of nature: First, the common category of nature; second, the nature with axiological meaning, which is a rational stipulation against the feudal economy by the bourgeoisie; third, the nature that presents the so-called "authentic humanity."[68]

The second conception of nature will be analyzed. For Lukacs, people in feudalism cannot conceive their social existence because their social relations are still mainly natural ones; but feudalist society contains a mandatory subjectivity, which is combated by the bourgeoisie holding the banner of "objectivity" or "natural laws." He believes that "'nature' has been heavily marked by the revolutionary struggle of the bourgeoisie: the 'ordered', calculable, formal and abstract character of the approaching bourgeois society appears natural by the side of the artifice, the caprice and the disorder of feudalism and absolutism."[69]

However, the young Lukacs asserts that the bourgeois nature is actually the "second nature" with specific meanings in social history formed during the materialized process of the capitalist market economy[70]. Different from the original nature, it is the *new man-made economic reality*. "They erect around themselves in the reality they have created and 'made,' a kind of second nature which evolves with exactly the same inexorable necessity as was the case earlier on with irrational forces of nature (more exactly: the social relations which appear in this form). 'To them, their own social action,' says Marx, 'takes the form of the action of objects, which rule the producers instead of being ruled by them.'"[71] The "nature" in capitalism refers to the following specific phenomenon: "What is of central importance here is that because of this situation a man's own activity, his own labour becomes something objective and independent of him. something that controls him by virtue of an autonomy alien to man."[72] Behind this are the "social laws of nature" and the implication that all the human relations are degraded to such conceived level of natural laws, assimilated to such a level envisaged in the laws of nature. Therefore, the classical bourgeois economists often treat man as the object. "It is concerned with relations that are completely unconnected with man's humanity and indeed with any anthropomorphisms – be they religious, ethical, aesthetic or anything else. Man appears in it only as an abstract number, as something which can be

---

68   *Ibid.*, p. 136.
69   *Ibid.*, p. 136.
70   *Ibid.*, p.128.
71   *Ibid.*, p.128.
72   *Ibid.*, p. 87.

reduce to number or to numerical relations."[73] The economy's "complete independence of human will, knowledge and purpose, forms the objective precondition" of human activities[74].

The Young Lukacs believes, "nature" is given an ideological sense because "social institutions (reification) strip man of his human essence and that the more culture and civilisation (i.e. capitalism and reification) take possession of him, the less able he is to be a human being. And with a reversal of meanings that never becomes apparent, nature becomes the repository of all these inner tendencies opposing the growth of mechanisation, dehumanisation and reification."[75] In capitalism, "man finds himself confronted by purely natural relations or social forms mystified into natural relations. They appear to be fixed, complete and immutable entities which can be manipulated and even comprehended, but never overthrown."[76]

> **For the individual, whether capitalist or proletarian, his environment, his social milieu (including Nature which is the theoretical reflection and projection of that milieu) must appear the servant of a brutal and senseless fate which is eternally alien to him. This world can only be understood by means of a theory which postulates 'eternal laws of nature.'**[77]

The Young Lukacs repeatedly makes the metaphorical use of Hegel's "cunning of reason" for the "laws of nature" that are firmly independent of men's will in capitalism. In his opinion, "there is an antagonistic process that is not guided by a consciousness but is instead driven forward by its own immanent, blind dynamic and that this process stands revealed in all its immediate manifestations as the rule of the past over the present, the rule of capital over labour."[78] Here, the economic laws in human social history "are able to function as 'pure laws of nature' by virtue of their purely economic power, that is, with the aid of non-economic factors."[79]

> **But they must not be governed by a law in the sense in which 'laws' govern individual phenomena; they must not under any circumstances be rationally organised through and through. This does not mean, of course, that there can be no 'law' governing the whole. But such a 'law' would have to be the 'unconscious'**

---

73 *Ibid.*, p. 232.
74 *Ibid.*, p. 231.
75 *Ibid.*, p. 136.
76 *Ibid.*, p. 19.
77 *Ibid.*, p. 38.
78 *Ibid.*, p. 181.
79 *Ibid.*, p. 229.

product of the activity of the different commodity owners acting independently of one another, i.e. a law of mutually interacting 'coincidences' rather than one of truly rational organisation. Furthermore, such a law must not merely impose itself despite the wishes of individuals; it may not even be fully and adequately knowable. For the complete knowledge of the whole would vouchsafe the knower a monopoly that would amount to the virtual abolition of the capitalist economy.[80]

Thus, there are two trends in the bourgeois reason: 1) The object of history is represented as immutable, eternal natural laws, by which, history itself becomes a zombie and man, a puppet. For the Young Lukacs, the bourgeois scholars fall into "a formalism incapable of comprehending that the real nature of socio-historical institutions is that they consist of relations between men."[81] 2) History is changed to an irrational control by blind power, "which is embodied at best in the 'spirit of the people' or in 'great men'."[82] This is a *heroic* view of history.

At the same time, the Young Lukacs certainly notices changes in modern capitalism. For example, the bourgeoisie immediately accept the concept of conscious organization and there is already interference into or control of the economic process, in some cartels and trusts. "The idea of a 'planned' economy has gained ground at least among the more progressive elements of the bourgeoisie,"[83] which reflects the surrender of the bourgeois class consciousness before the proletariat class consciousness. Anyway, it is just the last means accessible for capitalism before its internal contradictions disintegrates.

The Young Lukacs basically adopts the standpoint of Marxist historical dialectics to criticize the capitalist "laws of nature." Nevertheless, he fails to notice the figurative use of the phrase by Marx and Engels, which makes him lose a logical dialectic and unable to sublate socio-historical 'naturalness' on a new level to welcome the true development of human history. And still, his theoretical points are better than those in our traditional framework of philosophical interpretation.

---

80 *Ibid.*, p. 102.
81 *Ibid.*, p. 48.
82 *Ibid.*, p. 48.
83 *Ibid.*, p. 67.

C. THE IDEOLOGICAL MYTH OF "NATIVISM"

Fredric Jameson, the contemporary Western Marxian, assigns an entire sub-section titled "Nature as Ideology" in his book *Postmodernism and Cultural Theories*, which directly expresses what is metaphorically used by the Young Lukacs.

According to Jameson, the concept of nature is one of the most important ideologies in the arsenal of the bourgeois revolution. In his analysis, if observed from a historical perspective, nativism in the bourgeois ideology has two interpretations, both positive and negative; progressive and reactionary. As the Young Lukacs notes before, the stress of non-human "nature" has revolutionary significance in the struggle against feudalism. Here, Jameson's analysis slightly differs. In his view, the bourgeois knowledge of nature is active and progressive when it fights against aristocracy and caste system because the hierarchy of the feudal society is based on a natural family/blood origin, in which various social groups, such as the middle-class businessmen, farmers, high noblemen, are born with separation and difference in blood. To break off the "legitimate myth" of the feudal hierarchy, the bourgeoisie must set up a natural and common nature for all the people. To confirm a universal human nature, the true equality between people is a subversive act, a revolutionary behaviour with very profound significance. Moreover, this assertive statement will lead to an ideology, for which men will willingly fight and even sacrifice. The new ideological flint strikes the fire of "humanity," which then lights the lamp of "equality," which again, illuminates the road of "revolution," and finally paves the way to brightness. These are the progressive steps of the bourgeois ideology in history.

History tends to repeat itself, only in an opposite way. Once the bourgeoisie rise to power, the ideology of nature undergoes a fundamental change. Now, without the feudal nobles, the hierarchical blood origin disappears before the natural humanity and innate rights. So does the previous privileges in politics and laws. In capitalist society, people are equal in political life as each worker has the same vote as a capitalist does but the proletarians are actually being subjugated and exploited in their actual economic existence. The bourgeoisie, of course, cannot allow the working class to change their status and must prevent them from joining a revolution that might in turn seize power from the bourgeoisie themselves. Hence, the nature of the bourgeois ideology and the nature of man undergo big semantic changes: The meanings of these thoughts become completely different, which means the equal value of people in the market system, the equal exchange value and the equal commoditized value of labour. Accordingly, man possesses the liberty of selling his labour in the market.

The bourgeois ideology intends to perpetualize the capitalist mode of production through its conception of nature. The goal is obtained in a capitalism-is-nature-and-thus-humanity metaphor. In the eyes of Jameson, the bourgeois justifies that the market, exchange and commodities are a part of human nature and an immutable content of any imaginable social life. Thus, people do not believe their individual experience of the class reality. In the market system, we do not apparently face the dialectical class relations but the "atomized" competitions among groups composed of individuals with equivalent values. Therefore, the belief in nature and human nature will be legalized to combat collectivism or class consciousness in advance. According to Jameson, Marx has a profound criticism of the bourgeois ideology in the guise of "nature": Those economists employs confirmation of nature to make the "economic man" in capitalist society enter all other social forms and modes of production, whether they are the past or the future societies. In this regard, the bourgeois conception of nature reaches the peak with its ideological function and *discourse of power* for the reason that if capitalism is in line with nature (human nature) and humanity is always itself no matter when and where, the illusion of human nature will be drastically changed and the present system will be replaced accordingly, which is but a fancied Utopia. As a result, capitalism becomes the thing that will never be changed while *any attempt against it is a violation of human nature and the laws of nature*! In my opinion, Jameson carries out an important critical analysis here.

III. THE "HUMANIST" MARXISM AND THE THEORY OF MATERIAL-SUBJUGATION

In addition to the notice of Marx's theory of 'natural-ness', the "humanist" Marxism is concerned about the phenomenon of material-subjugation in capitalism, especially, the new situation and the dominant forms of people in the bourgeois ideology, which is of certain theoretical value and worth our attention.

A. THE YOUNG LUKACS'S CRITIQUE OF THE NON-SUBJECTIVE "REIFICATION"

Besides the critique of the "laws of nature" analyzed before, *History and Class Consciousness* by the Young Lukacs also criticizes the specific non-subjective "materialization" during the capitalist economic process. Unlike Marx, he does not distinguish reification from material-subjugation or, the early differentiation of objectification and alienation due to the reason that he is unaware of Marx's *1844 Manuscripts*. His category of "reification" is used in the sense of Marx's material-subjugation and confirmed as the nature of the entire capitalist economic life.

In the article titled "Reification and the Consciousness of the Proletariat," he writes, "Reification is, then, the necessary, immediate reality of every person living in capitalist society."[84] In the capitalist process of production, the essence of commodity-structure has often been pointed out.

Its basis is that a relation between people takes on the character of a thing and thus acquires a 'phantom objectivity', an autonomy that seems so strictly rational and all-embracing as to conceal every trace of its fundamental nature[85].

It is clear that the Young Lukacs still adopts the subjective perspective of commodity fetishism in the bourgeois ideology to interpret "reification." He acknowledges that it is not a universal phenomenon during the whole history but a special situation after the commodity spreads as a common structure in human society.

Firstly, the "reification" of the subjective activities. In capitalist production, man's "own labour becomes something objective and independent of him, something that controls him by virtue of an autonomy alien to man."[86] Human labour becomes a process of reification outside men and their activities are turned to objective commodities attached to the social laws of nature.

Secondly, the "reification" of the subject. Due to the labour reification, the labourers themselves are transformed to the attachment of material production, reified to a passive material factor. "Neither objectively nor in his relation to his work does man appear as the authentic master of the process."[87] "The split between the worker's labour-power and his personality, its metamorphosis into a thing, an object that he sells on the market is repeated here too."[88] Meanwhile, men in capitalist society are still dominated by the external forces. "Man in capitalist society confronts a reality 'made' by himself (as a class) which appears to him to be a natural phenomenon alien to himself; he is wholly at the mercy of its 'laws', his

---

84   Lukács, Georg. *History and Class Consciousness: Studies in Marxist Dialectics.* MIT Press, 1972. p. 197.
85   *Ibid.,* p. 89.
86   *Ibid.,* p. 87.
87   *Ibid.,* p. 89.
88   *Ibid.,* p. 99.

activity is confined to the exploitation of the inexorable fulfillment of certain individual laws for his own (egoistic) interests."[89] Therefore, "for the individual, whether capitalist or proletarian, his environment, his social milieu (including Nature which is the theoretical reflection and projection of that milieu) must appear the servant of a brutal and senseless fate which is eternally alien to him."[90]

Thirdly, the "reification" of the relationship among people. With the reification of the production structure, the previous simple relationship between men is expressed between objects and things; naturally, their exchange of labour is cast with a material veil. "In them the relations between men that lie hidden in the immediate commodity relation, as well as the relations between men and the objects that should really gratify their needs, have faded to the point where they can be neither recognised nor even perceived."[91]

Fourthly, the reification of man's consciousness. The Young Georg Lukacs claims, when the capitalist system makes continual production and reproduction of itself on higher and higher levels, the reification structure gradually, deeply and finally infiltrates into human consciousness. "The transformation of the commodity relation into a thing of 'ghostly objectivity' cannot therefore content itself with the reduction of all objects for the gratification of human needs to commodities. It stamps its imprint upon the whole consciousness of man."[92] During the process of labour production in modern capitalism, the labourer loses his own subjective consciousness; everything is increasingly processed in a formalized and standardized manner; the spiritual ability of the workers is mechanically oppressed and separated from personality, being an object, a commodity. Hence, the subject's knowledge, interest and expression are "reduced to an abstract mechanism functioning autonomously."[93]

In short, the Young Lukacs judges, the commodity relations in capitalism make everything reified.

His qualities and abilities are no longer an organic part of his personality, they are things which he can 'own' or 'dispose of' like the various objects of the external world. And there is no natural form in which human relations can be cast, no way in

---

89   *Ibid.*, p. 135.
90   *Ibid.*, p. 38.
91   *Ibid.*, p. 93.
92   *Ibid.*, p. 100.
93   *Ibid.*, p. 100.

which man can bring his physical and psychic 'qualities' into play without their being subjected increasingly to this reifying process[94].

The social reification in capitalism is covered by the bourgeois fetishism. "The fetishistic illusions enveloping all phenomena in capitalist society succeed in concealing reality, but more is concealed than the historical, i.e. transitory, ephemeral nature of phenomena."[95] They attempt to pass the capitalist "reification" off as eternal natural laws. "For only this conception dissolves the fetishistic forms necessarily produced by the capitalist mode of production and enables us to see them as mere illusions which are not less illusory for being seen to be necessary. These unmediated concepts, these 'laws' sprout just as inevitably from the soil of capitalism and veil the real relations between objects."[96] "They can all be seen as ideas necessarily held by the agents of the capitalist system of production. They are, there-fore...the ideology of its ruling class. Only when this veil is torn aside does historical knowledge become possible."[97]

For the first time, the young Lukacs relates the three major aspects of Marx's theory of material-subjugation (although he is not aware of the labour alienation theory of the Young Marx because the *1844 Manuscripts* have not been published at that time). The other important point of his is the rational "reification" behind science and technology brought out by the capitalist industrial production, which presents a new condition for the reification of man's consciousness and *ushers the Frankfurt School's critique of instrumental rationality.*

B. THE YOUNG LUKACS'S "RATIONAL" CRITIQUE OF SCIENCE AND TECHNOLOGY

The capitalist process of production faced by the Young Lukacs is already the modern industry represented by Taylor's automatic assembly line. He grasps an important point on a new level, namely, science and technology in the capitalist production; to be more precise, he defines the role of sci-ence and technology in the promotion of the reification of labourers. In his opinion, in capitalism, "the fetishistic character of economic forms, the rei-fication of all human relations, the constant expansion and extension of the division of labour which subjects the process of production to an abstract, rational analysis, without regard to the human potentialities and abilities of

---

94   *Ibid.,* p. 100.
95   *Ibid.,* p. 14.
96   *Ibid.,* p. 13.
97   *Ibid.,* pp. 13-14.

the immediate producers, all these things transform the phenomena of society and with them the way in which they are perceived."[98] At the same time, the scientific change of the productive forms makes the capitalist reification process more objective and justified. When scientific knowledge "is applied to society, it turns out to be an ideological weapon of the bourgeoisie."[99]

The Young Lukacs sees "a continuous trend towards greater rationalisation" with the application of science and technology in automated production[100]. It is the progressive elimination of the qualitative, human and individual attributes of the worker. On one hand, the process of labour is progressively broken down into abstract, rational, specialised operations. "On the other hand, the period of time necessary for work to be accomplished (which forms the basis of rational calculation) is converted, as mechanisation and rationalisation are intensified, from a merely empirical average figure to an objectively calculable work-stint that confronts the worker as a fixed and established reality."[101] Therefore, "with the modern 'psychological' analysis of the work-process (in Taylorism) this rational mechanisation extends right into the worker's 'soul.'"[102] In consequence of the objective, scientific rationalisation and mechanization, "the human qualities and idiosyncrasies of the worker appear increasingly as mere sources of error."[103]

Here, the Young Lukacs makes a new important discovery: The major aspect of the material-subjugation in present capitalist industrial production transcends the old dead labour (capital) to the *rationality* per se that emerges as a rational scientific law. As we know, Marx is aware that science and technology is distorted to the forces against the workers in the capitalist system. The Young Lukacs goes further. He immediately grasps the innate contradiction of man in the rationality of science and technology, which undoubtedly hits the mark. In my view, it results from the rationality of the capitalist industrial technology proposed by Max Weber, who conceives the rationality centred on objective technology is the fundamental principle of the survival of capitalism, and even the "spirit of capitalism."[104] Indeed, the Young Lukacs quotes Weber's another state-

---

98   *Ibid.*, p. 6.
99   *Ibid.*, p. 10.
100 *Ibid.*, p. 88.
101 *Ibid.*, p. 88.
102 *Ibid.*, p. 88.
103 *Ibid.*, p. 89.
104 Weber, Max, and Talcott Parsons. *The Protestant Ethic and the Spirit of Capitalism.* New York: Courier Dover Publications, 2003.

ment, in which the modern economic process in capitalism is compared to an operating machine based on rational calculations and "fixed general laws," different from "a patriarchal administration" that maintains "the irrational tradition."[105] "What is specific to modern capitalism as distinct from the age-old capitalist forms of acquisition is that the strictly rational organisation of work on the basis of rational technology did not come into being anywhere within such irrationally constituted political systems nor could it have done so."[106] As a bourgeois scholar, Weber certainly makes use of science and technology to validate the rationality of capitalism. On the contrary, the Young Lukacs finds an inherent paradox in it: This process of instrumental rationality that drives forward the productive forces is premised on an even higher cost, the subjugation of the workers and the loss of subjectivity. The bourgeoisie is using scientific rationality to enhance the capitalist process of "reification."

According to the Young Lukacs, the bourgeoisie conceals the nature of "reification" with science and technology in a calculable, abstract and numerical way. "It is concerned to make it permanent by 'scientifically deepening' the laws at work."[107] Today's capitalism makes man adopt "the contemplative stance adopted towards a process mechanically conforming to fixed laws and enacted independently of man's consciousness and impervious to human intervention, i.e. a perfectly closed system."[108] *As for the subjugation of people, the rationality from objective and impartial scientific technology is more serious and difficult to eradicate than the earlier material domination.* This conclusion of the Young Lukacs is important to understand the exploitative nature of the modern capitalist economic processes. He is acutely aware of the new phenomenon in the capitalist production: *Transference from the subjugation of man by the man-made object to the self-subjugation by the subject's own nature, rationality.* This is closely related to the changing circumstances in the early 20th century when science and technology dominated the structure of practice in the developed countries of the West. It is what we should be concerned about. Later, this point becomes a theoretical beginning for the Frankfurt School to criticize contemporary capitalism.

---

105   *Ibid.*, p. 96.
106   Lukács, Georg. *History and Class Consciousness: Studies in Marxist Dialectics.* MIT Press, 1972. p. 96.
107   *Ibid.*, p. 89.
108   *Ibid.*, p. 89.

For the Young Lukacs, the bourgeois "pretence that society is regulated by 'eternal, iron' laws which branch off into the different special laws applying to particular areas is finally revealed for what it is: a pretence."[109] By these words, he firmly stands by the proletarians and negates the anti-human and non-subjective phenomenon of "reification" in capitalist society. With the aim of beating down capitalism and advocating communism, he holds that it is Marxist historical realism that discovers the law: The "reification" of man's social relations is a specific phenomenon particular to capitalism, as well as a transient historical one. Thus, he corrects the Second International's error of extending the historical phenomenon of the economic domination over man to a general law in social history.

The Young Lukacs believes "vulgar Marxist theory" (mainly, Austrian Marxism) fails to understand Marx's scientific view of history. As a result, "it mistook purely historical categories, moreover categories relevant only to capitalist society, for eternally valid ones."[110] For Marx, the capitalist circumstance where the human subject is subjugated by the external economic forces is only a historical phenomenon, which will eventually be eliminated with the development of productive forces and the realization of communism. At that time, the winter snow will slowly thaw; the spring thunders will begin to roar; the sweet rain will timely fall; and human social history will certainly take a leap forward. The subject will gain the social "totality" in his conscious action and firmly grasp the necessity of the economic process. Thus, human society will change from the previous "process of social nature" to that under the conscious guide of the human subject, with its ultimate home, "in intention and basis," as "the realm of freedom."[111] Finally, humans will achieve their liberation, when "the 'realm of freedom,' the end of the 'prehistory of mankind' means precisely that the power of the objectified, reified relations between men begins to revert to *man*."[112]

It should be recognized and praised that the Young Lukacs takes a general Marxist point of view to analyze the capitalist thought of "reification" with the proletarian revolution in mind. His major idea rightly follows Marx's thought of material-subjugation. However, he does not differentiate reification (objectification) from "alienation" (material-subjugation), which he later admits as a Hegelian mistake. Later, in his self-criticism, Lukacs says, the text of *History and Class Consciousness* makes a Hegelian

109   Ibid., p. 101.
110   *Ibid.*, p. 239.
111   *Ibid.*, p. 250.
112   *Ibid.*, p. 69.

error, not to "make a terminological distinction between alienation and objectification."[113] This logical error changes the historical alienation into an eternal human condition. Secondly, the Young Lukacs makes a logical confusion of theoretical objectivity with subjective definition. He equals the phenomenon of material-subjugation in the capitalist production with the bourgeois ideology of fetishism. The last and the most important thing is that he fails to offer different treatment to the objective historical significance of the development of productive forces (science and technology) and the distorted nature of the ensuing improvement under the capitalist condition, making his critique mixed with a romantic hue that is to influence the Frankfurt School later.

C. THE FRANKFURT SCHOOL:
THE INSTRUMENTAL RATIONALITY AND
THE IDEOLOGY OF TECHNOLOGY

If the Young Lukacs shares quite a few points with Marx in the criticism of the capitalist "laws of nature" and the non-subjective "reification," the late Frankfurt School (since the establishment of the so-called "post-humanist" framework) has new changes in its critique of the material-subjugation in contemporary capitalism.

The Frankfurt School starts where the Young Lukacs ends but its analysis itself is *greatly advanced from the material alienation of the human subject in the economic life.* The scholars of the Frankfurt School believe that the absolute poor status in the concerns of Marx, Engels and the Young Lukacs cannot be found any more. "In advanced capitalist countries, the standard of living has, in any case, risen to such an extent, at least among broad strata of the population, that the interest in the emancipation of society can no longer be articulate directly in economic terms. 'Alienation' has been deprived of its palpable economic form as misery."[114] In their view, the former material-subjugation characterized by poverty is only inferior alienation. If it means *man's created material does not belong to himself.* The modern capitalist alienation already erodes the depths of the human heart, implying that *man's self does not belong to himself.* It has become the alienation of rationality, the alienation of alienation, or the alienation "squared."[115] In my opinion, the significance of this theory is less of a

---

113   Lukács, Georg and John Rees. *A Defence of History and Class Consciousness: Tailism and the Dialectic.* Verso, 2002. p. 34.

114   Habermas, Jürgen. *Theory and Practice.* Boston: Beacon Press, 1988. p. 195.

115   Zhang Yibing. *Broken Wings of Reason—Criticism of Western Marxism.* Nanjing: Nanjing Publishing House, 1990.

gradual logical advance than a new perception of the social man's *reality* in contemporary capitalism.

The criticism seizes the most important character of the human subject, rationality, and shows that human rationality is distorted to a non-subjective anti-human instrumental rationality. I think this opinion inherits and continues the Young Lukacs's critique of the capitalist science and technology, on both higher theoretical and practical levels.

For the Frankfurt School, human rationality is born out of the fight against divinity. It initially comes out as an "antidote" to myths, holding high the banner of the human "spirit of enlightenment" by which the *conquering and ruling knowledge* of nature becomes the categorical order of Western civilization because rationality is the ability to supervise nature and society for the satisfactions of people as well as a critical power for the subject's transcendence over reality. The nature of rationality is supposed to enable man to control nature, from which he can be liberated. However, in capitalism, it goes to its opposite, from commanding nature to subjugating himself. The subjective rationality turns itself into an instrumental objective means. The original aim of dominating nature gradually loses its function of emancipation, being more and more confined to technical performance. It is not concerned with the purpose but the methods; it receives not freedom but an instrumental chain; it serves not the spirit of the subject but the material or social techniques. The darkening process is premised on the exclusion of man's subjective reason by instrumental rationality.

By criticizing the capitalist instrumental rationality and reasonability, the Young Lukacs stands in the forefront of the Frankfurt School. As mentioned before, he notices the argument of the capitalist rationality by Max Weber, who positively explains the "ideal mode" (the mode of act) inside the social functioning of capitalism, namely, the paradigm of rationality. Weber conceives the innate drive of capitalist society is to appreciate the objective rationality, request the rules and laws operated outside the individual will to create a legal machine-like society independent of man. To oppose this opinion, the Young Lukacs sharply and lethally points out that Weber leaves the reification process of capitalism to discuss rationality while judging from the relationship between the human subject and object, the capitalist rationality is nothing else but the alienation of the subject, hidden with a deeper logic of anti-rationality. This view is endorsed by Habermas' comment. "What Weber called 'rationalization' realizes not rationality as such but rather, in the name of rationality, a specific form of unacknowledged political domination."[116] The act with rational purpose is to control both man and nature. And the overall generalization of this rationality in capitalist society leads to "the result that criteria of instrumental action also penetrate into other areas of life."[117] Therefore, there is the *paradox* in the development of rationality: "The liberating force of technology – the instrumentalization of things – turns into a fetter of liberation; the instrumentalization of man."[118] Indeed, the Frankfurt School has disproved the traditional rationalistic thought of totality by the Young Lukacs here.

In modern capitalist society, on the one hand is the situation that "man encounters nature as transformed by society, subjected to a specific rationality which became, to an ever-increasing extent, technological, instrumentalist rationality, bent to the requirements of capitalism. And this rationality was also brought to bear on man's own nature, on his primary drives."[119] "The society which projects and undertakes the technological transformation of nature alters the base of domination by gradually replacing personal dependence (of the slave on the master, the serf on the lord of the manor, the lord on the donor of the fief, etc.) with dependence on the "objective order of things" (on economic laws, the market etc.)."[120] On the other hand, the human subject per se is self-alienated in the technical process that should have been oriented towards the object.

The technical process, to which the subject has been reified after the eradication of that process from consciousness, is as free from the ambiguous meanings of mythical thought as from meaning altogether, since reason itself has become merely an aid to the all-encompassing economic apparatus. Reason serves as a universal tool for the fabrication of all other tools, rigidly purpose-directed and as calamitous as the precisely calculated operations of material production, the results of which for human beings escape all calculation[121].

---

116   Habermas, Jürgen. *Toward a Rational Society: Student Protest, Science, and Politics.* Boston: Beacon Press, 1971. p. 82.

117   *Ibid.*, p. 81.

118   Marcuse, Herbert. *One-dimensional Man: Studies in the Ideology of Advanced Industrial Society.* Psychology Press, 2002. p.163.

119   Marcuse, Herbert. *Counterrevolution and Revolt.* Boston: Beacon Press, 1972. pp. 59-60.

120   Marcuse, Herbert. *One-dimensional Man: Studies in the Ideology of Advanced Industrial Society.* Psychology Press, 2002. p. 147.

121   Horkheimer, Adorno, and Gunzelin Schmidt Noerr. *Dialectic of Enlightenment: Philosophical Fragments.* Stanford University Press, 2002. p. 23.

Therefore, "the more complex and sensitive the social, economic, and scientific mechanism, to the operation of which the system of production has long since attuned the body, the more impoverished are the experiences of which the body is capable."[122]

The rationality of automation technology comes into being. Through the control of natural rationality and the bureaucratic rule of the working process, it makes the economic and political operation of the whole capitalist society an automated non-subjective process. *With integration and effective suppression of deviation, a deeper alienation of man is made.*

It seems that even as technical knowledge expands the horizon of man's thought and activity, his autonomy as an individual, his ability to resist the growing apparatus of mass manipulation, his power of imagination, his independent judgment appear to be reduced. Advance in technical facilities for enlightenment is accompanied by a process of dehumanization[123].

Therefore, "human beings are being turned back into precisely what the developmental law of society, the principle of the self, had opposed: mere examples of the species, identical to one another through isolation within the compulsively controlled collectivity," like the rowers who are unable to speak to one another[124]. In contemporary capitalist production, "man becomes completely dumb and only science speaks out."[125] Science and technology replace the traditional capitalists to become the *objective subject* of controlling the workers. At the same time, to oppose such views of the "end of ideology" and "non-ideology," advocated by the Western bourgeois scholars in the 1950s and 60s, the Frankfurt School argues that *science and technology is the biggest ideology of contemporary capitalism*[126]. According to them, technology, as a cultural form, has substituted the old political ideology in its defense of the present social system. Habermas believes that the state intervention and the increasing legal status of science and technology

---

122   *Ibid.*, p. 81.
123   Horkheimer, Max. *Eclipse of Reason.* New York: Oxford University Press, 1947. p. V-VI.
124   Horkheimer, Adorno, and Gunzelin Schmidt Noerr. *Dialectic of Enlightenment: Philosophical Fragments.* Stanford University Press, 2002. p. 29.
125   Horkheimer, Max. *Critical Theory: Selected Essays.* New York: Continuum International Publishing Group, 1982. p. 186.
126   The alleged view of the "end of ideology" is proposed in the 1950s by some Western scholars. It mainly indicates the decline of the previous political opinions, such as Marxism and the communist revolution upheld by various radical movements in the West. It is mainly represented by Edward Shils's "The End of Ideology?" in *The End of Ideology Debate*, Volume 196 (Funk & Wagnalls, 1969) and Daniel Bell's *End of Ideology: On the Exhaustion of Political Ideas in the Fifties* (New York: Free Press, 1960).

have become the major directions of the development of late capitalism. With the scientific and technological advance, Weber's rationalization has been greatly universalized and the ruler has successfully transformed the political issue into a "technical" one.

In their eyes, modern capitalism is a controlling machine with the help of an objective, justified, scientific and technical rationality.

> **At the base of the pyramid atomization prevails. It converts the entire individual – body and soul – into an instrument, or even part of an instrument: active or passive, productive or receptive, in working time and free time, he serves the system... Behind the technological veil, behind the political veil of democracy, appears the reality, the universal servitude, the loss of human dignity in a prefabricated freedom of choice[127].**

Run over by the machine, the body is voided and the soul is repressed. This repression, so different from that which characterized the preceding, less developed stages of our society, operates today not from a position of natural and technical immaturity but rather from a position of strength. The capabilities (intellectual and material) of contemporary society are immeasurably greater than ever before – which means that the scope of society's domination over the individual is immeasurably greater than ever before. "Our society distinguishes itself by conquering the centrifugal social forces with Technology rather than Terror, on the dual basis of an overwhelming efficiency and an increasing standard of living."[128] And "it thus obliterates the Opposition between the private and public existence, between individual and social needs. Technology serves to institute new, more effective, and more pleasant forms of social control and social cohesion. The totalitarian tendency of these controls seems to assert itself."[129] In that sacred halo of science, the human subject further loses himself. No fairy tales, no magic flute, no amazing fantasies, and no magnificent poetry! Everything operates to the scientific laws. For the human subject, "as long as they are kept incapable of being autonomous, as long as they are indoctrinated and manipulated (down to their very instincts), their answer to this question cannot be taken as their own."[130]

---

127 Marcuse, Herbert. *Counterrevolution and Revolt*. Boston: Beacon Press, 1972. p.14.
128 Marcuse, Herbert. *One-Dimensional Man: Studies in the Ideology of Advanced Industrial Society*. Psychology Press, 2002. p. XL.
129 *Ibid.*, p. XLVI.
130 *Ibid.*, p. 8.

In today's capitalist society, technology is no longer a "neutral" concept. "Technological rationality has become political rationality."[131] Now, "the technological society is a system of domination, which operates already in the concept and construction of techniques."[132] It reflects the inherent contradictions of capitalist civilization: "The irrational element in its rationality."[133] Unfortunately, people tend to agree with this new fallacious ideology. In consequence, the technological ideology of contemporary capitalism is "more ideological" than the old political ideology. Habermas conceives that it has become a "background ideology" that modern capitalism cannot get rid of.

According to the Frankfurt School, we have a new "anonymous authority": The science and technology used by the bourgeoisie. In traditional societies, "it is clear that there is an order and who gives it: one can fight against the authority," like the landlord, the capitalist or the king[134]. Now, they are replaced by a new anonymous authority in the guise of scientific and technological rationality, which is more powerful than a public ruler because it springs from the depths of heart, caters to our psychological needs. People worship it as they do science, faith and justice. Society transforms to an automatic machine; the ruler is just the spokesperson of the rationality of science; and the control is euphemized as management that is again based on the objective necessity of social function. More importantly, it is impossible for people to oppose this new ruler. Under the control of the "anonymous authority," one is left in the dark, like being shot but unable to know who shoots. "There is nobody and nothing to fight back against."[135] There seems to be no necessary redemption and no need to face the consequence. As if we were getting ready to take the fight but losing the name of action: Where is the enemy?

Lastly, the Frankfurt School holds that the form of the ontological existence of the subjective rationality in contemporary capitalist society, the spiritual culture, viz., the *subjective vision that best represents the subject's personality is also completely distorted.* Alienation of man spreads from the process of production to the workers' free time because "the whole world is passed through the filter of the cultural industry."[136]

---

131 *Ibid.*, p. XLVII.
132 *Ibid.*, p. XLII.
133 Ibid., p. 19.
134 Fromm, Erich. *Escape from Freedom.* New York: Macmillan, 1994. p.166.
135 *Ibid.*, p. 166.
136 Horkheimer, Adorno, and Gunzelin Schmidt Noerr. *Dialectic of Enlightenment: Philosophical Fragments.* Stanford University Press, 2002. p. 99.

The products of the culture industry are such that they can be alertly consumed even in a state of distraction. But each one is a model of the gigantic economic machinery, which, from the first, keeps everyone on their toes, both at work and in the leisure time which resembles it. In any sound film or any radio broadcast something is discernible which cannot be attributed as a social effect to any one of them, but to all together. Each single manifestation of the culture industry inescapably reproduces human beings as what the whole has made them[137].

In this way, the reality of contemporary capitalism constitutes a more advanced phase of alienation. It is in various forms and in everywhere. Among them, modern mass media becomes the biggest tool of this high-level alienation in capitalism.

The means of mass transportation and communication, the commodities of lodging, food, and clothing, the irresistible output of the entertainment and information industry carry with them prescribed attitudes and habits, certain intellectual and emotional reactions which bind the consumers more or less pleasantly to the producers and, through the latter, to the whole. The products indoctrinate and manipulate; they promote a false consciousness which is immune against its falsehood. And as these beneficial products become available to more individuals in more social classes, the indoctrination they carry ceases to be publicity; it becomes a way of life[138].

The whole concept of contemporary capitalism has deteriorated into ideology: "Mere words take the place of the human reality; these words are administered by a bureaucracy which thus succeeds in controlling people and gaining power and influence."[139] Hence, according to Lefebvre, even the little things of daily life have been alienated because everything is immersed in the overall alienation; man becomes non-human; he is alienated into an involuntary objective status, and even transformed into a puppet of false life.

The Frankfurt School takes an example from the distortion of cultural art that best expresses the freedom of the human subject. "Art becomes a species of commodity, worked up and adapted to industrial production,

---

137   *Ibid.*, p. 100.
138   Marcuse, Herbert. *One-Dimensional Man: Studies in the Ideology of Advanced Industrial Society.* Psychology Press, 2002. p. 14.
139   Fromm, Erich. *Beyond the Chains of Illusion: My Encounter with Marx and Freud.* New York: Continuum International Publishing Group, 2001. p. 135.

saleable and exchangeable."[140] It expressly conveys commodity fetishism, only concerned with the attendance and profits instead of the pursuit of artistic values. And the artistic individuality is killed in the standardization and homogeneity of mass culture. The free subject disintegrates before the replicas of the cultural industries. For example, the pop music, with simplistic structure, repetitious rhythms, mechanical beats, foresees every effect it has, just producing mechanical responses from the audience. Thus, mass culture possesses a coercive nature. "Even during the leisure time, consumers must orient themselves according to the unity of production."[141]

The cultural Centre are becoming a fitting part of the shopping centre... It is good that almost everyone can now have the fine arts at his fingertips, by just turning a knob on his set, or by just stepping into his drugstore. In this diffusion, however, they become cogs in a cultural-machine which remakes their content[142].

No longer is there an exit for escape; nor the other side is attainable. In contemporary capitalist society, art has become the slave of the employer; whether artistic achievement or appreciation is distilled through pre-design to withstand competition in the market; the technological development makes gaudy garments conspicuously seen in busy streets out of cheap art that only marks an artistic depravity; the rationality of technology virtually cancels fine arts; they are mercilessly objectified, deprived of the original critical nature, and degraded to the accomplice of the technological rationality that destroys individuality.

D. ANALYSIS AND CONCLUSION

I believe that the Frankfurt School is very important in their critiques of the new situation where man is subjugated in contemporary capitalist society. They make valuable contributions to notice the new problems of modern capitalism. In their criticism of instrumental rationality, the scientific and technological rationality in capitalist society is distorted from man's reform of the object of nature into something anti-human. When science and technology are used to *contend with* people in capitalism, it is imposed as a man-made (economic and empirical) law (rationality) imposed on the existence of human beings, whether in the process of production or the

---

140 Horkheimer, Adorno, and Gunzelin Schmidt Noerr. D*ialectic of Enlightenment: Philosophical Fragments.* Stanford University Press, 2002. p. 128.
141 *Ibid.,* p. 98.
142 Marcuse, Herbert. *One-Dimensional Man: Studies in the Ideology of Advanced Industrial Society.* Psychology Press, 2002. p. 68.

reality of life. The application of the natural laws to man necessarily leads to a subjective *material-subjugation stemming from the objective rationality*, which, of course, has grown out of the "past labour" and the product's subjugation of man observed by Marx and Engels into a rational *self-subjugation* of the subject (labour). Like a boomerang, it almost returns to what Hegel once describes as the *conceptual* "cunning reason" that dominates man in the background.

On the other hand, it is worth our attention to the "real alienation" in contemporary capitalist society put forward by the Frankfurt School: The spiritual and cultural phenomenon of non-subjectivity, which is no longer a simple reversal of the *material force* but the *full hearted* subjugation of self by rationality per se and *the resultant validation of the material-subjugation of the capital in reality*, identified later by Agger as the Frankfurt School's logical conversion from the paradigm of "alienation" to that of "domination" in their social criticism. In fact, it is an important aspect of the "postmodern turn" I have mentioned before. In the eyes of Agger, this domination displays a mode in which man cannot detect his own alienation but can appreciate the capitalist productive forces and material affluence. Domination thus becomes the alienation imposed on man under the false consciousness. This view of the Frankfurt School, according to Agger, aims to adapt to the new reality of the state intervention into the post-war capitalist economy, of the apparent wealth for all classes and of the expanded consumerism. For example, Habermas focuses on the "theory of communicative action." Based on Marx's theory of the realm of freedom and the realm of necessity, he puts forward the real free *communicative* theory, different from the *labour* (work) driven by the necessity of the material life and the technological interest dominated by the means. Here, Habermas *fundamentally opposes to all forms of domination and control*. He advocates an ontological existence of the *dialogue* of the *mutually identified or recognized subjects*. He even opposes man's control or conquest of nature (it is consistent with the postmodernist thought and under the contemporary ecological impact. See relevant discussion in next chapter), despite his later stance of maintaining the capitalist system. For Adorno, Marx's proposition of the realm of freedom that *fully dominates nature* is also imprecise since he claims against any conquest and uniformity. Also, Fromm makes considerable effort in his later years to think about the "non-possessive" human existence and mentality.

It should be admitted that such early Western Marxians as the Frankfurt School and the Young Lukacs are largely relevant in their studies of the practice of the European proletarian revolution and the new circumstance of contemporary capitalism. For example, their conceptions are similar in regard to the question why the proletariat in Western Europe does not rise for revolution. The Young Lukacs and Gramsci put their emphasis on weakening the subjective consciousness of the working class who face a strong state machine of capitalism. In the latest development of capitalist society, with the post-war state intervention in the economy and the wide implementation of welfare policies, the class conflict appears to be "mediated" and the capitalist economy and political reality seem to eradicate the innate contradictions and crises. But the Frankfurt School leaves the economic life for the spiritual and cultural phenomena, practically making a logical negation and theoretical "critique" of the abstract subjective dialectics out of Marxism once again.

It is getting clearer when we turn to the premise of the Frankfurt School (Horkheimer's critical theory of society and Adorno's "atonal" philosophy and negative dialectics). Adorno says that Marx's dialectics should be "negative dialectics," which aims to break down the positive ideology in capitalist reality, expose and criticize the external domination over man, instead of exploring a practical strategy for the liberation based on classes. Later, Agger comments that dialectics have lost the element of practice in Adorno's illustrative system, which is a very insightful statement.

It is the initial deviation of the Frankfurt School that renders their theory pale. Although they see the new issues of the capitalist development, they exaggerate its absolute sense on a social level. The *dominant position* of science and technology in social history is changed into a *basic status* to substitute material production; the *prominent* cultural factors in contemporary bourgeois ruling are turned into the *only* means of control, causing their effort of "restructuring historical materialism" (Habermas) fall into the pit of concealed historical idealism. Therefore, for the Frankfurt School, the proletarian revolution of contemporary capitalist society is unsurprisingly reduced to a subjective "cultural revolution." It just goes back to the old *armchair criticism* disapproved by Marx and Engels a century ago.

CHAPTER VII

MODERN NATURAL SCIENCE AND THE MARXIST DIALECTICS OF SOCIAL HISTORY

1 *The Modern Scientific Revolution and the Marxist View of History*
2 *Self-Organizing Theory of Complex Systems and ‚Natural-ness'*
3 *The Deep Logic of the Contemporary Ecological Horizon and Marxist Historical Dialectics*

CHAPTER SEVEN

INTRODUCTION

Since Marx's foundation of the scientific view of history, one and a half centuries have past with huge social changes and great advances of natural science, as William Blake describes in *Auguries of Innocence*, "To see a world in a grain of sand and a Heaven in a wild flower. Hold **Infinity** in the palm of your hand and **Eternity** in an hour." In particular, the scientific revolution started from the 1930s and 40s provides not only the new theoretical base for science and technology but also novel angles and even new methodologies to explore the nature of social history. In this case, we cannot afford ignoring the issues of recognizing Marxist theory of historical development, understanding the relationship between historical dialectics and modern natural science. This chapter is mainly about the issues of natural science related to the Marxist view of history.

I. THE MODERN SCIENTIFIC REVOLUTION AND THE MARXIST VIEW OF HISTORY

Since the 1920s, especially, the 1930s and 40s, modern natural science has undergone enormous changes in the greatest revolution of scientific thoughts. Undoubtedly, this leap forward is also a direct foundation for the development of Marxism because the philosophical advance must be achieved by tackling new questions raised by natural science instead of going back to the heaps of old books. First of all, there is the question of the basic attitude, that is, how should we use the Marxist view of history to deal with the achievement of natural science? In other words, how can we level up the theoretical provisions of natural science to the logic of philosophical view of history? It is a matter of principle that must be solved before our concrete discussions are to be carried out.

A. THE MODERN SCIENTIFIC REVOLUTION AND THE MARXIST PHILOSOPHICAL REVOLUTION

The early 20th century witnessed a revolution of physics that lasted for up to 30 years. After that, the theories of relativity and quantum mechanics replaced the classical physics established by Galileo and Newton to become the pillars of modern physics, promoting radical changes in our understandings of matter, energy, space, time, movement and causality. After the 1950s, the whole natural science and technology entered a revolutionary state. Numerous ideas and theories sprang up, like the chemical bonding, the celestial evolution, the Big Bang, continental drift, etc; on the technological level, there were such advances as the electronic technology (computers and system control engineering), aviation and aerospace, laser, bio-engineering and marine engineering. In short, it was a *comprehensive scientific revolution* centred on a Geostatic scientific theory.

Philosophical rationality is based on natural science, whose rapid progress certainly makes philosophy flourish. Therefore, recognizing the overall transformation of contemporary natural science means confirming the *new development faced by* philosophical knowledge. Against the background of the Marxist development enhanced by natural science, there is a rather typical view that Marxism, born in the mid-19th century when natural science was mainly based on Newton's classical physics, must be pushed from the "classical phase" to the "modern stage," even be "reconstructed" because the great advance of natural science has already brought forth an overall revolution. This belief indicates an unspoken proposition: Marxist philosophy is *outdated* as far as its *scientific base* is concerned. Frankly speaking, I cannot accept this view.

A fundamental theoretical question must be validated at first: What is the real relationship between the *Marxist philosophy and modern natural science*? Or, Is Marxist philosophy really contrary to the new ideas of natural science? It should be a theoretical premise for our discussion.

As we know, the practical development of many important disciplines gradually began from the early 20th century. In general, people think that scientific framework centred on Newton's mechanics represents the traditional science, a scientific mapping with its essential features based on the idealized mechanical determinism. Its basic rules consist of the so-called *universality, absoluteness* and *eternality*, which is, in fact, erroneous. The old scientific framework provides foundation for the entire modern experimental science. The modern scientific revolution, represented by Albert Einstein, is in its essence a *process of historical, practical, dialectical view of history replacing the mechanical vision of history. Judging from the whole process of human thought, this great revolution is composed of three historical and complementary phases.*

First of all, it is the *objective process of practice* that started in the first half of the 19th century. In my opinion, the golden age of the classical framework of science was the turning period of the 17th and 18th centuries. From then on and till the 19th century, the old science was full of problems. The direct negation of the mechanical view of history dated back to the revolutionary practice of science in the mid-19th century, mainly represented by the Kant-Laplace nebular hypothesis, Charles Lyell's geologic evolution, and so on while the three big discoveries of the conservation of energy, cells and evolution wielded a heavy blow to the old scientific framework. When it came to the latter half of the 19th century, the development of the theories of electro-magnetics in physics, especially, the "ether" theory that was contrary to Newton's mechanics, left the crisis-ridden mechanical view of nature on the brink of collapse. It was nothing else but the general negativity of the new revolution of science contained in the old framework. These progresses inside sounded the death knell for the old view of history. Therefore, this revolution of natural science was the result of the development of scientific practice.

The first challenge against the old view of history was not from natural science but the modern *philosophical revolution*. In fact, every time when science enters the era of transformation, it is always the philosophical reflection that captures the factors of negativity on deeper theoretical levels to confront the old framework. Historically, it is the same with the relationship between the empirical philosophy and classical science, between the modern philosophical revolution and the contemporary scientific revolution. As early as the birth of German classical philosophy, especially, the formation of Marxism, the end of the mechanical view of nature was announced from a philosophical perspective. Marxist philosophy, centred on practical materialism, radically negates the theoretical framework of the mechanical view of history. Thus, we have reason to conceive this philosophical revolution of Marxism as the antecedent to the theoretical revolution of natural science. They are but two historical stages of one revolution on a larger scale.

Of course, the great philosophical advance is not equivalent to the revolution of science itself; nor can it replace the change of the scientific framework. Despite the scientific leap forward after the mid-19th century, the old theoretical system has still dominated natural science. It was not until over a critical point that the revolution of modern natural science occurred. It was another side of the general revolution, the most important ontological aspect. In my opinion, the modern revolution of science is a general transformation of thought that posits its logical starting point in Einstein's theory of relativity and includes a series of grand scientific changes in theoretical paradigms. If Marxism offers philosophy a scientific form, the formation of the new theoretical framework of modern natural science is its real form of development. It is a *completely new scientific framework of science* that essentially surpasses the old system. The theoretical framework of modern natural science is established with the same significance as that of Marxism in that both of them end the "pre-historical" period of human thought and make the movement of the general human cognition become a conscious process of scientific reality. The shared point for natural science and philosophy is a "continual transcendence over the starting point." Thus, here lies the most profound meaning of the two great revolutions in modern history of thought.

Now we can see that the process of scientific practice, the philosophical change and the revolution of the scientific conception do not necessarily happen simultaneously within an overall transformation of human cognition. They are all common progresses of the different cognitive aspects of science. It is their systematic movement that drives the overall transformation of human knowledge. At the same time, we see that Marxist philosophy *essentially agrees* with modern natural science in the direction of progression. Their theoretical frameworks are *isomorphic*. It needs to be noted that Marxist philosophy was not only born out of and based on natural science but also reliant on modern social practice, to be exact,

Marxism is not a certain historical dogma but the *scientific movement of thought* corresponding to the continual development of natural science and social practice.

Therefore, the recognition of today's development of Marxist philosophy, especially, with the advance of modern natural science indicates that it is by no means to undergo a thorough change and even abandonment caused by the "obsolete" foundation on which it is built. As mentioned earlier, it is Marxism that first makes the study of history an open movement of thought based on practice and scientific cognition. Its theoretical structure is not the same as that of a theoretical dogma but a *dynamic functioning*, a *process of scientific integration* always full of vitality.

B. ACHIEVEMENT IN MODERN NATURAL SCIENCES AND THE RESEARCH OF MARXIST HISTORICAL DIALECTICS

It is obviously undesirable to take either a blind or a simplistic attitude towards the development and new discoveries of natural science. The research of Marxist historical dialectics requires the basic stance of upholding and developing Marxism. Hence, we need to be both sober-minded and enthusiastic at heart, adherent to the scientific principle and serious about specific analysis. In general, there are two basic aspects as follows.

Firstly, it is by natural science that people have proved the facts, invented practical instruments, carried out successful experiments, and established new scientific theories. However, people have not made an effective philosophical summary, for example, the continual scientific achievements in the fields of elementary particles, DNA, artificial intelligence, and even new methodologies of complex systems science, etc. We should actively make our research and identify these new scientific stipulations and paradigms with the logic of philosophy. Admittedly, the new laws and methodologies of natural science cannot be directly moved into philosophy; there is the issue of philosophical integration, assimilation and sublimation. Otherwise, various drawbacks will come, like the rules of experimental science unable to enter the level of philosophical logic, the new scientific paradigms incompatible to the old philosophical discourse, or a far-fetched attachment of the new paradigm to the philosophical knowledge.

For instance, some theoreticians simply attribute the basic categories of complex systems science to the old philosophical framework, only adding an attributive "systematic" before the previous categories of historical dialectics, which is not a scientific approach, only a change of addressing.

As we know, not a few paradigms in complex systems science are irreconcilable with or contrary to the previous philosophical categories. We often define something by recognizing the external quality identical to its own existence as the essential stipulation to differentiate it from others because the content (totality) is the sum of elements expressed through a fixed form. While in systems science discipline, things are not the mechanical combination of elements. It is the qualitative stipulation that the system quality rejects as the identification of things. As the name suggests, the system quality refers to the overall character of the elements systematically organized, not the external identification. It certainly has its relative stability, but different from a fixed status that the general quality simply maintains; it means the dynamic stability out of the system's functional removal of interference, which constitutes an internal structure, the systematic structure. Obviously, complex systems science reaches a new level of human cognition. And it is incorrect to take a nihilistic attitude in understanding the whole process of philosophy. What we can do is to rightly attribute these new achievements of science to the history of human thought, explain their new content (values) added to human knowledge, and make an organic integration with the previous paradigms. Only in this way can we form a truly successful philosophical recognition.

Indeed, researchers of natural science usually make some hypotheses about the phenomena that cannot be explained at present but must be explored, for example, the doctrines of Big Bang, quark confinement, black holes and anti-matter. Due to further exploration in practice and theory, they may not possess a real challenge to the philosophical thought now but we need in-depth theoretical thinking because hypotheses often precede scientific discoveries and contain the prediction of truths. However, we cannot jump from hypothesis to conclusion; otherwise, we shall be lead astray. For example, some believe that the theory of "quark confinement" (simply put, it means quarks cannot be isolated) necessarily leads to the conclusion that there is no free state for fundamental particles beneath the level of quarks. Therefore, people cannot have perceptual experience of these particles; they face an insurmountable "barrier." Moreover, due to the limited information transmission coupled with the "uncertainty principle" during observation, we have to admit the existence of the "thing in itself," that is, the admission of agnosticism.

I think this kind of philosophical argument is based on uncertain hypotheses. Moreover, this view is not anything new, just repeating the erroneous philosophical thought of many natural scientists. As Engels comments,

"The number and succession of hypotheses supplanting one another – given the lack of logical and dialectical education among natural scientists – easily gives rise to the idea that we cannot know the *essence* of things."[1] Even in Engels' time, there were people who claimed to re-recognize the "thing-in-itself" due to the limitations of the human senses. Engels precisely points out, man's senses are not the absolute limits of human knowledge and only mechanical materialism interprets thinking just as the sensual phenomena of hearing, seeing and touching. "On the other hand, modern natural science has extended the principle of the origin of all thought content from experience in a way that breaks down its old metaphysical limitation and formulation."[2]

In fact, that quarks are not isolable elementary particles is only a hypothesis. Even if they do not have free states, their nature can be measured or concluded through other means with further development of science and technology. As for the uncertainty principle, it means the result, after being observed through certain instruments, must contain the impact of the instrument itself. If interpreted in philosophical discourse, it indicates that the object, after being affected by the subject, necessarily bears the subjective marks. As a Chinese saying goes, the sweet orange in the South grows into the bitter one in the North. The result differs according to intermediary means. However, it would be coward to lose the courage of Kuafu the god in the pursuit of the running sun just for fear of being burned down to ashes; it would be ignorant to give up the dream of Chang'e the goddess rising to the moon for the worry of being scorned as a fantasy; it would also be sad and ridiculous to stop exploring the world or fall into agnosticism for the reason of subjective or historical limitations of truths. Engels says it is unacceptable to draw an agnostic conclusion by the relativity of scientific knowledge. "In the first place, this assertion that we cannot know the thing-in-itself passes out of science into fantasy. In the second place, it does not add a word to our scientific knowledge, for if we cannot occupy ourselves with things, they do not exist for us."[3]

During our probe into the world nature, it is true that there are historical restrictions or many "uncertainty principles" and that every sensual experience or thought is marked by the subjective influence but all these cannot make us to pray for the "thing-in-itself" again. What would be the use of

---

1   Engels, and John Burdon Sanderson Haldane. *Dialektik der Natur.* New York: International Publishers, 1940. p. 159.
2   *Ibid.*, p. 383.
3   Selsam, and Harry Martel. *Reader in Marxist Philosophy.* New York: International Publishers Co, 1987. p. 144.

science and struggle for truth if the world were in absolute transparency? This is neither an issue of feelings nor a question of faith; it is a basic point about socio-historical progress.

With the above theoretical premise, our discussion of the relationship between the Marxist view of history and the advance of modern natural science can smoothly enter a micro-theoretical level. In this regard, some researchers of natural science have already applied a number of important achievements and methodologies into the study of society and history. Admittedly, their attempt is sometimes reasonable and insightful. At the same time, there are questions worthy of our attention.

Firstly, the new scientific results are often *mechanically applied* into the research categories of the social history, which causes a serious theoretical confusion instead of pushing our research forward. For instance, the new discoveries of natural science are put in opposition to Marxist historical dialectics; thus, some researchers claim that historical materialism should be "outdated"; so they attempt to reconstruct the view of social history with the new "scientific provisions." Without doubt, all these intentions end in failure. They neither know the scientific view of history in Marxist philosophy (perhaps, their comprehension is confined in one or two popular textbooks) nor understand the historical significance of modern natural science. For some other scholars, the theories of natural science, without any philosophical mediation and definition, expressly slip into the research of social history. Although their original intention is to develop the Marxist view of history, they fail to notice the different logical levels of specific sciences and philosophical theories.

Secondly, an important reason why the methods of natural science cannot be simply extended and applied in social science is that social history has *special features*. As mentioned earlier, in comparison to nature, society involves not only the object but also the human subject in history, not only a common material process but also the dynamic practice by the subject's creative function, not only the aspect of objective existence but also the content of conscious activities. Social history is both objective and historical/temporary because it abides by the rules of the subjective activities under certain historical conditions in constant changes. This is a serious issue when we apply the achievements of natural science into the research of social and historical phenomena. In my opinion, a considerable number of scholars engaged in the study of natural science, especially in the West, just make an inertial movement of thought in their shift to the fields of social history. They do not notice the possible features that might be different from those in natural phenomena. This mistake gravely affects the efficient application of the fruit of natural science in socio-historical dialectics.

Thirdly, I would like to point out that the introduction of new methodologies into social history must avoid repeating the old path of the *idealistic* conception of history. It is noteworthy that those successful in natural science turn out to be the "minute philosophers" when they enter the field of philosophy, especially, the research of historical dialectics in social history. For example, Erich Jantsch, the famous American system scientist gives a wonderful description of the most important advance achieved in complex systems science in his *Self-Organizing Universe*. However, in his conclusion of the conception of history, only reductionism preaches materialism that interprets human history according to the material process. According to Jantsch, in the field of human beings, more generally, on other various levels of the living field, history is the history of consciousness, which is the true meaning of this word[4]. This complex situation requires us to maintain our subjectivity of independent thinking and preclude blind *conformist* behaviour when faced with the achievement of natural science.

I have an example right at hand for it. In a discussion several years ago, a scholar, holding high the banner that "science and technology constitutes the primary productive force," stepped onto a wrong way. His thought goes as follows: The premise is that science and technology is the primary productive force as well as the foundation for the development of social history. The nature of science is information, of which the essence is negative entropy, which then comes from the idea and motivation in the mind of people because the external material does not take the initiative to create it. Therefore, man's idea and motivation (scientific theories) become the nature of socio-historical development (the "primary productive force"). In my opinion, this misinterprets the historical, *dominant* role (not the *initial and basic* status) of science and technology in the certain structure of productive forces during the progress of social history. It is thus a wrong conclusion of historical *idealism*.

It is impossible to exhaust all the details of these issues here. Next, I am going to deal with the scientific research relevant to the Marxist view of socio-history centred on the main line of this book.

---

4 Jantsch, Erich. The Self-Organizing Universe: *Scientific and Human Implications of the Emerging Paradigm of Evolution*. Pergamon Press, 1980. p. 181.

II. SELF-ORGANIZING THEORY OF COMPLEX SYSTEMS AND 'NATURAL-NESS'

Today is the era of great progress for humanity. With the material world entering the new stages in its long evolutionary history, human beings make continual advances equipped with numerous scientific accomplishments. Among them, one of the most profound developments is the science of complex systems, which can be said as a pivot of the theoretical framework of modern natural science. Mankind will once again face a new comprehensive understanding of science and rationality. Considering the intuitive knowledge of the ancient and the empirical science in modern times, the current tide is the third level of scientific cognition, viz., the rational comprehension on an exact scientific level. In this regard, llya Prigogine, Ervin László and others made considerable progress in the general evolutionary theory.

A. GENERAL EVOLUTION OF THE SELF-ORGANIZING THEORY OF COMPLEX SYSTEMS SCIENCE

In classical science, linear causal determinism composes the latitude and longitude lines of the spinning world that is but a sum of entities. Now, it is proved as a rough, idealized, and flat vision. The new scientific cognition originates in the theory that tends to regard the world as a functional organization of certain *relations* and *interactions* of elements. (llya Prigogine observes that this conception is logically identical to the ancient Chinese culture.) This time, the general dialectical thought of human intuition and philosophical speculation demonstrates itself in natural science again. If philosophy is to blow the horn of future, the validation from science itself can be the real progress. In my opinion, Albert Einstein is the first to send the classical science to the present altar of rationality. His theory of relativity removes the sacred aura from the old scientific framework that is a complete and direct description of the external laws according to the opinion of Newton. And man, as the observer, gets involved in making the scientific mapping of the world based on the evolution of the relative, historical science. Thus, the scientific truth is a specific reflection of the objective laws on a certain cognitive level while science itself becomes the evolution of the progressive cognition. Although Einstein's theory is still unconsciously half-dipped in the old science, his revolutionary thought shines with dazzling light.

The road of science in the 20th century was not smooth. There were many difficulties and even obstacles that highlighted the process of the scientific revolution. Since Einstein and quantum mechanics, nearly every theoretical paradigm has experienced Gestalt transformation. In this revolutionary process, the newly emerging science of complex systems stands out as the *rational logics of the new scientific world mapping*[5].

The complex systems science is a methodological framework to describe the world. It is a new narrative schema, in which, people's eyes start to turn from entities to relations, to "information" and to "time."[6] The material world is seen moving in a certain direction with integrated systematic association and functional structure, which composes the inside frame for all new sciences. This multiple, temporary and complex framework includes man's effort to remap the new world. Thus, a new rational view grows out of the development of the scientific domain. Human beings have really reached a new philosophical height in summarization and integration. The initial steps have been taken by Ervin Laszlo and others. GES, -the grand evolutionary synthesis-, is an important test of the cognitive progress of scientific rationality, in which, the basic logics of the complex systems science are used to illustrate the evolution of the whole material world. Here, rational cognition has undergone tremendous changes. Despite that it smoothly maps the object in natural science (including the artificial nature), we also notice that GES gets clumsy and far-fetched in the field of human society. I think this is the special quality of social strata in the general world evolution. If we fail to truly grasp the essence of social life and only depend on such borrowed words as "nonlinear," "bifurcations" and "fluctuations," we cannot gain insight into the deep structure of social strata.

As we all know, complex systems science bears two advances in its logics of scientific cognition: One, it offers a more microscopic and specific conception of the true structure of the world; two, it reveals the nature of evolution, that is, the internal mechanism that leads to the order and progression of the material world. Here, the sub-stratum of the world is constant. Obviously, evolution does not result in the continuous replacement of the material substratum but brings about the qualitative change

---

5   It needs to be noted that whether it is information theory, system theory, cybernetics, non-equilibrium thermodynamics, self-organization theory or catastrophe theory, all can found corresponding mother science. Nevertheless, the general logic of complex systems science surpasses specific disciplines.

6   Prigogine, and Isabelle Stengers. *Order out of Chaos: Man's New Dialogue with Nature, Part 2.* Toronto; New York, N.Y.: Bantam Books, 1984. p. 8.

of the *organized status* of the material substratum. In essence, the nature of evolution is not the emergence of a different entity but the *formation of a new order*. It reminds us of Henri Bergson's metaphor of the falling material and the gushing life. If applied here, it is not the material entity but the matter as objective existence that falls down; it is not the abstract animistic impulse of life but the dimensional internal structure of matter itself that gushes forward and accounts for the existence and irreversible evolution of the world system. In this way, the evolutionary impulse is not an external force or something mysterious but the function of the world's self-organizing mechanism. Laszlo carries out a brilliant logical analysis with GES.

When Laszlo, along with Prigogine and others, achieves the theoretical establishment in the research of nature, i.e. open systems and non-equilibrium, they turn to the field of society and human beings, probably because it is another open system just on a higher level. In my view, the application of complex systems science in this area is still unsatisfactory because it is more or less of a logical inertia in which the mechanism confirmed in the system of nature is assumed to be functional in social life in the same way. Meanwhile, due to the ignorance of the complexity of society, this theoretical validation is characterized by arbitrariness. In my view, understanding of the complex mechanism of evolution from the perspective of social existence should be based on the function and practice under certain conditions of social history, not on mere theoretical logics, the sequence of which cannot be reversed. Hence, we need to know the nature of social stratums again.

B. WHAT IS THE SELF-ORGANIZING PROCESS IN THE EVOLUTION OF HUMAN SOCIAL HISTORY?

According to Laszlo and Prigogine, the evolution of human society is a very typical dynamic and open system. Humans almost jump into social existence from the break of biological evolution and abide by the general rules of the system of the material world on a "specific social level" beyond the singular members of society, that is, the biological degree of the individuals. Obviously, society is the system formed by groups of people in certain relations. The functioning of society generates special control parameters due to the conscious activities of humans and the use of tools. Meanwhile, society is not reduced to the sum effect of the individual activities; social life is the advanced existence with special features on a new level. So far, I generally agree with Laszlo's description of social existence.

However, I have to point out that this confirmation of the evolution of social existence by Laszlo and others contain a profound logical paradox. It raises the following questions.

(1) The individual, as the component of society, has consciousness along with will. And society forms a certain system of total consciousness. Nevertheless, social existence is not the product of a conscious human design but results from the impact of man's activities. As a result, the total social life and evolution generally produces a natural and spontaneous order, which is organic rather than organized. The question is: Where does man's will dissolve since society functions and evolves like an organic whole of its own? Or, is man still the subject of social history?

(2) The spontaneous evolution of social organism contains such characters as self-replication, self-renewal and self-organization. Then, who is carrying out the self-evolution on earth? The thing, the man, or their combination? The issue is whether man can see the social evolution and control it.

(2) The overall social progress is driven by technology, which must be included in the above provisions of (1) and (2). Should technology be understood in a general sense or as the means in all the human activities? Since the means is the external thing objectified by the subjective activities, the driving force of social evolution can be validated. Hence, the question: Can the tool perform self-evolution as the means of activities?

(4) Social evolution is a general change of society triggered by the revolution of technology (the driving force that alters the configuration of relations between human beings as well as between man and nature). In an instant bifurcation of social mutations, the configuration of relations here undergoes fundamental changes that lead to the emergence of a new social evolutionary level. If the so-called "configuration" refers to the most elementary structure of social existence, who creates and promotes the structure?

In the nutshell is the issue: What is the nature of social existence? And then what is the social foothold of complex systems science that describes the general evolution of the material world? Can it be integrated with the objective historical dialectics?

First of all, we have to admit that in a certain sense, social life is one of the most important objects that complex systems science covers. The theories of dissipative structure, irreversible evolution, self-organization, mutations and restructuring can be found in their corresponding points in social life. We can even conclude that it is the complex and systematic evolution of society itself that highlights complex systems science today. Admittedly, the scientific validation of the evolution of social strata is not easy. It needs a new foundation to make a breakthrough.

I find that confirming the error of social development is often associated with the determination of the nature of social existence. In my opinion, the essence of social existence (the socio-sphere, or the social strata in the general material process) is not a piling up of material objects. It cannot lead to social life by simply mixing up the natural environment, population, various artificial tools and products. Moreover, social existence is not a self-organizing and self-moving process of materials without man. Precisely, as we criticized Althusser before, social development is not an absolute non-subjective process. The humanistic transcendental subject of social history is indeed an illusion but the process of social development can only be made with concrete activities of human beings. Social existence is essentially the process of the well-ordered social activities as a whole. The activity is not simply dependent on human thought; nor can it be classified as the abstract action of the subject. As a kind of creative movement to historically change the material environment and the human conditions, it is *historically loaded and woven with specific structures, and the subjective social practice with a consciousness-controlled system*. Practice is a constructional historical activity, which forms the only source for social development[7].

The original material entity in natural existence "declines" in social life, but it is not a passive falling down in the eyes of Bergson. Because of the emergence of the self-created controlling subject of the "negative entropy source," the system of total human activities (*not of ideological motives but the creative evolution of practice*), social existence stands out. Now, the previous subjective status of the material entity in natural existence is lost and presented as the premise and aim of man's historical activities. Although still existent in human activities, they *logically* retreat to the rear of social practice and historically *absorb the self-functioning role* of man's creative activities while being repelled all the time. In my view, the material entity has become the carrier of subjective activities and been sublated to the material level of social existence. Similarly, the subjectivity of human society cannot be attributed to the movement of individual life in a natural sense. The operation of human life system is only on the secondary substratum of social existence instead of social operation itself. In other words, man's natural environment (including the artificial "nature") and his natural existence

---

7 Zhang Yibing. "Construction of Practice." *Fujian Tribune*. 1 (1992).

result from the substantial basis of the indirect social existence and the accumulation of material activities.

It needs to be noted that the real occurrence of social existence assumes the form of a protruding *system of the objective multi-level functions*. This system of material movement on a higher level of social existence is not a direct substantial entity and its new status of being organized but the activities and material objects of man, the historical subject. We call it the field of social practice[8], which does not have a definition in the strict sense of physics but refers to a *network of objective functions similar to the field existence*. It is the immediate foundation for the advanced social existence established on the artificial "nature" and the natural population. The appearance of social history is mainly the historical conversion of the field of social practice while the material entity is only the historical accumulation and the present material of the field of social practice, which, as the major content of social existence, should not be confined to the subjective activities but be regarded as the objective process of loading man's creative interactions and weaving the material reality. Both the aspects of material and man demonstrate an objectified realization of *man's creative activities of construction*. Obviously, social behaviour is built by the dynamic activities of the individuals, which, under certain historical conditions, objectively makes up an orderly whole of practice in some way[9]. It is this system of objective material activities independent of man's will that makes the basic aspect of social existence.

Furthermore, the essential aspect of social existence is neither matter nor the abstract activities of the subject but the deep functional structure of the socio-historical practice, that is, the historical *pattern of social practice*, on which, Laszlo comments that social existence self-maintains and self-repairs the specific configuration of the parts and relations in the system. Marx also says, man's activities happen in "a definite form" and this structure of practice is "a definite form of expressing their life, a definite mode of life on their part."[10] As we know, any human activity in social life is actually structural, which, on the general level of social existence, is represented as the dynamic and orderly organization of human survival and evolution in certain historical conditions. It is this specific practice pattern that forms the *real nature* concealed on the level of social existence. The pattern is a functional structure of the dominance of certain social practice

8   Zhang Yibing. "Field of Social Practice." *Jiang Hai Xue Kan*. 5 (1988).
9   Zhang Yibing. "Integration of Practice." *Seeking Truth*. 5 (1989).
10   Marx, and Friedrich Engels. *The German Ideology*. Ed. Christopher John Arthur. New York: International Publishers Co, 1970. p. 42.

field and the foundation of structural constraints on which the real social life integrates certain practice.

To be specific, man creates social life and thus human history *differs* from that of nature. The major source for the irreversible organization of social history is provided by the constructional activities generated in the creative evolution of the subject. However, triggered by the general social practice integrated and structured in certain conditions, it cannot be simply equated with the individual behaviour of people (Heidegger's "Being"). Therefore, its nature is the human practice construction and self-creativity whereas this practice construction of overall social interactions amounts to the structural creative evolution of the subject. It is thus safe to say the evolution of social history is not that of materials but of man's historical activities, mainly demonstrated by what organization man uses to carry out production, social contacts and conscious exchanges. If there is a "dissipative structure" in social life, it must be a functional structure of interaction and integration for the general human activities. Self-organization and self-replication can only occur in the general functional activities of the human subject. Here, the physical tools become the *objectified load* ("fossils") of the practice pattern, instead of the historical subject. Hence, science and technology (the paradigms) can only be taken as a *particular dominant aspect* of the human practice pattern during certain historical periods.

In fact, the practice pattern represents a relational composition of objective activities; it is not an entity or substantial material but a functional system; it is not a real form external to human existence (like Newton's construction of space and time) but an orderly structure itself! During the operation of historical process, the practice pattern mainly represents the dynamic relationship between man and nature, and the dynamic relationship between man and man. The orderly composition of this dual relationship forms the evolutionary scale setting of the human social existence. Therefore, as a structural and constructional activity of creative evolution, the practice pattern naturally becomes the "ontology" of social existence, on which Prigogine's structural ontology and Whitehead's relational ontology display their profound aspects. It is also the objective logic of historical dialectics.

We can see that the physical entities do not make social history a creative evolution; man in the biological sense does not create social life; only the human social entity as a whole actively constructs social practice and thus becomes the true subject and promoter of social history. Humankind makes history through specific practice patterns, which displays a fundamental difference between the orderly social practice and the natural order. When the construction of this objective structure is put in comparison with the individual action, the practice pattern seemingly represents a *pre-given* constraint (not the a priori structure of the subject in Weber's "ideal type" and Piaget's "schema") and makes the will of the human individual melt into a *sub-will integrated into* the social whole as if there was an "invisible hand" combining part of the individual activities into a concerted action and then incorporating it into a higher system with other actions. Thus, there seems to be a certain evolutionary unconsciousness of social history, with social existence being a non-subjective "natural system." Meanwhile, the human social relationship is historically alienated to the material relationship, and the development of history spontaneously presents some non-subjectivity and "self-organization" similar to that of nature. (Laszlo does not offer a detailed analysis. We shall discuss latter that it is not the essence of social existence.)

Another important character of social stratum is its progressiveness as the foundation of social existence is the practical activities of humans. Only when these activities operate can the non-substantial social practice pattern be *protrusively constructed*. Social existence merely occurs in the "contemporary" subject-subject and subject-object contacts of certain historical conditions. Its disappearance will *de-construct* the specific practice pattern and the previous social life will disintegrate. This new orderly swinging between the construction and de-construction of the new relations is the process of social history. It is also the socio-historical development in the vision of Marxist historical dialectics.

C. THE SELF-ORGANIZATION AND 'NATURAL-NESS' OF SOCIAL EVOLUTION

I believe that a keynoted scientific understanding of social history is to integrate historicality, reality and concreteness. In the description of social existence and evolution by Laszlo and Prigogine, those pre-set general rules of society are not eternally possessed by certain social stratum but are evolved by themselves in history. Laszlo fails to notice that his picture of social network only reflects the *present* society while unable to explain the essence of the ancient and future social lives. True, Laszlo describes the historical process of social evolution, but he lets go of the historical conversion of practice patterns. Consequently, his mapping of the evolutionary social strata *just misses the important link of evolution*, in particular, the evolution of the historical human subject. In this regard, we can adopt the subjective dimension of Marxist historical dialectics to analyze the two aspects of the innate structure (practice patterns) of social existence.

Firstly, the orderly association between man and nature refers to the ability by which he dominates and uses nature as certain functionality of practice. This relationship is not iron fixed. Instead, it is a dynamic structure of order in constant historical changes. In ancient times, people just struggle out of Mother Nature and still depend on the natural umbilical cord. Man is the son of nature (indicating the blood relationship) and the slave of material evolution. The practice pattern at this moment only represents an immediate acceptance and use of nature. The overall force and behaviour of man are very small and simple. Unsurprisingly, nature is worshipped as God (pantheistic religion and totems). This situation is not caused by natural materials or the physical existence of human bodies but by the low-level creative evolution of the practical construction in human society. It is thus safe to conclude that social practice or even the entire social strata is in the primitive phase. When the practical construction of human society gradually develops, man shakes off his direct dependency on nature and makes it his object of labour. People attempt to establish the basic necessities that nature does not directly provide and control the object of nature in their subjective work (practice and creations). Before the real power of man gets strong, the coercive impulsion towards nature is already represented by the supernatural God (the alienation of man), who is an illusory power of man but reflects man's paleness. Although man already creates social economy at that time, that agricultural social existence cannot be separated from nature yet.

Experimental science is a powerful construction of practice by *man to conquest nature*. Technology and industrial production is the organized realization and objectification of man's social practice. With science and industries, the natural materials on Earth are ruled by man, which is a new general pattern of man and nature to embody the real establishment of the subjective status in material evolution. The historical development of human society does not turn into a true paradise but becomes a catastrophe of the material evolution and, ultimately, the disaster of human social existence and development. We are going to lose the beautiful situation described in the verse, "after rain the empty mountain stands autumnal in the evening," the comfortable feeling when "I pick fence-side chrysanthemums at will and leisurely I see the southern hill," or the graceful leisure with which "I walk till the water checks my path, then sit and watch the rising clouds." People are too arrogant and over-confidential in their ability of controlling nature. We have to re-examine the relationship between nature and man. When man transcends and controls nature, it is easy to forget that he is basically belonging to the same material system. The coercive construction of the human subject just means the destruction of the organic evolution and the general disorder of nature. Although we claim man's social existence is higher than that of nature, the latter is always a prerequisite for human survival. How can human beings survive if their living condition is destroyed? It should also be the philosophical significance of contemporary ecology (including the "instrumental reason" of the Frankfurt school). Obviously, there is no need for the abstracted ethical criticism and a simplified judgment of "should-not." Indeed, it is to establish the scientific concept of historical development because there would not be today's social development were there not the first and second phases of the organized structure of man and nature. The conquest of nature is a necessary part of historical development, which should be followed by a higher view of the holistic eco-system that transcends itself. (It will be discussed in the next section in detail.)

Secondly, the interpersonal relationship is more complex than that between man and nature. Composing the structural interactions of human society, this dynamic relationship is based on the specific functions of man and nature but highlighted as the direct and major aspect of social existence.

The internal human relationship bears its fault from the outset. In the early period of clan life, man's subjectivity of pastoral equality and love only exists within the narrow blood relationship of "me" (the clan) while people outside "me" are seen as inhuman objects and animals. This reversal and contradiction of the personal relationship continues in later social coercion (slaves are living objects of nature) and becomes the immediate force to drive the historical development. At this time, the self-regulating system of social life corresponds to the low status of man before nature. It is a conventional system in which a few governing kings only follow the "heavenly (natural) rules" to represent the strength of man's initiative. When it comes to modern industrial society, the new situation of social existence and subjective structure takes shape. The present economic system of materialization makes the internal human relations alienated to the relations of materials, in which the nature of social life appears to be a *material self-organization*. However, human subjectivity is established and reflected through the integration of the anti-natural actions of economy, which should have belonged to man but now represents some materialized self-growth outside man. In the first two historical stages, the individual wills or intentions melt in the objective integration of materials (nature and the artificial nature) and man's self-structure differs from the holistic pattern of the class. He cannot control his own action and the things created by himself, even kneeling down before a subjective fetishism of material-subjugation. In human social life, there appears the animal-like fight for natural objects. Man in social existence becomes an economic animal. Social evolution deprives people of their common independent creation. Hence, all these factors make social history a natural process ('naturalness') that presents a "spontaneous" non-subjectivity. However, it is not a universal law of social history but a specific historical phenomenon.

With the new development of social practice, the construction of the human subject will undergo another Gestalt change. Man begins to wake up from his blind and endless extortion of nature, taking a new ecological view with positive interactions with it. And in the subjective structure, man relies on his mature understanding of social science to grasp that "invisible hand" while the natural integration of the individual action transforms to a natural assimilation. Finally, man will eliminate material-subjugation, gradually detach from his natural process and becomes his own mater. In this way, all social strata pull the curtain of a real development of *subjective* self-organization, self-creation and self-evolution. Starting from this point of reform and innovation, humans will enter a new social stratum. Finally, man will become the master of himself, the designer of blueprint social existence, and the real controller of the long historical development. This also turns a new page of the movement of social-historical dialectics.

In my opinion, the historical progress of modern society is in agreement to our discussion of Marxist historical dialectics here. Marx's view of 'naturalness' and material-subjugation is also validated by today's practice and science, which is undoubtedly an encouraging achievement.

III. THE DEEP LOGIC OF THE CONTEMPORARY ECOLOGICAL HORIZON AND MARXIST HISTORICAL DIALECTICS

In recent years, ecology features on unique philosophical conversion among various natural and social sciences. It reflects a very novel and meaningful introspection on the relationship between the survival of humans and the external world with the level of practice greatly improved. In this regard, scholars have made much exploration. However, amid these ecological studies, the so-called "ecological Marxism" shakes its spear towards Marxist philosophy, especially, at the doctrine upheld in current China that "science and technology constitutes the primary productive force" of social development. Then, what is the real point behind the ecological philosophy? It is not a simple question to be solved by upgrading the achievement of natural science to the philosophical logics.

A. THE LOGICAL INTENTION OF THE CONTEMPORARY ECOLOGICAL HORIZON

Since Ernst Haeckel, a German scientist, created the concept of ecology in his book *Generelle Morphologie der Organismen* (1866), more than a century has passed. The contemporary science of ecology as a new discipline was not started until the 1960s. From an etymological point of view, the word ecology is derived from the Greek οἶκος, "house" or "home," which just means nature in ecology but indicates an ironic allegory: *We are treating our living "home" as the object of control and subjugation.* An immediate shock and clear warning will follow if we look back from a philosophical perspective. To revere nature or to conquer nature becomes the options of death and life. How does modern ecology construct the new vision of "nature as home"?

Firstly, modern ecology emerges in a problematic background. It does not establish itself as an abstract set of theories but self-criticizes the pain of man's ultimate practice at the moment. Now, ecology focuses not on the general relationship between man and nature or between the subject and the object, but rather on the reflection of the consequences caused by the subject's over-reforming of nature. In the old time of agricultural society, there was no such "ecological" conflict between man and nature, nor a subsequent theory. In fact, as Marx says, "Each principle has had its own century in which to manifest itself"[11], ecology just belongs to the *modern* age.

---

11   Marx, and Friedrich Engels. *Karl Marx, Friedrich Engels: Collected Works.* New York: International Publishers, 1975. p. 170.

In this connection, we must get clear what exactly happens between man and nature today. From a philosophical point of view, the issue of ecology mainly arises out of the *functional aberration* during man's development of productive forces to change nature. People no longer rely on the simple tools made of wood and stone to have a superficial change. Instead, a systematic materialization of science and technology takes place, which already makes a great change, leading to the overall *dysfunction and damage* of our natural surroundings. In such a functional imbalance, nature loses the objective power against man and become a helpless object to be trampled on. Moreover, man, unaware of the subjective errors, sadly finds that the wand of science and technology pointed at nature only hurts himself. The pain is already felt in the social development of Western countries. It is the so-called "ecological crisis."

As we know, the post-industrial society driven by science and technology obtains rapid, even wild growth, after the Second World War. The development of productive forces centred on new scientific and technological revolution opens a wider and deeper prospect than before, making man's scientific and technological power unmatched to that of nature and fostering the functionality of practice for man to move forward by throwing his weight around. On one hand, man has a philosophical sense of victory in which he is the master of nature and in charge of everything; on the other hand, the pompous man sees a potential spectre out of Pandora's box: The rolling wheels of human technology leaves an increasing deterioration of environment, the steady depletion of natural resources, the groaning earth under the weight of population explosion... Under these dreadful circumstances, man finds the real root of trouble: The ecological crisis is essentially the emergency of human existence because its consequences, the destruction of earth, is the end of the human world. At this point, man is awakened to find that the sword of science and technology is wielded to inexorably destroy his own "house" and "home of nature." The umbilical cord to supply nutrients for him is cut and Mother Nature is bleeding. The human subject is almost led to a tragic homeless end. It is against this miserable background that ecology is highlighted. Obviously, the ecological thought of philosophy is a theoretical reflection of problems, a *self-criticism* of the subject himself, and a critical introspection of the abusive subject capabilities.

Secondly, what constitute the major content of the philosophical thought of ecological problems? From a general view, one is its premise, or the *rule of association in systems science*. Simply put, as a new perspective to take the world as a whole, it is no longer the old philosophical principle of "universal connections" but direct confirmation by modern science. Systems science and complexity science appeared after the 1940s and has brought about a new scientific methodology of nature, the theory of systematic existence, which does not agree with the practice of isolating things but takes everything as constituted by the interactive multi-functional elements. The integrated whole is not a sum of the elements that will lose their systematic existential status once separated from the interactions within the system. It is a dynamic but stable status with the elements interacting with and relying on each other. The association of systems actually reflects the anthropocentric and egoistic view, which also accounts for the theoretical support of postmodernist thought. The reason is that man is sure to be destroyed in the total destruction of the ecological system if he separates himself and then casually hurts the other elements in the system. In the famous poem, John Donne writes,

> **No man is an island entire of itself; every man is a piece of the continent [...] any man's death diminishes me, because I am involved in mankind. And therefore never send to know for whom the bell tolls; it tolls for thee.**

In the new context, it should be:

> **There is no island entire of itself; every man or every leaf is a piece of the continent [...] any man or tree's death diminishes me, because we are all involved in the world. And therefore never send to know for what the bell tolls; it tolls for thee, me or any debris.**

In fact, the loss of human beings should not be deemed as the only important thing. We should value the whole world and learn experience from our damage of nature to walk out of such disaster. This is the methodological precondition of modern ecology.

Next, it is the theoretical point of ecology itself. In my understanding, the ecological study is based on the whole life circles on earth, concerned about the internal association and interdependency of the ecological systems, against the over-use of the subjective ability and the pervasive ecological damage done by the development of modern industries, especially the advance of science and technology, and for the ultimate purpose of establishing a benign structure of human survival. Here are three interrelated concepts: The human ecological environment, the ecosystem and the ecological balance. The human ecological environment refers to the total natural elements around us, which makes the cradle for human survival and development; the ecosystem is a functional unity of biological and environmental interactions; the ecological balance is actually a steady state achieved by exchanges between the creatures themselves and the environment, which is fundamental to the operation of the entire ecosystem. In short, the core of ecology is to study and maintain the balance that means life or death to human beings.

The human ecological system was believed to be a well-operated system several decades ago, composed by the basic elements, nature, human beings and society. It even remained so until the middle industrial period. However, with ongoing revolution of modern science and technology, the previous human ecosystem has undergone significant changes. Contemporary technology makes an exponential growth of the productive forces. The original dynamic pattern of human existence has been thoroughly changed. The pattern of nature, society and man suddenly mutates to an alienated spinning movement around the axis of technology. Man creates technology but cannot effectively control the technological tension, whose endless expansion distorts nature, society and man into a new attachment (See the aforementioned "dialectic of enlightenment" of the Frankfurt school). Most importantly, technology may have broken through the limits of the natural environment. Our surroundings are polluted; the resources are depleted; population increases to an unbearable amount; and the man-made nuclear weapons are ready to destroy the whole world. The ecological balance is upset, garbage floods, blue sky is swallowed by merciless smokes, the area of fertile soil shrinks and Mother Nature is dying. The human society seems to be doomed. All this is produced by the killer of technology originated in man himself. Therefore, ecology requires the control of technology, the restriction of the productive forces, the re-examination of the relations among nature, technology and the ecological system for a new set of *ecological values* without the anthropocentric influence.

Three, this ecological theme highlights the radical social reform among the economic crisis, energy crisis and environmental pollution in the advanced capitalist countries in the 1960s, that is, the "ecological revolution." From then on, it gradually forms the influential "Green Movement," in which, nature, society and man are regarded as an integrated ecological entity with interactive and interdependent components. Were any part of this system damaged, the ecological whole would have internal imbalance. In Green Politics, the famous "Ecological wisdom" goes: "How can we operate human societies with the understanding that we are part of nature, not on top of it? How can we live within the ecological and resource limits of the planet, applying our technological knowledge to the challenge of an energy-efficient economy? [...] How can we further bio-centric wisdom in all spheres of life?"[12]

Hence, the purpose of the eco-revolution is to prevent the destruction of natural resources by the development of modern industrial society, stop poisoning the biosphere, avoid the threat of nuclear technology, advance the renewable production, promote the appropriate techniques of mutual benefit for man and nature, and thus essentially protect human survival.

It is in this trend of "green politics" that the latest "ecological Marxism"[13] questions the logics of Marxist philosophy. In their eyes, the 19th century social process presents a false image of an inexhaustible nature so that Marx follows the old non-ecological industrialism by Ricardo, in which the human subject *dominates* and *conquers* nature. The endless growth of the productive forces is the principal content of historical development. Marx makes the same mistake as capitalism does in the development of production/technology to control nature. He puts hope in the productive forces and faith in the elimination of exploitation and alienation by transferring the public property to the hands of workers. But Marx fails to notice that technology is demanding control. In the contemporary development of production, the subjective productive forces lose their own "virginity." The advances of science and technology increasingly harm the environment, even to the level of an overall ecological crisis. Thus, "his theory had had to undergo additions and modifications, one of the most essential of which is the revelation of mastery over nature"[14], as well as the focus on the development of the productive forces.

Thus, in their view, we must respect the limits set by nature and face the reality of today's social development. In this way, we can correct Marx's error of conquering nature and rebuild the new horizon of Marxist philosophy with an ecological vision. The relationship between man and nature will appear in a systematic interdependence. A limited positive circle of production will become the foundation for the existence and development of new society. The essence of such fresh view of history is to put the human interest above the class interest, to provide a non-alienated, creative

---

12   Spretnak, Capra, and Wulf-Rüdiger Lutz. *Green Politics.* Santa Fe, NM : Bear, 1986. p. 230.

13   Also called "Green Marxism." See "Chapter 15" in Zhang Yibing's *Broken Wings of Reason - Criticism of Western Marxism.* Nanjing: Nanjing Publishing House, 1990.

14   Leiss, William. *The Domination of Nature.* Montréal: McGill-Queen's Press–MQUP, 1994. p. 86.

labour so that people can escape the consumer attitude that is both un-necessary and harmful to the ecosystem, and the development of society can be rooted in the complete harmonious relationship between human beings and nature. The eco-Marxist even holds that historical changes have rendered the old theories of the capitalist production and crisis ineffective because today's trend is shifted to the field of consumption and the eco-nomic crisis is replaced by the ecological crisis. Eco-Marxism intends for a third road different from modern capitalism and socialism with funda-mental ecological consciousness.

Admittedly, it is a really profound criticism from the perspective of natural science and a radical negation of Marxist philosophy, in particular, the logic of *historical dialectics* in Marxism. There seems to be a dilemma. If we accept the real advancement of the productive forces is the essence of the social-historical progress, the Marxist view of history seems unable to hold its basic point; if the development of science and technology is philosophi-cally negated, today's socialism theories summarized in China as Chinese characteristics which focus on technological advances will lose its rational-ity. Therefore, we have to be very clear on this issue.

B. MARX'S SOCIO-HISTORICAL DIALECTICS AND ECOLOGY

As noted above, Marx always emphasizes the subjective status in socio-historical development. The Young Marx defines the difference of man and animals as the transcendence of natural limits in his high school the-sis; later, he stresses the subjective sublation of the external natural ne-cessity through the "self-consciousness" demonstrated by the Epicurean atoms within Hegel's framework when he writes his doctoral dissertation. At that time, Marx seems to take a depreciative attitude towards nature as man's opponent to conquer. While in the *1844 Manuscripts*, Marx already adopts the standpoint of humanistic materialism and seems to be ready for changes. On one hand, he discovers that the non-subjective status is not caused by nature but the economic monster created by man himself. Thus, he puts forward the famous theory of labour alienation. From then on, Marx becomes gradually more tolerant with nature, believing that man's essence is nature, nature is humanized and man is naturalized. History is the true history of nature. In fact, Marx still takes nature as man's object of conquest but through a beautified expansion of natural humanism and the subjective dialectics of a speculative humanism.

After 1845, Marx abandons his previous conception, the humanistic logic of the abstract subject in his scientific philosophical vision; he makes a correct restoration of the base of human history to the materialized subjective activity of reforming the external object, in short, practice. Together with Engels, he finds the key to understand the historical development of human society, the objective movement of the material productive forces by man. Labour makes the real and historical change of external nature and it is the labour of production that creates man, society and history. Man's life and ideology only stem from the specific productive forces under certain historical conditions. This is the most important principle to guide their practice of historical materialism and the sole starting point for a scientific explanation of the relationship between man and nature from the perspective of historical dialects.

Firstly, historical dialectics adhere to the *historical view* of dealing with the relationship between man and the nature surrounding us. In the *Theses on Feuerbach*, the object of nature is interpreted as man's critical, revolutionary sensual activity; in the *German Ideology*, Marx and Engels require us to "set out from these natural bases and their modification in the course of history through the action of men."[15] Man's productive activity to reform nature is regarded as the qualitative difference from the animals. Marx and Engels criticize Feuerbach's abstract conclusion that man is in harmony with "nature which has not yet been subdued by men."[16] For today's civil society, it does not exist. "At the same time it is consciousness of nature, which first appears to men as a completely alien, all-powerful and unassailable force, with which men's relations are purely animal and by which they are overawed like beasts."[17]

Marx believes this type of relations is narrow because "nature is as yet hardly modified historically."[18] Man's existence in reality is very small when compared to nature. In his attempt to dominate nature, he only ends in myths/imagination. By this objective "struggle" of man or man's constant development of the productive forces to historically change the natural surroundings, man creates the new material foundation for existence. Therefore, the human subject survives in the nature mediated through practice instead of the original crude nature. Man's environment, the "sensuous world" that includes nature, "is, not a thing given direct from all

---

15   Marx, Engels, and Christopher John Arthur. *The German Ideology*. New York: International Publishers Co, 1970. p. 42.

16   *Ibid.*, p. 61.

17   *Ibid.*, p. 51.

18   *Ibid.*, p. 51.

eternity, remaining ever the same, but the product of industry and of the state of society; and, indeed, in the sense that it is an historical product, the result of the activity of a whole succession of generations."[19]

Next, in historical dialectics, Marx and Engels always treat nature as the object of man's reform and conquest. In addition, the historical development of labour that is implemented for this reform is regarded as the essence of and the general foundation for the social history of humankind. In their new worldview, the productive forces represent the essence of social development and man's functional ability to reform nature, "as practical power over nature."[20] "All production is appropriation of nature on the part of an individual within and through a specific form of society."[21] "Labour is, in the first place, a process in which both man and Nature participate, and in which man of his own accord starts, regulates, and controls the material re-actions between himself and Nature."[22] Here, nature as the object of labour and production is not "as mere natural objects (as such, they are never capital), but as natural objects already transformed by human activity."[23] More importantly, as for this real possession of nature by man, "it is the necessary condition for effecting exchange of matter between man and Nature; it is the everlasting Nature-imposed condition of human existence, and therefore is independent of every social phase of that existence, or rather, is common to every such phase." [24]If this unceasing sensuous labour and creation were "interrupted only for a year," human beings will lose all their foundation of survival.[25]

In the new philosophical vision founded by Marx and Engels, the direct production and reproduction of the human subject is both the historical (and the logical) starting point and the ultimate basis for the existence and development of human society. Man establishes his subjectivity via the material production that reforms nature and transcends animals to enter into the social-historical phase. The essence of human society is the mode of production (the practice pattern) used to change nature and social life;

19   *Ibid.*, p. 62.

20   Marx, Karl. *Grundrisse: Foundations of the Critique of Political Economy (rough draft)*. Trans. Martin Nicolaus. London; New York: Penguin, 1993. p.542.

21   *Ibid.*, p. 87.

22   Marx, and Friedrich Engels. *Capital: A Critique of Political Economy (Vol. I-Part I): The Process of Capitalist Production*. New York: Cosimo, Inc., 2007. p.197.

23   Marx and Friedrich Engels. *Collected Works*. London: Lawrence & Wishart, 1989. p. 397.

24   Marx, and Friedrich Engels. *Capital: A Critique of Political Economy (Vol. I-Part I): The Process of Capitalist Production*. New York: Cosimo, Inc., 2007. p.205.

25   Marx, and Friedrich Engels. *The German Ideology*. Ed. Christopher John Arthur. New York: International Publishers Co, 1970. p. 63.

thus, history means that the human subject constantly creates new dimensions of social life through his persistent changes and reorganization of external nature in a real, historical, concrete way, and through an orderly restructuring of the subjective interactions (practical construction).

Obviously, were there no man's transformation of external nature and the real development of the material productive forces, there would be no human existence and the progress of social history, let alone the harmonious partnership of man and nature. Therefore, Marx's and Engels' view that the advancement of the productive forces promote the historical development of social history forms the theoretical core of their – historical, real, concrete, practical materialism –, and the general foundation of their new view of history, which is also the first scientific explanation of the relationship between man and nature in the world.

Thirdly, Marx and Engels attach real importance to science and technology in their historical dialectics, taking it as the important drive in the development of the modern productive forces. In their eyes, science and technology comes into being under the conditions of modern industrial production, signifying the greatest revolutionary leap in the historical development of the productive forces. Marx believes that science is a driving and revolutionary force in history. However, it does not mean science always plays the critical role in any era; that science becomes the drive of the productive forces is historical in itself. It is in the capitalist industrial production that "the productiveness of labour develops continually with the uninterrupted advance of science and technology."[26] To be exact, "since steam, machinery, and the making of machines by machinery transformed the older manufacture into modern industry, the productive forces evolved under the guidance of the bourgeoisie developed with a rapidity and in a degree unheard of before."[27] In the opinion of Lenin, the emergence and development of science has greatly expanded the control of man over nature. Obviously, the classic Marxists fully recognize the significance of science and technology at the new stage of social history. They even talk about the *dominant* revolutionary role of science and technology in the new historical period.

It must be reminded that Marx believes material production is the universal and eternal natural necessity for the entire social existence and development, which cannot be changed as long as mankind exists. At the same

---

26   Marx, Karl. *Capital: Marx and Engels.* New York: International Publishers, 1984. p. 605.
27   Marx, and Friedrich Engels. *Karl Marx and Friedrich Engels: Selected Works in One Volume.* New York: International Publishers, 1968. p. 417.

time, Marx notices the issue of the changed dominant elements (not those in the subjective dimension of historical dialectics) in the structure of the productive forces, that is, the functional role of science and technology has shifted to a decisive status with the further development of large-scale social production. However, even if the decisive position gets more and more emphasized today, it cannot replace the basic station of the material production per se. We should pay special attention to this point; otherwise, we shall just repeat the mistake of the idealist conception of history.

I insist that the Marxist view of history advocating the human conquest of nature relies on the material productiveness as the nature of socio-historical development; science and technology still promotes the progress of human society. The era of Marx and Engels does not offer the ecological perspective or consciousness to make nature as man's partner. Nevertheless, the contemporary ecological thought does not alter the scientific theory of the productive forces in Marxist philosophy because the material productive forces used to reform the object of nature validated by Marx and Engels are indeed the true basis for human survival, and will always drive the development of human society. As long as society exists, the productive forces must move forward, which means that man will *forever take nature as the object to reform and the base of material living conditions*. Without the real change of nature, there would be no beginning of human history and the transformation from the primitive animal-like life into modern civilization; without the development of science and technology, the human subjects cannot hold his head high out of the natural progress. It is undeniable that the productive forces and contemporary science and technology created and discovered by humans are the pride of humanity. Any non-historical attitude towards the productive forces and science and technology is wrongly against the objective historical dialectics.

C. THE CONTROL OF MAN'S SOCIAL SUBJECTIVE ACTION AND THE THEORY OF 'NATURAL-NESS'

However, does this mean that Marxist historical dialectics refuse to accept the reflections of modern ecology? The answer is, of course, no. After careful analysis, I think the Marxist scientific view of history is essentially consistent with the mentality of modern ecologists who, in my opinion, do not deny the catalytic role of material production, including modern technologies, in the development of social history but oppose the *overexploitation* of nature by the human technological system and a certain imbalance of man's relations with nature. As science, ecology neither makes an abstract negation of man's reform of nature nor takes a romantic ethical impulse as its theoretical base. It can analyze the inevitable development and conversion of the relations between man and nature, that is, the historical dynamic relationship in which nature turns from an enemy to an example, from an example to an object, and from an object to a partner for man[28]. When humans first emerge from the natural world, they are faced with the powerful and mysterious forces and have to be hostile after a series of blows and injuries. The human development is associated with the exploration and study of the natural rules, which, for a long period, leaves nature our example. When man's maturity is established on the conquest and reform of the object of nature, it shows the highly developed productive forces of human society. Ecology acknowledges this historical relationship but finds man's overuse of technology to change nature in the third qualitative point, that is, the specific incongruence of man and nature caused by the great development of the productive forces dominated by highly advanced science and technology. For the *only purpose of opposing such abuse*, Ecology suggests the fourth mode of the man-nature relationship: The ecological "partnership," which indicates that ecology is not to make an abstract negation of the historical development of the productive forces but correct a certain deviation in its process. *It is not contrary to the general logic of Marxist historical dialectics.*

On the other hand, we can see that Marx and Engels are also against the "destructive" relationship with nature in their view of history, which is not a contemporary ecological opinion but indeed a bigger concept of nature to protect the environment. This view is related to the theory of socio-historical 'natural-ness' in the subjective dimension of Marxist historical dialectics mentioned above. For Marx, the development of social history at a certain stage presents a similar situation to that blind movement of nature (of course, Marx is discussing the phenomenon of the human subject being subjugated and driven by the material forces outside himself), and results in the *destructive aspect* of man against nature (especially, in the development of capitalist production). Marx says, "In the development of productive forces there comes a stage when productive forces and means of intercourse are brought into being, which, under the existing relationships, only cause mischief, and are no longer productive but destructive forces."[29] Marx does not simply negate the development of the productive forces but criticizes the particular situation and usage of them

---

28   Sachsse, Hans. *Ökologische Philosophie*. Wissenschaftliche Buchgesellschaft, 1984.
29   Marx, and Friedrich Engels. *The German Ideology*. Ed. Christopher John Arthur. New York: International Publishers Co, 1970. p. 94.

(technologies) within the *capitalist relations of production*. In capitalism, "machinery, gifted with the wonderful power of shortening and fructifying human labour, we behold starving and overworking it; The victories of art seem bought by the loss of character. At the same pace that mankind masters nature, man seems to become enslaved to other men or to his own infamy."[30] He even says, "Science appears as a potentiality alien to labour, hostile to it and dominant over it."[31] In Marx's view, it is true that science and technology do push the development of the productive forces in large-scale industrial production but the blind pursuit of profit in capitalism makes science and technology generate harmful outcomes for both man and nature. Engels seems closer to the modern ecological vision than Marx does by making very profound discussions on the relationship between man and nature, the negative aspects of man's disordered transformation of nature. He warned to treat and cherish nature more than a century ago. Despite the subjective victory over nature through developing the productive forces, especially, since the birth of modern science and technology, he says:

> **Let us not, however, flatter ourselves overmuch on account of our human victories over nature. For each such victory nature takes its revenge on us. Each victory, it is true, in the first place brings about the results we expected, but in the second and third places it has quite different, unforeseen effects which only too often cancel the first[32].**

Engels then takes a few examples. "The people who in Mesopotamia, Greece, Asia Minor and elsewhere, destroyed the forests to obtain cultivable land, never dreamed that by removing along with the forests the collecting centres and reservoirs of moisture they were laying the basis for the present forlorn state of those countries."[33] Similarly, "when the Italians of the Alps used up the pine forests on the southern slopes, so carefully cherished on the northern slopes, they had no inkling that by doing so they were cutting at the roots of the dairy industry in their region; they had still less inkling that they were thereby depriving their mountain springs of water for the greater part of the year, and making it possible for them to

---

30   Marx, and Friedrich Engels. *Karl Marx and Friedrich Engels: Selected Works in One Volume*. New York: International Publishers, 1975. p. 655.

31   Marx, and Friedrich Engels. *Karl Marx, Friedrich Engels: Collected Works, Volume 34*. London: Lawrence & Wishart, 1994. p. 34.

32   Engels, Friedrich. *The Origin of the Family, Private Property and the State*. New York: International Publishers Co, 1972. p. 260.

33   *Ibid.*, p. 12.

pour still more furious torrents on the plains during the rainy seasons."[34] In another example, Engels complains that the industrial development in capitalism "transforms all water into stinking manure," which undermines the condition for human activities[35]. For this, he sharply points out:

> **In the most advanced industrial countries we have subdued the forces of nature and pressed them into the service of mankind; we have thereby infinitely multiplied production, so that a child now produces more than a hundred adults previously did. And what is the result? Increasing overwork and increasing misery of the masses, and every ten years a great collapse[36].**

Here, Engels seems to adopt a contemporary ecological perspective. "Thus at every step we are reminded that we by no means rule over nature like a conqueror over a foreign people, like someone standing outside nature – but that we, with flesh, blood and brain, belong to nature, and exist in its midst, and that all our mastery of it consists in the fact that we have the advantage over all other creatures of being able to learn its laws and apply them correctly."[37] It just displays the consubstantial relationship between human survival and nature. The question is: How can we correctly recognize and utilize the natural rules? According to Engels, "we are acquiring a better understanding of these laws and getting to perceive both the more immediate and the more remote consequences of our interference with the traditional course of nature."[38] In particular, he emphasizes that since the great progress of natural science in the 20th century, we have learned "to control, also the more remote natural consequences of at least our day-to-day production activities."[39] Furthermore, he points out, "But the more this progress the more will men not only feel but also know their oneness with nature, and the more impossible will become the senseless and un-natural idea of a contrast between mind and matter, man and nature, soul and body." It is undoubtedly an insightful opinion.

As early as a century ago, Engels knows "in this sphere too, by long and often cruel experience and by collecting and analyzing historical material, we are gradually learning to get a clear view of the indirect, more remote social

---

34   Marx, and Friedrich Engels. *Karl Marx and Friedrich Engels: Selected Works in One Volume.* New York: International Publishers, 1968. p. 366.
35   Engels, Friedrich. *Anti-Dühring: Herr Eugen Dühring's Revolution in Science.* Moscow: Foreign Languages Pub. House, 1959. p. 408.
36   Engels, and John Burdon Sanderson Haldane. *Dialektik der Natur.* , 1940. p. 19.
37   Marx, and Friedrich Engels. *Karl Marx and Friedrich Engels: Selected Works in One Volume.* New York: International Publishers, 1968. p. 366.
38   *Ibid.*, p. 366.
39   *Ibid.*, p. 366.

effects of our production activity, and so are afforded an opportunity to control and regulate these effects as well."[40] It does not mean anybody can make the adjustment at any time because it is not just an issue of understanding. After all, it involves the development of the mode of production. "All hitherto existing modes of production have aimed merely at achieving the most immediately and directly useful effect of labour. The further consequences, which appear only later and become effective through gradual repetition and accumulation, were totally neglected."[41] Here, Engels starts with Marx's philosophical view of nature to have a far-reaching observation of the theoretical standpoint for contemporary ecology. However, his perception is not based on the problematic studies but established on the scientific practical dialectics of social history.

At that time when the ecological environment was not fundamentally damaged, the entire eco-system did not face a substantial crisis, and ecology was not born as an independent discipline, Marx and Engels correctly foresaw the important issues in their subjective dimension of historical dialectics, which has been just confirmed by today's ecology.

D. ANALYSIS OF THE RELATIONSHIP BETWEEN MAN AND NATURE

As analyzed above, it is safe to say that the alleged attacks at Marxist historical dialectics by "eco-Marxism" are indefensible. It does not mean Western "eco-Marxism" is devoid of any merit. For example, its basis on contemporary ecological theory is correct. It is also right to criticize the damage to nature caused by today's technological productive forces and the ecological imbalance due to the economic overgrowth. It just ends in error when turning the theoretical thought into a radical negation of Marxist historical dialectics, or, when it starts from contemporary ecology to make an a-historical negation of the scientific principle that man transforms and utilizes nature through material production.

It is easy to find that the so-called eco-Marxism is actually a modern branch of the Western Marxian humanist school. In particular, it has intrinsic connections with the Frankfurt School, in whose critique of contemporary capitalism, the capitalist ideology is the science and technology centred on the "instrumental reason." The Frankfurt School believes that human reason should have been a sober critical force beyond reality to transform the object and reform itself but the utility of instrumental science and

---

40   *Ibid.*, p. 367.
41   *Ibid.*, p. 367.

technology in modern society replaces the critical reason with specifically oriented values. People only care about the controlled and operated object, instead of the purpose and consequences. In today's capitalist society, science and technology have an undisputed reign over everything. The Frankfurt philosophers speak from a political point of view that science and technology lead to the false rationality of contemporary capitalism but cunningly conceal their substantive irrationality. They thus become the biggest ideology for the capitalist control on people. Therefore, they strongly oppose the bourgeois scholars who advocate technocracy with all-around discussions of the negative aspects of science and technology in modern capitalist society, which is, admittedly, correct. Nevertheless their basic thought is not scientific when they take the romantic stance to negate the progressive significance of modern science and technology. In fact, today's "eco-Marxism" is similar to the Frankfurt School, only with the difference of the natural (ecological) basis. Similarly, when their limited negation of the over-use of the natural object by the scientific productive forces in modern times is extended to a fundamental negation of the general foundation of developing the productive forces in social history, they inadvertently fall into the pit against the Marxist scientific view of history. It is also wrong for the philosophical reflection of modern ecology to put the ecological consciousness in antithesis to the Marxist view that the development of the productive forces is the general foundation of social existence and development.

Lastly, we must clearly realize that this issue is not purely theoretical or a battle of words about the philosophical or logical trends; instead, it is a significant practical problem for China today. As we all know, science and technology is our major drive of the practice of opening and reform in the current building of socialism. Deng Xiaoping has called science and technology as the "primary productive force." Therefore, it is of grand significance to determine the real position of ecology in the economical development on a philosophical level.

The possible theoretical questions are: Is there serious imbalance between man and nature at present if perceived from the overall Chinese social history? Is China's economic and productive growth beyond certain limits today? Should we put the promotion of science and technology before everything else? What is the deserved status of ecology for China's development today? These questions remind me of a philosophical fable in ancient China. It is about a person eating bread. He eats 6 pieces of bread but still feels hungry. When he just finishes half the 7th piece, he is full. This man cannot help feeling regretful: Why should I have eaten the first 6 pieces instead of the half of the last one? The relationship between the first six and the last half has a modern sense in the discussion of the above questions. In my view, all the important issues here boil down to one point: Should the Chinese eat the last half of the "ecological bread" to avoid the hunger of the underdeveloped economy?

As we all know, the ancient Chinese philosophy follows the logic of unity between man and nature. The early Chinese people attempted to establish a "nature-and-man-in-one" partnership in which the human subject complied with nature. And the Chinese culture almost lives in a natural "home" of ethics that stresses self-control among the human subjects. Generally, it coincides with today's ecological requirement. The problem is that the Chinese people did not obtain real social progress from such relationship for hundreds of years, less to mention the real subjective liberation, precisely because for a long period, including in the "Cultural Revolution," we could not walk out of the enclosed natural economy to really develop material productivity; we did not substantially and gradually reform nature to achieve the modernization of our national economy. No matter how harmonious or "unified" we were with nature, how good the natural environment was, it could not change the underdeveloped situation of the Chinese people. We should not be proud of it. One may argue that why we should repeat the same road as that of Western capitalism whose industrial development has brought about damage to the ecological environment. It reminds me of the critique of religion in the new century by Marx and Engels, who think that it is very sad to make commendations about the directness of nature to maintain the pre-capitalist modes of production against the background of modern productivity and technologies for "modern natural science, which, with modern industry, has revolutionised the whole of nature and put an end to man's childish attitude towards nature."[42] They point out that the primitive rural economy (of course, it accords with ecological balance) "should at last be ploughed up by modern cultivation and modern machines."[43] The slash-and-burn cultivation cannot represent the reclusive glory; striking sparks from a flint cannot be associated with a romantic candlelight dinner; and wearing rags cannot become a fashion of returning to nature. Perhaps, we should not retreat but move forward after reflection. It is the same with the development of the productive forces: We should avoid praising the "partnership" between man and nature with an underdeveloped economy.

---

42   Marx and Friedrich Engels. *Collected Works*. London: Lawrence & Wishart, 1978. p. 245.
43   *Ibid.*, p. 245.

Certain Western ecological works also mention the relationship between man and nature in ancient Chinese philosophy. It is believed that Tai Chi diagram is the symbol of Chinese culture to represent a typical Eastern relationship. In this dynamic schema, man and nature are equally opposite with each containing a core of the other in the centre but the whole is peaceful, unconscious of directions and requiring no human action. Therefore, for the Chinese philosophy, the subjective activity is characterized by inward ethical procedure rather than an actual operation pointed to the outside. From a philosophical view, it indicates the Chinese society enters an enclosed loop after it reaches certain historical progress. It is worth noting that the basic schema of man and nature in ancient China is different from the Western symbol of "cross," which breaks the rounded closeness, presents assertive edges and corners, and highlights the actual human initiative of transforming the objects and nature. "Cross represents a wake-up cry." It is this materialized practical spirit that prompts the Western pragmatism to develop the productive forces, leading to their economic take-off relying on modern science and technology. In comparison, the Chinese holistic thinking as a fundamental attitude towards life lacks of power. Today, the West is very concerned about the uncontrolled development so that they are interested in the Chinese wisdom. However, the Chinese example shows that it is not enough to deal with life only with wisdom. The universal criticism at present against various growths perhaps forgets or excludes how many abundant opportunities and how much development the technological development has brought to the West.

Frankly, I agree to this view despite a simplified interpretation of the Chinese culture. I find that there is an obvious mistake in the philosophical thought of present ecology: China's development of economy, utilization of science and technology, and speeding up of the productive forces are contrary to contemporary ecological protection. The Chinese are said to have abandoned their partnership with nature in the traditional culture and strayed into the Western mistake of "technocracy." I am afraid I cannot go along with this opinion. Today, a vigorous and effective reform of nature is still the primary object in the general development of China's social history. "Development must be the first and foremost concern of us!" The basic principle of Marxist historical view puts material production as the prerequisite of all social existence and high-level development. Without this premise, everything else is out of the question. The view is almost as absurd as the criticism of China's "human rights" by some Western scholars. At present, the biggest Chinese human right is the right of survival. It is not a proper time for the Chinese people to talk such things as "man cannot conquer and transform nature," "we must avoid mentioning the speeding up of the economic growth," or "we should depend on the ecological partnership to limit the development." Promoting the productive forces is still the first problem that China has to address. As our major task today, it just represents the first 6 pieces of bread mentioned before. Only after that can we have the last "half" piece to develop the partnership between man and nature. If ecological problems become a dominant factor in contemporary Western economic development, they are only an important guide and reference that should not be exaggerated with its corresponding significance in China. It is right for the people in the developed capitalist countries to oppose the economic yardstick and endorse "Buddhist economics" and the scale of "human values."[44] However, in today's China, the abstract promotion of man's values will certainly end in non-scientific failures, which we shall see more clearly in the next chapter.

Of course, it does not mean that the philosophical thought of contemporary ecological thinking in China should not have important practical impact. What I mean is a historical and scientific logical relationship between the economic development and the ecological perspective. In fact, the ecological environment is a very important link for the social development of every developing country. It has become an indispensable reference framework for each nationality in their economy because it directly affects the arrangement of their short- and long- term development. However, it is not the concern of this book here.

---

44   Schumacher, Ernst Friedrich. *Small is Beautiful: Economics as if People Mattered.* New York: Harper & Row, 1975. p. 50.

CHAPTER VIII

CONTEMPORARY PRACTICES OF SOCIALISM AND HISTORICAL DIALECTICS

1 *A Historical Reflection on the Road of Socialist Practices*
2 *The Philosophical Thought behind Deng Xiaoping's Socialist Road*

CHAPTER EIGHT

INTRODUCTION

Since the Establishment of Marx's scientific view of history one and a half centuries ago, the historical development of human society itself has undergone profound and significant changes. Scientific socialism once again strides into reality from theory while the real practice begins to be reflected after numerous difficulties and setbacks. Following Chinese Marxists' hard exploration in China between 1950 to 70ies, we are now on the road with Chinese characteristics designed by Deng Xiaoping. In this process, there have been new situations and problems beyond the expectations of those classical scholars, which should not be avoided in today's research of Marxist socio-historical view. In this chapter, we shall further get into the reality of socialist practices and seek the new logical position of Marxist historical dialectics.

I. A HISTORICAL REFLECTION ON THE ROAD OF SOCIALIST PRACTICES

After a long historical development, today's socialism is no longer a theoretical discourse existent only in books by Marx and Engels, nor a "ghost" wandering in practice but a living reality. Vladimir Lenin was the first to turn socialist theory into reality. The October Revolution blazed a trail for the real historical development of socialism. Mao Zedong was the first to lead China on the socialist road. He proved with practice that socialism was the choice of history for the development of Chinese society in modern times. And the real and big socialist progress based on material development has been made by Deng Xiaoping's socialism with Chinese characteristics. Thus, it is necessary to adopt Marx's socio-historical view to have a serious examination of the theoretical and logical sequence of these ideas and events.

A. A PHILOSOPHICAL INTROSPECTION ON THE PROCESS OF SOCIALIST PRACTICES

As we know, Marx and Engels unmistakably demonstrate an important prerequisite for realizing the proletarian revolution and socialism, that is, only on the apex of the development of capitalist productive forces can socialism occur. Thus, its entire economic and political base is the high-level development of material production. This is because the real liberation of man must *first* be established on his true domination over the natural and socio-economic forces from which the human subject *can* obtain full development and liberation.

Marx and Engels never assumed that socialism was to be achieved on a historical section with underdeveloped productive forces. They mainly focused on the developed capitalist countries in Europe for the final victory of the proletarian revolution, even saying that the socialist revolution could only succeed by occurring simultaneously in several European countries[1] because with the development of almost all capitalist countries at a similar level in the period of free competition stage, the bourgeoisie would unite to suppress the proletarian revolution in one country and thus the revolutionary task of the working class "is not accomplished anywhere

---

1   It seems that Marx's late research of the Russian communes and primitive social history should not be exaggerated and over-extended. From the basic logic of Marxist historical dialectics, the undeveloped productive forces cannot produce true socialism, even with the apparent alteration of social forms. The precious socialist practices by China and the USSR have already fully proved the scientific Marxist historical dialectics.

within the national boundaries."[2] Here, it means the chain of revolutions that happen one after another in countries during a certain period. Marx and Engels even talked about the possibility that the French give a signal fire and the Germans go into the battle. Although Marx noticed the particular Eastern social history in his later studies, he generally hoped for the West to realize socialism. However, his expectation of the revolutionary upsurge of the whole European proletarians did not come true even when Marx and Engels died. Moreover, the *actual development* of socialism later is *not entirely consistent with* (even contrary to) their theoretical thought.

In previous discussions of the Western Marxist view of history, we have had an important discovery that the Second International has a big mistake in understanding the development of Marxist social history after the death of Engels. They turn Marx's scientific view of history into a mechanical determinism merely examined by its economic aspect. The theorists, represented by Karl Kautsky, in the Second International seriously consider themselves upholding the primacy of developing material production in Marxist view of history and the prerequisite significance in the reality of the proletarian revolution. They have major theoretical arguments with Lenin's Bolshevik Party as to the direction of real struggles, in particular, the Russian Revolution at that time.

In their eyes, Marx's theory of the socialist revolution must be premised on the material production level in reality, that is, the highly developed productive forces in the large-scale industries of capitalist society that constitutes an *absolute* objective condition. Consequently, the Russian proletarian revolution is *unqualified*. Meanwhile, the proletariat cannot first form within one country, less to say an underdeveloped country. This opinion is shared by Georgi Plekhanov, "the father of Russian Marxism," and Julius Martov, who believe that Russia at that time "is not enough for the complete victory of socialism"[3] as the revolution "would make sense only if the objective conditions necessary for a social revolution prevailed. These conditions do not exist yet."[4] Their doubt continues even until the last moment of the October Revolution, when Plekhanov keeps questioning again and again whether "it is too early to 'introduce' socialism" in an underdeveloped and semi-Asian country as Russia[5].

---

2   Marx, Karl. *The Karl Marx Library, Volume 1*. New York: McGraw-Hill, 1977. p. 216.
3   Lenin, Vladimir Il'ich. *Democracy and Revolution*. Sydney: Resistance Books, 2000. p. 91.
4   Lenin, Vladimir Il'ich. *Collected Works: Apr.-June 1917*. London: Lawrence & Wishart, 1977. p. 192.
5   Lenin, Vladimir Il'ich. *Selected Works, Volume 2*. New York: International Publishers, 1967. p. 268.

On the contrary, Lenin not only upholds the integrity of Marxist world-view and historical materialism but also highlights the subject's dynamic role of practice and historical dialectics, especially, its *subjective dimension*. He sharply points out, "Whoever expects a 'pure' social revolution will never live to see it. Such a person pays lip-service to revolution without understanding what revolution is."[6] In his opinion, the proletarian revolution is premised not only on a *certain* objective level of material productivity but also on the subjective condition of the proletariat and other working people, that is, the conscious, dynamic and active will of the revolutionary groups because any revolution occurs as a result of changing objective conditions combined with the subjective situations. Therefore, Lenin believes that with certain capitalist development in Russia, plus the proletariat who have already got mature in their struggle against the bourgeoisie, in particular, the enormous impact of Marxism in certain historical conditions, they are already well equipped with the revolutionary *consciousness*. What's more, the world at that time is on a special historical section of imperialist hegemony and Russia just represents a weak link in the uneven development of capitalist politics and economy; all these catalytic conditions make it possible for the *breakthrough* of the proletarian revolution in Russia.

The victory of the October Revolution proves Lenin's new conclusion of Marxist and socialist revolution (later known as the doctrine that "socialism can first win victory among a few states or even in a single country) is right. From then on, his interpretation of Marxist and socialist revolution has a tremendous *practical attraction*. In my opinion, it is precisely a great victory of Marxist scientific historical dialectics (its subjective dimension!) in the practice of proletarian revolution. Were it to abide by the mechanical points of the Second International scholars, socialism would have never been seen until today. However, as to the transcendence of practice in the October Revolution, people do not emphasize its *specific* historical significance in reality and exaggerate it into *a general rule of socialist revolution and construction*. Hence, a logical paradox occurs. Behind Kautsky's and Plekhanov's mechanical view of history and socialist theories hides the reasonable premise for the theoretical process of Marxist historical dialectics, in particular, the general base of historical materialism and the objective dimension of historical dialectics, that is, *any economic-historical stage is impossible to be overstepped (NOT indicating the inevitability of capitalism)* and the full development of productive forces constitutes the necessary objective material preconditions for the establishment of socialism. However,

---

6   Lenin, Vladimir Il'ich. *British Labour and British Imperialism: A Compilation of Writings by Lenin on Britain.* London: Lawrence & Wishart, 1969. p. 166.

several mistakes have been made in respect of this point. One, the difference and significance of the two dimensions of historical dialectics are neglected; two, that the practice of socialism in reality transgresses certain historicality is overlooked. Thus, a tragic practice of socialism is doomed later.

Although the October Revolution is won, theoretical battles continued. Three days after the revolution, Plekhanov publishes an article to claim that people should ask themselves: "Do the working class get ready for the establishment of their own regime? ... Anyone with a little knowledge of what kind of economic condition necessary for the proletarian dictatorship will answer this question in a firm and negative attitude."[7] Another Menshevik also says: Russia, as an underdeveloped capitalist country, cannot leap from the tragic realm of necessity to the bright realm of socialism. At the same time, Kautsky believes that with the poor Russian economy, the October Revolution does not meet the socialist requirement of material production. It cannot be socialist in nature. If indiscriminately distorted into the category of socialist revolution, it would be like "a pregnant woman, who performs the most foolish exercises in order to shorten the period of gestation, which makes her impatient, and thereby causes a premature birth. The result of such proceedings is, as a rule, a child incapable of life."[8] These opinions are previously treated as opposite to the October Revolution and thus wrong. However, it is time to make a serious reflection on the innate theoretical discourse under these apparently erroneous points, such as the objective condition for the transition from the realm of necessity of the capitalist economy ('natural-ness' and material-subjugation) to the realm of freedom. To be exact, can socialism be truly established on the social base of low economic production? Can the change of ownership replace the transcendence over economic necessity in the social infrastructure? What are the concerns of a socialist country whose productive forces are undeveloped? On what social aspects does socialism demonstrate its superiority? All this makes a task that is not easy to finish.

Admittedly, Lenin does not fail to notice the above questions in his theoretical consideration. He repeatedly says, when the proletariat seize power and begin to hit the socialist road with their revolutionary initiative, it only requires certain qualitative and quantitative development of material productivity; but when socialism is already established and further

---

7   The English here is translated from the Chinese version of Georgi Valentinovich *Plekhanov's A Year in the Homeland.* Trans. Wang Yinting & Yang Yongze. Shanghai: Sdxjoint Publishing Company, 1980. p. 464.
8   Kautsky, Karl. *The Dictatorship of the Proletariat.* University of Michigan Press, 1964. p. 98.

advanced, the previous development is far from enough. He makes it clear that the major aspect to build socialism is already the objective level of material productivity, which returns to the objective dimension of historical dialectics. He writes, "It was easier for the Russians than for the advanced countries to begin the great proletarian revolution, but that it will be more difficult for them to continue it and carry it to final victory, in the sense of the complete organisation of a socialist society."[9] Accordingly, shortly after the victory of the revolution in Russia, Lenin makes the proposal of "a whole period of transition from capitalism to socialism" with the development of commodity production[10].

However, due to the particular state of civil war and the imperialist assault after Lenin's Bolshevik Party seizes power, the capitalist economic system is cancelled; commodity circulation is cut; basic necessities are assigned by the government and the peasants' grain is directly collected by the special workers' team sent to the rural areas. Lenin now proclaims that "socialism cannot be built if it is not, for that means building a centralised economic system, an economic system directed from the centre."[11] This "experience of direct socialist construction"[12] results in a great theoretical and practical illusion: Russia is in the *direct transition to socialism*! With lightning flashing by and thunders rolling ahead, Marx's expectation of communism in the *Critique of the Gotha Program* seems to suddenly come into being.

Nevertheless, reality is cruel. The new social system and policies fail in resolving the problems of material production, even aggravating the economic and political crisis in Russia's new socialism. Lenin is still the first to find this mistake. He openly acknowledges the error that he and the Party commit, that is, they try to go beyond the stage of the economic development. In reflecting on the wartime communism, he says:

> **We expected – or perhaps it would be truer to say that we presumed without having given it adequate consideration – to be able to organise the state production and the state distribution of products on communist lines in a small-peasant country directly as ordered by the proletarian state[13].**

---

9   Lenin, Vladimir Il'ich. *Collected works, Volume 29*. Trans. Institut Marksizma-Leninizma (Moscow, Russia). London: Lawrence & Wishart, 1970. p. 310.

10   Lenin, Vladimir Il'ich. *Selected Works, Volume 3*. Moscow: Progress Publishers, 1971. p. 17.

11   Lenin, Vladimir Il'ich. *Коллестед воркс, Volume 28*. Trans. Institut Marksizma-Leninizma (Moscow, Russia). Форейгн Лангуагес Пуб. Хусе, 1970. p. 400.

12   Lenin, Vladimir Il'ich. *Коллестед воркс, Volume 33*. Trans. Institut Marksizma-Leninizma (Moscow, Russia). Форейгн Лангуагес Пуб. Хусе, 1970. p. 94.

13   Lenin, Vladimir Il'ich. *Collected Works, Volume 33*. London: Lawrence & Wishart, 1978. p. 58.

Hence, Lenin quickly adjusts his thoughts and the socialist program in practice, making the significant "New Economic Policy," in which the measure of surplus-grain appropriation is substituted by grain tax, the direct control of economy by state adjustment is withdrawn into the commodity production and monetary circulation under state capitalism, and trade is allowed in the market. The New Economic Policy leases or returns the small and medium enterprises to the capitalists. Lenin asserts that state capitalism is the bridge and means to socialism in Russia.

Inasmuch as we are as yet unable to pass directly from small production to socialism, some capitalism is inevitable as the elemental product of small production and exchange; so that we must utilise capitalism (particularly by directing it into the channels of state capitalism) as the intermediary link between small production and socialism, as a means, a path, and a method of increasing the productive forces[14].

The implementation of the new policy is welcomed by the people and Russia's economy is rapidly restored and developed.

I judge that Lenin sees the major problem faced by the painful reality: The historical transition from the economic realm of necessity to the real realm of freedom cannot be simply completed by a general *conversion of social systems*; the nature of socialism is *not political and conceptual*. Clearly, Lenin senses that there is a *gap* of objective productive forces between reality and the possibility of implementing socialism. Without doubt, Lenin understands the contemporary Russia undergoes a real socialist revolution (the particular perspective of the subjective dimension of historical dialectics) but the social progress is far behind the economic stage when the human subject transcends historical 'natural-ness' and material-subjugation and makes man the master of history. He needs the socialist state capitalism to make up the missed lessons (Not those of capitalism but the high-level development generated by commodity economy! In other words, socialism must have an objective condition of advanced large-scale production, which is precisely the indispensable base of the subjective dimension of historical dialectics). This point is echoed by Deng Xiaoping half a century later. Today, it is not wrong for some to believe that Deng's socialist economic reform *originates in* Lenin's New Economic Policy, but that is some way down the line.

---

14 Lenin, Vladimir Il'ich. *Коллестед воркс, Volume 32*. Trans. Institut Marksizma-Leninizma (Moscow, Russia). Форейгн Лангуагес Пуб. Хусе, 1970. p. 350.

However, for various reasons, state capitalism does not obtain extensive development in Russia; in particular, this important idea of Lenin's is not really implemented in the socialist construction of the Soviet Union. ("Perhaps Lenin had a good idea when he adopted the New Economic Policy. But as time went on, the Soviet pattern became ossified."[15]) Later, Stalin also makes great achievements in many political and economic aspects, but he never fully understands the profound significance of Lenin's New Economic Policy on the aspect of the real foundation of socialist economy and the process of historical development. Moreover, Stalin establishes the socialist planned economy and the highly centralized model of social development envisioned in Marx's future society ideas, which has a huge historical influence on later development of socialism. This is the historical premise for our theoretical reflection on China's socialist road.

B. MAO ZEDONG'S PHILOSOPHICAL LOGIC AND THE REVOLUTIONARY ROAD OF PRACTICE

In my opinion, to clarify the road of China's socialist development, we need to shift from the previous concern of the general historical experience to a deep theoretical reflection on the aftermaths in historical reality. The key issue here is about the originality of the socialist practice and the logical reflection of China's road of socialism.

First of all, it is necessary to deeply understand Mao Zedong's philosophical logics, which cannot be achieved only through a common textual interpretation in the Western style but should be comprehended in accordance with the background of the Chinese culture. Thus, I think we may discover a new thread of theoretical thinking.

In his early years, Mao Zedong was deeply influenced by the pragmatic rationality in traditional Chinese philosophy that emphasized human ethics and action. His structure of worldview was strongly characterized by a human-*oriented* intention. In 1917, he read the Friedrich Paulsen's *A System of Ethics*. He considered the mind-material dualism (some logical inclination towards idealism) "very innovative and reasonable" and gives off his own sparks of thought[16]. As to Paulsen's moral norm that subject should comply with the object, the Young Mao Zedong says, "that something is good or bad is freely called by man according to its relationship with his

---

15   Xiaoping, Deng. *Selected Works of Deng Xiaoping, Volumes 1-3*. Trans. Bureau de Compilation et Traduction des Oeuvres de Marx, Lénine et Staline. Beijing: Foreign Languages Press, 1994. p. 153.

16   Translated from *Mao Zedong's Early Documents*. Chang Sha: Hunan Publishing House, 1990. p. 276.

life, instead of by its entity."[17] In the eyes of Mao, the theoretical stipulation of ethics is neither the ontological quality of an external object nor a mind creature but the real relationship between man and object (event). It is "something that possesses the a priori goodness because it is associated with life."[18] Here, we can feel Mao's theoretical intention to emphasize the relationship between man and object, especially, the actual relationship in which man's initiative intervenes the object. This is an important theoretical point to be developed.

Around 1920, the Young Mao Zedong turned to the standpoint of communism and accepted the Marxist scientific worldview. *The attention to the dynamic role of man's action (practice)* was still the main line of his logics. At this time, Mao was very concerned about how to achieve the revolutionary goal of communism in China, or even in the world. The purpose of "transforming China and even the world" is very clear. He just hopes to find a way for this aim. In comparison with some scholars who proclaim the educational methods and moderate forms to obtain the socialist reforms, Mao is in favour of Cai Hesen's view to first organize the communist party and then completely smash the old world by the practical way of the October Revolution. In his eyes, "all human life is the expansion of desire in reality."[19] The capitalists and imperialists "will certainly not withdraw except being overthrown"; they must be struck down by the practice of revolution; only practice can make the ideal of communism a reality. In his opinion, "ideal is critical but reality is particularly critical"; "the fact exists at present, impossible to be eliminated and necessary to be taken into action after man's recognition."[20] Hence, practice is the essential point to understand and change the world. This idea based on real life and society points to the same direction with the practical materialism in Marx's establishment of the new worldview in 1845 and Lenin's writing of his *Philosophical Notes*[21]. Obviously, Mao's thought is also founded on the *subjective dimension* of historical dialectics. This is a crucial entrance to the comprehension of China's revolution. In my opinion, the Young Mao still does not attach enough *theoretical* importance to the *real objective condition* for the practice of the human subject.

---

17   Translated from *Mao Zedong's Correspondence*. Beijing: People's Publishing House. 1983. p. 6.
18   Translated from *Mao Zedong's Early Documents*. Chang Sha: Hunan Publishing House, 1990. p. 154.
19   Translated from *Mao Zedong's Correspondence*. Beijing: People's Publishing House. 1983. p. 6.
20   *Ibid.*, p. 7.
21   See Bi Jianheng's *Mao Zedong and the Traditional Chinese Culture*. Chengdu: Sichuan People's Publishing House, 1990. p. 68.

After the mid-1930s, Mao became a mature Marxist and combined it with the reality of the Chinese revolution. A number of his glorious works reflect the critical spirit of Marxism, especially, the living, objective, practical thought of historical dialectics, such as the *Problems of Strategy in China's Revolutionary War* and *On Protracted War*. On the other hand, during the busy practice of fighting the war, he spared no effort to read the philosophical literature, like a hungry man enjoying a feast, and made a lot of very important notes. In the recently published literature, we clearly see the basis of his philosophical logics.

Mao Zedong fully understands and grasps the true essence of Marxist philosophy, firmly opposing any idealism and agnosticism, in particular, mechanical materialism. He exactly sees the unique practical quality of Marxist philosophy. For him, the old materialism recognizes the material nature of the world but ignores the role of human practice by taking man as a passive existence in nature, thus leading to a passive, mechanical and sensual intuition of the external world. Mao displays his insight by saying that "mechanical materialism cannot overcome idealism in that it neglects the subjective initiative."[22] Later, he also puts forward that the conscious initiative is the human character. Nevertheless, we are not for the subjectivism exaggerated in idealism because man's initiative is established on the foundation of objective practice. Mao cites a particular example to analyze the importance of the initiative. "Confucius focuses on name/form; we emphasize the substance, which explains the difference between us."[23]

In addition, Mao makes a comment on Feuerbach during his extensive readings. He thinks in Feuerbach's materialism "the subject and the object are not historically existent or developed and knowledge is the constant reflection of the same nature; the two is united in an unchanged state."[24] Feuerbach does not understand the important role of practice for man to face the external world. Nature does not change and man only reflects the external object by his sensual intuition like a mirror. Feuerbach is unaware of the "dialectical unity of the subject and the object," that is, only when man dynamically affects nature can the external object be included in a certain mapping of the functionality of practice and reflected into the subjective consciousness. It also accounts for Marx's conclusion that Feuerbach fails to grasp the significance of the external sensual activities and practice.

---

22 Translated from *Mao Zedong's Correspondence*. Beijing: People's Publishing House. 1983. p. 145.
23 *Ibid.*, p. 145.
24 Translated from *The Philosophical Notes of Mao Zedong*. Beijing: Central Party Literature Press, 1988. p. 17.

In Mao's opinion, "before Marx, materialism examined the problem of knowledge apart from the social nature of man and apart from his historical development, and was therefore incapable of understanding the dependence of knowledge on social practice."[25] Mao stresses the concrete and historical reliance of consciousness on social practice instead of on material, which forms the fundamental difference between Marxism and all other materialist doctrines. In his eyes, man's consciousness cannot directly reflect the object; "all his knowledge results from the struggles of production and classes."[26] Only through a certain angle of the prism of specific social practice can the external object be historically reflected. In the words of Marx, "Each principle has had its own century in which to manifest itself."[27] Hence, Mao puts forward a very profound question: Why does the materialist philosophy with a correct reflection of the external world only appear in ancient Greek and not before? His careful answer is as follows. Firstly, the right comprehension of natural rules must wait till certain historical development of practice (the level of productive technologies), when people can gradually and objectively lift the veil of nature; secondly, handicrafts and commerce can only be developed on a certain basis of social practice, after which, with the expansion of man's activities and observation in commodity exchanges, it is possible to provide abstract thinking and a more general spiritual vision necessary for the growth of materialist philosophy; lastly, only with the initial development of natural science can the general rules of the external world be recognized in materialism[28]. Above is the specific historical basis on which the materialist worldview is built. Obviously, "recognition is conditioned by the state of practice and social history."[29] Mao's theoretical analysis here is very brilliant.

Furthermore, he points out that even some Marxist philosophers slip to the old materialism due to their ignorance of the basic status of practice. For example, Russia's "Father of Marxism," Georgi Plekhanov and later, Abram Deborin. The former translates and introduces many basic Marxist principles and theoretical points but does not fundamentally understand the dialectics of objective practice, giving rise to a serious anti-historicism: "The unification of the subject and the object with the intuition that has

---

25 Zedong, Mao *Selected Works, Volume 1*. Beijing: Foreign Languages Press, 1964. p. 295.
26 Translated from *The Philosophical Notes of Mao Zedong*. Beijing: Central Party Literature Press, 1988. p. 145-146.
27 Marx, Karl. *The Poverty of Philosophy*. New York: International Publishers, 1963. p. 110.
28 Translated from *The Philosophical Notes of Mao Zedong*. Beijing: Central Party Literature Press, 1988. p. 145.
29 *Ibid.*, p. 71.

nothing to do with the activities of practice."[30] And Deborin does "not understand that the mutual penetration of the subject and the object is realized in social practice."[31]

This is one of the important reasons for their mistakes about the issue of socialist revolution and construction. In fact, Mao's criticism is very insightful. The nature of Marxist philosophy does not just recognize a general materialist principle that matter is primary and spirit secondary; instead, the idealized opposition of the two cannot really overcome idealism because the subjective *initiative of practice* is not realized, which corresponds to Marx's opinion expressed in the *Theses on Feuerbach* that the essence of the new worldview must be understood "subjectively"[32], that is, to turn the object from the intuitive material in the old materialism to the object of practice and take objective practice as the "profound foundation of the whole existent world." Mao is always paying attention to the subjective initiative. He even proposes that Marxist philosophy has *initiative as its most important aspect*[33]. It of course refers to the initiative of practice. In his eyes, Marxism does not repeat the old materialism, nor play with philosophical terms. Fundamentally, it is "not to satisfy one's curiosity but to change the world." Mao believes in an ancient philosophical proposition in China: Man can conquer nature! Of course, it does not mean the external world is melted in the subjective mind ("All things are in me") but that "man practically struggles with nature so nature is in his charge."[34] Man creates social history through practice and historically becomes the real master of it. This is an objective socio-historical view of *practical* materialism as well as the *subjective dimension* of historical dialectics with the emphasis of the subjective initiative confirmed by Marx and Engels (later, Mao's practical materialism attaches more importance to the objective political practice of the human subject, rather than the practice of *material production* as the *elementary basis* of politics. This point gradually reveals its deep harm in later socialist practice.) It should be noted that this idea runs through Mao's deep historical view and theoretical discourse during the revolution of China's New democracy; moreover, it is consistent with Marxist scientific view of history.

---

30 *Ibid.*, p. 20.
31 *Ibid.*, p. 21.
32 Marx, Karl. *Early Writings by Karl Marx*. Harmondsworth: Penguin Books, 1992. p. 421.
33 Translated from *The Philosophical Notes of Mao Zedong*. Beijing: Central Party Literature Press, 1988. p. 311.
34 *Ibid.*, pp. 262-263.

As we all know, in the beginning of the social revolution in modern China, there was a similar debate as that of Russia, in which Chen Duxiu believed China's real development lacked the *necessary foundation of material productivity* for the proletarian revolution. Just like Kautsky and Plekhanov, Chen could not have a comprehensive understanding of the revolutionary nature of Marxist historical dialectics, considering submission to the economic nature of history and even claiming to give up the Communist Party's leadership in modern Chinese social revolution. In contrast, Mao was closer to Lenin with his own focus on the philosophical thought of the subjective dimension of historical dialectics. It was this original spirit of the subjective revolutionary initiative and the deep and *actual* understanding of China's specific situation that made Mao Zedong's successful combination of the general truth of Marxism with the Chinese revolution, leading to the victory of the New Democracy under the leadership of the Communist Party of China. However, I must point out that Mao's philosophical thought correctly understands man's practical initiative based on historical dialectics in Marxist view of history but puts too much emphasis on man's *subjective* initiative (interpreted merely as opposite to the objective rules) while relatively overlooking the objective *practice*, in particular, the *objective condition* (the objective dimension of historical materialism and historical dialectics) necessary for man's practical initiative to work, which foreshadows the deviation of the socialist construction in China later.

C. A PERSPECTIVE ON MAO ZEDONG'S EXPLORATION OF SOCIALISM WITH "CHINESE CHARACTERISTICS"

As early as in 1940, Mao proposed the doctrine of New Democracy to guide the future development of China. Here, he adhered to the principle that "depends not on subjective boasting but on objective practice."[35] For him, the future economic mode in Chinese society is still mainly about the socialist state-owned economy (by expropriation from the big capitalists), with other bourgeois private properties "for China's economy is still very backward."[36] In the "Report to the Second Plenary Session of the Seventh Central Committee of the communist Party of China (March 5, 1949)," he declares that "the state-owned economy is socialist in character and the co-operative economy is semi-socialist; these plus private capitalism, plus the individual economy, plus the state-capitalist economy in which the state and private capitalists work jointly, will be the chief sectors of the

---

35   Zedong, Mao. *Selected Works*. Beijing: Foreign Languages Press, 1961. p. 339.
36   *Ibid.*, p. 353.

economy of the people's republic and will constitute the new-democratic economic structure."[37] This is decided by the objective socio-economic backwardness in China. Mao Zedong does not think the immediate condition for socialism is ready. In fact, China has to pass through a special period of New Democracy to fully develop the productive forces and create a real foundation necessary for socialism, finally achieving the transformation from new democracy to socialism. He is completely right in this point.

Mao accurately sees the historical process of modern Chinese society. As we know, China's option for the road of socialist revolution is not a result of the highly developed capitalist economy as Marx and Engels forecast, or, the objective trend to break off the internal relations of production in the capitalist mode of production and clear the path for the new productive forces of socialism. On every aspect, China's economic development is even worse than that of Russia. Generally, the socialist revolutions after the October Revolution are *more associated with the struggles against foreign oppression and for national independence and liberation in the backward regions and nationalities*, which accounts for a specific practice of socialism in reality. More importantly, in China's modern socio-historical development, *capitalism is the first road to be explored.* From Chiang Kai-shek to Sun Yat-sen, all the attempts to achieve national independence and social progress failed. "That the Chinese people accept the leadership of the Communist Party of China and walk on the road of New Democracy to Socialism is their serious historical choice. It is historically inevitable."[38] It is not a theoretical question. China's socialism is in reality and it is not right to negate the historical necessity of socialism in China only by Marx's specific imagination of the future socialist society. Were it not for such concrete socialist practices in Russia and China, Marx's and Engels' ideal of communism would still be a wandering "ghost" today. In addition, the 1949 revolutionary victory marked a great leap forward for the development of modern Chinese society. It ended the 100-year history of colonialism and imperialism combined with feudalism in the enslavement of the Chinese people; it also ended the history of frequent civil wars in a divided country. For the first time, the Chinese people stood up. It is an objective historical reality that cannot be ignored.

---

37   *Ibid.*, p. 369.
38   Hu Sheng, ed. Seventy Years for the Communist Party of China. Beijing: The CPC History Publishing House, 1991. p. 268.

After entering the period of socialist construction, Mao still attempts to integrate Marxism with China's reality for a road of socialism with Chinese characteristics.

He writes:

That understanding the laws of socialist construction must pass through a process. It must take practice as its starting-point, passing from having no experience to having some experience; from having little experience to having more experience; from the construction of socialism, which is in the realm of necessity as yet not understood, to the gradual overcoming of our blindness and the understanding of objective laws, thereby attaining freedom, achieving a flying leap in our knowledge and reaching the realm of freedom[39].

At the same time, "China is a big Eastern country, which determines its own respective characters in the process of democratic revolution, socialist reform and construction, and the future socialist society."[40] Later, Mao always attempts at a road with Chinese characteristics in the practice of socialism. It is his understanding of "characteristics" that require our deep thought.

Firstly, in accordance with the above idea, China's socialism is "disqualified" in material productivity from the very beginning. Hence, there is a special but critical period of transition, the New Democracy[41], during which time, the political reform must be achieved before our focus on the development of the productive forces (including utilizing the capitalist economic sectors) to establish the objective material foundation for socialism, that is, the necessary material condition advocated by Marx and Engels, for example, the real possibility for the large-scale socialized production on

---

39   Zedong Mao. *Chairman Mao Talks to the People: Talks and Letters: 1956-1971*. Ed. Stuart R. Schram. New York: Pantheon Books, 1975. p. 173.

40   Zedong, Mao. *Mao Zedong's Documents Since the Founding of the Nation, Book 6*. Beijing: Central Party Literature Press, 1992. p. 143.

41   This is a very complex issue in the real socialist practice of historical dialectics. I think the actual occurrence of the Russian and Chinese socialist reality must be the special examples of Marxism because Socialism does not happen as the necessary result of the socio-historical process but appears as an ideal guide, a historical result of the mixture of the subjective initiative of historical dialectics with the specific movement of national liberation, which is a reasonable transcendence by the subjective dimension of historical dialectics over the objective dimension . However, we fail to see that this transcendence is limited. Only by returning to the objective material production can it be historically combined with Marx's socialism and finally established.

the economic aspect and the resultant comprehensive development of the subject. This is a concrete return to the objective dimension of historical dialectics. In a letter to Bo Gu in 1944, Mao says.

> **The New Democratic society is based on factories (social production: the state-owned and the private sectors) and the co-operatives (including the temporary labourers), not on scattered individual economy, which, composed of peasant agriculture and cottage industry, is the foundation for feudalism instead of a democratic society (including all the Old Democracy, the New Democracy and socialism). It is also the difference between Marxism and populism. Simply put, the New Democratic society is based on machinery instead of on hand. We have not obtained machinery; we have not won. If we never get them, we shall never succeed and we shall perish[42].**

It is a very profound view of the necessary foundation for socialized productivity in the future society of socialism.

However, Mao misses the key aspect of this issue after seizing power. He understands the order of the two dimensions of historical dialectics, criticizes the error of accomplishing the whole task of the democratic revolution and the socialist revolution at one stroke, and repeatedly states in the early founding years of the state that it must take a long time from New Democracy to the *future* socialism and communism. Only after a certain development of the industries and the state-owned economy can we take *serious steps to socialism*, which, in his estimation, should range from nearly 20 to 30 years. It is a suspicious assessment in the very beginning because China's real level of productive forces at that time requires much longer time to reach the necessary stage of large-scale socialized production. Despite that, the transition period is seriously shortened. Shortly after three years of economic recovery, China began to transit to socialism in 1952, which was called the *phase of New Democracy Construction* but it has already entered socialism. This kind of transition is not a *real social development* based on material productivity but the *conversion of the relations of production* premised on a well-intentional theoretical design and political will. In Mao's words, "I pay more attention to the issues of system and the production relations. As for the aspect of productive forces, I have little knowledge."[43] *Entering socialism* in the absence of the necessary material

---

42   Translated from *Mao Zedong's Correspondence*. Beijing: People's Publishing House. 1983. p. 238-239.
43   Translated from *Mao Zedong's Selected Works, Book 2*. Beijing: People's Publishing House, 1986. p. 829.

basis is the first *unreasonable* transgression of the New Democracy, the essence of which is our confirmation of the production relations overstep the *real* level of the productive forces.

Secondly, it is about the issue of the socialist economic structure. According to China's actual level of productive forces, it lies in the transition from Marx's first great social form (the socio-historical phase of man's dependence when the necessity of nature dominates) to the second great social form (the socio-historical phase of material dependence when the necessity of economy dominates). In accordance with the objective laws of the economic development and the inevitable economic stage, China must enter the second great social form, building the market economy centered on commodity production and developing the productive forces for the necessary material basis of socialism. However, we do not start from the reality of China's historical stage but emphasize the theoretical presumption of the socialist "ought" (a general principle of socialism in the eyes of the classical Marxist scholars). In 1953, China started to implement the *planned* economy and began a *conscious control* of the economic development. After that, the economic construction continued in the mode led by the subjective intention and operated through political/administrative measures.

If observed from a deep philosophical perspective, China *immediately transits* from the period of natural necessity in the social development of human history to what Marx imagines the independent economic stage after eliminating 'natural-ness' in the second period of economic necessity, namely, the phase of communism (socialism). We just recognize the "planned, proportionate" system of socialist economy as the *necessary association* with the socialist political system while failing to understand Marx's conclusion that planning material production and the economic life is an *objective economic requirement stemming from the productive process* only at the stage of large-scale social production. Planning is not the subjective requirement without appropriate material condition. For Marx, economic 'natural-ness' (market economy) is certainly a historical progress in comparison with the subjective economy with the underdeveloped productive forces. Our building of the socialist planned economy on the lower level of material productivity is essentially different from Marx's design, which only results from the original product economy of high concentration. At first glance, we seem to eliminate the economic spontaneity. However, it leads to a more serious economic subjectivity and blindness. This is the second unreasonable transgression.

Moreover, the low productivity is not fundamentally changed while Marx's historical materialism holds that the economic structure in certain society can only be determined by a specific level of productive forces (which is an objective foundation independent of man's will). Hence, there is a strange situation in our social system: Politically, we have built the socialist "advanced" production relations and structure, but these advantages are *unconsciously* and inevitably turned by the underdeveloped conditions of productive forces into a "stagnant" development without proper innate drives (to the simple commodity production under the planned system), a "poor socialism" without enough necessaries (the shrinking circulation under the economic shortage), and a "communal pot" filled with lazy flocks (the abstract egalitarian system of distribution). The deformation and distortion reached the peak in the mistaken practice of the Cultural Revolution, which almost amounted to the primitive, poor socialism criticized by Marx in 1844. Here, I do not negate the major achievement and success of the socialist construction in contrast to the poor status of Old China but intend to illustrate the mistakes due to the neglect of the productive forces from the angle of the objective dimension of historical dialectics.

Thirdly, the principal contradiction in the socialist construction. When New China was founded, we were aware of the gap between the socialist construction and the low economic development. In the reform of the means of production before 1956, China gradually recovered and got ready for further development with rather great achievements. In the Eighth Congress of the Party, we realized that the principal contradiction of the socio-historical development in China's socialist construction was: "The one resulted from the need of the people for rapid economic and cultural development which fell short of their requirements. The chief task confronting the entire nation was to concentrate all efforts on developing the productive forces, industrializing the country and gradually meeting the people's growing economic and cultural needs. The essence of the contradiction is the conflict between the advanced socialist system and the low development of social productive forces."[44] The statement reflects the conscious understanding of the actually undeveloped productivity. It is certainly correct to take the economic improvement as the method to solve the major contradiction. However, we are not aware of the essential aspect of the socialist "advanced relations of production." In this connection, I do not concur with the view that the "Eighth Congress" is not totally right about the theory of the primary contradiction because it fails to indicate

---

44   Quoted from the official translation of the speech in the 8h National Congress of the Communist Party of China, 1956.

the "socialist relations of production have been established and are in correspondence with the growth of the productive forces, but these relations
are still far from perfect, and this imperfection stands in contradiction to
the growth of the productive forces."[45] In my opinion, it shows that the
process of establishing the socialist system is somewhat separated from the
actual development of the productive forces. Later, the actual situation
proved that it was this separation and unreasonable transcendence that
affected the development of the productive forces. Thus, today's reform is
not about the problems of the socialist system but of that unrealistic "transcendence." It is the same from the people's commune to the contracted responsibility system with remuneration linked to output, from the planned
system to the market system.

However, this important theoretical recognition of the primary social
contradiction is seriously distorted due to the specific international and
domestic context. The 20th Congress of the Soviet Communist Party, the
Poland-Hungary Incident in 1957 and the "anti-rightist" movement at
home all have made a deep impact on Mao Zedong. When he reads the
Soviet Textbook of Political Economics (the socialism part), he criticizes
Stalin's idea of socialist construction as "seeing things but not people," that
is, ignoring the superstructure. He wants to avoid the Soviet-style socialist
road by exploring a way of socialism with *Chinese characteristics*. What are
they, then? In Mao's eyes, it is "to continue the revolution under the dictatorship of the proletariat" with the emphasis on political and cultural struggles. His opinion undergoes a big transformation, sees shift from the *relations of production to the super structure*. Based on his judgment, the Second
Plenum of the Eighth CPC Central Committee concludes: "During the
whole transitional period before the completion of socialist society, the
struggles between the proletariat and the bourgeoisie, between the socialist
road and the capitalist way make up our internal primary contradiction."
After "Lushan Conference" and the big debate between China and the
Soviet Union, the Tenth Plenum of the Eighth CPC Central Committee
in 1962 presses forward with the idea. "During the proletarian revolution
and dictatorship, the transition from capitalism into communism (it may
take decades or even more time) is accompanied by the class struggle between the proletariat and the bourgeoisie, between the road of socialism
and that of capitalism."[46] As to the issue of class struggle and the danger of
capitalist restoration, we must give warnings from now on, year after year,

---

45   Zedong, Mao. *Selected Works, Volume 1*. Beijing: Foreign Languages Press, 1965. p. 394.
46   Zedong, Mao. Mao Zedong's *Documents Since the Founding of the Nation, Book 10*. Beijing:
Central Party Literature Press, 1992. p. 196.

and month after month. This view reaches the peak during the movement of "Four Cleanings," the proletarian "Cultural Revolution" under the control of Lin Biao and the "Gang of Four." The primary contradiction in socialism becomes the "great criticism" in thought[47].

Fourthly, in the subsequent socialist construction, Mao's dominant philosophical thinking is *changed from the previous objective historical dialectics based on reality into the subjective dialectics that highlight man's initiative.* He adopts the thought of practical materialism emphasizing the subject's initiative, which, through the democratic revolution, correctly opposes Chen Duxiu's mechanical understanding of Marxist historical dialectics and Wang Ming's dogmatic stubbornness about Marxism, fully exerts the revolutionary initiative of the proletariat on a *specific level* of combining socialism with China's national and democratic liberation, and achieves the revolutionary victory with precise recognition of the specific Chinese social history (the agricultural, peasantry and rural way). It belongs to the great victory of Marxist historical dialectics! Lies in the centre of Mao's road of New Democracy with Chinese characteristics is man's dynamic "class struggle," which experiences a great change in its objectified practice after entering the period of socialist construction.

In my understanding, Mao does not make light of practice (his "practical materialism") but only fails to observe that, *the practice of material production, along with the objective dimension of historical dialectics, is the foundation for the subjective dimension* of historical dialectics. It also explains why Marx's and Engels' illustration of the new philosophical vision is started from the material production and reproduction under certain historical conditions instead of the abstract practice. Mao pays the same attention to man as well as man's *objective* action but he puts the practice of political struggles on top of the practice of material production. Hence, his practical materialism slips from Marx's historical dialectics (material production as the general foundation for the existence and development of social history) to the subjective dialectics separated from historical reality (Politics and conception, although following the scientific wordings of Marx). He does not realize it by himself, which is, unfortunately, a historical tragedy[48].

---

47   See Deng Xiaoping's *Selected Works, Volume 3*. Beijing: People's Publishing House, 1993. p. 227-228.

48   In a conversation with Edgar Snow at the early stage of the "Cultural Revolution," Mao mentioned the mistakes of Liu Shaoqi and Deng Xiaoping. "They only pay attention to economy, instead of people; they are fully engaged in material stimulation instead of class struggle; they focus on production and rely on the 'specialists' to improve the techniques. In short, they make politics serve the economic and technical powers." See *The Essays of Snow, the Friendly American*. Beijing: Sdxjoint Publishing Company, 1971. p. 5.

On the other hand, we should note a reasonable part in the deep logics of Mao Zedong Thought, that is, a *strong demand to pursue human liberation*, which is also what we have discussed previously as the important practical content of the subjective dimension of Marxist historical dialectics. The concern for the realization of man's subjective liberation runs through the development of his philosophical logics. He is consistent with Marx at this point. And it is an innate driving force for the victory of the Party's democratic revolution. Mao's concept of socialism contains his constant attention to the problem of man's liberation, which is not only seen during the socialist transformation in the early years of New China but also found in "people's commune" and the movement of "Great Leap Forward," especially, in the "Cultural Revolution" later. For the change into a revisionist Soviet Union and the "danger of the capitalist restoration" in China, he wages a "people's war" under the dictatorship of the proletariat to eliminate the *newborn* human *inequality*, which is only led to the opposite direction.

Mao likes the statement by Marx and Engels: The proletariat need not only to liberate themselves but also the whole humankind. Without liberating of all human beings, the proletariat class cannot be finally liberated. He always attaches importance to the subjective status but opposes the bourgeois view of the abstract "human nature." (In this point, he is very close to the Young Marx writing the *1844 Manuscripts*.) In his eyes, the subject refers to the proletariat and the working masses. ("Everybody belongs to a class, without any exception.") He believes that there is *new oppression* of the socialist subject, the working people, in the socialist system; therefore, we have to "carry on the revolution under the condition of the proletariat dictatorship." He wants to use an "open, comprehensive, bottom-up approach to mobilize the broad masses to expose the dark side." He calls on the masses and students to "rebel" (slogans such as "Beat down the capitalist roaders," "Against the technical authority") and attempts to make the working people the direct masters of society ("All should be put under the leadership of the working class!" "The revolutionary committees!" "The workers, peasants and soldiers should go to college and manage colleges."). Interestingly, Mao is actually opposing the subjective "political alienation" on a new historical level! In his consideration, people's power is usurped by the "revisionists" and turned on the people themselves under the specific socialist condition. Hence, it is necessary to "re-seize power" ("Who give us the power?" The working class, the poor peasants, the working people occupying more than 90% of the population! We should act against the "revisionists who are only jacks-in-office." Cadres must be the "semi-official and semi-ordinary people.")[49] In addition, Mao wants to delete the urban and rural difference, for example, to let people "receive re-education by the poor and middle peasants." In his famous "Instructions on 7th May," we see the *free and comprehensive development of humans* (People should be "military-educational, military-agricultural, military-industrial and military-civilian." At the same time, the bourgeois must be criticized. In the respect, he is very close to Marx's definition of man's free development in communism in *German Ideology*.[50]

In my view, Mao's real intention is to climb to the summit of human liberation as soon as possible. He is very serious about the "pioneering work of revolution" with Chinese characteristics (before his death, he regards the Cultural Revolution, together with "driving Chiang Kai-shek to the island," as the "two major events in life"). He even takes this "revolution" as the new revolutionary starting point of the proletarians across the world. He believes that the world revolution enters a great new era. "The proletarians and the working people across Europe, North America and Oceania are just awakening." What's more, the "Red Storm in May" guided by Western Marxian humanism in Europe in 1968 is unbelievably consistent with China's Revolution with its *cultural characters far separated from the economic reality*[51].

I think that Mao is no doubt well-intentioned from the aspect of considering and exploring China's socialist progress. His efforts to completely liberate humankind under socialist conditions cannot be viewed as totally wrong. It at least points to the *same direction* as the subjective dimension of Marxist historical dialectics. But, this "revolution" of his is only a *thoughtful* result of the subjective dialectics and axiology, which is not *premised* on the objective historical dialectics and the material production of China's social development. In my view, Mao is generally distracted in the understanding of the nature of socialism in China's *characteristic* reality. He does not make the development of productive forces as the general foundation in the objective dimension of historical dialectics but leaves the material basis to wage a "revolution" (the subjective hyperbola and distortion of historical dialectics) based on the relations of production and the superstructure. In this way, no matter how this revolution appears reasonable, it

---

49   In the mid-1960s, Zhou Yang mentioned that Mao was very interested when he reported to him Marx's view of the estrangement of labor in the *1844 Manuscripts*.

50   Quoted from Mao's statements in *People's Daily* from 1965 to 1969.

51   See Chapter 15 in Zhang Yibing's *Broken Wings of Reason - Criticism of Western Marxism*. Nanjing: Nanjing Publishing House, 1990.

must be contrary to the objective historical dialectics[52]. He forcefully turns the objective 'natural-ness' existent in certain socio-historical process into a subjective planning; he notices man's political liberation but ignores the inevitable material-subjugation in certain economic process. Later, Deng Xiaoping correctly recognizes this problem. Therefore, from a deep philosophy logic view, there is a return from the subjective dialectics to Marxist historical dialectics from Mao Zedong to Deng Xiaoping.

II. PHILOSOPHICAL THOUGHT BEHIND DENG XIAOPING'S SOCIALIST ROAD

From the very beginning, the real occurrence and historical development of socialism in China has its peculiar features. How to realize Marx's and Engels' beautiful ideal in such an underdeveloped country? It is through the setbacks in practice that the Chinese people gradually find the answer to this question. China's socialist construction has undergone an important return from the bookish theories to the historical reality of the material productive forces. And the new hope of the socialist victory in China emerges in the process of the objective restoration of Marxist historical dialectics. Of course, the practice of socialism with Chinese characteristics is still a long way that extends ahead as we go.

A. THE DUAL STRUCTURE OF THE LOGIC OF DENG XIAOPING'S HISTORICAL DIALECTICS OF PRACTICAL MATERIALISM

Deng Xiaoping is a great revolutionary practicer, whose philosophical thought is composed of the rationality of historical, real and concrete practice. This is certainly *practical materialism*! Different than that of Mao Zedong, Deng Xiaoping's practical materialism starts from neither "man," the subjective dimension, nor the subject's political practice (struggles) but rather from the objective logic that emphasizes the general foundation of social history in Marx's and Engels' historical materialism and historical dialectics. To be specific, it is based on the *process of the material production* in the objective practice structure of social history, which becomes a *deeper level* of the theoretical nature of his historical dialectics. In this sense, we can say that Deng's philosophical thought is established through rebuilding Mao's subjective dialectics into the *objective* historical dialectics. This point is crucial for the practical road of socialism with Chinese characteristics later.

---

52   This view is expressed also by Deng Xiaoping in the Chinese version of the *Selected Works of Deng Xiaoping, Volume 3*. Beijing: People's Publishing House, 1993. pp. 116, 140.

Deng's objective logic that we should treat anything based on reality did not only appear in later socialist period. Early in the democratic period, he said, "The Communist Party works for the development of the productive forces; to do otherwise would run counter to Marxist theory."[53] This is the fundamental principal of Marxist scientific view of history (the objective logic). Accordingly, our guideline of production and construction must be: "First, to face up to the actual conditions of the country. We should never divorce ourselves from China's actual conditions."[54] That is, "we must not forget for a moment the fact that ours is a poor country beset with difficulties."[55] "Second, to face the needs of the masses. We should consider the needs of the masses in the course of development, finding out what their problems are and helping them to solve these problems."[56] Deng seldom proceeds from the abstract theories ("ought"); he always constructs Marx's historical dialectics on the actual level of social development. His *idea of facing reality, facing the people and facing the productive forces* provides the most important principles in his practice of historical dialectics and unique philosophical thinking. When Liu-Deng Army entered the Central Plains in 1948, Deng gave an example to the cadres about whether the few factories and markets in Dabie Mountain should be kept. If they were simply shut down for political reasons, there would be thousands of people unable to live on. Then, he asked, "Whom have we overthrown, the capitalists or the common people? I don't think we have overthrown the capitalists; instead, we have stripped the common people of their means of livelihood."[57] This is an important historical point to be developed on a theoretical level.

Deng's philosophical theory of China's socialist road was gradually built up after he became the core of the second-generation leadership. In my view, there are actually two related and incremental aspects in this process.

His first thing is to restore and confirm the *objective* premise for Mao's practical materialism in the New Democratic period, that is, the scientific ideological line of emancipating the mind, seeking truth from facts and proceeding from reality to deal with everything. In 1977, Deng required us to have a comprehensive and accurate understanding of Marxism. He opposes the dogmatic interpretation, like the "Two Whatevers," and adheres

---

53 Xiaoping, Deng. *Selected Works of Deng Xiaoping, 1938-1965*. Beijing: Foreign Languages Press, 1992. p. 149.
54 *Ibid.*, p. 248.
55 *Ibid.*, p. 248.
56 *Ibid.*, p. 248.
57 *Ibid.*, p. 105.

to the scientific *practical materialism* that takes criterion of practice as the base of one's worldview. He points out, "When everything has to be done by the book, when thinking turns rigid and blind faith is the fashion, it is impossible for a party or a nation to make progress. Its life will cease and that party or nation will perish."[58] "Only if we emancipate our minds, seek truth from facts, proceed from reality in everything and integrate theory with practice, can we carry out our socialist modernization programme smoothly, and only then can our Party further develop Marxism-Leninism and Mao Zedong Thought."[59] Not to do everything by the book (including the bookish Marxism) but to proceed from practice is a grand "ideological issue" proposed by Deng.

There is a profound theoretical point here: Deng is not *generally* against materialism but against a covert idealism. Why? Because the "Gang of Four" speaks about Marxism and materialism every day but *unconsciously* commit the idealistic error in actual life (the field of social history). Unfortunately, their mistake is still *inadvertently* continued among some of us. Doesn't it mean that *the secret idealism and metaphysics are the big enemies of our socialist practice today*? To be fair, Deng's revalidation of practical materialism is even more difficult than Marx does in his *Theses on Feuerbach*. As Lenin does in the *Philosophical Notes*, Deng is fully qualified to warn us: What is socialism and what is Marxism? We were not quite clear about this in the past[60].

Later, Deng says, "But the experience of the last 20 years has taught us one very important principle: to build socialism we must adhere to Marxist dialectical materialism and historical materialism or, as Comrade Mao Zedong put it, in everything we do we must seek truth from facts – in other words, we must proceed from reality."[61] "The reform and the opening policy have been successful not because we relied on books, but because we relied on practice and sought truth from facts."[62] Finally, it is from Deng that we correctly understand the critical *relationship* in the socialist practice, including the practice of the former Soviet Union and other Eastern European countries, the *relationship between Marxist scientific principles and the objective reality of social practice*. In the years after Lenin's socialist

58 Xiaoping, Deng. *Selected Works of Deng Xiaoping, 1975-1982*. Beijing: Foreign Languages Press, 1984. p. 154.
59 *Ibid.*, p. 154.
60 Quoted from the official translation of "Building a Socialism with a Specifically Chinese Character" issued on June 30, 1984.
61 Quoted from the official translation of *Selected Works of Deng Xiaoping, Volume 3*. Beijing: People's Publishing House, 1993. p. 118.
62 *Ibid.*, p. 382.

practice, we proceed more from Marxist "books" (and our good wishes) rather than from objective practice. As a result, we fall into the pit of rigid rules and lose flexibility. It is an unfortunate logical reversal[63]. In the road of building Marxism and socialism, we act against the most general rule of Marxist practical materialism that social existence should determine the concept instead of vice versa.

The reason why Marxism is the scientific truth is precisely that it is based on practice to reveal the rule of the development of the objective material world and the movement of historical dialectics. It provides us a guide to move forward but we should not take it as our only source and even a copy to *mold* the objective reality accordingly. Otherwise, we shall be trapped in it and achieve little development.

> **We cannot expect Marx to provide ready answers to questions that arise a hundred or several hundred years after his death, nor can we ask Lenin to give answers to questions that arise fifty or a hundred years after his death. A true Marxist-Leninist must understand, carry on and develop Marxism-Leninism in light of the current situation. The world changes every day, and modern science and technology in particular develop rapidly. A year today is the equivalent of several decades, a century or even a longer period in ancient times. Anyone who fails to carry Marxism forward with new thinking and a new viewpoint is not a true Marxist[64].**

Most scholars believe that Deng's philosophical thought almost ends here, as if it essentially returns from the subjective to the objective, from theory to practice. However, this view only reveals the outer level of Deng's philosophy but fails to grasp its *fundamental character* that contains a *deeper level, to proceed from reality (practice) is implemented on the socio-historical base of material production*. Without this understanding, it is impossible to truly understand Deng's thought. In fact, Mao does not oppose proceeding from reality or giving up the *practical* materialism but interprets China's reality as a revolution of culture in his later years and his advocacy of "practical materialism" just deviates from political practice[65]. Therefore,

---

63   the period of the Cultural Revolution, China's real practice is carried out by a conceptual scale, that is, the column of the "utmost directive" in the upper-right corner of *People's Daily*.

64   Quoted from the official translation of *Selected Works of Deng Xiaoping, Volume 3*. Beijing: People's Publishing House, 1993. p. 291-292.

65   Are not some of us who advocate the "practical materialism" today actually leaving practice for the abstract human subjectivity (the "ontology of practice," the "monism of practice," and the "humanistic practice")?

he focuses on "man" while abandoning the premise of the material foundation of historical materialism and the objective dimension of historical dialectics. Or, it will inevitably lead to failure to require the *abstract* social equality and the free comprehensive development on this poor land. Different than Mao, Deng opposes to proceed from political struggles, from the abstract subjectivity. Unsurprisingly, he is also against the abstract concepts of humanism and "alienation." He profoundly comments that who hold "that in the course of its development socialism constantly gives rise to a force of alienation, as a result of the activities of the main body of the society"[66] is "not advancing in their thinking but going backwards, back to pre-Marxist times."[67] Here, Deng openly opposes the subjective dialectic because it, along with the subjective dimension of historical dialectics, will be transformed to a subjective "magic" once separated from the reality of the material productive forces, and become harmful to the progress of social history no matter how beautiful it is in appearance[68].

The philosophical nature of Deng's practical materialism is the *objective logic* of Marxist historical materialism and historical dialectics: "We are historical materialists, and when we study a problem and try to solve it we cannot do so in isolation from the given historical conditions."[69]

Our revolutionary teachers Marx, Lenin and Comrade Mao always stressed the importance of concrete historical conditions and the need to study those of both the past and the present in order to ascertain objective laws to help us guide the revolution. To ignore the new historical conditions is to cut things off from their historical context, to divorce oneself from reality, and to abandon dialectics for metaphysics[70].

In other words, we cannot mechanically copy and indiscriminately apply the theoretical principles. We have to "proceed from reality," "seek truth from facts," and face the specific conditions and characteristics of the

---

66   Xiaoping, Deng. *Fundamental Issues in Present-Day China.* Beijing: Foreign Languages Press, 1987. p. 32.

67   *Ibid.*, p. 32. I also find that this idea of "alienation" logically answers late Mao Zedong's statements like that the bourgeois is inside the communist party and that to change from the "public servants" to "loads."

68   It is noticed that Deng always opposes the empty talks of "human values," "democracy," or "freedom" that are separated from the development of the productive forces in reality. He believes it just inherits from the Cultural Revolution. These seemingly opposite statements are actually consistent in logics. See *Selected Works of Deng Xiaoping, Volume 3.* Beijing: People's Publishing House, 1993. p. 41, 123-124.

69   Xiaoping, Deng. *Selected Works of Deng Xiaoping, 1975-1982.* Beijing: Foreign Languages Press, 1984. p. 133.

70   *Ibid.*, p. 135.

historical period of China's socialism. Following Mao, Deng goes on with the practical materialism. And more importantly, he restores the *objective foundation* for the practical *materialism* and historical dialectics, laying the most critical general foundation that practice should be the *material production* in the socio-historical process. At this point, he is consistent with the theoretical focus of Marx's and Engels' *German Ideology*, the objective dimension of historical dialectics. His *theoretical starting* point here (not the *logical start* of the generally abstracted practice) rightly negates Mao's understanding of the socialist nature as the relations of production and political revolution. Deng believes that the nature of socialism is to produce the more advanced productive forces than those in capitalism. Mao's subjective dialectics emphasizing man's initiative are replaced by the objective dialectics of economic development founded on material production.

In this sense, Deng says, "Actually, Marxism is not abstruse. It is a plain thing, a very plain truth. Using historical materialism, it has uncovered the laws governing the development of human society."[71] These words echo what Marx and Engels say in *German Ideology* that man has to first need the *material* things in life, such as eating, drinking and getting clothes and shelter before turning to other things, like political and cultural activities. Therefore, "the production of material life itself" is the first "historical act" and "a fundamental condition of all history."[72] Engels writes, "According to the materialist conception of history, the ultimately determining element in history is the production and reproduction of real life. Other than this neither Marx nor I have ever asserted."[73] Marx also considers it a truth even clear to a child. However, this "simple truth" of Marxist historical materialism is only to be fully recognized by Deng Xiaoping after numerous sufferings in practice. Thus, Deng's proceeding from reality, from practice has no *general reference to all the specific nature of objective reality in China's socio-historical development* but a particular indication of the real material productivity under certain historical conditions. This is also the first need of *material life* for the Chinese people.

From reality (practice) to the material life, and then from this direct condition of survival to the productive forces form the innate process of Deng's philosophical structure. Only a profound understanding of this point can

---

71   Quote from the official translation of *Selected Works of Deng Xiaoping, Volume 3*. Beijing: People's Publishing House, 1993. p. 382.

72   Marx, and Friedrich Engels. *The German Ideology*. Ed. Christopher John Arthur. New York: International Publishers Co, 1970. p. 48.

73   Marx, and Friedrich Engels. *Karl Marx and Friedrich Engels: Selected Works in One Volume*. New York: International Publishers, 1968. p. 692.

we grasp the essence of the *special truth* of his practical materialism. It is the *objective logic* of Marxist historical materialism and historical dialectics confirmed in this book as well. Otherwise, we cannot truly comprehend the scientific significance of Deng's socialist road with Chinese characteristics based on an *innate theoretical association*.

B. THREE SUCCESSIVE LAYERS OF THE COGNITIVE PROCESS OF DENG XIAOPING'S SOCIALISM PARADIGM

With Deng's philosophical logics analyzed above, it will be more convenient to further investigate his "Socialist Road with Chinese Characteristics" as termed in China's politics. After a careful research of the theoretical process, we know that this idea did not come into being overnight. It underwent an ongoing process of growth and enhancement. In my opinion, the process is composed of three interrelated and progressive cognitive levels: The clarification of confusions and restoration of Marxist ideas; the primary stage idea and reforming China's socialism; and the socialist market economy. All of them are centred on a core, the material productive forces as the general objective foundation for the existence and development of social history in historical dialectics. This is the theoretical nature of Deng Xiaoping's theory of socialism with Chinese characteristics.

Firstly, Deng's exploration starts by *re-examining* the perspective of the theoretical observation. It leads to the restoration of a scientific guideline, the practical materialism with the core of the material productive forces. On this new theoretical horizon, his view of socialist reality is bound to be enhanced and greatly improved. Obviously, Deng still adheres to Mao's principle of combining the universal truth of Marxism with the specific Chinese revolution and begins his own reflections on the specialty of China's social history. However, this time he avoids *Mao's "erroneous estimation" of reality with political characters but comprehends from the level of the material productive forces in the current situation of China*, that is, on the basis of the undeveloped productivity and poor economy to build socialism.

Deng's question is enlightening:

> **We are a socialist country. The basic expression of the superiority of our socialist system is that it allows the productive forces of our society to grow at a rapid rate unknown in old China, and that it permits us gradually to satisfy our people's constantly growing material and cultural needs. After all, from the historical materialist point of view correct political leadership should**

**result in the growth of the productive forces and the improve-
ment of the material and cultural life of the people. If the rate
of growth of the productive forces in a socialist country lags
behind that in capitalist countries over an extended historical
period, how can we talk about the superiority of the socialist
system? We should ponder the question: What have we really
done for the people?**[74]

His first attention is put on the reality of China's socialist construction.
Unless we "develop our productive forces and thus strengthen our country
and improve the material and cultural life of our people – unless we do
all this, our socialist political and economic system cannot be fully consolidated, and there can be no sure guarantee for the country's security."[75]
Obviously, Deng's thinking of socialism is always based on the material life
of the people and the subsequent *real level* of the productive forces.

I note an important *re-reversal* here. In the objective dimension of Marxist
historical materialism and historical dialectics, the development of productivity determines the nature of certain relations of production and
then the order of the entire superstructure, which is *irreversible* under any
historical conditions, including the socialist condition. That is to say, the
historical particularity of China to build real socialism requires a great
development of the productive forces at first, to enhance the economic
improvement and to strengthen the advantageous socialist relations of production. Otherwise, the socialist relations of production not only lose their
superiority but also degrade into the barrier of the productive forces due
to the poor economic level (like the failed "all eating from big-pot" system
in China). It is an objective law *independent of the political will by our relations of production.* Deng clearly follows this law of historical materialism
and historical dialectics. He takes it as an important theoretical criterion to
understand the socialist practice, that is, to see whether the socialist nature
is based on the enhancement of the productive forces.

Therefore, Mao's later determination that the class struggle should be the
primary contradiction of China's socialist society is changed to the statement that "our development of the productive forces is still very low and
far from meeting the needs of the people and the country." Why? Because
productivity is falling behind, the socialist superiority of the production
relations is consequently "of little effect." Without the advantageous relations of production, there is no abstract "superiority." It is not to negate

---

74   Xiaoping, Deng. *Selected Works of Deng Xiaoping, 1975-1982.* Beijing: Foreign Languages
Press, 1984. p. 154.
75   *Ibid.,* p. 102.

socialism. *"Although our socialist system is still imperfect and suffered disruption, it is much better than the capitalist system based on the law of the jungle and the principle of* 'getting ahead' at the expense of others."[76] For this, Deng goes out of his way to put forward the "Four Cardinal Principles."[77]

Deng's scientific thinking precisely corrects our previous understanding of socialism; it is also a logical continuation of Lenin's last thought of socialist construction[78]. On the other hand, it is a profound reflection on the mistaken socialist practice for decades. Deng stands high and says it is not the *personal* fault of Mao but our *historical* error.

In line of that thought, Deng develops the productive forces, promotes the economic development and regards them as the nature and main task of China's socialism. To be specific, it is to realize the "Four Modernizations," a highly developed socialist material culture. He profoundly points out:

This is a great revolution in which China's economic and technological backwardness will be overcome and the dictatorship of the proletariat further consolidated. Since its goal is to transform the present backward state of our productive forces, it inevitably entails many changes in the relations of production, the superstructure and the forms of management in industrial and agricultural enterprises, as well as changes in the state administration over these enterprises so as to meet the needs of modern large-scale production[79].

This is "our biggest politics at present"!

Thus, it is no more natural for Deng to criticize the view that communism is mainly a spiritual thing. "That is sheer nonsense! How is socialism superior, when our people have so many difficulties in their lives?"[80] He requires that "the focus of our work should be rapidly shifted to economic development."[81]

76   *Beijing Review,* Volume 26. 1983.

77   Four Cardinal principles were first declared by Deng to be taken as ideological and political guide for all the reform period: "Upholding the socialist path, upholding the people's democratic dictatorship, upholding the leadership of the Communist Party of China, upholding Marxism- Leninism-Mao Zedong Thought."

78   Deng says, "Perhaps Lenin had a good idea when he adopted the New Economic Policy." Quoted from the official translation of the *Selected Works of Deng Xiaoping, Volume 3.* Beijing: People's Publishing House, 1993. p. 139.

79   Xiaoping, Deng. *Selected Works of Deng Xiaoping, 1975-1982.* Beijing: Foreign Languages Press, 1984. p. 146.

80   Xiaoping, Deng. *Ideology and Economic Reform Under Deng Xiaoping, 1978-1993.* Ed. Wei-Wei Zhang. London: Kegan Paul International, 1996. p. 52.

81   Quoted from the official translation of the *Selected Works of Deng Xiaoping, Volume 3.* Beijing: People's Publishing House, 1993. p. 11.

> **Marxism attaches utmost importance to developing the productive forces. Therefore, the fundamental task for the socialist stage is to develop the productive forces. The superiority of the socialist system is demonstrated, in the final analysis, by faster and greater development of those forces than under the capitalist system. [...] One of our shortcomings after the founding of the People's Republic was that we didn't pay enough attention to developing the productive forces. Socialism means eliminating poverty. Pauperism is not socialism, still less communism[82].**

It goes without saying that it is a very profound understanding.

This is the first cognitive level of Deng Xiaoping's exploration of socialism with Chinese characteristics. With a new theoretical premise, he *re-confirms* that the special nature of socialism in China is its backward economic development that will not change with our socialist relations of production and cultural "reform" for two decades; he re-confirms that the primary contradiction is the low level of productivity, rather than the political and ideological class struggles under the socialist condition; and thus he re-confirms that the socialist task is to develop the productive forces, and realize the "Four Modernizations" instead of the "Cultural Revolution" under the proletariat dictatorship. His biggest contribution to the Chinese socialist revolution is to restore the objective logic of Marxist historical dialectics and the right direction of China's socialist practice. Accordingly, economic construction becomes the core of our socialist development.

After the "Third Plenary Session of the Eleventh Central Committee of CPC," the Party put all the effort into the development of the productive forces and the promotion of the economic growth. Deng said that "a genuinely Marxist ruling party must devote itself to developing the productive forces and, on that basis, gradually raise the people's living standards."[83] Mao was certainly a great leader who successfully led the Chinese revolution. However, his major drawback was to neglect the development of the social productive forces. "I do not mean he didn't want to develop them. The point is, not all of the methods he used were correct. For instance, neither the initiation of the Great Leap Forward nor the establishment of the people's communes conformed to the laws governing socio-economic development."[84] But the basic principle of Marxism is to develop the productive forces. The ultimate aim of Marxism is to achieve communism that is based on the highly developed productive forces. "Our experience

---

82   *Ibid.*, pp. 63-64.
83   See *Selected Works of Deng Xiaoping, Volumes 1-3.* Beijing: Foreign Languages Press, 1994.
84   *Ibid.*

in the 20 years from 1958 to 1978 teaches us that poverty is not socialism, that socialism means eliminating poverty."[85]

We summed up our experience in building socialism over the past few decades. We had not been quite clear about what socialism is and what Marxism is. Another term for Marxism is communism. A Communist society is one in which there is no exploitation of man by man, there is great material abundance and the principle of from each according to his ability, to each according to his needs is applied. It is impossible to apply that principle without overwhelming material wealth. In order to realize communism, we have to accomplish the tasks set in the socialist stage. They are legion, but the fundamental one is to develop the productive forces so as to demonstrate the superiority of socialism over capitalism and provide the material basis for communism[86].

I find that Deng's socialism with Chinese characteristics is always centred on the objective logic of Marxist historical materialism and historical dialectics that the material production must be the general foundation for the existence and development of social history. He reiterates that "our experience has enabled us to answer new questions that have arisen under new circumstances. We have been stressing the need to uphold the Four Cardinal Principles, haven't we? That is truly upholding socialism."[87] "Our principle is that we should integrate Marxism with Chinese practice and blaze a path of our own. That is what we call building socialism with Chinese characteristics."[88]

As I have noted, Deng's view of social history is fundamentally based on reality rather than abstract theories, which makes his comprehension goes deeper with further practice. A theoretical issue gradually emerges during the implementation of the bottom-up rural economic reform in China: Can the productive forces develop fast in the previous relations of production and the corresponding economic structure (system) built on it? In other words, can the "Four Modernizations" be achieved in accordance with the production relations system set by the principles of Marx and Engels? These theoretical questions must be answered. And Deng's answer

---

85   Xiaoping, Deng. *Fundamental Issues in Present-Day China*. Beijing: Foreign Languages Press, 1987. p. 107.
86   Quoted from Debra E Soled's China: *A Nation in Transition*. Congressional Quarterly, 1995. p. 436.
87   Xiaoping, Deng. *Deng Xiaoping on the Question of Hong Kong*. Beijing: Foreign Languages Press, 1993. p. 38.
88   See *Selected Works of Deng Xiaoping, Volumes 1-3*. Beijing: Foreign Languages Press, 1994.

to them forms the second important cognitive aspect of his reflection on socialism with Chinese characteristics, in which, not only the Marxist scientific principles are restored and generally applied to the observation of the reality of China's socialist construction but also Marxist scientific historical dialectics are used for the *new issues*.

Here, the first important result is the theoretical conclusion that China's socialism is *still at a primary stage (under-developed)*, which reflects Deng's deepened thought of the specialty of China. He repeatedly says, "True, we are building socialism, but that doesn't mean that what we have achieved so far is up to the socialist standard. Not until the middle of the next century, when we have reached the level of the moderately developed countries, shall we be able to say that we have really built socialism and to declare convincingly that it is superior to capitalism."[89] That we have not yet lived "up to the socialist standard" is a rather significant confirmation in theory. It expressly negates our abstract expansion of socialism in the "Cultural Revolution." Certainly, it does not mean we are *not* doing socialism but indicates that we are not qualified from the perspective of socialist material development. The practice of socialism for several decades in China does historically produce a better living condition than that of the old China. However, the undeveloped social economy, especially the natural economy in rural areas, is not radically changed[90]. And from an *open perspective of cross-border comparison*, our socialist economic development lags far behind the advanced capitalist countries in the world (this *gulf* is extremely important). Thus, Deng believes that we *should never prove the superiority of socialism with pauperism and backwardness*. Socialism is not something abstract but a *concrete* advantage to socialism in any aspect of social life (first of all, the economic aspect). Therefore, our socialism is unqualified for the gap between the present level of the material productivity and the possible superiority of socialism. We are a socialist country but an underdeveloped one at the primary stage of its development. Socialism itself is the first stage of communism, and here in China we are still in the *primary stage* of socialism – that is, the underdeveloped stage. In everything we do we must proceed from this reality[91]. Socialism must have highly developed material productivity. With this goal in mind, we must develop the productive forces. This is a new scientific determination of our socio-historical stage.

---

89   *Ibid.*
90   See the *Report in the Thirteenth Congress of the Communist Part of China*.
91   See *Selected Works of Deng Xiaoping, Volumes 1-3*. Beijing: Foreign Languages Press, 1994.

In my opinion, this idea of Deng's accords with Lenin's thought of the practice of socialism in his late years. His theory of the primary stage of socialism truly reflects the reality of the October Revolution and the Chinese revolution. As a real return to Marxism, it is of far-reaching historical significance.

The second important cognition is about the socialist reform and opening-up. People agree on the necessity and importance of reform but have doubt about the nature of reform. In the traditional interpretation, reform is a "self-improvement of the socialist system," which is basically correct. However, what on earth does reform change? What is the real meaning of it? And what is its historical relationship with the past socialist construction? Few would have thought of these questions. I think that Deng's socialist reform is not aimed at the *system per se* but a *historical fallback* of the relations of production that have surpassed the present level of productivity, which can be detected from the starting point of the reform.

As we know, Deng's first cognitive process is turned to the development of economy, the realization of the "Four Modernizations" in reality. It should be noted that it is in the *original* economic structure to *develop* the productive forces, which, especially the rural economy, result in the previous "advanced" relations of production (the *communist* "people's commune") being broken and the natural growth of the household contract responsibility system corresponding to the rural productive forces (the local individual labour in natural economy). *It is not the abstract change of an imperfect system but a correction of the relations of production that transcend the present productivity level.* Observed from a historical perspective, it appears like a regressive step. However, it is a return and retreat to the actual level of the productive forces to enhance their development, eliminating the barrier caused by the alleged "advanced relations of production." Hence, our rural productivity and economic development have achieved unprecedented improvement ever since. This is not based on the previous "advantage" of the people's commune but on the undeveloped *individual form of realization* that has been naturally formed and developed at present. It is the nature of our reform. Ultimately, our reform should be directed to follow the exploration of what can really enhance the relations of production and the economic system that is built on the low level of socialist productive forces.

Deng is great in that he pushes the crucial change of the economic structure of the productivity level. Certainly aware of the revolutionary significance of this reform, he regards the relations of production corresponding to the present productive forces (the "fallback") as the premise for China's socialism to develop economy and realize the "Four Modernizations." The previous production relations and economic structure can never boost the productive forces. They must be reformed first. This is Deng's second cognitive process of China's socialism. He says:

> **Revolution means the emancipation of the productive forces, and so does reform. The overthrow of the reactionary rule of imperialism, feudalism and bureaucrat-capitalism helped release the productive forces of the Chinese people. This was revolution, so revolution means the emancipation of the productive forces. After the basic socialist system has been established, it is necessary to fundamentally change the economic structure that has hampered the development of the productive This is reform, so reform also means the emancipation of the productive forces. In the past, we only stressed expansion of the productive forces under socialism, without mentioning the need to liberate them through reform. That conception was incomplete[92].**

Therefore, he reiterates that "reform is China's second revolution."[93] "Just like our past revolutions, the reform is designed to clear away the obstacles to the development of the productive forces and to lift China out of poverty and backwardness. In this sense, the reform may also be called a revolutionary change."[94]

In the last decade practice of the socialist reforms and opening-up, "the reform has stimulated the development of the productive forces and has resulted in a series of profound changes in economic life, social life, people's work style and their mentality. This reform is part of the self-perfecting process of the socialist system, and in certain areas and to a certain extent it is also a revolutionary change. It is a major undertaking that shows we have begun to find a way of building socialism with Chinese characteristics."[95] In the eyes of Deng, the reform becomes the critical coordinates of the socialist road with Chinese characteristics.

Meanwhile, I find that Deng's thought of the socialist reform is closely associated with the *idea of opening-up*, which possesses two important features: 1) it provides the *necessary coordinates of reference* for a scientific and historical comprehension of our actual socialist development as noted

---

92   *Ibid.*

93   *Ibid.*

94   Quoted from Hu Sheng's *Reflections on China's Road to Development: Nine Essays by Hu Sheng*, 1983-1996. Commercial Press, 1997. p. 155.

95   Xiaoping, Deng. *Fundamental Issues in Present-Day China*. Beijing: Foreign Languages Press, 1987. p. 127.

above; 2) it offers the necessary condition for a systematic development of the productive forces today. Deng says, "The present world is open. One important reason for China's backwardness after the industrial revolution in Western countries was its closed-door policy. After the founding of the People's Republic we were blockaded by others, so the country remained virtually closed, which created difficulties for us. The experience of the past thirty or so years has demonstrated that a closed-door policy would hinder construction and inhibit development."[96] The world is an open system, outside which socialism is not possible to obtain true development. This is the negation of the negation of the enclosed abstract self-affirmation, such as in the "Cultural Revolution." Socialism "should not erect barriers to isolate itself from the rest of the world."[97] The socialist *modernization* is a fully open system itself. We must embrace all that conducive to the development of the socialist productive forces. "While giving play to the advantages inherent in socialism, we are also employing some capitalist methods – but only as methods of accelerating the growth of the productive forces."[98] That is to say, "our decision to introduce the open policy and assimilate useful things from capitalist societies was made only to supplement the development of our socialist productive forces."[99] Even when faced with certain problems in the socialist process of reform, we must never turn China back into a country that keeps its doors closed. "A closed-door policy would be greatly to our disadvantage; we would not even have quick access to information."[100] "We cannot keep the door closed to the outside world. If we hadn't opened up, we would still be hammering out automobile parts the way we did in the past. Now things are vastly different; there has been a qualitative change."[101]

Thus, Deng forms his basic theoretical framework of the socialist construction with Chinese characteristics. "The main points were that we should shift the focus of our work from class struggle to expansion of the productive forces, that we should replace the closed-door policy with an open policy and that we should abandon old conventions and carry out reform in every field."[102] At the same time, "in carrying out the reform and

---

96   Quoted from *Alan Lawrance's China since 1919: Revolution and Reform : A Sourcebook*. Routledge, 2004. p. 232.
97   Deng Xiaoping. *Selected Works of Deng Xiaoping, Volumes 1-3*. Beijing: Foreign Languages Press, 1994.
98   *Ibid.*
99   *Ibid.*
100 *Ibid.*
101 *Ibid.*
102 *Ibid.*

the open policy and in shifting the focus of our work to economic development, we are not abandoning Marx, Lenin and Mao Zedong. We cannot forget our forefathers!"[103] And we shall not forget the "Four Cardinal Principles." These points are summed up as "One Centre with Two Basic Points" grand strategy.

The third important cognition is about the socialist planned commodity economy. It is the inevitable theoretical point of Deng's thinking of the socialist reform as well as the third scientific cognitive aspect, a theoretical transition to the *socialist market economy*.

For an accurate perception, I shall expand the scope of this issue. As mentioned earlier, Marx criticizes the socio-historical anarchy brought about by the capitalist commodity economy, negates the objective phenomena of 'natural-ness' and material-subjugation under the law of values (the "invisible hand"), and then replaces capitalism with communism (socialism) that is validated as the conscious and full development of human social history. Only when people scientifically master the objective economic laws *can they rely on the foundation of the large-scale social industrial production* to "proportionately plan" a conscious creation of social history. This point of Marx's is *nothing wrong*. However, the assumption of the socialist planned economy must be premised on the full development of the material productive forces. And Marx never expects to implement the planned economy in an underdeveloped country. However, in reality socialism mostly occurs in the less developed or backward countries later. We only see the necessary association between socialism and the planned economic structure but fail to understand the objective prerequisite for the reality of planning. This groundless "planning" (without the foundation of the large-scale social production) is bound for the subjective and administrative economy. As a result, the socialist economic structure deteriorates into a rigid system and even the alienated object to be reformed.

For a long period, we are accustomed to defining socialism by the relations of production. Once we are required to understand vice versa, to observe the real situation from the level of productive forces in social history, it is found that China is still in the transitional period from the first to the second phase in Marx's view of the three great social forms although its socialist revolution is achieved. Hence, the actual level of productivity does not offer the objective conditions for the planned economy of the communist (socialist) realm of freedom in the third great social form. From a general historical perspective, China has to undergo the capitalist commodity

---

103   *Ibid.*

economy to break the enclosed, backward and slow development of the productive forces. The historical reality of striving for national independence and liberation makes the Chinese people step on the road of socialism. Due to the errors of understanding and practice (which is, in a certain sense, historically unavoidable), we have established an economic system separated from the actual development of the productive forces. There was a time when a beautiful but empty illusion substituted the social reality; now, it is time to return to the real progress of history by reform. Only commodity production is carried out in this backward productivity can we greatly promote the productive forces, which, of course, does not mean capitalism is inevitable but indicates the unavoidable stage of the commodity economy. The orthodox Marxists believe that the commodity economy is directly related to capitalism and Marx would not imagine a socialist commodity economy! But this is where Deng Xiaoping's creativity matters, which does not deviate from Marxism but actually develops it. Indeed, in the beginning of this exploration, we only take the commodity and the market as supplementary to the planned economy, that is, the "socialist planned commodity economy."

There is no fundamental contradiction between socialism and a market economy. The problem is how to develop the productive forces more effectively. We used to have a planned economy, but our experience over the years has proved that having a totally planned economy hampers the development of the productive forces to a certain extent. If we combine a planned economy with a market economy, we shall be in a better position to liberate the productive forces and speed up economic growth[104].

Deng's third cognition of socialism with Chinese characteristics is the concept of China's socialist market economy. It is a complete new beginning as well as a more complex and hard exploration.

As we know, the socialist planned commodity economy is still centred on the structure of planning with a "supplementary" role played by the market, which means an incomplete reform in the old economic system and a subsequent confusing two-track system in the economy. It is harmful to the development of the productive forces. Again, it is Deng Xiaoping who breaks the ideal shackles at last. "The chief criterion for making that judgment should be whether it promotes the growth of the productive forces in a socialist society, increases the overall strength of the socialist state and

---

104   *Ibid.*

raises living standards."[105] With that criterion in mind, he proposes the new model of reforming the socialist market economy. He asks:

> **Why do some people always insist that the market is capitalist and only planning is socialist? Actually they are both means of developing the productive forces. So long as they serve that purpose, we should make use of them. Why do some people always insist that the market is capitalist and only planning is socialist? If they serve socialism they are socialist; if they serve capitalism they are capitalist. It is not correct to say that planning is only socialist, because there is a planning department in Japan and there is also planning in the United States. At one time we copied the Soviet model of economic development and had a planned economy. Later we said that in a socialist economy planning was primary. We should not say that any longer[106].**

In the famous "Speech of Southern Inspection," he says, "The proportion of planning to market forces is not the essential difference between socialism and capitalism. A planned economy is not equivalent to socialism, because there is planning under capitalism too; a market economy is not capitalism, because there are markets under socialism too. Planning and market forces are both means of controlling economic activity."[107] Clearly, it is with the reform and practice of socialism with Chinese characteristics that we turn to the commodity economy. At present, the world adopts the form of a planned market economy. Eventually, Deng's theory of socialist market economy comes into being. This is the third major leap of his understanding.

In Deng's cognitive process, there are two important theoretical points worthy of our serious attention. One, the traditional socialist concept connects socialism with the planned economy. Marx and Engels once oppose the "invisible hand" that is characteristic of capitalism (the market self-regulation of the law of value). Quite a few people cling on to the classical Marxist statement (the characteristic planning of future communism/socialism is *not wrong*) but they unfortunately start from only the "books." In contrast, Deng's focus is put on the development of the material productive forces. He believes that only commodity production (the innate objective function of the economic development in the second great social form) can really push the productive forces in the present process of social

---

105   *Ibid.*
106   *Ibid.*
107   Quote from the official translation of the *Selected Works of Deng Xiaoping, Volume 3.* Beijing: People's Publishing House, 1993. p. 373.

history. It shows Deng's real respect for the objective law and scientific adherence to Marxism. The Marxist "books" separate socialism from market economy, which is only a superficial understanding. In fact, judging from the foundation of the material productive forces in social history, the market economy and that "invisible hand" exactly form the unavoidable phase for our special socialism. This understanding of Deng Xiaoping's really reveals the objective law.

Two, the issue contains another profound issue, the regulation through planning in the present operation of the capitalist economy. It is a very complex theoretical problem. Indeed, with Marx and Lenin, the planned economy and the capitalist society are irreconcilable. Marx validates the phenomena of 'natural-ness' and material-subjugation in the subjective dimension of historical dialectics, which is nothing else but the criticism against the anarchical self-regulation of the market in the capitalist economy. He does not expect a planned economic operation (and to some extent, the existence of proportional development) in contemporary capitalism. However, does this mean the failure of Marxist historical dialectic? The answer of course is no. Instead, we can make a systematic illustration of this point. Marx and Lenin oppose the capitalist mode of production with a fundamental criticism, rather than a political assertion about superficial historical phenomena. They never expect capitalism will quickly perish but fully recognize the historical reason for the existence of the capitalist mode of production, in particular, the great capitalist civilization that generates the large-scale social production. At the same time, Marx profoundly exposes the deep contradiction within the capitalist mode of production, the confrontation between the large-scale social production and the private ownership of the means of production. As a result, the productive forces inside capitalism will blow up their own relations of production and then demise. Admittedly, Marx also sees that the bourgeoisie will not freeze their relations of production; instead, they will continue improving them within a certain range to adapt to the movement of the productive forces. Thus, he repeatedly stresses that "the historic character of wage labour is non-fixity."[108] "On the other hand, the capitalist mode of production, whose characteristic features are mobility of capital and labour and continual revolutions in the methods of production, and therefore in the relations of production and commerce and the way of life, leads to great mobility in the habits, modes of thinking, etc., of the people."[109] The reason is: "The bourgeoisie cannot exist without constantly revolutionising

---

108   Marx, Karl. *Grundrisse*. London; New York: Penguin, 1993. p. 891.
109   Marx, Karl. *Theories of Surplus Value, Volume 3*. London: Lawrence & Wishart, 1969. p. 444.

the instruments of production, and thereby the relations of production, and with them the whole relations of society. [...] Constant revolutionising of production, uninterrupted disturbance of all social conditions, everlasting uncertainty and agitation distinguish the bourgeois epoch from all earlier ones."[110] Moreover, as to the negative factor in the relations of production, the capital "is destructive towards all of this, and constantly revolutionizes it, tearing down all the barriers which hem in the development of the forces of production, the expansion of needs, the all-sided development of production, and the exploitation and exchange of natural and mental forces."[111] These statements seem to be targeted against the reality of capitalism today. By his thorough analysis, Marx illustrates that one of the natures of the capitalist mode of production is mobility and he never takes non-monopoly capitalism as its only form. And Lenin witnesses that capitalism is changing in the early 20th century! He finds that the free capitalism only relying on the spontaneous movement of the market moves towards another direction, the monopoly capitalism. Lenin rightly recognizes that the new changes of capitalism have, to a certain extent, produced something contrary to its own character.

In fact, after the 1930s, Lenin's view of monopoly capital was already developed to a new phase, state monopoly capitalism[112]. We must admit that present capitalism further modulates its relations of production and the large-scale social production, that is, *the state possession of the means of production to represent the entire bourgeoisie class* is used to loosen the noose around the neck of the bourgeoisie (the contradiction between the private ownership of the means of production and the large-scale social production). However, it displays the objective requirement of the large-scale production that the bourgeoisie must meet to mend their fraying relations of production. In this connection, they just *fall at the feet of Marx and Lenin*. This reform even adopts some factors of the socialist planned economy. For the general purpose of maintaining the private ownership, the bourgeoisie make patches and adaptations as possible as they. Indeed, this capitalist modulation is still very limited; it cannot fundamentally change the innate contradictions and completely eliminate the capitalist 'natural-ness' and material-subjugation. Contemporary capitalism virtually carries out a functional integration of the state monopoly, the planned regulation, the free market competition and other economic mechanisms, which amounts

---

110   Marx, Karl. *Karl Marx on Society and Social Change*. University of Chicago Press, 1973. p. 76.
111   Marx, Karl. *Grundrisse*. London; New York: Penguin, 1993. p. 410.
112   Zhang Yibing. "On the Scientific Base of the Contemporary Capitalist Research." *Social Sciences in Nanjing*. 2 (1990): 66.

to a "multi-flexible" overlapping of different things. In the words of the bourgeois scholars themselves, it is a "mixed economy" of planning and market. However, the "planning" in the contemporary capitalist economy is really the *objective requirement* of the economic development built on the large-scale social production (in a certain sense, the contemporary capitalist planning is more accurate than that of the socialist subjective mode; there is the basic question of the real material production). This is what Deng mentions: "capitalism also has planning."

Therefore, the purpose of our socialist reform must comply with the actual level of productivity, borrow the latest relations of production and economic patterns from the capitalist economic operation (the world-wide system of the market economy). This is the socialist market economy with commodity circulation being its major pattern.

The last point is, in the objective dimension of Marxist dialectics, the socialist market economy is the present aim of the socialist reform with Chinese characteristics, not the ultimate goal of the socialist development. Judging from the future direction of socialism (or the *subjective dimension* of Marxist historical dialectics), the socialist market economy is only a means to access the modernization of social economy and culture. It must be ultimately surpassed to obtain the goal of communism. At the same time, we should be aware of the complexity in the socialist construction brought about by the development of the commodity/market economy. In this process, it is necessary to pay some painful price on the social aspect.

Deng says, "The essence of socialism is liberation and development of the productive forces, elimination of exploitation and polarization, and the ultimate achievement of prosperity for all."[113] However, we can effectively develop the productive forces relying on the socialist market economy, "laying the foundation for the realization of communism in the future."[114] He emphasizes that "we should make it clear to the people, including our children, that we uphold socialism and communism and that the purpose of our policies in every field is to advance the socialist cause and eventually to realize communism."[115] We should clearly understand this point. Socialism with Chinese characteristics is precisely for the true liberation and the comprehensive free development of the human subject on a more

---

113   Wei-Wei, Zhang. *Ideology and Economic Reform under Deng Xiaoping, 1978-1993*. London: Kegan Paul International, 1996. p. 187.

114   See *Selected Works of Deng Xiaoping, Volumes 1-3*. Beijing: Foreign Languages Press, 1994.

115   Xiaoping, Deng. *Fundamental Issues in Present-Day China*. Beijing: Foreign Languages Press, 1987. p. 104.

solid and higher level of productive forces, which, again, reflects the unification of the objective dimension and the subjective dimension of historical dialectics.

The above analysis indicates that Deng's exploration of the road of socialism with Chinese characteristics has not come into being merely out of his mind but results from the reality of China's socialist practice and the movement of historical dialectics. It deeply reflects the general scientific understanding of the party and the people. It is the crystallization of our collective wisdom.

C. THE ECONOMIC DEVELOPMENT AT THE PRIMARY STAGE OF CHINA'S SOCIALISM IS A PROCESS OF NATURAL HISTORY

With the above discussion of Deng Xiaoping's socialism with Chinese characteristics, it is necessary to focus again on the basic clue of this book, that is, to carry on further philosophical validation based on the dual logical dimensions of Marxist historical dialectics and the theory of historical 'natural-ness' and material-subjugation.

As we know, Deng is the first to let socialism return to reality. His socialist practice aims at the historical process of social economy, starts from the general material foundation and social productivity at the present social stage in China, and truly turns our thought to the logics of historical materialism and the objective dimension of historical dialectics. In this respect, we just get rid of the *false socialist realm of freedom* founded on the undeveloped social economy and *re-enter* the realm of economic necessity[116]. Our socialist market economy is nothing else but the realm of necessity called by Marx as the economic necessity. The development of social economic life is the *process of natural history* independent of our will (the subjective intention and plan). During this period, there is the objective existence of socio-historical 'natural-ness' and material-subjugation, of which the primary social part is not capital any more but the social labour represented as the general social relations. These phenomena form a very complex theoretical system. Next, I am going to make a brief analysis. Today, China's social development is defined as the primary stage of socialism. It is scientific conclusion of our practice for several decades, mainly based on the reality of China's current socio-economic (productive) level and nature.

---

116   In fact, we never truly walked out of the realm of necessity nor entered the real realm of freedom. The "re-entering" here is rather a re-confirmation in theoretical logics and the direction of real practice.

China's road of socialism is a historical result but our several decades of economic and cultural development is still "unqualified" for the *necessary* level of the socialist productive forces required by Marx. Although our relations of production and political ideology once make a historical leap forward, reality shows that certain socio-historical phase must be based on the productive forces and must not be circumvented. After struggles of painful turns and turbulences, China's Marxists came to the clear recognition of the materialist "standard of the productive forces" with the admission of the backward productive forces and the *primary* stage of socialism. However, socialism should not have been poor and undeveloped. Hence, we would truly catch up on the road of the economic development and gradually go up the stairs towards the socialist *modernization*, walking from the canyon of the initial stage as early as possible. In a certain period of time, the "Four Modernizations" is simply interpreted as developing economy and production but we soon find that the *original system* cannot provide a quick growth for the socialist modernization, which is built on a highly developed social productive forces and thus in necessity of a new base, a new economic and political structure, only possible through "rebuilding on the ruins of the old system, that is, to "reform." Reform is a systematic project of social gestalt. It must shift from the "product economy" to the commodity economy, from the planned system to the market economy, and establish a corresponding new social political structure with a high degree of democracy and the rule of law in a new conceptual system. Accordingly, it is the second revolution of China's socialist practice. Starting with the material foundation of the mode of production itself, this revolution surpasses that in 1949 in a certain sense. To break the old social system and establish a new effective social structure to develop the productive forces, *reform provides the only entrance to modernization*. This is the historical logical relationship between the socialist *reform* in the primary stage and the *modernization of China*.

In 1949, we successfully carried out a political revolution and stepped into the period of socialist practice. In the normal process of historical development, any political revolution is an economic reform finished within the social superstructure but our political revolution occurs in a special contradiction of socio-historical dialectics. A crucial point is, when we claim for the socialist revolution, there is a huge economic hole in the base of society. The social economic reality falls far behind the possible development and maintenance of the socialist productive forces. The formal completion of a political revolution can be achieved through a swift qualitative and structural conversion but the economic development cannot be finished through mere change of forms. When we hope to quickly level up the productive forces for a socialist framework of economic planning regardless of reality (following the mode of Marx's conception of the future society but *without direct practicability*), it sadly results in a lifeless and rigid system. One hundred years ago, Marx foresaw that *revolution could not be created*. It must be a requirement of the objective social process. Similarly, he believed the economic phase as the process of natural history *could not be surpassed*, either. To remember this point is undoubtedly important. After the revolution in 1949, we should have developed the social production and constructed a new economic foundation so that a political revolution under certain conditions can become a truly *social revolution*. However, we were busily engaged in various revolutionary movements related to the production relations and superstructure, rather than taking a critical step to face reality. After 30 years of numerous detours, hardships and sufferings, the crucial step was finally taken by Deng Xiaoping to implement his socialist reform with Chinese characteristics. At last, gone with the winter of staggering trudges and here comes the ideal and poetic spring with great expectations. Today, we firmly face the historical reality by admitting that we are still in the primary stage of socialism. It is not enough. We should deepen this correct reflection in the theory of Marxist historical dialectics. In other words, the economic development of the primary stage of socialism is a *natural process of history*. Then, we can embark on the journey of sunshine.

We have learned that Marx divides the human social history into three great forms according to the historical functionality of practice in social economic development. In his vision, socialism ought to be an advanced stage after the pre-historical period (the natural "process of natural history"); therefore, it is naturally the period of the "realm of freedom" in human history. That is, socialism should transcend the phase in which the social economic laws work as the natural laws implemented through blind destruction. Then, the development of human history is no longer a process of natural history but a true history of human society; and man's historical subjective role no longer acts as the resultant of many blind forces but as a unified, conscious power of creativity. Human society will abandon the external economic necessity and step into the realm of freedom from the realm of necessity, which, of course, does not mean to disregard the economic development but requires a necessary economic condition as the premise for the comprehensive and free development with planning. Nevertheless, today's socialism does not belong to Marx's *advanced stage*. It is only "primary" due to the lack of necessary economic and social conditions. This is precisely a historical fallback after we fail in the formal entrance to the advanced stage. More importantly, we should understand that the present (*today's*) socialist primary stage does not belong to the third phase in Marx's division of the three great social forms. Indeed, we are in the transition from the first period (the natural economy) to the second period (the commodity economy) despite that it is the real socialism. This perspective is firmly based on the economic process and is more profound than that simplified structural division of capitalism and socialism. Thus, we are sure that the commodity economy can fully enhance the development of productive forces and cannot be bypassed (does *not mean capitalism is unavoidable*).

Meanwhile, according to the objective laws of historical dialectics revealed by Marx, the socialist market economy that we have just entered is generally a process of natural history, instead of a *subjective* "realm of freedom." This is a key premise for re-understanding socialism. Nevertheless, the commodity/market economy in the primary stage of socialism cannot avoid the phenomena of 'natural-ness' and material-subjugation on a certain level, which will not be demonstrated through *antagonistic* means like that in the capitalist mode of production. Under socialist conditions, the negative factors inherent in commodity economy can be reduced to a minimum, which is also a necessary price we have to pay for the historical advance on the undeveloped material level. Even so, we should take the scale of the innate logics of historical dialectics and aim at a highly developed society in the future. We should also be concerned with the *subjective dimension* of historical dialectics based on the highly developed material production. Otherwise, something more important than the economic development will be lost during the historical progress.

With such theoretical parameters for reference, we can re-understand the reform and modernization of socialism with Chinese characteristics. It is confirmed that the major economic part of socialism in the primary stage should be a socialist market economy. An essential connection should be noted here: As the primary socialist stage in natural history, its economic structure must be the commodity economy, in the charge of the "invisible hand" according to the historical development. But we are already in socialism. Therefore, it must be supplemented with the control of planning. In this way, a new historical economic form takes shape. For Marx, the socialist planning should come from the highly developed large-scale social production itself. However, our previous "planning" is based on the non-economic experience, which makes the guide of plan easily turned into the political action (or an administrative control) outside the function of economy. For this reason, the socialist planned commodity economy must undergo a substantial process of natural history to be rooted in the development of the productive forces and obtain the shift from arbitrary administrative means to abiding by the economic law.

In addition, the socialist reform is also the revolution of the relations of production, an economic transition. Different from the previous reforms, it does not focus on the relations of production themselves but on the true growth of the productive forces. The radical changes in the last 30 years have caused a *historical misplacement* of our productive forces and the economic forms (that is, the contradiction between the advanced relations of production and the undeveloped productive forces), which not only fails to enhance the productive forces but leads to a virtual economic stop[117]. Therefore, the reform is, first of all, a *fallback* to let the relations of production return to the *objective product* of the real economic movement from a *subjective creation* that forbids the productive forces to play the functional role of historical practice. Of course, the original economic system was not completely wrong since it was an unavoidable distortion of the underdeveloped economy itself. Today, there is still the economic reality that tends to deform the socialist relations of production. Only to find the appropriate economic form that consists/conforms with the productive forces and promote their development can we reach the goal of reforming. It should be noted that our reform is the result of a special history, different from the social changes in normal economic progress. It is to correct the economic relations and rebuild the historical perversion and mixture of the economic forms, for which, we are likely to regard the economic reform as a simple transference of forms and to slip into a new "Great Leap Forward" lead by subjective ideals. Deepening the reform is also an economic process. The new economic system can become practical only when it detects the growth points in the objective economic development and effectively operates. If the reform is turned again into a pure reconstruction of the relations of production separated from the status quo of the productive forces, it is likely to cause another historical perversion! Needless to say, it is a terrible thing, too.

Lastly, the development of the socialist productive forces and modernization is not an abstract indicator but the historical result of development of the productive forces. As for the advanced Western countries that have

---

117   The "product economy" in the old system, with its planning, actually has a miraculous correspondence with man's blood dependence in the natural economy of our society.

developed for hundreds of years, it is a natural historical process. Our socialist development of the productive forces cannot be achieved through such non-economic factors as exaggerated "running forward" and false "double figures." Modernization is the real economic growth independent of man's will. We cannot use our subjective imagination to make a fixed goal so that the process of modernization becomes a high-speed chase to overtake and double, which will inevitably repeat the hot-headed error in 1958. The understanding of the goal of modernization should be compared with the contemporary living standards of Western society. However, if it only stimulates the modernized needs and consumption while ignoring the emptiness of production/supply, we cannot achieve a real modernization, either. China's modernization can be obtained only through reforming and the hard development of economic production. Each step must be taken with the real progress of the productive forces; each hope must be made with the real progress of the productive forces; and each applause must be won with the real progress of the productive forces. There is not the slightest deception or artificial transcendence. It should be our strategic recognition.

The reform to develop the productive forces through the establishment of a socialist market economy is, without doubt, the only way for the Chinese people to stand up again. The socialist modernization with Chinese characteristics rightly complies with the historical trend. Any force cannot stop these rolling wheels of history. An andante passage of philosophical thought is to be played for our march ahead. Should any ideal music spread far over future, it must follow certain rhythms. We cannot blindly dash forward like before. Taking substantial and steady steps on the ground is better and faster than big strides interrupted by frequent falls. This is the historical requirement and the hope of our people. An ancient Chinese philosopher says, "An educated gentleman cannot but be resolute and broad-minded, for he has taken up a heavy responsibility and a long course." We should follow Deng Xiaoping to think and practice, shouldering the responsibility for the Chinese people.

APPENDIX 1

IS THE DEVELOPMENT OF HUMAN SOCIAL HISTORY ALWAYS A PROCESS OF NATURAL HISTORY?[1]

In contemporary research of historical materialism, the discussion of the objective social history will be generally begun by a statement in the preface of Marx's *Das Kapital* that "the evolution of the economic formation of society is viewed as a process of natural history."[2] In fact, this sentence is not completely correct in citation by itself and its adoption to represent a certain general character in the development of social history is even further digressed from Marx's original meaning. I shall first analyze the obvious errors and then draw some important theoretical issues from them to introduce a deep research of historical materialism.

In my opinion, a scientific study of Marxist philosophy must be premised on a *historical return to Marx*. First, the historical definition of the "economic formulation of society" is to be discussed. While Marx says that "the evolution of the economic formation of society is viewed as a process of natural history"[3], its translation changes from the original "economic formation of society" to the "formulation of social economy" in Russian, which is again mistakenly turned into the "social economic form" in Chinese. In our present research of historical materialism, the social economic form is defined as the economic base plus the superstructure (including the productive forces, sometimes), thus, generally indicating the social formation or structure. And a logical reference to Marx's statement above naturally reaches the conclusion that the development of social history is a process

---

1   The essay was first published in *Tian Fu New Idea.* 1 (1988).
2   Marx, and Friedrich Engels. *Capital: A Critique of Political Economy (Vol. I - Part I): The Process of Capitalist Production.* New York: Cosimo, Inc., 2007. p. 15.
3   *Ibid.*, p. 15.

of natural history. I think it is an erroneous theoretical interpretation. In fact, the laws of a *specific period* in the historical development of human society revealed by Marx, by which the conflicts in "the domain of history produce a state of affairs entirely analogous to that prevailing in the realm of unconscious nature"[4], are plainly equated with the general laws of social development. Hence, the *historical phenomenon* where the laws of human society are *alienated as the laws of nature* is universalized and eternalized.

However, Marx has a special connotation when he uses the "economic formulation of society" here. As to the division of historical stages, we are familiar with Marx's doctrine of the "Five Major Forms" that the development of human society is divided into primitive society, slave society, feudal society, capitalist society and communist (or socialist) society in the light of the relations of production in different developmental stages of human society (especially the Western social history), which forms a vital foundation of classical diachronic study of both the division of historical stages and historical materialism. To make an in-depth theoretical discussion, in his study of social history Marx divides the development of human society into *three basic forms (types)* in accordance with the practical and specific historical position of human beings as subjects in the development of social history. It is a doctrine on Marxist conception of social history that is of great importance but has been overlooked.

Marx expands his analysis from different theoretical perspectives as follows: Firstly, as to the issue of the *social subject*'s position in historical development, Marx comes up with the social forms of "the Relations of personal dependence," of "personal independence founded on objective dependence" and of "free individuality, based on the universal development of individuals and on their subordination of their communal, social productivity as their social wealth."[5] Next, in term of *human social relations*, society can be classified into that of "a local connection resting on blood ties, or on primeval, natural or master-servant relations"[6], that with the manifestation of "objective bond" as well as that of "universally developed individuals, whose social relations, as their own communal relations."[7] Thirdly, in view of the *objective laws* of social development, there can be the division of the "society of natural necessity," the "society of economic necessity" and the

---

4   Marx, & Engels. *K. Marx and F. Engels on Religion*. Moscow: Foreign Languages Pub. House, 1957. p. 253.

5   Marx, Karl. *Grundrisse: Foundations of the Critique of Political Economy (rough draft)*. Trans. Martin Nicolaus. London; New York: Penguin, 1993. p. 158.

6   *Ibid.*, p. 161.

7   *Ibid.*, p. 162.

"society of free human development." The first two are in the "realm of necessity" in the development of human society, while the last is the "realm of freedom." Here, the second great social form designated by Marx above is precisely the model of the economic formation of society.

For Marx, the economic formation of society is not the general form of the development of human history but the product of a specific phase of the development of human social history. In primitive society dominated by natural necessity, it is the production of humans themselves rather than material production that predominates in social existence and development, which, though, does not exclude material production from the general *decisive basis* of society. When the productive forces reach a certain point, material production will be independent of and then dominant over human production. It appears as a special economic power, forcing man, as the subject of history, subjected to the rule of external economic necessity. Although man is no longer a slave to natural necessity by his independence in the economic power, he becomes a slave to the new material force created by himself ("the invisible hand" arising from the pell-mell development of commodity economy). Human society exceeds nature (or animality) and creates history on its own but it is still of a restricted and blind activity-in-itself because humans remain "economic animals," history still occurs beyond humans as before, and the development of human social history still seems *analogous to the development of nature*. In Marx's earlier period (1844), he defines that phenomenon as the *alienation* of history. After the establishment of historical materialism, he still acknowledges the historic *alienation/materialization* according to the scientific conception of history. He then specifies further that the rule of economic necessity over man is not permanent but temporary. With the development of the productive forces, when personal production regains the predominance, then the economic force over individuals will not exist anymore. That is to say, by the end of the prehistoric phase of human society the *economic formation of society is bound to be transcended*.

Careful readers may find some similar ideas held by certain Western "humanistic Marxists": Lukacs's objection to the "economic priority" and the subsequent concept of "economic individuals" as well as such proposition by Lefebvre and Fromm as that it is the spontaneous domination of economic laws over social history that is supposed to be transcended. Others allege that the human liberation predicted by Marx precisely refers to the sublation of lopsided "economic individuals (animals)" in conjunction with the realization of universally developed individuals, and that the society in which economy predominates will certainly be replaced by a real historical stage of human society, and so on. We need to make a careful analysis of these opinions. On one hand, it should be acknowledged that western Marxists clearly see Marx's important statement on historical materialism that has been ignored for a long period; on the other hand, it is a mistake for them to go from the negation of economic necessity to the negation of material production, the general social base.

Now let us turn back to the true significance of Marx's argument that "the economic formation of society should be viewed as a process of natural history." Marx never concludes any society must be a "social economic form." Therefore, we cannot deduce that the whole development of social history becomes the process of natural history independent of man. Instead, this statement of Marx's simply confirms that after the emergence of private ownership, the society of class antagonism is the economic formation of society. Marx clearly says that "the Asiatic, ancient, feudal and modern bourgeois modes of production may be designated as epochs marking progress in the economic development of society."[8] In these social forms, there exist various blind external necessities, such as the laws of social history alienated as the laws of nature. As we know, Marx is always prudent in the issue of "natural laws." For one thing, he objects to the bourgeois classical economists' eternalization of the historical law of the development of capitalist society as "natural laws"; for another thing, he employs the "natural law" in a sense opposite to the real human social history[9]. What he states above evidently bears the second meaning. Marx argues that the pell-mell development of the economic formation of society (capitalist society in particular) similar to natural development is nothing but a transitional historical state, a certain stage of social development, which just accounts for the limitation and spontaneity of the development of capitalism. As the productive forces have improved, the "natural laws" implemented by means of blind destruction are bound to be substituted by the real "laws of social production". By then, the development of human social history will no more appear as a process of natural history but as the true *process of human social history*; moreover, the human role as the subject of history will not be fulfilled in a resultant form of blind multi-dimensional forces any more but in a unified conscious power of creativity. Sublating the external economic necessity, human society will enter the realm of freedom from the realm of necessity.

8   Marx, Karl. *Contribution to the Critique of Political Economy*. New York: International Publishers, 1979. p. 21.
9   Marx, Engels, Moore, etc. *Capital: The Process of Capitalist Production*. C. H. Kerr & Company, 1908. p. 533.

It should be equally specified that though Marx's view on the leap from the realm of necessity to the realm of freedom has been frequently cited in previous studies, the deep structure and true significance of such a key point have not been really grasped. The external necessity of social history, namely the economic laws "independent of man's will," have been mostly taken as eternal historical laws so that man seems to be permanently restricted by the objective world, which, however, is quite inaccurate. Generally speaking, historical laws are different from natural laws. The latter cannot be created; the former are spontaneous in prehistoric society – which is what Marx calls as the first and second social forms – and unlikely to be created consciously likewise. In this sense, man is locked in the social realm of necessity. However, in the future communist society as Marx imagines, a real human society with both highly developed material production and universal and free development of individuals, sublating and presupposing necessity, history will be on the threshold of the realm of freedom. At that point, man will become the master of his own history, not only correctly understanding and choosing historical laws but also consciously creating his own history in accordance with his own scientific will and practical intention.

That is exactly where communism essentially surpasses any previous society. Hence, a succession of Marx's discussion on the "true human society" (the overall historical process), "the Man" (the subject of history), the "realm of freedom" (the status and position of human beings in history), and "the union of free individuals"(social structure), all needs careful examination with a new discourse framework. Deepening that issue will certainly have considerable theoretical influence over grasping the essence of the development of social history on the basis of historical materialism, learning the basic differences between communism and all previous class societies, investigating the latest changes of capitalism as well as strategically studying the direction and historical course of contemporary socialist construction and the all-round reform with Chinese characteristics.

APPENDIX 2

ON MARX'S AD HOC STIPULATION OF 'NATURAL-NESS' IN THE DEVELOPMENT OF SOCIAL HISTORY[1]

For a long time in our study of historical materialism, there always hides a mistaken interpretation of Marx's general law about the development of social history to universalize some social characters in certain historical conditions similar to the process of natural history as the principle for the development of entire social history. In this regard, I proposed several questions and caused a lot of concerns. However, there are still some important theoretical knots necessary to be unfastened. Therefore, it is the task of this essay to discuss the historical clue of Marx's stipulation of 'natural-ness' in the development of social history as well as the true meaning of this stipulation for a further theoretical exploration of this issue.

I.

In my opinion, any confirmation of stipulation in Marx's scientific framework should first adhere to the principle of historicality, that is, we should not take some Marx's *ad hoc* logical points as the abstract laws that are *permanent and universal.* Thus, the preliminary historical clue of Marx's idea should be noticed in our understanding of the interactions between the historical development of human society and the process of natural history.

Early in his youth, Marx defines the difference between human and animals as the subjective self-transcendence and creativity. In his eyes at the time, nature is to limit man and thus the *survival of humanity is the history of constant struggle to free themselves from nature.* This idea seems to be a logical prelude or a point for Marx to develop relationship between man and the history of nature.

---

1   First published in *Philosophical Researches.* 2 (1991).

As we know, Hegel's philosophy paves the theoretical way for Marx but his philosophical thought is always an independent process of innate changes due to his strong sense of reality. In the early stage of the Young Marx's philosophical thought, we see a clear illustration of the internal law of social history, that is, the *logic of the alienation view of history*. Admittedly, this view of social history is a reverse perspective at first.

In his doctoral dissertation, Marx regards the alienation of spiritual entities (atoms) as the necessary way for self-realization because alienation is objectification and only objectification can reach the unification of essence and existence[2]. Obviously, he *logically approves* of the alienation of the subject's essence. Despite that, once his vision is put into history, there always emerges the opinion that in ancient times, people cannot get rid of their dependence on Mother Nature that restricts their existence; while as time goes by, man stands up with his own spirit (reason) and gradually becomes the master of nature. Hence, Marx says, "The premise of the ancients is the act of nature, that of the moderns the act of the spirit."[3] At that time, what dominates the Young Marx's thought is not Hegel's objective idealism but the emphasis on self-consciousness with the subjective idealism of the Young Hegelian School, which actually means the individual subjective initiative of *human beings*. By saying that "the nous is active and is resorted to where there is no natural determination. It is itself the non ens [Not-being] of the natural, the ideality"[4], the Young Marx highlights by what the human subject *transcends* nature. It is clear that he focuses on the socio-historical development of the human subject (spirit) and puts it in antithesis to the process of natural history.

During his work in "Rheinische Zeitung," Marx begins to contact social reality, besides pure theoretical concerns. Now, his idealistic framework is shaken. In his discovery, the alienation of spiritual nature in real life is not to realize the objectification of the Sublime by Hegel but is more presented as some unpleasant materialization of a despicable consciousness. On the one hand, Marx insists that "the essence of the spirit is always *truth* itself."[5] He thinks that a general independence of thought, viz., the "ought" of reason, is a fundamental requirement. On the other hand, he scorns this pursuit for material interest as "the erudition of a penny magazine," "the

---

2 Marx, and Friedrich Engels. *Karl Marx, Friedrich Engels: Collected Works*. London: Lawrence & Wishart, 1975. p. 53.

3 *Ibid.*, p. 431.

4 *Ibid.*, p. 435.

5 *Ibid.*, p. 112.

religion of sensuous desire."[6] This "abject materialism" and the "gold fetish" are produced in the period when "human history was part of *natural history*"[7], the feudal medieval ages. The feudal system makes the spiritual world of animals where *man's survival principles are under the mercy of the laws of natural materials.*

Here, we see a critical change in Marx's logics. If his dissertation still follows Hegel's confirmation of the alienation (objectification) value of the spiritual essence (atoms), he no longer regards the second part of the "essence-existence-essence" logic, viz., the estrangement of spirit or material reality as the realization of reason. Instead, he *negates* it as the sin that violates human spirit. Only *human history* is real while the historical materialization or the estrangement similar to nature is *anti-human*. Marx tends to make a consistent combination of the relation between human society and nature with the perspective of observing history (the view of alienation). In addition, the Young Marx has already admitted, although reluctantly, that the law is "outvoted" by the material interest[8]. It is a vital theoretical intuition and the starting point that anticipates his new scientific theory.

In fact, after 1842, the Young Marx begins to be influenced by Feuerbach's humanism. At first he only has a passing reference to Feuerbach, and gradually he feels the weakness of the "sublime" slogan of the Hegelian reason, equality and freedom before reality, unable to sublate those spiritual alienations. From the summer in 1843 to early 1844, Marx writes the *Critique of Hegel's 'Philosophy of Right'*, and publishes *On the Jewish Question* and the *Introduction to the Critique of Hegel's 'Philosophy of Right'*. This time, his critique of Hegel's idealism changes to the position of Feuerbach's materialism. Nevertheless, the main line of his philosophical thought is only the Feuerbachian framework of natural humanism; especially his view of history is still the structure of historical idealism centred on the theory of humanistic alienation.

As we know, Marx quickly abandons his previous hypothesis based on the "law of reason" and fully embraces the view centred on "man." By Feuerbach's materialism, he criticizes Hegel's reversed subject-predicate relation of spirit and material, that is, the relation between law, nation and civil society, and exposes the mystical nature of the Hegelian philosophy. In his criticism of Hegel's argument for the authoritarian state and social alienation, he says, "Man is the world of man – state, society. This state

6   *Ibid.*, p. 189.
7   *Ibid.*, p. 230.
8   *Ibid.*, p. 261.

and this society produce religion, which is an inverted consciousness of the world, because they are an *inverted world*."[9] More importantly, "it separates man from his universal nature; it makes him an animal whose being coincides immediately with its determinate character."[10] This is the man "who has lost himself, been alienated, and handed over to the rule of inhuman conditions and elements – in short, man who is not yet a real species-being."[11] If in the Middle Ages, the constraint in reality comes from nature that, together with his natural determination, has deprived him of the subjective status. Here, the non-subjectification of man is dominated by a non-human force. It is thus very important for Marx to first discover that *man is dominated by the material created by himself!*

If the above philosophical idea is a theoretical insight based on political analysis, the critical thinking that man is conditioned by his own creation gets more profound once he steps into the reality of social economy. It is the theory of labour estrangement and Marx is influenced by Moses Hess from the very beginning. In "On the Jewish Question" of 1843, the new theory of estrangement comes up. And in his notes addressing James Mill's book, *Elements of Political Economy*, we find this theory greatly extended. Marx firmly grasps a very important issue at the beginning of his economic studies, that is, man *changes from the slave of nature to that of the material created by himself* in the development of modern society. In either condition, *man is not the master of his own fate*. It is clear to see a strong ethical and romantic hue in the humanistic view of history held by the Young Marx.

This idea is fully expanded in the last works of his early theoretical development, the *1844 Manuscripts*, when he turns from democratism to the proletarian position although he is not a scientific socialist. In order to seek the foundation for the proletarian revolution, he naturally combines this analysis with the struggle for communism. In the manuscript, Marx has formed his important opinion that in modern society man cannot be man not because he is subject to external nature or the power outside him but that he is *enslaved by the power made by himself*. "Not the gods, not nature, but only man himself can be this alien power over men."[12] The sentence inherits the critical reflection on the religious and authoritarian rule; it also demonstrates that Marx eventually sees the *power of the non-subjective*

9   Marx, Karl. *Early Writings*. Harmondsworth: Penguin Books, 1992. p. 244.

10   Marx, Karl. *Critique of Hegel's 'Philosophy of Right.'* Trans. Joseph O'Malley. Cambridge University Press Archive, 1977. p. 82.

11   See Stephen Perkins's *Marxism and the Proletariat: a Lukácsian Perspective*. London: Pluto Press, 1993. p. 30.

12   Marx, Karl. *Early Writings*. Harmondsworth: Penguin Books, 1992. p. cccxxxiii.

alienation of the objective economic world made by man. Meanwhile, he finds that it is labour–instead of the previous spiritual power of reason –that creates the huge material world; therefore, all this de-subjective estrangement stems *from the estrangement of man's creative evolution.* "The domination of the land as an alien power over men is already inherent in feudal landed property."[13] Today, this dominating force is neither the land nor the illusory god, but an objective materialized world of economy created by man.

It should be noted that Marx thinks the inevitable result of the estranged labour is private ownership, which means the estranged labour provides the foundation to beat down the unreasonable "human slavery." Therefore, "the transcendence of human self-estrangement" is communism[14].

We notice a significant flash of thought in his philosophical logic here. Firstly, when he puts nature from human history into the logical structure, he begins to esteem nature. Man's essence is nature; the personified nature, naturalized man and history is the true natural history of man. Nature is now honoured as the *conquered object of man,* which is but an *inflated natural humanism,* not contradictory to Marx's previous negation of man constrained by nature.

Secondly, we find the impact of classical economics in this book, which reveals the non-subjective problem that is characteristic of the capitalist economy from the angle of positive economics. For example, he once confirms that Ricardo exposes the "blind control of the world" by the capitalist economic laws, that is, "it is precisely through competition that the way is cleared for this natural disposition of capital."[15] The "natural disposition" here refers to the non-human power out of man's control. It should be noted that it is an economic fact instead of a humanistic logical conclusion. This idea undergoes a major theoretical expansion later.

II.

In the eyes of Althusser, the *1844 Manuscripts* represents the darkness before dawn for Marx[16]. He means that the book, despite its closeness in time to the beginning of Marx's new worldview, is logically the most distant from the sun of truth. Although I am not in total agreement with

---

13   Marx, Karl and Friedrich Engels. *The Economic and Philosophic Manuscripts of 1844: and the Communist Manifesto.* Buffalo, N.Y: Prometheus Books, 1988. p. 63.
14   *Ibid.,* p. 102.
15   Oakley, Allen. *Marx's Critique of Political Economy: 1844 to 1860.* London: Routledge, 1984. p. 57.
16   Althusser, Louis. *For Marx.* London: Verso, 2005. p. 36.

Althusser's opinion, I think the *1844 Manuscripts* is written during the most chaotic period when Marx's dominant logical framework and power discourse is, without doubt, still the humanistic estrangement view of history, a paradigm *proceeding from the main logic of the "subjective" essence*. As we know, at that time, Marx is also seeking the foundation for the proletarian revolution. However, the more he is rooted in reality, the further he is forced to comply with another line of thought that is *historically oriented towards the real foundation of social history*. We can see the traces of this potential logical conflict abound in the *1844 Manuscripts*. It should be noted that they are not *equivalent* and parallel logics. The former is Marx's logical framework per se while the latter is a new general negativity included in the former. But Marx does not realize it himself. Once he knows, a fundamental theoretical change naturally ensues.

Marx's philosophical vision achieves a breakthrough in 1845, when he writes the *Theses on Feuerbach* and *German Ideology*, marking the birth of his new worldview. It is not a simplistic logical continuation of the *1844 Manuscripts* but a major qualitative leap forward, a "break," as the French philosopher Louis Althusser describes in an almost metaphysical expression, because now the logical framework of Marx's philosophy experiences a grand Gestalt transformation, that is, he generally abandons the basic logical context of the estrangement view of history based on the transcendental essence of the human subject and discovers a different foundation—the *historical, actual social practice*. At the same time, due to the innate stipulation of practice, the new philosophical line begins with the specific historical conditions. He gives up the rational logic (philosophy) to assess nature and social history and engages himself in revealing the laws of the material world. Hence, the history of human society is no longer the process of man's estrangement and restoration but the actual development of human social practice, the history of the objective human production. In this way, Marx eventually overcomes the hidden nub of historical idealism. It should be noted that Marx's focus on the criticism of historical idealism, especially of those "semi-materialists," does not indicate that spirit simply *generates* the reality of social history but refers to the abstract *doctrine that human will is the drive*. In other words, since the essential difference between human society and nature lies with the fact that social history is composed of human activities dominated by human will, social history transcends nature in that society is always driven by man's spirit. It is through a truthful description of the rules of historical development that Marx's historical materialism corrects this erroneous view of history and reveals such scientific principles as that *man's* social existence (the material practice) decides his ideology, that the development of the subject's social practice, or the productive forces, is what drives the historical movement, and that the masses are the creators and masters of social history. However, for a long time, in the traditional framework of philosophical interpretation, Marx's difference from the idealistic will-driving doctrine is defined as an *external process that is forever independent of man's will*; and his "process of natural history" is taken as the theoretical foundation for this mistake. It is all but a misunderstanding of Marx.

I have made a preliminary explanation about the old interpretative error of Marx's statement in the preface to *Das Kapital* that the "economic formulation of society is a process of natural history."[17] Here, I would like to mention that the traditional framework also ignores a crucial point in Marx's *scientific historical view*, the issue of '*natural-ness*' presented in certain phases of the development of social history. It is of great significance to understand this for an accurate grasp of the development of social history in Marx's historical materialism.

The humanistic framework based on a transcendental subjective essence no longer exists in Marx's new horizon of historical materialism centred on practice; instead, there is a scientific mapping of the specific conditions of social history. Here, Marx no longer makes an ethical negation of the *unreasonable* alienation of man by the social-economic forms of the human historical development, especially, the capitalist society, which is regarded, instead, as a more "reasonable" and advanced mode of production than that of the previous historical periods from the perspective of the development of social production. This view is quite different from that in the *1844 Manuscripts*. Marx further points out that with the development of the social productive forces, the capitalist mode of production starts to transform from the *historically reasonable* to the *historically unreasonable* due to its deep innate contradictions, which leads to its replacement by communism. It is not a logical conclusion that the sublation of man's estranged labour essence is communism but the exposition of the necessary trend of the *objective social laws*. Here, we find his initial explanation of 'natural-ness' in the development of social history.

It needs to be noted that Marx's reference to nature and the law of nature has multiple semantic interpretations in his works. For the latter, it is a scientific explanation of the natural development, without any semantic connotation or metaphoric inclination, which does not need special validation

---

17   See "Is Human Social History a Natural Historical Process Forever?" *Tian Fu New Idea.* 1 (1988).

and can be temporarily put into brackets. Otherwise, there will be some theoretical distraction in our interpretation[18].

Marx's initial validation of the stipulation of 'natural-ness' begins from defining the historicality of the capitalist mode of production. He first wages his critical sword toward the bourgeois economists who stand for the system and ideology of capitalism. In classical economics, the bourgeois scholars defend their ideology and celebrate capitalism as an eternal system. The task of the economics is to find the rules of production, distribution and exchange that decide the material wealth. As we know, early in the *1844 Manuscripts*, Marx employs the labour-estrangement theory against the postulation that the bourgeois private ownership is a natural and eternal condition. In later works, he further explains that it is unscientific for the bourgeois scholars to view the capitalist mode of production as "fixed, immutable, eternal categories."[19] For the bourgeois economists, there are two social systems: The artificial feudal system and the *natural* capitalist system. This natural capitalist mode of production seems to be "encased in eternal natural laws independent of history, at which opportunity bourgeois relations are then quietly smuggled in as the inviolable natural laws on which society in the abstract is founded."[20] Marx expounds very clearly: "When the economists say that present-day relations – the relations of bourgeois production – are natural ... These relations therefore are themselves natural laws independent of the influence of time. They are eternal laws which must always govern society. Thus, there has been history, but there is no longer any."[21] Please note that the above use of "natural laws" is Marx's quote from the bourgeois scholars to express his second meaning of nature, the natural status in antithesis to the man-made things, which is not the same with Marx's stipulation of 'natural-ness' in the development of social history.

Marx firmly argues against the aforementioned bourgeois view. He sharply points out that "the mode of production, the relations in which productive forces are developed, are anything but eternal laws, but that they correspond to a definite development of men and of their productive forces, and that a change in men's productive forces necessarily brings about a

---

18   See Chen Zhiliang and Yang Geng. "Re-Understanding the 'Natural Historical Process' of Society." *Philosophical Researches.* 2 (1989).

19   Marx, and Friedrich Engels. *Karl Marx, Friedrich Engels: Collected Works.* London: Lawrence & Wishart, 1975. p. 162.

20   Marx, Karl. *Early Writings.* Harmondsworth: Penguin Books, 1992. p. 27.

21   Marx, Karl. *Selected Writings in Sociology & Social Philosophy.* New York: McGraw-Hill, 1964. p. 63.

change in their relations of production."[22] It is the same with the capitalist system. The internal contradictions of the capitalist mode of production will inevitably lead to the demise of this mode and then be replaced by the socialist/communist system adapted to the advanced productive forces. In his later positive analysis, Marx's use of the natural laws has a new semantic change. In the *Economic Manuscripts of 1861-63*, a new logical line is revealed. "The bourgeois economists who regard capital as an eternal and natural (not historical) form of production then attempt at the same time to legitimize it."[23] Then, Marx stresses that the law of nature refer to the bourgeois production, that is, the law abided by under certain historical conditions. Without such law, the bourgeois production system would be unimaginable. Of course, it means the nature of the mode of production here, and thus, the issue of the natural law.

It is necessary to point out that Marx's "natural law" is endowed with a new metonymic sense rather than a mere negation of the bourgeois view. In other words, the capitalist mode of production is not a natural law forever but one *similar to the blind natural movement* during a certain period of social development. It is the most immediate meaning of Marx's stipulation of 'natural-ness'. And obviously, it is not a universal character but an *ad hoc* explanation of a certain historical period in human social history.

Marx shrewdly argues that the capitalist system has indeed some characters similar to the law of nature with its economy appearing in a status of the non-subjective development dominated by the blind forces. It shows that man still remains in the realm of animals, only being more an advanced economic animal, which is another continuation of his previous historical view. In Marx's theoretical vision, the phenomenon of 'natural-ness' in the capitalist economic development exposes the historicality and "incompleteness" of the capitalist mode of production. Marx thinks that in capitalism, social production reflects an uncontrollable blindness. It is "a mode of production whose inherent laws impose themselves only as the mean of apparently lawless irregularities that compensate one another."[24] Here, the "lawless" "laws" refer to those of socio-historical development while the "mean" "laws" can be viewed as the movement similar to the natural laws. Hence, the laws of production are represented by the "natural laws

22   Marx, Karl. *Selected Writings, Volume 1977, Part 2*. Ed. David McLellan. Oxford University Press, 1977. p. 210.
23   Marx, Karl. *Grundrisse: Foundations of the Critique of Political Economy (rough draft)*. Trans. Martin Nicolaus. London; New York: Penguin, 1993. p. 460.
24   Marx, and Friedrich Engels. *Capital: A Critique of Political Economy (Vol. I-Part I)*: The Process of Capitalist Production. New York: Cosimo, Inc., 2007. p. 115.

of production."[25] "Only as an inner law, vis-à-vis the individual agents, as a blind law of Nature, does the law of value exert its influence here and maintain the social equilibrium of production amidst its accidental fluctuations"[26] because "variation of work at present imposes itself after the manner of an overpowering natural law, and with the blindly destructive action of a natural law that meets with resistance at all points."[27] Marx believes that these capitalist "forms conform to its nature and have come into being in the natural evolution of competition."[28]

After validating the existence of 'natural-ness' in the capitalist mode of production, he further identifies that the mutation of social history into a natural movement is not unique in capitalism but a common character of the pre-historical periods of human beings. For a deep analogical examination, we can draw on his theoretical analysis of the three major forms of socio-historical development. Early in *German Ideology*, Marx starts from the nature of the productive tools to relate three major social forms: The pre-capitalist society with "natural instruments of production," the modern capitalist society with tools "created by civilization" and the future communist society[29]. For Marx, the first and second social forms present certain characters similar to nature, but with different qualities.

In the first case, that of the natural instrument of production, individuals are subservient to nature; in the second, to a product of labour. In the first case, therefore, property (landed property) appears as direct natural domination, in the second, as domination of labour, particularly of accumulated labour, capital[30].

Marx further develops the above idea in *Das Kapital* and other Manuscripts. Here, he adopts multiple perspectives to reaffirms different qualities of the major elements of human social history in three great social forms. First of all, *judging from the subjective role in historical development*, man's activity is based on the dependent relationship that is "entirely spontaneous at the outset" in the first social form; in the second social form, there is the

---

25 *Ibid.*, p. 809.

26 Marx, Karl. Capital: *A Critique of Political Economy, Volume 2*. New York: International Publishers, 1974. p. 880.

27 Marx, and Friedrich Engels. *Collected Works, Volume 35*. London: Lawrence & Wishart, 1996. p. 490.

28 Marx, and Friedrich Engels. *Karl Marx, Friedrich Engels: Collected Works*. New York: International Publishers, 1975. p. 514.

29 Marx, and Friedrich Engels. *The German Ideology*. Ed. Christopher John Arthur. New York: International Publishers Co, 1970. p. 68.

30 *Ibid.*, p. 68.

"personal independence founded on objective [sachlicher] dependence"; and the "free individuality, based on the universal development of individuals and on their subordination of their communal, social productivity as their social wealth, is the third stage."[31] For Marx, that in the first social form, man's natural production (including the human multiplication and use of raw materials) dominates and the production of the material means of subsistence is at most "a peripheral matter."[32] In the second form, man's material production takes the lead and drives the social development. At the same time, Marx discovers that the passive man is still determined by the external condition. The process of society itself is "a natural relation, as it were, external to the individuals and independent of them."[33]

However, when Marx turns to take the perspective of social relations of people, the three great social forms respectively take on "a merely local connection resting on blood ties, or on primeval, natural or master-servant relations," a form that misrepresents the human social relations with the "objective bond" and the "universally developed individuals, whose social relations, as their own communal [gemeinschaftlich] relations."[34] The later social form is certainly more advanced than the former; in particular, these material links are no longer "spontaneous" and become the *non-natural relations* created by people. Marx further explains that "these conditions, in turn, are independent of the individuals and, although created by society, appear as if they were natural conditions, not controllable by individuals."[35]

The third point is that Marx starts from the *objective laws of social history* to propose three corresponding characters of social movement, the "natural necessity," the "economic necessity" and the dependent development of human freedom. Marx calls the status of the first social movement conditioned by the natural laws as natural necessity and the economic world of materialization where man is subjugated the economic necessity. In both conditions, the social and historical activities of human beings are posited in a controlled non-subjective status. In addition, Marx divides the existential aspects of the human subject itself into the "natural existence," the economic "participants" and the social "Freeman," matching the social structures of the "natural community", the "social formation" and the "free association." It is by defining the first two social forms that Marx uncovers

31   Marx, Karl. *Grundrisse: Foundations of the Critique of Political Economy (rough draft)*. Trans. Martin Nicolaus. London; New York: Penguin, 1993. p.158.
32   *Ibid.*, p. 223.
33   *Ibid.*, p. 158.
34   *Ibid.*, p. 162.
35   *Ibid.*, p. 164.

the early human status of being-in-itself in Mother Nature and the non-human status of a personified capital with the social structure presented in natural formation of blood relationship groups and the spontaneous composition of the economic relations in the market network.

As for Marx's three social forms, we find that people in the first period are so heavily reliant on nature that natural necessity dominates humans and their social activities (the phenomenon of 'natural-ness' can be viewed as sub-naturalness in the early social development); in the second period, the development of social productive forces generate a huge system of material production and the economic power becomes a supernatural force above man. In this new world, there is again an inverted quasi-religious image: Although man displays his independence of nature in the economic life, no longer a slave to nature, he is at the same time subjected to the material forces created by himself (the "invisible hand" caused by the blind economic movements). Undoubtedly, it is a new economic necessity that exists outside man himself. In a certain sense, human society surpasses nature (other animals) and begins creating their own history, which is but achieved through a resultant force of the blind and spontaneous activities. More importantly, he is still the economic animal abiding by the jungle laws. History has not become true yet (without any humanistic implication here) since it still runs outside the domain of human beings like nature. This is the real significance of Marx's ad hoc definition of 'natural-ness' in social history.

Now, we have to turn back to the previous question: Is 'natural-ness' in social history a general character of social movement? I think it is not necessary to elaborate on the famous statement in Marx's *Das Kapital*. He just means the bourgeois economic formulation of society should be understood as a process of natural history, or, more precisely, the capitalist mode of production is a social existence similar to natural history. Marx never indicates any social form is a process of natural history. He once clearly says, "the Asiatic, ancient, feudal and modern bourgeois modes of production may be designated as epochs marking progress in the economic development of society."[36] In these social forms, there exists the blind external necessity like that of nature, that is, the laws of social history alienated into the "natural laws." Marx adds that the natural laws in the Asiatic, ancient or feudal modes of production are actually different laws. He then points out that the historical phenomenon of 'natural-ness' in "pre-historical" social forms only accounts for the narrowness and historicality of these

---

36   Marx, Karl. *Early Writings by Karl Marx*. Harmondsworth: Penguin Books, 1992. p. 426.

forms, especially, of the capitalist system. With the development of the productive forces, this "natural laws" carried out in blind destruction are sure to be replaced by the true laws of social production. To be specific, it refers to the replacement of the blind commodity economy by the planned and proportional development of social production, the achievement of socialism (communism).

Here, it is perhaps easy to find that Marx's stipulation of 'natural-ness' continues his early thought of the relationship between the human history and the natural history on a new scientific foundation. But there are several important changes. First, he still attaches importance to the subjective status man should have in the development of society and negates the historical situation that nature decides man. Here, he no longer stresses that man is universally higher than nature but makes the historical explanation of the objective process for man's social history to escape nature. Second, Marx still negates the non-subject status dominated by the external forces. It is no longer regarded as the loss and alienation of man's transcendental nature but is scientifically explained and criticized from the perspective of materialization and fetishism. Third, most importantly, Marx's analysis of 'natural-ness' in the pre-historical societies, especially, capitalism, is a necessary part of his new worldview as well as a crucial theoretical pillar for his argument for the historicality of the capitalist mode of production.

III.

In my opinion, I think the most important logical point to explain the phenomenon of 'natural-ness' occurring in specific historical conditions during the socio-historical development of human beings is to validate the true meaning of this assumption in that it essentially puts in perspective the historicality and irrationality of capitalism so as to explore the inevitable trend of socialism or communism. Therefore, the logical provisions of 'natural-ness' precisely define the basic difference between the development of socialist society and the historical movement of capitalism, which is also very important and profound for today's ideological struggles.

It is necessary to confirm that the most significant meaning of Marx's 'natural-ness' lies in its collective embodiment of the objective logics of historical materialism, that is, the principle of historicality of social development. At the same time, it is also a fundamental point of Marxist historical materialism as scientific socialism. The first two social forms in the pre-historic period, especially, 'natural-ness' generated during the capitalist society (private ownership), rightly expose the temporary and historical nature of the capitalist mode of production and even all the exploitative systems; thus, only socialism (communism as the third great social form) that corresponds with the development of the new productive forces can really *start the fresh history of human society*. It is here that the development of human history finally ends its pre-historical period and thoroughly eliminates 'natural-ness'; hence, man completely escapes the animal domain (the economic animal or the economic man), and steps into the period of the true historical advancement. If human society was always a natural historical process, we would accept the eternity of the inverted materialization in capitalism and man would be subjugated by the external force forever, which is, of course, not Marx's intention.

According to Marx's own idea, ",history' is not, as it were, a person apart, using man as a means to achieve its own aims; history is nothing but the activity of man pursuing his aims."[37] However, for Marx, under certain historical conditions, for example, in the ancient times when the social productive forces are on a very low level of development, human history is fundamentally a part of the history of nature. With the economic improvement and the productive forces developed to a new level, material production protrudes and departs from the production of human beings. It then takes control of socio-historical development and makes man once again a slave to the economic power. As a result, social history is presented in a blind, non-subjective status, similar to that of the natural development. And the economic formulation of society is not equivalent to the general social form but a specific stage of human history. Therefore, that control over man by the economic power, that 'natural-ness' of historical development is not eternal but a temporary phenomenon. When the productive forces are developed and the production of human beings themselves rises again to dominance, the controlling role of the economic power over man no longer exists. In other words, with the end of human's pre-historical period, the phenomenon of 'natural-ness' is certain to be dialectically negated.

Marx explicitly says that "this consolidation of what we ourselves produce into an objective power above us, growing out of our control, thwarting our expectations, bringing to naught our calculations, is one of the chief factors in historical development up till now."[38] That is to say, after the pre-historical period, human social history really begins. This is a process

---

37   Marx, and Friedrich Engels. *Marx and Engels Collected Works 1844-45*. New York: International Publishers, 1975. p. 93.

38   Marx, and Friedrich Engels. *The German Ideology*. Ed. Christopher John Arthur. New York: International Publishers Co, 1970. p. 53.

from the realm of necessity (including both the natural necessity and the economic necessity) into the realm of freedom. The phenomenon of 'natural-ness' in the old social development will be substituted by Marx's new expectation of the future. The previous "all-round dependence, this natural form of the world-historical co-operation of individuals, will be transformed by this communist revolution into the control and conscious mastery of these powers."[39] Here, it is particularly important to validate the issue of the subject of socio-historical development.

Louis Althusser, a French Marxist scholar, argues that Marx's social history is an *objective process without a subject*, which seems to win quite a lot of agreement. Nevertheless, I doubt Althusser's view. His subjectless criticism against the humanistic tendencies of Western Marxism is only reasonable in that it refers to the subject without any a priori humanistic nature nor being mediated by idealistic elaboration. In fact, Althusser does not argue for the subjectless society but against the human subject because his theory takes social relationship and structure as the subject itself while the social subject is the pluralistic decision-making process of social structure. In my opinion, this historical process without a subject is never Marx's intention but the structuralist residues. It is true that Marx adopts historical materialism to oppose abstract humanism and idealism but he does not intend to negate the subject of social history, the *human beings engaged in real historical activities of production*. On the contrary, Marx always attaches importance to the *subjective status* in the development of social history, which is also the most important goal of the future communist liberation of humankind.

As I have mentioned before, some Western Marxian theoreticians are aware of the above issue. They oppose the mechanical economism by the Second International. In the eyes of Kautsky and others, the core of Marx's historical materialism is to regard the development of social history as a natural historical process. In their paranoiac emphasis, the social process independent of man's will and the material-subjugation of the economic power outside seem to become the eternal phenomena of social history. Therefore, they claim themselves following Marx's iron logics and opposing Lenin's socialist revolution in the undeveloped Russia because the revolutionary process must be the "process of natural history." As we all know, Lenin breaks the myth of the Second International with the October Revolution and makes socialism become practice from scientific theory for the first time. To support Lenin, Antonio Gramsci calls it the

---

39 *Ibid.*, p. 55.

"Revolution Against *Capital*," which further forms an important historical clue in Western Marxist research[40]. György Lukács also bases his theoretical structure on the opposition of the "economic priority." Later, scholars such as Erich Fromm and Henri Lefebvre propose the notion of the "whole" man against the "economic man," claiming that it is the spontaneous domination of economic laws over social history that is supposed to be transcended. These views contain reasonable explanations in comparison with those by the Second International and even some major Russian Marxist theorists[41].

As we all know, Marx does not expect the future communist society become a natural historical process separated from man; instead, he indicates a comprehensive free development for human beings without 'naturalness', when man truly obtain his subjective status and become the real master and creator of social history with scientific understanding and usage of the objective laws.

At this point, Engels totally agrees with Marx. He even further extends this idea. When dealing with Duhring's economics, Engels ridicules the non-historical eternalization of economic laws as "natural laws." "The more that human beings become removed from animals in the narrower sense of the word, the more they make their own history consciously, the less becomes the influence of unforeseen effects and uncontrolled forces of this."[42] The other important point is contained in Engel's criticism against the idealistic error that man's concept and thought create his living conditions. With Engels, this view is overthrown by all the past history. Result is always different from and even contrary to the wish in most cases of development in history. People will first recognize the changing necessity of social conditions generated by the change of relations and be willing to realize that change, instead of being forced to recognize and do it unconsciously.

---

40   Zhang Yibing. *Broken Wings of Reason – Criticism of Western Marxism.* Nanjing: Nanjing Publishing House, 1990. p. 13.

41   As we know, in Nikolai Bukharin's interpretation of historical materialism, social history is a natural historical process; society is only a material "combination"; the movement of history becomes a balance-imbalance process-in-itself independent of man's will. What makes it more deplorable is that he applies this interpretation to explain the socialist and communist movements, which just deviates further from Marx.

42   Engels, and John Burdon Sanderson Haldane. *Dialektik der Natur.* New York: International Publishers, 1940. p. 18.

Now, I have to make some ad hoc explanations of the crucial theoretical points to avoid some deep logical errors. Firstly, Marx's specific use of 'natural-ness' in the development of social history is nothing of subjectivism for a micro confirmation of such stipulation has a critical logical premise, the objective reality of human historical movement. Here, the logical domain of 'natural-ness' mainly points at such issues of status and role for man in the process of history instead of indicating that the development of society may have the alleged "subjective laws," which is but a major logical slip to historical idealism. Even after the elimination of the alienated realm of necessity (the natural economic necessity), it still sublates the objective necessity into the premise for its own free development. The future human society is also an objective process, only with the conscious, dominant material practice of the socio-historical subject.

Secondly, we must acknowledge that the development of contemporary capitalist society is undergoing changes, especially after the second world war when there emerges the conscious regulating system on a state level (representing all the capitalists as class), which seems to go beyond Marx's definition of 'natural-ness' in capitalist economy. State-monopoly capitalism takes the form of state control (the "revolution of Keynes") and partially adjusts its relations of production, which appears to control the macro blindness of production ('natural-ness') and consequently, the crisis is curbed and the social productive forces obtain additional room for development. It certainly proves the correctness of Marx's conclusion of social history. The contemporary capitalist adjustment of the mode of production is conditioned by the necessity of the social productive forces. It just reveals that the capitalist is keeling down before Marx's scientific thought[43]. On the other hand, we should notice that this modification in contemporary capitalism is not an essential change of its mode of production but a temporary policy to loosen the rope around the neck of capitalism. More importantly, capitalism remains a contradictory system of exploitation. Under the surface of macro-social control is still the blind economic movement, which is the nature of capital. The only way to eliminate 'natural-ness' in the development of capitalist society is a thorough self-negation of this mode of production.

Thirdly, socialism in China today has not developed into the third phase in Marx's great social forms. For the lack of necessary economic and social conditions, we regard ourselves as "primary stage" socialism. The economic

---

43   Zhang Yibing. "On the Scientific Base of the Contemporary Capitalist Research." *Social Sciences in Nanjing*. 2 (1990): 66.

stages of social development is not to be bypassed (does not mean capitalism is unavoidable). According to the objective laws discovered by Marx, the economic operation in China's socialist society today is co-determined by planning and the natural market, which should be a theoretical standpoint for the socialist reform and modernization. In this regard, we have had enough bitter lessons.

BIBLIOGRAPHY

Adorno, Theodor W. *Negative Dialectics*. London: Routledge, 1990.

Agger, Ben. *Western Marxism, an Introduction: Classical and Contemporary Sources*. Santa Monica, Calif. : Goodyear Pub. Co., 1979.

Althusser, Louis. "Marx's Relation to Hegel." *Politics and History*: Montesquieu, Rousseau, Marx. London: NLB, 1972.

---. *For Marx*. London: Verso, 2005.

---. *Lenin and Philosophy and Other Essays*. Trans. Ben Brewster. New York: Monthly Review Press, 1971.

---. *Louis Althusser Essays in Self-Criticism*. Trans. Grahame Lock. London: NLB, 1976.

---. *Louis Althusser Philosophy and the Spontaneous Philosophy of the Scientists & Other Essays*. Ed. Gregory Elliot. London: Verso, 1990.

Althusser, Louis. *Reading Capital*. Trans. Étienne Balibar. London: Verso, 1997.

Bidet, David Fernbach, and Alex Callinicos. *Exploring Marx's Capital: Philosophical, Economic and Political Dimensions*. Boston: BRILL, 2007.

Bredel, Ralf. *The Ethical Economy of Conflict Prevention and Development: towards a Model for International Organizations*. Boston: Martinus Nijhoff Publishers, 2007.

Collingwood, Robin George. *The Idea of History*. Oxford University Press, 1956.

Cunow, Heinrich. *Marx's Theories of History, Society and State*.

Dussel, and Fred Moseley. *Towards an Unknown Marx: A Commentary on the Manuscripts of 1861-63*. London; New York: Routledge, 2001.

Engels, Friedrich. *Anti-Dühring: Herr Eugen Dühring's Revolution in Science*. Moscow: Foreign Languages Pub. House, 1959.

---. *Dialectics of Nature*. Moscow: Foreign Languages Pub. House, 1954.

---. *Society and Revolution: Essays in Honour of Engels*. People's Pub. House, 1971.

---. *The Origin of the Family, Private Property and the State*. New York: International Publishers Co, 1972.

Engels, West, and Eleanor Burke Leacock. *The Origin of the Family, Private Property, and the State, in the Light of the Researches of Lewis H. Morgan*. New York: International Publishers Co, 1972.

Fromm, Erich. *Beyond the Chains of Illusion: My Encounter with Marx and Freud*. New York: Continuum International Publishing Group, 2001.

---. *Escape from Freedom*. New York: Macmillan, 1994.

---. *Marx's Concept of Man*. New York: Continuum International Publishing Group, 2004.

---. *To Have or To Be?* New York: Continuum International Publishing Group, 2005.

Gerhardt, Eike, and Andrew Arato. *The Essential Frankfurt School Reader*. New York: Urizen Books, 1978.

Gramsci, Antonio. *Antonio Gramsci: Pre-Prison Writings*. London: Cambridge University Press, 1994.

---. *Further Selections from the Prison Notebooks*. London: Cambridge University Press, 1995.

---. *Selections from the Prison Notebooks*. New York: International Publishers, 1992.

Habermas, Jürgen. *Theory and Practice*. Boston: Beacon Press, 1988.

---. *Toward a Rational Society: Student Protest, Science, and Politics*. Boston: Beacon Press, 1971.

Hegel, Georg Wilhelm Friedrich. *Philosophy of History*. New York: Barnes & Noble Publishing, 2004.

Horkheimer, Adorno, and Gunzelin Schmidt Noerr. *Dialectic of Enlightenment: Philosophical Fragments*. Stanford University Press, 2002.

Horkheimer, Max. *Critical Theory: Selected Essays*. New York: Continuum International Publishing Group, 1982.

---. *Eclipse of Reason*. New York: Oxford University Press, 1947.

Jantsch, Erich. *The Self-Organizing Universe: Scientific and Human Implications of the Emerging Paradigm of Evolution*. Pergamon Press, 1980.

Jianheng, Bi. *Mao Zedong and the Traditional Chinese Culture*. Chengdu: Sichuan People's Publishing House, 1990.

Jinfu, Wang. "Another Discussion on the True Significance of the 'Natural Historical Process' by Marx." *Journal of Suzhou University*. 3 (1993).

Kant, Immanuel. *Kant's Collected Writings, Vol. 8* (Chinese Version). The Berlin-Brandenburg Academy of Sciences and Humanities, 1968.

Kautsky, Karl. *The Dictatorship of the Proletariat*. University of Michigan Press, 1964.

Kiss, Artúr. *Marxism and Democracy: A Contribution to the Problems of the Marxist Interpretation of Democracy*. Akadémiai Kiadó, 1982.

Korsch, Karl. *Karl Marx*. Chapman & Hall, 1938.

Korsch, Karl. *Marxism and Philosophy*. London: NLB, 1970.

Lawrance, Alan. *China since 1919: Revolution and Reform : A Sourcebook*. Routledge, 2004.

Lefebvre, Henri. *Survival of Capitalism*. London: Allison & Busby, 1976.

Lefebvre, Sturrock, and Kipfer. *Dialectical Materialism*. University of Minnesota Press, 2009.

Leiss, William. *The Domination of Nature*. Montréal: McGill-Queen's Press - MQUP, 1994.

---. *The Domination of Nature*. Montréal: McGill-Queen's Press - MQUP, 1994.

Lenin, Vladimir Il'ich. *British Labour and British Imperialism: A Compilation of Writings by Lenin on Britain*. London: Lawrence & Wishart, 1969.

---. *Collected Works*. 1978.

---. *Democracy and Revolution*. Sydney: Resistance Books, 2000.

---. *Selected Works*. Moscow: Progress Publishers, 1971.

Liang, Bo. "Special and General Understandings of Historical Materialism from the Theoretical Perspective of 'Two Kinds of Production.'" *Academic Journal of Jinyang*. 5 (1982).

Liang, Qi. "The Anthropological Notes of Marx and Historical Materialism." *Contentions (Zheng Ming)*. 4 (1990).

Löwy, Michael. *The Theory of Revolution in the Young Marx*. Chicago: Haymarket Books, 2005.

Lukács, Georg and John Rees. *A Defence of History and Class Consciousness: Tailism and the Dialectic*. Verso, 2002.

Lukács, Georg. *History and Class Consciousness: Studies in Marxist Dialectics.* MIT Press, 1972.

Marcuse, Herbert. *Counterrevolution and Revolt.* Boston: Beacon Press, 1972.

---. *One-dimensional Man: Studies in the Ideology of Advanced Industrial Society.* Psychology Press, 2002.

Marcuse, Wolin, and John Abromeit. *Heideggerian Marxism.* University of Nebraska Press, 2005.

Marx, Karl. *Early Writings.* Harmondsworth: Penguin Books, 1992.

Marx, and Friedrich Engels. *Marx and Engels Collected Works.* New York: International Publishers. 1975-2005.

Marx, and Friedrich Engels. *Marx and Engels Collected Works.* London: Lawrence & Wishart. 1975-2005.

Marx, and Friedrich Engels. *Capital: A Critical Analysis of Capitalist Production.* Moscow: Foreign Languages Pub. House, 1959.

Marx, and Friedrich Engels. *On Religion.* Chicago: Scholars Press, 1982.

Marx, and Friedrich Engels. *The German Ideology.* Ed. Christopher John Arthur. New York: International Publishers Co, 1970.

Marx, and Friedrich Engels. *The Economic and Philosophic Manuscripts of 1844: and the Communist Manifesto.* Buffalo, N.Y: Prometheus Books, 1988.

---. *The Letters of Karl Marx.* Ed. Saul Kussiel Padover. Englewood Cliffs, N.J.: Prentice-Hall, 1979.

---. *Grundrisse: Foundations of the Critique of Political Economy (rough draft).* Trans. Martin Nicolaus. London; New York: Penguin, 1993.

---. *Marx: Later Political Writings.* Ed. Terrell Carver. Cambridge University Press, 2002.

Mishra, Girish. *Malthus and his Ghost.* New Delhi: Manak Publications, 2001.

Oakley, Allen. *Marx's Critique of Political Economy: Intellectual Sources and Evolution.* London: Routledge & Kegan Paul, 1985.

Perkins, Stephen. *Marxism and the Proletariat: a Lukácsian Perspective.* London: Pluto Press, 1993.

Plekhanov, Georgiĭ Valentinovich. *The Development of the Monist View of History.* Прогресс Публишерс, 1972.

Prigogine, and Isabelle Stengers. *Order out of Chaos: Man's New Dialogue with Nature, Part 2.* Toronto ; New York, N.Y.: Bantam Books, 1984.

Rousseau, Jacques. *The Social Contract or Principles of Political Right.* Kessinger Publishing, 2004.

---. *Discourse on the Origin of Inequality*. Minneapolis: Filiquarian Publishing LLC., 2007.

---. *The Social Contract and the First and Second Discourses*. Yale University Press, 2002.

Sachsse, Hans. *Ökologische Philosophie*. Wissenschaftliche Buchgesellschaft, 1984.

Schmidt, Alfred. *The Concept of Nature in Marx*, London: NLB, 1973.

Schumacher, Ernst Friedrich. *Small is Beautiful: Economics as if People Mattered*. New York: Harper & Row, 1975.

Selsam, and Harry Marte. R*eader in Marxist Philosophy*. New York: International Publishers Co, 1987.

Shanin, Teodor. *Late Marx and the Russian Road*. London: Routledge & Kegan Paul, 1983. p103.

Sheng, Hu. Ed. *Seventy Years for the Communist Party of China*. Beijing: The CPC History Publishing House, 1991.

---. *Reflections on China's Road to Development: Nine Essays by Hu Sheng*, 1983-1996. Commercial Press, 1997.

Smart, Paul. *Mill and Marx: Individual Liberty and the Roads to Freedom*. Manchester University Press ND, 1991.

Smith, Adam. *The Theory of Moral Sentiments*. London: H. G. Bohn, 1853.

Smith, and Kathryn Sutherland. *An Inquiry into the Nature and Causes of the Wealth of Nations*. Oxford University Press, 1998.

Soled, Debra E. China: *A Nation in Transition*. Congressional Quarterly, 1995.

Spretnak, Capra, and Wulf-Rüdiger Lutz. *Green Politics*. Santa Fe, NM : Bear, 1986.

Ter-Akopian. "On the History of the Concept of 'Original Society.'" *Marxist-Leninist Study Materials*. 2 (1987).

Vico, Giambattista. *The New Science*. 1725.

Walter Benjamin. *Berlin Childhood Around 1900*. Harvard University Press, 2006.

Weber, Max, and Talcott Parsons. *The Protestant Ethic and the Spirit of Capitalism*. New York: Courier Dover Publications, 2003.

Wei-Wei, Zhang. *Ideology and Economic Reform under Deng Xiaoping, 1978-1993*. London: Kegan Paul International, 1996.

Xiaoping, Deng. *Deng Xiaoping on the Question of Hong Kong*. Beijing: Foreign Languages Press, 1993.

---. *Fundamental Issues in Present-Day China*. Beijing: Foreign Languages Press, 1987.

---. *Ideology and Economic Reform Under Deng Xiaoping, 1978-1993*. Ed. Wei-Wei Zhang. London: Kegan Paul International, 1996.

---. *Selected Works of Deng Xiaoping, Volumes 1-3*. Trans. Bureau de Compilation et Traduction des Oeuvres de Marx, Lénine et Staline. Beijing: Foreign Languages Press, 1994.

Yibing, Zhang. "A Big Leap for Lenin in His Deepened Understanding of Materialistic Dialectics: Notes of Philosophical Notes." *Philosophical Researches*. 5 (1992).

---. "An In-depth Interpretation: Western Marxism and Georg Lukács." *Philosophical Trends*. 8 (1999).

---. "Construction of Practice." *Fujian Tribune*. 1 (1992).

---. "Field of Social Practice." *Jiang Hai Xue Kan*. 5 (1988).

---. "Integration of Practice: The Functional System of the Orderly and Interactive Human Activities: A New Philosophical Vision." *Seeking Truth*. 5 (1989).

---. "On the Scientific Base of the Contemporary Capitalist Research." *Social Sciences in Nanjing*. 2 (1990): 66.

---. "The Historical Examination of the Logical Starting Point of Historical Materialism." *Journal of Nanjing University*. 2 (1982).

---. "The Relationship of Me to My Condition is My Consciousness." *Tianfu New Idea*. 5 (1992).

---. *Back to Marx: The Philosophical Discourse in the Context of Economics*. Nanjing: Jiangsu People's Press, 2009.

---. *Broken Wings of Reason - Criticism of Western Marxism*. Nanjing: Nanjing Publishing House, 1990.

Youcheng, Liu. *Three Forms of Social Development*. Zhejiang People's Publishing House, 1987.

Zedong, Mao. *Chairman Mao Talks to the People: Talks and Letters: 1956-1971*. Ed. Stuart R. Schram. New York: Pantheon Books, 1975.

---. *Correspondence*. Beijing: People's Publishing House. 1983.

---. *Early Documents*. Chang Sha: Hunan Publishing House, 1990.

---. Mao Zedong's Documents Since the Founding of the Nation, Book 10. Beijing: Central Party Literature Press, 1992.

---. *Selected Works*. Beijing: People's Publishing House, 1986.

---. *The Philosophical Notes of Mao Zedong*. Beijing: Central Party Literature Press, 1988.

Zhiliang, Chen and Geng, Yang. "Re-Understanding the 'Natural Historical Process' of Society." *Philosophical Researches*. 2 (1989).

ABOUT THE AUTHOR

Zhang Yibin, alias Zhang Yibing, male, born in 1956 in Nanjing, Jiangsu Province, graduated from the Department of Philosophy at Nanjing University in August 1981, Ph.D. He is now vice-president of Nanjing University, professor and doctorate tutor oriented in Marxism. His academic works focus on western Marxist philosophy study and textual investigation with a strong interest in the field of humanities. His main books besides abundant articles, include: *Research on Western Marxism and Contemporary Radical Thoughts in Mainland China* (2013); *Possession und vier Texttypen von Heidegger* (2013); *Back to Heidegger: Ereignis and Situating* (The Commercial Press, 2012); *Lenin Revisited - A Post-textological Reading on Lenin's Philosophical Notes* (Jiangsu People's Press, 2008); *Back to Marx: The Philosophical Discourse in the Context of Economics* (Jiangsu People's Press, 2009, Second edition); *Contra Baudrillard: Deconstruction of a Postmodern Myth* (Beijing: The Commercial Press, 2009); *The Problematic of Lacan's Philosophy* (2008); *The Impossible Truth of Being: Imago of Lacanian Philosophy* (The Commercial Press, 2006), *A Deep Plough. Unscrambling Major Post-marxist Texts form Adorno to Zizek* (Vol. 1, Renmin University of China Press, 2004; Vol. 2, RUC Press, 2008); *Problématique, Lecture Symptomale et Idéologie: A Textological Reading of Althusser* (Central Edition and Translation Press, 2003); *Atonal Dialectical Imagination: The Textual Reading of Adorno's Negative Dialectics* (Sanlian Bookstore Press, Beijing, 2001). His book *A Deep Plough: Unscrambling Major Post-Marxist Texts From Adorno to Zizek* and *Lenin Revisited - A Post-textological Reading on Lenin's Philosophical Notes* was translated and published in English in 2011 and 2012.

INDEX

abstract man 117, 126, 140, 325

Adorno 332, 333, 336, 352, 353, 355, 357, 358, 359, 477, 478

Agger 330, 338

alienation xv, xxxi, xxxv, 46, 50, 51, 52, 54, 60, 62, 63, 64, 74, 76, 77, 78, 79, 85,
      89, 92, 95, 97, 102, 105, 115, 116, 126, 153, 155, 168, 169, 183, 185, 191,
      192, 198, 200, 203, 213, 214, 216, 217, 218, 219, 220, 221, 227, 228, 241,
      242, 243, 253, 263, 268, 279, 290, 291, 323, 324, 330, 331, 332, 344, 346,
      349, 350, 351, 353, 356, 358, 380, 387, 388, 423, 429, 455, 460, 461, 463,
      465, 471

alienation of alienation 350

alienation view of history xv, 242, 331, 460

Althusser xx, xxii, xxxviii, xxxix, 109, 114, 124, 166, 298, 322, 323, 324, 325,
      326, 328, 329, 376, 463, 464, 473, 477

Annenkov 182, 187

anonymous authority 355

anthropocentrism 49, 53, 102, 191

anti-anthropocentrism 332

anti-human 73, 79, 117, 120, 300, 326, 349, 351, 357, 461

Asiatic mode of production 245, 250

axiological hypothesis 116, 126, 318, 329

Bacon 52

based on the subject 77, 159, 178, 244

basis xix, xxii, xxiii, xxvi, xxviii, xxxi, xxxiv, xxxv, xxxviii, 54, 56, 57, 61, 62,
      69, 79, 93, 115, 116, 120, 121, 122, 126, 127, 136, 145, 157, 161, 178,
      217, 219, 234, 251, 256, 260, 265, 266, 272, 277, 279, 280, 294, 301, 319,
      324, 335, 344, 347, 348, 349, 354, 377, 390, 392, 394, 396, 397, 412, 413,
      414, 419, 424, 431, 434, 435, 455, 457

Bauer 117, 130, 160

Bergson 374

Bloch 132, 306, 322

capital fetishism 228, 231

capitalism xiv, xv, xxix, xxxiv, xxxv, xxxviii, 51, 56, 58, 86, 87, 91, 94, 97, 102,
103, 115, 117, 119, 120, 122, 127, 130, 151, 153, 159, 166, 169, 171, 174,
175, 178, 181, 182, 185, 188, 200, 203, 204, 206, 207, 208, 209, 210, 211,
214, 215, 216, 217, 220, 224, 226, 228, 234, 235, 239, 242, 246, 248, 249,
251, 252, 262, 263, 264, 265, 270, 272, 274, 275, 276, 277, 278, 279, 289,
290, 300, 303, 308, 317, 319, 321, 330, 331, 332, 335, 336, 337, 338, 339,
340, 341, 343, 345, 346, 347, 348, 349, 350, 351, 352, 353, 354, 355, 356,
357, 359, 387, 388, 394, 395, 396, 397, 398, 406, 408, 409, 410, 415, 416,
421, 430, 435, 436, 438, 440, 441, 442, 443, 444, 445, 449, 456, 457, 466,
467, 468, 471, 472, 475, 476

Chen Duxiu 415, 422

civil society 81, 82, 83, 84, 86, 87, 89, 145, 157, 183, 242, 245, 254, 389, 461

classical economics 55, 57, 60, 110, 203, 463, 466

Cohen 326

Colletti 326

commodity fetishism 227, 230, 338, 344, 357

communism xxxiv, xxxv, xxxvii, 94, 103, 104, 107, 113, 115, 116, 117, 118,
122, 123, 129, 151, 153, 154, 158, 169, 170, 174, 176, 177, 178, 187, 199,
207, 220, 234, 235, 239, 241, 242, 244, 246, 248, 252, 259, 274, 275, 276,
277, 278, 279, 280, 287, 288, 304, 305, 311, 349, 408, 411, 416, 418, 419,
421, 424, 433, 434, 435, 436, 440, 442, 445, 457, 462, 463, 465, 471, 472

complex systems science 367, 368, 371, 373, 374, 375, 376

construction xix, xxiii, xxxiv, xxxviii, 91, 93, 95, 127, 128, 139, 152, 158, 161,
162, 184, 211, 216, 224, 355, 377, 378, 379, 380, 381, 382, 391, 406, 408,
410, 414, 415, 417, 419, 420, 421, 422, 425, 426, 432, 433, 434, 436, 437,
439, 445, 457

constructional 376, 378

creationism xxvi, 50, 191, 192

cunning of reason 60, 62, 63, 193, 266, 340

Deborin 413

Deconstruction xiv, 119, 326, 485

Democritus 75, 76

Deng Xiaoping xviii, 178, 397, 401, 403, 404, 409, 410, 422, 425, 426, 427,
428, 429, 430, 431, 432, 433, 434, 435, 436, 439, 441, 442, 443, 445, 446,
448, 451, 481, 482

diachronic 83, 95, 101, 144, 187, 454

dialectics of practice 125

discourse xvii, xix, xx, xxv, xxxiv, xxxviii, xxxix, xli, 54, 61, 68, 69, 72, 74, 79,
80, 82, 83, 87, 88, 89, 91, 95, 101, 102, 108, 109, 113, 114, 115, 116, 117,
120, 122, 123, 124, 125, 129, 138, 151, 152, 153, 166, 167, 169, 174, 181,
182, 195, 198, 202, 205, 209, 213, 215, 217, 220, 227, 228, 234, 236, 241,
242, 244, 261, 262, 267, 284, 287, 290, 306, 310, 322, 325, 331, 333, 343,
367, 369, 404, 407, 414, 457, 464

dissipative structure 375, 378

dominant xiv, xxii, xxiii, xxvi, xxviii, xxx, xxxi, xxxii, xxxvi, xxxviii, 53, 57, 62, 63, 69, 75, 80, 82, 83, 88, 91, 96, 97, 100, 107, 108, 109, 113, 114, 115, 117, 124, 128, 129, 132, 137, 138, 144, 150, 151, 153, 154, 157, 158, 159, 166, 167, 169, 172, 173, 174, 178, 185, 187, 188, 191, 195, 219, 224, 245, 248, 259, 260, 267, 274, 275, 287, 288, 289, 292, 293, 299, 300, 301, 305, 310, 316, 320, 321, 322, 327, 332, 343, 359, 371, 378, 391, 392, 394, 400, 422, 455, 464, 475

ecology xxxiv, 381, 383, 384, 385, 386, 392, 393, 396, 397, 399

economic formulation of society 453, 454, 465, 470, 472

economic necessity xxix, xxxi, xxxii, xxxiii, xxxv, 167, 174, 257, 258, 262, 263, 265, 269, 270, 271, 272, 275, 276, 277, 301, 407, 419, 446, 448, 454, 455, 456, 469, 470, 473, 475

Einstein 365, 366, 372, 373

Elster 252, 256, 263, 271, 277, 278, 326

Epicurus 75, 76, 77

external determinism 46

externalization 73, 213

fetishism xiv, 89, 206, 227, 228, 230, 231, 232, 233, 234, 293, 338, 344, 346, 350, 357, 382, 471

Feuerbach 47, 50, 63, 80, 81, 82, 83, 84, 85, 91, 92, 97, 102, 114, 115, 116, 117, 118, 123, 124, 125, 126, 130, 131, 132, 133, 134, 135, 136, 137, 146, 148, 151, 152, 153, 154, 155, 156, 157, 159, 160, 164, 166, 168, 186, 193, 194, 201, 220, 227, 280, 288, 291, 293, 298, 309, 325, 328, 329, 334, 389, 412, 414, 427, 461, 464

Fichte 60, 61, 63, 69, 70, 71, 72, 73

field of social practice 377

Fourier 56

Frankfurt School 54, 104, 137, 267, 332, 333, 335, 346, 348, 350, 351, 352, 353, 355, 356, 357, 358, 359, 396, 397, 478

freedom xxii, xxvii, xxxi, xxxiii, xxxiv, xli, 48, 53, 58, 59, 63, 64, 75, 78, 80, 96, 99, 107, 129, 165, 175, 193, 199, 226, 241, 247, 257, 259, 260, 261, 263, 264, 265, 266, 267, 268, 269, 270, 271, 273, 274, 276, 280, 284, 285, 286, 289, 298, 299, 300, 305, 310, 321, 322, 335, 349, 351, 354, 356, 358, 407, 409, 417, 429, 440, 446, 448, 449, 455, 456, 457, 461, 469, 473

Fromm xx, xxxii, 321, 322, 327, 328, 329, 333, 355, 356, 358, 455, 474, 478

from the subjective aspect 329

functionality of practice xix, 143, 292, 295, 307, 380, 384, 412, 448

Gans 71

general historical materialism xiii, xiv, xxiii, 152, 163, 164, 167, 186, 187, 188

Georg Lukacs 345

German classical philosophy 55, 58, 60, 366

Gestalt 114, 373, 382, 464

Gramsci 317, 318, 320, 326, 337, 359, 473, 478

Guizot 56

Habermas 336, 350, 351, 352, 353, 355, 358, 359, 478

Heraclitus 48, 49

hidden idealism 152

historical determinism 146, 183, 192, 292, 318

historical dialectics xv, xxii, xxiii, xxvi, xxviii, xxx, xxxii, xxxv, xxxvi, xxxviii, xli, 58, 61, 63, 67, 73, 94, 113, 122, 128, 129, 130, 132, 138, 139, 144, 146, 147, 150, 151, 152, 153, 154, 158, 159, 162, 163, 167, 169, 171, 172, 176, 178, 181, 182, 183, 185, 186, 188, 189, 190, 194, 195, 198, 199, 203, 209, 216, 217, 220, 225, 227, 234, 235, 239, 240, 241, 243, 244, 245, 246, 248, 253, 259, 260, 261, 262, 274, 275, 283, 292, 293, 297, 298, 299, 300, 305, 309, 310, 315, 317, 319, 320, 327, 328, 331, 332, 334, 341, 363, 367, 370, 371, 375, 378, 379, 380, 382, 388, 389, 390, 391, 392, 393, 396, 403, 404, 406, 407, 408, 409, 411, 412, 414, 415, 417, 418, 420, 422, 423, 424, 425, 426, 428, 429, 430, 431, 432, 434, 435, 436, 443, 445, 446, 447, 448, 449

historical division 241, 242, 243, 245, 246, 248, 273

historical materialism xiii, xiv, xv, xxi, xxii, xxiii, xxv, xxvi, xxvii, xxviii, xxx, xxxi, xxxii, xxxiv, xxxvi, xxxviii, 58, 108, 113, 115, 120, 128, 129, 130, 132, 138, 139, 144, 148, 150, 151, 152, 153, 154, 158, 159, 163, 164, 167, 174, 175, 178, 181, 182, 183, 186, 187, 188, 189, 190, 191, 194, 196, 198, 200, 209, 216, 217, 225, 235, 236, 240, 243, 244, 245, 247, 248, 249, 252, 253, 261, 262, 274, 275, 279, 283, 291, 292, 293, 298, 299, 305, 306, 308, 309, 316, 319, 320, 321, 326, 327, 328, 330, 359, 370, 389, 406, 415, 420, 425, 427, 429, 430, 431, 432, 435, 446, 453, 454, 455, 456, 457, 459, 464, 465, 471, 473, 474

Hobbes 54

Horkheimer 332, 336, 352, 353, 355, 357, 359, 478

humanist estrangement view of history 85

humanistic estrangement view of history 88, 108, 109, 114, 115, 116, 123, 128, 158, 168, 193, 464

human nature xxvi, 52, 61, 87, 92, 94, 117, 125, 155, 260, 267, 277, 288, 290, 342, 343, 423

ideology xiv, 87, 119, 129, 130, 149, 156, 166, 167, 173, 176, 203, 205, 209, 213, 216, 219, 227, 228, 233, 236, 259, 316, 320, 321, 323, 326, 328, 332, 342, 343, 344, 346, 350, 353, 355, 356, 359, 389, 396, 397, 447, 465, 466

Ideology of Technology 350

inhuman 85, 105, 106, 155, 156, 164, 166, 168, 172, 175, 176, 215, 289, 337, 381, 462

initiative xxii, xxvi, xxvii, xxviii, xxxvi, xxxviii, 46, 47, 50, 52, 59, 61, 69, 70, 71, 73, 74, 75, 76, 101, 102, 115, 116, 117, 124, 125, 126, 127, 129, 137, 139, 151, 190, 191, 195, 198, 209, 230, 244, 248, 284, 286, 287, 289, 292, 293, 295, 298, 317, 319, 320, 322, 327, 329, 334, 371, 381, 399, 407, 411, 412, 414, 415, 417, 422, 430, 460

initiative of practice 414

instrumental rationality 52, 137, 346, 348, 351, 357

Jameson 332, 342, 343

Jantsch 371, 479

Kant 55, 58, 59, 60, 63, 69, 70, 71, 72, 73, 125, 126, 136, 192, 193, 195, 288, 365, 479

Kautsky 317, 405, 406, 407, 415, 473, 479

Korsch xv, 318, 320, 327, 336, 337, 338, 479

labour 57, 88, 91, 92, 95, 96, 97, 98, 99, 100, 101, 102, 103, 104, 105, 108, 109, 115, 116, 118, 119, 120, 121, 122, 136, 142, 157, 158, 160, 165, 167, 169, 170, 171, 172, 175, 177, 194, 199, 202, 203, 204, 205, 210, 211, 213, 214, 215, 216, 218, 219, 220, 221, 222, 223, 224, 226, 227, 229, 230, 231, 232, 233, 241, 242, 250, 251, 253, 254, 260, 262, 263, 264, 268, 269, 270, 271, 272, 273, 277, 278, 279, 286, 289, 291, 304, 330, 339, 340, 343, 344, 345, 346, 347, 358, 380, 388, 389, 390, 391, 394, 396, 437, 443, 446, 462, 463, 465, 466, 468

leap from the realm of necessity to the realm of freedom xxxiii, 457

Lefebvre xxxii, 319, 327, 328, 334, 335, 356, 455, 474, 479

Leiss 332, 387, 479

Lenin xvii, xxxvi, 194, 317, 321, 324, 391, 404, 405, 406, 407, 408, 409, 410, 411, 415, 427, 428, 429, 433, 437, 440, 443, 444, 473, 477, 479, 482

Li Huayu xxv

List 119

logic of objective description 53, 245

Mao Zedong xxxvi, 404, 410, 411, 412, 413, 414, 415, 416, 417, 418, 421, 423, 425, 427, 429, 440, 479, 482, 483

Marcuse 327, 352, 354, 356, 357, 480

materialization 54, 78, 79, 193, 199, 213, 214, 215, 217, 218, 219, 275, 304, 319, 343, 381, 384, 455, 460, 461, 469, 471, 472

material production xxiii, xxvi, xxviii, xxxi, xxxii, xxxiii, xxxviii, 49, 109, 121, 138, 139, 140, 141, 145, 146, 148, 149, 152, 158, 163, 167, 168, 172, 187, 188, 189, 194, 198, 199, 202, 204, 231, 233, 251, 253, 255, 258, 260, 261, 262, 263, 266, 267, 268, 269, 270, 272, 273, 275, 276, 277, 279, 280, 292, 298, 305, 309, 310, 316, 317, 320, 327, 337, 344, 352, 359, 390, 391, 392, 396, 399, 404, 405, 407, 408, 414, 417, 419, 422, 424, 425, 428, 430, 435, 445, 449, 455, 456, 457, 469, 470, 472

material-subjugation xiii, xv, xxiii, xxviii, xxix, xxxi, xxxii, xxxiii, xxxiv, xxxv, xxxvi, xxxvii, xli, 47, 63, 178, 181, 200, 213, 217, 218, 220, 221, 222, 223, 224, 225, 226, 227, 228, 230, 232, 233, 234, 235, 236, 239, 244, 247, 249, 253, 254, 255, 257, 259, 260, 262, 266, 269, 270, 273, 274, 275, 277, 278, 279, 293, 297, 301, 302, 303, 308, 310, 315, 327, 332, 338, 343, 344, 346, 347, 349, 350, 358, 382, 407, 409, 425, 440, 443, 444, 446, 449, 473

Mill 90, 97, 101, 105, 107, 110, 178, 203, 462

mode of production xv, xxxiv, xxxv, xxxvi, 51, 88, 103, 121, 143, 144, 145, 156, 162, 163, 164, 168, 169, 175, 177, 181, 182, 184, 185, 186, 189, 190, 195, 197, 198, 199, 201, 203, 205, 206, 207, 208, 212, 219, 220, 222, 223, 226, 227, 228, 231, 232, 233, 234, 235, 240, 245, 246, 248, 250, 251, 252, 274, 276, 343, 346, 390, 396, 416, 443, 444, 447, 449, 465, 466, 467, 468, 470, 471, 472, 475

money fetishism 227, 228, 230

natural determinism xxvi, 49, 191, 335
natural intention 59, 60
natural materialism 82, 83, 132, 288
natural necessity xiv, xxxi, 167, 187, 192, 202, 204, 205, 257, 258, 263, 264,
    266, 269, 275, 277, 301, 303, 337, 388, 391, 419, 454, 455, 469, 470, 473
natural realm of necessity 263, 264
naturoidity xxviii, xxix, xxxiv, xxxvii, 178, 199, 201, 207, 208, 234, 259, 274,
    293, 299, 304, 306, 310, 334, 338, 343, 382, 407, 467, 472, 474, 475
negation of the negation 94, 101, 102, 122, 127, 128, 168, 185, 199, 213, 242,
    439
New Philosophical Horizon 111, 129, 163
Nietzsche 50
non-human 62, 64, 83, 85, 110, 192, 258, 290, 329, 342, 356, 462, 463, 470
objectification 63, 73, 74, 78, 81, 97, 98, 99, 104, 118, 213, 218, 219, 263, 267,
    268, 271, 344, 349, 350, 380, 460, 461
objective dialectics xxxvi, 72, 125, 152, 158, 430
objective dimension of historical dialectics xxxv, 144, 152, 163, 172, 195, 198,
    235, 292, 406, 408, 418, 420, 422, 424, 429, 430, 446
orderly whole of practice 377
parallelogram 308, 311
pattern of social practice 377
Plato 48, 49, 323
Plekhanov 57, 405, 406, 407, 413, 415, 480
political alienation 423
positivism 326, 329, 333
postmodernism 332
practical construction 152, 380, 391
practical materialism xxi, xxvii, xxviii, xxxvi, xxxvii, 114, 125, 126, 128, 129,
    130, 132, 136, 137, 138, 150, 151, 152, 153, 183, 194, 199, 240, 293, 298,
    300, 366, 391, 411, 414, 422, 425, 426, 427, 428, 429, 430, 431
practical ontology 136, 139
Practice 136
practice pattern 377, 378, 379, 380, 390
Prigogine 372, 373, 374, 378, 379, 480
prism of practice 125, 133, 296
problematic 328, 383, 396
process of natural history xxii, xxv, xxvii, xxviii, xxix, xxx, xxxii, xxxiii, xxxiv,
    xxxv, 182, 195, 196, 197, 198, 208, 210, 250, 274, 275, 277, 336, 446,
    448, 449, 450, 453, 456, 459, 460, 465, 470, 473
Process Without a Subject 322
productive forces xxvi, xxviii, xxix, xxxi, xxxiii, 47, 118, 120, 122, 129, 135,
    137, 142, 143, 144, 146, 147, 148, 150, 156, 165, 170, 171, 172, 173, 174,
    175, 176, 177, 178, 183, 184, 185, 186, 187, 188, 189, 197, 198, 199, 204,
    206, 207, 211, 214, 216, 219, 221, 222, 223, 226, 234, 240, 244, 245, 246,
    247, 250, 252, 258, 259, 267, 268, 269, 270, 271, 273, 274, 275, 276, 278,
    279, 280, 304, 310, 348, 349, 350, 358, 371, 384, 386, 387, 388, 389, 390,

391, 392, 393, 394, 396, 397, 398, 399, 400, 404, 405, 406, 407, 409, 416,
    417, 418, 419, 420, 421, 424, 425, 426, 429, 430, 431, 432, 433, 434, 435,
    436, 437, 438, 439, 440, 441, 442, 443, 445, 446, 447, 448, 449, 450, 451,.
    453, 455, 456, 465, 466, 467, 470, 471, 472, 475
Proudhon 182, 184, 185, 204, 210, 212
quantum mechanics 364, 373
quark confinement 368
Quesnay 58
rationality 52, 103, 107, 115, 137, 169, 184, 242, 245, 252, 326, 328, 332, 346,
    347, 348, 350, 351, 352, 353, 354, 355, 357, 358, 364, 372, 373, 388, 397,
    410, 425
realm of freedom xxii, xxvii, xxxi, xxxiii, xxxiv, xli, 63, 193, 241, 247, 259, 260,
    261, 266, 267, 269, 270, 271, 273, 274, 276, 298, 300, 305, 310, 349, 358,
    407, 409, 417, 440, 446, 448, 449, 455, 456, 457, 473
realm of necessity xxvii, xxxi, xxxiii, xli, 63, 193, 199, 241, 247, 259, 260, 261,
    262, 263, 264, 265, 266, 267, 269, 270, 271, 272, 273, 275, 298, 358, 407,
    409, 417, 446, 448, 455, 456, 457, 473, 475
relations of production xxvi, 142, 143, 165, 178, 184, 186, 187, 188, 197, 206,
    232, 233, 245, 256, 279, 325, 326, 394, 416, 418, 420, 421, 424, 430, 432,
    433, 434, 435, 437, 440, 443, 444, 445, 447, 450, 454, 467, 475
revolution of modern science 386
Ricardo 107, 110, 205, 338, 387, 463
Rousseau 53, 54, 64, 85, 215, 323, 477, 480
Sachsse 393, 481
Sartre xxii, 322
Schelling 60, 61
Schmidt 335, 336
Schumacher 400, 481
Scientific socialism 403
Second International xiv, xv, xxix, xxxvi, 166, 209, 292, 316, 317, 318, 319,
    320, 321, 322, 326, 327, 330, 349, 405, 406, 473, 474
second nature 335, 339
Self-alienation 126, 213, 332
self-organization 373, 375, 379, 381, 382
Smith 57, 58, 204, 209, 481
social criticism xiii, xxviii, 153, 178, 182, 203, 208, 220, 221, 228, 234, 291,
    358
social existence xiv, xv, xxii, 81, 82, 104, 129, 134, 135, 137, 139, 140, 141, 143,
    146, 147, 148, 152, 159, 161, 162, 163, 164, 167, 187, 198, 202, 235, 255,
    265, 269, 291, 292, 305, 310, 334, 335, 339, 374, 375, 376, 377, 378, 379,
    380, 381, 382, 391, 397, 399, 428, 455, 464, 470
socialism with Chinese characteristics 404, 417, 421, 425, 431, 434, 435, 436,
    438, 441, 442, 446, 449
special historical materialism xiii, xiv, xxiii, xxx, 58, 151, 153, 158, 186
Stirner 130, 134, 154, 155, 168
structuralism xxxix, 326, 329

subjective dialectics xxxii, 54, 67, 69, 74, 79, 80, 83, 85, 86, 87, 88, 94, 101,
102, 104, 108, 109, 122, 127, 128, 157, 158, 166, 168, 191, 220, 242, 243,
244, 284, 286, 290, 291, 293, 320, 322, 327, 331, 359, 388, 422, 424, 425,
430
Subjective dimension of historical dialectics xxxvi, xxxviii, xli, 58, 144, 151,
153, 154, 158, 167, 172, 178, 181, 188, 190, 195, 199, 203, 216, 217, 220,
227, 234, 235, 240, 245, 246, 248, 253, 261, 262, 292, 298, 299, 300, 305,
310, 392, 396, 409, 411, 414, 415, 417, 422, 429, 443, 446, 449
subjective initiative xxvi, xxvii, xxxvi, 46, 47, 52, 69, 70, 71, 73, 75, 101, 116,
151, 195, 248, 284, 286, 319, 320, 322, 327, 412, 414, 415, 417, 460
subjectivity xxii, xxiii, xxviii, 46, 47, 48, 50, 52, 68, 73, 74, 77, 78, 83, 116, 124,
125, 140, 162, 163, 192, 194, 209, 251, 255, 263, 265, 274, 287, 289, 290,
292, 293, 319, 322, 327, 339, 348, 358, 371, 376, 379, 381, 382, 390, 419,
428, 429
subjectless 194, 333, 473
sub-naturalness 470
sub-natural period 250
Sun Bokui xxvii, xxxviii, 141, 249
systems science 367, 368, 371, 373, 374, 375, 376, 384
Taylorism 347
teleology 50, 54, 55, 322, 323, 324
theory of alienation 60, 85, 330, 331
theory of humanistic alienation 461
Thiers 56
Three Great Social Forms 240, 253
totality 61, 162, 165, 172, 175, 186, 192, 225, 259, 271, 319, 320, 327, 333, 349,
352, 368
traditional framework of philosophical interpretation xiv, xv, xvii, xxii, xxiii,
xxv, xxvi, xxvii, xxviii, xxix, xxxiv, xxxv, xxxvi, xxxvii, xxxviii, 151, 200,
201, 248, 260, 299, 306, 310, 326, 327, 329, 341, 465
uncertainty principle 368, 369
Vico 55, 57, 60, 63, 191, 192, 481
Volpe 326
vulgar materialism 89
Weber 347, 348, 351, 354, 379, 481
Western Marxism xv, xx, xxi, xxiii, 313, 316, 318, 320, 322, 326, 330, 350, 387,
424, 473, 474, 477, 482
Young Engels 207, 284, 286, 287, 289, 290, 291, 297
Young Hegelians 64, 286, 287, 288
Young Mao Zedong 410, 411
Young Marx xx, xxix, 64, 65, 68, 69, 70, 71, 72, 73, 74, 75, 76, 77, 78, 79, 80,
81, 82, 83, 84, 85, 86, 87, 88, 89, 90, 91, 92, 93, 94, 95, 96, 97, 98, 99,
100, 101, 102, 103, 104, 105, 106, 107, 108, 109, 110, 114, 115, 157, 169,
185, 190, 201, 203, 207, 213, 227, 241, 242, 243, 284, 287, 322, 328, 346,
388, 423, 460, 461, 462, 479
Zasulich 241, 247
Zeno 48

www.ingramcontent.com/pod-product-compliance
Lightning Source LLC
Chambersburg PA
CBHW030348130626
46549CB00004B/1415